HOMELAND SECURITY

Larry K. Gaines

California State University at San Bernardino

Victor E. Kappeler

Eastern Kentucky University

Prentice Hall

Boston   Columbus   Indianapolis   New York   San Francisco   Upper Saddle River
Amsterdam   Cape Town   Dubai   London   Madrid   Milan   Munich   Paris   Montreal   Toronto
Delhi   Mexico City   Sao Paulo   Sydney   Hong Kong   Seoul   Singapore   Taipei   Tokyo

Editorial Director: Vernon Anthony
Senior Acquisitions Editor: Eric Krassow
Editorial Assistant: Lynda Cramer
Director of Marketing: David Gesell
Senior Marketing Manager: Adam Kloza
Senior Marketing Assistant: Crystal Hernandez
Project Manager: Holly Shufeldt
Art Director: Jayne Conte
Cover Designer: Suzanne Behnke
Cover Photo: Fotolia
Full-Service Project Management and Composition: Integra Software Services Pvt. Ltd.
Text and Cover Printer/Binder: Edwards Brothers Malloy
Text Font: Minion

Credits and acknowledgments for materials borrowed from other sources and reproduced, with permission, in this textbook appear on the appropriate page within text.

Library of Congress Cataloging-in-Publication Data

Gaines, Larry K.
   Homeland security / Larry K. Gaines, Victor E. Kappeler.
     p. cm.
   Includes bibliographical references and index.
   ISBN-13: 978-0-13-511192-5
   ISBN-10: 0-13-511192-7
   1. United States. Office of Homeland Security.   2. Terrorism—United States—
Prevention.   3. National security—United States.   4. Internal security—United States.
I. Kappeler, Victor E.   II. Title.
HV6432.4.G35 2012
363.3250973—dc22

                        2011000345

10 9 8 7 6 5   V031

Prentice Hall
is an imprint of

www.pearsonhighered.com

ISBN 10:   0-13-511192-7
ISBN 13: 978-0-13-511192-5

Dedication

*This book is dedicated to the fine men and women
in the military, federal agencies, state agencies, and local
governments who protect us.*

CONTENTS

Part III   Defeating Terrorists and Their Activities

PREFACE

On September 11, 2001, operatives of the terrorist group al Qaeda attacked the World Trade Center in New York City and the Pentagon in Arlington, Virginia, using hijacked passenger airliners. It was a wakeup call for America. It was the most significant terrorist attack on the United States, and it had a quashing impact on our country and our public psyche. Terrorism has existed throughout the world since there were nation-states, but the 9/11 attacks made Americans acutely aware of the problem and our country's vulnerability. Although there had been numerous minor terrorist attacks in the United States, primarily by right-wing and left-wing radicals, no previous attacks came close to the magnitude of the 9/11 attacks.

President George W. Bush immediately took action. The United States invaded Afghanistan, the originating country of the attacks, closely examined our intelligence apparatus, and created the Department of Homeland Security. Although the U.S. government had long been involved in counterterrorism, the 9/11 attacks spawned a new era in which homeland security became a primary governmental objective. As with any new initiative, there were mistakes and much of what we did was trial and error. Nonetheless, we now are engaged in homeland security, and we are constantly making adjustments so that we can better deter attacks and respond to any attacks that might not be prevented. Thus, homeland security is a work in progress.

This text examines our efforts to secure our homeland, and it critically examines some of the problems that have occurred in the past. Since homeland security primarily is a response to the threat of terrorism, this threat is intertwined throughout the text. In order to understand homeland security, one must first understand the threat and operations of terrorist organizations. To a large extent, the organization and operation of homeland security are dictated by the terrorist threat. We therefore attempt to address both concerns so that the reader has a firm grasp of both terrorism and homeland security.

Both of these are complex issues with many facets to each. Homeland security includes a number of agencies within the Department of Homeland Security as well as agencies in other federal departments and state and local agencies. Homeland security has had an impact on every federal department as new initiatives and mandates have been developed. As an example, the creation of the Department of Homeland Security was the result of moving 22 agencies from other federal departments into the new department. The Department of Defense and the 16 agencies in our intelligence community are now more actively involved in counterterrorism. More federal agencies are involved in counterterrorism than in addressing America's crime problem. Homeland security is a monumental undertaking.

ORGANIZATION OF THE TEXT

The text contains 14 chapters organized into four major parts examining a variety of topics and issues that are important in understanding homeland security and terrorism. Each chapter begins with learning objectives that provide a roadmap for the chapter. Additionally, key terms are provided. The key terms represent important concepts or ideas that are critical to understanding the chapter material. Embedded in each chapter are HS Web Links and HS Analysis Boxes. The HS Web Links point to materials the reader can access in order to clarify points or obtain additional information about an area in the chapter. The HS Analysis Boxes are analytical situations that apply information in the chapter. They are designed to get the reader to analyze and critically think about important problems or issues in homeland security and terrorism. Discussion questions are also provided to assist the reader in identifying some of the key issues in each chapter. Finally, each chapter contains an extensive up-to-date reference list. These references serve to provide additional information about specific topics in the chapter.

PART I: THE FOUNDATION FOR HOMELAND SECURITY

Part I provides an in-depth foundation for understanding homeland security. Homeland security encompasses a wide range of agencies and activities. The chapters in Part I examine the various activities that constitute homeland security, the various agencies involved in securing our homeland, critical infrastructure or potential terrorist targets, and the laws that are used to counter terrorism.

Chapter 1: Introduction to Homeland Security

Chapter 1 provides a foundation for understanding the mechanics of homeland security. Essentially, homeland security was developed using two important documents. The first was the 9/11 Commission Report, which provided a great deal of information about our homeland security shortcomings. These shortcomings later evolved into objectives for government homeland security operations. For the most part, they focused on our intelligence establishment and our response to the 9/11 attacks. The second document was the *National Strategy for Homeland Security* developed by the Office of Homeland Security in 2002. The *National Strategy* was expansive in that it detailed a number of areas in need of development. The areas ranged from prevention to recovery. It resulted in a number of new programs and agency requirements.

Chapter 2: The Homeland Security Apparatus

Chapter 2 examines the various agencies involved in homeland security. When the Department of Homeland Security was organized, 22 agencies from other federal departments were transferred into the new department. This resulted in a great deal of confusion as agencies assumed new responsibilities in addition to old mandates. Also, a great deal of politics was involved in the creation of the department. Members of Congress and the administration in the White House had differing ideas about how homeland security should function. This led to a number of problems and a waste of energy and time. When we consider homeland security, we often focus exclusively on the federal government. However, if a terrorist attack occurs, it will directly affect a local jurisdiction and a state. Homeland security at the local and state levels is also examined in this chapter. It provides a comprehensive overview of agencies and their relationships.

Chapter 3: Overview of National Infrastructure Protection

Terrorists focus on targets. These targets are critical infrastructure and key assets. Critical infrastructure refers to industries, business, and activities that are of great importance to our economy and safety. Critical infrastructure includes mass transit, the Internet, banking, criminal justice agencies, businesses, and public gatherings such as the Super Bowl or college and high school sports events. Key assets refer to government monuments such as the Washington Monument or icons such as the Golden Gate Bridge. Their destruction might not result in a significant loss of lives or monetary loss, but it would certainly have a psychological impact on our country. The National Infrastructure Protection Plan was developed to provide guidance on protecting our infrastructure and key assets. This plan is examined in depth in Chapter 3.

Chapter 4: Legal Aspects of Homeland Security

The United States is a democracy that is guided by laws. This premise separates us from many other countries in the world. As such, the mechanics of combating terrorism must be grounded in law. A number of laws have been passed that assist us with counterterrorism. Additionally, presidents have signed presidential directives and presidential orders that are legally binding and are used to supplement laws. The directives and orders of Presidents George H. W. Bush, Bill Clinton, George W. Bush, and Barack Obama are discussed. Additionally, important anti-terrorism laws such as the USA PATRIOT Act are examined. This discussion demonstrates the complicated nature of counterterrorism. We have laws ranging in topics from terrorist finances to weapons of mass destruction to immigration policy. These laws and presidential directives and orders provide a comprehensive legal framework for protecting our country.

PART II: HOMELAND SECURITY AND TERRORISM

Part II focuses primarily on terrorism. Terrorism is the primary justification for homeland security—it drives this important governmental initiative. In order to develop an effective homeland security apparatus, it is important to understand the nature of terrorism. The chapters in Part II provide this foundation by defining terrorism and examining the various terrorist groups and their activities.

Chapter 5: Political and Social Foundations of Terrorism

If effective counterterrorism policies and operations are to be implemented, it is critical that we understand terrorism. First, this chapter defines terrorism and distinguishes it from other types of conflicts. The chapter provides a history of terrorism. Many people today think that terrorism is a new phenomenon; however, it has existed as long as there have been nation-states. It is used by countries and political or religious groups. Essentially, terrorism is used to undermine groups involved in a particular religion or countries that are seen as enemies as exemplified by al Qaeda's attacks on the United States. This chapter provides a political and social understanding of terrorist groups in terms of their formation and activities.

Chapter 6: The Nature and Geography of Terrorist Groups, State Sponsors of Terror, and Safe Havens

Today, many Americans focus exclusively on the terrorists who exist in the Middle East, since this is where several attacks on Americans have originated. Indeed, there are numerous terrorist groups in that part of the world. However, terrorism is not the exclusive domain of the Middle East. There are terrorist groups throughout the world. This chapter addresses the primary and active terrorist groups in terms of their activities and objectives. The discussion demonstrates that there are all sorts of groups and motivations. Additionally, several terrorist groups operate in the United States. These groups are identified and discussed in terms of their recent terrorist activities.

Chapter 7: Transnational Organized Crime and Terrorism

Transnational organized crime refers to organized criminal syndicates that operate across international borders. They represent large criminal organizations that are involved in a variety of criminal activities. They are a threat to countries since they depend on corruption and violence to achieve their illegal ends. We often think about terrorism and organized crime as two distinct problems. However, it should be noted that transnational organized crime groups exist in many of the same areas where terrorist groups exist. Terrorists often use organized crime groups to facilitate their attacks, and transnational organized crime groups sometimes use terrorist groups to accomplish their criminal ends. The relationship between transnational organized crime groups and terrorist groups is particularly problematic in that these relationships can facilitate more deadly attacks and more caustic criminal operations. We must focus on these relationships if we are to effectively deal with both groups. This chapter provides an understanding of them, their activities, and possible countermeasures to use against them.

PART III: DEFEATING TERRORISTS AND THEIR ACTIVITIES

When considering counterterrorism, we too often focus exclusively on the battlefield. However, the battlefield is only one aspect or area of concern. Homeland security requires a full, direct attack on a variety of fronts. The chapters in this part examine several important issues, including intelligence, weapons of mass destruction, cyber terrorism, and terrorist finances. Each of these areas must be considered in developing effective counterterrorism measures.

Chapter 8: Intelligence and Counterintelligence and Terrorism

In the past, intelligence focused on countries and their activities. For example, during the cold war, our intelligence community closely monitored the activities of the Soviet Union and the countries that were part of the Soviet bloc or were aligned with the Soviet Union. Today, we still collect intelligence about different countries' activities, but at the same time, we are also concerned with the activities of radical or terrorist groups that may reside in those countries. Moreover, since terrorists have likely infiltrated our borders, we must monitor activities in the United States. There are 16 agencies comprising the intelligence community. They have specific tasks and areas of responsibilities, but each now focuses on counterterrorism. Each agency's activities are addressed in this chapter.

Chapter 9: Homeland Security and Weapons of Mass Destruction

The most significant threat to our nation is weapons of mass destruction. The deployment of such a weapon could result in massive casualties and reverberating economic effects. This chapter provides a history of weapons of mass destruction. It also provides a discussion of each type: chemical, biological, and radiological or nuclear. Each type of weapon presents unique challenges in terms of prevention and response. The chapter examines the likelihood of their deployment in terms of constraints on terrorists. Some of the countermeasures are also discussed.

Chapter 10: Cyber Crime and Terrorism

Cyber crime is the fastest-growing criminal activity in the United States and the world. It consists of cyber fraud and identity theft. A number of homeland security experts advise that cyber terrorism is second only to weapons of mass destruction in terms of threat. In this chapter, we distinguish among cyber crime, cyber terrorism, and cyber warfare. Although each is associated with cyber space, each is unique in presenting different challenges. There is sparse evidence that there has been extensive cyber terrorism. However, cyber warfare is increasingly being used by countries or governments against other countries and political groups. Finally, terrorists are extensively using the Internet to facilitate their activities. They use the web to espouse propaganda, recruit new members, solicit donations, and generate support for their activities. A number of terrorist groups have websites in a variety of languages. Such websites must be monitored as they often provide intelligence about different groups' activities.

Chapter 11: Terrorist Financing

One of the issues examined by the 9/11 Commission was terrorist financing. Al Qaeda operatives used a variety of mechanisms to funnel money to the 9/11 hijackers. Since then, our policy has been to attempt to cut off funding to terrorist groups whenever possible in an effort to starve them or restrict their activities. The United States and other countries have implemented laws and policies designed to prevent terrorist financing. This chapter examines the methods by which terrorist groups secure financing. Raising money, moving money, and banking money are discussed. It is interesting that terrorists use a variety of mechanisms. The chapter also examines countermeasures that have been implemented. Special attention is given to Saudi Arabia since a substantial amount of terrorist financing originates there. Finally, the financial needs of terrorist groups are discussed.

PART IV: HOMELAND SECURITY'S RESPONSE TO TERRORIST THREATS

Part IV examines the endgame in homeland security. It examines several topics, including immigration and border control, the response to homeland security incidents, and policing and homeland security. Border control and immigration are hotly contested political issues that have implications for homeland security in terms of preventing terrorists from entering the United States. This part also examines the framework for responding to terrorist attacks, including the role of the police and counterterrorism

Chapter 12: Border Security and Immigration

Border security and immigration have become important political issues as a result of the threat of terrorism and the number of illegal aliens coming to our country. It is important to realize that these are two distinct issues that must be addressed. This chapter examines patterns of immigration in terms of the numbers of illegal immigrants and their points of origin. The methods by which we have attempted to seal our borders and their effectiveness are examined. It is noted that a number of people from a variety of countries have entered the United States illegally across our southern and northern borders. As such, border control policies are discussed in some detail. The United States has implemented a number of programs to better screen people, vehicles, and cargo entering our country. These programs are examined.

Chapter 13: The Response to Homeland Security Incidents

It is important that we have the capacity and organization to respond to any homeland security incident. The response to Hurricane Katrina is examined, since this event represents one of the largest disasters in our history, and lessons have been learned from the response. A delayed, inadequate response to a similar event likely would result in a larger number of casualties and more destruction. As such, the federal government has developed a number of plans that serve as a template for response. The plans integrate federal, state, and local resources. These plans are discussed in detail.

Chapter 14: Homeland Security and Policing

Chapter 14 examines the police in terms of their homeland security role. Any incident or terrorist attack will occur in a local community. As such, the police will be the first responders to the incident. The local police also play an important role in preventing terrorism by collecting information about activities and people in the community—police officers gather locally based intelligence. Fusion centers and intelligence-led policing are examined, as these are the primary programs used in policing to gather terror-related intelligence. Police organization is discussed since a number of police departments have developed homeland security units and made other alterations to their departments' structure. The importance of community policing relative to counterterrorism is examined. The special case of New York City is examined since that city has been attacked twice by terrorists and likely will be a target in the future.

ACKNOWLEDGMENTS

We thank the following individuals for reviewing the manuscript and making helpful comments:

Danny Davis, Keiser University; Vanessa Escalante, LA College International; Mohamad A. Khatibloo, Westwood College/AITA Colleges; John Brian Murphy, Goodwin College; Bobby B. Polk, Metropolitan Community College; Paul Scarborough, Sanford Brown College; Paul Scauzillo, Platt College; David Sexton, LA College International/State Center Community College District; Barbara J. Smith, Metropolitan Community College; and Joel Woods, ACR-Clawson.

1

Introduction to Homeland Security

LEARNING OBJECTIVES

1. Discuss the impact of the 9/11 attacks on the United States and its citizens.
2. Know the extent and meaning of homeland security especially given that it has a number of definitions.
3. Understand the findings and implications of the 9/11 Commission Report.
4. Know the direction of homeland security as articulated in the National Strategy for Homeland Security.

KEY TERMS

Fear of terrorism

Homeland security

National Commission on Terrorist Attacks Upon the United States

National Strategy for Homeland Security

Critical infrastructure

Homeland security advisory system

Dual use analysis

Smart borders

Enhanced Border Security and Visa Entry Act

Counterterrorism

Joint Terrorism Task Forces

National Infrastructure Protection Plan

Select Agent Program

National incident management system

Radio inoperability

Push packs

Northern Command

INTRODUCTION

The September 11, 2001, attacks on the World Trade Center in New York City and the Pentagon in northern Virginia altered the American political landscape. The attacks resulted in 3,030 deaths and 2,337 people were injured. Moreover, 343 firefighters and 75 police officers were killed while responding to the aftermath of the tragedy. The event had a significant impact on politics. National security and the threat of terrorism became the most prominent issues in American politics and did not subside as the preeminent issues until 2008 when the economy became depressed as a result of personal and governmental debt, the crash of the loan industry, and the essential bottoming of housing prices. The 9/11 attacks affected business. For example, several of the major airlines subsequently declared Chapter 11 bankruptcy. Restrictions were placed on international commerce, and foreign travel into the United States was restricted and became more difficult for many.

The American psyche was changed. America woke up that day in September and became acutely aware that the world could be a dangerous place, and the United States was not immune from attacks originating on foreign soil. America was no different from many other countries that had experienced acts of terrorism. **Fear of terrorism** became a critical political and social issue. To some extent, the level of fear was stoked by the federal government's color-coded alert system, which was repeatedly broadcast and reported by the news media. Fear of a terrorist attack, however, took on new proportions. For example, in 2007, in a national crime survey, fear of being a victim of terrorism ranked third behind a residential burglary and theft of one's auto, as displayed in Figure 1-1 (University of Albany, 2007).

The level of fear of being a victim of a terrorist attack was greater for females as compared to males. In terms of race, white respondents were less fearful of a terrorist attack as compared to

Respondents reporting concern about crime victimization By sex and race, United States, 2007 Question: "How often do you, yourself, worry about the following things – frequently, occasionally, rarely or never?" (Percent responding "frequently" or "occasionally")		Sex		Race		
	Total	Male	Female	White	Non-White	Black
Your home being burglarized when you are not there	47%	47%	46%	46%	50%	49%
Having your car stolen or broken into	44	40	47	42	51	50
Being a victim of terrorism	36	30	41	34	41	43
Having a school-aged child of yours physically harmed while attending school	34	33	35	28	55	62
Getting mugged	29	24	34	27	36	44
Your home being burglarized when you are there	29	21	37	27	32	27
Being attacked while driving your car	24	17	30	22	30	31
Being sexually assaulted	19	4	32	16	29	31
Being the victim of a hate crime	18	14	21	12	37	57
Getting murdered	19	16	22	15	31	40
Being assaulted or killed by a co-worker or other employee where you work	6	5	5	5	8	8

FIGURE 1-1 Fear of Crime by Type of Crime. *Source:* University of Albany. (2007). *Sourcebook of Criminal Justice Statistics.* Washington, DC: Bureau of Justice Statistics.

Analysis Box 1-1

It is curious that fear of being a victim of a terrorist attack is quite high in comparison to other the fear of crimes that are more common. Many of these crimes are serious. Fear of crime and drugs has been a leading political and media phenomenon for several decades. Why do you think that fear of a terrorist attack is so high?

other racial groups. It is interesting that there had been only a few "terrorist" attacks in the United States and only two perpetrated by terrorists from outside the country (both World Trade Center attacks), but the level of fear relative to that for a common crime was quite high. For example, although it varies from year to year, recently there have been approximately 16,000 homicides a year, a crime significantly more prevalent than terrorism, but fear of a terrorist victimization was rated much higher. Only burglary and auto theft were ranked higher on the fear index than terrorism victimization. Realistically, the probability of an American citizen being killed or injured as a result of a terrorist attack is quite low compared to all other crimes.

Sporadic and isolated terrorist events have occurred in the United States in the past, but they, for the most part, were homegrown. In the 1960s and 1970s, left-wing groups protesting the Vietnam War and various social issues were involved in a number of activities that today might be characterized as terrorist acts. These included bombings, kidnappings, bank robberies, and acts of sabotage. The most notable of these groups was the Symbionese Liberation Army, which, in addition to committing robberies and attacks on the police, kidnapped newspaper heiress Patti Hearst, who later became a part of the group and participated in several of their crimes. Most Americans viewed these acts as nothing more than common crimes. Terrorism was not part of the mental equation.

Alfred P. Murrah Federal Building after the bombing.   *Source:* FEMA http://www.fema.gov/photodata/low/1545.jpg

America and Terrorist Attacks

The most significant terrorist attack in the United States prior to the 9/11 attacks was the 1995 Oklahoma City bombing. Timothy McVeigh and Terry Nichols, using a truckload of fertilizer, blew up the Alfred P. Murrah Federal Building, killing 168 and injuring 674 people (Michel and Herbeck, 2001). This attack was perpetrated by American right-wing extremists, and although most people were appalled by the act, it did not have a lasting impact on American perceptions of safety or on the political landscape. It was viewed as an anomaly or common crime. There was no rush to increase the levels of homeland security. There was little or no public discourse about targeting or monitoring extremist groups to prevent future attacks.

HS Web link: To learn more about the Oklahoma City Bombing and Timothy McVeigh, go to *http://www. law.umkc.edu/faculty/ projects/ftrials/mcveigh/ mcveightrial.html*

Prior to 9/11, the only terrorist attack on American soil perpetrated by offenders from another country was the first World Trade Center attack on February 26, 1993. Ramzi Yousef and several coconspirators detonated a bomb made from 500 pounds of urea nitrate-hydrogen. The bomb was planted in the North Tower parking garage with the intent of destroying the North Tower and causing it to collapse or topple onto the South Tower, knocking it down (Wright, 2006). The plan did not succeed, but the explosion resulted in the deaths of six people and 1,042 were injured. Even though the 1993 attack was significant in terms of loss of life, injuries, and destruction, it had little impact on the American people or U.S. policy. Again, the terrorist act was treated as an anomaly and a crime. It was not seen as a wakeup call.

Previously, Middle Eastern terrorists had staged attacks against American interests in other parts of the world. In October 2000, al-Qaeda terrorists attacked the USS *Cole* in Aden Harbor, Yemen, while the ship made a routine fuel stop. The terrorists approached the ship in a small boat and exploded a large bomb once they were in close proximity to the ship. The explosion resulted in 17 sailors being killed and 39 others were injured. Al Qaeda had previously perpetrated two other attacks. On August 7, 1998, al-Qaeda operatives used car bombs to attack the U.S. embassies in Dar es Salaam, Tanzania, and Nairobi, Kenya. The bombings were coordinated and exploded almost simultaneously. In Dar es Salaam, 11 people were killed and 85 injured, and in Nairobi, 212 people including 12 Americans were killed and an estimated 4,000 people were injured. Osama bin Laden took credit for the bombings, stating that they were a response to the American invasion of Somali (Wright, 2006).

The most deadly terrorist attack on Americans prior to the 9/11 attacks occurred in 1988 when terrorists planted explosives on Pan Am flight 103 leaving London's Heathrow International Airport destined for New York. The Boeing 747 exploded and crashed in Lockerbie, Scotland. All 243 passengers and 16 crewmembers were killed. One hundred eighty-nine of the victims were Americans (Emerson and Duffy, 1990). Several years later, Abdel Basset Ali al-Megrahi was convicted of the crime. Al-Megrahi was a Libyan intelligence officer (Carrell, 2007). Suffering from terminal cancer, he was released from a Scottish prison and returned to Libya in August 2009. The release and his homecoming were extensively covered by the American media and caused outrage in the United States.

HS Web Link: To learn more about the Pan Am Flight 103 bombing, go to *http://history 1900s.about.com/od/1980s/a/ flight103.htm*

Historically, small, isolated groups with the wherewithal to engineer a few isolated events or attacks have initiated terrorist activities. Many of the attacks were overseas, such as the embassy bombings and the attack on the USS *Cole*; therefore, they raised little interest among the American people. Many Americans saw these events as isolated "foreign problems" and not constant threats. The 9/11 attacks, however, were prosecuted by an outside terrorist group that had international standing, support, funding, and a history of attacking Americans. As one politician summed it, historically, the United States was protected by friendly neighbors to the north and south and by oceans on the east and west (see Clarke, 2008). Until the two World Trade Center attacks and the attack on the Pentagon, Americans had not experienced an attack from an outside

World Trade Center after the 9/11 attack.   *Source:* http://www.fema.
gov/graphics/remember9/11/09.jpg

enemy since Pearl Harbor at the beginning of World War II. Previous to that, the last attack on American soil by another country occurred during the War of 1812.

The 9/11 attacks resulted in new thinking at all levels of government. President George W. Bush immediately went to war. He declared a "war on terrorism." As part of that war, he ordered America troops to invade Afghanistan and Iraq. The 9/11 attacks were said to have originated from Afghanistan, and the Bush administration advanced the idea that Saddam Hussein, the leader of Iraq, was amassing weapons of mass destruction and would provide them to terrorists to attack the United States. While engaged in overseas military operations, the public was told it faced the possibility of a "shadow enemy" within the United States. The nation had to be prepared to thwart an enemy attack on American soil, and if not successful in this endeavor, preparation needed to be made to adequately respond to the consequences of an attack. This is the essence of homeland security: preparation for an attack that could come at any time, affect any number of targets, and result in untold casualties and damage to people and national infrastructure. A climate of fear was promoted that portrayed an unprecedented level of danger coming from both external and internal enemies who could mount an attack at any time and in any place in the country.

When the 9/11 attacks occurred, America was not only vulnerable to attack, but the country was also woefully unprepared to prevent it. There previously had been a number of terrorist attacks throughout the world, including a few in the United States, but guarding against attack had been a low priority (Clarke, 2008). The 9/11 attacks and the fear in their aftermath significantly changed the national philosophy and ushered in a new strategy and American defense system. Nonetheless, the country had little foundation from which to build a national prevention strategy. The country essentially started at zero, or near zero, and was told it needed to build defenses to the possibility of asymmetric terrorist attacks.

WHAT IS HOMELAND SECURITY?

There is substantial confusion over the phrase **homeland security**. Much that has been written about homeland security focuses singularly on potential terrorist attacks. Some of the discourse, however, also examines responses to natural disasters and other catastrophes. When natural disasters and catastrophes are included within the homeland security purview, it obviously broadens the mission. While recognizing that there are definitional issues relating to homeland security operations, here we primarily focus on homeland security and terrorist attacks. To a large extent, homeland security is the protection of people and assets within national borders through preventive efforts, and when a terrorist event occurs, responding to that event to mitigate loss of life and damage. For example, the Office of Homeland Security (2007) defines *homeland security* as "a concerted national effort to prevent terrorist attacks within the United States, reduce America's vulnerability to terrorism, and minimize the damage and recover from attacks that do occur" (p. 3). The *National Strategy for Homeland Security* (Office of Homeland Security, 2002) provides a framework for accomplishing homeland security. It consists of four basic goals:

1. ***Prevent and disrupt terrorist attacks.***   To prevent and disrupt terrorist attacks, the federal government is working to deny terrorists and terrorist-related weapons and materials entry into the United States and across all international borders. Efforts will be made to disrupt terrorists' ability to operate within the United States. Moreover, efforts will be made to prevent the emergence of violent Islamic radicalization in order to deny terrorists future recruits and to defeat homegrown extremism. This goal infers both national and international interventions.
2. ***Protect the American people, critical infrastructure, and key resources.***   There are numerous targets for terrorist attacks. Efforts should be made to protect the lives and livelihoods of the American people. The threat of terrorism must be negated or reduced. Additionally, efforts should be made to mitigate the nation's vulnerability to acts of terror and the full range of human-made and natural catastrophes and to minimize the consequences of an attack or disaster should it occur.
3. ***Respond to and recover from incidents that do occur.***   To save lives, mitigate suffering, and protect property in future catastrophes, an effective, coordinated response system across all levels of government should be developed and implemented. This includes clarifying roles and responsibilities across all levels of government and the private and nonprofit sectors. The focus should be on ensuring that operational capabilities and flexibility necessary to facilitate both short-term recovery and an effective transition to long-term rebuilding and revitalization efforts are in place.
4. ***Continue to strengthen the foundation to ensure long-term success.***   To fulfill these responsibilities over the long term, principles, systems, structures, and institutions that cut across the homeland security enterprise must be evaluated and evolve as deficiencies or problems are identified (Office of Homeland Security, 2007).

The goals of homeland security as enumerated in the *National Strategy for Homeland Security* focus on prevention, protection, response, and continued strengthening of homeland security efforts. They represent a dynamic, ever-changing response to terrorist threats. Referring to our earlier discussion on homeland security definitional problems, the *National Strategy* does not focus on catastrophes or hazards per se.

HS Web Link: To read the National Strategy for Homeland Security, go to *http://www.dhs.gov/ xlibrary/assets/nat_strat_ homelandsecurity_2007.pdf*

Definitional Issues and Homeland Security

Although terrorism has been around as long as there have been tribes and nation-states, homeland security is a relatively new concept or government function in the United States. Many other countries, however, have long been concerned with homeland security. For example, it has been a national imperative and a matter of survival in Israel throughout its more than 60 years of existence, and England has dealt with terrorism for decades. In the past, the U.S. government attempted to protect its borders, but the motivation was not to keep terrorists out of the country. For the most part, border security focused on illegal drug trafficking and importation, preventing undocumented people from entering the country, ensuring that tariffs were collected on imported goods from other countries, and preventing illegal goods such as counterfeit name-brand clothing and prescription drugs from entering the United States. Little thought was given to intercepting terrorists or weapons of mass destruction. Consequently, few homeland security mechanisms were in place prior to the 9/11 attacks.

Since homeland security is relatively new, at least as an administrative imperative, it does not have a distinct operational definition. Everyone has an idea as to what it constitutes, but there is little consistency among constituent groups. Most definitions are formed by the duties and responsibilities of those charged with performing homeland security functions. They tend to define it based on organizational purposes. Obviously, if it is not well defined operationally, efforts may be off target, creating excessive expenditures, cracks or creases in coverage, and overall inefficiency. This is not only wasteful, but it also results in a more dangerous America. A uniform definition should guide the government's efforts to make the nation more secure.

Bellavita (2008) examined the homeland security literature and noted that a number of definitions have evolved over the past few years. These definitions vary based on events that are targeted by homeland security programming:

1. *Terrorism*—the prevention and response by federal, state, and local governments and by the private sector to terrorist acts and to mitigate their impact on American society.
2. *All Hazards*—concerted efforts to prevent and disrupt attacks, protect against natural and human-made hazards, and respond to and recover from such incidents.
3. *Terrorism and Catastrophes*—efforts by the Department of Homeland Security and other governmental agencies to respond to and recover from terrorist and catastrophic events that affect security.
4. *Jurisdictional Hazards*—each political jurisdiction in the United States may have different perceptions as to what constitutes homeland security. A mayor in a small city in Kansas likely will view it differently as compared to the mayor of New York City.
5. *Meta Hazards*—efforts to mitigate or prevent any social trend or threat that disrupts the American way of life, for example, global warming or shortages of petroleum.
6. *National Security*—governmental efforts to protect the sovereignty, territory, domestic population, and critical infrastructure in the United States.
7. *Security Uber Alles*—used by governmental officials to justify the curtailment of American civil liberties and personal freedom; emphasis of process over outcomes.

Although there is substantial overlap across several of these views of homeland security, a number of subtle and not so subtle differences do exist. First, many of the definitions focus on terrorism, whereas others also include catastrophes and hazards; a catastrophe is an event that has occurred, whereas hazards are conditions that may lead to a catastrophe. With the Federal Emergency Management Agency (FEMA) as part of the Department of Homeland Security (DHS), it would appear that homeland security would de facto include catastrophes and hazards. Yet, a majority of government pronouncements focus solely on terrorism, whereas others include natural and human-made hazards such as industrial accidents, tornados, earthquakes, floods, and hurricanes. Are there differences in the structure of homeland security if it is intended to respond to catastrophes and hazards?

The use of the terms *hazards* and *catastrophes* raises another issue. To what extent or magnitude does an event fit within the scope of homeland security? For example, in 2008, a bridge across the Mississippi River on Interstate 35W in Minneapolis, Minnesota, collapsed, resulting in 13 deaths and approximately 100 people injured. The bridge collapse certainly resulted in significant economic damage to the area economy as well as casualties. Was a catastrophe of this magnitude to be included within the rubric of homeland security? A terrorist attack of the same magnitude certainly would receive the attention of the homeland security apparatus. The inclusion of catastrophes and hazards in the definition of homeland security at this point is nebulous at best, and it clouds the organization of the homeland security apparatus and its operation. Even so, events such as these are routinely included within homeland security's scope, but it remains unanswered as to which criteria or demarcation should result in an event becoming a homeland security issue. Local officials obviously will have a more inclusive view of these terms as compared to officials at the federal level.

Second, the scope of homeland security, according to some authorities, has been expanded to include social trends (meta hazards) thought to affect national security. For example, in 2008, a National Intelligence Estimate (NIE) was released that detailed the impact of global warming on national security. It was forcefully argued that ultimately global warming would negatively affect national security as many unstable countries experience flooding, famine, and population migration and shifts. These changes could result in terrorist attacks and the overthrow of governments in a number of nation-states. If meta hazards are included in the definition of homeland security, what resources should be devoted to them, and which meta hazards should receive attention? It should be remembered that at the time of the NIE report, many in the Presidents Bush's administration did not believe that global warming was a real threat.

Another meta hazard deserving attention is the nation's dependence on foreign oil. In the 1970s, America faced an energy shortage. President Jimmy Carter took minor steps to abate the problem, but President Reagan promptly reversed direction and consumption of energy resources continued unabated. The energy and automotive industries ran roughshod over national interests to maximize their profits. The lack of a coherent, workable energy policy haunts us today, and the Congress and the White House continue to do little to solve the problem in the near or long-term future. It is unquestionable that energy is a national security issue, but should it fall within the rubric and organizational arrangement of homeland security, and if so, how should the homeland security apparatus be involved in mitigating the problem?

Third, to a great extent, homeland security has become operationalized as preventing and mitigating the possible use of weapons of mass destruction (WMD) with little regard for catastrophes or hazards. Although the homeland security rhetoric includes discussions of responses to hazards and catastrophes, the primary focus remains on WMDs. This is particularly problematic for the DHS since FEMA is located under its organizational umbrella, and there are far more natural disasters than terrorist attacks. For example, although President George W. Bush was particularly strong in the area of homeland security, his popularity and successes of his presidency seemed to have ended with the failed response to Hurricane Katrina and the devastation in New Orleans and the Gulf Coast. From September 11, 2001, through December 31, 2007, FEMA recorded four terrorist attacks in the United States, whereas there were 105 hurricanes, 78 tornados, and five earthquakes (see Bellavita, 2008). The sheer number of natural disasters will impact homeland security's organization and operational imperatives.

Finally, homeland security has come to be defined as a limitation on and a tool to adversely affect personal freedoms and rights. Those focusing on the expansion of government powers tend to emphasize processes over outcomes. It is reasoned that if homeland security operatives have the proper authority, then they will be able to establish security for the country. The USA PATRIOT Act gave expansive powers to the federal government in terms of spying on suspected terrorists. White House and U.S. Justice Department memoranda routinely, if not explicitly, approved the use of torture when dealing with so-called enemy combatants. Foreigners are routinely prohibited from coming to the United States, and American travelers are routinely subjected to intrusive inspections and restrictions. The average citizen seems oblivious to or unconcerned with these limitations on their freedoms. Perhaps such measures can be justified should they result in America being safer. There is little evidence, however, that draconian measures have resulted in a reduction of terrorist acts in the United States, led to the capture of any terrorists, or in any way made Americans safer. Indeed, they likely made America more vulnerable to attack as extremists view some of these practices as an attack on their faith, culture, and sovereignty. Such acts certainly have had an adverse impact on how other countries across the globe view the United States.

Homeland security definitional issues abound. The inability to properly or accurately define the scope of homeland security makes it questionable whether workable policies can be promulgated at the federal, state, or local level, creating a social and political abyss. A lack of workable policies results in incomplete or deficient homeland security actions, and it likely increases vulnerabilities to attacks, catastrophes, and hazards. In the following sections, we examine homeland security in terms of terrorist attacks while realizing that natural and human-made disasters play a key role in homeland security.

The enhancement of homeland security and response capabilities provides other benefits. The experience with Hurricane Katrina in 2005 demonstrated that the United States needs the ability to respond to a variety of natural disasters. In addition to hurricanes, there are earthquakes, tornados, fires, and floods. Enhanced homeland security allows the nation to more effectively respond to these events. The same response channels are utilized in both terrorist attacks and natural disasters. Experts contend that as a result of global warming, we will be experiencing an increase in weather events such as flooding and hurricanes.

Ghamari-Tabrizi (2006) notes that to some extent political leaders and government officials may be overemphasizing responses to terrorist attacks and should give greater consideration to

---

Analysis Box 1-2

Given that there are numerous definitions of homeland security and that homeland security is expected to respond to a wide spectrum of events, the idea of homeland security becomes somewhat confusing. The inclusion of these events changes the direction and perspective of homeland security. Does the inclusion of all the different events strengthen or weaken homeland security and why? Second, which of these definitions should dominate national policy making?

FIGURE 1-2 Evolution of Homeland Security. *Source:* Department of Homeland Security. (2010). *Quadrennial Homeland Security Review Report: A Strategic Framework for a Secure Homeland.* Washington, D.C.: Author, p. 14.

responding to natural and human-made disasters. Currently, planning emphasizes terrorist attacks with the belief that such planning will better enable the federal and state governments to respond to natural disasters. As noted earlier, natural disasters are more likely to occur and occur more frequently. Ghamari-Tabrizi suggests that perhaps homeland security should be approached from the other direction. That is, plan for natural disasters and use the resultant mechanisms to respond to terrorist attacks should they occur. This, to some extent, would result in a change in priorities and affect agencies' roles. Such a reversal of roles likely would increase agencies' ability to respond to natural disasters, and it is questionable if it would detract from the ability to respond to terrorist attacks. This shift in policy, however, is not politically acceptable since homeland security and defense against terrorism are two of today's primary political mantras.

In 2010, the *Quadrennial Homeland Security Review: Report* (DHS, 2010) was released. This report attempted to provide further direction for the homeland security apparatus. As shown in Figure 1-2, the core homeland security mission is composed of mission areas that are derived from traditional responsibilities and newer threats and evolving hazards. The *Report* emphasizes (1) preventing terrorism, (2) managing our borders, (3) enforcing immigration laws, (4) safeguarding cyberspace, and (5) resilience to disasters as the primary mission areas.

THE SCOPE OF HOMELAND SECURITY

Many people, when contemplating homeland security, focus on governmental efforts and programs implemented to protect the country from terrorists. However, referring to the goals enumerated in the *National Strategy for Homeland Security* (Office of Homeland Security, 2007), it becomes obvious that homeland security is much more encompassing and is international in scope. For example, the strategy's goals discuss activities such as the international interdiction of terrorists and weapons and the prevention of the emergence of violent radicalization around the world. Homeland security for America is seen as an international prerogative involving American agencies and agencies from a number of foreign governments. The United States has developed working and cooperative relationships with numerous countries. An example of such cooperation was the arrest by British authorities of alleged terrorists who had plotted to blow up several transatlantic flights to the United States. On August 9, 2006, authorities arrested 24 suspects who allegedly planned to use a peroxide-based explosive to destroy the planes while they were over the Atlantic Ocean. Several American governmental agencies worked with British authorities during the investigation and subsequent arrests.

Homeland security is an international, multilayered effort. Figure 1-3 provides a breakdown of the umbrella homeland security activities.

Primary Agency	Relationship Agency	Activities
American Intelligence Agencies, for example, CIA, NSA, State Dept.	Foreign Intelligence and Police Agencies	Identify international terrorist groups Identify individual terrorists in other countries Uncover and investigate possible terror plots Track terrorists as they move from one country to another Compile databases of terrorists and activities
Federal Bureau of Investigation	Foreign Intelligence and Police Agencies	Work with American intelligence agencies and foreign intelligence and police agencies in monitoring foreign terrorists that may be attempting to enter the United States Maintain case files on possible terrorists and activities in the United States Investigate terrorist acts at home and abroad Monitor suspicious persons and activities Coordinate activities with state and local police agencies
Department of Homeland Security	Foreign Governments Other Federal, State, and Local Agencies	Monitor persons entering and leaving the United States Reduce passport, visa, and other document fraud Monitor shipments of material into and out of the United States Respond to acts of terrorism to mitigate impact Coordinate with the states on protecting national infrastructure assets Secure our borders from illegal entry Coordinate port, airline, and transportation security Respond to and investigate terrorist events
State Governments (state police, civil defense, national guard, and disaster)	Department of Homeland Security	Develop and implement state homeland security plans Respond to terrorist events
Local Governments (police, fire, civil defense, paramedics, and hospitals)	State Governments and Federal Agencies	First responder to terrorist events Collect intelligence in conjunction with state agencies and FBI

FIGURE 1-3 National and International Homeland Security Activities.

As can be seen in Figure 1-3, homeland security involves a variety of agencies from across the world. It involves more than activities restricted to American soil. It also involves numerous federal, state, and local agencies. Moreover, they are involved in a variety of activities ranging from intelligence to law enforcement to responding to terrorist events. These activities result in the task of homeland security being extremely complicated and requiring a substantial amount of coordination across various governments and numerous levels of government.

Today all levels of government are immersed in homeland security. As noted earlier, numerous definitional issues surround homeland security. Nonetheless, strategies and tactics need to be developed to institute greater levels of safety for people, and a number of these efforts are underway. Strategically, these efforts have been guided by the *9/11 Commission Report* (National Commission on Terrorist Attacks Upon the United States, 2004) and the *National Strategy for Homeland Security*. The 9/11 Commission document critiqued national security efforts and established milestones or benchmarks for progress, whereas the *National Strategy for Homeland Security* provided detailed program direction. These two documents essentially provided a roadmap for future developments in homeland security.

THE 9/11 COMMISSION REPORT

The 9/11 attacks resulted in substantial turmoil in the nation's capital with the two primary political parties, interest groups, and political factions blaming one another for the security failure. It became clear that there was a need to evaluate the country's vulnerability to terrorist attacks and to determine the contributing mistakes that had been made in the past. Consequently, the **National Commission on Terrorist Attacks Upon the United States** (9/11 Commission) was created to examine past policies and make recommendation for establishing security. The bipartisan commission interviewed current and former government officials to gauge readiness. The report provided a comprehensive and detailed account of the 9/11 attacks and a fairly unbiased review of the failings of the existing national security apparatus. The *9/11 Commission Report* is especially telling since the 9/11 Commission found that several intelligence agencies had information concerning possible attacks and the attackers, but no one agency put the pieces together. These mistakes occurred at the highest level of government. For example, George Tenet, director of the CIA, stated that he briefed a number of high-level officials in the Bush White House including Secretary of State Condoleezza Rice, but no action was taken and the possible impending attacks were given little consideration (Eggen and Wright, 2006). Essentially, not only were intelligence agencies unprepared or inadequately briefed, there were vast caverns between each of the agencies and the executive branch whereby information was seldom shared or properly vetted. Indeed, the agencies tended to compete with one another as opposed to cooperating toward a shared goal—safeguarding America.

HS Web Link: To view the 9/11 Commission Report, go to *http://govinfo.library.unt.edu/9/11/report/9/11Report.*

As a result of its work, the 9/11 Commission made 41 recommendations that can be found in Chapters 12 and 13 of the report (summarized in Figure 1-4). The recommendations were divided into three broad areas: (1) homeland security and emergency response, (2) intelligence and congressional reform, and (3) foreign policy and nonproliferation (9/11 Commission, 2004).

A number of recommendations concerned homeland security. The 9/11 Commission recommended that Congress create one committee to oversee homeland security. It noted that emergency response agencies should adopt the Federal Emergency Management Agency's incident command system resulting in uniformity when responding to terrorist events. Homeland security funding to the states and local governments should be based on potential

Homeland Security and Emergency Response

Radio spectrum for first responders	F/C*
Incident command system	C
Risk-based homeland security funds	F/A*
Critical infrastructure assessment	D
Private sector preparedness	C
National strategy for transportation security	C–
Airline passenger prescreening	C
Airline passenger explosive screening	C
Checked bag and cargo screening	D
Terrorist travel strategy	I
Comprehensive screening system	C
Biometric entry-exist screening system	B
International collaboration on borders & document security	D
Standardize secure identification	B

Intelligence and Congressional Reform

Director of national intelligence	B
National Counterterrorism Center	B
FBI national security workforce	C
New missions for CIA director	I
Incentives for information sharing	D
Government-wide information sharing	D
Northern Command planning for homeland defense	B–
Full debate on PATRIOT Act	B
Privacy and civil liberties oversight board	D
Guidelines for government sharing of personal information	D
Intelligence oversight reform	D
Homeland security committees	B
Unclassified top-line intelligence budget	F
Security clearance reform	B

Foreign Policy and Nonproliferation

Maximum effort to prevent terrorist from acquiring WMD	D
Afghanistan	B
Pakistan	C+
Saudi Arabia	D
Terrorist sanctuaries	B
Coalition strategy against Islamist terrorism	C
Coalition detention standards	F
Economic policies	B+
Terrorist financing	A–
Clear U.S. message abroad	C
International broadcasting	B
Scholarship, exchange, and library programs	D
Secular education in Muslim countries	D

FIGURE 1-4 9/11 Commission Recommendation and Progress Grades.

The 9/11 Commission. *Source:* http://www.9-11commission.gov/press/photos/index.htm

targets as opposed to some other formula. It noted that the Transportation Security Administration (TSA) should make screening of passengers, cargo, and luggage for explosives a priority. Screening should be improved at the borders and at sites of critical infrastructure.

The 9/11 Commission was extremely critical of the government's intelligence apparatus. It noted that the intelligence community needed reorganization. It recommended the position of national intelligence director be created to oversee and manage national intelligence operations. Most important, the national intelligence director would ensure that the various intelligence agencies cooperated and shared information. It recommended that the director of the CIA rebuild that organization, incorporating more human intelligence capabilities and ensuring that information from all sources is analyzed more effectively, and take steps to ensure that intelligence is shared with other consumers of the information. It recommended the creation of a National Counterterrorism Center staffed by personnel from the intelligence agencies. The center would facilitate counterterrorism planning and operations as well as facilitate the flow of information among agencies. The Commission also noted that congressional oversight of intelligence was dysfunctional, which contributed to a number of problems.

The Commission made recommendations about foreign policy and nuclear nonproliferation. An examination of the recommendations regarding U.S. relationships with other countries made it obvious that the United States had to develop a new foreign policy that considered terrorism. Many pre-9/11 international relationships were predicated on cold war thinking, and economic relationships, primarily the acquisition of petroleum, drove a great deal of foreign policy. For example, the Commission recommended a reconsideration of the relationship with Saudi Arabia, noting the need for political and economic reform in that country. The Commission advised that the United States support Pakistan President Musharraf if the government was to

---

Analysis Box 1-3

The 9/11 Commission examined a number of areas relating to the 9/11 attacks on New York City and Washington, D.C. and found a number of deficiencies. The federal government has continually moved to make improvements across the board. Of the areas identified by the Commission, in your opinion, which ones are the most critical to homeland security? Which of the areas should receive the highest priority in terms of completion?

---

effectively deal with extremists in that country; Musharraf has subsequently resigned and Pakistan is close to a state of turmoil. Several recommendations centered on economic development in those countries thought of as breeding grounds for terrorists. The Commission recommended creating alliances with other countries to fight global terrorism. In other words, America needed to confront, not contribute to, the conditions that spawned terrorists.

The 9/11 Commission made numerous recommendations and provided a playbook by which to improve homeland security. Unfortunately, the federal government has been slow to implement a number of these recommendations. The Commission completed its work in August 2004. Several members of the Commission monitored the government's progress toward accomplishing the 41 goals it identified. In December 2005, 16 months after the report was issued, these members issued another report grading the federal government's success in achieving the goals (Public Discourse Project, 2005). Figure 1-4 provides a listing of the topical areas and the grades the Commission members awarded the government.

The 9/11 Commission provided a comprehensive assessment of where America was in terms of homeland security. It also provided direction and goals that were critical to safeguarding the country. As noted in Figure 1-4, the nation was slowly making progress toward some of these goals, but progress in many areas was unsatisfactory.

The Commission called for a maximum effort to protect America from WMD attacks, and as noted in Figure 1-4, the Public Discourse Project gave efforts a grade of D. In 2008, the Partnership for a Secure America, which included several members of the 9/11 Commission and the Public Discourse Project, released a follow-up report evaluating these efforts. The Partnership assigned a grade of C for efforts to prevent a nuclear attack, a B– for efforts to combat chemical terrorism, and a grade of C– for efforts to prevent a biological attack. About the same time, the Majority Staffs of the Committee on Homeland Security and the Committee on Foreign Affairs of the U.S. House of Representatives (2008) issued a report examining the U.S. government's and the DHS's progress in achieving the goals outlined by the 9/11 Commission. The committees noted a number of failures, and in several cases, congressional mandates had been missed or disregarded. Clearly, progress has been made, but much needs to be done. Efforts have not been maximized to prevent a WMD attack or secure the country.

THE NATIONAL STRATEGY FOR HOMELAND SECURITY

The 9/11 Commission was not the sole governmental body examining homeland security. The Office of Homeland Security in the White House was also examining the nation's security and plotting a roadmap for the future. In 2002, the office issued the **National Strategy for Homeland Security**. This report was subsequently updated in 2007, but the original document provided a comprehensive, detailed roadmap with many of its recommendations mirroring those of the 9/11 Commission. Today, the *National Strategy for Homeland Security* provides primary guidance for homeland security strategies and tactics.

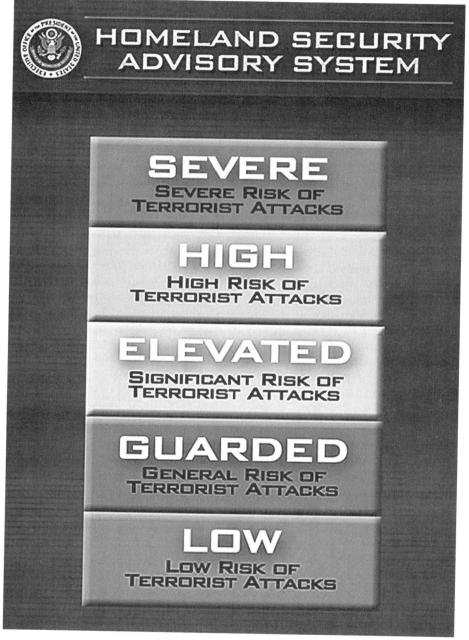

Homeland Security Advisory System.   *Source:* http://www.dhs.gov/files/programs/
Copy_of_press_release_0046.shtm

The Office of Homeland Security (2006) identified a number of critical mission areas: (1) intelligence and warning, (2) border and transportation security, (3) domestic counterterrorism, (4) protecting critical infrastructure, (5) defending against catastrophic terrorism, and (6) emergency preparedness and response. In addition, several foundational areas were identified. These areas represented supportive changes needed to facilitate homeland security. They included (1) law, (2) science and technology, (3) information sharing and systems, and (4) international cooperation.

Intelligence and Warning

Terrorists are often successful when they conduct a surprise attack. Therefore, the discovery of information about an impending attack could lead to preventative action. Alternatively, if the attack did occur, its consequences could be mitigated. Thus, it would seem imperative that the U.S. government create the capacity to gather intelligence on terrorists and terrorist organizations and use that information to prevent attacks. The *National Strategy for Homeland Security* identified a number of initiatives that should be pursued, including the following:

- *Enhance the Analytic Capabilities of the FBI.*   This included hiring more agents to enhance the collection and analysis of terror-related intelligence.
- *Build New Capabilities Through Information Analysis and Infrastructure Protection.* The DHS was tapped to increase our ability to collect information and provide guidelines to better protect our **critical infrastructure**.
- *Implement a* **Homeland Security Advisory System.**   A color-coded system was developed to advise citizens for potential terrorist-related dangers.
- *Dual Use Analysis to Prevent Attacks.*   **Dual use analysis** refers to monitoring the purchase and use of material, equipment, and chemicals that have legitimate social purposes, but that can also be used by terrorists to mount an attack. Such materials should be identified and their sale and transfer, especially in large quantities, should be monitored and, in some cases, investigated to prevent their importation to terrorist groups.
- *Employ Red Team Techniques.*   Red teams are used to conduct mock attacks on facilities to test their security systems and measure their preparedness.

HS Web Link: To read more about the Homeland Security Advisory System, go to *http://www.dhs.gov/files/ programs/Copy_of_ press_release_0046.shtm*

Border and Transportation Security

The *National Strategy* identified several objectives to enhance border and transportation security. The United States is part of a global community in which substantial amounts of commerce, imports, and exports are international. For example, the North American Free Trade Agreement (NAFTA) essentially opened the northern and southern borders to uncountable traffic. A global economy demands the efficient flow of people and goods, but at the same time, security measures need to be implemented to ensure safety particularly regarding terrorists and WMD materials. Measures identified in the strategy included the following:

- *Ensure Accountability in Border and Transportation Security.*   In the past, numerous federal and state agencies were involved in border and transportation inspection, regulation, and control resulting in little accountability. A number of federal agencies have been transferred to the DHS, resulting in all border security and inspection agencies being located in one department.
- *Create Smart Borders.*   **Smart borders** enhance our capacity to keep illegal aliens from entering our country and consist of a multilayered composition of land, sea, and air surveillance, supplemented with electronic surveillance such as radar capable of identifying people attempting to cross the border illegally.

- *Increase Security for International Shipping Containers.* Nearly half of the imports brought into the United States arrive by container, with approximately 5.7 million containers entering the country each year (Office of Homeland Security, 2002). More effective efforts should be made to screen them for WMDs and WMD materials.
- *Implement the Aviation and Transportation Act of 2001.* This law emphasizes security in a number of transportation areas including commercial airlines, interstate transportation of hazardous materials, shipping container security, critical infrastructure security, and information sharing across agencies involved in the enhancement of security.
- *Expand the role of the U.S. Coast Guard.* The U.S. Coast Guard plays a key role in national defense, maritime safety, the flow of shipping and vessels, and the protection of natural resources. The Coast Guard now has an expanded role of intercepting ships to inspect them for undocumented people, contraband, or weapons of mass destruction.
- *Reform Immigration Services.* These services were reorganized in the DHS to make them more efficient when processing the more than 7 million immigration and visa applications each year. It also allows for more focused enforcement of immigration laws. As a part of this reform, the DHS implemented the **Enhanced Border Security and Visa Entry Act.** One of the requirements of this act was that foreign visitors possess travel documents that contain biometric information such as fingerprints. This requirement helps reduce the use of forged documents by visitors and possible terrorists. Reforms have also concentrated on deporting undocumented people.

Domestic Counterterrorism

Counterterrorism is now a critical component of government action at all levels—federal, state, and local. Heretofore, local and state governments did not play much of a role in counterterrorism; these activities were seen as falling under the purview of the federal government. Today, there is a need for new programs and better coordination with federal agencies in the DHS and the FBI in the area of counterterrorism. Along these lines, federal agencies must enhance cooperation, information sharing, and tactical operations:

- *Improving Intergovernmental Law Enforcement Coordination.* A primary initiative endorsed in the *Strategy* was the expansion of the FBI's **Joint Terrorism Task Forces** (JTTFs). The JTTFs represent a coordinating body at the federal level to integrate law enforcement counterterrorism efforts. The JTTFs consist of representatives from federal law enforcement, international law enforcement, and state and local police. The JTTFs represent a strategic overarching mechanism to coordinate enforcement and intelligence activities. The JTTFs represent a systematic continuous coordination of efforts and a flow of counterterrorism information at all levels of government.
- *Facilitating the Apprehension of Potential Terrorists.* The FBI extended its efforts to provide information to local law enforcement agencies to facilitate the capture of "potential" terrorists and to enhance these investigations. The FBI expanded the information contained in the National Crime Information Center (NCIC) database to include information about terrorists and possible terrorist activities. The FBI is working with the State Department to add information about suspected terrorists and make the database available to immigration and consular officers. It is also in the process of developing a consolidated terrorist watch list. An inclusive list used by all agencies is thought to result in a more accurate listing and one that is more useful to officials involved in screening people coming into the country. The FBI is also working with foreign governments to collect information on terrorists in those countries.

Customs officers inspect seaport containers.   *Source:* http://www.
cbp.gov/xp/cgov/newsroom/multimedia/photo_gallery/archives/
2002_newsphotos/miami_insp.xml

• ***Enhancing Investigations and Prosecutions.***   Counterterrorism, the investigating of terrorists and their activities, represents one of the most complicated investigations that can be conducted. These investigations attempt to discover law violators or terrorists before they are able to perpetrate their crimes. A greater emphasis must be placed on these investigations if national security is to be achieved. This will entail closer working relationships among a variety of federal, state, and local agencies.

• ***Restructuring the FBI to Emphasize the Prevention of Terrorist Attacks.***   In the past, the FBI's effort to combat terrorism or foreign espionage was one of several offenses investigated by the agency. Today, the FBI has been reorganized to make these offenses a higher priority. It has created a number of new counterterrorism positions and has shifted hundreds of agents from criminal investigation to anti-terror investigations. It is also deploying squads of anti-terrorist experts who can assist field offices in investigations. The National Joint Terrorism Task Force headquartered at the FBI serves as the primary investigative terrorism countermeasure on American soil.

• *Targeting and Attacking Terrorist Financing.* Targeting terrorist financing and money laundering remains a high priority at the federal level. The FBI has a Financial Review Group, which is a multiagency effort to review and investigate suspicious financial transactions. Here, the FBI attempts to uncover terrorist financing mechanisms, destroy them, and arrest and prosecute people involved in these activities.

Protecting Critical Infrastructure

When most people think of homeland security, they think of protective measures implemented to keep them safe when they travel, when they are in their homes or at work, and when they shop or are involved in recreational or entertainment activities. They see the baseline of homeland security as preventing an attack in the United States. As such, the *National Strategy for Homeland Security* has identified a number of initiatives designed to provide Americans better levels of physical protection:

• *Unify Responsibility for Infrastructure Protection in the Department of Homeland Security.* The creation of the DHS consolidated responsibility for protecting national critical infrastructure and placed many of these operations within the DHS. Even though a number of federal agencies remain involved in protecting critical physical and human assets, the efforts are coordinated by the DHS.

• *Build and Maintain a Complete and Accurate Assessment of Critical Infrastructure and Key Assets.* America has numerous critical infrastructure and key assets. These assets are thought to be the targets of future terrorist attacks. The DHS must identify and assess vulnerabilities (as discussed in more detail in Chapter 3). This assessment consists of identifying protection levels required for various assets and key targets.

• *Develop Partnerships with State and Local Governments and the Private Sector.* Effective protection of critical infrastructure depends on the federal government working closely with the private sector as well as with state and local governments. The private sector controls approximately 85 percent of America's critical infrastructure (Office of Homeland Security, 2002). The firms controlling this infrastructure have the technical expertise to target harden the infrastructure, and they must initiate protective measures such as barriers, fencing, access controls, and so on to make it more difficult for possible terrorists to infiltrate infrastructure. State and local police departments are responsible for providing security to local communities, and as such, they are not only first responders to terrorist attacks, but they also deter attacks through effective policing measures. The federal government, private sector, and state and local governments provide layered protection for infrastructure.

• *Develop a National Infrastructure Protection Plan.* In 2006, the DHS released the **National Infrastructure Protection Plan** (NIPP), which is discussed in detail in Chapter 3. The NIPP provides a model to provide critical infrastructure protection. Although developed several years ago, the plan has not been fully implemented. There is a need to constantly review how well assets are being protected and how protective levels can be improved.

• *Secure Cyberspace.* The use of electronic data powers the American economy. It is the foundation for commerce. Indeed, identity fraud and other cyber crimes constitute the fastest-growing criminal problem in the United States (Allison, Schuck, and Lersch, 2005). Efforts must be made to ensure the security of these systems. In addition to the DHS and the FBI, a number of federal agencies are currently working to improve cyber security.

• *Develop Models for Effective Protective Solutions.* Protective measures must be prioritized by focusing first on those infrastructure assets that are critical to the economy and the safety of citizens. Destruction of some of these assets would have a greater negative effect as compared to the destruction of others. First, analytical models can be developed to show which assets are most critical. This assists in identifying priorities. Second, these analytical models can identify shortfalls in security systems and possibly identify points of attacks on various assets.

• *Guard Critical Infrastructure from Inside Threats.* Past history demonstrates that insiders, including current or former disgruntled employees, have participated in acts that can cripple or negatively affect parts of critical infrastructure. The Office of Homeland Security (2002) advises that in the food-processing industry, these insiders have been responsible for nearly all the previous incidents of food tampering. The DHS is now establishing protocols or standards for conducting background investigations of potential employees. Facilities should establish security zones where key operations are conducted. These security zones would be controlled areas with limited access by employees. Only those employees who have security clearances would be allowed to enter.

• *Partner with the International Community to Protect Transnational Infrastructure.* We now live in a global economy and critical infrastructure is tied to and connected with that of other countries. The North American Free Trade Agreement has opened up the northern and southern borders of the United States. The nation receives a substantial amount of electricity from Canada and natural gas and petroleum products from Mexico and South America. These resources are vital to keep commerce operating. It is advisable for the American government to work with these nations in protecting international resources and assets. Dependency on international markets results in homeland security reaching well beyond the nation's borders.

Defend Against Catastrophic Events

Homeland security involves defense against catastrophic events such as radiological, biological, chemical, and nuclear attacks. Such attacks can significantly damage America. Additionally, such defenses better enable a response to natural catastrophes such as earthquakes, floods, tornados, or hurricanes. The *National Strategy for Homeland Security* has identified several initiatives in this area:

• *Prevent Terrorist Use of Nuclear Weapons Through Better Sensors and Procedures.* Effective homeland security involves the development and deployment of more effective sensors that detect nuclear or radiological materials that could enter the country or be transported within the borders. The DHS is charged with not only the development of these sensors, but also the development of procedures to strategically deploy them to ensure maximum protection from attacks. The DHS is working with the Department of Transportation to deploy sensor systems throughout the national transportation infrastructure.

• *Detect Chemical and Biological Materials and Attacks.* Security demands the ability to detect the use of biological and chemical weapons. The Environmental Protection Agency is currently upgrading air-monitoring stations to detect biological, chemical, and radiological substances. It is also important for officials to recognize and report any suspicious diseases that may be the result of the release of WMDs. The Centers for Disease Control and Prevention (CDC) is expanding its efforts to detect and diagnose bioterrorism threats. The CDC is also working with state and local health departments to ensure early detection and notification. The DHS is working with the Department of Agriculture to establish monitoring systems for livestock. There are a number of diseases that could cripple farming industries.

• *Develop a Broad Spectrum of Vaccines, Antimicrobials, and Antidotes.* Preparation for a biological or chemical attack requires stockpiling medicines necessary to treat those who might come into contact with a biological or chemical agent. Although the country possesses the medicines needed to deal with some of the chemical or biological agents that could be used in a terrorist attack, new and more effective agents must be developed. The inventory of these agents must also be expanded. Development abilities must also be enhanced within the biotech field to increase the production of agents and to develop new more effective agents. Ample supplies must also be kept on hand should there be an attack that affects large numbers of people.

• *Implement the Select Agent Program.*   Numerous civilian medical, pharmaceutical, and medical research laboratories across the country house dangerous viruses and bacteria. These private and governmental installations work with a number of biological agents that could be used in a terrorist attack. These laboratories are working to develop antidotes to the associated diseases and to learn how these various bacteria and viruses attack human and animal hosts. These biological agents could be accidentally released or someone working in one of the labs could purposively release them. As an example, in September 2001, a number of letters laced with anthrax were mailed to several media news offices, two Democratic senators' offices, and private citizens. The attacks resulted in five deaths and 17 others became ill. The alleged perpetrator was identified six years later in 2008 (Willman, 2008). As a result of the attacks, anthrax vaccine was stockpiled and administered to a number of people who had come into contract with the spores and to people who potentially could have come into contact with them. The **Select Agent Program** attempts to regulate the shipment of biological organisms and toxins. Many of the laboratories have only minimum security. It is obvious that there must be a measure of control to prevent their release.

Emergency Preparedness and Response

One of the primary objectives of homeland security is to mitigate the consequences of any terrorist attack. This requires adequate preparation to effectively respond to an incident. The Federal Emergency Management Agency is the lead federal agency in responding to terrorist attacks and natural disasters and catastrophes. Other agencies, however, can be involved, including the military and various federal homeland security agencies. Since any attack would occur at the local level, state and local agencies must be prepared to respond. The *National Strategy for Homeland Security* outlines a number of initiatives designed to better prepare for possible catastrophes:

• *Integrate Federal Response Plans.*   The DHS is charged with developing a master plan that includes all disciplines or agencies in an all-hazards response plan (discussed in more detail in Chapter 13). The plan would guide federal action in any type of terrorist attack, natural disaster, or catastrophe. In the past, each agency had its own plan, and in totality, these plans constituted a patchwork response.

• *Create a National Incident Management System.*   As noted earlier, state and local governments and agencies are involved in any response to a catastrophe. A number of private entities, such as the Red Cross, Salvation Army, and churches, also become involved in responding to catastrophes. The DHS was charged with developing a **national incident management system** that not only coordinates activities of federal agencies, but also those of state and local agencies as well as private organizations. This is discussed in more detail in Chapter 13.

• *Improve Tactical Counterterrorism Capabilities.*   There are federal, state, and local law enforcement assets that are available to intercede in possible terrorist attacks. These assets include local SWAT teams, emergency response medical teams, and hostage negotiators. Several federal agencies also have first responders who can be dispatched to a scene. A national incident management plan is required to develop deployment protocols and incident management.

- *Seamless Communications Among All Responders.* A critical problem area identified as a result of the response to the 9/11 attacks was that first responders often could not communicate with one another because they used different radio frequencies. This resulted in a lack of coordination in their responses. Nationally, first responders must be able to communicate with one another in these situations. This **radio inoperability**, inconsistent radio frequencies among first responders, must be eliminated.
- *Prepare Health Care Providers for Catastrophic Terrorism.* A WMD attack would certainly overwhelm local hospital and health care facilities. Various federal agencies are now preparing surge capabilities to assist local assets in the event of an incident. Elements include disaster medical assistance teams and national medical response teams.
- *Augment America's Pharmaceutical and Vaccine Stockpiles.* A surge in casualties as a result of a biological, chemical, or radiological attack would result in an explosive demand for medications. The DHS in conjunction with the Department of Health and Human Services will maintain 12 strategically located sites that will contain **push packs** containing 600 tons of antibiotics, vaccines, and medical supplies. The push packs can be deployed to a site in less than 12 hours. Additionally, critical vaccines and antibiotics will continue to be stockpiled.
- *Prepare for Chemical, Biological, and Radiological Decontamination.* The DHS will require annual certification of first responder preparedness to ensure that first responders will be able to work safely in contaminated areas. A number of government grants have become available for local and state agencies to train, equip, and conduct exercises or simulations for first responders.
- *Plan for Military Support of Civil Authorities.* The military has extensive personnel, equipment, and expertise that can be utilized in a catastrophe. Additionally, the National Guard is a significant force that can be fairly quickly deployed in an emergency. The military's **Northern Command** coordinates National Guard and Reserve responses to catastrophes. This represents a unified command that can coordinate resources and respond quickly to situations.

Legal Initiatives

The new environment of homeland security assumes that there is a constant threat. In addition to program changes and the realignment of government agencies and services, the legal system is being altered to respond to these newly perceived threats. The Office of Homeland Security has identified a number of legal measures that could be incorporated as a response to terrorism:

- *Enable Critical Infrastructure Information Sharing.* The *National Strategy for Homeland Security* contains numerous recommendations advocating that governmental agencies and the private sector be able to quickly share vital information with other units of government. This is particularly important when establishing protocols for the protection of critical infrastructure. Many businesses and industries have been unwilling to share information for fear that public knowledge could provide proprietary information to competitors or could be used by the public to attack their integrity or operating processes. Some advocate that laws must allow for the communication of information to appropriate governmental agencies, but at the same time, protect its integrity and limit its dissemination. This information could be used to evaluate levels of protection and vulnerability and the location of materials that could be used as weapons of mass destruction.

• *Streamline Information Sharing Among Intelligence and Law Enforcement.*   The 9/11 Commission (2004), in the wake of the 9/11 attacks, found that intelligence information sharing and cooperation were major problems. In the past, numerous legal requirements forbid government law enforcement and intelligence agencies from sharing information. The USA PATRIOT Act addressed a number of these problems, but legal guidelines in conjunction with operational procedures must be constantly evaluated to ensure that they allow agencies to share important information. In some cases, cooperative relationships must be mandated to overcome past organizational cultures that relied on secrecy and operational independence. The director of national intelligence has the primarily responsible for ensuring cooperation.

• *Review the Authority for Military Assistance in Domestic Security.*   Federal law prohibits the military from becoming involved in civil law enforcement except when authorized by the Constitution or by Congress. For example, federal laws were changed to allow the military to become involved in drug interdiction. Should there be a terrorist attack, the military could play a key role in the response in terms of mitigation. Federal laws should be reviewed and revised when appropriate to ensure that the military can be quickly dispatched and its services utilized.

HS Web Link: To learn more about the proposed standards for state drivers' licenses, go to *http://www.dhs.gov/files/laws/gc_1172765386179.shtm*

• *Coordinate Minimum Standards for State Driver's Licenses.*   The minimum requirements to obtain a driver's license and the information contained on it vary across the 50 states; there is no standard format. Terrorists, including members of al Qaeda involved in the 9/11 attacks, have exploited the inconsistencies. The United States should have a uniform driver's license.

• *Suppress Money Laundering.*   The Money Laundering Suppression Act (P.L 103-325) urges the states to adopt uniform laws to license and regulate financial institutions. The USA PATRIOT Act encourages the states to adopt laws to control or prevent money laundering. The adoption of these laws will make it more difficult for terrorist organizations to launder their money, and it will protect law-abiding citizens engaging in legitimate financial transactions

• *Review Quarantine Authority.*   Many state quarantine laws are well over 100 years old and do not adequately address the possibility of biological attacks. The state laws should be reviewed and evaluated in terms of their ability to adequately deal with a biological attack and prevent the spread of diseases.

Science and Technology

There is a need to increase the ability to respond to the deployment of weapons of mass destruction. WMDs remain a real threat to the populace. Consequently, more effective technology needs to be developed in a number of areas. The Office of Homeland Security has identified several areas that require technological and scientific advances:

• *Develop Chemical, Biological, and Radiological Countermeasures.*   Mechanisms need to be developed that prevent terrorists from using WMD. This includes developing sensors for detecting radioactive, chemical, and biological materials that allow agents to intercede before their deployment. There is also a need to develop more effective antivirals to treat citizens who might become exposed to biological weapons. Finally, more effective tracking systems must be implemented to ensure that these materials are not stolen or otherwise lost or unaccounted for in labs or during transportation.

• *Develop Systems for Detecting Hostile Intent.*   Behavioral science must be applied more quickly to the war on terrorism. Law enforcement must have the tools to predict terrorist behavior. Perhaps there are behavioral precursors or activities that can identify those potentially involved in terrorism. Such systems would be most useful to augment airport

FBI agent using an automated fingerprint identification system.   *Source:* http://www.fbi.gov/hq/cjisd/iafis.htm

security. Similar systems could be implemented at borders to screen people as they enter the United States.

• *Apply Biometric Technology to Identification Devices.*   Fingerprints have been used as the primary means of identification for more than a century. Today, law enforcement uses DNA to investigate crimes. More effective and efficient identity devices such as retinal scanning need to be developed. Terrorists or other persons of interest who are on the FBI's watch list may obtain false documents, but an effective biometric system would result in their identification.

• *Improve the Technical Capabilities of First Responders.*   Police, fire, and emergency medical personnel are the first to respond to an attack, and some future attack could involve weapons of mass destruction. Systems must be developed that ensure first responders' safety. More effective sensing devices are needed to alert first responders to potential radiological, biological, or chemical hazards. There is a need for more effective protective gear so that first responders are not injured when responding to a WMD catastrophe. Effective decontamination equipment and treatment procedures are needed to ensure their safety. There is a need for substantial technology innovation in this area.

• *Technological Research in Homeland Security.*   The DHS needs to develop a research capacity to usher in greater innovations. As a start, there is a need to coordinate this research. The DHS must establish a bureaucracy that facilitates the timely development of innovative technology. A national laboratory should be established with the mission to facilitate research in this area, and simultaneously, the DHS should work with the national laboratories and private contractors to develop new technology.

Information Sharing and Systems

The preceding sections identified a need for substantial new programming. The DHS has approximately 180,000 employees and coordinates its operations with other federal, state, and local agencies as well as with the private sector. This massive structure requires command, control, and coordination. A number of informational needs have been identified. In the "Information Sharing and Systems" section of the *National Strategy for Homeland Security*, the Office of Homeland Security (2002) reiterates a number of these needs, including the integration of information sharing across state and local governments and within the federal government, as well as the need to improve public safety communications. Additionally, the *Strategy* suggests the adoption of common meta-data standards for electronic information relative to homeland security. One problem that currently exists is that data are kept by a number of agencies using different data management systems. This makes it extremely difficult to merge data sets to perform sophisticated analyses. It makes it difficult for one agency to pass raw data to another agency. If data are stored using consistent frameworks, it will allow for more data mining and better analyses.

There also is a need to improve the quality and dissemination of public health information. Some health records are on paper, whereas others are stored electronically. Even with electronic records, there is little consistency in terms of systems and systems integration across health care providers. There is a need to be able to analyze large numbers of records across large geographical areas to identify any trends or problems that might suggest that a biological weapon has been deployed.

International Cooperation

Terrorism does not know any boundaries. Countries on every continent have been attacked by terrorists, some struggles having been waged for decades. Indeed, it is a global war on terrorism, and success requires international cooperation. Additionally, shared borders with Mexico and Canada make it likely that terrorists will attempt to enter the United States by crossing a border. A number of initiatives have previously been examined, including the need for smart borders, combating fraudulent travel documents, and inspection and control of international shipping containers. There are other international issues that must be pursued:

• *Intensify International Law Enforcement Cooperation.* There have been terrorist attacks in Europe and elsewhere committed by the same groups that could attack the United States. American law enforcement officials must cooperate with police officials in foreign countries. This includes sharing intelligence information, information about terrorist attacks and investigations, and information about terrorist groups. This cooperation can provide a wealth of information beneficial to all countries. The sum of this information is greater than what comes from examining only the various parts or pieces of intelligence. When the United States works with other nations that have been attacked, it not only provides mitigation assistance, but intelligence information is also gained about groups with the capacity and wherewithal to mount an attack in America.

• *Help Foreign Nations Fight Terrorism.* The United States must assist foreign countries fighting terrorism, especially countries in the Middle East and Europe. The United States can provide foreign governments with training, military assistance, and equipment to help secure their borders. Government officials must identify programs that can be applied internationally and assist in their implementation.

Analysis Box 1-4

The *9/11 Commission Report* and the *National Strategy for Homeland Security* provide a roadmap for implementing homeland security. The federal government has expended a great deal of resources in implementing the various recommendations. What are the areas of overlap between these two documents? The *National Strategy* is comprehensive in addressing issues across a wide range of deficiencies. Are there any areas that you recognize that are not addressed in the *National Strategy*, but should be?

• *Review Obligations and Limitations Associated with Treaties and International Law.* The overwhelming majority of international treaties and laws limiting U.S. law enforcement and intelligence operations in foreign countries were approved under the Cold war paradigm. This new era of terrorism has substantially altered the world and international relations. This means that new methods are required to combat this new enemy. The federal government must examine existing international relationships and limitations posed by treaties and international laws. These must be changed to ensure maximum cooperation with other counties in the war on terrorism. The United States must implement mutual legal assistance treaties with other counties and work with the United Nations to enact proposals that hinder terrorist activities and facilitate international cooperation.

The previous sections provide a detailed examination of the *National Strategy for Homeland Security*. Although issued in 2002, it represents one of the most comprehensive roadmaps to homeland security, and it serves as the foundation for decisions and policy making today. It details a number of needs across the complete spectrum of homeland security requirements.

COSTS OF HOMELAND SECURITY

With increased homeland security activity come increased costs. The federal government has been running an expansive deficit for the past 10 years. The wars in Iraq and Afghanistan, the bailout of American financial institutions, and tax reforms have contributed to this burgeoning deficit. The United States now has a deficit of approximately $11 trillion. As a result of this deficit, government officials, taxpayers, and the people are concerned with the costs of governmental programming, including homeland security, especially considering other priorities such as health care, the wars in Iraq and Afghanistan, education, infrastructure, and the like.

As a result of the end of the cold war in the 1990s, the federal government reduced the amount spent on the military budget. The diminished possibility of war with the old Soviet Union reduced the need for military expenditures. This peace dividend allowed for the expansion of a number of other domestic programs. Some fear that the war on terrorism will cut into this peace dividend and negatively affect the U.S. economy. However, Hobijn and Sager (2007) examined expenditures for homeland security and found that overall spending rose from $56.0 billion in 2001 to about $99.5 billion in 2005. Federal expenditures accounted for $34.2 billion of this increase, whereas expenditures in the private sector accounted for approximately $9.4 billion. Hobijn and Sager noted that these increases had only a modest impact on the economy. They found that homeland security expenditures accounted for less than 1 percent of the gross domestic product (GDP). Nonetheless, these expenditures result in reduced funding of domestic social programs.

Figure 1-5 shows where these expenditures have occurred and also, to some degree, federal priorities. Protecting critical infrastructure received more than one-third of allocated monies, followed by border and transportation security. A substantial part of the expenditures in critical infrastructure was for airline security stimulated by the 9/11 attacks. Border security and immigration have become significant political issues, which has pushed them to the forefront in terms of funding priorities. It is noteworthy that the government has spent the least amount on intelligence and domestic counterterrorism. Current events and politics to a great extent often guide homeland security expenditure patterns.

The United States is not the only country that has substantially increased homeland security expenditures. European nations have been reorganizing their homeland security apparatuses and devoting more resources to them. Lipowicz (2008) reports that Saudi Arabia is drastically increasing its homeland security and antiterrorism allocations. Lipowicz notes that the Saudis will spend $115 billion during the next decade and will be second only to the United States in homeland security expenditures. Today, Saudi Arabia has 24 agencies devoted to homeland security with an estimated 250,000 employees. Costs will continue to rise as countries attempt to protect themselves from terrorist attacks.

Harvey (2007) notes that these expenditures are paradoxical in that higher levels of expenditures often beget ever-increasing levels of government investment. First, such expenditures represent a substantial amount of costs, public sacrifice, and political capital. He suggests that as expenditures increase there will be an increase in people's expectation of safety. When failures or attacks

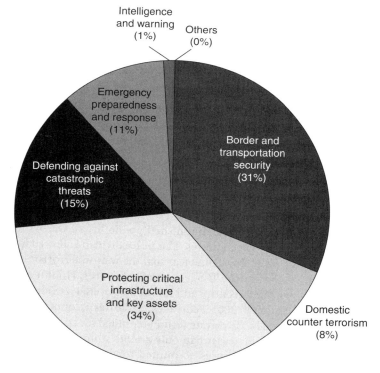

FIGURE 1-5   Homeland Security Expenditures by Area.   *Source:* U.S. Office of Management and Budget (2006).

occur, public outrage could increase. This results in greater political commitment to higher levels of protection and substantial increases in spending. In other words, failure drives expenditures. Success seldom enters the picture in terms of funding. More substantial costs can be anticipated in the future.

Indirect Costs

In addition to the direct costs associated with homeland security, there are indirect costs that are not considered when calculating the total cost of homeland security. One significant indirect cost is the increase in government spending outside the rubric of homeland security. The Northern Command, a major military command, was created to provide homeland defense on American soil, so a significant amount of its budget can be attributed to homeland security. Homeland security functions have been enhanced in many federal governmental departments, and it is likely that their costs are not included in any calculations of homeland security costs.

Other indirect costs should be considered. First, security costs at airports have increased because of Transportation Security Administration operations. It has also resulted in numerous passenger delays and additional costs. People likely are spending thousands, if not millions, of hours at airports, which results in a loss of productivity. Second, the government has increased restrictions on international travel, making it difficult for many businesspeople to travel to the United States, and in some cases, some of these people are not allowed to enter. Given the global economy, these restrictions negatively affect business arrangements and productivity. Third, the government is more closely screening imports coming into the United States for weapons of mass destruction. This results in delays and substantially increased transportation costs. The cost of security produces numerous indirect costs the affect the economy.

Summary

Homeland security is now a critical political and practical part of the American landscape. The 9/11 attacks resulted in substantial changes in a number of areas. Homeland security has become a way of life, and this is unlikely to change anytime in the foreseeable future.

This chapter provided an introduction to homeland security and the definitional issues surrounding it. Although most people see homeland security as a defense against terrorist attacks, the homeland security apparatus is concerned with catastrophes and future hazards as well as terrorist attacks. Homeland security requires a response to a host of disasters, including terrorist attacks. The fact that disasters such as hurricanes and earthquakes are included in the response protocols complicates the direction and organization of homeland security. The all-hazards approach may complicate effective responses to terrorism.

After the 9/11 attacks, the United States had little in terms of government organization or enterprise to counter future attacks. The formation of homeland security essentially started at zero, and bureaucracies were developed that could effectively respond to threats. Essentially, the Department of Homeland Security was created and became the lead agency in preparing for terrorist events. However, since this was a relatively new phenomenon, there was no foundation for organizing homeland security efforts. Two documents have served as roadmaps for homeland security, the *9/11 Commission Report* and the *National Strategy for Homeland Security*. The *9/11 Commission Report* basically provided an assessment of the problems with security arrangements at the time and made a number of suggestions for improvement. The *National Strategy for Homeland Security*, on the other hand, provided a detailed map as to how to proceed with establishing security. It was comprehensive and detailed a number of critical areas requiring immediate and long-term development. Today, the *National Strategy* document serves as the primary policy guide for homeland security. Numerous federal agencies are engaged in fulfilling the recommendations it enumerated.

Discussion Questions

1. An examination of fear of crime studies shows that fear of being a victim of a terrorist attack is high, higher than that of more common crimes and homicide. Given the limited number of terrorist attacks on American soil and the limited number of deaths and injuries, why does fear of a terrorist attack rank so high?

2. There is a debate over what problems should be covered or addressed by homeland security. How does this debate affect the organization and operations of homeland security?

3. The *9/11 Commission Report* and the *National Strategy for Homeland Security* form the foundation for homeland security. Compare and contrast these two documents in terms of scope and direction.

4. The Homeland Security Advisory System has been used to alert Americans about terrorist activities and impending attacks. How effective is this system and why?

5. The *National Strategy for Homeland Security* addresses an expansive array of homeland security activities and objectives. Which three areas do you believe are the most critical? Why?

6. In 2009, the world was threatened by a swine flu (N1H1) pandemic. Did homeland security efforts improve our capacity to deal with the threat? How?

7. Describe why it is important for state and local officials to be involved in homeland security.

References

Allison, S., A. Schuck, and K. Lersch. (2005). "Exploring the crime of identity theft: Prevalence, clearance rates, and victim/offender characteristics." *Journal of Criminal Justice*, 33: 19–29.

Bellavita, C. (2008). "Changing homeland security: What is homeland security?" *Homeland Security Affairs*, 4(2): 1–30.

Carrell, S. (2007). "Lybian jailed over Lockerbie wins right to appeal." *The Guardian* (June 29). http://www.guardian.co.uk/uk/2007/jun/29/lockerbie.scotland (Accessed August 7, 2008).

Clarke, R. (2008). *Your Government Failed You: Breaking the Cycle of National Security Disasters*. New York: HarperCollins.

Department of Homeland Security. (2010). *Quadrennial Homeland Security Review Report: A Strategic Framework for a Security Homeland*. Washington, D.C.: Author.

Department of Homeland Security. (2008). *National Response Framework*. Washington, D.C.: Author.

Eggen, D. and R. Wright. (2006). "Tenet recalled warning Rice." The Washington Post, http://www.washingtonpost.com/wp-dyn/content/article/2006/10/02/AR2006100200187.html

Emerson, S. and B. Duffy. (1990). *The Fall of Pan Am 103: Inside the Lockerbie Investigation*. New York: Putnum.

Ghamari-Tabrizi, S. (2006). "Lethal fantasies: With its eye on the 'universal adversary,' homeland security catastrophes." *Bulletin of the Atomic Scientists*, 62(1): 20–22.

Harvey, F. (2007). "The homeland security dilemma: Imagination, failure, and the escalating costs of perfecting security." *Canadian Journal of Political Science*, 40: 283–316.

Hobijn, B. and E. Sager. (2007). "What has homeland security cost? An assessment: 2001–2005." *Current Issues in Economics and Finance*, 13(2): 1–7.

Lipowicz, A. (2008). "Saudi homeland security costs spike." *WashingtonTechnology*. http://www.washingtontechnology.com/online/1_1/32891-1.html (Accessed August 6, 2008).

Michel, L. and D. Herbeck. (2001). *American Terrorist: Timothy McVeigh and the Oklahoma City Bombing*. New York: Regan Books.

National Commission on Terrorist Attacks Upon the United States. (2004). *The 9/11 Commission Report*. New York: W.W. Norton.

Office of Homeland Security. (2007). *The National Strategy for Homeland Security*. Washington, D.C.: Author.

Office of Homeland Security. (2006). *National Infrastructure Protection Plan*. Washington, D.C.: Author.

Office of Homeland Security. (2002). *The National Strategy for Homeland Security*. Washington, D.C.: Author.

Public Discourse Project. (2005). *The 9/11 Commission Report: The Unfinished Agenda*. Washington, D.C.: Author. http://www.9-11pdp.org/ (Accessed January 6, 2011).

University of Albany. (2007). *Sourcebook of Criminal Justice Statistics*. Washington, D.C.: Bureau of Justice Statistics. http://www.albany.edu/sourcebook/pdf/t239.pdf (Accessed September 19, 2008).

U.S. House of Representatives Majority Staffs of the Committee on Homeland Security and Committee on Foreign Affairs. (2008). *Wasted Lessons of 9/11: How the Bush Administration Has Ignored the Law and Squandered Its Opportunities to Make Our Country Safer*. Washington, D.C.: Author.

Willman, D. (2008). "Suspect stood to gain from anthrax panic." *Los Angeles Times* (August 2), pp. A1, A10.

Wright, L. (2006). *Looming Tower*. New York: Knopf.

The Homeland Security Apparatus

LEARNING OBJECTIVES

1. Analyze the development of homeland security in the United States.
2. Understand the Department of Homeland Security's organization.
3. Know the various agencies within the Department of Homeland Security.
4. Know the roles of agencies outside the Department of Homeland Security.
5. Understand the role of the Department of Defense in homeland security and defense.
6. Discuss the role of state governments in homeland security.

KEY TERMS

Department of Homeland Security

Office of Homeland Security in the White House

Mission distortion

Transportation Security Administration

Known Shippers Program

Federal Air Marshal Program

Customs and Border Protection

U.S. Citizenship and Immigration Services

Immigration and Customs Enforcement

Office of Federal Protective Services

Office of Detention and Removal

Office of Investigations

U.S. Secret Service

Uniform Division

U.S. Coast Guard

Federal Emergency Management Agency

Federal Law Enforcement Training Center

Science and Technology Directorate

Department of Defense

Homeland defense

NORTHCOM

Chemical and Biological Rapid Response Team

National Guard Weapons of Mass Destruction–Civil Support Teams

INTRODUCTION

Since 2001, homeland security has become a significant governmental and private sector enterprise. New governmental bureaucracies were created with the primary mission of providing homeland security. The **Department of Homeland Security** (DHS) is the primary federal agency changed with providing security, although other federal departments are involved, and states have developed agencies charged with implementing homeland security programs. This chapter examines the homeland security apparatus. It discusses the federal agencies and some of the state initiatives designed to effectuate homeland security. The DHS serves as the hub of operations or the primary point organization for homeland security.

HS Web Link: To learn more about the Department of Homeland Security, go to *http://www. dhs.gov/index.shtm*

Department of Homeland Security

Before the creation of the DHS, homeland security was coordinated by the **Office of Homeland Security in the White House**. It was headed by Tom Ridge, whose title was assistant to the president for homeland security. When the DHS was created, Ridge transitioned into the newly created cabinet position. The DHS was created as a result of the Homeland Security Act of 2002 (Public Law 107-296) and was officially inaugurated on March 1, 2003 (DHS, 2008). The DHS was given the responsibility to be the lead federal agency in securing the country. Although at first glance this appears to have been a simple, straightforward task, it was in reality very complicated, involving a matrix of programs and agencies. The creation of DHS was accomplished by reorganizing a number of departments in the federal government. More than 100 units and bureaus from other departments were transferred to the new DHS. After its creation, the DHS became the third largest department in the federal government with more than180,000 employees (DHS, 2008). Only the Departments of Defense and Veterans' Affairs are larger. It represented the largest federal government reorganization since President Harry Truman merged the various branches of the military into the Department of Defense. Figure 2-1 provides a listing of the units and agencies that were shifted to the newly organized DHS.

As noted in Figure 2-1, a number of agencies and subagencies were reorganized in the DHS. Independent agencies such as the U.S. Coast Guard and the U.S. Secret Service were placed under the DHS umbrella. Several agencies from the Departments of Energy, Justice, and Treasury were moved to the DHS. The Federal Emergency Management Agency (FEMA), which had been independent, was consumed within the DHS. A review of the agencies moved to the DHS demonstrates the complexity and comprehensiveness of the consolidation.

POLITICAL CONSIDERATIONS IN THE CREATION OF THE DEPARTMENT OF HOMELAND SECURITY

The Department of Homeland Security was created in 2003 with much fanfare from Congress and the White House. Its creation indicated to the American populace that the federal government was making a substantial effort to increase security. After the 9/11 attacks, fear of terrorist attacks dominated public opinion. People visually and emotionally witnessed the destruction of the World Trade Center Towers and part of the Pentagon. This moved national security to the forefront of people's thinking and fears. The dramatic nature of the event and the devastation of the attacks ensured that there would be a response.

However, the creation of the DHS was, in the minds of many politicians and bureaucrats, not an effective solution to the problem of homeland security. Many believed that adequate

Original Agency (Department)	Current Agency/Office
The U.S. Customs Service (Treasury)	U.S. Customs and Border Protection–inspection, border and ports of entry responsibilities
	U.S. Immigration and Customs Enforcement–customs law enforcement responsibilities
The Immigration and Naturalization Service (Justice)	U.S. Customs and Border Protection—inspection functions and the U.S. Border Patrol
	U.S. Immigration and Customs Enforcement—immigration law enforcement: detention and removal, intelligence, and investigations
	U.S. Citizenship and Immigration Services—adjudications and benefits programs
The Federal Protective Service	U.S. Immigration and Customs Enforcement
The Transportation Security Administration (Transportation)	Transportation Security Administration
Federal Law Enforcement Training Center (Treasury)	Federal Law Enforcement Training Center
Animal and Plant Health Inspection Service (part) (Agriculture)	U.S. Customs and Border Protection—agricultural imports and entry inspections
Office for Domestic Preparedness (Justice)	Responsibilities distributed within FEMA
The Federal Emergency Management Agency (FEMA)	Federal Emergency Management Agency
Strategic National Stockpile and the National Disaster Medical System (HHS)	Returned to Health and Human Services, July 2004
Nuclear Incident Response Team (Energy)	Responsibilities distributed within FEMA
Domestic Emergency Support Teams (Justice)	Responsibilities distributed within FEMA
National Domestic Preparedness Office (FBI)	Responsibilities distributed within FEMA
CBRN Countermeasures Programs (Energy)	Science & Technology Directorate
Environmental Measurements Laboratory (Energy)	Science & Technology Directorate
National BW Defense Analysis Center (Defense)	Science & Technology Directorate
Plum Island Animal Disease Center (Agriculture)	Science & Technology Directorate
Federal Computer Incident Response Center (GSA)	US-CERT, Office of Cybersecurity and Communications in the National Programs and Preparedness Directorate
National Communications System (Defense)	Office of Cybersecurity and Communications in the National Programs and Preparedness Directorate
National Infrastructure Protection Center (FBI)	Dispersed throughout the department, including Office of Operations Coordination and Office of Infrastructure Protection
Energy Security and Assurance Program (Energy)	Integrated into the Office of Infrastructure Protection
U.S. Coast Guard	U.S. Coast Guard
U.S. Secret Service	U.S. Secret Service

FIGURE 2-1   Agencies Transferred to the DHS.

governmental apparatuses were in place, but they lacked proper coordination (Clarke, 2008). Coordination would provide better results as compared to developing a new bureaucracy. Indeed, coordination had existed across various departments when dealing with a number of significant problems in the past. For example, the National Security Council has been responsible for coordinating national security efforts across a variety of agencies and across federal government departments for approximately 50 years.

In actuality, the DHS's creation had its impetus from Connecticut Senator Joe Lieberman. Initially, President George W. Bush's administration was opposed to the creation of such a department. Lieberman, a Democrat at the time, proposed the department's creation in the U.S. Senate. When the proposal began to get widespread support and traction from Democrats and Republicans alike, the White House offered its own version to prevent the Democrats from gaining political mileage or advantage in the homeland security political arena (Clarke, 2008). The creation of the DHS was initially problematic, as it required substantial time, energy, and resources being spent on developing a bureaucracy as opposed to dealing directly with homeland security problems. Moreover, the reorganization did not completely deal with the coordination problem. Even though a number of agencies were moved to the DHS, numerous agencies outside it retained homeland security responsibilities, for example, the Federal Bureau of Investigation or the Central Intelligence Agency, but were not merged into the new department. Further, the DHS included a number of agencies with dissimilar missions, for example, FEMA, Customs, and the Coast Guard, complicating coordination and contributing to **mission distortion** within the DHS.

Richard Clarke (2008), who held a number of high-level positions in intelligence in the State and Defense Departments, perhaps best summarized the creation of the new DHS:

> The creation and subsequent dysfunction of the Department of Homeland Security is revealing of many of the reasons why the U.S. government so often fails at national security. For several years, over two administrations of different political parties, people who were engaged in federal management and national security tried to resist a politically motivated drive to be seen to "do something" about security through bureaucratic reorganization. When, after 9/11, that drive became irresistible, the chief criteria in designing and managing the major new government enterprise were appearance and politics, not problem solving. The largest federal department created in more than fifty years was slammed together with insufficient resources and regulatory powers. Worse yet, far from recruiting the best managers that government and industry could assemble, it was laced with political hacks and contractors to a degree never seen in any federal agency. (p. 204)

Clarke is not alone in his criticism. Shapiro (2007) argues,

> Policy discussions of homeland security issues are driven not by rigorous analysis but by fear, perceptions of past mistakes, pork-barrel politics, and insistence on an invulnerability that cannot possibly be achieved. It is time for a more analytic, threat-based approach, grounded in concepts of sufficiency, prioritization, and measured effectiveness... ...[F]ive years into the apparently endless war on terrorism, homeland security should evolve from a set of emergency measures into a permanent field of important government policy that, like any other, must justify its allocation of taxpayer funds through solid analysis. (pp. 1–2)

White House Chief of Staff Andrew Card and White House Personnel Chief Clay Johnson were the principal engineers behind the Bush administration's new DHS. Clarke (2008) notes that they had four interests as they created the new bureaucracy. First, they wanted to cut federal expenditures. Thus, the budget for the new DHS was less than the combined budgets for the agencies that were transferred into it, which substantially weakened the department's ability to fulfill its mandates. Second, they emphasized political appointments in the department as opposed to recruiting career experts. Third, they sought to reduce the role of organized federal labor groups, so the enabling legislation prohibited unionization. Finally, they wanted to ensure that the new bureaucracy was created as quickly as possible, which eliminated requisite planning and criticism from bureaucrats who could identify problems or deficiencies with the new organizational plan. In essence, politics and ideology had a significant impact on the department during its early stages of development, which resulted in a number of problems in later years.

Kamarck (2007) has identified a number of issues that question the effectiveness of today's DHS. First, as of May 2007, one-quarter of the executive positions in the department remained vacant, as did more than one-third of the policy-making positions. She also advises that the bureaucracy is too cumbersome and expansive and that some functions should be moved to other departments. For example, should FEMA be a part of the DHS? Perrow (2002) argues that homeland security has resulted in FEMA's budget being diverted from its original mission, making the agency less responsive and effective. Prior to the creation of the DHS, FEMA was an independent agency. The merging of border protection agencies with emergency response agencies has resulted in coordination and mission diffusion problems and perhaps has weakened both agencies. The DHS should focus on border protection and as a conduit for integrating and sharing homeland security intelligence with state and local governments and the private sector. Although well intended, the merging of many agencies into an expansive DHS certainly has resulted in many control, coordination, and management problems. In 2006, the Office of Personnel and Management performed a job satisfaction survey for all the federal agencies and found that job satisfaction was lowest in the DHS (Chan, cited in Kamarck, 2007).

Since its inception, a number of problems have plagued the DHS, which is typical when new agencies are created or when there is a massive reorganization. The following sections discuss some of those problems.

White House and Congressional Oversight

Homeland security remains a prominent political issue, and as such, it draws the interest of politicians. Oftentimes, political interests overrode organizational imperative. Politicians were all too often more interested in managing appearances as opposed to solving real problems. It would seem that the secretary of the Department of Homeland Security would have exclusive domain over its operation and long-term objectives. However, the White House and Congress have substantial oversight responsibilities and exert substantial influence and control over the DHS. The White House is responsible for promulgating a national strategy regarding homeland security. This responsibility resides with the White House since a coherent strategy would include numerous other federal departments as well as the DHS. Obviously, the DHS would be involved in policy development, but final authority rests with the White House. Wermuth (2005) notes that little progress has been made on developing a national strategy. Furthermore, the executive branch has been more interested in tinkering with the day-to-day operations of the DHS as opposed to policy development. A coherent strategy is necessary for short- and long-range planning.

Congress has fared no better in terms of providing guidance to the DHS. Some 80 committees and subcommittees in the House and Senate have some degree of oversight of homeland security. This diffusion results in inconsistency and a general lack of cohesiveness in terms of congressional oversight, appropriations, and the submission and passage of important homeland security–related legislation. Given the number of congressional committees the secretary reports to, it is surprising that the secretary has time to manage the department. It would make more sense for one committee in the House and Senate to have this oversight responsibility, but too often committee chairs and members are unwilling to defer their authority. Authority over some aspect of homeland security always plays well with their electorates.

This problem has been recognized by a number of authorities. For example, the *National Strategy for Homeland Security* (Office of the White House, 2002) recommended that the secretary have more latitude in reorganizing the DHS, and Kamarck (2007) recommended that congressional oversight be consolidated into one committee in the House of Representatives and one committee in the Senate. Given the fluid nature of terrorism and the department's many and varied range of responsibilities, it is obvious that the DHS, as the primary response mechanism, should have increased flexibility. However, the political tethers binding the department have not been loosened. This remains a formable problem.

Agency Confusion and Mission Distortion

The manner in which the DHS was created led to a number of problems not only for the department, but also for the individual agencies subsumed within it. In terms of the DHS, its rapid organization and deployment resulted in substantial confusion. At first glance, it would appear that the DHS has proprietary responsibility for homeland security. However, a number of agencies outside the DHS have significant security roles and responsibilities, for example, agencies within the Department of Defense, the Federal Bureau of Investigation, the Treasury Department, and the Energy Department to name a few. This diffusion of interests ultimately results in coordination and command issues (see Wermuth, 2005). An event or case may involve confusion over jurisdiction and the appropriate application of law.

At the same time, the reorganization resulted in agencies acquiring new responsibilities generally without a reduction in old mandates. This resulted in **mission distortion** or confusion regarding individual agencies' missions and priorities. For example, the U.S. Customs and Border Protection (CBP) is charged with interdicting terrorists entering the United States. Additionally, the agency is responsible for protecting American agriculture from harmful pests and agricultural diseases, stemming the flow of drugs and other contraband, and collecting import duties. These duties are wide ranging and asymmetric. How should the CBP's duties be prioritized? How do the antiterrorism duties fit within its organizational structure and operations? These became critical questions and resulted in substantial bureaucratic confusion within many of the agencies in the DHS. Homeland security duties, for the most part, were simply added to the agencies' original or traditional responsibilities. The creation of the DHS did not result in clear and tight operational procedures to guide lower-level managers and supervisors.

Agency managers were not experienced with or knowledgeable about the new mandates, which reduced the agencies' ability to quickly get off the ground. Many of these managers had a steep learning curve, even those who had previously worked with the old agencies. Also, these managers, generally as a result of their lack of experience, did not have the capacity to "think outside the box." A new department and new problems require a degree of nonconformity and innovative thinking (see Bellavita, 2005). The terrorism problem could not be effectively countered using tactics that were left over from the cold war. Success required new thinking and new strategies. As an

Analysis Box 2-1

The previous discussion shows that politics were heavily involved in the creation of the Department of Homeland Security. It also shows that during its inception, there were numerous organizational and operational problems.

Of course, this is consistent with many governmental endeavors. Given the political history of the DHS and the current political atmosphere in the United States, do you believe that we have improved homeland security? Why?

example, successes were not experienced in Iraq until a troop surge was initiated, tacticians began to use more counterinsurgency tactics, and coalitions with various tribes or groups were forged.

The initial development of the DHS resulted in numerous problems, and this occurs when a new agency is developed or undergoes significant changes. We have made progress with regard to a number of these problems, but the executive branch should continue to focus on improving the DHS's overall operating effectiveness.

THE STRUCTURE OF THE DEPARTMENT OF HOMELAND SECURITY

As suggested, the DHS was created by hobbling together a number of agencies from throughout the federal government into the new department. Additionally, a number of other agencies were added as new responsibilities were identified. Complex organizations are constantly evolving. Working relationships among agencies must be refined, and in some cases, agencies must be reorganized. To a great extent, the DHS is a work in progress. As homeland security matures as a federal imperative, the DHS will certainly continue to change. It is a natural part of organizational evolution, and if change does not occur, most likely the DHS will in some regards become less effective in pursuing its various missions.

Figure 2-2 provides an organizational chart depicting those agencies in the DHS and their reporting chain of command. As noted, the DHS has approximately 180,000 employees dispersed across a number of agencies.

The DHS is a cabinet-level agency within the executive branch. It is headed by a secretary, who reports to the president. The department contains a number of support units as well as operational units that generally are headed by an assistant secretary or a director. Some of the DHS support units include Policy, General Counsel, Legislative Affairs, Public Relations, Management, Operations Coordination, and Civil Rights & Civil Liberties Officer. These offices work with other federal agencies, the Congress, the White House, and the public in terms of planning and advocating for the department.

The following sections provide an overview of some of the operational units within the DHS. Notice that there are a number of agencies that in their aggregate have a wide range of responsibilities and activities.

Transportation Security Administration

The **Transportation Security Administration** (TSA) was moved to the DHS from the Department of Transportation. When most people think of the TSA, they focus on airport security. However, the TSA's mandate is much broader. The primary responsibilities of the TSA are to protect the nation's entire transportation system, including aviation, waterways, rail, highways, public transportation, and pipelines. Thus, the agency has a substantial responsibility, with aviation being only a small portion of the overall mandate.

HS Web Link: To learn more about the TSA, visit *http://www.tsa.gov/*

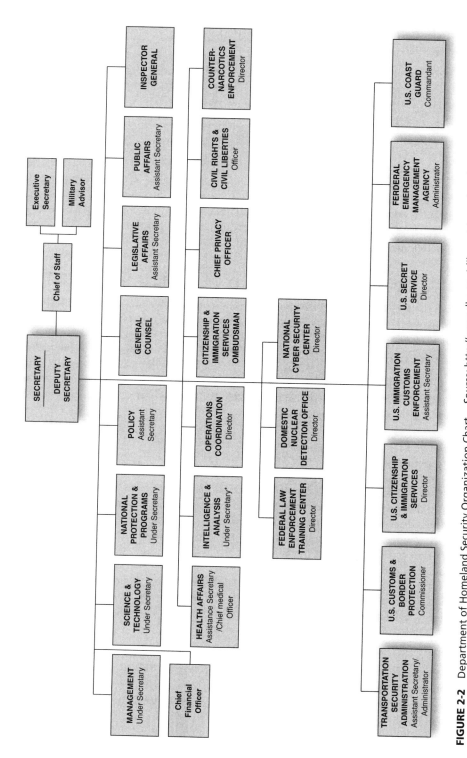

FIGURE 2-2 Department of Homeland Security Organization Chart. *Source:* http://www.dhs.gov/xlibrary/photos/orgchart-web-520.png

The TSA attempts to ensure freedom of movement for people and commerce. The most visible members of the TSA are in airports. There are 450 airports from Guam to Alaska employing about 50,000 screeners (GAO, 2003). TSA air travel responsibilities include the screening of luggage and passengers for destructive devices. The TSA deploys several systems to accomplish this monumental task. First, it uses explosive detection machines when screening checked luggage. These machines determine if there are trace explosives in the luggage or on the luggage. Second, carry-on baggage is screened in a similar manner. TSA officers collect samples of residue and analyze them for trace explosive materials. The agency is deploying newer machines that blow air onto passengers and the air is collected and analyzed for explosive materials. TSA officers also use bomb-sniffing dogs. There are about 450 dog-sniffing teams stationed in 80 different airports (TSA, 2008).

The TSA is in the process of upgrading its technology for screening passengers. The agency is experimenting with backsider technology that projects X-ray beams over the body to create a reflection of the body displayed on the monitor, as well as millimeter wave technology that bounces harmless electromagnetic waves off the body to create a black-and-white three-dimensional image (TSA, 2010a). These technologies are controversial since they display a passenger's body.

The TSA has concentrated on air travel security, but the technology is beginning to be deployed in other travel sectors. For example, the TSA is using some of its bomb-sniffing dogs in subways. This is a critical move given the number of people who travel using mass transit systems and because in other countries terrorists have detonated bombs in subways and on buses and trains (e.g., in Great Britain and Spain). The TSA has teamed with the New York City Transit Authority to test passive millimeter wave technology. The system screens for explosives as passengers enter the Staten Island ferry.

After the 9/11 attacks, new regulations allowed pilots to carry firearms in the cockpit of their aircraft. The TSA is responsible for training pilots on how to use firearms. All flight crew members are provided with self-defense training to improve their ability to control situations on aircraft. A substantial amount of cargo is transported by air, much of which is on passenger planes. The TSA monitors and regulates cargo that is being shipped by air, and the agency audits shippers to ensure that only approved cargo is transported. The **Known Shippers Program** ensures that only cargo from approved or known shippers can be transported in certain instances. It is planned that in the future, the TSA will X-ray all cargo that is shipped by air.

The TSA has made efforts to secure hazardous materials and explosives that are transported on the nation's highways. Drivers who transport such materials now must obtain a hazardous materials endorsement (HME) for their commercial driver's license. The TSA conducts background investigations prior to the issuing of the HMEs. In 2006, the TSA began to require similar background checks for drivers from Canada and Mexico who transported dangerous materials into the United States. To date, TSA has had more than 200,000 new applications for HMEs and has conducted checks on approximately 3 million applicants since the program was implemented (TSA, 2008).

One of the law enforcement components within the TSA is the **Federal Air Marshal Program**, which deploys armed officers on civilian aircraft whose purpose is to intervene in possible hijackings or other terrorist activities. When the 9/11 attacks occurred, there were only 50 air marshals, and they were assigned primarily to international flights. Even though the program has been expanded, only about 1 percent of the 28,000 daily flights have an air marshal onboard (TSA, 2010b). The air marshals also work with local law enforcement, the Federal Bureau of Investigation, and other federal agencies coordinating antiterrorism activities.

TSA officers screen passengers prior to boarding aircraft.   *Source:* http://www.tsa.gov/graphics/images/press/houston_reopens4.jpg

U.S. Customs and Border Protection

Customs was created in 1789 to collect tariffs on goods imported into the United States. The tariffs collected by Customs essentially supported the federal government for more than 125 years and funded a substantial amount of the country's early infrastructure. **Customs and Border Protection** (CBP) was organized by merging inspectors from the Agriculture Quarantine Inspection Program, Immigration and Naturalization Services, Inspection Services, Border Patrol, and the Customs Service. Today, CBP has more than 40,000 employees. According to the CBP, the primary law enforcement responsibilities for the agency are (1) apprehending criminals and others who illegally attempt to enter the United States, (2) seizing illegal drugs and other contraband, and (3) protecting U.S. agriculture from harmful pests and diseases. The three areas of focus include border protection and port security. The agency has more than 40,000 employees with 21,000 officers, 20,000 border patrol agents, 2,400 agriculture specialists, and 1,200 air and marine officers (CBP, 2010.)

HS Web Link: To learn more about the Customs and Border Protection, go to *http://www.cbp.gov/*

The national debate over undocumented immigration has resulted in additional personnel and the development of new technology to help secure the country's borders. A primary mission of the CBP is to prevent terrorists and terrorist weapons, including weapons of mass destruction, from entering the United States. Included in this mission is the apprehension of undocumented immigrants and smugglers. Since 1994, the agency has made more than 15.6 million apprehensions of people attempting to enter the United States illegally. The CBP is also involved in seizing drugs coming into the United States across the borders.

The CBP is responsible for patrolling more than 7,000 miles of the Canadian and 2,000 miles of the Mexican borders. The most substantial obstacle is the terrain, especially along the Mexican border, which is where the largest number of smuggling and illegal alien activities occurs. The border is primary desert and mountains, which makes patrolling and observation extremely difficult. The CBP uses air and vehicular patrols. In some cases, all-terrain vehicles and horses are used. The patrols look for illegal aliens or evidence that they are using a particular route. In some cases, fences have been constructed in areas that have high traffic. The fences alter illegal immigrants' routes and reduce the amount of area that must be constantly patrolled. A number of virtual fences are being constructed to stem the tide of people crossing the borders. These virtual fences are equipped with radar and motion detection devices, which alert officers when crossings are being attempted. Additionally, the CBP has checkpoints where people crossing the border are stopped to ensure that they have proper documentation. Automobiles, buses, freight trains, and marine craft entering the United States are checked. It is anticipated that over the next several years, the resources and activities of the CBP will increase substantially as the United States attempts to provide greater security for its borders.

CBP officers are also responsible for air and sea ports. Ports not only include the primary sea ports, but also points of entry for international aircraft coming into the United States. With the expanded emphasis on preventing terrorists from entering the United States, the CBP has taken a more proactive role in screening people and cargo entering the country. This includes checking the documentation of people arriving and leaving the United States, including passports and visas, and checking cargo for contraband.

CBP agents check unloaded cargo.   *Source:* http://www.cbp.gov/xp/cgov/newsroom/multimedia/
photo_gallery/afc/field_ops/inspectors_seaports/cs_photo06.xml

The CBP (2008) reports that on a typical day during 2006, officers were involved in the following activities:

Processed—

- 1.1 million passengers and pedestrians, including 680,000 undocumented people
- 70,900 truck, rail, and sea containers
- 240,737 incoming international air passengers
- 71,151 passengers/crew arriving by ship
- 327,042 incoming privately owned vehicles
- 85,300 shipments of goods approved for entry
- $84,400,000 in fees, duties, and tariffs

Executed—

- 63 arrests at ports of entry
- 2,984 apprehensions between ports for illegal entry

Seized—

- 1,769 pounds of narcotics in 63 seizures at ports of entry
- 3,788 pounds of narcotics in 20 seizures between ports of entry
- $157,800 in undeclared or illicit currency
- $646,900 worth of fraudulent commercial merchandise at ports of entry
- 4,462 prohibited meat, plant materials, or animal products, including 147 agricultural pests at ports of entry

Refused entry of—

- 574 noncitizens at ports of entry
- 63 criminal attempting to enter the United States

Intercepted—

- 71 fraudulent documents
- 20 smuggled people
- 1.5 travelers for terrorism/national security concerns

These statistics show that the CBP is involved in a substantial number of activities across a broad spectrum of security areas. They demonstrate that the agency is involved in a variety of measures that are critical to national security, particularly screening terrorists who may attempt to enter the United States. The CBP is responsible for points of entry, the border, and ports, be they marine or airports. Once undocumented people have entered the United States or traveled beyond points of entry, U.S. Immigration and Customs Enforcement assumes jurisdiction (this agency is discussed next).

Analysis Box 2-2

Looking at the activities performed by the CBP, it is evident that the agency is involved in a wide range of activities that do not relate to homeland security. Based on the agency's performance, as reviewed, which of these activities do you believe are the most important? Are there activities that should be assigned to another agency? Do you think these activities take away from the agency's ability to perform homeland security duties?

U.S. Citizenship and Immigration Services

In 2003, the services and functions of the U.S. Immigration and Naturalization Service (INS) were transferred to the Department of Homeland Security as the **U.S. Citizenship and Immigration Services** (USCIS). The enforcement and inspection functions within the INS were transferred to the Customs and Border Protection Agency. The USCIS is responsible for the administration of immigration and naturalization adjudication functions and establishing immigration services policies and priorities. These functions include

1. Adjudication of immigrant visa petitions
2. Adjudication of naturalization petitions
3. Adjudication of asylum and refugee applications
4. Adjudications performed at the service centers
5. all other adjudications performed by the INS

The USCIS has 15,000 employees and contractors working in approximately 250 headquarters and field offices around the world. As a result of the 9/11 terrorist attacks, governmental agencies have more closely examined the legality of numerous people's status. Many people have overstayed their visas and otherwise entered the United States illegally. The USCIS is responsible for hearing appeals when deportation proceedings begin. On a typical day, the USCIS will

- Process 30,000 applications for immigration benefits
- Issue 6,000 permanent resident cards (green cards)
- Adjudicate 230 asylum applications
- Naturalize 3,000 new civilians and 27 new citizens who are members of the armed forces (USCIS, 2008)

These statistics demonstrate that the USCIS is involved in a number of investigations. For example, the agency will also conduct 135,000 background checks each day and process approximately 11,000 sets of fingerprints. These activities have become much more critical since 9/11. For example, Customs and Border Protection agents are apprehending larger numbers of undocumented people as they cross the border and are employed in the United States. USCIS must adjudicate all those who fight deportation. They sometimes must adjudicate suspected terrorists or those who may have ties to terrorists who are being deported. They also are involved in cases in which undocumented criminals are being deported from the United States. Thus, they play a key role in keeping the country safe (USCIS, 2008).

HS Web Link: To learn more about the USCIS, go to *http://www.uscis.gov/portal/site/uscis*

U.S. Immigration and Customs Enforcement

Immigration and Customs Enforcement (ICE) was created by combining the law enforcement arm of the Naturalization Service, the intelligence and investigative sections of the former Customs Service, and the U.S. Federal Protective Services. It is headed by an assistant secretary, and it is the largest investigative branch within the Department of Homeland Security. The inclusion of the U.S. Federal Protective Services resulted in ICE being responsible for the protection of 8,800 federal properties. One of its primary purposes is to protect the United States from terrorist and criminal attack by investigating people, money, materials, and criminal activities that might be a threat to the United States. ICE attempts to identify criminal activities and vulnerabilities that pose a threat to the nation, as well as enforcing economic, transportation, and infrastructure security. Whereas Customs and Border Protection secures our borders, ICE has immigration and other responsibilities beyond the borders or inside the interior of the United States. Consequently, ICE has a range of investigative responsibilities:

1. Dismantling gang organizations by targeting their members, seizing their financial assets, and disrupting their criminal operations.
2. Investigating employers and targeting undocumented workers who have gained access to critical infrastructure worksites (such as nuclear and chemical plants, military installations, seaports, and airports).
3. Investigating fraudulent immigration benefit applications and fraudulent illegal document manufacturing.
4. Investigating the illegal export of U.S. munitions and sensitive technology.
5. Investigating criminal organizations that smuggle and traffic in humans across our borders.
6. Ensuring that people ordered removed depart the United States as quickly as possible.
7. Destroying the financial infrastructure that criminal organizations use to earn, move, and store illicit funds.
8. Targeting and intercepting counterfeit products smuggled into the United States.
9. Providing support to state and local law enforcement communities in the areas of forensic documents and cyber crimes (ICE, 2009).

ICE has several divisions that focus on specific crimes or types of investigations. First is the **Office of Federal Protective Services** (FPS). This division is responsible for protecting federal properties and buildings. It has uniformed officers stationed at the facilities, and there are investigators who respond to calls, conduct investigations of crimes that occur at facilities, and participate in crime prevention planning. FPS personnel also conduct security surveys for facilities so that security measures remain current and effective.

HS Web Link: To learn more about ICE, go to *http://www.ice.gov/*

ICE agents escort a suspected illegal alien. *Source:* http://www.ice.gov/pi/news/gallery/#big-freeze2_lg

The **Office of Detention and Removal** (DRO) is responsible for enforcing the nation's immigration laws and ensuring the departure of all removable people from the United States. When undocumented aliens are apprehended, the DRO has the responsibility for deporting them. In some cases, they volunteer to be deported; when the undocumented aliens contest deportation, the case is heard by the U.S. Bureau of Citizenship and Immigration Services. If the undocumented alien is ordered to be deported, the DRO is responsible for the actual deportation. In 2006, more than 187,000 illegal aliens were removed from the United States (ICE, 2010). The DRO is working more closely with the nation's jails and prisons to deport undocumented immigrants who have committed crimes. As a result of these partnerships, several thousand inmates have been deported, easing jail overpopulation and reducing costs to the criminal justice system. Officers of the DRO also prosecute undocumented aliens who reenter the United States after being deported.

The **Office of Investigations** within the ICE investigates a wide range of criminal activities. These offenses include human smuggling; drug trafficking and smuggling; various financial crimes; cyber crimes, including child pornography; and the exportation of classified information and material, especially weapons and weapons technology. It is notable that some of these crimes specifically relate to terrorism. The Office of Investigations works with a variety of other agencies. For example, it has worked with the Drug Enforcement Administration in countering large-scale drug-smuggling rings in South and Central America. It has made a number of arrests when Americans or foreign nationals have attempted to sell prohibited arms to foreign countries. It has arrested a number of cyber child pornographers and predators.

The Office of Investigations collects and analyzes intelligence information, coordinating its efforts with other ICE and Homeland Security agencies. The intelligence focuses on people, particularly undocumented aliens, money, and materials moving in and out of the United States. For example, the unit is concerned with the importation and exportation of classified technology or materials that could be used in building weapons of mass destruction. This office works with the Federal Bureau of Investigation and the Central Intelligence Agency in collecting and analyzing intelligence on potential terrorists and transnational criminal syndicates.

U.S. Secret Service

The **U.S. Secret Service** was established in 1865, and its primary mission at the time was to capture counterfeiters and reduce counterfeiting. During the Civil War, approximately one-third of all the money in circulation was counterfeit. Today, countries such as North Korea are counterfeiting American money to raise hard currency. Counterfeiting undermines our economic system and national security.

HS Web Link: To learn more about the U.S. Secret Service, go to *http://www. secretservice.gov/*

In 1901, after President McKinley was assassinated, Congress directed the Secret Service to provide protection for the president. Prior to that time, there was no federal agency responsible for presidential protection. This remains the primary responsibility of the Secret Service. In 1922, during the administration of President Warren G. Harding, the Secret Service created the **Uniform Division**, which provides protection for the White House, the Treasury Building, presidential offices, the vice president's residence, and foreign diplomatic missions. In 2002, when President George W. Bush reorganized federal law enforcement, the Secret Service was moved from the Treasury Department to the Department of Homeland Security.

In addition to investigating the counterfeiting of currency, the Secret Service has authority to investigate credit card and computer fraud. In 1984, Congress enacted legislation making the fraudulent use of credit cards a federal violation. The Secret Service also investigates unauthorized access to automated teller machines and the possession and trafficking of counterfeit or stolen credit cards. "The Secret Service is charged with the detection and arrest of any person committing any offense

Secret Service agents provide executive protection.   *Source:* http://www.secretservice.gov/protection.shtml

against the laws of the United States relating to coins, currency, stamps, government bonds, checks, credit/debit card fraud, computer fraud, false identification crimes, and other obligations or securities of the United States" (Secret Service, 1998: 1). The USA PATRIOT Act increased the Secret Service's role in investigating fraud and related activity in connection with computers. The act also authorizes the director of the Secret Service to establish nationwide electronic crimes task forces to assist the law enforcement and private sectors and academia in detecting and suppressing computer-based crime. The act increased the statutory penalties for the manufacturing, possessing, dealing, and passing of counterfeit U.S. or foreign obligations. It also allows enforcement action to be taken to protect financial payment systems while combating transnational financial crimes directed by terrorists or other criminals.

Today, the Secret Service employs more than 4,256 enforcement agents (Reaves, 2006. The Secret Service provides protection to the president, vice president, their immediate families, former presidents and their wives and children (up to the age of 16), visiting heads of foreign states and other distinguished visitors, and presidential and vice presidential candidates within 120 days of the general presidential election.

Analysis Box 2-3

In terms of homeland security, it appears that the U.S. Secret Service has three primary objectives: (1) executive protection, (2) stop counterfeiting, and (3) stop the counterfeiting of financial documents and credit card fraud. How do these three objectives relate to homeland security?

U.S. Coast Guard

Historically, the primary responsibility of the **U.S. Coast Guard** was the enforcement of maritime laws. This responsibility included ensuring the safe flow of maritime traffic, maritime security including the interdiction of drugs coming into the United States, protection of natural resources including fishing and protected environmental areas, and maritime safety by ensuring that craft abided by laws and regulations. As an example, in 2010, the U.S. Coast Guard was given the responsibility of coordinating the mitigation of the oil platform explosion and oil spill in the Gulf of Mexico near Louisiana. Today, the mission of the U.S. Coast Guard has been expanded to watch for threats to national security. The agency is responsible for protecting more than 361 ports and 12,383 miles of coastline, America's longest border. In fact, port and waterway security consume more than half of the Coast Guard's budget (O'Rourke, 2006).

The U.S. Coast Guard's mission includes the following:

1. Maintain maritime border security against illegal drugs, illegal aliens, firearms, and weapons of mass destruction.
2. Ensure that we can rapidly deploy and re-supply our military assets, both by keeping Coast Guard units at a high state of readiness and by keeping marine transportation open for the transit assets and personnel from other branches of the armed forces. (U.S. Coast Guard, 2008)

The U.S. Coast Guard coordinates its activities with civilian law enforcement and the U.S. military. Whereas the U.S. Customs and Border Protection protects points of entry, the U.S. Coast Guard provides a parameter defense. This is accomplished by interdicting and investigating suspicious vessels prior to their entering maritime ports. As such, the U.S. Coast Guard investigates people and activities especially as they relate to terrorism, narcotics smuggling, undocumented aliens attempting to enter the United States, and transnational crime.

U.S. Coast Guard, in conjunction with the military, practices antiterrorist maneuvers.   *Source:* http://www.northcom.mil/Images/Images_2010/061010/100518-N-8069G-163.jpg

The previous sections detailed the activities of the enforcement and security units within the DHS. In addition to enforcement and security, the DHS has a number of units that provide support and mitigation should there be a terrorist attack or some type of catastrophe. The following sections describe some of these units.

Federal Emergency Management Agency

In 2001, the **Federal Emergency Management Agency** (FEMA) became part of the DHS. It is the federal agency responsible for responding to and mitigating disasters and catastrophes in the United States. The agency derives its authority from the Robert T. Stafford Relief and Disaster Act (1988) and has about 2,600 employees. FEMA is activated once the president declares an area a disaster. Historically, the agency has responded to numerous natural disasters such as hurricanes, floods, tornados, and earthquakes. FEMA is responsible for a quick and long-term response. In terms of an immediate response, FEMA is a first responder that attempts to meet disaster victims' water, food, and shelter needs. FEMA personnel coordinate activities with state and local personnel and largely depend on contractors to provide immediate services and supplies. In the long term, FEMA is responsible for providing support during the rebuilding of a disaster area. This is accomplished through grants and low-interest loans to affected people.

HS Web Link: To learn more about FEMA, go to *http://www.fema.gov/*

The agency received substantial criticism for its reaction to the Hurricane Katrina, which struck the Gulf Coast and New Orleans in 2005. Critics argued that the response was slow and inadequate. A number of congressional investigations were conducted, and ultimately, the director of FEMA was forced to resign. This was not the first time the agency was criticized for a failed response. After Hurricane Hugo devastated South Carolina and the disaster relief was woefully deficient, South Carolina Senator Ernest Hollings called FEMA, "the sorriest bunch of bureaucratic jackasses I've ever seen." After failed responses to disasters in California, Representative Norman Mineta noted that the agency could "screw up a two car parade." In 1992, Hurricane Andrew struck the South Florida coast resulting in significant damage. The response was so inadequate that Congress directed FEMA to make changes and improve or face being abolished (Roberts, 2006).

It should be realized, however, that the United States had never faced a natural disaster of the magnitude of Katrina. Regardless, the experience did show a number of problems with governments' ability to react to disaster. A major problem with FEMA is that the agency does not have the power to force states to better prepare for future natural disasters. This often results in the effects of natural and other disasters falling squarely on FEMA's shoulders. This obviously has implications should there be a biological, chemical, or radiological attack. Such an attack could be of the magnitude of Hurricane Katrina. FEMA's past failures show that the country is not prepared, and that better coordination of services is needed. FEMA should be given more operational authority, and it should have the budget enabling it to maximally respond to catastrophes.

Federal Law Enforcement Training Center

The **Federal Law Enforcement Training Center** (FLETC) is located in Brunswick, Georgia. FLETC is responsible for training law enforcement officers from about 80 federal agencies as well as officers from state and local departments. The addition of FLETC to the DHS enabled the DHS to rapidly increase terrorist-related training. Moreover, it allowed a number of federal agencies to receive integrated and coordinated training. That is, there is terrorist-related curriculum that is consistent across all agencies in addition to specialized training for individual agencies. Having all the training housed in one location results in a more efficient training program across the board.

FEMA National Response and Coordination Center operated on a 24 / 7 schedule when tropical storm Ernesto threatened South Florida.   *Source:* http://www.fema.gov/photodata/low/26061.jpg

Science and Technology Directorate

The **Science and Technology Directorate** is one of the primary technical assistance and technology units within the DHS. The threat of terrorism has resulted in a need for a number of new technologies—technologies that will enable the DHS and other agencies to identify threats and mitigate attacks. The DHS, in conjunction with the National Laboratories, private contractors, military research centers, universities, and its own research facilities, is involved in applied research in a number of areas:

- Border security
- Maritime security
- Cargo security
- Chemical and biological defense
- Cyber security
- Transportation security
- Incident management
- Information sharing and management
- Infrastructure protection
- Communications interoperability
- People screening
- Counter improvised explosive devices (DHS, 2008: 14)

This list demonstrates the wide range of research and development needed in homeland security. It shows that there are numerous vulnerabilities, and that new technology may be able to reduce those vulnerabilities. It also means that we must continue to develop new technology as we face terrorist threats.

Figure 2-3 provides a list of some of the accomplishments reported by the Science and Technology Directorate. As can be seen from Figure 2-3, the agency has made inroads in a

- Chemical, biological, radiological, nuclear, and enhanced explosives sensors and detection equipment standards
- X-ray and gamma-ray technical performance standards, including detection standards for bulk explosives, weapons, and contraband
- Interagency standards for decontamination technologies, protocols, and training
- Standards supporting first responders; incident management standards; communications standards; and chemical, biological, radiological, and nuclear (CBRN) protective equipment and urban search-and-rescue robots standards
- Standards for biometrics including latent fingerprint analysis standards, rapid biometric evaluation standards, and biometric image and physical feature quality standards for identity cards and travel documents
- Test and evaluation policies and processes

FIGURE 2-3   DHS Science and Technology Accomplishments.

number of areas. For example, standards for the production of sensors to detect chemicals, biological matter, and nuclear materials have been developed. Standards for biometric imaging were also established. These standards represent benchmarks for industry and ensure that those sensors and imaging devices that are ultimately placed into use will adequately detect WMD materials. The Science and Technology Directorate also established test and evaluation standards to ensure that new technologies meet operational needs.

DEPARTMENT OF DEFENSE AND HOMELAND SECURITY

Today, the **Department of Defense** (DoD) is extensively involved in security efforts. Given that the DoD is responsible for protecting the nation from attacks by other nations and the magnitude of possible terrorist attacks, it is natural that the resources from the DoD be enlisted in homeland security or defense efforts. The DoD is familiar with terrorist tactics, has the organizational capacity to deal with such problems, and has a wealth of personnel and technology to devote to mitigating a terrorist attack or assisting the DHS in preventing such an attack.

The DoD plays a support or secondary role in homeland security. For the most part, the DoD is involved in homeland defense as opposed to homeland security (Erckenbrack and Scholer, 2004). **Homeland defense** refers to deterrence and support as opposed to security. This distinction allows the DoD to avoid becoming involved in missions that are under the purview of the DHS and other agencies. Instead, the DoD provides support to the DHS and other agencies involved in homeland security. Therefore, the DoD's involvement is limited to specific types of situations. Former Secretary of Defense Donald Rumsfeld identified three such situations: (1) extraordinary situations or circumstances that require traditional military action or missions, (2) emergency situations or catastrophes as a result of terrorist attacks or some natural disaster, and (3) provision of security assistance at National Security Special Events such as the Olympics (see Bowman, 2003). For the most part, the DHS and other agencies are primarily involved in homeland security, and DoD personnel become involved only in limited situations.

HS Web Link: To learn more about the DoD's homeland defense role, go to *http://www.fas.org/man/ crs/RL31615.pdf*

Because of potential terrorist attacks and a need for the military to become involved in some homeland security situations, the DoD created a new command, the Northern Command (NORTHCOM). **NORTHCOM**'s area of responsibility includes the continental United States, Alaska, Canada, Puerto Rico, and the Virgin Islands. Hawaii and the U.S. territories remain under the control of the Pacific Command. Additionally, NORTHCOM's authority includes a 500-mile sea and air approach to the United States. NORTHCOM has subsumed the North American Aerospace Defense Command (NORAD) since the 9/11 attacks involved aircraft. NORAD would be involved in intercepting and neutralizing any attack involving aircraft. Here, NORAD would coordinate activities with the Federal Aviation Administration. NORTHCOM would also command any National Guard units that are federally activated for homeland security purposes. NORTHCOM does not have a large contingent of personnel but depends on other military units that have designated terrorist prevention or response missions.

The military has a number of assets that are indispensible in homeland security. First, it has units that can respond to a chemical, biological, radiological, or nuclear (CBRN) incident. The DoD has a joint service **Chemical and Biological Rapid Response Team** (CB-RRT) that is designed to support civilian authorities in the event of a chemical or biological attack or catastrophe. This unit is activated once such an incident has occurred. The DoD has also authorized 55 **National Guard Weapons of Mass Destruction–Civil Support Teams** that can be federally activated should there be a CBRN incident. The CB-RRT and other military units can advise civilians on how to respond to attacks, diagnose attacks to determine the types of agents used, measure the scope and dangers associated with an attack, and assist in mitigating the impact of an attack. The DoD plays an important role if WMDs are used.

A second role in homeland security is intelligence. A majority of America's intelligence expenditures occur in the DoD, and the DoD has a number of agencies that are involved in collecting intelligence information. DoD agencies include the National Security Agency, National Reconnaissance Office, National Imagery and Mapping Agency, Defense Intelligence Agency, and the intelligence and security units within the three branches of the military. The DoD intelligence agencies coordinate with other intelligence agencies such as the Federal Bureau of Investigation and the Central Intelligence Agency. The intelligence function is addressed in more detail in Chapter 8.

STATE-LEVEL HOMELAND SECURITY

Most if not all states now have a state-level office or department devoted to homeland security. These offices have four primary responsibilities: (1) coordinate state efforts with the DHS, (2) coordinate the homeland security efforts within the state, (3) coordinate state and federal homeland security grants and expenditures, and (4) provide education and training to people involved in homeland security activities. Larger states tend to have more sophisticated homeland security apparatuses as compared to smaller states. Nonetheless, these state agencies play a key role in prevention, mitigation, and response should a terrorist attack or other catastrophe occur.

As an example, the state of New York has a fairly comprehensive homeland security apparatus. The state's primary agency is the Office of Homeland Security. In 2007, the state distributed $98 million for transit security projects. The office coordinated the expansion of the number of National Guard members patrolling in transit stations. It provided training on terrorist attacks on schools based on information from the terrorist attack on a Beslan, Russia, school. It supported legislation requiring security for pipelines and fueling networks. It conducted training and public forums on new hazardous materials security. Training to prevent agro-terrorism (crops and livestock tainted with poisons, viruses, or bacteria) was presented in three New York counties. The office partnered with the Transportation Security Administration to conduct more rail transportation baggage screening. It also worked with a variety of other agencies to develop a response to pandemic influenza and increase local medical and first responder assets (Office of Homeland Security, 2007).

HS Web Link: To learn more about New York's homeland security program, go to *http://www. security.state.ny.us/*

Analysis Box 2-4

All states are now involved in homeland security, and some states have progressed at a more rapid rate as compared to others. New York, since it has been attacked twice, likely is more advanced than other states. Locate your state's homeland security website. How does your home state compare to New York? If you are a resident of New York, compare New York to another state. Can you identify and deficiencies?

In addition to the prevention activities, the office works with criminal justice agencies to collect and share counterterrorism information. It also works with a variety of other state agencies to develop a database of critical infrastructure and associated threats. It provided agencies with intelligence advisories and worked with law enforcement to develop better public awareness in reporting potential terrorist activities. In conjunction with the DHS and the New York City, the agency equipped police officers with radiological detection devices. Finally, New York officials worked with Canadian officials in securing border crossings into and out of the United States (Office of Homeland Security, 2007).

These activities demonstrate that state agencies are actively involved in homeland security operations. Even though the federal government has primary responsibility for safeguarding the nation, it falls on the states to develop plans and apparatuses for responding to terrorist threats. The states are actually on the frontline for many of these threats. Activities in each state represent another layer that terrorists must penetrate before successfully committing an attack.

Summary

This chapter presented an overview of the apparatus that is involved in providing homeland security. The primary federal agency is the DHS, which was created in reaction to the 9/11 attacks on our country. The attacks resulted in substantial changes at the federal and state government levels. The DHS was created by combining a number of agencies from throughout the federal government into one department that could coordinate our homeland security efforts. The creation of the DHS was not without problems, including all sorts of issues with regard to command and control, and a number of problems existed in terms of coordinating the agencies within the new department. White House and congressional politics also provided a number of obstacles. Nonetheless, the DHS continues to mature and evolve, continuously improving in terms of affording the American people protection from terrorist attacks.

The various agencies housed in the DHS were described. These agencies and their missions demonstrate the complexity of homeland security. The TSA is not only responsible for airline safety, but it also is involved in all other transportation safety initiatives.

The customs agencies, ICE, CBP, and USCIS, essentially are charged with protecting our nation from terrorists who try to enter the United States. Additionally, these agencies safeguard the nation by attempting to intercept any WMDs or WMD materials before they can be imported into the country.

The Department of Defense is also involved in homeland security. If there is a biological, chemical, or radiological attack, the DoD has the resources that can best deal with the situation. These resources are under the command of NORTHCOM, which coordinates all DoD homeland security efforts. Additionally, the DoD has several intelligence agencies that, as a part of their mission, collect intelligence information on terrorists and their potential activities. The DoD coordinates its activities with those of the DHS.

Finally, the individual states have homeland security offices or agencies. These entities coordinate all homeland security efforts in the state. These activities range from public education and governmental employee training to assisting with the implementation of homeland security programming. The New York

Office of Homeland Security was discussed in some detail. New York City has been attacked twice by terrorists and the state likely will be targeted in the future. The New York state agency must successfully coordinate the state's activities with those of local governments and the federal government.

Discussion Questions

1. Politics played a key role in the formation of the Department of Homeland Security. What impact did this have in terms of the department's overall effectiveness in the short and long term?

2. Given that there are 22 agencies in the Department of Homeland Security, how well do you think they work together given their diverse roles and responsibilities?

3. Of the 22 agencies that comprise the Department of Homeland Security, which ones are you familiar with based on your consumption of news and current events?

4. What role does the Department of Defense play in homeland security?

5. Do you believe that immigration and border security are major homeland security issues? Why?

6. Since FEMA is the only agency that responds to natural disasters, do you believe it should be placed in another federal department? Why?

References

Bellavita, C. (2005). "What is preventing homeland security?" *Homland Security Affairs*. 1(1): 1–11.

Bowman, S. (2003). "Homeland security: The Department of Defense's role." *Report for Congress*. Washington, D.C.: Congressional Research Service.

CBP. (2010). *Snapshot: A Summary of CBP Facts and Figures*. http://www.cbp.gov/linkhandler/cgov/about/accomplish/snapshot.ctt/snapshot.pdf (Accessed June 21, 2010).

CBP. (2008). CBP website. http://www.cbp.gov/xp/cgov/about/mission/cbp_is.xml (Accessed July 12, 2008).

Clarke, R. (2008). *Your Government Failed You: Breaking the Cycle of National Security Disasters*. New York: HarperCollins.

Department of Homeland Security. (2008). *Homepage*. http://www.dhs.gov/index.shtm (Accessed July 7, 2008).

Erckenbrack, A. and A. Scholer. (2004). "The DOD role in homeland security." *Joint Force Quarterly*, 35: 34–41.

Government Accounting Office. (2003). *Airport Passenger Screening: Preliminary Observations on Progress Made and Challenges Remaining*. Washington, D.C.: Author.

Immigration and Customs Enforcement. (2009). Homepage. http://www.ice.gov/ (Accessed January 10, 2009).

Immigration and Customs Enforcement. (2010). *ICE Office of Detention and Removal*. http://www.ice.gov/pi/news/factsheets/dro110206.htm (Accessed June 21, 2010).

Kamarck, E. (2007, November). "Fixing the Department of Homeland Security." *Progressive Policy Institute*. http://www.ppionline.org/documents/FixingDHS11142007.pdf (Accessed August 10, 2008).

Office of Homeland Security State of New York. (2007). *Annual Report, 2007*. Albany, NY: Author.

O'Rourke, R. (2006). *Homeland Security: Coast Guard Operations—Background and Issues for Congress*. Washington, D.C.: Congressional Research Service.

Perrow, C. (2002). "Using organizations: The case of FEMA." *Homeland Security Affairs*, 1(2): 1–8.

Reaves, B. (2006). *Federal Law Enforcement Officers, 2004*. Washington, D.C.: Bureau of Justice Statistics.

Roberts, P. (2006). "FEMA after Katrina." *Policy Review*, 137: 15–33.

Shapiro, J. (2007). *Managing Homeland Security: Develop a Threat-Based Strategy*. (Opportunity 08 Paper). Washington, D.C.: Brookings Institution.

TSA. (2010a). *Imaging Technology: Innovation & Technology*. http://www.tsa.gov/approach/tech/imaging_technology.shtm (Accessed May 20, 2010).

TSA. (2010b). *Federal Air Marshal Shortage?* http://www.tsa.gov/approach/mythbusters/fams_shortage.shtm (Accessed June 21, 2010).

TSA. (2008). Transportation Security Administration website. http://www.tsa.gov/5th/index.shtm (Accessed July 11, 2008).

USA Patriot Act (PL 107-56).

U.S. Citizenship and Customs Service. (2008). Website. http://www.uscis.gov/portal/site/uscis (Accessed August 11, 2008).

U.S. Coast Guard. (2008). Website. http://www.uscg.mil/ (Accessed August 11, 2008).

Wermuth, M. (2005). "The Department of Homeland Security: The road ahead." *Testimony Presented to the Senate Committee on Homeland Security and Governmental Affairs*. Santa Monica, CA: Rand Corp.

Overview of National Infrastructure Protection

LEARNING OBJECTIVES

1. Understand the meaning of critical infrastructure.
2. Know the three categories of critical infrastructure.
3. Be able to critique the National Critical Infrastructure Database.
4. Know the National Infrastructure Protection Plan framework.
5. Describe the problems associated with different types of critical infrastructure assets.
6. Understand how terrorists view and possibly target various critical infrastructure assets.

KEY TERMS

Critical infrastructure assets
Human assets
Physical infrastructure
Cyber infrastructure
National Asset Database
Operation Liberty Shield
Risk management model
Operations research
Program evaluation
Security goals

Risk
Consequences of an attack
Vulnerability of the target
Security priorities
Effective protective measures
Target hardening
Effectiveness
Bottom-up approach
Big bang theory of asset protection

INTRODUCTION

Homeland security is a governmental effort to protect national **critical infrastructure assets**. According to the Department of Homeland Security (2006), there are three primary categories of critical infrastructure: (1) human, (2) physical, and (3) cyber. **Human assets** refer the large numbers of people who congregate because of living situations, working conditions, or social events and who need to be protected. Homeland security efforts focus on protecting groups of people to prevent a large number of casualties. Thus, numbers of people drive protection decisions. Although people can be the targets of terrorist attacks, infrastructure is also important. **Physical infrastructure** refers to transportation (air, rail, waterway, and roadway infrastructure); manufacturing facilities, especially petrochemical facilities; large employers; and nuclear facilities, such as reactors, storage devices, and materials being transported regionally or nationally. In essence, a strike at a physical infrastructure facility may not result in a large number of deaths, but it could have a significant economic impact in the region or country. Finally, **cyber infrastructure** refers to information networks used to transfer vast amounts of information and to coordinate business, industry, banking, and to a large degree, people's daily lives. It also refers to keeping information secure from those who would access and steal it for illegal or illegitimate uses.

HS Web Link: To learn more about our national infrastructure protection, go to *http://www.dhs.gov/ files/programs/editorial_ 0827.shtm*

The protection of people may include individuals such as government officials at the federal, state, or local level or high-profile individuals such as Hollywood actors, business or corporate leaders, or politicians. These people are potential targets as their deaths would create a great deal of publicity for the terrorist act, or the deaths could result in governmental or private sector inefficiency at some level resulting in economic loss. Groups of people are also possible targets. A sporting event or entertainment venue may be targeted. A busy shopping area or mall is another potential target as are schools, churches, government assemblies, or rallies. For example, the majority of bombs targeting civilians detonated during the Iraq War are usually in shopping venues. These types of attacks result in publicity and tend to have a greater impact on the population by affecting travel, personal freedom, and commerce.

In terms of physical infrastructure, there are literally millions of potential targets. A given city, of nearly any size, may have hundreds of potential targets. Every city and town in America at least periodically has substantial population gatherings, whether they are town meetings, high school sporting events, or local celebrations such as parades or festivals. Many cities have manufacturing facilities associated with the petrochemical industry, which if attacked, could result in the release of dangerous chemicals. The destruction of roadways or bridges in metropolitan areas could have an economic impact since it would impede work and commerce. Dangerous chemicals and petroleum products are often transported by rail or the trucking industry, which are potential targets. Communications, banking centers, and postal or shipping facilities are also viable targets.

Other areas of concern that have not been given adequate attention by homeland security policy makers are food and water supply chains. For example, in 2008 an outbreak of salmonella was associated with fresh tomatoes in several states. The outbreak resulted in a number of people becoming ill. It also resulted in substantial economic loss to agribusiness. In the past, criminals have used biological weapons on food. In 1984, the biotoxin *salmonella typhimurium* was deposited in several restaurant salad bars in Dalles, Oregon. Although no deaths were reported, there were 715 cases of poisoning and another 117 people exhibited symptoms (Weaver, 1985). The possibility also exists that someone could introduce toxins into water sources, potentially

Every city has numerous potential physical infrastructure targets.

causing deaths, illness, and a loss of public confidence in government. The point is that numerous critical infrastructure assets are potential targets, and homeland security necessitates that they be considered when planning for attacks and taking preventive measures. This results in a vast and complex endeavor.

FEDERAL AGENCIES INVOLVED IN THE PROTECTION OF AMERICAN ASSETS

A number of federal agencies are involved in the protection of critical infrastructure. Departments and agencies within the federal government are charged with specific sector responsibilities. These departments and agencies have some level of homeland security protective responsibility for those assets that fall within their purview. Figure 3-1 provides a breakdown of these agencies and their areas of responsibilities.

As shown in Figure 3-1, a number of departmental-level federal agencies are involved in homeland security. Many are cabinet-level departments; thus, numerous lower-level agencies within each of these departments play a role in security. The task of homeland security is divided among the agencies according to industries that are regulated or controlled by the various departments and by general governmental responsibilities. Homeland security is an encompassing task requiring a coordinated effort not only within the federal government, but also among state and local agencies that are involved in the security framework. Thus, a central questions are, "How well will these agencies cooperate and provide an optimal response or solution to a homeland security event?" and "Are there gaps in security as a result of the decentralization of some security responsibilities?" Response becomes complicated and bureaucratic.

Sector-Specific Agency	Critical Infrastructure/Key Resources Sector
Department of Agriculture Department of Health and Human Services	Agriculture and Food
Department of Defense	Defense Industrial Base
Department of Energy	Energy
Department of Health and Human Services	Public Health and Healthcare
Department of the Interior	National Monuments and Icons
Department of the Treasury	Banking and Finance
Environmental Protection Agency	Drinking Water and Water Treatment Systems
Department of Homeland Security *Office of Infrastructure Protection*	Chemical Commercial Facilities Dams Emergency Services Commercial Nuclear Reactors, Materials, and Waste
Office of Cyber Security and Telecommunications	Information Technology Telecommunications
Transportation Security Administration	Postal and Shipping
Transportation Security Administration, United States Coast Guard	Transportation Systems
Immigration and Customs Enforcement, Federal Protective Service	Government Facilities

FIGURE 3-1 Federal Agencies Responsible for Nation's Critical Infrastructure. *Source:* Department of Homeland Security. (2006). *National Infrastructure Protection Plan.* Washington, D.C.: Author, p. 2.

Attempts have been made to assign primary responsibility for securing specific infrastructure assets or terrorist targets to specific federal departments. For example, the Transportation Security Administration (TSA) is responsible for transportation systems. This includes not only airports, but also other transportation systems, including trucking and rail. The TSA is also charged with protecting our shipping and postal services. The Coast Guard protects water transportation lanes and ports in the Atlantic and Pacific Oceans and the Gulf of

Analysis Box 3-1

Numerous federal agencies are involved in homeland security. Each of these agencies has specific responsibilities or areas that it attempts to control or prevent terrorist activities. Many are outside the Department of Homeland Security. Do you believe that there are other federal agencies that should have responsibilities? Do you believe there will be coordination problems? Coordination is important to ensure that all possible targets are protected.

Mexico. The Department of the Treasury secures our banking and finance systems. One of the duties here is to stop terrorist financing. The Department of the Interior plays a homeland security role by protecting our national monuments and icons such as the Lincoln Memorial or Grant's Tomb. The Department of Energy has an expansive role in homeland security, as it is responsible for acquiring energy and protecting our energy sources. Since terrorists may attempt to acquire nuclear materials from an American facility or attack such a facility to create a radiological catastrophe, the Department of Energy is on the front line of homeland security. These examples demonstrate how homeland security responsibilities are dispersed throughout the federal government.

SCOPE OF AMERICAN CRITICAL INFRASTRUCTURE ASSESTS

Given that a primary task of homeland security is the protection of critical infrastructure assets, it becomes important to identify those assets. This is a monumental task given that there are thousands assets spread across the United States. The first task in identifying them is to define critical infrastructure assets. For the purposes of compiling a list of such assets and providing guidance to the DHS, **critical infrastructure assets** were defined in the USA PATROIT Act (P.L. 107-56) as follows:

> Systems and assets . . . so vital to the United States that the incapacity or destruction of such systems and assets would have a debilitating impact on security, national economy security, national public health and safety, or any combination of those matters.

This definition suggests that the assets to be included in any listing or database should possess several qualities. First, they should be of national importance. Their attack, destruction, or disabling should have a significant negative impact on the country. This impact can be related to economics, security, health, or safety. This definition, of course, fails to provide specific criteria and remains open for interpretation. For example, if terrorists attacked and destroyed a chemical facility, it obviously would be a significant event, but does it fall within the scope of the definition of critical infrastructure as enumerated in the USA PATRIOT Act? In other words, hard and fast working criteria do not exist based on the legislation. The absence of workable criteria complicates the task of identifying critical infrastructure and makes securing them more difficult. Workable and understandable criteria must ultimately be developed.

Regardless, Congress directed the Department of Homeland Security to develop a national critical infrastructure database, the **National Asset Database**. The database would list all assets deemed to meet the criteria outlined in the USA PATRIOT Act. The process was initiated in 2003 with **Operation Liberty Shield**, which consisted of a number of programs that operated in conjunction and concurrently with the invasion of Iraq. The initial list contained 160 assets, including chemical and hazardous materials plants, nuclear plants, energy facilities, business and financial centers, and other assets that were considered of extreme importance in light of the criteria established in the USA PATRIOT Act.

HS Web Link: To learn more about the National Critical Infrastructure Asset Database, go to *http://www. fas.org/sgp/crs/homesec/ RL33648.pdf*

In developing the *National Strategy for the Physical Protection of Critical Infrastructure and Key Assets*, the Office of the President (2003) provided a listing of the key areas that should receive consideration in the development of the list:

- Information technology
- Telecommunications
- Chemicals
- Transportation
- Emergency services
- Postal and shipping services
- Agriculture and food
- Public health and health care
- Drinking water and water treatment
- Energy
- Banking and finance
- National monuments and icons
- Defense industrial complex
- Key industry/technology sites
- Large gatherings of people

The DHS continued to collect information about assets and by 2006, the list had grown to 77,069. Several sources were used in constructing the National Assets Database, including federal agencies, the states, and industries. In addition to the DHS compiling a list of assets, it relied on the states and industries to provide items for inclusion in the database. The DHS attempted to provide some criteria to the contributors to the database. For example, oil refineries with a refining capacity of more than 225,000 barrels of oil per day, commercial centers with a potential economic loss of $10 billion, or events or activities with a population gathering of 35,000 people were to be included in the database (Moteff, 2007). Assets meeting these criteria obviously were of vital importance. Figure 3-2 provides a breakdown by sector of the assets listed in the database.

Collection of critical infrastructure assets began in 2003, and since its inception, a great deal of criticism has been leveled at the project. As noted earlier, it appears that the DHS is using unclear or inconsistent standards when compiling the list. For example, Moteff (2007) notes that the database not only included duly recognized assets consistent with the definition enumerated in the USA PATRIOT Act and the *National Strategy for the Physical Protection of Critical Infrastructure and Key Assets*, but it also included assets that on their face should not be in the listing. There were events and locations such as petting zoos, parades, and local festivals, which are dubious in terms of national security priorities. Nonetheless, if a petting zoo in middle

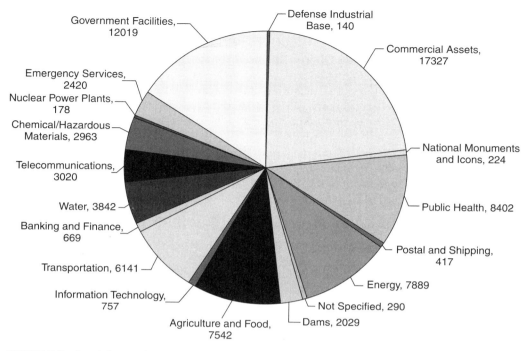

FIGURE 3-2 Breakdown of Critical Infrastructure Assets by Industry. *Source:* Moteff, J. (2007). *Critical Infrastructure: The National Asset Database.* Washington, D.C.: Congressional Research Service.

America was attacked resulting in several deaths, but not of the magnitude as outlined in the *National Strategy*, it would still have repercussions across the nation. This demonstrates the difficulty in developing workable guidelines.

Another problem with the database were inconsistencies across states and cities. Moteff notes that Indiana had 8,000 assets in the database, more than larger states such as California, Texas, and New York. These states obviously have a larger number of critical infrastructure assets, and it appears that those reporting Indiana's assets were using less rigid criteria to determine inclusion. California listed the Bay Area Regional Transit System as a single asset, whereas New York City included 739 separate subway stations. Fewer banking centers were listed for New York as compared to North Dakota. These inconsistencies demonstrate the problems associated with compiling a list of critical infrastructure. Nonetheless, it is a task that must be accomplished with a level of accuracy. It serves as the foundation for future security efforts.

Analysis Box 3-2

A number of problems have been associated with building the National Asset Database. It appears that various states or jurisdictions used different criteria to decide if an asset should be included. Based on the work and problems associated with the database, what assets in your community should be included in the database? How would the assets that you identify compare with some of the assets described earlier?

THE NATIONAL INFRASTRUCTURE PROTECTION PLAN: CONCEPTUAL OPERATION OF HOMELAND SECURITY PROTECTION

Thus far, this chapter has examined efforts to determine or identify those critical infrastructure assets that should receive a high priority in terms of deploying protective measures. Once assets are identified, measures must be taken to ensure their safety. Woodbury (2005) advises that a system needs to be developed that maximally protects infrastructure assets; it is the *raison d'etre* for homeland security. Furthermore, he advises that a measurement of the effort needs to be conducted. First, measurement allows for accountability. Today, billions of dollars are being spent on homeland security, and evaluation provides information on whether these expenditures result in enhanced safety. Second, measurement should guide future expenditures. Investments should be made in security activities and processes that are proven to be successful. Finally, measurement provides an estimate of success—knowledge of the level of safety afforded as a result of expenditures and efforts.

Even though accurate identification or appropriate prioritization of these assets is lacking, the Department of Homeland Security has devised a conceptual model for affording some assets proper levels of protection and security. The *National Infrastructure Protection Plan and Risk Management Framework* (DHS, 2006) provides a measurement and evaluation model that allows us to measure success. It represents a national model for implementing homeland security for infrastructure assets. Figure 3-3 provides a conceptual or policy view of homeland security as it is implemented in the United States. The model is constructed to ensure continuous evaluation in an effort to identify deficiencies and to constantly enhance effectiveness.

The model is grounded in risk management, operations research, and program evaluation. It requires that all possible risks are identified and considered in decision making. It is a highly structured approach that attempts to control or account for the environment and remove or reduce uncertainty related to some threat. Given the enormous number of potential human, physical, and cyber targets, protecting them requires the development of a priority system. That is, not all potential targets are of equal value to terrorists or the economic or social well-being of the country, and not all targets are equally vulnerable to attack. Theoretically, homeland security, then, is based on a **risk management model** whereby decisions are made about where to apply scarce resources in the security of critical infrastructure based on perceived risk.

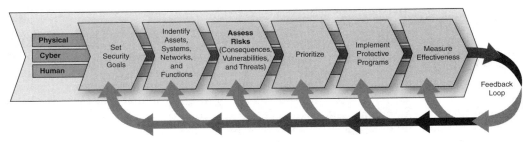

FIGURE 3-3   National Infrastructure Protection Plan Framework.   *Source:* Department of Homeland Security. (2006). *National Infrastructure Protection Plan.* Washington, D.C.: Author.

The model is grounded in **operations research**, which is based on systems theory and is a process whereby mathematical equations or scenarios are used to determine the impact of some occurrence. Operations research, for example, allows researchers to determine the impact on communications should a communications center be attacked and destroyed. Not all attacks or losses will have the same results, and operations research allows for the identification of the magnitude of loss, which plays an important role in prioritizing protective measures. Those assets that could result in the greatest human or economic loss should receive a higher priority.

Program evaluation plays a key role in protective measures. Once priorities are established, protective measures are implemented. Critical questions here are, "Do the protective measures work–provide protection?" and "Do they provide the appropriate level of protection?" Answers to these questions are of critical importance. If protective efforts are not evaluated, critical infrastructure may remain at risk. Furthermore, the results of program evaluations guide future efforts and expenditures.

The model displayed in Figure 3-3 consists of six distinct actions that lead to the security of human, physical, and cyber assets (see DHS, 2006). Each action is dependent on the others to implement an effective security system. Moreover, the model has a continuous feedback loop so that evaluation and adjustments can be made at each level to enhance protection. The following sections examine each of the six actions.

Set Security Goals

The establishment of **security goals** refers to determining a level of security for the human, physical, and cyber assets. The DHS (2006) advises that security goals "define specific outcomes, conditions, endpoints, or performance targets that collectively constitute an effective protective posture" (p. 30). A police analogy here may be informative. If a police department receives intelligence information that a particular bank will be robbed in the immediate future, police officers may be asked to conduct additional patrols around the bank, or the department may deploy a stakeout unit to intercept the robbers. The additional patrols constitute a lesser level of security as opposed to officers staking out the bank. In terms of homeland security, how formable or protected should the various targets be considering the costs associated with hardening or protecting targets? In our example, the stakeout officers provide more security, but at an increased cost, as compared to the additional patrols. Obviously, resources are limited and policy decisions must be made. Nonetheless, security goals with specific performance targets or benchmarks should be established. Without such goals, security likely will be haphazard and incomplete. An objective, identified level of security is required to advise security policy for a given critical asset. These security goals represent minimum standards that must be achieved by governmental bodies and industries.

Corollary questions are, "Should there be different security levels associated with different industries or categories of potential targets?" "Which potential targets within a category should receive more consideration relative to others?" and "What criteria should be used to make these decisions?" For example, should nuclear reactors receive more attention than petrochemical facilities? If so, how much more protection should they receive? These become critical questions since the answers provide the foundation for policy formulation. They establish security standards that become concrete objectives for various industries. This becomes a complex question that thus far has not been addressed in a number of industries or social situations. For example, a number of industries do not have protection benchmarks and others have minimal standards.

Another important question in developing security goals is what should be the primary criterion that drives their establishment. For example, one criterion might be that security goals should emphasize the minimization of damage that might be incurred should an attack occur. Another equally plausible criterion would be to implement security measures that make attacks more difficult or expensive for potential terrorists. These two different approaches can yield very different conclusions. This demonstrates the need to set well-thought-out security goals.

Identify Assets, Systems, Networks, and Functions

As discussed earlier, the DHS has been involved in developing an inventory of critical infrastructure assets. The DHS depends on industries and the states to provide the list assets. Additionally, a number of assets have been identified as a result of natural disasters in the past. However, there have been a number of problems with these efforts.

Although there is a partial list, its accuracy or usefulness is questionable. Accordingly, it is a major impediment to homeland security if as required in the *National Infrastructure Protection Plan* critical infrastructure assets are improperly collected and cataloged. Currently, a number of assets that are not vital to the country are contained on the list. At the same time, it must be reasoned that some vital assets have been omitted from the database. These problems also imply that officials are not at the point at which various assets can be prioritized. Some assets will require greater levels of security as compared to others. The national database remains a weak link in security. Moreover, officials have not developed the necessary priority system and the criteria used to make prioritization decisions.

Assess Risks

The potential risk associated with each asset must be established. The methodology used by the DHS (2006) is based on risk management. It attempts to determine a target's level of risk relative to other targets by quantifying each target's risk. Risk can be calculated as follows:

$$R = f(C, V, T)$$

- R is the level of risk and establishes a priority for a given critical infrastructure asset. **Risk** is based on the consequences of a particular asset being destroyed or damaged, how vulnerable the asset is, and the threats to the particular asset. The calculation of risk facilitates the establishment of response and prevention priorities.
- C is the **consequences of an attack** on a particular target in terms of public health, the economy, public confidence in institutions, and the functioning of government that would result from an attack or natural disaster. Consequences are estimated by examining a specific target and estimating how valuable it is in terms of human, physical, or cyber losses should the target be attacked.
- V is an assessment of the **vulnerability of the target**. That is, some targets are more easily attacked than others. Some industries are "hardened" or better secured, making them less susceptible to attack. For example, today it would be easier for terrorists to attack a post office or a petrochemical facility as compared to commandeering a commercial airplane. Generally, vulnerability will be established using common threat scenarios. In some cases, red teams, teams that conduct a simulated attack on an asset, will be used when specialists attempt to penetrate an asset to test its vulnerability.

These threat scenarios are based on previous attacks or disasters that a particular type of asset has previously experienced.

- T is the *threat* or the likelihood that a specific target will suffer an attack or disaster. In terms of terrorist attacks, this means that America's intelligence and law enforcement apparatus must identify who the likely terrorists are, their capabilities, and their desired targets. Some potential targets are more susceptible to attack than others—more desirable from the terrorists' point of view.

Once the information about the consequences of an attack on a target, its vulnerability, and threat level is collected, the mathematical formula will provide a risk quotient. Lewis and Darken (2005) provide an example of how the calculation of risk may be applied by comparing a car bomb and a cyber attack on a bank.

Threat	Vulnerability	Consequences or Damage	Risk
Bomb	10%	$10 million	$1 million
Cyber	60%	$1 million	$600,000

The risk of a car bomb on the bank is about one in ten or 10 percent, whereas there is a 60 percent chance of a cyber attack. The bomb possibly would result in $10 million in damage, whereas the cyber attack would cost about $1 million. Thus, the risk (costs) associated with a cyber attack becomes greater as a result of greater vulnerability to the cyber attack. This calculation does not include threat since no information exists for the overwhelming majority of potential targets. Nonetheless, this formula allows for the comparison of the importance of various targets and can be used to establish priorities.

Another issue is that critical infrastructure assets are not equally dispersed geographically. There are concentrations of these assets, and many are interdependent. An attack on one asset may adversely affect a number of other assets in the region or cripple the whole economy. For example, 30 percent of all waterborne container shipments pass through the ports of Los Angeles and Long Beach (Army Corps of Engineers, 2006). Parfomak (2007) notes that these concentrations of assets represent systems that if attacked would have a greater impact on the national economy as compared to attacks on singular assets. These concentrations also may become inviting to possible terrorists—they allow terrorists to select the most vulnerable target from a number of potential targets. Essentially, officials must understand the systemic nature of assets as they attempt to calculate the consequences of their being attacked.

In terms of estimating or assessing risks, former Defense Secretary Donald Rumsfeld once eloquently stated that, "we do not know what we do not know." It is questionable if one can quantify to any degree of accuracy the consequences of attacks, the vulnerability of individual assets, or the threat. For example, it is not known which targets or types of targets are of interest to terrorists, and there are virtually thousands of targets to select. Therefore, it is difficult if not impossible to estimate risk for a target or particular set of targets. There are no standards or criteria by which to rate critical infrastructure assets in terms of their vulnerability. Officials likely do not have the information necessary to calculate potential risk. This is a substantial challenge to homeland security, and it appears to be more of a theoretical perspective as opposed to an operational initiative. The DHS's risk assessment formula may be useful in obtaining a partial picture of risk, but it falls short of providing definitive across-the-board answers.

Prioritize

Once security goals or standards have been established and risk has been assessed, the next step is to establish **security priorities**. These should guide planning and coordination among different agencies within the government and with the private sector and provide guidance in resource allocation. Nonetheless, once risk is calculated, it will advise policy makers in terms of which industries, industry segments, or systems are at the highest risk. For example, one can examine the aggregate security risk associated with different industries as well as individual facilities. According to the DHS (2006), those segments that are at greatest risk should receive the most attention and resources in order to enhance protection and mitigation. Second, the risk assessment should provide guidance in terms of which mitigation and prevention systems are the most cost efficient and effective. Here risk assessment allows us to measure the impact of protective systems by evaluating their overall effects.

Prevention and mitigation efforts can include an array of processes and security approaches or a combination of measures. The various measures used across an industry can be evaluated using the risk assessment model to determine those that are most efficient and effective. This information can be used in the establishment of industry-wide standards and cost containment. Experimentation with security measures is best accomplished by the industries themselves, which can provide feedback to the DHS in terms of levels of success. This process will provide substantial information relative to securing critical infrastructure assets as well as prodding the implementation of cost effective security measures.

Is it possible to prioritize critical infrastructure?   *Source:* AP (05012602495)

Implement Protective Programs

The implementation of **effective protective programs** can have a number of benefits to an industry. The DHS (2006) lists the following benefits:

1. Deter attacks—programs may result in attackers believing the risk is greater than the potential effects of a planned attack.
2. Devalue—levels of security may result in less damage from a possible attack; another disincentive to possible terrorists.
3. Detection—implementation of security programs not only harden targets, they also enhance protectors' ability to detect attacks. Most likely, facility administrators will deploy some intelligence operations as well as target-hardening tactics, which may assist in uncovering potential attackers. For example, video cameras not only serve to deter, but they also allow for the collection of information about people in the immediate area.
4. Defend—as the homeland security processes mature, they will include more defensive measures. For example, primary security measures will be supplemented with perimeter hardening, fencing, access control, and other defensive measures that expand security concentrically around possible targets.

For the most part, the discussion in this section has focused on hardware and target hardening. **Target hardening** refers to the implementation of access control, video cameras, fencing and buffer zones around targets, and structural changes that enhance security. There are also human elements in an effective security plan. First, training programs must be developed and provided to employees. These training programs should indoctrinate employees on the need for security. Too often employees are not committed to the importance of security issues. Annual or biannual training can reinforce their importance. Second, organizational policies and procedures that enforce security should be developed. Security policies and procedures would help ensure that security is a part of the organizational culture. Third, middle management and supervisors should be given greater authority and responsibilities in security matters. Security should become an important part of their jobs. Finally, security measures, both human and physical, can be reinforced through periodic inspections. Regular inspections should be conducted by supervisors, managers, and risk management personnel to ensure that policies and procedures are being followed and to examine physical security measures to determine their effectiveness.

Measure Effectiveness

The final action in the homeland security risk management framework is the measurement of **effectiveness**. Woodbury (2005) notes that there must be accountability in protective measures and systems to ensure that they function as envisioned. The *National Infrastructure Protection Plan* attempts to quantify each of the six actions in the plan, resulting in data and information that can be used to evaluate effectiveness or instill accountability. The DHS (2006) advises that three types of measures can be produced: (1) descriptive measures, (2) process or output measures, and (3) outcome measures. In terms of descriptive measures, the system will lead to the development of a more comprehensive and accurate inventory of critical infrastructure assets geographically and by industry. It will also provide information about system relationships or the interdependency of particular assets on other assets. Not only do we live in a global economy, but nationally, numerous industries depend on supplies provided by other industries. An attack on one industry can have a domino effect resulting in a massive economic disruption across several sectors.

Process evaluations focus on security efficacy. First, they examine how well security measures meet stated security goals: Do we have the desired level of protection? The various security measures are examined to ensure that they achieve desired results. Second, these evaluations attempt to determine if security measures are implemented as envisioned by policy makers. There often are significant differences or deviations between what is actually implemented and what has been designed or envisioned. A process evaluation will ensure that security measures meet standards or requirements and require adjustments when there are inconsistencies. To a large extent, process evaluations ensure that programs are operating as expected.

Finally, outcome measures attempt to measure whether the facility has the desired level of security. We noted that the first step in the homeland security process is the development and articulation of security goals or standards: Is the potential target or critical infrastructure sufficiently safe from an attack? This is usually accomplished by applying standard attack scenarios based on intelligence from previous attacks on similar facilities. Deficiencies noted in the evaluation can be the result of two factors. First, the security plan that was implemented at the facility was deficient—it did not result in adequate levels of security. Second, it may be the result of the plan not being implemented correctly—process evaluation issues. The outcome measures are the key indicators of a facility's readiness and ability to withstand an attempted breach; when outcomes are less than satisfactory, remedial action must be taken.

When these evaluations are conducted across all critical infrastructure assets, in the result is a database that can provide an overview of America's security. Moreover, individual industry evaluations can be aggregated to determine an industry's relative safety from attack. Such a database allows us to rank various industries in terms of their ability to withstand or thwart an attack. This process also results in core metrics. That is, there will be some security measures that can be applied to all assets. On the other hand, some protective measures may be applicable to a particular group of assets. Once these core measures are identified, their application can be generally applied to a particular industry or set of assets, which facilitates security implementation and evaluation. Of course, there are instances when unique security measures will be applied to specific assets. Nonetheless, planning, implementation, and evaluation are expedited as a result of this process.

CRITIQUE OF THE *NATIONAL INFRASTRUCTURE PROTECTION PLAN* MODEL

The six-phased model of the homeland security risk management framework as outlined in the *National Infrastructure Protection Plan* is a comprehensive model based on data collection at a number of levels. It is based on rational comprehensive planning and decision making that assumes the planner or decision maker has all the necessary information and is able to process all the information before making a decision. However, a substantial amount of information is unavailable to decision makers when using the risk management model envisioned in the *National Infrastructure Protection Plan*. Problems are not clearly enumerated, and officials do not have complete information by which to make decisions. First, there are no firmly established security goals. An examination of many security goals demonstrates that they are general statements and global in nature, for example, provide security, prevent attack, or mitigate problems, but realistically, they are not useful when attempting to understand the level of security that is required for critical infrastructure assets; for example, what level of security should exist for a petrochemical facility, electric transmission line, or a federal reserve bank? Precise security standards have not been established across all industries. Realistically, we cannot have security without security goals or performance standards.

Second, in terms of identifying assets, the DHS has been working on a National Asset Database for a number of years. However, it remains questionable if the database is accurate—how many nonessential assets are included in the database and how many essential assets are excluded? Moteff (2007) found a number of such inconsistencies. Nonetheless, the database does provide a starting point and, perhaps, is the strongest link in the protection chain. Further efforts are needed to ensure the accuracy of the database. This involves the development of clear criteria for inclusion in the database.

Although the National Asset Database contains more than 28,000 assets, the actual number likely is infinite. It may be possible to provide adequate security for the most important assets, but many others of less importance will remain viable targets. Attacking a shopping mall or exploding a car bomb may not have as profound an impact; nonetheless, it would significantly affect the American population at a number of levels. Protection levels for some assets may lead to displacement whereby terrorists simply attack targets that are more vulnerable. Ellig, Guiora, and McKenzie (2006) examined suicide bombers in Israel and found that they often detonated their bombs on busy streets because shopping malls had more security. Mueller (2008) recommends that officials abandon compiling a critical infrastructure asset list altogether or at least identify only the most important or most critical economic assets and concentrate efforts on those assets. He also advises that the probability of any given asset being attacked is zero and rather than spending billions on asset protection, it may be more economical to rebuild any assets that are destroyed by terrorists.

Third, and likely the most problematic, is assessing risks. To perform this function, one must have accurate information about (1) consequences of an attack or destruction of a particular asset, (2) vulnerability of an asset, and (3) the level of threat. Officials have not adequately determined the consequences of attacks on specific assets. Currently, security standards do not exist for much of the critical infrastructure, and without such standards, it is somewhat difficult to determine a potential target's or a group of targets' vulnerability. Even with standards, a determination of vulnerability is quite subjective with a degree of inherent error. The threat level is even more complicated. There have been relatively few terrorist attacks, but there are multiple terrorist organizations that would do America harm. We, in essence, do not know which of the thousands of possible targets is the focus of terrorists' planning. Risk assessment becomes little more than subjective judgments.

Perhaps a good example is the threat system that currently is used by the DHS. Generally, the threat level is orange, and in fact it remains at this level most of the time. There have been occasions when the threat level has been raised from orange to red, indicating that a threat is more probable. In most cases, if not all, a rise in the threat level by the DHS is the result of Middle Eastern "chatter," that is, an increase in Internet and other communications coming from those areas where large numbers of terrorist groups exist. It is assumed that the chatter is a precursor to a terrorist attack. However, when the threat system is raised, no information is provided to the public or law enforcement agencies relative to possible or potential targets. In other words, when a threat level is raised, local responders and law enforcement are given no guidance or information to plan their reactions.

A corollary to this problem is that regardless of the levels of security imposed for a particular asset, it remains quite easy to inflict some level of damage. When people think of maximum security, they generally envision military bases or military research complexes. Even with the levels of security at these installations, there is a degree of vulnerability. A motivated terrorist or group of terrorists likely can discover an avenue of attack. When levels of security and types of measures are identified for an industry or type of facility, it is likely that the costs will prohibit their complete implementation. Critical infrastructure asset protection likely will not meet standards nor will it measure up to the absolute standards often imposed at military and scientific installations. Thus, there always will be a measure of vulnerability. This issue is at the heart of setting security goals as discussed earlier.

The fourth step in the model is to establish priorities, which is driven by risk assessment. As noted, risk assessment's efficacy remains in question. Nonetheless, one must attempt to identify those assets or industries that pose the greatest risk. Once this is done, one must develop and implement policies and procedures that result in greater levels of security. The problem is that not only are there a large number of assets, but also a multitude of industries and individual facilities or assets. Regulatory agencies have not implemented enhanced security requirements except in a few cases, and when such requirements exist, it is questionable if they meet the identified security goals. For example, nuclear facilities are highly regulated in terms of security, but petroleum, water, and natural gas facilities are not, and when standards exist, they are only haphazardly enforced. Most critical assets are owned by private corporations, and they likely are not willing to implement expensive security measures that detract from profits without being required to do so through governmental regulation.

The fifth step in the model is to implement security measures. As noted, there are numerous security measures that can be implemented. How will it be determined which of the standards should be applied to a particular industry? Should all the assets in a particular industry be required to implement the same security measures? This assumes that there are few differences across assets in an industry and core measures can be used throughout. In many industries, there are newer and older facilities that in terms of security and construction are very different. There may be so many differences within particular industries that so-called core standards will be of little use.

The sixth step in the model is feedback and evaluation. Governments in general do not comprehend the idea of evaluation. An examination of programs across all sectors of the economy and society would show that government focuses on "output" or "effort." Members of Congress, the president, and other members of the executive branch often discuss new programs, how much is being spent on a given problem, or the number of citizens being served. Much of this programming is guided by pork barrel politics, interest groups, or the need to appear to be doing something that is important. The point is that politicians and government in general seldom examine a program or activity to evaluate whether it accomplishes what it is supposed to be accomplished: Does the program solve the problem (outcomes)? Cost effectiveness is often discussed in government, but seldom implemented.

The *National Infrastructure Protection Plan* as detailed here represents a comprehensive strategy by which to protect the American people and critical assets. It is a rational comprehensive model that examines protective standards, infrastructure assets, threats, protection, and feedback to determine how well assets individually and collectively are protected from terrorist attacks. However, it is questionable as how effective the plan is. At this juncture, it appears to be a more conceptual than realistic model. At best, it has been applied piecemeal across some of America's industries. Many of these protective measures were mandated prior to the plan, so it is questionable if the model has had much effect in protecting America. It appears to be a theoretical or conceptual plan that presents an "ideal" benchmark for the future.

A BOTTOM-UP APPROACH

As noted, numerous problems are associated with the *National Infrastructure Protection Plan*. It represents a comprehensive, top-down approach to developing protection for infrastructure. It seems that actual protection mechanics are lost in its complexity and comprehensiveness.

Analysis Box 3-3

The *National Infrastructure Protection Plan* outlines a comprehensive model to safeguard our critical infrastructure assets. However, it appears to be extremely complicated, requiring a great deal of data and information. On the other hand, the bottom-up approach appears to be less complicated and depends to some extent on current industry standards. What are the differences between these two approaches? Which approach do you believe would result in the highest levels of security? Why?

The process is unwieldy. Woodbury (2005) suggests that perhaps the first step in infrastructure protection is to identify the protective measures that are in place. This **bottom-up approach** would allow us to determine which security measures are in place across various industries. It would lead to the identification of core security systems across the various industries. Second, once systems or measures have been identified, they should be evaluated in terms of their costs and effectiveness. What levels of security do they provide? This could lead to the development of an inventory of best practices that can be shared with various industries. It would also provide information about the protective levels of assets and industries, which is a necessary next step in future policy formulation. A simpler bottom-up approach likely will lead to higher levels of security at least in terms of asset protection.

There has been some movement toward a bottom-up approach. In 2009, the Federal Emergency Management Agency issued a draft copy of the *Target Capabilities List: User Guide*. This document is intended to implement more capabilities-based preparedness, in essence supplementing the *National Preparedness Guidelines* and the *National Infrastructure Protection Plan*. The stated goal of the *Target Capabilities List* is to "provide more user-friendly, accessible, and credible capacity targets with which to link all preparedness cycle activities to strengthen preparedness across prevention, protection, response, and hazard mitigation capabilities" (p. 3). It requires that government and private entities identify "credible targets" and link them to homeland security processes—a bottom-up approach. It is interesting that the document discusses potential targets in terms of classes or industries. Each class is then directly linked to stated capabilities and responsible parties. In other words, protection and response goals are established for each class of potential target or critical infrastructure asset. This appears to be a more efficient method or approach to critical infrastructure protection.

THE REALITY OF CRITICAL INFRASTRUCTURE PROTECTION: STATES' RESPONSIBILITIES

Most of this chapter has examined the federal framework for protecting the nation's critical infrastructure assets. Conspicuously absent from this discussion has been state and local governments' collective responsibilities. However, when a disaster or terrorist attack occurs, the target of the attack will be an asset located in a local jurisdiction within a state. Therefore, the states and local governments have substantial responsibility for the protection of infrastructure assets. *National Infrastructure Protection Plan* (2006) discusses the importance of state and local governments' involvement in homeland security. Their responsibilities mirror the federal government in that they should organize and plan for homeland security events, be involved in infrastructure risk management, share information with the private sector and other governmental bodies, and coordinate activities with agencies involved in homeland security.

HS Web Link: To learn how the DHS is providing grants to the states to improve homeland security, go to http://www.dhs.gov/ynews/releases/pr_1260283102665.shtm

The states have a large measure of responsibility in critical infrastructure asset protection. Indeed, given the federal responses to natural disasters in the past, the states and localities are saddled with substantial responsibility, and it likely will be no different in the event of a future terrorist attack. The central question here is, "What is the demarcation line between federal and state responsibilities?" There is some likelihood that the federal government will define its role as supportive as opposed to being primarily responsible for mitigation. Given this situation, it is important for the states to understand their roles in the event of a catastrophe.

Lewis and Darken (2005) note that the federal government should provide the states with guidance and funding for securing critical infrastructure assets since the states are primarily responsible for securing and defending these assets. Local and state law enforcement agencies have the personnel who patrol and respond to infrastructure problems or threats Federal officials are generally called upon after the problem has occurred. State and local authorities are in a better position to provide protection. However, it is currently unclear as to whether state and local governments have the guidance to make asset protection decisions. The *National Infrastructure Protection Plan* certainly is in place, but for the most part it is abstract and has not consistently been equated to operational policies.

Part of this problem is that state and local officials may not comprehend the degree of risk associated with specific targets. Large facilities are located in local jurisdictions, but local authorities often do not understand or have knowledge of their importance to the economy, nor do they always have information about their vulnerability. A corollary to this is that if local jurisdictions are involved in developing the primary security plans for asset protection, what criteria will be used to establish a priority list? The *National Infrastructure Protection Plan* discusses some of these criteria, but local jurisdictions likely will evaluate assets based on their importance to the community as opposed to the nation as a whole. Local jurisdictions likely will give greater credence to a facility that employs a large number of people as compared to a firm that handles several states' communications.

Another problem is that most critical infrastructure is owned by private enterprise. Infrastructure sectors are generally regulated by the federal government. Therefore, local and state officials have little authority or ability to impose infrastructure protection requirements. Such requirements normally are imposed by Congress or by federal regulatory agencies. This implies that the federal government's role must be larger than advisory or supportive. Only the federal government can force industries to implement safeguards. State and local units of government do not have the tools to implement all the necessary preventive measures. There must be greater coordination between the levels of government.

The DHS has operated under the **big bang theory of asset protection** (Lewis and Darken, 2005). Here, the most attention, efforts, and resources have been assigned to the high-value targets, but in most cases, these are targets that are the least likely to be attacked. For example, a nuclear reactor is a high-value but well-protected target. On the other hand, a chemical plant is of lessor value as a target, but also less secure. As noted in the National Asset Database, thousands of other targets are geographically dispersed across the United States, and their protection falls squarely on state and local officials who realistically do not have the expertise and resources to provide adequate protection. It is obvious that one must consider in greater detail how assets are to be protected and state in concrete terms the responsibilities of the federal, state, and local governments.

KEY CRITICAL INFRASTRURE SECTORS

A discussion of potential targets of terrorist attacks generally distinguishes between soft and hard targets. *Hard targets* are generally but not always military in nature and are hardened with a variety of security measures. *Soft targets*, on the other hand, generally refer to civilian targets that have little protection and are vulnerable to attack. The primary purpose of the *National Infrastructure Protection Plan* (DHS, 2006) is to enhance security around soft targets. Unfortunately, there are numerous such targets that are vulnerable to attack.

When most Americans think of terrorists, they focus almost exclusively on Middle Eastern terrorist groups such as al Qaeda, Hamas, or Hezbollah. There certainly are a number of global jihadist groups that desire to attack U.S. infrastructure. However, they are not alone. For example, Ackerman, Bale, and Moran (2006) identify American radical right-wing groups and ecology or "eco-terrorist" groups as also having motive to attack infrastructure. In some ways, members of these groups see some infrastructures as epitomizing their perceived injustices in America, and their destruction would make an important political statement. Thus, there are many threats to infrastructure assets. The following sections examine some of the critical infrastructure and their vulnerabilities.

Water

There are approximately 170,000 water systems in the United States (Bullock et al., 2005). Moreover, these water supply systems are concentrated in specific geographical areas. Zimmerman (2006) advises that 45 percent of the American population is served by 6.8 percent of the water systems. Terrorists can disrupt water supplies in two ways. First, the computer networks that control water systems could be hacked or fall prey to a cyber attack. Such an attack could cause the release of water out of reservoirs or other containment facilities or contaminate the water through faulty or inadequate treatment. Second, the water could be contaminated with the release of toxins, bacteria, or other contagion. Although there have been no documented terrorist attacks on the nation's water supplies to date, there have been documented cases of sabotage. In one case, a water tower in Spokane, Washington, was broken into and the water was contaminated with bacteria; at the same time, a water reservoir in nearby Idaho was contaminated with the same bacteria. Two other water supplies were contaminated, one with bacteria and the other with toxic chemicals (Forest, 2006). These examples demonstrate the potential for attacks on water supplies. It points to the need for officials to constantly monitor water quality and ensure that automated controls are secured.

Energy

Energy—oil, gas, and electricity—has become a cogent political issue as demands have increased, sometimes stripping availability and increasing the threat of global warming. The United States has a massive energy infrastructure. The electric industry serves 130 million households and the nation consumes approximately 3.6 trillion kilowatt hours of electricity annually. The electricity is distributed through an extensive power grid that touches every corner of the country. There are more than 300,000 producing oil wells in the United States and 153 refineries and more than 7,500 petroleum storage facilities. There are 278,000 miles of natural gas lines serving the American people (Bullock et al., 2005).

The energy infrastructure is vast and geographically dispersed, and for the most part, it is unguarded. This makes the energy infrastructure vulnerable to terrorist attacks. Although there

Water systems are vulnerable to attacks.   *Source:* http://www.dhs.gov/xlibrary/assets/NIPP_Plan.pdf

have not been any terrorist attacks on these assets to date, there have been acts of vandalism and sabotage (see Forest, 2006). Industrial accidents and natural disaster events also have destroyed facilities, causing supply disruptions. In 2008, a severe gasoline shortage in the Southeastern United States was one result of a hurricane that destroyed a primary refinery in Louisiana, and there have been numerous blackouts and brownouts, some severe and lasting for long periods of time. The most common problem is deteriorating or overburdened infrastructure. Potential terrorist attacks, realistically, would have little impact on this infrastructure, as witnessed by the effects of the industrial accidents and natural disasters. This infrastructure is fairly redundant, and when there is a disruption, facilities are quickly repaired or resources are rerouted to the affected area.

However, some of these facilities should receive special consideration. First, since most of the energy supply movement is controlled by computer systems, it must be ensured that these automated control systems are secure from hacking and other cyber attacks—security software and hardware should be constantly evaluated and updated. Second, some facilities store or contain large amounts of natural gas or petroleum products, and their destruction could result in a shortage of supplies for consumers and environmental and economic problems for those residing in the immediate area. Also, nuclear facilities are a special case since an attack on these facilities could have drastic results as discussed in Chapter 9. These types of facilities should receive some level of enhanced security.

Our energy grid is vast and open and may become a target for terrorists.

Airline Security

The 9/11 attacks dramatically pointed to a significant security problem with the national aviation network. Airplanes were commandeered and used as bombs, resulting in the loss of 3,000 lives and billions of dollars of damage. In 1988, Libyan intelligence officials placed a bomb on Pan Am Flight 103, causing the plane to explode and crash in Lockerbie, Scotland. These and other attacks across the world dramatize the need for better airline security. In the wake of the 9/11 attacks, the Aviation and Transportation Act was passed. The act accomplished three security tasks: (1) It established the Transportation Security Administration (TSA) charged with security of the national transportation system, (2) mandated that TSA employees screen passenger luggage and air freight, and (3) by December 2002 screen all passenger baggage using X-ray equipment. Today, passengers are screened using electromagnetic devices that detect metal (possible weapons). The TSA is in the process of installing millimeter-wave passenger-screening technology. This machine transmits radio waves that are reflected off the passenger, producing a detailed image to identify any possible weapons or explosives. The new technology is more effective compared to electromagnetic screening. Even though the TSA is responsible for screening, the individual airport authorities and the airlines are ultimately responsible for overall security, which often is coordinated by the Federal Aviation Administration.

Cargo has become another security issue. Even though passengers and their baggage are screened, not all cargo is being screened for explosive devices. About 22 percent or 2.8 million tons of domestic cargo travels via passenger airline service each year (Lipton, 2007). Congress has mandated that cargo be screened, but this objective has not been fully met. At the time of the mandate, only about one-third of cargo was screened. The TSA has worked to achieve 100 percent screening. Another potential airline security problem is surface-to-air missiles. In 2002, al Qaeda attacked an Israeli airliner in Mombassa, Kenya (Flynn and Kosatka, 2006).

Clarke (2008) notes that missile attacks on airliners are a real problem and that the government has not done enough to protect air travel from these attacks. He notes that it would cost approximately $1 billion to equip airliners with protective devices, and it would cost the U.S. economy about $1 trillion should an airliner be shot down with a surface-to-air missile. Only Air Force One is currently equipped with this technology.

One final threat to air travel security is physical attacks on airports. In 1999, Ahmed Ressam was arrested as he entered the United States from Canada with the intent to set off a bomb at the Los Angeles Airport. In 1997, four Muslim men were arrested in New Jersey for planning to attack JFK International Airport. They had planned to bomb jet fuel supply tanks and a major fuel pipeline. In 2002, Hesham Mohamed Hadayet, an Egyptian, killed two people and wounded several others at an El Al ticketing station in Los Angeles before being killed by security personnel. These incidents serve notice that airport security must go beyond screening passengers, baggage, and cargo. A number of parameter issues must be considered.

Hotel Security

Terrorists often attack soft targets such as hotels, restaurants, schools, and hospitals. Robbins (2006) found that between 1968 and 2005, 73 percent of terrorists' targets were soft targets. Hotels are one of the most common targets of terrorist attacks. They are prime targets because the terrorists often are able to inflict large numbers of casualties, invoke panic and other psychological consequences, and adversely affect a community and possibly a country's economy. Also, hotels are likely targets because there generally are large numbers of hotels in large urban areas, allowing the terrorists to choose a high-value target that is readily accessible and allows for escape. Hotels generally have little or no security, which also facilitates attack. They have a constant flow of people, allowing the terrorists to mingle and fit in with the clientele. Figure 3-4 provides a partial listing of major hotel bombings across the globe.

An examination of hotel bombings shows a number of trends. First, the attackers generally concentrate on luxury hotels (Jenkins, 2009). Many of the hotels were owned by Hilton and Marriott. Hotel attacks seem to be a tactic that is used by a variety of terrorist groups. The hotels are often frequented by government, international, and military leaders. In some cases, the terrorists struck when such dignitaries were in the hotel, scheduled to be at the hotel, or had recently stayed in the hotel. It appears that suicide bombings are the most common mode of

City	Year	Type of Attack	Casualties	Group Responsible
Algiers	2008	Suicide Bombing	31 deaths	Algerian Islamic Group
Kabul	2008	Suicide Bombing	6 deaths	Taliban
Islamabad	2008	Vehicle Bomb	56 deaths	Unknown Islamic Terrorist Group
Pattani, Thailand	2008	Vehicle Bomb	2 deaths	Muslim Separatists
Peshawar, Pakistan	2007	Planted Bomb	25 deaths	Unknown Islamic Terrorist Group
Baghdad	2007	Suicide Bombing	9 deaths	Unknown Islamic Terrorist Group
Amman	2005	Suicide Bombing	57 deaths	Al Qaeda
Istanbul	2004	Suicide Bombing	2 deaths	Kurdish Separatists
Jakarta	2003	Vehicle Bomb	12 deaths	Muslim Extremists

FIGURE 3-4 Sample of Terrorist Attacks on International Hotels. *Source:* Information collected from a variety of international news outlets.

Indian troops rally as the Taj Mahal Hotel burns during a gun battle between troops and terrorists inside the hotel.   *Source:* AP (081128039393)

attack. This seems to indicate that many hotels have security measures that prevent vehicle bombings or terrorists planting bombs—security measures that must be adopted by American hotels. An overwhelming majority of the bombings occur in areas wrought with political strife and terrorist activities.

THE SPECIAL CASE OF MUMBAI: AN ARMED ASSAULT   In the past, as noted in Figure 3-4, most hotel attacks were a single attack on a particular hotel. In some cases, the hotels were attacked in conjunction with other targets. On November 26, 2008, Pakistani terrorists conducted a multi-target attack in Mumbai, India, India's largest city and South Asia's financial capital. The attacks resulted in at least 173 deaths and 308 injured. The attack was made by a commando-like force that simultaneously attacked multiple targets, including the luxury hotels the Taj Mahal Palace and the Oberoi. In addition to attacking the hotels, the terrorists attacked a railway station, a popular café, and the Orthodox Jewish–owned Nariman House. It was estimated that the attacks included at least 16 groups of attackers. The attackers used automatic assault rifles and grenades. Once in the hotels, they went from floor to floor killing the lodgers. In many cases, they would check passports and other identification documents to determine nationality. The attackers primarily targeted American and British hotel guests (Magnier and Sharma, 2008).

The attacks were carried out by a militant Pakistani group, TashKar-e-Toiba. Its members traveled from Karachi, Pakistan, by boat across the Arabian Sea. The attacks immediately affected relations between India and Pakistan, which have been engaged in a decades-long conflict over the Kashmir region of India. India and Pakistan quickly moved additional troops to the border. Moreover, international intelligence officials reported that the terrorist group had received support from the Pakistani intelligence service, which further exacerbated relations between the two countries. The attacks also provided terrorist organizations, especially those in Pakistan, with a recruitment tool. In fact, al Qaeda warned India not to attack Pakistan after the Mumbai attacks (NDTV, 2009). The terrorists essentially showed that they could successfully conduct a major attack on India.

The Mumbai attacks represented the first time that terrorists had used this tactic: suicide commando units attacking multiple targets using small arms. However, in February 2009, Taliban fighters used a similar tactic in Kabul. The attackers simultaneously attacked three locations, including the Justice Ministry, using suicide bombers and automatic rifles. The attacks left at least 20 people dead. During the attack on the Justice Ministry, the attackers went floor to floor killing as many people as possible (Sachtman, 2009). It appears that commando attacks may have become a new tactic in the terrorists' arsenal.

Transportation

The United States has an extensive transportation system that includes roadways and rail. Both of these conduits carry massive numbers of passengers and cargo, including hazardous materials. They are concentrated in large urban areas and present challenges to homeland security. Numerous transportation disasters have killed and injured people, and a number of incidents have involved hazardous materials. Although there have not been terrorist attacks on these sectors, past experience points out that there always is that potential. For example, a number of terrorist attacks on Israeli citizens have been by suicide bombers detonating bombs on buses. The subway attacks in Madrid in 2004, Moscow in 2004, and London in 2005 provide credence to transportation being a likely target for terrorists. These incidents resulted in large numbers of casualties.

Rail transportation is vital in our metropolitan areas.

Analysis Box 3-4

Numerous types of physical infrastructure are considered when establishing a homeland security program. Of the various industries or types of infrastructure discussed in this section, which ones should receive the highest priority? How did you arrive at your decision?

People and hazardous materials are the two primary considerations in transportation systems. Regarding the safeguarding of people, some precautions have been implemented in the United States (see Forest, 2006). A number of transportation authorities have installed cameras to detect suspicious persons and activities. Trash cans or trash receptacles have been removed from transit stations as terrorists have planted bombs in these receptacles in other countries. In some cities, such as New York City, passengers and their belongings are subject to random searches to deter terrorists from carrying bombs onto buses and subways. The Department of Homeland Security is working to develop explosive detection sensors for installation in mass transit facilities. The Transportation Security Administration has been training explosive detection canines that are being deployed in airports and mass transit terminals. In the wake of the 2005 London bombings, British authorities have deployed millimeter-wave passenger-screening technology to screen passengers at mass transit terminals. Thus, it appears that mass transit security is being ramped up in some locations. The major problem facing transit authority officials is a lack of funding. Many of these systems operate in the red or their budgets are at a breakeven point.

The transportation of hazardous chemicals and material presents different problems. All sorts of hazardous materials are transported by rail and trucks throughout the United States. The U.S. Department of Transportation advises that there are 1.2 million daily shipments of hazardous materials by truck, rail, and air. These shipments range in size from several ounces to several tons (McGuire, 2005). Moreover, unlike mass transit, the shipment of hazardous materials occurs literally everywhere throughout the country. Hitherto, little consideration had been given to the transportation of hazardous materials unless there was some accident or incident involving them, and there are numerous major incidents each year occurring in rural and urban areas. For the most part, the Department of Homeland Security and the Transportation Department have initiated programs with haulers and shippers to better track hazardous materials while in transit. This will add a measure of accountability in the shipping of hazardous materials. Nonetheless, these materials present a significant hazard. Trucks or railcars containing hazardous materials can be blown up or tampered with to cause leakage in highly populated areas. At this point, monitoring seems to be the primary strategy to prevent terrorist attacks.

INFRASTRUCTURE FROM THE TERRORISTS' VIEWPOINT

The preceding sections outlined the many issues surrounding the protection of America's critical infrastructure. This section examines critical infrastructure from the terrorist's perspective. Even though there are literally thousands of potential targets in the United States, not all are equally inviting to the terrorist as a potential target. Indeed, some critical infrastructures are secured or located in such a manner that their attack would be quite difficult. Others may be located in geographical areas that make their attack difficult because of potential logistical problems for terrorists. Theoretically, some critical infrastructures are not potential targets because terrorists do not have the opportunity to mount a successful attack. If we better understand the limitations or constrictions placed on terrorists, we may be better able to identify those targets that are at greater risk.

Clarke and Newman (2006) have examined the opportunity for terrorist attacks in detail. They note that the commission of a terrorist act, like a criminal act, requires that terrorists have the opportunity to carry it out. As such, there are conditions that must exist for terrorists to be able to attack a specific target. They identified four factors or conditions that must exist for an attack to occur, as shown in Figure 3-5.

As can be seen in Figure 3-5, there are limitations on terrorists' target choices. Not all targets are created equal—some have natural inhibitors that cause them to be disregarded by potential terrorists. This information allows us to examine critical infrastructure from the terrorists' perspective and provides two important advantages when attempting to secure our infrastructure. First, if we apply the four conditions or requirements to critical infrastructure, we can make a rough determination about the infrastructure's vulnerability or its potential as a target. For example, a high-value target located in mid-America has a lower level of risk since it is inherently more difficult for terrorists to travel there undetected and acquire the tools and weapons to mount an attack. Thus, we can limit the number of potential targets that can be considered by terrorists. In fact, we can reasonably surmise that terrorists are more likely to attack a target in urban areas, especially those that have larger Middle Eastern populations—they must be able to blend in with the population to avoid suspicion. Second, it advises us on how to deploy additional security measures for high-value targets. We can apply the four conditions to a location and make an estimate of the probability of attack. The criteria outlined in Figure 3-5 likely will produce better estimates as compared to the formula outlined in the *National Strategy for Homeland Security*. Moreover, it likely will provide more information about how to safeguard some high-value targets.

Conditions	
1. Targets	Although there are multiple targets, many are not worthy or suitable for a variety of reasons: (a) destruction of target does not achieve terrorists' objectives; (b) located in an area where strangers, especially Middle Easterners, would be observed; (c) target is too well guarded; and (d) the size or nature of the target makes total destruction difficult.
2. Weapons	Not all weapons are appropriate for a given target. Weapons required to attack a specific target may not be available. For example, some targets are more suitable for attack with biological weapons, but if these are not available, an attack cannot be effectively mounted. Today, it is difficult to obtain large amounts of explosives to attack a large target. The attack on a potential target can be mounted only with the appropriate weapons.
3. Tools	Terrorists must acquire a number of tools, including vehicles, pilot's license, proper identity papers, identification allowing access to a target, and so on. These tools are necessary to conduct an attack. If they cannot be obtained, an attack cannot occur.
4. Facilitating Conditions	Terrorists often exploit security lapses, loopholes, and so on when choosing a target. If these do not exist, it is inherently more difficult to mount an attack. The degree of security often is not known until immediately prior to an attack, which serves to dissuade an attack.

FIGURE 3-5 Conditions Necessary to Facilitate a Terrorist Attack.

Analysis Box 3-5

Clarke and Newman examine the selection of targets from the terrorists' perspective. They recognize that terrorists have limitations, especially logistical issues.

Based on their analysis, do you reside in an area that is more or less susceptible to terrorist attacks? How should this affect homeland security planning in your area?

It is informative to apply Clarke and Newman's conditions to an actual situation. An examination of Gaza in Palestine shows that Hamas has been conducting a war with the Israelis for a number of years. Its primary modes of attacks have been suicide bombers and rocket attacks. The Israelis have attempted to thwart suicide bombers by walling off Gaza and searching Palestinians who leave the area and enter Israel. This essentially affects potential terrorists' tools and weapons. Since the Palestinians are inhibited, some of the facilitating conditions are also limited. The walling off of Gaza has prevented most weapons from entering the area, although some weapons are smuggled into Gaza through tunnels from Egypt. Moreover, the Israelis frequently target and attack suspected rocket launching locations and storage facilities, making such attacks difficult. Even though Hamas has launched hundreds of rockets into Israel, they have been crude and have produced few casualties. The bottom line is that there are conditions that limit Hamas's modes and methods of attack. Limitations should be a part of the calculus as we decide on infrastructure protection.

Summary

Homeland security has been a governmental initiative for generations, but the 9/11 attacks in New York City and Washington, D.C., made it a national prerogative. Americans were acutely aware that they could be attacked and were in danger from foreign extremists. Currently, there is no clear definition of homeland security. It includes a number of problems or conditions centering on terrorist attacks, catastrophes, and hazards. This lack of definition leads to operational problems and an unclear path for implementation. Upon examining the literature, it appears that homeland security essentially consists of three primary objectives: (1) prevention of terrorist attacks, (2) protection of American citizens and infrastructural resources, and (3) response and recovery from incidents that do occur. It is all encompassing in that numerous federal, state, and local agencies are involved in implementing homeland security. The primary concern, however, is the protection of people and infrastructure.

The framework for implementing homeland security is enumerated in the *National Infrastructure Protection Plan*. It is a national imperative that is applicable to all infrastructure and human resources. It represents the foundation for planning and security implementation. It consists of six steps or phases:

1. Establishment of security or protection goals
2. Identification of critical infrastructure assets
3. Assess risks to various assets and industries
4. Prioritize security measures and assets
5. Implement protection programs
6. Measure the effectiveness of measures that have been implemented

Numerous issues are associated with the model. For the most part, it is too comprehensive and complicated. It is questionable as to what degree the model has been implemented. That is, it may remain as a theoretical perspective or idea type that is unachievable across many infrastructure sectors. The relative responsibilities of the local, state, and federal governments have not been solidified. Nonetheless, we must develop a national strategy for protecting people and infrastructure, one that can be implemented clearly and comprehensively. It seems a first step should be an inventory of current modes of protection and an evaluation of their effectiveness. This would provide a solid foundation from which to build in the future.

Discussion Questions

1. What is critical infrastructure?
2. How is the federal government organized in terms of responsibility for safeguarding critical infrastructure assets?
3. Discuss the National Asset Database and its effectiveness in contributing to homeland security.
4. What are the elements in the *National Infrastructure Protection Plan and Risk Management Framework* and how do they function?
5. What is the bottom-up approach to infrastructure protection and how does it compare to the *National Infrastructure Protection Plan and Risk Management Framework*?
6. Water is an important critical infrastructure asset. How can water systems be attacked?
7. From a terrorist's standpoint, what conditions must exist for an attack to be successful?
8. What is the big bang theory of asset protection?

References

Ackerman, G., J. Bale, and K. Moran. (2006). "Assessing the threat to critical infrastructure." In *Homeland Security: Protecting America's Targets*, Vol. 3, pp. 33–60. Westport, CT: Praeger Security International.

Army Corps of Engineers. (2006). "Waterborne commerce statistics center." http://www.iwr.usace.army.mil/ndc/wcsc/by_portname04.htm (Accessed July 13, 2008).

Bullock, J., G. Haddow, D. Coppola, E. Ergin, L. Westerman, and S. Yeletaysi. (2005). *Introduction to Homeland Security*. Burlington, MA: Elsevier.

Clarke, R. (2008). *Your Government Failed You: Breaking the Cycle of National Security Disasters*. New York: HarperCollins.

Clarke, R. and G. Newman. (2006). *Outsmarting the Terrorists*. Westport, CT: Praeger Security International.

Department of Homeland Security. (2006). *National Infrastructure Protection Plan*. Washington, D.C.: Author.

Ellig, J., A. Guiora, and K. McKenzie. (2006). *A Framework for Evaluating Counterterrorism Regulations*. Washington, D.C.: Mercatus Center, George Mason University.

Emerson, S. and B. Duffy. (1990). *The Fall of Pan Am 103: Inside the Lackerbie Investigation*. New York: Putnum.

FEMA. (2009). *Target Capabilities List: User Guide*. Washington, D.C.: Author.

Flynn, G. and A. Kosatka. (2006). "Civil aviation in the United States: Security before and after 9/11." In *The McGraw-Hill Homeland Security Handbook,* ed. G. Kamien, pp. 613–30. New York: McGraw-Hill.

Forest, J. (2006). "Protecting America's critical infrastructure: An introduction." In *Homeland Security: Protecting America's Targets*, Vol. 3, ed. J. Forest, pp. 1–29. Westport, CT: Praeger Security International.

Jenkins, B. (2009). *Terrorists Can Think Strategically: Lessons Learned from the Mumbai Attacks*. Santa Monica, CA: RAND Corp.

Lewis, T. and R. Darken. (2005). "Potholds and detours in the road to critical infrastructure protection policy." *Homeland Security Affairs*, 1(2): 1–15.

Lipton, E. (2007). "New security for air cargo screening." *International Herald Tribune* (February 8). http://www.iht.com/articles/2007/02/08/news/security.php (Accessed December 8, 2008).

Looney, R. (2002). "Economic costs to the United States stemming from the 9/11 attacks." *Strategic Insights*, 1(6): 1–4.

Magnier, M. and S. Sharma. (2008). "Terror attacks ravage Mumbai: At least 101 die; Americans and Britons apparently sought as hostages." *Los Angeles Times* (November 27), pp. A1, A8, A10.

McGuire, R. (2005). Statement before the Committee on Homeland Security, Subcommittee on Economic Security, Infrastructure Protection, and Cybersecurity, U.S. House of Representatives (November 1). http://testimony.ost.dot.gov/test/passtest/05test/McGuire1.htm (Accessed December 9, 2008).

Moteff, J. (2007). *Critical Infrastructure: The National Asset Database*. CRS Report for Congress. Washington, D.C.: Congressional Research Service.

Mueller, J. (2008, March). "The quixotic quest for invulnerability: Assessing the costs, benefits, and probabilities of protecting the homeland." Paper presented at the National Convention of the International Studies Association, San Francisco.

NDTV. (2009). *Al Qaeda Warns India of Any Attack on Pakistan* (February 10). http://www.ndtv.com/convergence/ndtv/mumbaiterrorstrike/Story.aspx?ID=NEWEN20090083079 (Accessed February 11, 2009).

Office of Homeland Security. (2007). *The National Strategy for Homeland Security*. Washington, D.C.: Author.

Office of Homeland Security. (2002). *The National Strategy for Homeland Security*. Washington, D.C.: Author.

Office of the President. (2003). *The National Strategy for the Physical Protection of Critical Infrastructure and Key Assets.* Washington, D.C.: Author.

Performak, P. (2007). *Vulnerability of Concentrated Critical Infrastructure: Background and Policy Options.* Washington, D.C.: Congressional Research Service.

Robbins, J. (2006). "Soft targets, hard choices." In *Homeland Security: Protecting America's Targets,* Vol. 2, pp. 37–50. Westport, CT: Praeger Security International.

Sachtman, N. (2009). "Mumbai-style attack in Kabul leaves 20 dead." http://blog.wired.com/defense/2009/ 02/mumbai-style-at.html (Accessed February 11, 2009).

Weaver, J. (1985). "Statement." *Congressional Record (Procedures and Debates, 99th Congress,* 131(3–4) (February 28, 1985): 4185–89.

Woodbury, G. (2005). "Measuring prevention." *Homeland Security Affairs,* 1(1): 1–9.

Zimmerman, R. (2006). "Critical infrastructure and interdependency." In *The McGraw-Hill Homeland Security Handbook,* ed. G. Kamien, pp. 523–45. New York: McGraw-Hill.

Legal Aspects of Homeland Security

LEARNING OBJECTIVES

1. Understand the legality and role of presidential orders.
2. Know the progression of executive orders as they relate to homeland security and counterterrorism.
3. Be able to discuss the Foreign Intelligence Surveillance Act Court.
4. Be familiar with the USA PATRIOT Act and its scope.

KEY TERMS

Executive orders

Proliferation of Weapons of Mass Destruction

Blocking Property of Weapons of Mass Destruction Proliferators and Their Supporters

Prohibiting Transactions with Terrorists Who Threaten to Disrupt the Middle East Peace Process

Blocking Property and Prohibiting Transactions with Persons Who Commit, Threaten to Commit, or Support Terrorism

National Counterterrorism Center

Interpretation of the Geneva Conventions Common Article 3 as Applied to a Program of Detention and Interrogation Operated by the Central Intelligence Agency

Homeland Security Information Sharing

Strengthening the Sharing of Terrorism Information to Protect Americans

Establishing the President's Homeland Security Advisory Council and Senior Advisory Committees for Homeland Security.

Public Alert and Warning System

Review and Disposition of Individuals Detained at the Guantánamo Bay Naval Base and Closure of Detention Facilities

Special Interagency Task Force on Detainee Disposition

Antiterrorism and Effective Death Penalty Act of 1996

USA PATRIOT Act

Foreign Intelligence Surveillance Act of 1978

INTRODUCTION

In the aftermath of the terrorist attacks on September 11, 2001, the United States Congress enacted a series of laws designed to curb the possibility of another attack on American soil. These laws were passed with great speed and much public and media attention. The speed at which these laws were enacted is evidenced by the fact that the most well-known legislation, the USA PATRIOT Act, was passed by the U.S. House of Representatives with only one representative having read the bill before it was voted into law (Abourezk, 2008). Although well intended, many of the provisions of the new federal anti-terrorist legislation were so sweeping, unclear, and susceptible to abuse by government officials that corrective orders, new legislation, or judicial action was taken to address some of their many shortcomings.

Concern with terrorism and terrorist groups was not merely the product of the attacks of September 11th, nor was it limited to the legislative branch of government. Long before the attacks on Washington, D.C., and New York City, U.S. presidents have been issuing executive orders and directives designed to address the threat of terrorism. President Bill Clinton, for example, issued numerous executive orders that either directly or indirectly dealt with many of the issues surrounding terrorism. President George W. Bush was perhaps the most prolific issuer of orders addressing terrorism. President Barack Obama has also issued executive orders providing new directions in homeland security and terrorism. In all, a growing body of executive orders needs to be considered along with legislation passed by the Congress of the United States.

This chapter considers some of the most essential presidential executive orders, congressional legislation, and law enforcement authorizations and practices that have been crafted to combat terrorism and create a safe homeland. As can be seen, they provide a legal foundation for strengthening our ability to fight terrorism and respond to terrorist acts.

PRESIDENTIAL EXECUTIVE ORDERS AND DIRECTIVES

Presidents of the United States have the authority to issue a variety of executive orders, directives, and military orders (Relyea, 2008). Perhaps the oldest and best-known of these presidential instructions are **executive orders**. Executive orders are instructions to federal officials and agencies and are designed to govern the execution of public policy. When exercising presidential authority under emergency conditions, however, executive orders can take on a much more serious quality: "For example, President Roosevelt used an executive order on February 19, 1942, to require the internment of American citizens of Japanese ancestry who were living in certain designated Pacific coast defense areas" (citation omitted, Relyea, 2008: 8–9). Following the terrorist attacks of September 11, 2001, President George W. Bush began issuing executive orders and a new series of presidential directives called *Homeland Security Presidential Directives* (HSPDs). During his presidency, Bush issued at least 24 of these directives (Relyea, 2008) and numerous executive orders. Executive orders and directive can have far-reaching consequences. For example, HSPD-6 issued by President Bush created an elaborate terrorist identification and watch system as illustrated in Figure 4-1.

Executive orders and directives, although not legislation, have the force of law depending on their substantive effect. The contents of an executive order links policy statements and judgments of the executive branch of government to existing legislation. In essence, unlike a law enacted by Congress, a presidential order or directive itself does not carry the force of law, but rather the contents of the order and its relationship to existing authorities is determinative of its

HS Web Link: To learn more about presidential executive orders, go to *http://www.thisnation.com/question/040.html*

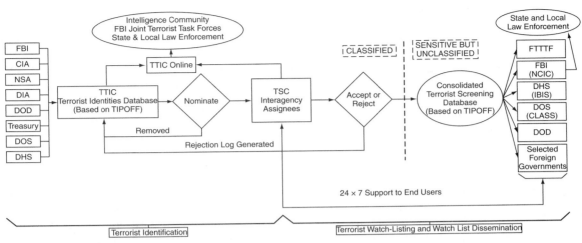

FIGURE 4-1   Terrorist Identification, watch-listing, and Watch List Dissemination under HSPD-6   *Source:* Krouse, W. J. (2004). *Terrorist Identification, Screening, and Tracking Under Homeland Security Presidential Directive 6.* CRS Report for Congress, April 21, 2004, p. 16.

legal effect. Executive orders and directives are policy statements that link governmental policy to existing legislation by drawing upon existing statutes for their authority or by providing direction for the application of the statutes they draw upon for their authority. An executive order remains in effect until a president changes it.

In the following section of this chapter, we review the provisions of several executive orders and directives issued by U.S. presidents that were designed to combat terrorism or provide a legal basis for developing homeland security measures.

President Clinton issued many early anti-terrorism executive orders.   *Source:* http://www. whitehouse.gov/photos-and-video/photogallery/the-presidents

Executive Orders of President Clinton

Although the public generally does not associate President Clinton with the "war on terrorism" or even the development of homeland security, he issued a number of executive orders that laid much of the policy foundation for the prevention of terrorism. President Clinton's orders evidence concern with four broad areas of government policy relating to homeland security: (1) control over the proliferation of weapons of mass destruction (WMDs), (2) control of financial transactions that could be used to support terrorism, (3) collection of intelligence information, and (4) protection of the nation's critical infrastructure. We consider each of these areas in the following sections that review executive orders.

PROLIFERATION OF WEAPONS OF MASS DESTRUCTION   President Clinton issued Executive Order #12938, **Proliferation of Weapons of Mass Destruction**, on November 14, 1994, under the International Emergency Economic Powers Act (50 U.S.C. 1701) and the National Emergencies Act (50 U.S.C. 1601), which enabled him to enact orders and directives during emergency situations. Declaring that the proliferation of nuclear, biological, and chemical weapons (WMDs) and their deliver systems constituted "an unusual and extraordinary threat to the national security," the president issued an executive order against their proliferation. The order (1) established multilateral international coordination to control the proliferation of WMDs and their delivery systems; (2) established a system for controlling exports of WMDs and any goods, technology, or services that could be used to "develop, produce, stockpile, deliver, or use weapons of mass destruction or their means of delivery"; (3) imposed sanctions on foreign persons and any foreign country that "use, develop, produce, stockpile, or otherwise acquire chemical or biological

National security cases often are adjudicated in the U.S. Supreme Court.   *Source:* http://www.supremecourt.gov/

weapons" in violation of international law; and (4) prohibited any government agency from procuring or entering into "any contract for the procurement of" WMD materials.

On June 28, 2005, President George H. Bush issued Executive Order #13382, **Blocking Property of Weapons of Mass Destruction Proliferators and Their Supporters**, designed to take additional steps to control the proliferation of WMDs by expanding the orders issued by President Clinton. The new order allowed blocking of the property and financial assets of any person or group thought to have given support for or

> Engaged, or attempted to engage, in activities or transactions that have materially contributed to, or pose a risk of materially contributing to, the proliferation of weapons of mass destruction or their means of delivery (including missiles capable of delivering such weapons), including any efforts to manufacture, acquire, possess, develop, transport, transfer or use such items, by any person or foreign country of proliferation concern.

These Orders provided operating agencies with guidance on how to prevent the proliferation of WMD materials. Since the threat posed by WMDs was so great, President Bush and President Clinton issued orders not only to prevent them from entering the United States, but also to prevent other countries from facilitating terrorists' acquisition of WMDs and WMD materials. They also enabled the federal government to take action against anyone who violated these orders.

PROHIBITING TRANSACTIONS WITH TERRORISTS WHO THREATEN TO DISRUPT THE MIDDLE EAST PEACE PROCESS President Clinton issued Executive Order #12947, **Prohibiting Transactions with Terrorists Who Threaten to Disrupt the Middle East Peace Process**, on January 23, 1995, to control acts of violence by certain Middle Eastern groups. The president was concerned that "foreign terrorists that disrupt the Middle East peace process constitute an unusual and extraordinary threat to the national security, foreign policy, and economy of the United States." The executive order prohibited financial transactions between U.S. citizens and any group of foreign persons designated by the secretary of state, the secretary of the treasury or the attorney general as constituting a "significant risk of committing acts of violence that have the purpose or effect of disrupting the Middle East peace process, or to assist in, sponsor, or provide financial, material, or technological support for, or services in support of, such acts of violence." The order prohibited donations to groups that engage in acts of violence and specifically prohibits "the making or receiving of any contribution of funds, goods, or services to or for the benefit of" people designated under the order. The order charged the FBI with investigating violations of its prohibitions.

This order was modified on August 20, 1998, by Executive Order #13099, which purposefully broadened its scope and directed its provisions against terrorist groups and specifically named

---

Analysis Box 4-1

Weapons of mass destruction are the greatest danger to homeland security. Executive Order #13382 attempts to prevent WMDs from falling in the hands of terrorists. It is an effort by the United States to prevent other countries from sharing technology.

Do you believe that financial punishment as proscribed in the executive order has the ability to stop nations from sharing technology? Does the executive order have any effect on terrorist groups or rogue nations?

Osama bin Laden and al Qaeda among other groups and individuals as terrorists. Later, on September 23, 2001, President Bush further bolstered the provisions of these orders by issuing Executive Order #13224, **Blocking Property and Prohibiting Transactions with Persons Who Commit, Threaten to Commit, or Support Terrorism**, which expanded the number of people designated as posing a significant risk of committing acts of terrorism that threaten the security of the United States.

The United States and other countries have been attempting to broker Middle East peace for decades. For example, President Clinton held the Wye River Talks in 1998, resulting in minor concessions on both sides, and he coordinated additional talks in 2000 (Migdalovitz, 2005). The Israeli-Palestinian issue has long served as a flashpoint for terrorism. There are numerous groups that are opposed to any peace settlement. Presidents Clinton and Bush provided a legal foundation by which to deal with individuals, countries, and groups that interfere with the peace process.

BLOCKING PROPERTY AND PROHIBITING TRANSACTIONS WITH THE TALIBAN   On July 4, 1999, President Clinton issued an executive order prohibiting transactions with the Taliban in Afghanistan and blocking the movement of their financial assets. The order stemmed from the president's concern that territory under Taliban control was being used as a safe haven and base of operations for Osama bin Laden and the al Qaeda organization and that their continued threats of violence "against the United States and its nationals constitute an unusual and extraordinary threat to the national security." The president ordered that all assets of the Taliban or of people who controlled or provided "financial, material, or technological support for" the Taliban be frozen. The order also prohibited any transaction, including the exporting or importing, of "any contribution of funds, goods, or services to or for the benefit of the Taliban" or "the exportation, re-exportation, sale, or supply, directly or indirectly, from the United States . . . of any goods, software, technology (including technical data), or services to the territory of Afghanistan controlled by the Taliban."

President Bush later terminated this executive order on July 2, 2002, commenting that the ability of the Taliban, al Qaeda, and Osama bin Laden to use Afghanistan as a safe haven and base of operation had been "significantly altered given the success of the military campaign in Afghanistan" (Executive Order #13268). Ironically, during the first year of President Barak Obama's term, the Taliban and al Qaeda's ability to use Afghanistan as a safe haven became a national security issue, demonstrating how rapidly conditions can change.

FOREIGN INTELLIGENCE PHYSICAL SEARCHES   On February 9, 1995, President Clinton issued an executive order authorizing the attorney general "to approve physical searches, without a court order, to acquire foreign intelligence information for periods of up to one year" and "to approve applications to the Foreign Intelligence Surveillance Court . . . to obtain orders for physical searches for the purpose of collecting foreign intelligence information." The order, based on the Foreign Intelligence Surveillance Act of 1978 (50 U.S.C. 1801 et seq., as amended by Public Law 103- 359), also authorized select government officials heading national security or defense agencies "to make the certifications required by . . . the Act in support of applications to conduct physical searches." The order was twice modified by President Bush following creation of the Office of Director of National Intelligence and after amendment of the Foreign Intelligence Surveillance Act of 1978 (50 U.S.C. 1801 et seq.).

The original order and its modifications set the stage for controversy surrounding our domestic surveillance program during the Bush administration. Civil libertarians attacked wiretaps that were conducted as a result of the order. Later it was mandated that such searches be reviewed by the court that was established to consider wiretaps. Little public information is available on the extent to which the Clinton administration used the provisions of the order.

CRITICAL INFRASTRUCTURE PROTECTION   Recognizing that national infrastructure is vital to the safe and efficient operation of the nation and "that their incapacity or destruction would have a debilitating impact on the defense or economic security of the United States," President Clinton issued an executive order on July 15,1996, to protect and ensure their operation. Critical infrastructures included "telecommunications, electrical power systems, gas and oil storage and transportation, banking and finance, transportation, water supply systems, emergency services (including medical, police, fire, and rescue), and continuity of government." The order recognized that critical infrastructure threats included both physical threats to real material property and electronic threats to radio frequencies, information systems, and communications systems. The order also acknowledged that much of the nation's infrastructure was under the control of the private sector.

The order established the *President's Commission on Critical Infrastructure Protection*, which was changed with (1) identifying and consulting with members of the public and private sectors having interests in critical infrastructure assurance, (2) assessing the scope and nature of threats to critical infrastructure, (3) determining legal and policy issues arising from efforts to secure critical infrastructure, and (4) making recommendations for a "comprehensive national policy and implementation strategy to protect critical infrastructures from physical and cyber threats."

To ensure the protection of critical infrastructure while the commission was carrying out its work, the president established an *Infrastructure Protection Task Force* (IPTF) in the Department of Justice. The IPTF's function was to

(i)   provide, or facilitate and coordinate the provision of, expert guidance to critical infrastructures to detect, prevent, halt, or confine an attack and to recover and restore service;

(ii) issue threat and warning notices in the event advance information is obtained about a threat;

(iii) provide training and education on methods of reducing vulnerabilities and responding to attacks on critical infrastructures;

(iv) conduct after-action analysis to determine possible future threats, targets, or methods of attack; and

(v)   coordinate with the pertinent law enforcement authorities during or after an attack to facilitate any resulting criminal investigation. (See also Executive Order #13025; Executive Order #13041)

This executive order and the work done by the commission and task force provided a foundation for much of the work that went into the development of the National Infrastructure Protection Plan that was discussed in Chapter 3. The plan now serves as the foundation for protecting our critical infrastructure assets.

In all, President Clinton issued several executive orders that laid the foundation for developing executive policy on combating the threat of terrorism. Many of these orders provided the basis for subsequent decisions made by the executive branch. Key among this policy foundation were concerns with WMDs, intelligence collection, financial transactions, and protection of infrastructure.

President Bush issued a substantial number of executive orders establishing our homeland security operations. *Source:* http://www.whitehouse.gov/photos-and-video/photogallery/the-presidents

Executive Orders of President George W. Bush

The 9/11 attacks occurred early in President Bush's administration. After the attacks, he issued a number of executive orders to strengthen our ability to combat possible terrorist attacks and to strengthen homeland security.

ESTABLISHING THE OFFICE OF HOMELAND SECURITY AND THE HOMELAND SECURITY COUNCIL   Perhaps the most important executive order issued by President George W. Bush was that of October 8, 2001, establishing an *Office of Homeland Security* (OHS) and the Homeland Security Council. The Homeland Security Council consisted of representatives from several executive branch departments and was charged with making policy and advising the president on homeland security matters.

The mission of the OHS was to "develop and coordinate the implementation of a comprehensive national strategy to secure the United States from terrorist threats or attacks." The OHS was to work with federal, state, and local agencies to "coordinate the executive branch's efforts to detect, prepare for, prevent, protect against, respond to, and recover from terrorist attacks within the United States." The order charged the newly created OHS with at least five basic responsibilities: (1) work with federal, state and local agencies; (2) prepare for and mitigate the consequences of terrorist threats and attacks; (3) coordinate efforts to prevent terrorist attacks within the United States; (4) protect critical infrastructure from the consequences of terrorist attacks; and (5) respond to and promote recovery from any terrorist threats or attacks on the United States. In addition to these major responsibilities, the OHS was charged with providing incident management, continuity of government, and the development of programs for educating the public about terrorism. This order established the foundation for the development of the Department of Homeland Security.

This proved to be an important step in developing our homeland security apparatus. The OHS later evolved into the Department of Homeland Security (Scardaville and Spencer, 2002). Prior to this change, the OHS developed a number of reports that remain crucial to homeland security operations—for example, the *National Strategy for Homeland Security*, which outlined our plan for homeland security (as discussed in Chapter 1).

NATIONAL COUNTERTERRORISM CENTER On August 27, 2004, President Bush issued Executive Order #13354, creating the **National Counterterrorism Center** (NCTS) to

a. serve as the primary organization in the United States Government for analyzing and integrating all intelligence possessed or acquired by the United States Government pertaining to terrorism and counterterrorism, excepting purely domestic counterterrorism information . . . ;

b. conduct strategic operational planning for counterterrorism activities, integrating all instruments of national power, including diplomatic, financial, military, intelligence, homeland security, and law enforcement activities within and among agencies;

c. assign operational responsibilities to lead agencies for counterterrorism activities that are consistent with applicable law and that support strategic plans to counter terrorism . . . ;

d. serve as the central and shared knowledge bank on known and suspected terrorists and international terror groups, as well as their goals, strategies, capabilities, and networks of contacts and support; and

e. ensure that agencies, as appropriate, have access to and receive all-source intelligence support needed to execute their counterterrorism plans or perform independent, alternative analysis.

The NCTC served as an important step in coordinating our intelligence operations. The 9/11 Commission (2004) found that a significant intelligence problem was the lack of communications and sharing of intelligence information across our domestic intelligence agencies. The NCTC is composed of representatives of all the intelligence agencies, helping to ensure better coordination. The body coordinates all counterterrorism activities on U.S. soil.

HS Web Link: To learn more about the executive order establishing the NCTC, go to *http://www. fas.org/irp/offdocs/eo/ eo-13354.htm*

INTERROGATION OF TERRORIST SUSPECTS Perhaps the most controversial order issued by President Bush was the one directing the manner of detention and methods of interrogation to be used against detainees in the "war on terror," Executive Order #13440, **Interpretation of the Geneva Conventions Common Article 3 as Applied to a Program of Detention and Interrogation Operated by the Central Intelligence Agency**. Because the country was engaged in an armed conflict with al Qaeda and that group was responsible for the attacks on the United States on September 11, 2001, President Bush issued an executive order specially designating members of al Qaeda, the Taliban, and associated forces as "unlawful enemy combatants" and stripping them of the protections afforded under the Third Geneva Convention. The Geneva Conventions provide prisoners of war with certain protections and prohibits abuse and torture.

Under the provisions of the order, the Central Intelligence Agency (CIA) was allowed to carry out a program of detention and interrogation outside of the rules of the Third Geneva Convention. This included "enhanced interrogation" practices. These interrogations and detentions were to be applied to any "alien detainee who is determined by the Director of the Central Intelligence Agency,"

(A) to be a member or part of or supporting al Qaeda, the Taliban, or associated organizations; and (B) likely to be in possession of information that:

1. could assist in detecting, mitigating, or preventing terrorist attacks, such as attacks within the United States or against its Armed Forces or other personnel, citizens, or facilities, or against allies or other countries cooperating in the war on terror with the United States, or their armed forces or other personnel, citizens, or facilities; or
2. could assist in locating the senior leadership of al Qaeda, the Taliban, or associated forces.

The order allowed the director of the CIA to determine interrogation practices as long as he viewed them as "safe for use with each detainee" and that detainees received "the basic necessities of life, including adequate food and water, shelter from the elements, necessary clothing, protection from extremes of heat and cold, and essential medical care." The CIA director was also given the authority to develop and approve a "plan of interrogation tailored for each detainee in the program . . . , train all interrogators and personnel in the program, monitor the program, and, determine the program's compliance with applicable law." In essence, the CIA director was given total control over the detention and interrogation of any person he designated as an "unlawful enemy combatant," including the determination of the legality of interrogation practices.

Controversy surrounding the order, including allegations of detainee abuse and torture as well as national and international outrage, led President Obama to revoke Executive Order #13440 by issuing Executive Order #13491). President Obama argued that the practices undermined national security and justice.

PRESIDENTIAL DIRECTIVES ENHANCING HOMELAND SECURITY   Over the course of his presidency, George W. Bush issued a series of executive orders designed to enhance homeland security and protect against the threat of terrorism. These included Executive Order #13311, **Homeland Security Information Sharing**, and Executive Order # 13356, **Strengthening the Sharing of Terrorism Information to Protect Americans**. These executive orders allowed various federal agencies to share information about potential terrorists and terrorist activities. Prior to the issuance of these executive orders, federal laws prohibited some intelligence agencies from sharing this information. President Bush issued Executive Order #13260, **Establishing the President's Homeland Security Advisory Council and Senior Advisory Committees for Homeland Security**. These bodies provided the initial planning for our homeland security organization. Executive Order #13407, **Public Alert and Warning System**, created the color-coded warning system to advise the public of terrorist threat levels.

In addition to these executive orders President Bush issued at least 24 "Homeland Security Directives," which are presented in Figure 4-2.

Analysis Box 4-2

There has been substantial controversy over the handling of noncombatant terrorists. The CIA and other entities performed rendition whereby suspected terrorists were taken against their will to other countries and interrogated, and sometimes tortured. Civil libertarians decried such policies for violating prisoners' rights. On the other hand, our country was attacked and the threat of additional attacks remains. How do we balance the rule of law with national security?

Number	Title	Date
HSPD 1	Organization and Operation of the Homeland Security Council	29 Oct 01
HSPD 2	Combating Terrorism Through Immigration Policies	29 Oct 01
HSPD 3	Homeland Security Advisory System	11 March 02
HSPD 4	National Strategy to Combat Weapons of Mass Destruction	11 December 02
HSPD 5	Management of Domestic Incidents	30 September 03
HSPD 6	Integration of Screening Information to Protect Against Terrorism	16 September 03
HSPD 7	Critical Infrastructure Identification, Prioritization, and Protection	17 December 03
HSPD 8	National Preparedness	17 December 03
HSPD 9	Defense of United States Agriculture and Food	30 January 04
HSPD 10	Biodefense for the 21st Century	28 April 04
HSPD 11	Comprehensive Terrorist-Related Screening Procedures	27 August 04
HSPD 12	Identification Standard for Federal Employees and Contractors	27 August 04
HSPD 13	Maritime Security Policy	21 December 2004
HSPD 14	Domestic Nuclear Detection	15 April 2005
HSPD 15	U.S. Strategy and Policy in the War on Terror (classified)	6 March 2006
HSPD 16	National Strategy for Aviation Security	22 June 2006
HSPD 17	Nuclear Materials Information Program	28 August 2006
HSPD 18	Medical Countermeasures Against Weapons of Mass Destruction	31 January 2007
HSPD 19	Combating Terrorist Use of Explosives in the United States	12 February 2007
HSPD 20	National Continuity Policy	4 April 2007
HSPD 21	Public Health and Medical Preparedness	18 October 2007
HSPD 22	Domestic Chemical Defense	Classified
HSPD 23	Cyber Security and Monitoring	8 January 2008
HSPD 24	Biometrics for Identification and Screening to Enhance National Security	5 June 2008

FIGURE 4-2   Homeland Security Presidential Directives   *Source:* DHS. (2010). Homeland Security Directives. http://www.dhs.gov/xabout/laws/editorial_0607.shtm (Accessed October 4, 2010).

Radvanovsky (2006) notes that the Department of Homeland Security was directed to immediately implement these Homeland Security Presidential Directives. Essentially, they provide an organization or framework for implementing homeland security with each directive focusing on a specific content area. They provide direction to each of the departments that are involved in an area. They assist in ensuring that there are no gaps in our coverage or protection.

HS Web Link: To learn more about the Homeland Security Presidential Directives, go to *http://www.dhs.gov/xabout/laws/editorial_0607.shtm*

Executive Orders of President Barack Obama

GUANTANAMO BAY REVIEW   President Barack Obama issued Executive Order #13492, **Review and Disposition of Individuals Detained at the Guantánamo Bay Naval Base and Closure of Detention Facilities**, on January 22, 2009, requiring review and disposition of all pending cases against prisoners held by the Department of Defense at the Guantánamo Bay Naval Base. The order required closure of that detention facility. Approximately 800 individuals had been detained in the facility for more than seven years. Controversy over these detentions and the circumstances and conditions in which detainees were confined led the president to determine that the disposition of these cases and the closure of the facility would

President Obama has issued several national security executive orders building on those issued by Presidents Bush and Clinton.   *Source:* http://www.whitehouse.gov/photos-and-video/photogallery/the-presidents

"further the national security and foreign policy interests of the United States and the interests of justice."

The order required an immediate review of all Guantánamo detentions and the disposition of their cases by (1) a determination of transfer, (2) a determination of prosecution, or (3) an alternative determination. The order also required that during the review period that all U.S. government officials act in conformity with all applicable laws governing conditions of confinement, including the Geneva Conventions.

On the same day that President Obama issued the Guantánamo executive order, he issued another executive order establishing a **Special Interagency Task Force on Detainee Disposition**

> to conduct a comprehensive review of the lawful options available to the Federal Government with respect to the apprehension, detention, trial, transfer, release, or other disposition of individuals captured or apprehended in connection with armed conflicts and counterterrorism operations, and to identify such options as are consistent with the national security and foreign policy interests of the United States and the interests of justice.

Although President Obama issued the order in 2009, a year later Guantánamo was still in operation. It could not be determined legally or practically how to deal with the remaining prisoners in the facility.

ENSURING LAWFUL INTERROGATIONS   On January 22, 2009, President Obama issued an executive order revoking President Bush's Executive Order #13440 of July 20, 2007. The order countermanded "All executive directives, orders, and regulations inconsistent with this order, including but not limited to those issued to or by the Central Intelligence Agency (CIA) from September 11, 2001, to January 20, 2009, concerning detention or the interrogation of detained individuals." The order essentially required federal agencies to follow the interrogation

---

Analysis Box 4-3

The detention facility at Guantánamo Bay has proven to be extremely controversial over the years. President Bush created the facility to keep terrorists out of the United States and to try them using military tribunals. Regardless of intent, the facility created worldwide controversy and presidential candidate Obama pledged to close it once elected president. After taking office, President Obama was not able to close the facility. Should the United States maintain Guantánamo Bay or a similar facility? How do we balance the rule of law and public opinion with national security?

---

techniques outlined in the Army Field Manual (2 22.3). The order directed the CIA to "close as expeditiously as possible any detention facilities that it currently operates" and prohibited it from operating detention facilities in the future. The order also directed federal officials to

> provide the International Committee of the Red Cross with notification of, and timely access to, any individual detained in any armed conflict in the custody or under the effective control of an officer, employee, or other agent of the United States Government or detained within a facility owned, operated, or controlled by a department or agency of the United States Government.

This order was controversial in that there had been a significant public debate on how the United States should treat enemy combatants and others suspected of being involved in terrorist activities. It established new guidelines for agencies.

Presidents Clinton, Bush, and Obama have issued a number of executive orders pertaining to homeland security. In total, they outline a number of policy decisions and programs that strengthen our ability to combat terrorism and enhance safeguarding our homeland. Certainly, additional new orders or modifications of existing orders will be used in the future and will help shape the development and direction of national security.

FEDERAL ANTITERRORISM STATUTES

In addition to the executive orders, Congress has passed a number of federal statutes relating to terrorism and homeland security. Several of the key statutes are addressed here.

Antiterrorism and Effective Death Penalty Act of 1996

On April 24, 1996, following the bombing of the Alfred P. Murrah Federal Building in Oklahoma City, Congress enacted the **Antiterrorism and Effective Death Penalty Act of 1996** (AEDPA; Pub. L. No. 104-132, 110 Stat. 1214) with broad-based bipartisan political support. The AEDPA, signed into law by President Clinton, was intended to prevent terrorism by (1) streamlining the implementation of the death penalty, (2) modifying the law on restitution to the victims of terrorism, (3) making it more difficult for terrorists to secure sources of financial and material support, (4) making it easier to exclude and remove foreign terrorists from the United States, and (5) placing greater restrictions on the possession and use of materials capable of producing catastrophic damage by terrorists (Doyle, 1996).

One of the main provisions of the law is the reduction of the power of federal judges to grant relief for habeas corpus abuses. Habeas corpus is the legal procedure by which, under the United States Constitution, detainees may seek relief from unlawful imprisonment through judicial review. Article 1, Section 9, of the Constitution states: "The privilege of the writ of habeas corpus shall not be suspended, unless when in cases of rebellion or invasion the public safety may require it." Under Title I of AEDPA, federal courts are restricted from granting detainees relief from violations of habeas corpus unless a state court makes a decision that is "(1) contrary to, or involved an unreasonable application of, clearly established Federal law, as determined by the Supreme Court of the United States; or (2) resulted in a decision that was based on an unreasonable determination of the facts in light of the evidence presented in the State court proceeding" (Pub. L. No. 104-132, 110 Stat. 1214). A second provision of the act is a reduction in the number of subsequent habeas petitions a detainee can present to the courts. The law created an absolute bar on second or successive petitions by a detainee once a judicial determination is made. The act also prevents the U.S. Supreme Court from reviewing a denial of a habeas petition by a federal court of appeals.

The Antiterrorism and Effective Death Penalty Act of 1996 was an effort to deal more effectively with terrorists. Although the act was passed as a result of an attack by a right-wing domestic terrorist, it became useful in the wake of the 9/11 attacks.

The USA PATRIOT Act

Perhaps the most well-known and controversial law enacted by the U.S. Congress in the aftermath of the terrorist attacks of September 11, 2001, is the **USA PATRIOT Act**. The legislation was passed by the Senate on October 11, 2001, and subsequently passed by the House on October 24, 2001. President George W. Bush signed the bill into law on October 26, 2001. The "act was based on a Department of Justice proposal that was modified by the Congress before it was enacted into law. The purpose of the act was to grant greater powers and authority to federal enforcement officials to investigate and prosecute those responsible for the September 11, 2001, attacks and to protect the country from future attacks like those carried out in New York and Washington, D.C. The act, whose full title is "Uniting and Strengthening America by Providing Appropriate Tools Required to Intercept and Obstruct Terrorism" (USA PATRIOT Act), was a sweeping law that modified or amended more than a dozen other federal statutes and greatly expanded the powers of members of the federal executive branch of government and federal law enforcement officials. The breath of changes made by the act is illustrated in Figure 4-3, which shows selected federal statutes modified by the law.

HS Web Link: To learn more about the USA PATRIOT Act, go to *http:// www.fas.org/irp/crs/ RS21203.pdf*

The act contains some 10 titles and more than 1,000 sections. An examination of the statutes that were modified as listed in Figure 4-3 shows how sweeping the act was. It addressed a number of areas including intelligence, investigations, controlled substances, crime, privacy, and financial transactions. It modified a number of governmental functions to enhance terrorism investigations and to prevent terrorist attacks.

A comprehensive treatment of the legislation would require a book-length work that is well beyond the scope of this chapter. There are, however, several key areas that require some individual attention and should be of interest to students of homeland security. The act addresses four key areas of concern for homeland security: (1) the collection of communication information and data, (2) conducting foreign intelligence investigations, (3) controlling money laundering, and (4) funding and enhancing national border security (Doyle, 2002). We will consider each of these areas in the sections that follow.

COLLECTION OF COMMUNICATIONS   To understand how the act changed the ability of federal officials to collect communications information used in criminal investigations, especially those involving suspected terrorism and terror-related activities, it is necessary to look back at the provisions of Title III of the Omnibus Crime Control and Safe Streets Act of 1968, 18 U.S.C. 2510-2522

Bank Holding Company Act of 1956, 12 U.S.C. 1841
Communications Act of 1934, 47 U.S.C. 151
Controlled Substance Import and Export Act, 21 U.S.C. 951
Controlled Substances Act, 21 U.S.C. 826
Electronic Communications Privacy Act of 1986 (ECPA), 18 U.S.C. 2510
Fair Credit Reporting Act (FCRA), 15 U.S.C. 1681
Federal Deposit Insurance Act, 12 U.S.C. 1811
Federal Wiretap Statute, 18 USC 119
Foreign Assistance Act of 1961, 22 U.S.C. 2291
Foreign Intelligence Surveillance Act (FISA) 50 U.S.C. 1805
Intelligence Reform and Terrorism Prevention Act of 2004, Public Law 108–458; 118 Stat. 3742
National Security Act, 50 U.S.C. 401
Omnibus Crime Control and Safe Streets Act of 1968, 42 U.S.C. 3797
Right to Financial Privacy Act of 1978, 12 U.S.C. 3401
Title III of the Omnibus Crime Control and Safe Streets Act of 1968, 18 U.S.C. 2510
Violent Crime Control and Law Enforcement Act of 1994, Public Law 103–322; 49 USC 46502

FIGURE 4-3   Selected Federal Statutes and Sections Modified by the USA PATRIOT Act and Its Reauthorization.

(Title III). Title III was substantially altered by the passage of the act. As a result of Supreme Court decisions restricting the government's ability to conduct investigations based on electronic surveillance, Congress enacted Title III to generally restrict eavesdropping on telephone, face-to-face, and computer forms of communication.

Title III created a three-tier system of protection from governmental surveillance. Under the first and most protective tier of the schema, federal law enforcement officers needed permission of senior members of the Justice Department to seek a court order authorizing the collection of private communications. Under the law, these permissions could be granted only when investigating a selected number of crimes listed in the statute. The law carefully restricted the process of the surveillance by law enforcement officers, limited the communication that could be seized, and controlled the duration and breath of surveillance activities. Additionally, the statute required courts to notify the parties involved in the communications that the activities had occurred following the collection of the communications.

At the second and next lower level of protection, federal law enforcement officials could seek a court order for telephone records and e-mails for any crime without Justice Department approval.

At the third and lowest tier of protection, federal law enforcement officials could themselves certify the need for surveillance, rather than getting a court order approving the use of pen registers and trap and trace devices that capture the identity and source of communications rather their actual content. Government intrusion at the lowest tier of protection did not need to be reported to the parties involved in the communication.

Passage of the USA PATRIOT Act in 2002 substantially altered each of these three tiers of protection. Provisions of the act:

- Permit pen register and trap and trace orders for electronic communications (e.g., e-mail);
- Authorize nationwide execution of court orders for pen registers, trap and trace devices, and access to stored e-mail or communication records;
- Treat stored voice mail like stored e-mail (rather than like telephone conversations);
- Permit authorities to intercept communications to and from a trespasser within a computer system (with the permission of the system's owner);

- Add terrorist and computer crimes to Title III's predicate offense list;
- Reinforce protection for those who help execute Title III, ch. 121, and ch. 206 orders;
- Encourage cooperation between law enforcement and foreign intelligence investigators;
- Establish a claim against the U.S. for certain communications privacy violations by government personnel; and
- Terminate the authority found in many of these provisions and several of the foreign intelligence amendments with a sunset provision. (Doyle, 2002: 2–3)

In essence the act, under certain circumstances, allows law enforcement officials greater liberty to collect and review communications records and stored e-mails, treats voice mail as if it were e-mail, reduces the requirement of probable cause necessary to secure a warrant, and in some cases allows federal officials to bypass the judiciary entirely. The act also expands the types of information federal officials can collect from communication service providers, including credit card and banking records. The act also adds to an already expansive list of crimes, outlined under Title II, which do not require a warrant or court order for monitoring. Cyber crime, terrorist-related crimes, the activities of hackers, and crimes involving interstate and foreign commerce were added to the list of crimes.

FOREIGN INTELLIGENCE INVESTIGATIONS The USA PATRIOT Act amended the Foreign Intelligence Surveillance Act (FISA). FISA originally required that federal law enforcement officials certify for special courts that "the purpose for the surveillance is to obtain foreign intelligence information." Under this provision, although evidence of a crime might be uncovered during a foreign intelligence investigation, the legislation was to be used for intelligence gathering

A number of foreign intelligence cases have been presented in the courts.   *Source:* AP (06011107414)

and not for "fishing" for evidence of a crime or as a way of getting around the offenses listed in Title III. The act also allowed for physical searches based on lower standards.

The act expanded the authority of federal officials to collect information on foreign intelligence within the United State when conducting investigations. It also allowed the sharing of intelligence information among federal agencies. Sauter and Carafano (2005) note that this provision tore down the wall that hampered investigations prior to the 9/11 attacks. Prior to the act, several federal agencies involved in intelligence and counterterrorism were not allowed to share information. The act also lowered the consequence for officials who abuse privacy and third parties who assist authorities in collecting information. According to Doyle (2002), the act:

- Permits "roving" surveillance (court orders omitting the identification of the particular instrument, facilities, or places where the surveillance is to occur when the court finds the target is likely to thwart identification);
- Increases the number of judges on the Foreign Intelligence Surveillance Act (FISA) court from 7 to 11;
- Allows application for a FISA surveillance or search order when gathering foreign intelligence is *a significant* reason for the application rather than *the* reason;
- Authorizes pen register and trap & trace device orders for e-mail as well as telephone conversations;
- Sanctions court-ordered access to any tangible item rather than only business records held by lodging, car rental, and locker rental businesses;
- Carries a sunset provision;
- Establishes a claim against the U.S. for certain communications privacy violations by government personnel; and
- Expands the prohibition against FISA orders based solely on an American's exercise of his or her First Amendment rights. (p. 3)

MONEY LAUNDERING   *Money laundering* is the illegal movement of cash or items of value that are derived from the commission of a crime or valuables that are intended to assist in the commission of a crime (discussed in more detail in Chapter 11). Money laundering involves the movement or concealment of the movement of valuables in a manner as to elude detection or cover up a crime. These practices can range from structuring financial transactions in certain ways to limiting the amount of money that is transferred as well as moving valuables through multiple institutions to conceal sources. Money laundering can be used in association with traditional crimes or used to support or fund terrorist activities. Money laundering has been historically controlled through the creation of a complex array of regulations, reporting requirements, and criminal laws.

Passage of the USA PATRIOT Act addressed the problem of money laundering in three basic areas. First, it expanded the authority of the secretary of the treasury to regulate U.S. financial institutions. Under the regulatory provisions of the act, the secretary of the treasury was to propagate rules:

- Under which securities brokers and dealers as well as commodity merchants, and advisors must file suspicious activity reports (SARs);
- Requiring businesses, which were only to report cash transactions involving more than $10,000 to the IRS, to file SARs as well;
- Imposing additional "special measures" and "due diligence" requirements to combat foreign money laundering;

- Prohibiting U.S. financial institutions from maintaining correspondent accounts for foreign shell banks;
- Preventing financial institutions from allowing their customers to conceal their financial activities:
- Establishing minimum new customer identification standards and recordkeeping and recommending an effective means to verify the identity of foreign customers;
- Encouraging financial institutions and law enforcement agencies to share information concerning suspected money laundering and terrorist activities; and
- Requiring financial institutions to maintain anti–money laundering programs which must include at least a compliance officer; an employee training program; the development of internal policies, procedures and controls; and an independent audit feature. (Doyle, 2002: 3–4)

Second, the act created new crimes to control money laundering and enhanced punishment for this crime. The act

- Outlaws laundering (in the U.S.) any of the proceeds from foreign crimes of violence or political corruption;
- Prohibits laundering the proceeds from cybercrime or supporting a terrorist organization;
- Increases the penalties for counterfeiting;
- Seeks to overcome a Supreme Court decision finding that the confiscation of over $300,000 (or attempt to leave the country without reporting it to customs) constituted an unconstitutionally excessive fine;
- Provides explicit authority to prosecute overseas fraud involving American credit cards; and
- Endeavors to permit prosecution of money laundering in the place where the predicate offense occurs. (Doyle, 2002: 4)

Third, the act modified the ways forfeitures could be carried out and granted the government greater power to confiscate the property of anyone thought to support, plan, aid, authorize, or participate in an act of domestic or international terrorism. Under the provisions of the act, the government can present its evidence for forfeiture in secret and the person having his or her property confiscated bears the burden of proving his or her innocence. No criminal conviction for terrorism is required for the confiscation of property and in some cases all of a person's or organization's assets can be seized regardless of whether or not the individual's assets can be linked to an act associated with terrorism. The act

- Establishes a mechanism to acquire extended jurisdiction, for purposes of forfeiture proceedings, over individuals and entities;
- Allows confiscation of property located in this country for a wider range of crimes committed in violation of foreign law;
- Permits U.S. enforcement of foreign forfeiture orders;
- Calls for the seizure of correspondent accounts held in U.S. financial institutions for foreign banks [that] are in turn holding forfeitable assets overseas; and
- Denies corporate entities the right to contest a confiscation if their principal shareholder is a fugitive. (Doyle, 2002: 4–5)

FUNDING AND ENHANCING NATIONAL BORDER SECURITY The USA PATRIOT Act provides for changes in the ways in which foreign nationals can be treated under the laws of the United States and the amount of funding and types of security used to control the national borders, and it creates new crimes and procedures for dealing with the potential for terrorism. Provisions of the act designed to enhanced funding of border security do the following:

- Authorize the appropriations necessary to triple the number of Border Patrol, Customs Service, and Immigration and Naturalization Service (INS) personnel stationed along the Northern Border, section 401;
- Authorize appropriations of an additional $50 million for both INS and the Customers Service to upgrade their border surveillance equipment, section 402;
- Remove the $30,000 ceiling on INS overtime pay for border duty, section 404;
- Authorize appropriations of $2 million for a report to be prepared by the Attorney General on the feasibility of enhancing the FBI's Integrated Automated Fingerprint Identification System (IAFIS) and similar systems to improve the reliability of visa applicant screening, section 405;
- Authorize the appropriations necessary to provide the State Department and INS with criminal record identification information relating to visa applicants and other applicants for admission to the United States, section 403; and
- Authorize appropriations of $250,000 for the FBI to determine the feasibility of providing airlines with computer access to the names of suspected terrorists, section 1009. (Doyle, 2002: 40–50)

Enhanced monitoring along the nation's borders is provided for by the act with these provisions:

- Instruct the Attorney General to report on the feasibility of the use of a biometric identifier scanning system with access to IAFIS for overseas consular posts and points of entry into the United States, section 1007;
- Express the sense of the Congress that the Administration should implement the integrated entry and exit data system called for by the Illegal Immigration Reform and Immigrant Responsibility Act of 1996 (8 U.S.C. 1365a), section 414;
- Add the White House Office of Homeland Security to the Integrated Entry and Exit Data System Task Force (8 U.S.C. 1365a note), section 415;
- Call for the implementation and expansion of the foreign student visa monitoring program (8 U.S.C. 1372), section 416;
- Limit countries eligible to participate in the visa waiver program to those with machine-readable passports as of October 1, 2003 (8 U.S.C. 1187(c)), section 417;
- Instruct the Attorney General to report on the feasibility of using biometric scanners to help prevent terrorists and other foreign criminals from entering the country, section 1008;
- Authorize reciprocal sharing of the State Department's visa lookout data and related information with other nations in order to prevent terrorism, drug trafficking, slave marketing, and gun running, section 413. (Doyle, 2002: 49–50)

United States Foreign Intelligence Surveillance Court

As a result of domestic spying by federal law enforcement officials during the Vietnam era, Congress passed the **Foreign Intelligence Surveillance Act of 1978** (FISA; 50 U.S.C. § 1803). The act was designed to control foreign agents involved in espionage within the United States and also to protect U.S. citizens from governmental abuses. The law authorized the creation of the United States Foreign Intelligence Surveillance Court (FISC). The basic function of the FISC is to monitor and control the surveillance activities of federal law enforcement officials who are investigating suspected foreign intelligence operatives in the United States. Passage of the USA

HS Web Link: To learn more about the FISA Court, go to *http://usgovinfo.about.com/od/uscourtsystem/a/fiscourt.htm*

PATRIOT Act, however, extended the surveillance to U.S. citizens under certain circumstances and expanded provision of the law to include the collection of intelligence on terrorism and terrorist activities.

One of the primary functions of the court is to review requests for electronic surveillance warrants. Because the work of the court involves national security issues, the FISC is basically a "secret" court that operates outside public observation and review. Although the court keeps records of its activities, these records are not available to the public and the court does not operate in a public forum. According to Lee Tien (2001) of the Electronic Frontier Foundation,

> The records and files of the cases are sealed and may not be revealed even to persons whose prosecutions are based on evidence obtained under FISA warrants, except to a limited degree set by district judges' rulings on motions to suppress. There is no provision for the return of each executed warrant to the FISC, much less with an inventory of items taken, nor for certification that the surveillance was conducted according to the warrant and its "minimization" requirements. (p. 1)

The court can meet any time of day or night and any day of the week. Also there is always at least one judge available to review warrant requests. The only parties involved in the court's processes are government officials.

Although the FISA legislation and the FISC were born out of a concern over privacy abuses by federal law enforcement officials, both are clearly designed to favor the government and the issuance of investigative warrants, not to protect citizens' privacy and liberty interests. If the attorney general (AG) decides that an emergency situation exists, he or she is authorized to begin a program of surveillance without a FISC warrant. The AG must, however, inform the court of the operation within 72 hours. If a member of the FISC rejects a search application, the decision can be appealed to United States Foreign Intelligence Surveillance Court of Review. Based on existing information, the rejection of a warrant application by the FISC is a rare happening and more often than not warrant applications are modified and issued by the court rather than being rejected. According to a Department of Justice memorandum (Moschella, 2004),

> During calendar year 2003, 1727 applications were made to the Foreign Intelligence Surveillance Court for electronic surveillance and physical search. The 1727 applications include applications made solely for electronic surveillance, applications made solely for physical search, and combined applications requesting authority for electronic surveillance and physical search simultaneously. The Court approved, in whole or in part, 1724 applications. (pp. 1–2)

Controversy arose when it was learned that

> Under a presidential order signed in 2002, the intelligence agency [NSA] has monitored the international telephone calls and international e-mail messages of hundreds, perhaps thousands, of people inside the United States without warrants over the past three years in an effort to track possible "dirty numbers" linked to Al Qaeda. (Risen, Lichtblau, and Walsh, 2005)

Analysis Box 4-4

The FISA court, like a number of anti-terrorism laws and procedures, has been controversial. Essentially, the court hears requests for government surveillance secretly and none of the courts findings are made public. Do you believe the U.S. government should have the power to secretly conduct electronic surveillance on American citizens when there is probable cause to believe the citizen is involved in terrorist activities? Do you believe government agencies may spy on Americans using the FISA procedure for other purposes?

It is possible that the program, conducted by the National Security Agency (NSA), was designed to collect information that was later used to seek warrants from the FISA court. The practice was sufficiently serious to cause one FISAC judge to resign his position (Leonning and Linzer, 2005). Although controversial, the Foreign Intelligence Surveillance Court, as a result of the act, has expanded electronic intelligence gathering. It is seen as a method by which to identify possible terrorists and terrorist plots.

Summary

This chapter reviewed some of the many sweeping legal changes that have taken place since the terrorist attacks of September 11, 2001. These changes were not merely limited to new legislation, but included changes in executive orders and the operations of the courts. Most of these changes were directed at giving law enforcement and intelligence officials greater power to combat the possibility of terrorism.

The chapter considered executive orders issued beginning with President Clinton's and through President Obama's administration. Executive orders are presidential instructions to federal officials and agencies that are written to govern the execution of public policy. Many of the executive orders issued by Presidents Clinton, Bush, and Obama have been implemented either to prevent the possibility of a terrorist attack or to correct overreaches of the executive branch of government. Most of these orders were designed to assist in establishing a higher level of homeland security. Controlling WMDs, limiting transactions that could be used to facilitate terrorist activities, enhancing the collection of intelligence, and providing protection of the nation's infrastructure were the main areas in which policy changes have been developed.

Since the terrorist attacks of 9/11, Congress has enacted or modified a substantial number of laws designed to prevent terrorism and establish home-land security. Perhaps the most well-known and controversial law enacted by the U.S. Congress in the aftermath of the terrorist attacks of September 11, 2001, is the USA PATRIOT Act. The act addressed four key areas of concern: (1) collecting communication information and data, (2) conducting foreign intelligence investigations, (3) controlling money laundering, and (4) funding and enhancing national border security.

Finally the chapter addressed the United States Foreign Intelligence Surveillance Court, which was designed to control foreign agents involved in espionage within the United States and also to protect U.S. citizens from governmental abuses. Passage of the USA Patriot Act, however, extended the surveillance to U.S. citizens under certain circumstances and expanded provision of the law to include the collection of intelligence on terrorism and terrorist activities. Although the FISA legislation and the FISC were born out of a concern over privacy abuses by federal law enforcement officials, both are clearly designed to favor the government and the issuance of investigative warrants, not to protect citizens' privacy and liberty interests. Most of the legal changes that have taken place since 9/11 have been controversial because they upset the historic balance between security and law enforcement needs on the one hand and privacy and liberty interests on the other.

Discussion Questions

1. What is the legal standing of presidential executive orders and directives and how do presidents use them?
2. Given the executive orders issued by Presidents Clinton, Bush, and Obama, what issues were paramount for each president? Where there any trends?
3. What are the primary initiatives implemented as a result of the USA PATRIOT Act?
4. What are FISA Courts? What are the legal controversies surrounding them?
5. What actions have been taken affecting terrorist financing?

References

Abourezk, J. G. (2008). "Another 'surge' is needed–this time, of common sense." *Washington Report on Middle East Affairs*, 27(1): 35–37.

Doyle, C. (1996). *Antiterrorism and Effective Death Penalty Act of 1996: A Summary.* American Law Division, Federation of American Scientists. http://www.fas.org/irp/crs/96-499.htm (Accessed February 2, 2011).

Doyle, C. (2002). *CRS Report for Congress: The USA PATRIOT Act: A Sketch.* Washington, D.C.: Congressional Research Service. Executive Order #13025 Amendment to Executive Order 13010, The President's Commission on Critical Infrastructure Protection, November 13, 1995.

Executive Order #13041 Further Amendment to Executive Order 13010, As Amended, April 3, 1997.

Executive Order #12885 Amendment to Executive Order No. 12829, December 14, 1993.

Executive Order #12938 Proliferation of Weapons of Mass Destruction, November 14, 1994.

Executive Order #12947 Prohibiting Transactions with Terrorists Who Threaten to Disrupt the Middle East Peace Process, January 23, 1995.

Executive Order #12949 Foreign Intelligence Physical Searches, February 9, 1995.

Executive Order #13010 Critical Infrastructure Protection, July 15, 1996.

Executive Order #13025 Amendment to Executive Order 13010, The President's Commission on Critical Infrastructure Protection, November 13, 1996.

Executive Order #13064 Further Amendment to Executive Order 13010, As Amended, Critical Infrastructure Protection, October 11, 1997.

Executive Order #13064 Further Amendment to Executive Order 13010, as Amended, Critical Infrastructure Protection, October 11, 1997.

Executive Order #13099 Prohibiting Transactions with Terrorists Who Threaten to Disrupt the Middle East Peace Process, August 22, 1998.

Executive Order #13224 Blocking Property And Prohibiting Transactions With Persons Who Commit, Threaten to Commit, or Support Terrorism, September 23, 2001.

Executive Order #13228 Establishing the Office of Homeland Security and the Homeland Security Council, October 8, 2001.

Executive Order #13260 Establishing the President's Homeland Security Advisory Council and Senior Advisory Committees for Homeland Security, March 19, 2002.

Executive Order #13268 Termination of Emergency with Respect to the Taliban and Amendment of Executive Order 13224 of September 23, 2001, July 2, 2002.

Executive Order #13311 Homeland Security Information Sharing, July 29, 2003.

Executive Order #13354 of August 27, 2004 National Counterterrorism Center, September 23, 2001.

Executive Order #13356 Strengthening the Sharing of Terrorism Information to Protect Americans, August 27, 2004.

Executive Order #13382 Blocking Property of Weapons of Mass Destruction Proliferators and Their Supporters, June 28, 2005.

Executive Order #13383 Amending Executive Orders 12139 and 12949 in Light of Establishment of the Office of Director of National Intelligence, July 15, 2005.

Executive Order #13388 Further Strengthening the Sharing of Terrorism Information to Protect Americans, October 25, 2005.

Executive Order #13407 Public Alert and Warning System, June 26, 2006.

Executive Order #13440 Interpretation of the Geneva Conventions Common Article 3 as Applied to a Program of Detention and Interrogation Operated by the Central Intelligence Agency, July 20, 2007.

Executive Order #13475 Further Amendments To Executive orders 12139 And 12949 In Light of the Foreign Intelligence Surveillance Act of 1978 Amendments Act of 2008, October 7, 2008.

Executive Order #13491 Ensuring Lawful Interrogations, January 22, 2009.

Executive Order #13492 Review and Disposition of Individuals Detained at the Guantánamo Bay Naval Base and Closure of Detention Facilities, January 22, 2009.

Executive Order 13129 Blocking Property and Prohibiting Transactions with the Taliban, July 4, 1999.

Hosenball, M. and M. Isikoff. (2008). "Unintended consequences." *Newsweek* (March 24), p. 47.

Leonning, C. D. and D. Linzer. (2005). "Spy court judge quits in protest: Jurist concerned Bush order tainted work of secret panel." *Washington Post* (December 21).

Migdalovitz, C. (2005). *The Middle East Peace Talks.* Washington, D.C.: Congressional Research Service.

Military Order Detention, Treatment, and Trial of Certain Non-Citizens in The War Against Terrorism. (2001). *Federal Register*, 66(222: 57831-57836).

Moschella, W. (2004). *Memo from Assistant Attorney General.* Washington, D.C.: U.S. Department of Justice, April 30. http://www.fas.org/irp/agency/doj/fisa/2003rept.pdf (Accessed April 29, 2010).

Moss, R. D. (2000). *Memorandum for the Counsel to the President.* Washington, D.C.: Office of Legal Counsel, Department of Justice.

National Commission on Terrorist Attacks Upon the United States. (2004). *The 9/11 Commission Report.* New York: W.W. Norton.

Olsen, K. (2007). "Patriot Act's wide net." *Nation* September 24), p. 8.

Radvanovsky, R. (2006). *Critical Infrastructure.* Boca Raton, FL: Taylor and Francis.

Relyea, H. C. (2008). *Presidential Directives: Background and Overview, Updated November 26, 2008.* CRS Report for Congress, Order Code 98-611 GOV.

Risen, J., E. Lichtblau, and B. Walsh. (2005). "Bush lets U.S. spy on callers without courts. *New York Times* (December 16). http://www.nytimes.com/2005/12/16/politics/16program.html?pagewanted=all (Accessed January 6, 2011).

Sauter, M. and J. Carafano. (2005). *Homeland Security.* New York: McGraw-Hill.

Scardaville, M. and J. Spencer. (2002). "Federal homeland security policy." The Heritage Foundation. http://www.heritage.org/Research/Reports/2002/06/Federal-Homeland-Security-Policy (Accessed April 26, 2010).

Tien, L. (2001). *Foreign Intelligence Surveillance Act: Frequently Asked Questions (and Answers).* Electronic Frontier Foundation (September 27).

Uniting and Strengthening America by Providing Appropriate Tools Required to Intercept and Obstruct Terrorism (USA PATRIOT Act). P.L. 107-56, 115 Stat. 272 (2001).

Yeh, B. T. and C. Doyle. (2006). *USA PATRIOT Improvement and Reauthorization Act of 2005: A Legal Analysis.* CRS Report for Congress, Updated December 21, 2006.

Political and Social Foundations of Terrorism

LEARNING OBJECTIVES

1. Understand the continuum of social conflict.
2. Know the definition of terrorism.
3. Be familiar with the history of terrorism.
4. Understand the causes of terrorism.
5. Know the types of terrorism.
6. Understand the strategies for dealing with terrorism.

KEY TERMS

Normative social conflict
Civil disorder and riots
Terrorist activities
Guerilla warfare
Civil war
Social construct
Terrorism
Premeditation
Political agenda
Noncombatants or civilians
Sub-national or clandestine groups
Sicari and Zeolots
Anarchists and socialists
State sponsored terrorism
Propaganda of the deed
Culture-based civilizations
Fault lines

Globalization
Frustration-aggression theory
Relative deprivation
Identity crisis
Narcissistic rage
Moral disengagement
Dissent terrorism
Left-wing and right-wing terrorism
Religious motivated terrorism
Criminal terrorism
Crush terrorist groups unilaterally
Crushing terrorist groups multilaterally
Containment
Defensive actions
Diversion
Delegitimation
Transforming terrorist breeding grounds

INTRODUCTION

Over the course of its short history, a substantial amount of confusion as to the primary objective for our system of homeland security has existed. For example, Bellavita (2008) examined the homeland security literature and notes that a number of definitions have evolved. He advises that the need for homeland security has been associated with terrorism; all types of hazards, including catastrophes, jurisdictional hazards, and meta-hazards (large scale or multiple hazards); national security; and government's desire to curb civil liberties. The Swine or N1H1Flu outbreak in 2009 was considered by many to be a homeland security threat as it was a virus that potentially could have infected large numbers of Americans. As discussed in Chapter 1, homeland security has acquired multiple meanings, ranging from dealing with all hazards to focusing solely on terrorist attacks. Even though the objectives and operation of homeland security have been debated, expanded, and sometimes contracted, the primary motivation for homeland security is the threat of terrorist attacks on American soil or on American interests abroad. Thus, it is important that we have a clear understanding of terrorism and its potential impact on the United States.

This chapter examines terrorism in terms of its roots, history, motivation, and political and social implications. It primarily focuses on terrorism that has developed and spread from the Middle East, since this form of terrorism poses the greatest threat to our homeland security. The different terrorist problems across the globe will be addressed in Chapter 6. Nonetheless, without a clear understanding of terrorism, it is difficult to develop and apply effective countermeasures or homeland security programming. In essence, we must understand and specify the problem before acting. Without doing so, our countermeasures may be unproductive or ineffective and a waste of valuable resources. This task is complicated by the numerous types or forms of terrorism and their different motivations. For example, terrorist acts in Latin American have different forms and motivations as compared to terrorism that occurs in the Middle East. American response to terrorism must be tailored to the underlying nature of the terrorists and their acts. However, before examining these issues, it is important to define terrorism. We must distinguish terrorism from war, insurgency, and other conflicts, even though these other forms of aggression sometimes intersect and overlap with terrorism. We must also distinguish terrorism from other forms of criminality. Terrorism indeed is a criminal act, and terrorists often resort to criminal acts to raise the funds required to perpetrate their acts, but terrorism is distinguishable from crime in that it represents a distinct type of activity requiring specific governmental and societal responses.

Continuum of Social Conflict

All societies, regardless of their level of civility, experience some conflict generally evolving around political, social, economic, or religious issues. Figure 5-1 shows the continuum of social conflict. The lowest level is normative social conflict, whereas the most extreme cases lead to civil war. For example, America has limited violence, but there is substantial conflict or consternation over a number of political and social issues. Americans are constantly experiencing **normative social conflict**. This level of conflict is also inherent to many Muslim countries in which Shiites and Sunnis vie for power. In some cases, this normative conflict will result in civil disobedience, such as work stoppages or strikes. A higher level of discontent results in **civil disorder and riots**, such as those that occurred in Iran 2009, after the announcement that President Mahmoud Ahmadinejad won a contested election. **Terrorist activities** occur when a significant number of

Palestinian Fatah supporters clash with Hamas supporters.   *Source:* AP (061215010333)

HS Web Link: To learn more about guerilla warfare, go to *http://smallwarsjournal.com/documents/guevara.pdf*

people are discontent with the social or government structure. They generally are highly committed to some cause and have a measure of support from the general population. If conditions persist and an increasing level of support is exhibited by the population, the terrorist activities may evolve into **guerilla warfare**. If conditions continue to worsen, the country or area may become embroiled in armed conflict or even a **civil war**. Thus, terrorism is an expression of social discontent and is one type of conflict that can occur.

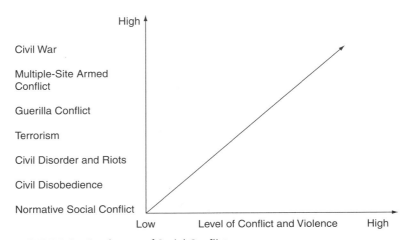

FIGURE 5-1 Continuum of Social Conflict.

DEFINING TERRORISM

To some extent, **terrorism** is a **social construct** in that different people have various definitions of the term. It is a pejorative term in that it has extremely negative associations and always connotes death and destruction. Society is constantly exposed to the term by the news media, politicians, and popular entertainment venues, and it is applied to a wide variety of actors, conditions, activities, and situations. As a social construct, the term is used to demonize people, societies, and actions. Its use solicits highly emotional responses. Politicians are able to garner support by attacking terrorists and anything remotely associated with them, regardless of guilt or involvement. The media are better able to increase subscribership or viewership when running stories about terrorists. It captivates people's attention.

HS Web Link: To learn more about the definitions of terrorism, go to *http://www.asap-spssi.org/pdf/asap019.pdf*

Labeling an act or a person a terrorist has a partisan dimension. For example, Israelis label Palestinian suicide bombers as terrorists whereas the Palestinians see such behavior as an act of defiance or retribution for acts perpetrated on the Palestinian people by the Israelis. The Palestinians see themselves as freedom fighters, not terrorists. The Israelis see their actions as a defense against attacks by the Palestinians. Right-wing extremists in the United States, such as Timothy McVeigh who blew up the federal building in Oklahoma City in 1995, do not see themselves or their organizations as terrorists. They see themselves as fighting government oppression, and these right-wing activities in the United States increased substantially after the election of President Barack Obama, the first African American president. For example, there was a substantial increase in the number of guns purchased by Americans. Thus, the terrorist label largely is dependent upon political perspective or whether one is the aggressor or the victim.

It is important to note that perspectives change over time. For example, Ahmad (2003) notes that members of the Jewish underground in Palestine in the 1930s and 1940s were described as terrorists, but by 1944 these terrorists were characterized as freedom fighters by the Western press. This change was largely due to the events of the Holocaust and Western liberal thinking. The result was support for a Jewish state, irrespective of previous terrorist activities or labels. In 1979, the Soviet Union invaded Afghanistan. The mujahedeen who fought the Soviets were characterized by President Reagan as "freedom fighters." Today, many of these same freedom fighters are aligned with or a part of al Qaeda or the Taliban, and we now characterize them as terrorists. Thus, at one point in history, a group may be seen as terrorists and at another point in time, freedom fighters. Perspective, like politics, can change. To some extent, activities only partially help define terrorism; whether a group is a friend or foe also contributes to the characterization.

Terrorism can originate from a variety of sources or directions. First, the state can sponsor or perpetrate it. There is a long history of states in Africa, Asia, and South America using terrorist tactics on their own people. The government of Sudan used terrorist activities to kill, starve, and create political refugees by attacking its citizens in the Darfur region. Several countries have launched terrorist campaigns in the Congo in the fight for that country's mineral resources. Right-wing and left-wing political groups in a variety of countries have created paramilitary groups that use terrorist activities to further their political agendas. Transnational organized crime groups such as the drug cartels in Mexico have used terror to undermine the rule of law and the legitimate government. A number of religious groups have resorted to terrorism, including radical Muslims in the Middle East who have terrorized legitimate governments and citizens who belong to other religious faiths or who are otherwise opposed to them. In the United States, radical Christians have bombed abortion clinics and murdered abortion doctors, and animal rights groups have burned university research centers and the personal property of researchers. Thus, all sorts of groups have been involved in promoting terrorism for their various objectives.

Some would argue that there is no such thing as terrorism; they argue that the term is so nebulous and fraught with political insinuations that it is of little use. They would argue that terrorists are involved in a variety of crimes: bombings, homicide, kidnapping, extortion, narcotics trafficking, tax evasion, and so forth. Terrorists who are involved in these activities actually are little more than organized criminals with a political agenda that is supported by criminal activity. Perhaps our focus should not be the politics, but the crime and criminal organizations. For example, Hoffman (2009a) advises that terrorists should be identified by their acts, not by their ideology or politics. Indeed, numerous politicians commit crimes to further their personal wealth and political agenda, and these activities may not have a direct effect on people, but they certainly almost always have an indirect impact. For example, the government of Afghanistan is ripe with corruption. To some extent, these politicians are no less criminal than some terrorists.

Nonetheless, given that terrorism is a socially constructed term with multiple meanings and dimensions, it is important to develop an operational definition—what does it mean within the context of governmental operations and responses? Whittacker (2001) complied a listing of governmental definitions:

> The unlawful use of force or violence against persons or property to intimidate or coerce government, a civilian population, or any segment thereof, in furtherance of political or social objectives (FBI).

> The calculated use of violence or threat of violence to inculcate fear, intended to coerce or intimidate governments or societies as to the pursuit of goals that are generally political, religious or ideological (U.S. Department of Defense).

> Premeditated, politically motivated violence perpetuated against noncombatant targets by sub-national groups or clandestine agents, usually intended to influence an audience (U.S. Department of State).

These institutional definitions demonstrate that there is no consistent definition of terrorism. This of course can contribute to inconsistent or hazy policy. However, the various definitions do have some common threads. Pillar (2003) examined a number of terrorism definitions and identified four consistent themes. First, terrorism involves **premeditation**. Terrorism generally is perpetrated through violent acts, but it can also involve other criminal acts. Regardless, these acts are planned and perpetrated with the intention of having some impact on victims or enemies. Second, terrorists and their acts are motivated by some **political agenda**. Terrorists' political agendas range from the religious to the cultural or social. Terrorists commit many of the same crimes as do ordinary criminals, but terrorists have a political agenda, whereas ordinary criminals commit their acts for financial gain. As an example, a number of politicians and the media have referred to the Central American gang Mara Salvatrucha 13, or MS-13, as a terrorist group. Its members certainly are violent and are involved in a wide variety of crimes including numerous homicides, but their motive is financial gain, not the overthrow of any government. Third, generally the terrorists' targets are **noncombatants or civilians**. Attacks on civilians have a more substantial psychological impact on terrorists' perceived enemies. Such attacks also demonstrate their power among supporters or potential supporters. Attacks on civilians help undermine or weaken governments, which, ultimately, is

Pakistani police gather shoes and clothing from victims of a suicide bombing. *Source:* AP (100417112594)

the terrorists' primary objective. When terrorists believe they have the capacity, they will attack military targets as a way of demonstrating that the government is ineffectual or inept. A final thread running through definitions of terrorism is that terrorists are generally **subnational or clandestine groups**. They are identified by their political cause, which is opposed to the government under attack.

Perhaps an example is illustrative. On June 10, 2009, James W. Von Brunn walked into the Holocaust Memorial Museum in Washington, D.C., and began firing a rifle at museum patrons, killing a security guard before he was seriously wounded. Von Brunn, according to the Anti-Defamation League, was a Holocaust denier. He was a notorious racist and anti-Semitic. In a previous publication, he praised Adolf Hitler (Hall, Bello, and Heath, 2009). Many viewed the shooting as another hate crime, whereas a few in the media viewed it as an act of terrorism. How would the reaction have been different if the shooting were performed by a Muslim as opposed to a neo-Nazi? Most likely the media would uniformly have handled the incident as an act of terrorism, touting the increase in terrorist incidents and fueling public fear even though the incident was isolated. Fear as a result of terrorist activities has had a substantial impact on public opinion.

Finally, it should be noted that there are different types of terrorism. For the most part, the configuration of a particular terrorist group is dependent upon environment, relationship with the state, motivation, and goals. Thus, there can be a variety of terrorist organization configurations. Forst (2009) notes that categories can be understood by examining these dimensions:

- Whether the group is politically motivated (left-wing or right-wing groups that attempt to topple a government)

Drawing of von Brunn at court hearing.   *Source:* AP
(090902016063)

- Whether the group is operating under state authority (state-sponsored terrorism such as in the 1970s when the Khmer Rouge killed nearly 2 million Cambodians)
- Level of affiliation with other terrorist organizations or networks (smaller groups associated with other terrorist organizations such as al Qaeda)
- The degree of planning and organization
- Whether the group is motivated by religious or ethnic factors
- The group's targets, people, or symbols of the state or perceived oppressors (terrorist groups generally have specific types of targets and focus on that type)
- Types of people targeted (are civilians or civilian groups or governmental officials targeted). (see p. 8)

Examining the various terrorist groups using these criteria can provide a better understanding of the group's motivations, activities, and operations. It can also result in more effective countermeasures.

Analysis Box 5-1

Forst identifies several dimensions associated with terrorist groups. Given what you know about al Qaeda, how well does al Qaeda meet or fit these dimensions. Identify other terrorist groups and compare them to Forst's dimensions. Forst's dimensions show that there are different kinds of terrorist groups operating throughout the world.

A BRIEF HISTORY OF TERRORISM

Given that it is difficult to define terrorism because it is socially constructed and the meaning one associates with the term is subjective and dependent upon perspective, it is illuminating to provide a brief history of the subject. A history of terrorism provides perspective and a better understanding of its origins. This enables one to develop a more concrete understanding of it and its implications. Since the term terrorism is socially constructed, it is largely defined by past terrorist acts.

Early Forms of Terrorism

Terrorism is not a new phenomenon. It likely has existed since people began to combine into political collectives and states. Burgess (2003) advises that some of the earliest examples include the **Sicari and Zeolots,** Jewish groups that were active during the Roman occupation of the Middle East during the first century. The Sicari attacked and primarily killed Jews they deemed to have abandoned their faith whereas the Zeolots killed Romans and Greeks. Many of the killings occurred in daylight in front of witnesses. These highly visual killings were meant to send messages to the Romans and the Jews who collaborated with them. Highly visual and public attacks remain one of terrorists' primary weapons today. Later, other groups began to use the tactics of the Sicari and Zeolots. For example, in the eleventh century, a Shiite Muslim sect killed politicians and other religious persons who did not subscribe to their version of Islam. They became known as *assassins*, a term that is still in use today.

HS Web Link: To learn more about early terrorism, go to *http://www.terrorism-research.com/history/early.php*

The French Revolution

The term *terrorist* or *terrorism* comes from the French Revolution or the *regime de la terreur* (reign of terror) that prevailed in France from 1793 to 1794. The Revolution leader, Maximilien Robespierre set out to rid France of the enemies of the Revolution and killed large numbers of Frenchmen. As Burgess (2003) notes, "The Revolution devoured itself in an orgy of paranoiac bloodletting" (p. 3). According to Robespierre, "Terror is nothing other than justice, prompt, severe, inflexible; it is therefore an emanation of virtue; it is not so much a special principle as it is a consequence of the general principle of democracy applied to our country's most urgent needs" (Quoted in Halsall, 1997). Robespierre believed that the "ends justified the means," even though the result was the execution of 40,000 of his fellow citizens. It represented a mentality that is prevalent among terrorists today—human life is less important as compared to the collective cause.

Late Nineteenth- and Early Twentieth-Century Terrorism

Beginning in the 1800s and extending into the early 1900s, a substantial amount of terrorism was conducted by **anarchists and socialists** who were interested in social justice and were anti-capitalist and anti-government. The overwhelming majority of their acts were aimed at government officials and others who were seen as supporters of a social order that oppressed the poor. Their aim was to destroy the ruling governments and replace them with a new social order. In Russia, a populist group opposed to the Tsarist regime assassinated government officials, including Tsar Alexander II. Nationalist groups in Ireland, India, Japan, the Ottoman Empire, and the Balkans also attacked government officials (Burgess, 2003). In 1894, French President Carnot was killed by an Italian anarchist. In 1897, the Austrian empress and the Spanish prime minister were killed. The United States was not immune from these anti-government forces as two U.S. presidents (Garfield and McKinley) were assassinated during this period. Laqueur (1996) points out that if world leaders had assembled in 1900, their primary concern would have been terrorism.

During this period, **state-sponsored terrorism** emerged whereby governments assisted terrorist groups in attacking political opponents or other countries. For example, Serbia armed and trained a number of terrorists, one of whom killed Archduke Franz Ferdinand, heir to the Austrian throne on June 28, 1914. This assassination resulted in the start of World War I. Bulgaria used terrorists to try to undermine the government of Yugoslavia. Immediately prior to World War II, Nazi Germany, Fascist Italy, and Stalinist Russia used terror tactics somewhat similar to those used by Robespierre to control their own populations. Governments quickly learned that terrorism was a useful tool to undermine other governments and to control their own populations.

After World War II, a number of conflicts broke out throughout the Middle East, Europe, Asia, and Africa in countries such as Kenya, Malaysia, Cyprus, Palestine, Ireland, and Algeria. These conflicts were in reaction to colonization, mainly by the French and English, and a variety of groups in a number of countries fought to gain their independence. They primarily used terrorist tactics to fight the colonialists. For example, the State of Israel grew out of such a conflict. In many cases, these conflicts consisted of guerilla warfare. Although these guerillas often used terrorist tactics against their enemies, they differed from terrorists in that the conflicts often involved irregular paramilitary groups fighting colonial powers. Nonetheless, these groups fully understood the power of terrorism and tended to use it when it served their needs. Hoffman (2006) notes,

> They also began to target innocent civilians from other countries who often had little if anything to do with the terrorists' cause or grievance, simply in order to endow their acts with the power to attract attention and publicity that the attacks against their declared or avowed enemies often lacked. Their intent was to shock and, by shocking, to stimulate worldwide fear and alarm. These dramatic tactical changes in terrorism were facilitated by the technological advances of the time that had transformed the speed and ease of international commercial air travel and vastly improved both the quality of television news footage and the promptness with which that footage could be broadcast around the globe. Accordingly, terrorists rapidly came to appreciate that operations perpetrated in countries other than their own and directly involving or affecting foreign nationals were a reliable means of attracting attention to themselves and their cause. (p. 64)

Terrorism in the Late Twentieth Century

In the 1960s and 1970s, the nature of terrorism changed direction in that terrorist groups included not only nationalists, but also a number of left-wing groups that emerged across the globe. For example, the Red Brigades in Italy; the Red Army Faction in West Germany, and a number of groups in the United States, such as the Black Panthers, the Weather Underground or Weathermen, and the Symbionese Liberation Army. These left-wing groups essentially reacted to capitalism and the perceived injustices perpetrated on the poor. They became notorious as a result of their bombings, gun battles with police officers, and bank robberies. At the same time, a number of nationalist groups came to the forefront, including the Provisional Irish Republican Army, the Basque ETA in Spain, and the Palestinian Liberation Organization (PLO), that were fighting for nationalistic interests or independence. One group, the Black September conducted one of the most notorious terrorist attacks at the time when its members kidnapped and killed 11 Israeli athletes at the 1972 Olympic games in Germany.

State-sponsored terrorism also emerged. The Soviet Union, its eastern bloc allies, and China supported terrorist groups in countries throughout the world, and countries such as Iran, Syria, Libya, and Syria began to sponsor terrorist groups to support the Palestinians. For example, Hezbollah and Hamas receive substantial resources from Syria and Iran.

Terrorism Today

Today, American counterterrorism thinking and operations are dominated by al Qaeda, although numerous other groups are also a threat to American interests. Al Qaeda perpetrated the 9/11 attacks on New York and Washington and essentially has declared war on the United States. Al Qaeda, housed primarily in Afghanistan and Pakistan, has a worldwide network that is sophisticated and resilient relative to other terrorist groups. It is able to raise millions of dollars annually and has made political inroads in a number of countries. Relative to earlier terrorist groups or organizations, it is a "super power" because of its financing and influence. Its stated objective is to rid Muslim lands of American and Western influences. The organization also wants to install theocratic governments to promote the Islamic religion, especially in the Middle East.

French police officers scuffle with Basque activist.   *Source:* AP (100714028105)

There is one distinct difference between today's terrorists and those from the past. Today, terrorists seldom attack government officials; they attack civilian targets and attempt to create as many deaths and injuries as possible. This has been referred to as the **propaganda of the deed**. Here the attacks deliver strong messages to a larger audience. Although such attacks have a profound and direct impact on the victims, they also have a psychological impact on non-victims. As an example, in Chapter 1, we discussed fear of crime surveys in the United States. Even though there have been relatively few major attacks occurring in only three cities (New York, Washington, and Oklahoma City), fear of being a victim of a terrorist attack is ranked third relative to all other forms of victimization. Realistically, the probability for a given American to be a victim of such an attack is almost nonexistent.

A review of the history of terrorism shows a number of similarities with the "new" terrorism of today. Contemporary politicians, security experts, and the media treat today's threats as a new phenomenon. However, as Field (2009) points out, the actual behavior of terrorists has not changed to any degree over time. The tactics and motivations of today's terrorists are quite consistent with those of terrorists throughout history. Perhaps the only difference is that terrorists' weapons have become more deadly and destructive. Field advises that rather than attempting to develop new counterterrorism measures, we should examine those measures that have been successful in history. Their implementation may prove to be more fruitful as compared to new strategies.

THE ROOTS AND CAUSES OF TERRORISM

Here, we examine the etiology of terrorism. There is no singular cause of terrorism, but there are multiple causes that individually and in combination result in terrorist groups forming and attacking their perceived or actual enemies. Moreover, some causes affect particular groups or individuals, whereas other causes result in conflict and terrorism for other groups. Some of these causes are macro level, such as the clashes between civilizations or cultures and globalization, whereas others such as religious, ethnic, or tribal clashes are at a more micro level. On the level of the individual, a person may perceive that a group has wronged him or her and reacts by committing a terrorist act as a personal vendetta. Here, we examine the major causes or contributors to terrorism, especially Middle Eastern terrorism.

Civilization or Culture Clashes

According to Huntington (1996) the world is composed of **culture-based civilizations.** Each civilization is composed of primary or dominant countries (major powers) with spheres of influence over a number of supportive and subordinate countries. The subordinate countries' political and economic construction is largely molded by the primary countries' culture. For example, Western countries' political and economic institutions are different from China's largely because the Western and Chinese cultures are quite different. Huntington identifies the cultures that dominate today as Western, Japanese, Chinese, and the Orthodox headed by Russia. Since Huntington wrote his treatise, India rapidly has become a major world economic power and likely can be added to this list. This is not to say these are the only cultures, but these dominate the world today. They are powerful and have strong economies, political systems especially in terms of developing a contingency of satellite countries, and powerful militaries.

These dominant cultures compete with one another on the global stage. If one power begins to make strides militarily, economically, or socially, competing cultures or countries feel threatened and respond accordingly, often increasing their military might in order to ward off potential threats. Subsequently, there are escalations and counter-escalations. The intersection of these global powers results in **fault lines** that represent areas that are more conducive to conflict. For example, in recent years Russia has been attempting to reassert its dominance in the Balkans and Caucuses to prevent the westernization of those countries. China is rapidly increasing its global stature economically and is now increasing its military might and developing relations with a number of third-world countries in an effort to secure vital resources and world influence. This is counter to the interests of the United States and the West. Fault lines result in conflict that in some cases leads to military actions. For example, India and Pakistan have fought armed conflicts and remain enemies as a result of competing cultures. Even when there is no military intervention, groups may engage in extra-governmental conflict in some cases involving terrorist actions. For example, Pakistan's intelligence service has supported groups that commit terrorist acts against India. They also have provided some support for the Taliban.

These fault lines and problems were not evident during the cold war. During this period, the United States and the West were locked in an elongated conflict with the Soviet Union and its satellite states. Other emerging powers such as China, Japan, and India basically remained on the fringes of the mix. The conflict overshadowed all other fault lines and conflicts. For example, the Arab and Muslim world was just as concerned with Soviet influence and hegemony as was the West. However, the breakup of the Soviet Union and the end of the cold war reduced perceived threats and essentially unleashed groups, cultures, and in some cases countries to pursue their cultural identities. These groups have come into conflict with other groups or the state, which sometimes has led to terrorist activities.

Huntington's treatise examined culture clash at the macro level, but culture clashes also occur at the micro level. The societies and cultures in many countries in Africa, the Middle East, and Asia are dominated by tribes, clans, and similar groups. War, conflict, and terrorist activities have been waged among these various groups. These ethnocentric conflicts often involve terrorism with large numbers of civilians being killed and displaced. This was the case in Darfur where Arab Sudanese were fighting with African Sudanese.

Globalization

Globalization is an ever-increasing social phenomenon affecting nations and peoples across the globe. It is rapidly changing and transforming our world. As Nassar (2005) notes,

> Regardless of national birth, our global reality is one of interdependence and shared destiny. We have been interconnected and interdependent from time immemorial. This global interdependence has been growing at a fast pace during the past century. Consequently, today we find ourselves inhabiting a world that has become a seamless and invisible web of interconnected parts despite all the borders that divide its many states. (p. 2)

HS Web Link: To learn more about globalization, go to *http://youthink. worldbank.org/issues/ globalization//*

Analysis Box 5-2

Huntington notes that a substantial amount of the world's conflict is the result of culture clashes. This is especially likely to occur where a country dominated by one culture is close to another country with another culture (fault line). The United States has numerous cultures and groups of people. Do you know of examples where there have been culture clashes in America? When culture clashes occur in the United States, they are relatively minor compared to other countries. Why do you think this is so?

To some extent, globalization is seen as a force that is homogenizing the world—providing consistency and uniformity in a world composed of differences, inconsistencies, and conflict. It is reasoned that increased globalization will result in a global social and economic network with adherents from across many countries. This is not a new concept. After World War I, the League of Nations was formed, and later its successor, the United Nations, was seen as a vehicle to resolve world conflict. In essence, creation of these bodies was viewed by many as the foundation for a world government and a new world order. Other organizations embodying this unifying objective have been created including the World Trade Organization, the International Monetary Fund, and the World Bank. Globalization has come to mean many things, including interdependence, liberalization, secularization, consumerism, democratization, universalism, Westernization, and capitalism (see Nassar, 2005; Cronin, 2004). To some extent, some in third-world countries see it as a sophisticated effort to reestablish colonization. They see globalization as infringing upon their culture and way of life.

Today, however, one of the most commonly mentioned reasons for the growth of terrorism is globalization. It has contributed to terrorism in two ways. First, as noted, globalization has been an effort to homogenize the social and economic fabrics of countries. In essence, it has to a degree been an assault on long-standing, accepted cultures that have existed for hundreds of years in many countries, particularly the Middle East. To this end, Kay (2004) notes that globalization is a mechanism by which countries exert power and control. As a consequence, many of those who are the recipients or who are on the blunt end of globalization have objected to the "Westernization" of their cultures. Some see Westernization as demonic and as a crusade against their way of life. They also see globalization as a method by which Western industrialized nations can control their country and other nondeveloped countries. Western cultures assume that other cultures long for change and that this change is beneficial, an assumption not accepted by many of those who are the subject of Westernization.

Second, globalization has resulted in a more interconnected world. Today, borders do not inhibit communication, business transactions, or the transfer of money and commodities. Terrorists have seized these new opportunities or tools to facilitate their objectives and attacks. Terrorists now can more easily communicate with one another. They can quickly transfer funds from one country to another to finance operations. Modern technology has made it increasingly more difficult for governments to unearth and thwart such activities. To some extent, global terrorist groups now operate similarly to multinational corporations and governments in terms of their interconnectivity.

Religion

Religion, perhaps, has the deepest roots in terms of playing a role in terrorism. Religion is a primary component of many cultures and civilizations—in some cases, religion defines a culture or society. For example, government and everyday life in some Islamic countries are dictated by the Koran. Many Muslims long for theocracy to replace secular governments. Many Americans see themselves as Christians and believe that government should be operated consistent with Christian principles. Israel is a Jewish state and many others such as Muslims are afforded second-class status. The decades-long conflict in Northern Ireland primarily was between Irish Catholics and Irish Protestants. Thus, we see religion playing a key role in conflicts and terrorism. Religion plays a more important and dominate role in some people's lives than does their association with a country or nationalism. Hoffman (1995) advises that religion plays a much larger role in terrorism today than in the past. Religiously oriented terrorists of all sorts use religious precepts to legitimize violence. Hoffman (2006) advises that religious-based terrorism has increased substantially, and it now represents about one-half of the terrorist groups in the world:

> In 1994, for example, a third (sixteen) of the forty-nine identifiable international terrorist groups active that year could be classified as religious in character and/or motivation; and in 1995, their number grew yet again, to account for nearly half (twenty-six, or 46 percent) of the fifty-six known active international terrorist groups. A decade later, it is perhaps not surprising to find that this trend not only continued but solidified. In 2004, for instance, nearly half (fifty-two, or 46 percent) of the terrorist groups active that year were religious, while thirty-two (28 percent) were left-wing groups, and twenty-four (24 percent) were ethno-nationalist/separatist organizations. (p. 86)

Terrorism predicated on religion often leads to more violence as compared to terrorism that emerges for secular reasons. Martin (2003) notes that religious terrorists participate in unrestrained violence and are willing to use the most deadly weapons possible. Secular terrorists tend to be more restrained. Religious terrorists have an unrestricted choice of targets—anything or anyone who is not of their religious persuasion. Secular terrorists attack only those who are perceived as enemies, usually the government or government officials. Religious terrorist groups are confined to zealots or "true believers" who are more willing to attack perceived enemies with impunity. For example, al Qaeda has indiscriminately attacked citizens in numerous countries with the intent of inflicting as many casualties as possible.

HS Web Link: To learn more about religious-based terrorism, go to *http://terrorism.about.com/od/politicalislamterrorism/tp/Religious-terrorism.htm*

Israeli-Palestinian Conflict

An important underlying factor contributing to global terrorism is that the Israeli-Palestinian conflict has gone unresolved for so many years. As Nassar (2005) notes, "The Israeli-Palestinian conflict has been characterized by terrorist atrocities committed by both sides. The terror attacks demonstrate the full viciousness that accompanies the migration of nightmares between nations" (p. 59). Not only is it a long-standing conflict, it is one that has gained the world's attention, particularly in Arab and Muslim countries. The conflict serves as a backdrop for much of the angst that currently exists in the Middle East.

The foundation for the Israeli state was forged through terrorism. Prior to World War II, many Jews were migrating to Palestine with the idea of creating a homeland and escaping oppression in Europe. As the number of Jews increased, conflict emerged with the Palestinians and Arabs in the area. At the end of the war, larger numbers of Jews moved to the area, which enhanced the conflict and problems. At the time, the area was controlled by the British, who had restricted the entry of new Jewish settlers. The Jews waged a terror campaign against the British that culminated with the bombing of the King David Hotel, which housed the British Military Headquarters. Shortly thereafter, the British withdrew from the area and the State of Israel was formed. These rocky beginnings sowed the seeds of discontent, which remain today.

The Israelis and Palestinians initially lived in relative peace for a number of years, but as the number of Jews increased, infringing on Palestinian land, tension evolved into conflict. This conflict has resulted in several wars. Most notably, in 1967, Israel went to war with several of its

Analysis Box 5-3

Although there are several causes of terrorism, it seems that the Israeli-Palestinian conflict is directly or indirectly a part of the conflict. If there were a peace settlement, do you believe that it would have an impact on Muslim-based terrorism? How do you think it would affect terrorism?

Arab neighbors, including Egypt, Syria, and Jordan. The Six Day War, as it came to be known, resulted in Israel gaining substantial territory, including the Sinai Peninsula, the Gaza Strip, the West Bank, East Jerusalem, and the Golan Heights. Later Israel returned the Sinai Peninsula to Egypt but retained control over the other territories.

Today, Palestine and many of the Palestinian people, those who did not flee to other countries, are under Israeli rule. This relationship has resulted in a fairly constant war between the Palestinians and the Israelis with the Palestinians using terrorist tactics and the Israelis depending on conventional military might. Many in the Arab and Muslim world believe that the Palestinians have been unjustly subjected to tyrannical rule and conditions. It has spawned or contributed to several international terrorist organizations including Hamas and Hezbollah.

To a large extent, the plight of the Palestinian people has become a rallying call for all Muslims. It is a prism through which many Arabs and Muslims see the world and make judgments. Numerous Muslim terrorist groups use this conflict as a tool for recruitment, raising funds, and justifications for jihadist activities. The conflict is not so much a cause as it is a rationale for involvement. As long as the conditions in Palestine remain unresolved, it is much easier for numerous Muslim terrorist groups to obtain funding and recruit new fighters.

Russian Invasion of Afghanistan

In 1979, the Soviet Union invaded Afghanistan with the purpose of overthrowing the government and installing a Soviet-aligned government in the country. The Russian invasion was rather ruthless with the Russians killing scores of civilians, particularly women and children. Muslims throughout the region immediately began to garner support for the Afghans. Fighters arrived from other countries; Muslim charities began collecting large amounts of money to be used in the fight; and Afghan tribes were united in the effort to expel the Russians. Later, the United States and Saudi Arabia provided billions of dollars in military aid to the Afghans to facilitate their war efforts. The Russians were eventually defeated and left the country.

This war has a number of implications for terrorism today. First, it unified many of the radical Muslim groups in the country, and today, a number of these groups comprise the al Qaeda and Taliban organizations that are fighting the United States. Second, the war resulted in the construction of a fairly significant underground infrastructure that was used to fight the Russians; this infrastructure remains in place and is currently being used by al Qaeda and the Taliban to fight the American military and its allies. Third, the war resulted in the establishment of a fairly complex and comprehensive system of charities to raise funding for mujahedeen and jihadists. This fairly efficient charity system is used today by several terrorist groups, including al Qaeda. Finally, the defeat of the Russians showed the Muslim and Arab world that it could defeat large world powers. The war emboldened terrorists to take on the United States. Thus, the Russian invasion of Afghanistan did not necessarily cause terrorism, but its outcome has facilitated it.

Russian soldiers leaving Afghanistan after their defeat. *Source:* AP (8610171434)

INDIVIDUAL EXPLANATIONS OF TERRORISM

The causes of terrorism just discussed focus primarily on macro-level variables that have been used to explain the phenomenon. In addition to macro-level conditions, other factors also make some people more susceptible to becoming a terrorist as compared to others. Even though some members of a culture, area, or religious group become terrorists, others do not. Thus, there are individual factors that contribute to people joining terrorist causes. Several theories attempt to explain why an individual would be a terrorist.

Borgeson and Valeri (2009) identify five primary psychological theories or conditions that might explain people's involvement in terrorism: (1) frustration-aggression, (2) relative deprivation, (3) negative identity, (4) narcissistic rage, and (5) moral disengagement.

The **frustration-aggression theory** posits that stress often leads to frustration, and in turn, frustration that remains unabated can result in aggression. The lower classes in many countries, which are considerable in size, have large numbers of young people who are frustrated over their social conditions or livelihoods. Indeed, an examination of the nationalities of terrorists shows that many come from countries that are economically, socially, or politically oppressed. These societies have remained stagnant for generations, resulting in people who perceive that they have few if any opportunities to better themselves. This frustration sometimes leads to individuals striking out at those who they perceive as their oppressors.

Second, Borgson and Valeri identify **relative deprivation** as a contributor to terrorism. Relative deprivation occurs when individuals compare their station in life and opportunities with those of others and find a negative disparity and become frustrated as a result. In some cases, when they compare their station in life with that of others, they develop unrealistic expectations about what they can achieve or what they deserve. Of course, one of the contributing factors to these unrealistic expectations has been globalization, which has made many people aware of others' higher standards of living—the vast differences between Western societies and many third-world societies. The expansion of media outlets in many of these countries has made such differences blatantly apparent (Ahmed, 2007). The perceived inequity has resulted in resentment, anger, and aggression. For example, today many living in Muslim or Arab countries believe that Western nations are stealing or at a minimum not paying market value for scarce resources such as oil. They perceive that they are being deceived and disadvantaged by Western oil-consuming nations.

A third possible factor is a negative **identity crisis**. Here, individuals do not have a sense of belonging and come to identify with population subgroups or tribes rather than the country in which they reside. In some cases, these groups are radical or involved in criminal activities. Terrorist groups such as al Qaeda, Hamas, and Hezbollah become attractive to people with negative identity crises—adherents are easily recruited especially when they also feel that they have been deprived. For example, Osama bin Laden came from a rich Saudi family, but he came to identify with radical Islam and spent his wealth conducting jihad against the West, Saudi Arabia, and other countries he deemed to be enemies of his view of Islam. He effectively has identified with a subculture that is foreign to his family. Fourth, **narcissistic rage** refers to a personality complex with which individuals become egotistical, selfish, and conceited. They have little regard for others, and they generally become this way during their formative years. When they become offended or cannot have their way, they tend to lash out at those who they perceived harmed them. Terrorist organizations are particularly attractive to the narcissistic personality. They provide a forum to express their grievances and anger. Membership serves as a vehicle for them to feel important. It also provides a mode by which to punish or hurt those people or groups that they dislike. Belonging to a terrorist organization or being a terrorist essentially allows, to some extent, unrestrained behavior.

Finally, **moral disengagement** occurs when people move to a fantasy world—their worldview becomes distorted and unrealistic. They may see themselves as a hero with a cause. They believe their actions, although harmful to some, are overwhelmingly beneficial and appreciated by others—the ends justify the means. A prime example is Robespierre's slaughtering of several thousand French citizens during the French Revolution as discussed earlier. People who are morally disengaged are able to neutralize their negative actions by demonizing their victims. For example, today many jihadists see the American government as being evil, perpetrating crimes on Muslim people. Since the Koran prohibits the killing of innocent people, the jihadists advise that the American people elect their government, so therefore, the American people are evil, thus allowing Americans to be killed indiscriminately. This allows the jihadists to morally disengage from the evil acts that they commit.

This discussion demonstrates that there are numerous psychological and individual factors that might contribute to a person becoming a terrorist. Many terrorists come from a background or society that exemplifies strain, political and social repression, and deprivation. These social factors have a significant impact on people's psyche. Nonetheless, psychological condition is just one of many factors (cultural, economic, political, religious, and sociological) that contribute to terrorism. Indeed, there is no single psychological profile for terrorists (Long, 1990); they come from a wide range of backgrounds and possess a variety of perspectives and rationales for their involvement. Terrorist groups are able to attract large numbers of adherents who are uniquely dangerous and deadly.

TYPES OF TERRORISM

It is important to understand that there are a variety of terrorist organizations and terrorist activities across the globe. Today, most Americans exclusively associate al Qaeda with terrorism as a result of the 9/11 attacks and the President George W. Bush administration's linking of al Qaeda to the wars in Iraq and Afghanistan. It should be emphasized that al Qaeda is only one terrorist group, and it represents only one form of terrorism. Martin (2003) examined worldwide terrorism and developed a typology of terrorist groups, which is examined here. This typology perhaps more effectively allows for a more comprehensive understanding of terrorism. Martin identified five types of terrorism based on motivation: (1) state-sponsored terrorism, (2) dissident terrorism, (3) terrorists from the left and right, (4) religious terrorism, and (5) criminal terrorism.

State-Sponsored Terrorism

Terrorist activities that occur as a result of state-sponsored terrorism are similar to those perpetrated by other groups. The primary difference lies in their motivation. State-sponsored terrorism, as its name implies, consists of terrorist acts that occur at the direction, directly or indirectly, of the state or government. The targets of this type of terrorism can be politicians and political parties or groups within the host country, government leaders or politicians and groups in other countries, or other countries in general. For example, political regimes often use paramilitary terrorist groups to attack competing political opponents. Leaders in one country may use terrorism against another country that is seen as a political rival.

Currently, the U.S. Department of State has listed four countries that are state sponsors of terrorism: Iran, Syria, Sudan, and Cuba (U.S. Department of State, 2009). The U.S. State Department designation results in withholding U.S. foreign aid assistance, a ban on defense exports and sales, control over some dual-use items (items that can be used for defense and nondefense purposes), and financial restrictions. According to the State Department, the reasons for this designation are

> Sudan continued to take significant steps towards better counterterrorism cooperation. Iran and Syria have not renounced terrorism or made efforts to act against Foreign Terrorist Organizations and routinely provided safe haven, substantial resources, and guidance to terrorist organizations. Cuba continued to publicly defend the FARC and provide safe haven to some members of terrorist organizations, though some were in Cuba in connection with peace negotiations with the Governments of Spain and Colombia. (Chapter 3)

This is not intended to imply that other countries do not sponsor terrorism to further their objectives. In the case of Sudan, Syria, Iran, and Cuba, their actions are so grievous that they rise above those of other states. There a numerous instances when countries have meddled in other countries' business via terrorism or attempted to control some dissent group or population.

Dissent Terrorism   *Against their own Govt.*

Dissent terrorism refers to a dissent group using terrorist activities against its government. Prime examples include the Sri Lanka Tamil Tigers, who fought the government for independence; the Irish Republican Army, which fought the British government over control of Northern Ireland;

and the Basque Separatists in Spain, who have an on-going terrorist campaign for independence. Additionally, dissent terrorism is quite common on the continent of Africa where different dissent groups are constantly fighting governments for control. In some cases, these terrorist campaigns are waged for independence; in others, the fight is over power, wealth, and control.

Terrorists on the Left and Right

Left-wing and right-wing terrorism is rooted in political ideology, and it generally occurs in countries where one political philosophy dominates, generally in a repressive fashion, and ideological opponents juxtaposed to the rulers fight to overthrow the government. There are ample examples. Fidel Castro overthrew the Batista government in 1959, installing a communist government in the island state. The governments of Peru and Columbia have been fighting communist-inspired terrorist groups for a number of years. Many right-wing authoritarian rulers will use right-wing paramilitary organizations or groups to attack and terrorize their political opponents, usually socialists. In most cases, this form of terrorism pits capitalism against socialism.

Religious Terrorism

Today, **religious motivated terrorism** dominates the world stage, and it has been the primary motivational factor for world terrorism for the past several decades. This form of terrorism dominates the Middle East (Hoffman, 2006). The number of religious motivated terror groups outnumbers all other forms of terrorist groups. Even though many associate religious motivated terrorism with the Muslim religion, there are other religious groups that are engaged in terrorism. What makes this problem more difficult is that they are far more lethal or deadly as compared to secular groups. In many cases, they see or regard violence as a divine duty or sacramental act conveyed by sacred text and imparted by clerical authority (Hoffman, 1995). Consequently, there are no moral constraints on their activities. They kill innocent citizens including women and children with impunity.

As noted, this form of terrorism is not restricted to the Muslim faith. Some of the same attributes, violence legitimized by religious precepts, a preoccupation with perceived nonbeliever or sinner enemies, and isolation from mainstream society, drive other religious groups. For example, American Christian white supremacists have committed all sorts of crime as a result of their faith and hatred for other groups such as African Americans and Jews. Christian extremists have murdered doctors who perform abortions and have blown up abortion clinics. Radical Jewish messianic groups have used terrorism to further their religious tenants, which include the safeguarding of Israeli territory and preventing the government from relinquishing it to Palestinians. There are numerous Christians who endeavor to bring about the apocalypse by encouraging a war between the Muslims and Christians in order to facilitate the Second Coming.

Criminal Terrorism

Whereas the forms of terrorism just discussed are motivated by politics or religion, **criminal terrorism** refers to terrorist acts that are used to facilitate crime and criminal profits. Perhaps the most cogent example of criminal terrorism today is the drug cartels in Mexico. The majority of drugs coming into the United States today come through Mexico. The Mexican cartels produce large quantities of marijuana, black tar heroin, and methamphetamine. The immense size of the drug trade has resulted in the cartels amassing large amounts of money by which to raise large

Three men lie dead, victims of a rival drug cartel.   *Source:* AP (9605240648).

and sophisticated paramilitary groups; bribe police, military, judicial, and government officials; and essentially bring the state to its knees. As discussed earlier, terrorism is associated with political and religious motives, and crime a normally does not fall within the scope of the definition of terrorism. However, the case of the Mexican drug cartels demonstrates that there is a fine line that separates criminal organizations from terrorist organizations. In Mexico, the drug cartels' criminal actions now threaten to undermine the government, and indeed, many of the violent actions perpetrated by these cartels are aimed at making the government less effective in dealing with crime. In the case of Mexico, we can accurately classify the cartels as terrorist organizations because they are involved in political objectives, undermining the government, as well as profits. Chapter 7 examines transnational organized crime. As noted there, criminal terrorism exists throughout the world. It weakens legitimate governments and results in anarchy.

LEVEL OF TERRORIST ACTIVITIES

Terrorism is an ongoing, worldwide problem with attacks occurring in numerous countries. Of course, a large number of attacks are occurring in Iraq and Afghanistan as a result of the wars. Even so, there are numerous attacks in other countries. The U.S. Department of State and the National Counterterrorism Center attempt to maintain a count of terrorist attacks and the level of deaths associated with them. Figure 5-2 provides a breakdown of worldwide attacks for the years 2005 through 2008. It is divided into three sections. The first section provides information about the number of attacks and their impact, the second section focuses on the number of casualties as a result of attacks, and the third section breaks out the attacks in Iraq and Afghanistan since they are war zones where large numbers of attacks have occurred.

Numbers of Attacks	2005	2006	2007	2008
Attacks worldwide	11,157	14,545	14,506	11,770
Attacks resulting in death, injury, or kidnapping of at least one person	8,025	11,311	11,123	8,438
Attacks resulting in the death of at least one individual	5,127	7,428	7,255	5,067
Attacks resulting in the death of zero individuals	6,030	7,117	7,251	6,703
Attacks resulting in the death of only one individual	2,880	4,139	3,994	2,889
Attacks resulting in the death of at least 10 individuals	226	293	353	235
Attacks resulting in the injury of at least one individual	3,842	5,796	6,256	4,888
Attacks resulting in the kidnapping of at least one individual	1,475	1,733	1,459	1,125

Numbers of Casualties as a Result of Attacks	2005	2006	2007	2008
People killed, injured, or kidnapped as a result of terrorism	74,280	74,709	71,608	54,747
People worldwide killed as a result of terrorism	14,560	20,468	22,508	15,765
People worldwide injured as a result of terrorism	24,875	38,386	44,118	34,124
People worldwide kidnapped as a result of terrorism	34,845	15,855	4,982	4,858

Incidents of Terrorism in Iraq and Afghanistan	2005	2006	2007	2008
Terrorist attacks in Iraq	3,467	6,631	6,210	3,258
Attacks resulting in at least one death, injury, or kidnapping	2,837	6,028	5,573	2,902
People killed, injured, or kidnapped as a result of terrorism	20,722	38,878	44,012	19,083

FIGURE 5-2 Incidents of Terrorism Worldwide. *Source:* Office of the Coordinator for Counterterrorism. (2009). *National Counterterrorism Center: Annex of Statistical Information, Country Reports on Terrorism 2008*. U.S. Department of State. http://www.state.gov/s/ct/rls/crt/2008/122452.htm (Accessed May 5, 2009).

As noted in Figure 5-2, in 2008, there were 11,770 terrorist attacks worldwide with 3,258 occurring in Iraq and Afghanistan. The number of attacks in 2008 was about the same as 2005, representing a decline from 2007. A large measure of this decline is attributable to reduced levels of violence in Iraq. Thus, excluding Iraq and Afghanistan, there were just over 8,500 terrorist attacks worldwide. There were 235 attacks that resulted in the death of at least 10 people. Further, 6,703 attacks resulted in no deaths, and approximately 8,400 attacks resulted in at least one death, injury, or kidnapping. These statistics indicate that most of the attacks were relatively small.

The report also revealed that there were 15,765 people killed as a result of terrorist attacks in 2008—a little more than 1.3 deaths per attack. There were 34,124 people injured or about double the number of people killed. The report noted that more than 50 percent of the victims of terrorist attacks were Muslims, demonstrating that most attacks are in Arab and Islamic communities. Approximately 65 percent of the victims were civilians, which is consistent with today's terrorists' targets.

The report also examined modes of attack. As shown in Figure 5-3, most attacks used conventional weapons. They were carried out using conventional methods such as armed attacks, bombings, and kidnappings. In one instance, the Taliban claimed responsibility for a food poisoning attack on Afghani officials that resulted in 261 becoming ill. Otherwise, there were no other reported instances in which terrorists used any sort of weapons of mass destruction. The number of suicide bombings declined in 2008 to 405. Female suicide bombers accounted for

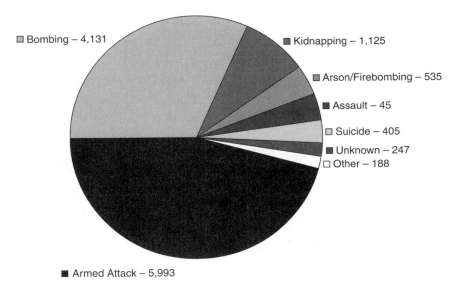

- ■ Bombing – 4,131
- ■ Kidnapping – 1,125
- ■ Arson/Firebombing – 535
- ■ Assault – 45
- ■ Suicide – 405
- ■ Unknown – 247
- □ Other – 188
- ■ Armed Attack – 5,993

11.770 attacks
Some double counting occured when multiple methods were used.

FIGURE 5-3 Methods of Terrorist Attacks *Source:* National Counterterrorism Center. (2009). *2008 Report on Terrorism.* Washington, D.C.: Author, p. 28.

about 9 percent of such bombings. Thus, it appears that the terrorist attacks in 2008 were consistent with past attacks and with our knowledge of terrorist attack methods. It is also important to note that historically, suicide bombings have resulted in larger numbers of deaths as compared to other forms of attack (Hoffman, 2009b).

Finally, it should be noted that terrorist attacks are occurring across the globe. We tend to focus on the Middle East, particularly Iraq and Afghanistan, because of the wars there and the fact that al Qaeda attacked us from its base in Afghanistan. Nonetheless, we must realize that terrorism is a worldwide problem. Figure 5-4 provides a breakdown of the deaths by country as a result of terrorist attacks in 2008.

Note that Iraq had the largest number of deaths and Afghanistan the third largest number of deaths as a result of terrorist attacks. Several other Middle Eastern countries, Pakistan, Algeria, and Lebanon had casualties as a result of attacks. Several East Asian countries also suffered casualties as a result of terrorist attacks: India, Thailand, Sri Lanka, and the Philippines. The African countries of Somalia, Congo, Sudan, and Chad suffered from such attacks. These statistics demonstrate that terrorism is a worldwide problem.

STRATEGIES FOR DEALING WITH TERRORISM

Essentially, the United States had an awakening as a result of the 9/11 attacks. These attacks were not the first ones on Americans by Islamic radicals, but they were the second and most devastating attack to occur on American soil. Subsequently, the United States has developed a much needed homeland security system. An important part of homeland security is to develop effective strategies that deal with or counter foreign terrorists. Obviously, there will be continued attacks, and the

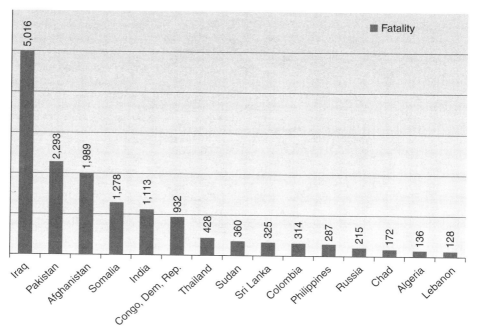

FIGURE 5-4   Deaths by Country as a Result of Terrorist Attacks.   *Source:* National Counterterrorism Center. (2009). *2008 Report on Terrorism.* Washington, D.C.: Author, p. 24.

attacks will increase both in frequency and magnitude of death and destruction if we do not implement effective strategies for dealing with the terrorists. This section elaborates on the strategies that are under consideration.

In years past, the United States has deployed a variety of strategies to combat worldwide terrorism. These have ranged from all-out military intervention such as in Iraq and Afghanistan to military and humanitarian aid in countries such as Pakistan. Some of these efforts have achieved moderate success, whereas others have been less fruitful. Byman (2009) Upon examining the terrorism landscape and government responses, Byman (2009) has identified seven strategies that cover the range of possible strategies. His focus was on al Qaeda, but the strategies could be appropriately applied or considered when dealing with other terrorist organizations. They include (1) crushing terrorist groups unilaterally, (2) crushing terrorist groups multilaterally, (3) containment, (4) defense, (5) diversion, (6) delegitimation, and (7) transforming terrorist breeding grounds. Obviously, we should carefully consider strategies, and we should select the strategies that produce the optimum outcomes for a given situation.

Crushing Terrorist Groups Unilaterally

Our national instinct is to attack and **crush terrorist groups unilaterally**. This means that one country or group battles a terrorist group by itself. After the 9/11 attacks, we sent armed forces into Afghanistan and later into Iraq. Initially, our strategy was to take out the al Qaeda and Taliban fighters—a strategy that was supported by a large number of politicians and citizens. This strategy results in high body counts and much destruction. The idea is that if you annihilate the enemy, his will to fight will be diminished. Scheuer (2004) advises that historically, our relations with the Muslim world have resulted in this being the most viable alternative; however, he does not advocate this method for dealing with terrorists and suggests that a number of our policies should be changed. Today, such a strategy would only antagonize the Muslim world and lead to an increase in terrorism and anti-American sentiment.

This philosophy, to a degree, dominated the Bush administration until we found that it did not work, particularly in Iraq. As an example, the administration supported a preemptive military doctrine whereby we attacked real or perceived enemies before they could attack us (see Howard, 2009). The preemptive military doctrine has been given credence as a result of weapons of mass destruction. Given the potential destructiveness of WMDs, we cannot wait to be attacked before taking decisive action. This rationale has been applied easily to terrorist groups even when there is no evidence that they possess weapons of mass destruction—they may acquire them in the future. The crushing terrorists alternative subjugates other alternatives that might prove to be more effective. Moreover, history advises that this means of dealing with terrorists has not been successful to any large degree.

Several examples of crushing terrorists strategies are available. Since 1983, the Tamil Liberation Tigers of Sri Lanka fought the government to create their own independent state on the island. The insurrection has claimed tens of thousands of lives over the years. In 2002, a peace was brokered, but shortly thereafter the conflict began again in earnest. In 2009, the government applied maximum military force including large-scale attacks on rebel strongholds to root out the separatists (CIA, 2009). Fighting resulted in large numbers of casualties and the displacement of thousands of citizens. Even though the government was able to defeat the rebels, it remains questionable if it will lead to lasting peace. Similarly, in 2006, Israeli troops invaded Lebanon with the intent of destroying Hezbollah military positions. The fighting killed well over 1,000 people and as many as 1 million people were displaced during the fighting. After over a month of fighting, the Israelis withdrew. Although the Israeli army inflicted substantial damage to Hezbollah positions, it had little effect on its operations in Lebanon. Similarly, the Israelis launched an attack on Hamas in the Gaza Strip in 2009. Hamas had fired hundreds of rockets from Gaza into Israel, and the invasion was intended to destroy Hamas's military capability. The attack resulted in several thousand Palestinian casualties, but in the end, it did not eliminate Hamas's capability to conduct terrorist attacks on Israel.

Crushing Terrorist Groups Multilaterally

The **crushing terrorist groups multilaterally** strategy is similar to the previous strategy, but it includes efforts to solicit political and military support from other countries. The intent is to crush the terrorist group, but it involves shared effort. For example, when the United States invaded Afghanistan after the 9/11 attacks and Iraq shortly thereafter, the United States attempted to build a coalition of countries. Multilaterally attacking a terrorist group has a number of advantages. First, it allows for sharing of the military operations. For example, the presence of a multinational force in Afghanistan and Iraq allowed the United States to send fewer troops to those countries. Second, it results in the sharing of expenses. Wars and conflicts, even against terrorist organizations, can be expensive. The involvement of several countries spreads the expense across several countries, thus reducing the expenses for a given country. Third, it provides a strategic advantage. When multiple countries are involved facilities, ports, bases, intelligence services, and so on can be shared, providing substantial strategic flexibility. Finally, when several countries are involved in a conflict, it is much easier to sway world public opinion. Al Qaeda has not only

A Palestinian girl at an Islamic jihad rally in Gaza holds a homemade rocket that reads "Israel" in Arabic and Hebrew. *Source:* AP (08073007002)

attacked the United States, but it has also attacked numerous countries across the globe. This has resulted in a multilateral front by which to combat bin Laden and his organization.

Containment

Containment is an alternative whereby nations do not attempt to defeat a particular terrorist group, but the idea is to restrict its movements and operations to confined areas. Here, antiterrorist forces concentrate on terrorist activities occurring outside their domain of control. For example, for years Philippine authorities have been fighting the abu sayyaf, an Islamic group fighting for an independent province in the Philippines. For the most part, the government has contained them to the southern portion of the country. Government countermeasures have focused primarily on the parameter, thus to some extent controlling the terrorists activities. Byman (2009) notes that this was the American strategy for decades. It is impossible to find every terrorist, making crushing a particular group difficult. On the other hand, efforts can be made to limit its operations, and these efforts often result in positive outcomes. Containment is a much less expensive alternative to attempting to crush or destroy a terrorist group in that it requires fewer resources. Containment also results in fewer political and public relations problems since the anti-terrorist forces focus on safeguarding and helping potential victims. For example, in 2009, Afghani officials were highly critical of U.S. forces because of civilian casualties. Containment, to a large extent, avoids this problem. Containment also results in terrorist organization stagnation—limiting their ability and successes—which can over time negatively affect recruitment, resources, and ability to operate. For example, since the 9/11 attacks, only a handful of Americans have been killed by al Qaeda outside Iraq and Afghanistan. The United States and other countries have been successful in destroying and containing many of its operations.

Defense

The first three alternatives discussed here are offensive in nature. In some cases, strong **defensive actions** have a significant impact on terrorist groups. In other words, if they are not able to wage successful attacks against their enemies, they become impotent or appear to be so, which makes it increasingly more difficult to recruit new fighters and raise money. A prime example of a defensive strategy is Israel's security barrier. The barrier separates most of the West Bank from Israel. After construction of the barrier, the number of suicide bombings in Israel diminished significantly. In Chapter 3, we discussed critical infrastructure protection, a primary initiative in homeland security. The primary purpose of critical infrastructure protection is to prevent terrorist attacks or make them much more difficult.

A primary problem with defense, as discussed in Chapter 3, is that it is difficult to identify what must be defended or protected. The United States literally has thousands of potential targets of varying value to the American public and to potential terrorists. It is questionable if homeland security experts have adequately identified or even made decisions about protection priorities. Thus far, homeland security programming has cost the United States billions of dollars. It is uncertain if our critical infrastructure is better protected today as compared to before the massive expenditures. Even when protection measures are implemented, they may result only in displacement whereby terrorists select new tactics or targets. Obviously, some potential targets are better protected than others, but we cannot achieve maximum levels of security to protect all potential targets. Effective defense is questionable and perhaps elusive.

Diversion

Diversion is a process whereby a victim or potential victim of terrorists attempts to divert terrorists' attention to another terrorist target or victim. It is somewhat of a "bait and switch" tactic. Byman (2009) notes that this is a fairly common tactic. For example, the United States criticized Russia for its handling of rebel groups in Chechnya. This criticism, at least to some extent, diverted terrorists' attention from the United States. Pakistan for decades used the Kashmir dispute with India to channel terrorists' actions in Pakistan. In the 1980s, a number of Middle Eastern countries sent their radicals or jihadists to Afghanistan to fight the Russians, thus relieving pressure in their own countries. The United States repeatedly speaks of human rights in a number of countries. The motivation of such statements comes into question. Are the statements a genuine effort to improve conditions in a targeted country, or are they more useful in helping focus terrorists' attention on a target other than the United States? Many terrorists and jihadists have come to despise the repressive governments of their own countries. When taken too far, a diversion policy likely will anger the government that is the target of the diversion. In some cases, it may result in the fall of a government that is friendly with the United States and its replacement with one that facilitates terrorism against our country.

Delegitimation

A long-range strategy for dealing with a terrorist group is **delegitimation.** Here, the government attacks the terrorist group along a number of fronts in an effort to cause citizens and potential supporters to question the group's motives, tactics, and ability to genuinely improve people's life conditions. In many cases, the government will employ moderate clerics, preachers, political leaders, media, and other groups to condemn the terrorists and their activities. The government will highlight its own programs and efforts that appeal to the citizenry. Of particular importance is the government's ability to highlight the innocent citizens that are the casualties of terrorist attacks. For example, after attacks in the kingdom in 2003, Saudi Arabia began to portray the gruesome impact of the attacks in the media. It damaged the credibility of the terrorists and lessened support for them (Byman, 2009). Of course, it should be realized that the terrorists are engaged in a similar campaign, using every opportunity to criticize their enemy and delegitimize it. For example, terrorist groups across the globe used the photos and American actions at the Abu Ghraib prison in Iraq to incite support and anti-Americanism. The Taliban in Pakistan and Afghanistan blame numerous civilian casualties on the United States in an effort to delegitimize America and the Pakistani and Afghan governments. In the end, the government or enemy must be able to show that it offers a better life and more opportunities as compared to the terrorist group. It becomes a battle for minds and hearts.

Transforming Terrorist Breeding Grounds

Transforming terrorist breeding grounds is a strategy that is similar to delegitimation except that it is more long term and comprehensive in nature. An examination of terrorist groups and organizations shows that they predominately, but not always, exist in countries or areas that are poor and repressed. For example, France and England have had Islamic terrorist problems, or at least substantial Muslim discontent, but these problems have been the result of these groups not being able to assimilate into the middle classes in those countries. Nevertheless, today most terrorist groups are located in third-world countries or areas where social and economic problems are endemic. The terrorists and those who affiliate with them often perceive that they have no choice but to wage war with those who oppress them.

As Gurr (1990) notes, democratic reforms can substantially reduce the support for terrorists and win over those who otherwise might be recruited by them. Inclusion is a far better tactic than exclusion. Indeed, Li (2005) found that democratic reform tended to reduce the incidence of terrorist events whereas government constraints tended to increase them. The RAND Corporation (Jones and Libicki, 2008) examined 648 terrorist groups between 1968 and 2006 and found that only 7 percent of the terrorist campaigns ended as a result of military force, whereas 43 percent of them ended as result of political transition. Political, social, and economic reform can be effective countermeasures to terrorism.

It must be remembered that the transformation of a terrorist breeding ground is difficult, wrought with pitfalls, and expensive. To transform an area, political institutions, economies, and social systems must be addressed successfully. Politically, those who are disenfranchised must become part of the government structure and their grievances must be addressed. The oppressed must be provided equal economic opportunities. Too often the economic and politically elite within a country see any social or economic changes as threatening their way of life, particularly their relative power and wealth. They tend to fight such reforms even though the reforms likely will create a safer and more peaceful environment. Nonetheless, systemic changes in some cases are the only way to deal with growing terrorism problems.

Transformation is a lesson that has been learned well by numerous terrorist organizations. For example, Hamas and Hezbollah, although labeled terrorist organizations, have considerable influence not only because of their military capabilities, but also because both of these organizations conduct considerable charitable campaigns. Many Arab and Muslim countries do not possess social safety nets for their citizens. Organizations such as Hamas and Hezbollah, however, fill these gaps in places such as Lebanon and Palestine. For example, after the 2006 Israeli invasion of Lebanon, Hezbollah immediately assisted the populace in rebuilding destroyed portions of the country. Hezbollah was more effective than the Lebanese government in providing assistance to the Lebanese people.

Analysis Box 5-4

As discussed earlier, several strategies can be used to defeat terrorists. Which of the strategies presented do you think would be most effective in dealing with the Taliban in Afghanistan and Pakistan? Which strategy do you believe would be the most ineffective? Why?

Helping citizens has a lasting impact, and it produces long-lasting loyalty. The terrorists have been successful in a number of areas in transforming citizens to support the terrorists and their objectives.

There are several alternative strategies by which to combat terrorism. Selection of a strategy must be based on the nature of the problem and intervention capabilities. Obviously, those strategies that assist people in affected areas tend to have the greatest potential for success.

Summary

This chapter examined the political and social foundations for terrorism. When examining homeland security, it is important to have an understanding of the primary threat to the homeland—terrorist acts committed against and in the United States. As noted, terrorism is not the only threat or problem that is subsumed within homeland security—for example, natural disasters, pandemic flu outbreaks, and other catastrophes—but, it is without question the most threatening given the possibility that terrorists will use some form of weapons of mass destruction when attacking America. In essence, homeland security necessitates that we prepare for all sorts of major problems.

Regarding terrorism, we noted that it is difficult to define it. Definitions abound; even different departments and agencies within the federal government have different definitions. What makes it difficult to define is that it is embodied in politics or perspective. For example, one person's terrorist is another person's freedom fighter. To some extent, terrorism can be viewed as the commission of crime, usually a horrific crime, to achieve political, social, or religious objectives as opposed to having a financial motive. Moreover, the majority of victims of terrorism are innocents, and oftentimes, the victim count includes large numbers of women and children. It is a premeditated act that attacks legitimate governments or competing groups.

Terrorism is not a new phenomenon; it has a long history, and there have been all sorts of groups involved in terrorist activities throughout the ages. A host of causes contribute to terrorism. Today, we have a particular mix of worldwide terrorist organizations and groups, and we can identify some of the causes. These include culture, globalization, religion, the Israeli-Palestine conflict, the Russian invasion of Afghanistan, and individual social psychological factors that affect individuals' decision to become terrorists. We cannot definitively point to any single factor or root cause.

There are also different types of terrorism. These types are distinguished by motivation. Essentially, there is state-sponsored terrorism whereby the state or state actors attempt to use terrorism against their enemies; dissent terrorism whereby groups within a country, usually ethnocentric, are disgruntled with the political arrangements and attempt to use terrorism to change the political landscape; left-wing and right-wing terrorists who are politically motivated to change government arrangements; religious terrorists who attempt to change the government into a theocratic state; and finally terrorism whereby criminal organizations attempt to affect a government in order to facilitate their criminal enterprises. These forms of terrorism crop up periodically and can be present in any country.

The U.S. Department of State and the National Counterterrorism Center attempt to monitor the levels of terrorist activities. A large portion of the terrorist acts today are committed in Iraq and Afghanistan as a result of the wars being conducted there. We are also witnessing an increase in attacks in Pakistan. Recently, Pakistan began to enact stronger measures against the

Taliban operating in that country, which has led to an increase in terrorist attacks. Even though weapons of mass destruction remain a frightening consideration, most terrorist attacks are conducted using conventional weapons and explosives, and a large percentage of attacks are performed via suicide bombers.

Finally, we addressed the various strategies for countering terrorism. They range in scope from military action to humanitarian aid. Militarily, a country can attempt to use force to destroy a terrorist threat by itself or in conjunction with a consortium of allies. Rather than destroying the terrorist group or organization, which is quite difficult, a country can attempt to use various tactics to contain it. Another strategy focuses on homeland security, whereby a country attempts to protect its borders and critical infrastructure from attack. A strategy that has been used with great frequency by a variety of governments has been to divert the wrath of the terrorists toward another enemy or target. This is generally accomplished by highlighting the injustices perpetrated by other countries. Delegitimation is a process whereby the victims of terrorism and other countries attempt to implement programs that provide citizens with greater benefits as opposed to any provided by the terrorists. They also point out the atrocities committed by the terrorists, especially on innocent civilians. The goal is to move public opinion away from the terrorists and gain support for the government. A final strategy is transforming terrorist breeding grounds. We can identify areas that produce large numbers of terrorists. If we can improve the social and economic conditions in these areas, we likely can reduce the appeal of terrorism and reduce the number of converts.

This chapter examined the political and social aspects of terrorism. It is important to understand the dynamics of terrorism if we are to construct effective homeland security programming. It is important that homeland security is achieved by a mix of programs that addresses every aspect of threats to the homeland.

Discussion Questions

1. What is the continuum of social conflict? Provide examples of current conflicts in the world that fit each of the categories within the continuum.
2. There are numerous definitions of terrorism. What are the various elements contained in these definitions?
3. Discuss the various causes of terrorism.
4. Which countries are involved in state-sponsored terrorism? Which groups or activities do they support?
5. Discuss the types of terrorism. Which types are the greatest threat to the United States?
6. Discuss the various ways of defeating terrorism. In your opinion, which method would be most effective in defeating terrorism in the Middle East?

References

Ahmad, E. (2003). "Terrorism: Theirs and ours." In *Terrorism and Counterterrorism: Understanding the New Security Environment*, eds. R. Howard and R. Sawyer, pp. 47–53. New York: McGraw-Hill.

Ahmed, A. (2007). *Journey into Islam: The Crisis of Globalization.* Washington, D.C.: Brookings Institution.

Bellavita, C. (2008). "Changing homeland security: What is homeland security?" *Homeland Security Affairs*, 4(2): 1–30.

Borgeson, K. and R. Valeri. (2009). *Terrorism in America.* Sudbury, MA: Jones and Bartlett.

Burgess, M. (2003). "A Brief History of Terrorism." CDI: Center for defense information. http://www.cdi.org/friendly-version/printversion.cfm?documentID=1502 (Accessed April 14, 2009).

Byman, D. (2009). "US counter-terrorism options: A taxonomy." In *Terrorism and Counterterrorism: Understanding the New Security Environment*, 3rd ed., eds. R. Howard, R. Sawyer, and N Bajema, pp. 460–82. New York: McGraw-Hill.

Central Intelligence Agency. (2009). *The World Fact Book.* http://www.cia.gov/library/publications/the-world-fact-book/geos/ce.html (Accessed May 14, 2009).

Cronin, A. (2004). "Behind the curve: Globalization and international terrorism." In *Defeating Terrorism: Shaping the New Security Environment*, eds. R. Howard and R. Sawyer, pp. 29–50. New York: McGraw-Hill.

Field, A. (2009). "The 'new terrorism': Revolution or evolution." *Political Science Review*, 7(2): 195–207.

Forst, B. (2009). *Terrorism, Crime, and Public Policy.* New York: Cambridge University Press.

Gurr, T. (1990). "Terrorism in democracies: Its social and political bases." In *Origins of Terrorism: Psychologies, Ideologies, Theologies, and States of Mind,* ed. W. Reich, pp. 87–98. New York: Cambridge University Press.

Hall, M., M. Bell, and B. Heath. (2009). "Shooting suspect was on anti-hate groups' radar." *USA Today.* http://www.usatoday.com/news/nation/2009-06-10-shooter_N.htm (Accessed August 18, 2009).

Halsall, P. (1997). "Maximilien Robespierre: Justification of the use of terror." http://www.fordham.edu/halsall/mod/robespierre-terror.html (Accessed April 14, 2009).

Hoffman, B. (2009a). "Defining terrorism." In *Terrorism and Counterterrorism: Understanding the New Security Environment,* eds. R. Howard and R. Sawyer, pp. 4–33. New York: McGraw-Hill.

Hoffman, B. (2009b). "The logic of suicide terrorism." In *Terrorism and Counterterrorism: Understanding the New Security Environment,* eds. R. Howard and R. Sawyer, pp. 311–22. New York: McGraw-Hill.

Hoffman, B. (2006). *Inside Terrorism.* New York: Columbia University Press.

Hoffman, B. (1995). "Holy terror: The implications of terrorism motivated by a religious imperative." *Studies in Conflict and Terrorism,* 18(4): 271–84.

Howard, R. (2009). "Preemptive military doctrine: No other choice." In *Terrorism and Counterterrorism: Understanding the New Security Environment,* 3rd ed., eds. R. Howard, R. Sawyer, and N Bajema, pp. 483–91. New York: McGraw-Hill.

Huntington, S. (1996). *The Clash of Civilizations and the Remaking of World Order.* New York: Simon & Schuster.

Jones, S. and M. Libicki. (2008). *How Terrorist Groups End: Lessons for Countering of Qa'ida.* Santa Monica, CA: RAND.

Kay, S. (2004). "Globalization, power, and security." *Security Dialogue,* 35(1): 9–25.

Laqueur, W. (1996). "Postmodern terrorism." *Foreign Affairs,* 75(5): 24–36.

Li, Q. (2005). "Does democracy promote or reduce transnational terrorism incidents?" *Journal of Conflict Resolution,* 49(2): 278–97.

Long, D. (1990). *The Anatomy of Terrorism.* New York: Free Press.

Martin, G. (2003). *Understanding Terrorism: Challenges, Perspectives, and Issues.* Thousand Oaks, CA: Sage.

Nassar, J. (2005). *Globalization & Terrorism: The Migration of Dreams and Nightmares.* New York: Rowman & Littlefield.

Pillar, P. (2003). "The dimensions of terrorism and counterterrorism." In *Terrorism and Counterterrorism: Understanding the New Security Environment,* eds. R. Howard and R. Sawyer, pp. 24–46. New York: McGraw-Hill.

Scheuer, M. (2004). *Imperial Hubris.* Washington, D.C.: Brassey's Inc.

U.S. Department of State. (2009). *Country Reports on Terrorism,* 2008. http://www.state.gov/s/ct/rls/crt/2008/122436.htm (Accessed May 15, 2009).

Whittacker, D. (2001). *The Terrorism Reader.* London: Routledge.

6

The Nature and Geography of Terrorist Groups, State Sponsors of Terror, and Safe Havens

LEARNING OBJECTIVES

1. Be familiar with the various terrorist groups in the world.
2. Be familiar with the terrorist groups operating in the United States.
3. Know the nation-states that sponsor terrorism.
4. Know the safe havens for terrorists.

KEY TERMS

Abu Nidal Organization
Al-Aqsa Martyrs' Brigade
Asbat Al-Ansar
Hamas
Palestine Liberation Front
Al Jihad
Muslim Brotherhood
Al-Gama'a al-Islamiyya
Ansar al-Islam
Kurdistan Workers Party
Hezbollah
Al Qaeda
Islamic Courts Union
Al-Shabaab
Pakistani Taliban

Lashkar-e-Tayyiba
Harakat ul-Mudjahidin
Jaish-e-Mohammed
Islamic Movement of Uzbekistan
Uighars
Hizb ul Tahrir
Jemaah Islamiyyah
Abu Sayyaf Group
Aum Shinrikyo
Autodefensas Unidas de Colombia
Ejército de Liberación Nacional
Revolutionary Armed Forces
   of Colombia
Shining Path
Basque Fatherland and Liberty

Political extremism

Single-issue

Lone wolf

Earth Liberation Front

Animal Liberation Front

State sponsor of terrorism

Safe haven for terrorism

Tri-Border Region

INTRODUCTION

As with the very definition of terrorism, foreign terrorist groups, the state sponsors of terror, and safe havens are all phrases fraught with conceptual difficulty (LaFree and Dugan, 2009; Symeonidou-Kastanidou, 2004). Whether a group of individuals is seen as a terrorist organization, an extremist group, or a band of radical freedom fighters is often a matter of perception and ideology. Although it may be trite to say, what one person may see as a terrorist organization, others may see as a group of freedom fighters, protectors, or guerilla resistors. One way of determining the status of a group is to look at a country's designation of the group. Several countries, including the United States, can formally designate a group a "foreign terrorist organization."

Likewise, nation states have the ability to designate other countries as "state sponsors of terror" and consider regions of the world as safe haven for terrorism. Although these designations provide some clarity in determining the differences among groups that are considered terrorist organizations, nations do not always agree on which groups they view as terrorists. In this chapter, we discuss the nature of terrorist groups, describing many of these groups, their principal mission, and their location of operation. We consider only the major and most active groups that are generally seen by Western governments as terrorist organizations. Many organizations designated by various governments as terrorist groups go under various names that often differ by the country describing them as well as by the groups themselves. Many of these groups merge over time with other groups, abandon their struggle, or become inactive for a variety of reasons. Figure 6-1 shows the various organizations that have been designated as terrorist by the governments of the United States, the European Union, Australia, and Canada.

In the first section of the chapter, we attempt to familiarize the reader with some of the basic information about these groups by their geographic area of operation. We then turn our attention to states that have been designated by the U.S. government as "state sponsors of terror." Following a discussion of these states and the problems associated with making this designation, we explore the concept of terrorist safe havens, looking at parts of the world that are said to be inviting for terrorism or extremist activities.

FOREIGN TERRORIST ORGANIZATIONS

Although terrorist groups exist throughout the world, a large number are located in the Middle East. This area has the highest concentration of groups and state sponsors of terror. Recently, these groups have become the most problematic and most active as a result of their attacks and violence. This section examines some of these terrorist organizations.

Middle East Groups

Several groups are located in the Middle East and reside in various countries. Here, we examine the most notable groups by country.

Terrorist Organization	US	EU	Canada	Australia
Abu Nidal Organization (ANO)	•	•	•	
Abu Sayyaf Group (ASG)	•		•	•
Al-Aqsa Martyrs Brigade (AAMB)	•	•	•	
Al-Shabaab	•			•
Ansar al-Islam (AI)	•		•	•
Armed Islamic Group (GIA)	•		•	
Asbat al-Ansar (AAA)	•		•	•
Aum Shinrikyo (AUM)	•	•	•	
Autodefensas Unidas de Colombia (AUC)			•	
Basque Fatherland and Liberty (ETA)	•	•		
Communist Party of the Philippines/New People's Army (CPP/NPA)	•	•		
Continuity Irish Republican Army (CIRA)	•	•		
Gama'a al-Islamiyya (IG Islamic Group)	•	•	•	
Hamas (Islamic Resistance Movement)	•	•	•	•
Harakat ul-Jihad-i-Islami/Bangladesh (HUJI-B)	•			
Harakat ul-Mujahidin (HUM)	•		•	
Hezbollah (Party of God)	•	•	•	•
Islamic Jihad Group	•	•		
Islamic Movement of Uzbekistan (IMU)	•		•	•
Jaish-e-Mohammed (JeM) (Army of Mohammed)	•		•	•
Jemaah Islamiya organization (JI)	•		•	•
al-Jihad (Egyptian Islamic Jihad)	•		•	
Kahane Chai (Kach)	•	•	•	
Kata'ib Hizballah	•			
Kongra-Gel (KGK, formerly Kurdistan Workers' Party, PKK, KADEK)	•	•	•	•
Lashkar-e Tayyiba (LeT) (Army of the Righteous)	•		•	•
Lashkar e Jhangvi (LeT)	•		•	•
Liberation Tigers of Tamil Eelam (LTTE)	•	•	•	
Libyan Islamic Fighting Group (LIFG)	•			
Moroccan Islamic Combatant Group (GICM)	•			
Mujahedin-e Khalq Organization (MEK)	•		•	
National Liberation Army (ELN)	•			
Palestine Liberation Front (PLF)	•	•	•	
Palestinian Islamic Jihad (PIJ)	•	•	•	•
Popular Front for the Liberation of Palestine (PFLF)	•	•	•	
PFLP-General Command (PFLP-GC)	•		•	
Tanzim Qa'idat al-Jihad fi Bilad al-Rafidayn (QJBR) (al Qaeda in Iraq) (formerly Jama'at al-Tawhid wa'al-Jihad, JTJ, al-Zarqawi Network)	•			
al Qaeda	•		•	•
al Qaeda in the Islamic Maghreb (formerly GSPC)	•		•	•
Real IRA	•	•		
Revolutionary Armed Forces of Colombia (FARC)	•	•		

FIGURE 6-1 Officially Designated Terrorist Organizations.

Terrorist Organization	US	EU	Canada	Australia
Revolutionary Nuclei (formerly ELA)	•	•		
Revolutionary Organization 17 November	•	•	•	
Revolutionary People's Liberation Party/Front (DHKP/C)	•	•	•	
Shining Path (Sendero Luminoso, SL)	•	•	•	
United Self-Defense Forces of Colombia (AUC)	•	•	•	

FIGURE 6-1 Continued *Sources:* U.S. Department of State. (2009). Foreign Terrorist Organizations. Office of the Coordinator For Counterterrorism, July 7, 2009 (the U.S. government listed 44 organizations); Australian Government. (2009). Listing of Terrorist Organisations. Attorney-General's Department, September 15, 2009 (as of September 2009, the Australian government listed 18 organizations); Public Safety Canada. (2009). publicsafety.gc.ca (Canada listed 40 organizations); Official Journal of the European Union. (2009). Council Common Position 2009/67/CFSP of 26 January 2009 (the European Union listed 47 organizations).

PALESTINE The **Abu Nidal Organization** (ANO) is also known as the Fatah Revolutionary Council. The mission of the group is said to be the destruction of Israel and the creation of an independent Palestinian state. The group was established in the 1970s after the Yom Kippur War when Israel defeated several countries that had attempted to invade it. The group split from the Palestinian Liberation Organization (PLO) because its leaders believed that Yasir Arafat was not dealing harshly enough with Israel (Martin, 2003; Public Safety Canada, 2009). After splitting with the PLO, the group moved to Baghdad, and then later to Syria and Libya. While in Syria, the ANO provided some intelligence services to the Syrians and engaged in terrorist attacks. Syria could not control the organization, resulting in strained relationships with its leaders. Libya welcomed the group and provided financial support and a base of operations.

The Abu Nidal Organization has been involved in more than 90 bombings, hijackings, and assassinations. The group is responsible for attacks in 20 countries, killing or injuring almost 900 persons, with the most significant attacks occurring in the Rome and Vienna airports in 1985 and the Neve Shalom synagogue in Istanbul. It was also responsible for the hijacking of Pan Am Flight 73 in Karachi in 1986 and the attack on the City of Poros day-excursion ship in Greece in 1988. The group also had large numbers of fighters involved in the Lebanese Civil War. It is currently thought to be inactive since its leader was killed in 2002. However, in 2008, a Jordanian official reported the apprehension of a member who planned to carry out attacks in Jordan (U.S. State Department, 2009; White 2009).

The **Al-Aqsa Martyrs' Brigade** was established in 2000 in the aftermath of armed conflicts between Palestinians and Israelis and was closely associated with Yasir Arafat's Fatah movement. The group's primary objective is the removal of all Israeli military forces and settlers from the West Bank, Gaza Strip, and Jerusalem. The group seeks to establish an independent Palestinian state and resist Israeli occupation. The group has used bombings, rocket attacks, and suicide bombings to achieve its mission. In 2008, the Brigade launched a number of rocket and mortar attacks into southern Israel from the Gaza Strip (U.S. State Department, 2009).

Rothem (2002) advises that Brigade's suicide attacks were some of the most deadly. It usually attacked secular targets where there were large crowds. This resulted in massive casualties. The group claimed responsibility for more than 300 attacks on Israelis. Also, the group was the first to use female suicide bombers in 2002. The Brigade became one of the most violent groups operating in Palestine.

Asbat Al-Ansar is based in a Palestinian refugee camp in Lebanon. It is composed primarily of Sunnis, and its goal is the eradication of anti-Islamic and Western influences in Lebanon. The group

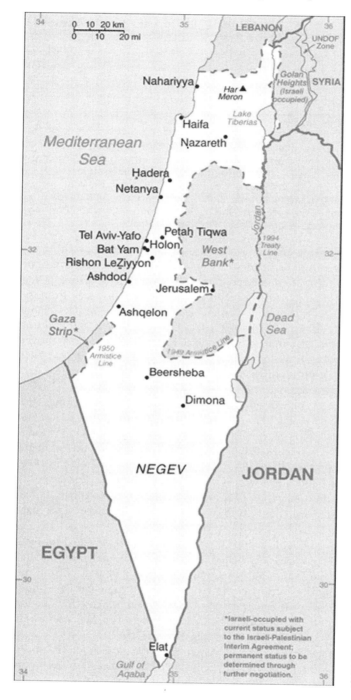

Map of Israel and the Palestinian Territories. *Source:* Central Intelligence Agency, World Factbook. https://www.cia.gov/library/publications/the-world-factbook/geos/is.html

seeks to establish an Islamic state. In the mid-1990s, the group assassinated Lebanese religious leaders and bombed secular targets such as nightclubs, theaters, and liquor stores. In 2000, Osama bin Laden began supplying the group with resources. It then carried out a rocket-propelled grenade attack on the Russian Embassy in Beirut in January 2000 in support of the Chechens who were fighting for independence (U.S. State Department, 2009). In 2001, the group attempted a coup in Lebanon, but it was defeated by government forces (Keats, 2002b). Asbat Al-Ansar operatives have been involved in fighting coalition forces in Iraq since at least 2005 (U.S. State Department, 2009).

Hamas is a Sunni terrorist organization that evolved from the Palestinian branch of the Muslim Brotherhood in late 1987 during the first Palestinian uprising. The group has the goal of establishing a Palestinian state. Hamas is one of the largest terrorist groups operating in the Middle East and is responsible for hundreds of attacks on military and civilian targets using suicide bombings, shootings, rockets, and improvised explosive devices (IEDs). Hamas fought a 23-day war with Israel from late December 2008 to January 2009, in an effort to break an international blockade on the Gaza Strip and force the openings of the international crossings (U.S. State Department, 2009). In 2005, the group curtailed its attacks as the result of a temporary ceasefire that was brokered by the Palestinian Authority. In 2006, Hamas won elections in the Gaza Strip and now militarily and politically controls the area.

Hamas has a military wing and a political wing. The military wing is responsible for maintaining control of its operations against Israel, whereas the political wing is extensively involved in providing social services to the Palestinian people. For example, in 2009, the Israelis invaded the Gaza Strip. Hamas provided most of the soldiers fighting the Israelis, and in the aftermath, Hamas provided much of the humanitarian aid to the Palestinian people who were affected by the invasion. Hamas operates a number of social programs, which results in a great deal of public support on the part of the Palestinian people. These humanitarian acts assist the group in raising large amounts of money. For example, Hamas has used American charities to raise money in the United States, as discussed in Chapter 11.

HS Web Link: To learn more about Hamas, go to *http://www.cfr.org/ publication/8968/hamas. html*

Hamas militants head for position for a gun battle with Fatah supporters.   *Source:* AP (06122208131)

Analysis Box 6-1

A substantial amount of terrorism and a number of terrorist groups are associated with Palestine. Most of the groups have similar objectives: defeating Israel and the purging of Western culture and values in Muslim lands. In 2010, President Obama initiated peace talks between the Israelis and the Palestinians. How important are these talks? If peace could be achieved, what impact would it have on the area?

The **Palestine Liberation Front (PLF)**, also known as the Front for the Liberation of Palestine (FLP), is a group allied with the PLO. The group was founded in 1961 with the objective of establishing an independent Palestinian state with Jerusalem as its capital. The group has carried out several attacks, including the 1985 hijacking of the Italian cruise ship *Achille Lauro* (U.S. State Department, 2009). The group is housed primarily in Palestinian refugee camps in Lebanon, where it has substantial support. Its leader, Abu Abbas, supported Saddam Hussein during the Gulf War. In 2004, he was captured by coalition forces in Iraq and died while in custody.

EGYPT   **Al Jihad** is also known as the Egyptian Islamic Jihad and was founded in the 1970s in Egypt. The organization is a splitter group of the **Muslim Brotherhood** and seeks to convert the state of Egypt into an Islamic nation. The Muslim Brotherhood has a significant following in Egypt and is politically active, attempting to overthrow Egyptian President Muhammad Hosni Mubarak. Al Jihad merged with al Qaeda in 2001. The group has attacked both U.S. and Israeli

Map of Egypt.   *Source:* Central Intelligence Agency, World Factbook. https://www.cia.gov/library/publications/the-world-factbook/geos/eg.html

interests and is responsible for the 1981 assassination of Egyptian President Anwar Sadat. The group was also responsible for the Egyptian Embassy bombing in Islamabad in 1995 and a disrupted plot against the U.S. Embassy in Albania in 1998. The group has not committed independent acts of terrorism since its merger with al Qaeda in 2001 (U.S. State Department, 2009).

Al-Gama'a al-Islamiyya is a militant Egyptian movement that seeks to change the Egyptian government to an Islamic state. At one time, the group was the largest militant group operating in Egypt, but it has transformed to a loose network of groups. This change was the result of President Mubarak's cracking down on militant Islamist groups in Egypt. In 1993, its leader, Sheikh Omar Abdel al-Rahman, was arrested in connection with the first World Trade Center bombing. In 1996, he and nine others members of the group were convicted for conspiring to destroy New York City landmarks, including the UN headquarters, the Federal Building, and the Lincoln and Holland Tunnels (Keats, 2002a). The group has attacked a number of civilian targets, including the 1997 Luxor attack that killed 62 people. It claimed responsibility for the June 1995 assassination attempt on Egyptian President Hosni Mubarak in Addis Ababa, Ethiopia (U.S. State Department, 2009). Today, the group is divided and consists of a number of small cells.

IRAQ **Ansar al-Islam**, also known as Partisans of Islam, is a Sunni military group made up of Iraqi Kurds and Arabs. The group was established in 2001 in the Kurdish region in northern Iraq (U.S. State Department, 2009). It is one of the largest Sunni groups operating in Iraq. The group is said to be responsible for attacks, kidnappings, and murders throughout Iraq and has conducted numerous attacks on government officials and coalition forces in Iraq. The group desires to install an Islamic

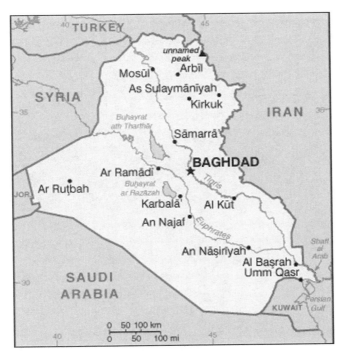

Map of Iraq. *Source:* Central Intelligence Agency, World Factbook. https://www.cia.gov/library/publications/the-world-factbook/geos/iz.html

government with fundamentalist values and is opposed to all things secular. The group has ties to and receives financial support from al Qaeda, which makes it more dangerous (Gregory, 2008). According to the State Department, some members of Ansar al-Isalm trained in al Qaeda camps in Afghanistan, and the group provided safe haven to affiliated terrorists before Operation Iraqi Freedom.

The **Kurdistan Workers Party** (PKK) is a Turkish political party that was founded in 1974. An estimated 12 million Kurds live in Turkey. The primary goal of the group is the establishment of independent Marxist Kurdish state in southeast Turkey and northern Iraq. Most recently, the group has been fighting the Turkish government to establish an autonomous region within Turkey. In the 1980s, the group killed an estimated 10,000 Kurds to solidify its control over the Kurdish movement. Since 1984, it is estimated that the group has killed at least 37,000 people (Spindove and Simonsen, 2010). The PKK raises large amounts of money through the heroin trade. It transports heroin from Afghanistan and Turkey to other countries.

PKK uses guerilla warfare in an attempt to achieve its objectives. The group has attacked Turkish military troops and political leaders. In 2008, PKK militants killed 15 Turkish soldiers at the Aktutun outpost on the Turkish-Iraqi border, and five days later the group killed several police officers and wounded 19 in an attack in southeastern Turkey (U.S. State Department, 2009). In the mid-1990s, the PKK bombed hotels and tourist destinations and kidnapped tourists in an effort to affect Turkey's tourist industry. Today, the PPK has moved its principal operations into Iraq. From Iraq, it mounts attacks inside Turkey. On several occasions in the late 2000s, Turkish troops crossed into Iraq to attack PPK strongholds. These actions strained relations among Turkey, Iraq, and the United States.

HS Web Link: To learn more about the PKK, go to *http://www.cfr.org/ publication/14576/inside_ the_kurdistan_workers_ party_pkk.html*

Map of Lebanon. *Source:* Central Intelligence Agency, World Factbook. https://www.cia.gov/library/publications/the-world-factbook/geos/le.html

LEBANON **Hezbollah**, the "Party of God," is a radical Islamic organization that operates in Lebanon. It formed in 1982, as a result of the Israeli invasion of Lebanon. It takes its ideological inspiration from the Iranian revolution and the teachings of the late Ayatollah Khomeini (U.S. State Department, 2009). The group seeks to eradicate Western influence in Lebanon and the Middle East and is dedicated to the destruction of the State of Israel, resistance to Israeli occupation of Palestine, and the liberation of the Palestinian people. The U.S. State Department advises that the group is the most sophisticated in providing television shows and distributing content via the Internet. It has strong influence in Lebanon's Shiite community as a result of its connections to Iran. It also receives substantial support from Syria. The Lebanese government as well as many others in the Arab world recognize Hezbollah as a legitimate "resistance group" and political party. Hezbollah plays a key role in the Lebanese government.

The group has been active in Europe, North and South America, and Africa and has been involved in numerous anti-U.S. and anti-Israeli terrorist attacks. Prior to September 11, 2001, it was responsible for more American deaths than any other terrorist group (U.S. State Department, 2009). The Council of Foreign Relations (2009) notes that the group's most significant terrorist activities included the 1983 suicide truck bombing of marines in Lebanon that killed more than 200, the 1992 bombing of the Israeli Embassy in Argentina, and a 2006 raid into Israel during which the group kidnapped two Israeli soldiers. The Israelis responded to the raid by invading southern Lebanon and battling Hezbollah fighters for 34 days. Although the Israelis inflicted substantial casualties on Hezbollah, they could not remove the group from the area.

Osama bin Laden remains on the U.S. most wanted list. *Source:* https://www.fbi.gov/wanted/terrorists/terbinladen.htm

INTERNATIONAL   **Al Qaeda,** "the Base," is a network of Sunni extremist groups that was founded in 1988 by Osama bin Laden. Originally, the group was made up of members who fought in Afghanistan against the Soviet Union. The organization was based primarily in Afghanistan and had developed close working relationships with the Taliban, who provided protection and sanctuary. After the American invasion of Afghanistan, al Qaeda moved its operations into the Taliban region of Pakistan. Al Qaeda acts as an organizer of associated groups that operate in the Middle East, Africa, and Central Asia. The group's primary mission is the overthrow of secular governments in Islamic countries and the eradication of Western influences in Islamic states.

Al Qaeda is the greatest threat to the United States and remains committed to attacking American interests across the globe. It is believed to focus its planning on targets that would produce mass casualties, dramatic destruction, and economic problems (U.S. State Department, 2009). The group is responsible for suicide attacks, bombings, kidnappings, and hijackings. The networks or their associates were responsible for the bombings of United States embassies, the bombing of the USS *Cole*, and the 9/11 attacks on the World Trade Center and the Pentagon. The United States has stepped up its operations in Afghanistan and the Pakistani government has taken a more active role in combating al Qaeda and the Taliban. There also has been an increase in al Qaeda activity in Yemen as a result of instability in the country.

During much of the war in Iraq, the al Qaeda organization in Iraq (AQI) had been active. It was composed of Sunni Arabs who lost control of the country after the American invasion. It primarily attacked Shiites and coalition forces using guerilla tactics such as car bombs, suicide bombings, and roadside explosives. In 2006, Abu Musab al Zarqawi, the group's leader, was killed after American warplanes dropped a 500-pound bomb on the house where he was meeting with other insurgents (Knickmeyer and Finer, 2006). This proved to be a major setback for the group. According to the U.S. State Department (2009), by 2008 much of AQI had been neutralized by coalition and Iraqi forces. Nonetheless, AQI continues to have a presence and continues its attacks and may become more active again in the future.

The central command of al Qaeda has been decimated as a result of coalition ground activities in Iraq and Afghanistan, drone attacks on al Qaeda leadership in Pakistan, and enhanced and multination cooperative intelligence operations across the world. These activities have resulted in a decentralized structure consisting of cells located throughout the world. Today, al Qaeda remains a problem, but it cannot mount actions similar to the 9/11 attacks.

HS Web Link: To learn more about al Qaeda, go to *http://www.cfr.org/publication/9126/alqaeda_aka_alqaida_alqaida.html*

As noted in Figure 6-1, numerous are groups involved in terrorist activities in the Middle East, and only a small sample of these groups is discussed here. The primary groups operating in the Middle East are al Qaeda, Hamas, and Hezbollah. Today, they tend to be the largest and most active. It is important to realize that many of these other groups are cooperating with one another, but others are competing and in some cases engaged in open conflict. There are constant power struggles as groups attempt to become more powerful militarily and politically. They all have one thing in common: their support for the Palestinians and their hatred for Israel. The Israeli-Palestinian problem continues to be a flashpoint resulting in numerous acts of terrorism.

The following section examines some of the terrorist groups that exist on the continent of Africa. A number of these conflicts involve Muslims, but some involve other groups with different agendas.

African Groups

Of particular interest to the United States is the Horn of Africa. This area is composed of Ethiopia, Somalia, Eritrea, and Kenya. A great deal of its instability is the result of Ethiopia and Somalia fighting over the Ogaden region of Ethiopia (Spindlove and Simonsen, 2010). In 1991, the government of Somalia was overthrown by clan warlords. Somalia has not had a functioning government since then. It has deteriorated with constant clan fighting and lawlessness. These conditions in the Horn are ripe for the creation of terrorist organizations.

Al Qaeda has had a number of cells in Kenya. Members of al Qaeda have blended in with the population and are relatively safe from Kenya's weak government. Al Qaeda launched attacks on the U.S. Embassy in Nairobi in 1998. A major problem with Kenya has been that it does not have any counterterrorism laws (U.S. State Department, 2009). This has made it difficult to deal with al Qaeda. Additionally, numerous Muslim groups openly support the al Qaeda. For the most part, operatives have slipped out of Kenya to participate in operations in neighboring countries.

Islamic Courts Union (ICU) controlled most of southern Somalia. It came into power after the government collapsed in 1991. The ICU essentially filled a void as a result of the anarchy and lack of organization in the country. It installed Sharia or Islamic law. The ICU consisted of Islamic clans that had aims similar to the goals of the Taliban in Afghanistan—it essentially forbid anything Western. The populace supported the ICU as it brought order and reduced the amount of lawlessness. In 2006, a transitional government was established in Somalia. With the support of the American CIA,

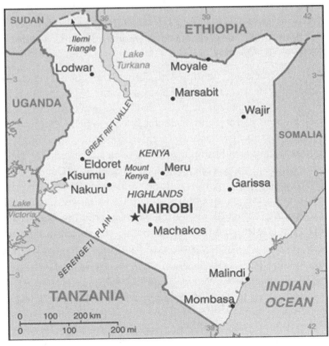

Map of Kenya.   *Source:* Central Intelligence Agency World Factbook. https://www.cia.gov/library/publications/the-world-factbook/geos/ke.html

Map of Somalia. *Source:* Central Intelligence Agency World Factbook. https://www.cia.gov/library/publications/the-world-factbook/geos/so.html

Ethiopian troops invaded Somalia and fighting with Somali Transitional Federal Government troops defeated the ICU. Although defeated and having lost power, the ICU remains a force in the country.

Al-Shabaab ("the youth") is a radical group that broke away from the Islamic Courts Union. The leader of the ICU was a moderate, and al-Shabaab leaders believed in more violent measures. The group has used terrorist tactics such as suicide bombings, shootings, and assassinations against the Somalia government and Ethiopians. It has been suggested that the group has ties with al Qaeda. In 2008, one of the group's leaders pledged allegiance to Osama bin Laden on a video. The group has forced young men to join as fighters, and there has been an influx of foreigners, including Americans, joining the group's ranks. In 2008, several young Somali men disappeared from Minneapolis. According to the FBI, one of the men was later involved in a suicide bombing in Somali (Hanson, 2009a). It is estimated that the group has several thousand fighters.

To counter al-Shabaab and other terrorist groups in the Horn, the United States created the Combined Joint Task Force, Horn of Africa (CJTF-HOA). The CJTF-HOA is a military operation that focuses on terrorists in the region. West (2005) and Feickert (2005) advise that the CJTF-HOA has been extremely successful. The task force has targeted several terrorist organizations and a number of terrorist leaders. The task force has killed a number of these high-value terrorists and essentially destroyed a considerable number of these groups' leaders. Feickert notes that the program has been so successful that it should be a model for fighting terrorists in other regions.

As in the Middle East, there are numerous other groups in Africa. The al Qaeda in the Islamic Maghreb operates in Algeria. This group's objective is to overthrow the government and install an Islamic government. It has attacked government officials and tourists. In 2007, the group detonated a car bomb near government officials killing 28, and in the same year, a suicide bomber attempted to kill the president. The blast killed 22 and injured 107 (ADL, 2010). Another Algerian group, the Armed Islamic Group, is also attempting to overthrow the Algerian government and has conducted numerous attacks in France, which had assisted the Algerian government in clamping down on terrorist organizations.

The Darfur region of Sudan continues to be problematic as government forces and Janjaweed (Arab militias) have committed genocide against African civilians in Darfur with thousands having been killed and displaced. The Muslim-controlled government of Sudan fought Christians who lived primarily in southern Sudan. In 2011, the south voted to separate from Sudan creating a new country. Although race and religion play a role in the tensions between the north and south, a key ingredient in the conflict has been control over the country's oil revenues.

There are numerous conflicts elsewhere in Africa. The Sub-Saharan region for decades has been in the throes of civil wars with terrorist tactics being one of the primary tools. The region is rich in minerals, including diamonds and oil, with fighting centering on control of those resources. Child armies, slavery, and starvation contribute to the problems. There is also tribal and ethnic fighting as different groups vie for political power and control. Many parts of Africa are in constant conflict and turmoil.

Asian Groups

Several terrorists groups operating in Asia are spread across several countries.

PAKISTAN Pakistan is a hotbed of terrorist groups and activities. After the coalition invasion of Afghanistan, Osama bin Laden and his al Qaeda forces moved to northern Pakistan. Now

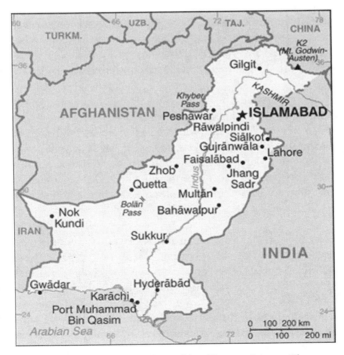

Map of Pakistan. *Source:* Central Intelligence Agency, The World Factbook. https://www.cia.gov/library/publications/the-world-factbook/geos/pk.html

al Qaeda coordinates its worldwide activities from the area. There, numerous tribes that support or are a part of the Taliban reside primarily in the South Waziristan region. Additionally, there are groups conducting terror operations against India as a result of the dispute over Kashmir.

The **Pakistani Taliban** consists of a group of tribes that are predominately Pashtun. In addition to having a large presence in northwest Pakistan, Pashtunis are the largest ethnic group in Afghanistan, constituting approximately 40 percent of the population. The Pashtunis also constitute the largest majority of Taliban. Although the Pakistani and Afghani Taliban are differentiated by command structure, they have close tribal relations and common goals. The goal of the Taliban is to install Sharia law; defeat the government, which it claims is ineffective; and remove Western influence from Pakistan and Afghanistan. It is believed that the Pakistani Taliban have 30,000 to 35,000 fighters, a considerable force to confront the Pakistani Army. Most recently, the group has increased its use of car bombings and suicide bombings. The most prominent was the bombing of the Marriott Hotel in Islamabad where 60 people were killed. The group primarily focuses on government and military targets (U.S. State Department, 2009). The Pakistani government has been taking a more active role in combating the Pakistani Taliban, and the United States has used drone missile attacks on suspected Taliban leaders. These attacks have resulted in the deaths of a number of high-ranking Taliban leaders.

Lashkar-e-Tayyiba or the Righteous Army is a Pakistani group that developed in the 1980s. It operates in the Indian states of Kashmir and Jammu. The main goal of the group is to end India's control of these states. The group has used suicide bombings and attacks against government officials and Indian security forces. The group received international attention in 2008, when it conducted a coordinated multi-target attack in Mumbai, India. The attack targeted a Jewish center, hotels, a cinema, and the port area. In the wake of the attack, 164 people were killed and scores were injured (Sabha, 2008). Only one attacker was captured alive. Pakistan has investigated the incident and made a number of arrests. Lashkar-e-Tayyiba is one of the largest of the traditionally Kashmiri-focused militant groups (U.S. State Department, 2009). The group has links with the Taliban and al Qaeda as well as extremist groups in Chechnya and the Philippines.

Numerous similar groups are operating in Pakistan. For example, **Harakat ul-Mudjahidin** and **Jaish-e-Mohammed** are Pakistani-based Kashmiri Islamic groups that seek Pakistani rule in the Indian territory of Kashmir. The Jaish-e-Mohammed is thought to be responsible for an attack on the Indian Parliament that killed nine and injured 18. In July 2004, Pakistani authorities arrested a Jaish-e-Mohammed member wanted in connection with the 2002 abduction and murder of U.S. journalist Daniel Pearl. In 2006, the Jaish-e-Mohammed claimed responsibility for a number of attacks, including the killing of several Indian police officials in the Indian-administered Kashmir capital of Srinagar (U.S. State Department, 2009).

CENTRAL ASIA Another area of concern are the central Asian countries of Turkmenistan, Uzbekistan, Tajikistan, Kyrgyzstan, and Kazakhstan. These countries once were part of the Soviet Union and are now independent. Many of these newly formed governments are corrupt and weak. They are impoverished countries and serve as transshipment routes for drugs. Their authoritarian governments have resulted in citizen unrest and disaffection. Several Islamic groups have formed in the area, and their close proximity to Iran, Afghanistan, and Pakistan likely will facilitate additional radical groups moving into the area. For example, the **Islamic Movement of Uzbekistan** is a radical organization that seeks to replace the government with one based on Islamic law. It conducted some of the first suicide bombings in central Asia (U.S. State

Map of Central Asia.   *Source:* Central Intelligence Agency, World Factbook. https://www.cia.gov/library/publications/the-world-factbook/geos/uz.html

Department, 2009). Also, in the Xinjiang province in China to the east, the **Uighars** are attempting to create an Islamic state. The **Hizb ul Tahrir** is a Palestinian organization that is growing in the area. The group initially came to the region to preach and convert the region's residents to Islam (White, 2009). Many of its members believe that a Muslim country or region can be formed in the area. The region has the beginnings of a new terrorism front.

PACIFIC RIM AREA   The Pacific Rim countries of the Philippines, Indonesia, and Malaysia have experienced an upswing in terrorism activities. One group, the **Jemaah Islamiyyah**, is intent on establishing an Islamic state incorporating Indonesia, Malaysia, the southern Philippines, Singapore, and Brunei. The group is considered one of the largest transnational groups in Southeast Asia and has links with al Qaeda. The group has staged a number of high-profile attacks, including the 2004 bombing outside the Australian Embassy in Jakarta, the 2003 bombing of the J.W. Marriott Hotel in Jakarta, and the 2002 Bali bombing that killed more than 200 people. The Bali bombing was one of the deadliest terrorist attacks since 9/11. In 2001, Singapore authorities uncovered a plot by the group to attack the U.S. and Israeli Embassies, and British and Australian diplomatic buildings in Singapore. The group has provided operational support and training for Philippine Muslim violent extremists (U.S. State Department, 2009).

The **Abu Sayyaf Group** is an extremist group that operates in the Southern Philippines. The group supports a separate Islamic state in the southern part of the country. A substantial portion of the country's Muslim population resides there, and many have the same aspirations as those of members of al Qaeda. The group has engaged in bombings, kidnappings, and assassinations primarily directed against security forces, businesses, and religious leaders (Public Safety Canada, 2009).

JAPAN   A somewhat unique terrorist group is the **Aum Shinrikyo**. It was established in 1987 as a religious group in Japan. The group is driven by an apocalyptic ideology and is

Map of Philippines and area. *Source:* Central Intelligence Agency, World Factbook. https://www.cia.gov/library/publications/the-world-factbook/geos/rp.html

Map of Japan. *Source:* Central Intelligence Agency, World Factbook. https://www.cia.gov/library/publications/the-world-factbook/geos/ja.html

thought to have a goal of bringing about nuclear Armageddon. The group believes that a nuclear war will bring about the Armageddon and only members of the cult will survive. Members of the group are responsible for the release of sarin gas in a Tokyo subway, causing 12 deaths and the hospitalization of more than 5,000 people in 1995 (Fletcher, 2008). The group had attempted several previous biological and chemical attacks. However, all the attacks have been in Japan.

The majority of terrorist groups operating in the Pacific area are Muslim in nature, and they direct their attacks against Israel, the United States, and Western culture. They are very similar to the groups operating in the Middle East and North Africa.

Analysis Box 6-2

Members of Aum Shinrikyo are the only terrorists to successfully kill a large number of people using a weapon of mass destruction—chemicals. Indeed, there are few examples of other terrorist groups using WMDs, and none have been effective. For the most part, terrorists use conventional weapons. Why do you believe this has occurred? Do you believe that other terrorist groups will attempt to use WMDs such as chemical weapons in the future?

Latin American Groups

Numerous terrorist groups are operating in Latin America. Their motivations are quite different as compared to the groups in Asia, Africa, and the Middle East. First, terrorism south of the United States is driven by politics. A number of countries historically have had inefficient, authoritarian governments. This has resulted in the formation of left-wing and right-wing groups that have used terrorism to advance their agendas. Second, several countries in the region have large oil reserves, and wealth from these operations has not been distributed equitably across the population. In many cases, conflicts have erupted between the rich and the poor. Finally, the transnational narcotics trade has resulted in substantial political corruption, violence, and organized criminal groups amassing substantial wealth. These groups have been destabilizing governments. A number of terrorist groups have become involved in the narcotics trade to finance their activities, and in some cases, to accumulate wealth. It is difficult to distinguish if some of these groups are organized crime groups or terrorist groups.

COLOMBIA   Several groups are operating in Colombia. The **Autodefensas Unidas de Colombia** is a right-wing terrorist group with the mission of protecting the economic interests of the elites and combatting left-wing groups such as FARC and ELN, which are discussed later. The group acts as an organizer and supporter for other paramilitary groups. It receives support from a number of Colombian politicians, drug traffickers, and communities that are provided protection. Although not directly involved in drug trafficking, the group often levies taxes on drug traffickers for protection (Global Security, 2010).

Map of Colombia.   *Source:* Central Intelligence Agency, World Factbook. https://www.cia.gov/library/publications/the-world-factbook/geos/co.html

FARC leaders in parade.   *Source:* AP (00042901501)

Two significant left-wing groups are operating in Colombia. The **Ejército de Liberación Nacional** (ELN) is also known as the National Liberation Army and the Army of National Liberation. Its primary mission was to establish a people's revolutionary government. Because of the exploitation of Colombia's natural oil resources, the group has targeted many of its attacks on the foreign-controlled oil industry. It is also involved in the narcotics trade and has been involved in a number of kidnappings and political assassinations. The **Revolutionary Armed Forces of Colombia** (FARC) is an armed rebel group that operates in Colombia. The group was established in the 1960s and is the largest left-wing group operating in that country. FARC's mission is to overthrow the Colombian government and replace it with a leftist government that would promote the interests of the people of the country and those of Latin America. As a rebel group, the organization has engaged in bombings, hijackings, assassinations, and the kidnapping of Colombian officials. It is extensively involved in the drug trade, working with some of Colombia's drug cartels. Venezuelan President Hugo Chavez has been accused of providing money and material support to the group. Chavez, the leftist president of Venezuela, has been supporting left-wing and anti-American governments in South America and across the globe (Hanson, 2009b). At this point, it is difficult to distinguish these two groups from drug trafficking or criminal organizations even though they are recognized as terrorist organizations. The Colombian government has had a number of successes countering these groups in recent years with financial and military assistance from the United States.

PERU   The **Shining Path** operates in Peru. It was founded in 1980 as a breakaway group from the Communist Party of Peru. The group's main objective is to overthrow the Peruvian government and replace it with a communist government. The group envisions a peasant revolution

Map of Peru.   *Source:* Central Intelligence Agency, World Factbook. https://www.cia.gov/library/publications/the-world-factbook/geos/pe.html

that would free the country from foreign influence and domination. The group has been responsible for bombings, political assassinations, and attacks throughout Peru. The Peruvian government, over the past several years, has successfully killed or captured a number of the group's leaders, substantially weakening it. According to the U.S. State Department (2009), the group carried out a number of attacks on officials in 2008. However, today, it appears that the drug trade has supplanted a number of its political activities.

European Groups

Historically, a number of terrorist groups have operated in Europe, especially during the cold war. Most of these groups were left-wing or socialist and communist. Examples include the Red Brigade in Italy, the Red Army Faction in Germany, and the Communist Combat Cells of

---

Analysis Box 6-3

Several potent terrorist groups are operating in South and Central America. Some are narco-terrorists, whereas others have a political agenda. Moreover, they have a long history of demonstrating that governments have not been able to effectively defeat them. Their operations have remained south of our border. Do you believe that it is possible for their operations to creep northward into the United States? Should we be as concerned with the southern terrorist groups as we are with the Middle Eastern groups?

Belgium. During the cold war, these groups were actively pursuing a socialist agenda through violence, including kidnappings, bombings, and other attacks. Essentially, left-wing terrorism in Western Europe has all but vanished. The departure of European left-wing radical and terrorist groups is attributable to the fall of the Soviet Union. The Soviets provided these groups with substantial support and funding. The fall of the Soviet Union also resulted in interest in socialism as a viable political framework to wain. The creation of the European Union also reduced terrorism by removing government boundaries and creating a more unified view of the world.

A few terrorist organizations are still operating in Western Europe, but the most substantial terrorist-related problem now is Islamic terrorists who are attacking Western ideas and Western countries that have interests in Muslim lands. Muslim terrorists have initiated attacks in Madrid and London. A number of Muslims have left Europe to join jihad movements in countries that are marked with ongoing terrorist fighting. There also is a considerable Muslim population in many Western European countries who might become more involved in terrorist activities in the future. This is a continuing threat.

One of the key terrorist organizations that remains is the **Basque Fatherland and Liberty** (ETA). It is a European group that was founded in 1959. The group operates in the Basque provinces of Spain and France. The group is devoted to establishing an independent Basque state in the six Basque provinces of Spain and France. Since its foundation, ETA has carried out numerous murders and attacks (U.S. State Department, 2009). This conflict is ethnically based as opposed to being politically or religiously based.

TERRORISM IN AMERICA

The previous section primarily addressed Muslim terrorists. These terrorists reside in a number of countries in the Middle East, Africa, and Asia. Islamic-inspired terrorism is a problem for the United States. LaFree, Yang, and Crenshaw (2009) examined international terrorist groups from 1970 to 2004 and identified 53 terrorist groups that were anti-American, of which 31 were radicalized Islamic groups. The remaining 22 groups were communist or socialist inspired or drug trafficking groups that engaged in terrorism. Only al Qaeda has successfully launched an attack on American soil. Nonetheless, in addition to radical Muslim terrorism, there are other forms including right-wing terrorists or militias and eco-terrorists operating in the United States.

The FBI (2002) has developed a classification for domestic terrorism. First is **political extremism**, whereby groups are using terrorism to affect political change. Second, **single-issue** terrorism refers to groups focusing on a particular issue such as animal rights activists or anti-abortion activists who resort to violence and other terrorist activities. Finally, the **lone wolf** is an individual who uses terrorist activities to attack people as a result of an issue or perceived injustice or political ideology.

Radical Muslim-Inspired Terrorism

Al Qaeda perpetrated the most significant terrorist attack on the United States with the 9/11 attacks on New York City and the Pentagon. Since the 9/11 attacks, there have not been any significant attacks by Muslim extremists, but there has been significant terrorist activity. In 2010, Faisal Shahzad left a car bomb in New York City's Times Square. The bomb was amateurish, consisting of gasoline and propane tanks with fireworks as a detonator. It did not explode

A schematic of the attempted car bomb is displayed, showing the positioning of the explosive charges that were placed in the vehicle.   *Source:* Photo by Craig Crawford for the Department of Justice. https://www.justice.gov/css-gallery/#3

(Newman and Moynihan, 2010). It was unclear as to whether he was a lone wolf or working in concert with other terrorists. There was evidence that he had some contact with possible terrorists in Pakistan (Rotella and Linzer, 2010). In a similarly unsuccessful plot, on Christmas day 2009, Umar Farouk Abdulmutallab attempted to blow up a commercial flight from Amsterdam to Detroit with a bomb he had hidden in his underwear. He was unable to ignite the explosive while in the restroom (Reuters, 2010).

HS Web Link: To read more about the Times Square bomber, go to *http://www.time.com/time/nation/article/0,8599,1986469,00.html*

There are numerous examples of Islamic-inspired terrorists being arrested in the United States, including the following:

- In 2010, Najibullah Zazi pleaded guilty to terrorism charges for conspiring to attack New York City with weapons of mass destruction. He had received training from al Qaeda in Pakistan (Winter, 2010).
- In 2009, Daniel Patrick Boyd and six others were arrested in South Carolina and charged with supporting violent jihad (Schrader, 2009).
- In 2009, David Headley, a Pakistani American, was arrested for planning terrorist attacks abroad. He also participated in the reconnaissance of Mumbai prior to the attacks in that city (Richey, 2010).
- In 2009, Colleen LaRose of Philadelphia who became known as GI Jane was arrested for using the Internet to recruit jihadists and help terrorists overseas (Dorell and Johnson, 2010).

- In 2009, Major Nidal Malik Hasan, an Army psychiatrist and devout Muslim at Ft. Hood in Texas, shot and killed 12 people and injured 31 others. Hasan was briefing soldiers bound for Iraq. Hasan was also about to deploy to Iraq (Abcarian, Powers, and Meyer, 2009).
- In 2009, five Muslim Americans from Virginia, Ulmar Farooq, Ramy Zamzam, Waqar Khan, Ahmad Mini, and Amein Yemer, were arrested in Pakistan where they had traveled seeking training as jihadist guerillas (Schulte, 2010).

Jenkins (2010) examined the radicalization of Americans. He found 46 cases of radicalization with 125 individuals between September 11, 2001, and the end of 2009. Some had plotted attacks in the United States; some had provided material support to terrorists or terrorist groups; still others plotted to become involved in jihad in other countries. There are approximately 3 million Muslims residing in the United States, so the number who succumbed to radicalization is rather small. Most of those arrested first became attracted to the jihadist rhetoric through the Internet. The jihadist messages resonated with and helped support their feelings of discontent and religious fervor. Many of the American jihadists had failed marriages or had failed economically or lost their jobs. The Internet allowed them to blame America as opposed to taking responsibility for their problems.

Jenkins advises that it is costly and dangerous to attempt to arrest jihadists after they have committed a terrorist attack; we should intervene before an attack occurs. Currently, our primary strategy is intelligence and law enforcement. He advises that we should expend considerable more effort on prevention by reaching out to the Muslim communities. Recently, an advisory commission headed by William Webster, former CIA and FBI director, recommended to the secretary of homeland security that community policing and other outreach programs likely would have a positive influence on disenfranchised Muslims (Dilanian, 2010). Today, a number of police departments are attempting to develop better relations with these communities by creating advisory boards, citizen-police forums, and so on. Some departments have employed Muslim chaplains. Outreach may result in the identification of community problems that can be resolved before there is radicalization. Such programs may result in Muslim Americans reporting suspicious activities or individuals in their communities.

Right-Wing Terrorists and Militias

In 2010, the police raided the homes of a Michigan militia group, arresting nine members of the group Hutaree, an apocalyptic Christian group. According to federal indictments, they had plotted to attack and kill a police officer and then use an improvised explosive device to attack the funeral caravan and kill other officers (Bunkley and Savage, 2010). Mark Potak (2010) of the Southern Poverty Law Center advises that the number of American hate groups has remained at record levels, approximately 1,000. The variety of right-wing hate groups includes militias, Ku Klux Klan, neo-Nazis, patriot groups, and skinhead groups. There are common threads running through all these groups. First, they often evoke the name of "God." To some extent, they believe that the "white man" is the chosen one and attack, verbally and physically, immigrants, Jews, Catholics, and minorities. Second, they believe that there is a government conspiracy to take our freedoms and guns and install a socialist government in the United States. They essentially want to arm themselves and be prepared for a holy war to be waged against the government and others who they see as threatening their values.

In 2010, the Office of Intelligence and Analysis in the Department of Homeland Security issued a report on right-wing extremism. The report notes that the economic crisis in America could enhance recruitment by right-wing groups; the recession in the 1990s resulted in a resurgence of right-wing extremism. The election of Barak Obama, the first African American president, has resulted in discontent, shoring up right-wing ideology and acceptance of its propaganda. This activity has resulted in an increase in violent attacks on government facilities, banks, police officers, and infrastructure.

HS Web Link: To learn more about right-wing militias, go to *http://www.adl.org/learn/ext_us/militia_m.asp?xpicked=4&item=19*

Although right-wing extremism initially diminished after the Oklahoma City bombing, there has been a significant increase over the past several years. They are anti-American in that they fail to accept the inclusive democratic values that are prevalent today. These groups have a history of attacking public officials and infrastructure targets. This makes these groups a primary concern in homeland security.

Eco-Terrorism and Animal Rights Groups

Today, a few left-wing terrorist groups are operating in the United States. One such group is the **Earth Liberation Front** (ELF). ELF formed in England in 1992 when eco-terrorists from Earth First and animal rights extremists associated with the **Animal Liberation Front** (ALF) joined together. The FBI has declared ELF as a terrorist organization since its members have used arson, bombings, and other violent acts to accomplish their ends (Jarboe, 2002). In 2002, the FBI estimated that damage as a result of the group's attacks had cost $45 million. ELF is one of the most active terrorist groups operating in the United States.

ELF has been most active in the western United States. Its members have attacked universities, professors, government facilities, and private businesses and corporations they see as being destructive to the environment or harming people or animals. Their primary mode of operation is arson or incendiary devices. They have attacked animal research laboratories at the University of California at Davis and Michigan State University. Other significant attacks include

Smoldering ruins of a restaurant in Vail, Colorado. ELF claimed responsibility for the fire.
Source: AP (98102001970)

Analysis Box 6-4

A variety of terrorists reside in the United States. There are different groups with different motives. At this point, which types of groups are the most dangerous?	Should homeland security officials be as concerned with right-wing and left-wing groups as they are with Muslim extremists?

---

a Bureau of Land Management wild horse facility near Burns, Oregon; a U.S. Department of Agriculture animal damage control building near Olympia, Washington; and the destruction of a Vail, Colorado, ski facility. ELF and other such groups normally attack property, not people. However, they are capable of violence (Jarboe, 2002).

STATE SPONSORS OF TERRORISM AND SAFE HAVENS FOR TERRORIST ORGANIZATIONS

Any discussion of the nature and geography of terrorist organizations in the context of homeland security requires consideration of two interrelated concepts—"state sponsors of terrorism" and "safe havens" for terrorist organizations and operations. As with all discussions of terrorism, objective definitions and designations are difficult to achieve. The complexity of designating which groups constitute terrorist organizations and in which geographical areas they operate is confounded because designations are derived, at least in part, from political and ideological considerations rather than being purely objective assessments. Matters are even more complicated when one considers the interrelated nature of state sponsors of terrorism and safe havens as well as the intentions and motivations of various state officials.

HS Web Link: To learn more about state sponsors of terrorism and terrorist safe havens, go to *http://www.state.gov/s/ct/rls/crt/2006/82736.htm*

State Sponsors of Terrorism

In the United States, the secretary of state has the legal authority to designate a nation-state a state sponsor of terrorism. A **state sponsor of terrorism** is any country "determined by the Secretary of State to have repeatedly provided support for acts of international terrorism" (U.S. State Department, 2010). This authority is granted under the provisions of three federal statutes: the Export Administration Act, the Arms Export Control Act, and the Foreign Assistance Act. The designation results in economic sanctions against the state and may include restrictions on foreign assistance, a ban on sales of defense and dual-use (military and civilian) materials, and other financial or trade restrictions. The designation not only affects the state so designated and its people, but also American citizens and businesses can be prosecuted for prohibited trade activities with nations designated as state sponsors of terror. Mark Sullivan (2005: 1) notes that,

> certain trade benefits, most foreign aid, support in the international financial institutions, and other benefits are restricted or denied to countries named as state sponsors of international terrorism. . . . [V]alidated licenses are required for exports of virtually all items to countries on the terrorism list, except items specially allowed by public law, such as informational materials, humanitarian assistance, and food and medicine.

In 2010, the United States had designated four nation-states as sponsors of terrorism: Cuba, Iran, Sudan, and Syria. The list previously included Libya, North Korea, and South Yemen,

Nation	Designation Date
Cuba	March 1, 1982
Iran	January 19, 1984
Sudan	August 12, 1993
Syria	December 29, 1979

FIGURE 6-2   Nation-States Designated as Sponsors of Terrorism by the United States. *Source:* U.S. State Department.

all of which have been removed. The president of the United States can remove a nation from the terrorist list by submitting a report to Congress showing that

> (1) there has been a fundamental change in the leadership and policies of the government of the country concerned; (2) the government is not supporting acts of international terrorism; and (3) the government has provided assurances that it will not support acts of international terrorism in the future [or] justifying the recision and certifying that (1) the government concerned has not provided any support for international terrorism during the preceding six-month period; and (2) the government has provided assurances that it will not support acts of international terrorism in the future. (Sullivan, 2005: 2)

Currently, the United States designates four nation-states as supporters of terrorism. These states are listed in Figure 6-2 along with their date of designation.

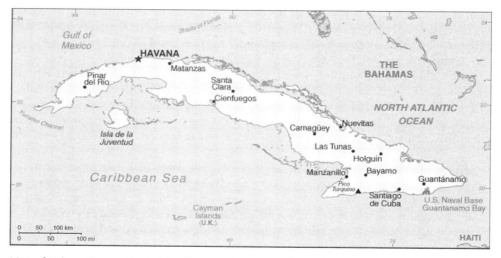

Map of Cuba.   *Source:* Central Intelligence Agency, World Factbook. https://www.cia.gov/library/publications/the-world-factbook/geos/cu.html

CUBA   Cuba is perhaps the best example of the problems associated with designating a nation-state a sponsor of terrorism. Cuba was designated a sponsor of terrorism by the United States in 1982 under the administration of President Ronald Regan because of its activities supporting the exportation of socialism internationally (Sullivan, 2005). Cuba had a history of supporting revolutionary movements and governments in Latin America and Africa, but in 1992 Fidel Castro stressed that his country's support for insurgents abroad was a thing of the past (Sullivan, 2005). Today, most analysts accept that Cuba's policy generally did change, largely because the breakup of the Soviet Union resulted in the loss of billions of dollars in subsidies and support (Sullivan, 2009). Essentially, Cuba without Soviet support does not have the resources to engage in international terrorism or the exportation of socialism.

The Council on Foreign Relations (2010) reports that even though Cuba is no longer exporting revolution to other countries in South and Central America and Africa, it continues to provide a safe haven for terrorists and criminals by refusing to extradite them to other countries. For example, Cuba has provided support for members of the separatist Basque group ETA even though the Spanish government demanded that Cuba stop providing its members sanctuary. The U.S. State Department also claimed that Cuba supported two Colombian rebel groups designated as terrorist groups—the National Liberation Army (ELN) and the Revolutionary Armed Forces of Colombia (FARC).

IRAN   Iran is much different from Cuba. According to official reports by the U.S. State Department (2009), Iran remains the most active state sponsor of terrorism. Most of the

Map of Iran. *Source:* Central Intelligence Agency, World Factbook. https://www.cia.gov/library/publications/the-world-factbook/geos/ir.html

terrorist activities carried out by Iran are attributable to the Qods Force (QF) that is composed of an elite group of men from the Islamic Revolutionary Guard Corps (IRGC). The QF is thought to provide training, funding, and planning for terrorist activities across the Persian Gulf and in Europe. The group has links to Hamas, Hezbollah Palestinian groups, and the Taliban. Iran is thought to support the Lebanese Hezbollah, Iraq-based resistors, and Taliban troops in Afghanistan.

For Palestinian groups, Iran has provided weapons and training to the Palestine Islamic Jihad and the Popular Front for the Liberation of Palestine–General Command (PFLP-GC). The U.S. State Department reports that in 2008, Iran provided more than $200 million in funding to Lebanese Hezbollah and trained more than 3,000 Hezbollah fighters at camps in Iran. Since the end of the 2006 Israeli-Hezbollah conflict, Iran has assisted Hezbollah in rearming.

Iran fueled the Iraqi conflict by providing weapons, training, funding, and guidance to Iraqi militant groups that targeted coalition and Iraqi forces. Iran's Qods Force continued to provide Iraqi militants with Iranian-produced advanced rockets, sniper rifles, automatic weapons, and mortars that have killed Iraqi and coalition forces as well as civilians. Iran has several al Qaeda members in custody but refuses to transfer them to the United States or to Iraqi officials. It appears that Iran is doing everything that it can to thwart any peace efforts in the Middle East.

SUDAN The U.S. State Department considers the Sudan an active partner in global counterterrorism efforts. However, Sudan's efforts are rather tenuous. The Sudanese government has

Map of Sudan. *Source:* Central Intelligence Agency, World Factbook. https://www.cia.gov/library/publications/the-world-factbook/geos/su.html

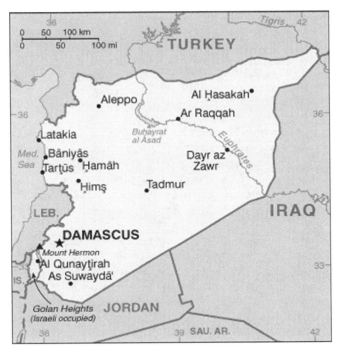

Map of Syria.   *Source:* Central Intelligence Agency, World Factbook. https://www.cia.gov/library/publications/the-world-factbook/geos/sy.html

pledged to work with the United States in oppressing terrorist groups, but these efforts have been lacking. This is perhaps because a number of hard-line Sudanese officials distrust the United States and do not see the benefit of bilateral cooperation. A large part of the problem may be the result of the Darfur problem and the civil war that raged between elements in the northern and southern parts of the country. The U.S. State Department (2009) advises that there are a number of terrorist groups in the Sudan, including al Qaeda, Palestine Islamic Jihad (PIJ), and Hamas. The Sudanese government does not recognize Hamas as a terrorist group; it sees Hamas members as freedom fighters. Other than Hamas, the Sudanese government does not support any terrorist groups. The Sudanese government is ineffective, which makes it safe for terrorist groups to reside in the country.

SYRIA   Syria has played a key role in a number of terrorist activities and organizations in the Middle East. Syria has close relations with Iran even though Syria is predominately Sunni and Iran is a Shiite Islamic state. Historically, Syria has provided support to a number of terrorist groups, including Hezbollah, Palestine Islamic Jihad (PIJ), the Popular Front for the Liberation of Palestine (PLFP), and the Popular Front for the Liberation of Palestine–General Command. Many of these groups' central commands are located and coordinate their activities from Syria. For a number of years, Syria occupied Lebanon and worked closely with Hezbollah during the occupation. Syria provides material support to Hezbollah and other groups by allowing Iran to ship arms and supplies to Hezbollah fighters. Syria is also a conduit through which foreign fighters have entered Iraq to fight coalition forces.

Safe Havens for Terrorism

Although determining which nation-states should objectively be included on a state sponsor of terrorism list is a complex task, the designation of a nation-state or geographical region of the world as a safe haven for terrorism is perhaps an even more daunting one. Nation-states designated as sponsors of terror can be, but are not necessarily, safe havens for terrorism. A nation-state can provide material support for terrorism without providing safe haven for terrorists within their country's territory.

The designation of a nation state or region in the world as a safe haven for terrorism is more complex than merely determining whether or not terrorists are present in some particular location or whether a state is supportive of the group. For example, it is quite likely that there are terrorists in the United States, but it can hardly be said that the United States is a "safe haven" for them. Moreover, it is also likely that groups within the United States either knowingly or unknowingly provide material support, in terms of financial resources, for groups designated as terrorist organizations.

Before we define a "safe haven," it is important to consider some of the difficulties in making this designation. Terrorist activities and operations are not affixed in our traditional understanding of political geography. That is to say, the borders of nation-states do not completely restrict the movement of people, materials, and ideas nor do they contain and isolate social relations and communications. Globalization has complicated this problem. This is the case both in terms of normal social activities as well as terrorist activities. Terrorist organizations carry out their activities in social and communication networks that traverse political geography. Terrorists and other criminals simply do not recognize political or legal jurisdictions nor do they recognize the borders of nations.

It is also difficult to draw a clear line between legal enterprises and state activities and those that funnel material support for terrorist activities. Confounding this observation is that many governments have little control of their international borders or no ability to establish, regulate, or maintain them. Whereas international borders are easily located on maps, they are much more difficult to establish and control in practice, which makes many of the international boundaries we take for granted porous and easy to traverse. In some parts of the world, national borders are almost impossible to physically locate. The existence of failed states, states with weak governments, and nations with little will to control the activities and movements of terrorists makes for geographic space that can harbor terrorists and their organizations. The United States government refers to these spaces as havens for terrorism.

The U.S. Department of State (2008) has defined a **terrorist safe haven** as "ungoverned, under-governed, or ill-governed areas of a country and non-physical areas where terrorists that constitute a threat to U.S. national security interests are able to organize, plan, raise funds, communicate, recruit, train, and operate in relative security because of inadequate governance capacity, political will, or both" (p. 196).

This sweeping definition is important for several reasons. First, it recognizes that both physical and virtual space can be conducive to carrying out activities that support or facilitate terrorism. The Internet as a means of communication provides an excellent example of how physical geography alone is an inadequate way of viewing terrorist activities. Second, it recognizes that a nation-state's ability to govern is directly related to the emergence of a terrorist safe haven. Many states simply do not have the resources to govern and can be inviting to terrorists. Third, there is recognition that the will of a government to eradicate terrorism is a determining factor in denying terrorists a safe haven. Having the "ability to govern" is not the same as having the "will to govern" and carry out counterterrorist activities. Finally, it acknowledges the fluidity of the concept of a safe haven. The ability of a nation-state to govern changes over time as do the aspirations of terrorist groups. This means that safe havens for terrorists also change over time. As nations rise and fall, as the will or ability to govern or eradicate terrorism ebbs and flows, and as the plans of terrorists change, so too do the spaces that can be said to constitute safe havens for terrorists.

Locations of Safe Havens

Reports by U.S. government officials recognize several geographic locations around the world as constituting safe havens for terrorists. These reports are most often constructed by using extremely broad geographical markers such as Africa, East Asia and the Pacific, the Middle East, South Asia, and the Western Hemisphere for beginning points of discussion. Consideration often then turns to discussion of a specific region or country within that geographical area. We will use this basic structure to present an overview of the geography of safe havens for terrorism in the sections that follow.

AFRICA   In Africa, two locations seem to be of the greatest concern to U.S. government officials—the nation of Somalia and the Trans-Sahara region. Somalia is a failed state as it does not have a functional government. The country is run by clans and tribes, resulting in fighting and conflicts. Also, it has a long and porous unprotected border, especially the coastal area. Al Qaeda currently has a small presence in the country, but this could change since there would be no governmental interference. Likewise, the nation's proximity to the Arabian Peninsula and the presence of a rather large extremist domestic population make the country an inviting place for terrorist activities.

The merger of several extremists groups in the African regions of Sahel and Maghreb has led to terrorist attacks and is a cause for concern. Because these are very remote and vast locations with sparse populations and because government in these locations is almost nonexistent, the area has become a training ground and supply point for some Islamic militant groups (U.S. State Department, 2009). This area has a great deal of potential for future problems.

EAST ASIA AND THE PACIFIC   Two areas in East Asia and the Pacific present a concern for U.S. government officials. The Sulu Archipelago and the Sulawesi Seas region and the southern Philippines are thought to be safe havens for terrorism. The Sulu Archipelago is made up of thousands of small islands, which make governance difficult and monitoring an impossibility. There is extensive migration and trade in the area—people and goods move in and out of the region with little regulation or documentation. The Sulu/Sulawesi Seas are thought to represent a safe haven for several extremists groups, including the Jemaah Islamiya and the Philippine Abu Sayyaf Group. Likewise, the southern Philippines areas are thought to be safe havens for terrorists. A lack of state control as well as a government that is hostile to its own Muslim minority population have lead to the emergence of several insurgent groups located in the area (U.S. State Department, 2009).

MIDDLE EAST   In the Middle East, Iraq, Lebanon, Pakistan, and Yemen are all countries of concern. Although most U.S. government officials are reluctant to view Iraq as a safe haven for terrorism because of the ongoing American military operations, they readily acknowledge that terrorist groups such as al Qaeda, Ansar al-Islam, and Ansar al-Sunna operate within the country. Although the capacity of al Qaeda in Iraq has been greatly diminished in terms of members, areas of operation, funding, and local support, many of its members are thought to have moved their operations from Baghdad and Anbar into the northern Iraqi provinces of Ninawa, Diyala, and Salah ad Din. Also, although there are indications that the levels of violence have been reduced around Baghdad and Anbar, it has yet to be determined whether this suppression can be sustained or if terrorists have merely moved their operations to other locations within the country.

Northern Iraq presents a particularly illustrative case of the difficulty of viewing safe havens in terms of traditional political geography. The primary group of concern in northern Iraq is the Kurdistan Worker's Party (PKK). The PKK has a strong presence in northern Iraq and moves back and forth across Iraq's border with Turkey. The PKK and the government of Turkey have had a long-running conflict. The PKK coordinates its activities out of northern Iraq and makes incursions into the Kurdish areas of southeastern Turkey, attacking security forces and Turkish political officials. Likewise, Turkish security forces conduct cross-border military operations against the PKK in northern Iraq. Although the PKK claims to be a political rebel group, it is viewed by Iraq, Turkey, the United States, and the Kurdistan Regional Government as a terrorist group.

Although a number of terrorist and extremist groups operate in Lebanon, the largest and most powerful group in that country is Hezbollah. Hezbollah operates primarily in southern Lebanon where it enjoys popular support among the people because of the social services it provides in the region. Hezbollah builds hospitals and schools and provides support the government fails to provide its people. Hezbollah gained worldwide attention and much local support when it fought Israel in southern Lebanon in 2006. Although Hezbollah is listed by the U.S. government as a terrorist organization, it holds elected seats in the Lebanese parliament, has recognized bases of operations, and is seen as a legitimate political party by the Lebanese government.

Yemen represents a continued and serious security threat and safe haven for terrorists. There are reports that al Qaeda members and other terrorists are fleeing the Pakistani-Afghan border region and the interior of Pakistan as a result of increased military and anti-terrorism activities and moving to Yemen (Bruno, 2009). Yemen has been the focus of terrorist attacks on the United States. In 2000, a navy destroyer, the USS *Cole*, was attacked by terrorists, causing several deaths and considerable damage to the ship (Whittaker, 2003). The attack occurred in Yemeni waters. On Christmas day 2009, Umar Farouk Abdulmutallab attempted to blow up a commercial flight from Amsterdam to Detroit with a bomb he had hidden in his underwear. He had received training in Yemen (Reuters, 2010). Anwar Al-Awlaki, an American-born Muslim cleric residing in Yemen, has declared jihad against the United States and called upon all American Muslims to respect their religion rather than their country (Elibiary, 2010).

Government reports indicated that the country's ability to control and contain terrorists continues to deteriorate. The primary terrorist group operating in Yemen is al Qaeda in Yemen. The group continues to carry out attacks against U.S. targets, tourists, and government officials. Despite attempts to increase security, which include numerous raids on terrorist cells, bolstering its maritime borders, and more coordinated counterterrorism activities between Yemen and Saudi Arabia, the country is still experiencing internal rebellion and terrorism.

SOUTH ASIA The Afghan-Pakistan border might well be viewed not only as a safe haven for terrorism but also as a hub for terrorist activities. Al Qaeda operates within and along the rugged Pakistan-Afghanistan border where it plans and stages attacks against U.S. and European interests. Additionally, a number of attacks on Pakistani targets come from the region. The United States military and Afghan and Pakistani security forces have targeted al Qaeda, reducing its operational and command and control capabilities, but it still maintains operational connections with al Qaeda–linked cells throughout the world (U.S. State Department, 2009). Additionally, numerous other terrorist groups are operating in Pakistan. Some of these groups were formed as a result of the conflict with India over the Kashmir region, whereas others are linked to the Taliban's attempts to install an Islamic state in the region.

Terrorism problems in Pakistan have increased. Over the past couple of years, assaults and bombings targeting the police, military, government officials, and civilians have increased. The Lashkar-e-Tayyiba, a Pakistani-based terrorist group, conducted a devastating attack in Mumbai, India. Elements of the Taliban are located in Pakistan. The Taliban conducts attacks on coalition troops in Afghanistan as well as fighting Pakistani government troops and officials. The Taliban has been linked to a number of bombings and attacks in Pakistan. The root of a substantial amount of this violence is Sunni-Shite tensions and the Taliban's desire to impose Sharia law in Afghanistan and maintain control of large parts of their Pakistani territory.

WESTERN HEMISPHERE   There is a range of terrorism problems in South and Central America. For the most part, the problems are related to narco-terrorism and conflicts between right-wing and left-wing groups. Historically, Colombia and Peru have witnessed substantial terrorism problems. Other countries have had difficulties in the past, but today most of these problems are under control. Mexico presents a special problem. Walsh (2009) reported that in Mexico in 2008 there were 5,367 homicides and approximately 65 people abducted and held for ransom each month. There is widespread corruption throughout all levels of Mexico's criminal justice and government apparatus. Mexico is close to becoming a failed state as a result of narco-terrorism. A weakened government in Mexico reduces our security at the border, which can result in terrorists more easily slipping across our southern border.

The **Tri-Border Region** or Ciudad del Este, Paraguay, is of particular concern to the United States. The Tri-Border Region encompasses parts of Paraguay, Brazil, and Argentina. It is a lawless region where government officials have little or no control. It is an area where terrorists, organized crime groups, and drug traffickers reside and conduct business. A number of Islamic terrorist groups have a presence in the region. Hudson (2003) advises that they include Egypt's Al-Gama'a al-Islamiyya and Al-Jihad, al Qaeda, Hamas, Hezbollah, and al-Muqawamah, which is a pro-Iran wing of the Lebanon-based Hezbollah. According to Boettcher (2002), a number of terrorist groups met in the region to plot attacks on American and Israeli diplomatic facilities. There is a large Arab population in the area, which is conducive to the formation of terrorist cells. Hezbollah evangelicals are preaching in the area in an effort to attract Lebanese residents to their cause.

HS Web Link: To learn more about the Tri-Border Region, go to *http://www. loc.gov/rr/frd/pdf-files/ TerrOrgCrime_TBA.pdf*

Islamic terrorist groups have used the region for fund-raising, drug trafficking, money laundering, plotting, and other activities in support of their organizations. The area is a major center for money laundering, with an estimated $12 billion being laundered each year (Hudson, 2003). In addition to terrorist groups, numerous transnational organized crime groups operate in the area, including syndicates from Chile, China, Colombia, Corsica, Ghana, Libya, Italy, Ivory Coast, Japan, Korea, Lebanon, Nigeria, Russia, and Taiwan. It is probable that the terrorist groups are working with the transnational organized crime groups especially in the areas of narcotics trafficking, arms smuggling, and money laundering—the crime groups can provide the terrorist groups with additional logistic support. The area is closely watched by the intelligence community, especially considering its close proximity to the United States.

Although the designations of state sponsors of terror and safe havens for terrorism are important concepts for the development of a global initiative for homeland security, the concepts are problematic. A lack of sufficient information and available intelligence on many areas hampers efforts for developing an understanding of the role state sponsors of terrorism and safe havens for terrorism can play in establishing a workable homeland security strategy. They nonetheless represent dangerous areas that require constant, focused attention.

Summary

In this chapter we reviewed some of the concepts involved in the geography of terrorism. First, we examined a number of terrorist groups and their bases of operations. Numerous such groups with different agendas are spread across the globe. However, there are concentrations, especially in the Middle East. These predominately consist of Muslim extremists and groups opposed to Israel. Second, we examined state sponsors of terrorism. In the United States, the secretary of state has the legal authority to designate a nation-state a state sponsor of terrorism. This authority is granted under the provisions of three federal statutes: the Export Administration Act, the Arms Export Control Act, and the Foreign Assistance Act. The designation of state sponsor of terrorism is based on evidence that a nation-state has repeatedly supported international acts of terrorism. State sponsors of terrorism are countries that as a matter of policy support different terrorist groups. They see terrorism as a way of furthering their political agendas or derive some other benefit from their support. Finally, we examined safe havens for terrorism. Some of these safe havens are located in countries that are sponsors of terrorism. Others are located in countries that have weak or dysfunctional governments. These governments cannot control their borders and have inadequate police or military forces to deal with the terrorists.

Discussion Questions

1. Terrorist groups are located throughout the world. Which of these groups poses the greatest danger to the United States?
2. There are right-wing and eco-terrorist groups located in the United States. Which type of group poses the greater danger to our country?
3. What is a state sponsor of terrorism, and which states are considered as such? Are there other countries that should be added to this list?
4. The Middle East contains the largest number of terrorist groups. What distinguishes these groups from other terrorist groups in the world?
5. Based on the information provided in this chapter, which terrorist groups should the United States target? Why?

References

Abcarian, R., A. Powers, and J. Meyer. (2009). "Suspect in Ft. Hood shooting faced Iraq deployment." *Los Angeles Times* (November 6). http://articles.latimes.com/2009/nov/06/nation/na-fort-hood-shootings6 (Accessed May 26, 2010).

ADL. (2010). *Al Qaeda in the Islamic Maghreb (AQIM)*. http://www.adl.org/terrorism/symbols/al_qaeda_maghreb.asp (Accessed May 7, 2010).

Australian Government. (2009). *Listing of Terrorist Organisations*. Attorney-General's Department, September 15, 2009.

Boettcher, M. (2002). "South America's 'tri-border' back on terrorism radar." CNN. http://articles.cnn.com/2002-11-07/world/terror.triborder_1_tri-border-israeli-targets-argentine-intelligence-documents?_s=PM:WORLD (Accessed January 10, 2011).

Bruno, G. (2009). "A fraying Yemen's terrorism problem." *Council on Foreign Relations.* http://www.cfr.org/publication/21082 (Accessed May 12, 2010).

Bunkley, N. and C. Savage. (2010). "Militia charged with plotting to murder officers." *Los Angles Times* (March 30). http://www.nytimes.com/2010/03/30/us/30militia.html (Accessed June 2, 2010).

Council on Foreign Relations. (2010). *State Sponsors: Cuba.* http://www.cfr.org/publication/9359/ (Accessed May 10, 2010).

Council on Foreign Relations. (2009). *Hezbollah.* http://www.cfr.org/publication/9155/ (Accessed May 5, 2010).

Dilanian, K. (2010). "Fighting threats from within." *Los Angeles Times.* (May 27, 2010), A1, A14.

Dorell, O. and K. Johnson. (2010). "Jihad Jane shows terrorism-case trend." *USA Today* (March 11). http://www.usatoday.com/news/nation/2010-03-10-jihad-jane_N.htm?csp=obinsite (Accessed May 25, 2010).

Elibiary, M. (2010). "It's a mistake to assassinate Anwar al-Awlaki." *Fox News* (April 16). http://www.foxnews.com/opinion/2010/04/16/mohamed-elibiary-alawlaki-assasinate-muslims-war-terror-nsc/ (Accessed May 12, 2010).

FBI. (2002). *Terrorism 2000/2001.* Washington, D.C.: Author.

Feickert, A. (2005). *U.S. Military Operations in the Global War on Terrorism: Afghanistan, Africa, the Philippines, and Columbia.* Washington, D.C.: Congressional Research Service.

Fletcher, H. (2008). "Aum Shinrikyo (Japan, cultists, Aleph, Aum Supreme Truth)." *Council on Foreign Relations.* http://www.cfr.org/publication/9238/ (Accessed May 10, 2010).

Global Security. (2010). *United Self-Defense Forces/Group of Colombia (AUC—Autodefensas Unidas de Colombia)* http://www.globalsecurity.org/military/world/para/auc.htm (Accessed May 10, 2010).

Gregory, K. (2008). "Ansar al-Islam (Iraq, Islamists/Kurdish Separatists), Ansar al-Sunnah." *Council on Foreign Relations.* http://www.cfr.org/publication/9237/ (Accessed May 5, 2010).

Hanson, S. (2009a). "Al-Shabaab." *Council on Foreign Relations.* http://www.cfr.org/publication/18650/ (Accessed May 6, 2010).

Hanson, S. (2009b). "FARC, ELN: Colombia's left-wing guerrillas." *Council on Foreign Relations.* http://www.cfr.org/publication/9272/ (Accessed May 10, 2010).

Hudson, R. (2003). *Terrorist and Organized Crime Groups in the Tri-Border Area (TBA) of South America.* Washington, D.C.: Federal Research Division, Library of Congress.

Jarboe, T. (2002). "The threat of eco-terrorism." Testimony before the House Resources Committee, Subcommittee on Forests and Forest Health. http://www.fbi.gov/congress/congress02/jarboe021202.htm (Accessed June 2, 2010).

Jenkins, M. (2010). *Would-Be Warriors: Incidents of Jihadist Terrorist Radicalization in the United States since September 11, 2001.* Santa Monica, CA: RAND.

Keats, A. (2002a). "Al-Gama'a al-Islamiyya—Islamic group." CDI. http://www.cdi.org/terrorism/algamaa.cfm (Accessed May 5, 2010).

Keats, A. (2002b). "Asbet al-Ansar (band of partisians)." CDI. http://www.cdi.org/terrorism/asbat.cfm (Accessed May 5, 2010).

Knickmeyer, E. and J. Finer. (2006). "Insurgent leader al Zarqawi killed in Iraq." *Washington Post* (June 8). http://www.washingtonpost.com/wp-dyn/content/article/2006/06/08/AR2006060800114.html (Accessed May 2, 2010).

LaFree, G. and L. Dugan. (2009). "Research on terrorism and countering terrorism." In *Crime and Justice: A Review of Research,* ed. M. Tonry, pp. 413–77. Chicago: University of Chicago Press.

LaFree, G., S. Yang, and M. Crenshaw. (2009). "Trajectories of terrorism: Attack patterns of foreign groups that have targeted the United States." *Criminology & Public Policy,* 8: 445–74.

Martin, G. (2003). *Understanding Terrorism: Challenges, Perspectives, and Issues.* Thousand Oaks, CA: Sage.

Newman, A. and C. Moynihan. (2010). "Faisal Shahzad arraigned on terror charges." *New York Times* (May 18). http://cityroom.blogs.nytimes.com/2010/05/18/faisal-shahzad-to-be-arraigned/ (Accessed May 24, 2010).

Office of Intelligence and Analysis. (2010). *Rightwing Extremism: Current Economic and Political Climate Fueling Resurgence in Radicalization and Recruitment.* Washington, D.C.: Author.

Potack, M. (2010). *Rage on the Right, the Year in Hate and Extremism.* http://www.splcenter.org/get-informed/intelligence-report/browse-all-issues/2010/spring/rage-on-the-right (Accessed June 2, 2010).

Public Safety Canada. (2009). *Public Safety Canada.* http://www.publicsafety.gc.ca/prg/ns/le/cle-eng.aspx (Accessed June 20, 2010).

Reuters. (2010). "U.S. reviewing tape of underwear bomber: Holder." *Reuters* (April 27). http://www.reuters.com/article/idUSTRE63Q5GZ20100427?feedType=RSS&feedName=domesticNews (Accessed May 12, 2010).

Richey, W. (2010). "David Headley pleads guilty in 2008 Mumbai attack." *Christian Science Monitor* (March 18). http://www.csmonitor.com/USA/Justice/2010/0318/David-Headley-pleads-guilty-in-2008-Mumbai-terrorist-attack (Accessed June 1, 2010).

Rotella, S. and D. Linzer. (2010). "Times Square bombing investigation focuses on suspected role of Pakistani army major." *Pro Publica*, http://www.propublica.org/article/times-square-bombing-investigation-focuses-on-pakistani-major (Accessed May 24, 2010).

Rothem, D. (2002). "In the spotlight: Al-Aqsa Martyrs Brigades." CDI. http://www.cdi.org/terrorism/aqsa.cfm (Accessed May 3, 2010).

Sahba, L. (2008). "HM announces measure to increase security." Indian Press Information Bureau. http://pib.nic.in/release/release.asp?relid=45446 (Accessed May 7, 2010).

Schrader, D. (2009). "Neighbors offer different portrait of N.C. terror suspects." *USA Today* (July 27). http://www.usatoday.com/news/nation/2009-07-27-north-carolina_N.htm (Accessed May 24, 2010).

Schulte, B. (2010). "5 Virginia men facing terrorism charges in Pakistan write of noble motivation." *Washington Post* (May 15). http://www.washingtonpost.com/wp-dyn/content/article/2010/05/15/AR2010051503548.html (Accessed June 1, 2010).

Spindlove, J. and C. Simonsen. (2010). *Terrorism Today.* Upper Saddle River, NJ: Prentice Hall.

Sullivan, M. P. (2009). *Latin America: Terrorism Issues.* Washington, D.C.: Congressional Research Service.

Sullivan. M. P. (2005). *Cuba and the State Sponsors of Terrorism List.* Washington, D.C.: Congressional Research Service.

Symeonidou-Kastanidou, E. (2004). "Defining terrorism." *European Journal of Crime, Criminal Law, and Criminal Justice*, 12: 14–35.

Treverton, G. F. (2009). *Film Piracy, Organized Crime, and Terrorism*, Sana Monica, CA: RAND.

U.S. Department of State. (2010). *State Sponsors of Terrorism.* http://www.state.gov/s/ct/c14151.htm (Accessed May 10, 2010).

U.S. Department of State. (2009). *Country Reports on Terrorism, 2008.* Washington, D.C.: Author. http://www.state.gov/s/ct/rls/crt/2008/index.htm (Accessed May 3, 2010).

U.S. Department of State. (2008). *Country Reports on Terrorism.* Washington, D.C.: Author.

Walsh, M. (2009). "Mexico murders soar as drug violence spirals out of control. *The Telegraph*, http://www.telegraph.co.uk/news/worldnews/centralamericaandthecaribbean/mexico/4217538/Mexico-murders-soar-as-drug-violence-spirals-out-of-control.html (Accessed January 11, 2011).

West, D. (2005). *Combating Terrorism in the Horn of Africa.* Boston: Harvard University, Belfer Center for Science and International Relations.

White, J. (2009). *Terrorism and Homeland Security.* Belmont, CA: Cengage.

Whitaker, B. (2003). "Bomb type and tactics point to al-Qaida." *The Guardian* (August 21). http://www.guardian.co.uk/world/2003/aug/21/alqaida.iraq (Accessed May 12, 2010).

Winter, M. (2010). "Afghan from Denver admits NYC terror plot." *On Deadline.* http://content.usatoday.com/communities/ondeadline/post/2010/02/afghan-from-denver-admits-nyc-terror-plot/1?csp=obnetwork (Accessed May 25, 2010).

7

Transnational Organized Crime and Terrorism

LEARNING OBJECTIVS

1. Understand the different kinds or types of crime.
2. Be able to define transnational organized crime.
3. Know the different models of transnational organized crime.
4. Know how the various transnational organized crime groups are structured.
5. Know the different crimes and activities associated with transnational organized crime.

KEY TERMS

Transnational organized crime

Supply-side economics

Illegal goods and services

Hierarchal, organized entities

Street crime

Organized crime

White-collar crime

Globalization of the economy

Increased numbers and heterogeneity of immigrants

Improved communications technology

Weak governments

Political models

Economic models

Market model

Enterprise model

Social models

Cultural model

Ethnic network model

Social network model

Standard hierarchies

Regional hierarchies

Clustered hierarchy

Core group configuration

Criminal networks

Drug trafficking

Narco-states

Human trafficking

Smuggling of technology and
 WMD materials

Arms trafficking

Gray market

Piracy

Non-drug contraband smuggling

Financial fraud

Environmental crimes

INTRODUCTION

This chapter examines **transnational organized crime** (TOC), which loosely defined refers to organized criminal groups that operate multinationally. TOC is examined in terms of criminal activities, focusing on key players or TOC groups, extent of the problem, structure, and operational activities. This chapter also examines the relationship between transnational crime and other forms of crime, particularly terrorism. It is important to examine TOC within the context of homeland security since there are numerous similarities between TOC and terrorism.

When examining terrorism, many people consider it to be an assault on people, society, or government. Government officials and political commentators often use the most negative terms possible to elicit maximum drama. Realistically, however, terrorism generally is the commission of a crime by a group of organized individuals. Their crimes often center on violence, but these violent acts nonetheless are criminal acts. Terrorists are also involved in other types of crime that are instrumental to their terrorist objectives. They are involved in accumulating wealth for the furtherance of their terrorist political objectives. Moreover, TOC and terrorist groups have parallel organizations that are sometimes cooperating or even integrated (Wagley, 2006). TOC groups often are used to strategically facilitate terrorism. As Mueller (1998) notes, terrorism is a form of TOC.

It is difficult to define TOC or organized crime precisely because there are numerous TOC groups or organizations spread across the globe involved in a variety of criminal and sometimes noncriminal activities. For this reason, some researchers argue that there is not a commonly accepted definition for organized crime or TOC (Small and Taylor, 2005). A description of organized crime likely serves to provide a better understanding of the phenomenon than attempting to develop a definition. Kenney and Finckenauer (1995) have identified several characteristics associated with organized crime groups, and these characteristics are applicable to TOC. They are listed in Figure 7-1.

Organized criminal organizations are nonideological in that they do not have a political or religious agenda; they pursue economic gain through criminal enterprises as opposed to political objectives. As Glenny (2005) notes, "International mobsters, unlike terrorists, don't seek to bring down the West; they just want to make a buck" (p. 1). They have organization since they often are engaged in several criminal activities that can cross multiple political jurisdictions. Van Dijk (2008) studied 40 organized crime groups and found that 70 percent were involved in activities in three or more countries and 58 percent were involved in multiple activities. This often requires a well-organized network. They are perpetual in that they are organized and operate to conduct criminal activities (e.g., narcotics trafficking, extortion, money laundering, economic crimes) for long periods of time. They rely on force to gain compliance from competitors, government officials, and, in some cases, client-citizens. They have restricted membership. Here, organized crime groups are similar to legitimate enterprises and terrorist organizations. They select or employ people who are competent or possess

- Are nonideological
- Have an organized hierarchy
- Are perpetual over time
- Use force or the threat of force
- Restrict membership
- Obtain profits through illegal enterprises or means
- Provide illegal goods and services that are desired by the public
- Use corruption to neutralize politicians
- Seek a monopoly or control over specific criminal enterprises
- Have job specialization or differentiation
- Adhere to a code of secrecy
- Utilize extensive planning to achieve long-term goals

FIGURE 7-1   Characteristics of Organized Crime Groups.

necessary skills or who can manage a criminal activity and these employees must be trustworthy. They provide illegal goods and services to the public. Organized crime uses **supply-side economics**, as does a legitimate business or enterprise (see Rengert, 2003). It provides illegal goods and services (drugs, prostitution, gambling, human subjects, etc.) that are desired by the public. Organized crime attempts to neutralize law enforcement and political systems through corruption, bribery, and coercion (see Van Dijk, 2008).

HS Web Link: To learn more about the FBI's organized crime unit, go to *http://www.fbi.gov/hq/cid/orgcrime/ocshome.htm*

Organized crime groups operate more effectively with the tacit or overt approval of political systems, which is why they generally are more prevalent in countries or areas that have weak governments. They often seek to monopolize a criminal enterprise in a geographic area, which may be a local community, region, or country. This monopoly is established through violence or intimidation and, to some extent, by allying with the political system and law enforcement officials. A prime example is Mexico, where many police, justice, and other governmental officials have been co-opted or corrupted by the drug cartels. In a number of cases, when the cartels were unable to co-opt officials, they simply killed them; this often results in a higher level of compliance by other officials. Monopolies result in larger profit margins for the organized crime group. Organized crime organizations have some level of specialization. That is, the soldiers or associates have specific duties, often working in groups and coordinated by managers or leaders. There is a strict code of secrecy. Members who violate this code are often killed or their families are killed. This reduces the possibility of law enforcement penetration into the organization, and it helps prevent competing organized crime groups from attacking the organization or making inroads into the criminal monopoly. Finally, organized crime groups plan extensively. They have long-term goals and are involved in complicated networks when conducting their activities. Planning is essential to perpetual successes.

Rather than defining TOC, Cockayne (2007) identifies two perspectives associated with TOC. First, he notes that TOC can be a set of activities that supply **illegal goods and services** to meet a demand. Simple TOC organizations often focus on a few illegal operations, whereas more complex TOC organizations will be involved in a host of interrelated criminal and legitimate activities. As TOC organizations grow, they tend to become more complex organizationally and involved in more activities to further their illicit economic agenda.

Analysis Box 7-1

We discuss organized crime as an economic enterprise. To some extent, it is similar to any other enterprise whether it be McDonalds, Ford, Wal-Mart, or some other business. What are the similarities between organized crime and these legitimate businesses? What are the differences? Can you analyze a criminal enterprise using economic terms and activities?

Second, TOC groups consist of **hierarchal, organized entities**, as discussed later in this chapter. They essentially are business-like organizations that operate in the shadows and outside government oversight. Like the private sector, they develop relationships with other TOC organizations, legitimate business entities, governments, and sometimes terrorist organizations to facilitate their criminal enterprises. Cockayne questions whether TOC is a set of activities or an entity or organization. He argues that perhaps this is irrelevant. Actions should be taken when criminal enterprises assume an international or transnational posture. When a group or organization achieves international status, it has the potential to negatively affect large numbers of people and even governments. It creates significant harm across multiple geographical boundaries. Finally, the United Nations has defined TOC as "offenses whose inception, prevention and/or direct or indirect effects involved more than on country" (United Nations, 1995, p. 4).

These definitions and descriptions demonstrate that TOC is a series of sophisticated and sometimes complicated crimes involving multiple actors across international boundaries. When an organized crime group stretches across several countries or large areas, it demonstrates the power, influence, and negative effects it may have on individual countries. It goes well beyond street thugs, local gangs, or localized criminal groups. In addition to criminal problems, TOC has a negative impact on government and social institutions as well as the daily lives of those who reside near its places of operation.

DISTINGUISHING TYPES OR CATEGORIES OF CRIME

One way to better understand TOC is to examine it in relation to other kinds of crime. Historically, government officials, policy makers, and crime researchers have attempted to distinguish among street crime, white-collar crime, and organized crime (Edwards and Gill, 2002). Vice crimes generally have been subsumed within the organized crime category since vice was these criminals' primary modus operandi. Some criminologists have developed typologies to better understand and study the types of crime (Clinard, Quinney, and Wildeman, 1994). Such typologies have been seen as useful to understanding criminal conduct since various types of crimes often are committed by different types of criminals with differing motives.

Society, especially American society, traditionally has viewed street crime as being more problematic and intrusive on people's lives relative to other forms of crime. **Street crime** results in visible deaths, injuries, and economic losses that are vividly portrayed in the news and popular media—there are observable victims. White-collar crime and organized crime generally have not had high visibility, and as such, most people have been unconcerned with these categories of crime. **Organized crime** is involved primarily in victimless crimes such as gambling, loan sharking, narcotics trafficking, and prostitution and the provision of desired illegal goods and services to the general public. **White-collar crime,** which includes numerous forms of fraud, for the most part, has been invisible to the public unless the government has made a case against some corporate entity. However, after the Enron scandal in 2001 and the deteriorating economic conditions in the United States in 2008 that resulted in home foreclosures, high unemployment, and the bailout of large financial institutions, the American people became more aware of white-collar crime and its impact on society.

An examination of these three general categories of crime shows that their differences are a matter of degree. For example, organized criminal syndicates often infiltrate legitimate businesses and, using white-collar crime techniques, destroy the business, absconding with its resources and capital or using them as a front for illegitimate enterprises. Organized crime figures and white-collar criminals have on occasion resorted to homicide, embezzlement, and other forms of street crime to further their criminal ends. White-collar criminals sometimes conspire with organized crime operatives, for example, in the illegal disposal of toxic waste and other environmental crimes. White-collar criminals frequently are involved in manipulating the costs of goods and services to increase profit. They circumvent work safety standards and produce substandard products. Some suggest that white-collar crime results in more deaths, injuries, and economic loss than do street crimes (Friedrichs, 1996). There is substantial participative overlap across these three forms of crime, and differentiating them sometimes can be difficult. For the most part, TOC participants generally are involved in all forms of crime, depending on the situation, environment, and criminal enterprise.

As noted earlier, terrorism represents a new category of crime that morally and politically is distinct from other types of crime. It is deemed reprehensible. Actually, it is not new, but it has received substantial public attention as a result of the 9/11 attacks and the subsequent concern with homeland security. As discussed in Chapter 1, it dominates the thinking of Americans and citizens worldwide. Like other forms of crime, terrorism includes street crimes, white-collar crime, and transnational organized crime that terrorists will use to accomplish their goals. Although there is a measure of overlap between "other criminals" and terrorists, there are some fundamental differences between these criminal types. Clarke and Newman (2006) enumerate several differences:

1. The motivations for crime and terrorism are vastly different—the former being committed for self-gratification, the latter for a higher cause.
2. Terrorists are so much more determined than criminals.
3. Terrorism requires much more planning and is much less opportunistic than most crime.
4. Terrorism depends on external funding.
5. Terrorism usually involves much larger-scale acts.
6. Terrorism can only be committed by organized groups, whereas crime is more often a solitary undertaking. (p. 5)

This chapter examines transnational organized crime, because it is a tool used by terrorists to further their objectives. A number of terrorist organizations mirror TOC organizations in terms of structure and some of the activities that are performed. They use criminal activities

---

Analysis Box 7-2

Here we discuss several forms of crime including street, white-collar, organized crime, and terrorism. All forms of crime receive public attention, but some are in the spotlight more than others. Which form of crime do you believe causes society the most harm? Do you believe public policy neglects any of these forms of crime? Which forms should receive the most government attention?

---

to raise capital for their maintenance and attacks. They sometimes use TOC groups to facilitate their various activities. TOC groups have extensive networks that can be used in partnership to facilitate attacks or raise funding. It is sometimes difficult to categorize crime by types and perpetrators since different groups will use all sorts of criminal activities depending on needs and opportunities. Nonetheless, there appear to be a number of connections between TOC and terrorist activities.

IMPACT OF TRANSNATIONAL ORGANIZED CRIME

Traditional street crimes have an impact on individuals, causing physical harm and monetary losses. A high volume of street crime may affect a city as victimization and fear override proper social functioning on the part of citizens. White-collar crime generally affects a particular business or perhaps an industry. TOC, on the other hand, can have an impact on nation-states and large numbers of citizens, especially when criminal activities dominate an area. Felbab-Brown (2008) examined TOC and found that it can result in several critical problems, especially for countries that are underdeveloped or have weak governments. Criminal organizations attempt to corrupt governments. They bribe the government officials, police, customs officials, judges, and financial institutions. Such activities further politically weaken governments, reduce legitimate economic opportunities for citizens, and result in the loss of tax and other revenues for the government.

When bribery does not work, criminal organizations often resort to violence and intimidation. Van Dijk (2008) found that 81 percent of the TOC groups he studied used violence extensively. Many police and military units in Mexico have been compromised or intimidated by the Mexican drug cartels. In some cases, officials have become directly involved with the drug cartels, participating in drug and other illegal activities as a result of intimidation or corruption; in other cases, they do not enforce laws or attempt to counter these unlawful activities. In some areas, there is almost a total absence of a justice system. This has led to anarchy and lawlessness. Felbab-Brown (2008) notes that in the 2007 Guatemala elections, TOC members murdered 50 political candidates and their supporters. They undertook a concerted effort to take control of Guatemala's political institutions. The same conditions now exist in Mexico. Essentially, TOC groups penetrated the governments with the intention of controlling certain governmental activities to promote their illicit activities. The situation is not limited to Guatemala and Mexico; there are numerous countries across the world where this is occurring with different degrees of success.

TOC intrusions into legitimate government and business activities become a slippery slope as state actors co-opt criminals and actively solicit direct involvement in criminal activities.

As such intrusions become successful, they result in officials reciprocating and seeking to establish informal and sometimes formal relations with TOC to share the wealth so to speak. Guatemalan military officials, for example, used profits derived from TOC relations to support their budgets and provide income for senior military officials (Felbab-Brown, 2008). In some cases, TOC soldiers organize into government-approved militias. These militias then protect corrupt officials, stamp out political opposition, and closely guard their illicit criminal operations. The TOC network becomes enmeshed in the political and social fabric of the country (U.S. Government Working Group, 2000). In some cases, the military and police are used to attack other competing cartels, further solidifying TOC's hold on the country.

HS Web Link: To learn more about how TOC is a threat, go to *http://www.unodc.org/unodc/en/organized-crime/index.html*

Third, TOC undermines and threatens the state not only in terms of justice and social order but also in terms of economic viability. Large-scale criminal activities in a state or area can have a number of negative microeconomic effects. Van Dijk (2008) discovered that 75 percent of the TOC groups he studied had penetrated the legitimate economy. Felbab-Brown (2008) notes that such activities can contribute to inflation, real estate speculation, currency instability, and the displacement of legal production. When large-scale TOC activities are present, the government frequently is less likely to invest in economic development and there generally is less foreign investment. For example, revived opium poppy production in Afghanistan has resulted in the reduction of foodstuff production. This negatively affects Afghanistan's economy and has led to severe food shortages in parts of the country. The government has had little success in moving the populace to food production and away from poppy production.

Finally, TOC and illicit criminal economies threaten the security of the state. These activities result in large-scale criminal groups and aligned militias that threaten the government. In the 1980s, the Shining Path in Peru and the FARC in Colombia controlled large swaths of those countries and essentially attempted to overthrow the legitimate governments. It took decades and substantial American assistance to bring these groups under control. They were extensively involved in drug cultivation and smuggling and a host of other crimes including kidnapping. Today, a number of legitimate governments are threatened by TOC groups.

Italian police arrest a suspected mobster.   *Source:* AP (08121603695)

CONDITIONS FACILITATING TRANSNATIONAL ORGANIZED CRIME

Although TOC has existed for decades, it has become more problematic recently, especially in light of the threat of terrorist attacks. TOC is ever-present, existing throughout the world. As Shelley (1999) notes, "There is no region of the world without criminal organizations operating on its territory. Even the most remote islands of the world now host transnational organized crime because many of these places provide the safe havens and offshore banking systems that allow organized crime to thrive" (p. 2). Today, there more TOC organizations, and they are much larger than in the past, span greater geographical areas often operating in several different countries, and are involved in larger amounts of crime both in terms of the number of criminal activities and the magnitude of their criminal activities (Van Dijk, 2008). These changes have resulted in new challenges for law enforcement. Moreover, as a result of its size and criminal enterprises, TOC poses a real threat to sovereign governments across the globe. As complex international organizations, they have become more difficult to counter, requiring international law enforcement cooperation and coordination.

Finckenauer (2000) and Reuter and Petrie (1999) have identified three factors that have contributed to this phenomenal growth: globalization, increased numbers and heterogeneity of immigrants, and improved communications technology. First, **globalization of the economy** has provided TOC new avenues by which to commit its criminal conspiracies. As the U.S. Government Interagency Working Group on International Crime Threat Assessment (2000) notes,

> The dynamics of globalization, however, particularly the reduction of barriers to movement of people, goods, and financial transactions across borders, have enabled international organized crime groups to expand both their global reach and criminal business interests. International organized crime groups are able to operate increasingly outside the traditional parameters, take quick advantage of new opportunities, and move more readily into new geographic areas. The major international organized crime groups have become more global in their operations, while many smaller and more local crime groups have expanded beyond their country's borders to become regional crime threats. (p. 4)

As the Working Group notes, the removal of borders resulting in the free flow of people, commodities, and information eliminated a number of barriers to TOC. Now, TOC groups can operate across a number of borders with impunity. It has also resulted in TOC groups aligning with other TOC groups to launder money; smuggle drugs, other contraband, and people; engage in criminal conspiracies; and become involved in financial fraud and other schemes. The removal of border restrictions has reduced TOC groups' risks and costs when conducting these criminal activities and enabled them to become engaged in larger numbers of criminal enterprises.

There is little official examination of TOC activities unless their criminal actions are discovered by law enforcement. When law enforcement does discover TOC involvement, it often is difficult for officials to take effective actions, especially when the TOC group is housed in another country that does not cooperate with international law enforcement or has been corrupted. Complicating this problem is that countries have different laws and criminal procedures, sometimes making it difficult for a country to take action against TOC groups in other countries. TOC groups oftentimes use borders to hide from or evade law enforcement officials.

Increased numbers and heterogeneity of immigrants refers to the fact that today there are larger numbers of cohesive immigrant populations in a number of countries. Globalization has resulted in the removal of borders, allowing groups to migrate unabated, and this migration often results in the importation of criminal activities that are culturally based. This has resulted in ethnic and religious enclaves in cities and countries. For example, Long Beach, California, has approximately 40,000 Cambodians, the largest concentration outside that country. Cities across America and the world have similar ethnic concentrations.

This migration and concentrations often result in the importation of a new class of criminals and victims. Crime that was common in their old countries becomes an accepted practice in the new country. The criminals often maintain contacts and relations with criminals in their old country, and these relationships often result in transnational criminal operations. There are numerous examples, including Russian and Eastern European organized crime groups, Asian triads (underground societies) operating out of Taiwan and China, and the Japanese Yakuja. Finckenauer and Waring (1998) observed that there are 200 large Russian organized crime groups operating in 58 countries. Crime at this point becomes entrepreneurial and multinational.

Improved communications technology has played a key role in the growth of TOC. Internationally dispersed TOC groups can now communicate more easily, facilitating the development and operation of criminal conspiracies and enhancing command and control across borders. Borders no longer serve to restrict activities. The era of enhanced communications also facilitates crime by reducing technical restrictions on the transfer of monies and the shipment of goods from one country to another. For example, cocaine shipments can be coordinated more effectively, and payments can be more easily transferred among individuals and across countries. It allows TOC to react to changing conditions more rapidly and become more efficient.

Finally, it should be noted that **weak governments** play a key role in the formation of TOC organizations; these governments do not have the wherewithal or the tools to combat large and sophisticated TOC groups. Weak governments not only are unable to muster the resources to tackle TOC groups but they are also susceptible to corruption that results in its facilitation. A prime example is Somali. There essentially is no functioning central government in that country. It is ruled by warlords who function by engaging in a wide range of criminal activities. Somali's coast has one of the largest concentrations of pirates in the world. As another example, Paraguay perhaps has the weakest government in South America, and the Ciudad del Este area, or the tri-border area, is lawless with dozens of criminal organizations from across the world operating there. Strong autocratic governments also are sometimes home to TOC organizations. These governments often are rife with corruption, resulting in cooperative relationships between TOC groups and governmental officials. The United States and Western Europe have strong, democratic governments, making them less susceptible to TOC, although organized criminal groups certainly exist in these countries. However, as the relative strength and ability of a government declines or diminishes, generally more TOC groups are in residence, and they grow and become more powerful.

Analysis Box 7-3

Over the past decade, gangs have become a major problem in cities in the United States and other countries. In many cases, these gangs form along ethnic and racial lines. Given your knowledge about gangs from the news media and other sources, can you identify some ethnically based gangs? Can you identify gangs that are not ethnically based? Where do the gangs you have identified reside and commit their crimes?

NETWORKING: THE ETIOLOGY OF TRANSNATIONAL ORGANIZED CRIME GROUPS

Criminal organizations, like everything else, have a beginning. There are conditions that facilitate the creation of TOC groups. Not all TOC groups have the same initiation. They form in a myriad of social milieus as a result of different social, political, and economic conditions. Some form as a result of familial ties, whereas others are constituted as a result of tribal connections and alliances. Business relationships often lead to criminal cabals; such relationships may result in opportunities for participants to acquire larger amounts of money faster. It is informative to examine the environmental conditions that result in the creation of TOC groups. An understanding of the conditions may lead to preventive or enforcement efforts when dealing with them.

Williams and Godson (2002) advise that the etiology of TOC groups can be explained using three models: (1) political models, (2) economic models, and (3) social models. The models identified by Williams and Godson do not necessarily represent distinct paths to the creation of TOC. Indeed, some TOC groups may originate as a result of factors that can be found in one or more models; however, Williams and Godson's models provide an understanding of TOC's origin in various locales.

Political Models

Political models refer to TOC groups forming as a result of weak nation-states. Weak nation-states generally are characterized by ethnic conflict or terrorist activity. This conflict often is due to different groups vying for power or control over the government and criminal and legitimate enterprises. These states have ineffective central governments that cannot cope with the conflict or terrorism. These states frequently are unable to meet consumer demand even for basic staples, creating a market for TOC groups. The state becomes a petri dish in which organized crime groups grow and spread like a bacterial culture. As Williams and Godson note, "States that are weak provide a congenial home base for criminal organizations" (p. 321). Democratic states have high acceptance levels of government control and the rule of law and tend to be more resistant to organized crime activities. They have the social and law enforcement institutions that are better able to deal with the criminal threat.

Economic Models

Economic models explain TOC groups' creation as a result of becoming involved in various enterprises. Two economic models help explain the emergence of TOC groups (Williams and Godson, 2002). First is the **market model,** whereby TOC groups focus on criminal or illegal markets. Arlacchi (1987) describes an illegal market as

> a place or situation in which there is a constant exchange of goods and services, whose production, marketing, and consumption are legally forbidden or severely restricted by the majority of states. Moreover, the activities of that illegal market are socially and institutionally condemned as an inherent threat to human dignity and the public good. Typical markets of this kind . . . include hard drugs, illicit arms sales, trade in economic or sexual slavery, capital originating from criminal activity, and deals involving secret information and intelligence. (p. 49)

When there is a demand for illegal goods and services, and if the demand is sufficient, illicit enterprises will evolve to fulfill the demand. The rapidity and extent of this evolution is often dependent upon the capacity of the nation-state to control such activities as well as the levels of demand. Initially, small groups emerge to fill the demand. When these groups are left alone, they continue to evolve. They form alliances with other groups, attempt to acquire more territory, co-opt governmental intervention via corruption, and often grow into larger criminal enterprises.

The second economic model facilitating the growth of TOC organizations is the **enterprise model**. Here, criminal organizations are no different from legitimate businesses in that they focus on business principles to conduct their criminal activities. Williams and Godson (2002) summarize this perspective as follows:

> They typically scan their environment for opportunities, seek to make rational judg-
> ments about opportunities and dangers, and seek to maximize their profits where this
> does not involve unacceptably high levels of risk. Not all criminal organizations engage
> in a formal planning process; nevertheless their thinking, intuitively or deliberately, will
> reflect standard business needs and take into account such factors as new products
> opportunities, product dominance, profit margin, market needs and opportunities,
> degree of competition, risk management, retirement strategy, and the like. (p. 325)

According to the enterprise model, a crime group will attempt to diversify its criminal activities and territory once it has reached a tipping point in terms of size and organization. This behavior is similar to that of any licit enterprise.

Social Models

Social models postulate that the growth of TOC groups is predicated on environmental factors. Williams and Godson (2002) have identified three social models that can be used to explain the emergence of TOC groups: (1) the cultural model, (2) the ethnic network model, and (3) the social network model. The **cultural model** refers to culturally based TOC groups. Some cultures are closed in that they have little regard for government; have strong communal, religious, and family ties; and generally are suspicious of outsiders, choosing to have little contact with them. The culture often exerts more control over its populace than the formal government or the rule of law. Loyalty to the culture is more important than loyalty to the country or state. The isolation, combative relationship with the larger society, and cultural dominance allow criminal-based norms to impregnate the culture over time. Examples of cultural-based TOC groups include the Sicilian Mafia and the Chinese Triads.

The **ethnic network model** is similar to the cultural model except that it refers to members of a tribe, culture, or ethnic group that is multinational. Members of the Sicilian Mafia and Chinese Triads migrated to the United States and other countries. Nigerian immigration to South Africa, the United States, Russia, Italy, and Brazil resulted in Nigerian criminal organizations in those countries. Once relocated, they maintain contact with the criminal groups in their previous homelands. In many cases, ethnic loyalties form the basis for recruiting new members into the criminal cabal. This facilitates the growth of criminal activities and enterprises in the countries where members of the network are located and spawns a large multinational TOC network.

The third social model explaining the emergence of TOC groups is the **social network model.** A number of organized crime scholars characterize organized crime organizations as being social networks regardless of culture or ethnicity (Potter, 1993). They observe that organized crime is fragmented, does not have sophisticated organizations, but is based on opportunity and patron–client relationships (Albini, 1971). Here, criminal organizations emerge as members develop contacts with other criminals and clients through social networking. Criminals who are proficient in their trade are able to avoid arrest and increase the number of participants within their social network and increase the amount of criminal activity that occurs across the network. Associations may be family based, clients, other criminals, members of ethnic groups, and so on. Membership within the network is the result of new members being able to contribute to the criminal enterprises. They are not geographically limited and often extend across borders. Involvement is based on convenience, facilitation, and acquaintanceship.

Williams and Godson (2002) have identified the various environments that can contribute to the creation of TOC groups. They also note that hybrid or composite models develop. These hybrid models have their etiology in some combination of business, economic, and social forces—numerous environmental factors contribute to their creation. Some of these organizations become global in nature, and they develop and are sustained through these various sources. Globalization has significantly contributed to this phenomenon by facilitating the migration of people, communications, movement of money, and the ability to take advantage of opportunities in other countries. As these groups become larger, they can search for opportunities and environmental conditions that facilitate their criminal activities. Moreover, if the political climate is too restrictive in one location, these multinational criminal organizations can more easily move or concentrate operations elsewhere.

Finally, it should be noted that the conditions that give rise to organized crime also can be used to explain the formation of a number of terrorist organizations. Terrorist organizations often are centered on religion or a political cause, but political, economic, and social conditions often contribute to their initial formation and growth.

HOW TRANSNATIONAL CRIME IS ORGANIZED

The commission of crime, especially by large-scale criminal operations, is not a simple matter. Large-scale operations are analogous to similarly sized business operations. As noted earlier, large-scale criminal enterprises are complex organizations and have some level of hierarchy and specialization. For example, Rush (1999) examined the Cali drug cartel in Colombia and found specialized positions such as financial advisors, cell or regional managers, bookkeepers, stash house sitters or guardians, cocaine handlers, money handlers, motor pool personnel, and others. Thus, TOC groups must organize and attract people with various skills or expertise; businesses face a similar task. Like legitimate businesses, they must develop working relationships with outside groups. These groups may be other TOC groups, legitimate businesses or individuals, and in some cases terrorist organizations. Cocaine cartels must work with growers, transportation personnel, and wholesale or retail sellers. Some terrorist groups raise money by selling drugs, thus intersecting with TOC groups. Arms dealers must work with arms manufacturers, transportation, and governments and other consumers. There are many similarities between business and TOC groups. Moreover, as the TOC organization expands its operations, its organizational structure becomes more complex.

Wagley (2006) differentiates traditional organized crime from what he terms "more modern networks." Traditional organized crime was hierarchical, used a family structure, and operated for an extended period, whereas the newer organizations are more decentralized, often using a cell structure. Shelly (1999) and Williams (1998) advise that criminal organizations of the new millennium can be characterized as flexible and somewhat fluid in structure. First, they must be able to pursue ever-changing environmental conditions and economic opportunities. The primary objective of TOC is financial gain; flexibility allows organizations to rapidly change and pursue new opportunities. Second, law enforcement awareness of the dangers posed by TOC has increased law enforcement scrutiny and enforcement actions. TOC groups must be flexible enough to avoid police interventions. Third, there is the constant threat of competition. These competitors often exert pressure through violent action and political associations to attack competitors. TOC groups must be able to adapt and change rapidly as a result of these threats.

In 2000, the United Nations Centre for International Crime Prevention examined 40 organized crime groups in 16 countries in terms of organization. The study found the following characteristics:

1. Two-thirds of the groups were organized around a hierarchy, while the remaining one-third were loosely organized.
2. Most of the groups studied were medium-sized with 20 to 50 members.
3. Most of the groups studied relied on violence to further their objectives.
4. Only about one-third of the groups were ethnically based and about one-half of the groups did not have any ethnic or social identity.
5. Many of the groups were involved in only one primary crime activity. Other research, however, shows that many are involved in multiple criminal enterprises (Van Dijk, 2008).
6. Most of the groups were involved in transnational criminal activities.
7. The majority of the groups used corruption to further their economic objectives. Here, Van Dijk found that 75 percent of the TOC groups he studied were involved in corruptive activities.
8. About one-third of the groups had developed political influence within the area or region.

The UN study demonstrates variability in TOC organization. It also shows that these organizations are involved in a variety of activities, and it is difficult to classify or make generalizations about the structure and functioning of TOC groups. Nevertheless, the UN developed a typology of TOC organizations or networks. The UN study identified five unique organizational structures used by TOC. An examination of these structures is informative since the organization of terrorist groups likely is similar.

HS Web Link: To learn more about the structure of Russian organized crime, go to *http://www.fas.org/irp/world/para/docs/rusorg3.htm*

Standard Hierarchy

Standard hierarchies mirror those found in many legitimate organizations and are generally found in the more sophisticated or developed TOC organizations. They generally have a single leader with subordinate managers who have clear operational responsibilities and control. There is some level of specialization whereby members are delegated different responsibilities and tasks. Leaders and managers maintain strict discipline and generally membership is ethnically homogeneous. In terms of size, the membership generally ranges from about 10 to several hundred members, but there are a number of drug trafficking organizations using the standard hierarchy that are much larger.

A number of TOC organizations are organized using the standard hierarchical format. Organized crime groups from China use this format. These groups center on a single individual and members are absolutely loyal. Most of the members are recruited from the criminal class. They enforce obedience by using violence and are involved in a variety of crimes and often invest in legitimate businesses. Many of the TOC groups from Eastern Europe and Russia also use this form of organization. The Russian and Eastern European TOC groups are involved in a blend of legitimate business and crime. They often are involved in banking, investments, and a number of criminal activities. Their criminogenic methods allow them to obtain capital and intimidate legitimate businesses when transacting with them. A number of Mexican and Colombian drug cartels are also structured in this fashion.

Regional Hierarchy

The second type of structure identified by the UN study was **regional hierarchies**. They are similar in structure to standard hierarchies except they have branches or structured groups in multiple locations. There is a centralized authority, and this authority exerts some level of control over the branches. Nonetheless, the branch leaders have a degree of autonomy in terms of controlling the branch and making decisions in terms of criminal and legitimate enterprises. A prime example of the regional hierarchy organization is outlaw motorcycle gangs. For example, the Hell's Angels are organized by chapters, but the chapter leaders maintain contact and coordination with the main chapter, and they have exported their format to a number of countries around the world. The UN study notes that the Italian mafia is organized similarly. These groups have a number of families. Within each family are middle-level managers who are responsible for controlling an area, but each manager reports to the head of the family. A number of Japanese-based organized crime groups, including Fuk Ching, Yamaguchi-Gumi, and the Yakuza, operate similarly. A number of prison gangs in the United States operate using this structure.

Clustered Hierarchy

The third type of organization identified in the UN study was the clustered hierarchy. The **clustered hierarchy** is similar to the regional hierarchy except that in the clustered hierarchy the various criminal groups have a larger measure of independence. Each group may have a different structure, but they all operate within an umbrella that is coordinated to some degree by a central authority. Each cluster or group has a high degree of autonomy. The overall organization may form to divide markets or areas to reduce conflict, or the arrangements may be forged in order to facilitate criminal activities. Clustered hierarchies are engaged in a wide range of criminal activities since the clusters are composed of groups spread over a large geographical area. Many American organized crime groups fit this model. Each family has its territory and is independent, but each one often coordinates some of its activities with other families. A number of American youth gangs also fit this category. Also, given that al Qaeda has been attacked on a number of fronts, it appears that today it utilizes this format.

Core Group

The fourth type of TOC structure identified by the UN is the **core group configuration.** Here, a small core group of individuals control the activities. The core membership is involved in all the organization's enterprise from management to conducting the criminal activities. The core is surrounded by a number of associates who may be called upon as needed. These groups are relatively small with about 20 members. Like other types of groups, they depend on violence and corruption to guard their activities. A number of these groups are working throughout the world. Some exist in Europe and North America. There are two such groups in the Netherlands that specialize in human trafficking. They often focus on a limited number of criminal activities.

Criminal Network

The final type of criminal organization identified in the UN study was the criminal network. **Criminal networks** consist of a group of individuals who are loosely connected as a result of a criminal activity. The criminal activity and personal loyalty tie the individuals together. The associations facilitate the criminal activity. They typically are involved in financial crimes such as forgery or large-scale fraud. Individuals or small groups within the network are chosen because of their abilities, connections, or expertise. Some of the members may be involved in money laundering, forging documents, and disposing of the financial instruments. The associations are constantly changing since new or different expertise may be needed as the crimes and scams morph into new areas.

This section has discussed five types of networks that are used by TOC groups. Since the 9/11 attacks, law enforcement organizations worldwide have been focusing on terrorist and TOC groups. TOC groups have been targeted because of the scope of their criminal activities and because terrorist groups often participate in TOC activities or work closely with TOC groups, especially at the cell level. This intensified enforcement in some cases has resulted in the destruction of standard and regionalized TOC organizations, forcing them to become decentralized. Moreover, the age of Internet communications and globalization has made decentralized operations more efficient.

When TOC and terrorist organizations become more decentralized, the leaders have less control over the geographically dispersed operations and cells, and the cells begin to act more independently. Dishman (2009) advises that as decentralization occurs and control is lost, criminal and terrorist organizations develop cooperative and symbiotic relationships, and the distinction between these two types of organizations becomes blurred. Stanislawski and Hermann (2004) go so far as to note, "In many respects, transnational organized crime has become the lifeblood for terrorist groups and networks" (p. 1). Even though terrorist groups have political motives and TOC groups have financial motives, cooperative relationships facilitate both groups achieving their objectives.

Decentralization of terrorist organizations often results in the broader organization not having the resources to fund each cell or core group at adequate levels, which results in greater decentralization, as the individual cells independently pursue economic opportunities. Additionally, even though terrorists are often religiously or politically motivated, they also have a desire to be financially successful or independent. In some cases, greed dominates or circumvents philosophy. This sometimes results in terrorists replacing or substituting their terrorist desires with criminal activities. Crime and the accumulation of wealth become more important than "the cause." We see terrorists involved in TOC for personal gain and to fund their terrorist activities. For example, Hezbollah has been involved in cocaine trafficking and al Qaeda has been involved in opium and heroin trafficking. It becomes difficult to differentiate terrorist organizations from TOC organizations.

Analysis Box 7-4

As discussed earlier, terrorist organizations are structured in a similar fashion as TOC groups. The most deadly and problematic terrorist group threatening the United States is al Qaeda. Given what you have learned in your classes and the news media about al Qaeda, which of the organizational formats best describes al Qaeda's organization? Why?

TRANSNATIONAL ORGANIZED CRIME ACTIVITIES

There are numerous TOC groups across the world. Indeed, it is likely that they exist in every country; some countries have larger numbers of such groups as compared to other countries. A number of studies have identified a wide range of criminal activities in which TOC groups are involved (United States Interagency Working Group, 2000; Wagley, 2006). Rabasa et al. (2006) and Sanderson (2004) examined the criminal activities of terrorist organizations, and they found that the two groups' activities were very similar and overlapped. The following provides an overview of the crimes committed by TOC groups.

Drug Trafficking

Drug trafficking is the largest and most extensive illegal activity for TOC groups. It is carried out worldwide and affects every country. TOC groups are involved in drug trafficking at several levels: (1) production, (2) smuggling and transportation, and (3) wholesale and retail operations. Some TOC groups are involved at all three levels; others are involved in only one or two levels of activities.

In terms of production, these activities take place worldwide and include a variety of drugs. For the most part, we are concerned with the production of cocaine, heroin, marijuana, and prescription or synthetic drugs. Cocaine is produced in South America, primarily in Peru, Bolivia, and Colombia (Lyman and Potter, 1998). Coca plants are harvested and the raw coca is refined into cocaine primarily in Colombia by the Colombian drug cartels. Opium production occurs primarily in Asia in the Golden Triangle (Laos, Myanmar, and Thailand) and the Golden Crescent (Afghanistan, Iran, and Pakistan). These countries supply most of the world's illicit

Drug-related cash confiscated by the DEA. *Source:* http://www.justice.gov/dea/photos/operations/xcellerator/xcellerator22.jpg

opium and heroin, although Colombian and Mexican drug cartels are now growing opium to supplement their cocaine operations.

Indeed, Afghanistan is the largest supplier of opium with a large portion of production being carried out or supervised by the Taliban and al Qaeda terrorist groups. In 2009, American intelligence agencies estimated that the Taliban received $40 million per year as a result of the heroin trade (Miller, 2009). In 1998, Afghanistan produced 62 percent of the world's opium, and by 2007, its portion of the world's supply was 93 percent. The Afghanistan and world opium production figures are presented in Figure 7-2.

Although a substantial amount of marijuana is grown in the United States, substantial quantities are also produced in South America and Mexico. Large amounts of marijuana also are grown in Morocco, Lebanon, Afghanistan, Thailand, and Cambodia and are transported to Europe and Asia. There is also a large underground market for prescription and synthetic drugs. The drug MDMA or ecstasy is manufactured in Europe, particularly in the Netherlands, and much of the methamphetamine coming into the United States is manufactured in South America and Mexico. These operations are controlled by a number of TOC groups.

TOC smuggling and transshipment operations are extensive. The Colombian drug cartels transship drugs to other countries where they are sold at the retail and wholesale levels by TOC groups. Much of the cocaine coming into the United States is smuggled in by Mexican drug cartels. Other TOC groups wholesale cocaine in other parts of the world. The Italian mafia based in southern Italy distributes a large amount of the drug to parts of Europe, and numerous other TOC groups based in Europe, Asia, and Africa distribute cocaine and other illegal drugs. The transportation of drugs in Europe has become fairly easy with the advent of the European Union. There no longer are borders or border inspections to inhibit drugs from moving from one country to another.

Wholesale and retail drug operations represent another layer or type of TOC group. These groups tend to be based in one or a few countries and are limited in terms of international connections and sophistication. They assume a variety of organizational configurations. They tend to be small or medium sized and focus on one primary criminal activity. As drugs move from one country to another, the drugs may move through several TOC groups. The retailers and wholesalers tend to be geographically based, controlling a specific area. They tend to be ruthless, using violence and political corruption to protect their trafficking operations.

	Afghanistan	World	Percentage of Production in Afghanistan
1998	2,693	4,346	62%
1999	4,565	5,764	79%
2000	3,276	4,691	70%
2001	185	1,596	12%
2002	3,400	4,491	76%
2003	3,600	4,765	76%
2004	4,200	4,850	87%
2005	4,100	4,620	89%
2006	6,100	6,610	92%
2007	8,200	8,847	93%

FIGURE 7-2   Afghan and Worldwide Opium Production in Tons.   *Source*: United Nations Office of Drugs and Crime. (2008). *Drug Trends the Fight against Drugs*. www.usdoj.gov/dea/pubs/pressrel/pr070708_presentation.ppt (Accessed June 17, 2009).

Drugs confiscated by the DEA.   *Source:* http://www.justice.gov/dea/photos/operations/coronado/7.jpg

One issue that complicates law enforcement efforts to intervene in the global transshipment of drugs is the development of narco-states. **Narco-states** are countries where drugs have become incorporated into the fabric of government and society. A 2003 Congressional Research Report identified 50 cases linking North Korean diplomats to international drug trafficking (Perl, 2003). In 1999, Egyptian authorities apprehended a North Korean diplomat with 506,000 rohypnol tablets, a date rape drug. In 1989, the United States invaded Panama because that country had become a central point in the transshipment of cocaine and other drugs into the United States and other countries. It was alleged that Manuel Noriega, the country's president, was directly involved in these operations. Today, violence is endemic in Mexico as drug trafficking cartels fight for control of drug markets. Many police and government officials have been corrupted and work with the drug cartels. Narco-states tend to be rife with corruption, and some officials may see facilitating terrorists as a way of increasing their wealth.

Human Trafficking

The movement of people who do not possess proper documentation (visas or passports) across international borders has become a major problem. This problem assumes two forms. First, there are large numbers of people who essentially decide to move from one country to another (migrate) and do so without documentation. In some cases, they simply avoid border restrictions and "sneak" into the new country; in other cases, they may hire someone to take them or to facilitate their journey and entry (these facilitators often are referred to as "mules"). They may use forged documentation or remain in a country after their visas have expired. These people voluntarily move from one country to another. The majority of illegal aliens in the United States fit this category. (This is discussed in more detail in Chapter 13.)

Human trafficking, on the other hand, refers to the forced migration of people. Article 3 of the UN Protocol to Prevent, Suppress and Punish Trafficking in Persons, Especially Women and Children, Supplementing the UN Convention Against Transnational Organized Crime, defines human trafficking as

The recruitment, transportation, transfer, harboring or receipt of persons, by means of threat, use of force or other means of coercion, of abduction, of fraud, of deception, of the abuse of power or of a position of vulnerability or of the receiving or giving of payment . . . to a person having control over another person, for the purpose of exploitation.

The U.S. Working Group (2000) further illuminates the problem,

Traffickers of women and children, much like narcotics traffickers, operate boldly across sovereign borders. They prey on women from countries where economic and employment prospects are bleak, organized crime is rampant, and females have a subordinate role in society. Often these women are tricked into leaving their countries by false promises of a better economic life abroad; traffickers lure victims with false advertisements and promises of jobs as models, dancers, waitresses, and maids. Once the women are abroad, traffickers use a variety of means to sell and enslave them. In other instances, traffickers buy young girls from their relatives. (p. 9)

Figure 7-3 helps distinguish regular migration from human trafficking.

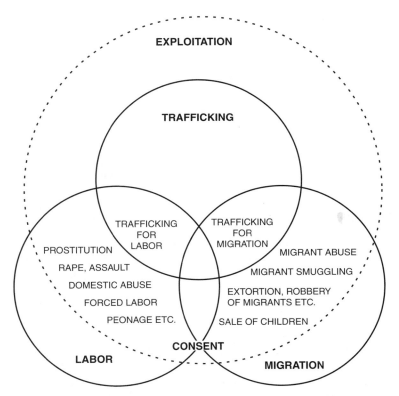

FIGURE 7-3 Schematic Representation of Relationships among Exploitation, Trafficking, Migration, Smuggling, Labor, and Consent *Source:* Newman, G. (2006). *The Exploitation of Trafficked Women.* Problem-Solving Guides Series No. 38. Washington, D.C.: Office of Community Oriented Policing Services.

Human trafficking has become a significant TOC activity. The International Organization for Migration (2008) estimates that there are 800,000 people smuggled internationally each year for the purpose of human trafficking. There are organizations that specialize in the trafficking of women and children. In these cases, the women and children are sold for forced-labor or sexual activities. The International Labor Organization (2005) estimates that at any given time, 2.5 million people are working as forced laborers, of whom 42 percent are in prostitution. A few organizations participate in both activities. The type of human trafficking engaged in by a TOC largely depends on its location and its connections or demand.

Of great concern from a homeland security standpoint is that these smuggling networks may bring terrorists into the United States. These networks are constantly moving people; thus, the ability to do so is present. As noted, a number of these networks are involved in other crimes such as narcotics smuggling. It is reasonable to assume that they would have no compulsion not to smuggle terrorists into the United States or other countries. Terrorist organizations certainly have the resources to pay for their passage. It is extremely dangerous when human smuggling rings and terrorist organizations intersect.

Smuggling of Technology and WMD Materials

Smuggling of technology and WMD materials refers to illegally transferring weapons technology from one country to another. In Chapter 9, we examine weapons of mass destruction. It is notable that there is a market for smuggling WMD materials and technology, and the smuggling of these materials appears to be increasing. Indeed, recently an international smuggling ring involved in the sale of nuclear technology and information was uncovered in Pakistan. A. C. Khan, the head of Pakistan's nuclear program, had sold technology to countries such as North Korea, Iran, and Libya (Frantz and Collins, 2007). The United States Interagency Working Group (2000) notes that there have been 14 confirmed seizures of smuggled fissile materials totaling 15.3 kilograms of weapons-usable uranium and 368.8 grams of plutonium. These seizures demonstrate the existence of smuggling operations, and these groups likely will continue to attempt to smuggle uranium and plutonium since there likely is a lucrative market for radiological materials. They probably will attempt to smuggle biological and chemical weapons materials as well. It is particularly problematic that technology-smuggling organizations exist throughout the world.

HS Web Link: To learn more about TOC groups, terrorists, and the smuggling of WMDs, go to *http://www.cidcm.umd.edu/ carnegie/papers/ stanislawski_hermann.pdf*

Arms Trafficking

The end of the cold war and several smaller wars throughout the world such as the one fought in Lebanon has resulted in an overabundance of weapons in circulation. When these weapons are not needed by governments, they become a commodity that can be sold on the black market. They represent a resource to their owners that can be converted into needed cash that can be used to rebuild in the aftermath of a conflict or for other purposes. **Arms trafficking** is the illegal selling of weapons to prohibited groups or countries, usually those in which conflicts are occurring. There are also a number of black marketeers who are constantly selling weapons around the world. Arms sales are an expansive industry with extremely high profits. These factors contribute to a global market with readily available arms; it makes making war easy and expedient.

A substantial portion of illegal arms are sold on the gray market. The **gray market** consists of individual arms dealers who subvert the legitimate arms licensing processes and requirements. Essentially, they illegally ship or smuggle arms to sanctioned countries by disguising the shipments as something other than arms. For example, they may ship arms under the guise of

Captured AK-47s that were being smuggled into Mexico.
Source: http://www.ice.gov/images/090106elpaso_fp.jpg

humanitarian aid or as farm equipment or other machinery. In some cases, the arms pass through several brokers and other handlers before they reach their final destination. The brokers who smuggle weapons sometimes develop intricate mazes of shipment points in an attempt to ensure that authorities do not discover the arms.

An array of weapons are sold on the black market. They include parts for larger and sophisticated weapons systems, assault rifles, portable anti-tank and anti-aircraft weapons, light artillery and mortars, military-grade explosives, and munitions. It is estimated that several million dollars worth of weapons are sold annually to countries and groups that are under United Nations embargos (U.S. Interagency Working Group, 2000). Many of these weapons fall into the hands of terrorists, insurgents, and organized crime groups such as drug cartels. Some of the increased violence in the Mexican drug battles is attributable to the drug cartels in that country obtaining more sophisticated weapons to protect their operations from the police and military and to defeat competing cartels that may attempt to conquer drug operations and territories. Many terrorist groups obtain their weapons from state sponsors. For example, many of the weapons used by insurgents and terrorists in Iraq and Afghanistan came from Iran and other countries opposed to the United States.

It is estimated that there are 500 million illicit weapons in circulation worldwide, with about 100 million in West Africa. There were 49 major conflicts in the 1990s, and 47 of these conflicts were waged with small arms. Small arms are responsible for more than a half million deaths a year, including 300,000 in armed conflict and 200,000 more from homicides and suicides (Bah, 2004). Although our primary concern is for weapons of mass destruction, it appears that small arms are the real weapons of mass destruction, because they result in the greatest number of deaths and pose a threat to state sovereignty, especially in underdeveloped nations with ongoing insurgencies. Whereas countries vigorously police chemical, biological, and radiological weapons, only minimal effort is exerted to control small weapons.

In some corners of the world, illegal arms dealing intermingles with other TOC activities. Rabasa and her colleagues (2006) identify several instances in which guns were traded for drugs. FARC insurgents from Colombia traded cocaine for guns with Paraguayan gunrunners. Hezbollah has been found to be active in Paraguay, obtaining drugs that ultimately would be used to fund some of its operations in the Middle East and possibly elsewhere. It seems that TOC and terrorist groups

Analysis Box 7-5

Gun control is a major political issue and controversy in the United States. Many Americans are afraid that the federal government will take their guns or restrict gun ownership. Currently, there are few gun laws in most states that restrict the sale of weapons, especially assault weapons. Given that large numbers of automatic weapons that are being used by Mexican drug cartels are being smuggled into Mexico from the United States, should we have stricter gun laws? Should we be concerned with guns going to Mexico since they are legal in the United States, and crime in Mexico is the Mexican government's problem?

devise economic models that oftentimes use the barter system to obtain money for their various purposes. They identify markets and work to obtain the goods that are needed in those markets. In some cases, they may acquire or trade goods several times before obtaining their objective.

Trafficking in Precious Gems

There is a large world market for precious gems and metals. Their opulence is valued by the rich and elite throughout the world, resulting in a substantial demand. The smuggling of precious gems has become a source of significant revenue for organized crime and warlords and insurgents, especially in Africa, which is home to a number of armed conflicts and insurgencies. For example, the UNITA insurgent group in Angola, rebels in the Democratic Republic of the Congo, and the Revolutionary United Front in Sierra Leone use black market gems to finance their wars.

Approximately three-quarters of the world's diamonds are mined in Africa, and in 1998, it was estimated that the value of the diamonds mined was $5.2 billion, and approximately 13 percent were

Miners dig for diamonds in Zimbabwe. *Source:* Canadian Press. AP (090626038211)

mined illegally, primarily by insurgent groups. In some gem-producing countries, insurgents control and mine larger quantities of diamonds than do the governments. This not only results in the availability of funds to fuel wars and conflicts, but it also results in substantial revenue losses for these governments, generally weak nation-states, making it more difficult for them to respond to insurgencies and economic problems plaguing the country (U.S. Government Interagency Working Group, 2000). Consequently, many of these diamonds are sold on the black market. Such diamonds and other gems have come to be called "blood diamonds" or "conflict diamonds" as they often are mined by slaves or captives and sold by warlords and insurgents to finance armed conflicts. The African diamond trade has made it intrinsically more difficult to solve these African conflicts.

Africa is not the only source of the black market gem and precious metal trade; Russian, Chinese, and Italian organized crime groups are extensively involved in this activity. Russian officials estimate that between $100 and $300 million worth of diamonds are smuggled out of Russia each year (U.S. Government Interagency Working Group, 2000). In many cases, the organized crime groups infiltrate legitimate mines and businesses, procure the commodities, smuggle them out of the country, and sell them on the black market. The high demand for gems and precious metals creates a substantial market and high profits for the groups.

Piracy

Piracy is an attack on ships by intruders who intend to steal cargo or ransom the ship, its contents, or crew and passengers. Most people have the impression that maritime piracy was abolished long ago. However, it remains a significant problem, especially off the coasts of Africa

Navy frigate assigned to East Africa to provide maritime security.   *Source:* http://www.navy.mil/management/photodb/webphoto/web_100221-N-8463W-096.jpg

and Asia and in some cases South America and the Caribbean. There are approximately 50,000 ships carrying about 80 percent of the world's traded cargo. This number does not include pleasure and other private non-cargo ships on the high seas. The large number of ships at sea at any given time represents multiple targets for pirates who see piracy as a lucrative business.

Piracy is a growing TOC activity. The frequency of piracy and the level of violence remain quite high even though several governments, including the United States, are making a concerted effort to reduce the problem. There were 406 incidents reported in 2009 with 153 vessels boarded, 49 vessels hijacked, and 84 attempted attacks. A total of 1,052 crewmembers were taken hostage with 68 injured and 8 killed (International Chamber of Commerce, 2010). The *Journal of Commerce* (2009) reports that bulk carriers and container ships are the most frequently attacked. Chemical tankers, product tankers, and general cargo ships are also attacked. Large ships are the primary targets of pirates. As an example, in 2008, pirates based in Somalia intercepted a Ukrainian freighter carrying Russian tanks, rocket-propelled grenades, and other munitions. The pirates demanded a $20 million ransom for the ship, its contents, and its 11-member crew. A few months later, pirates attacked and ransomed a Saudi Arabian oil tanker containing $100 million worth of oil. These attacks demonstrate that pirates are capable of attacking even the largest nonmilitary ships and their attacks are becoming more brazen.

Pirates have fairly sophisticated tactics. They generally attack a large ship using a "mother" ship or boat from which several smaller and faster craft are launched. The smaller boats surround the target ship. Once the target is surrounded, the pirates fire automatic weapons and sometimes rocket-propelled grenades over the ship. The larger ship cannot escape since the smaller craft are faster. The target ships often have a small number of crewmembers, making resistance fruitless. Even though a large number of ships are boarded at sea, most acts of piracy occur in port. Here, the pirates simply board the ship while in dock and unload its cargo. Piracy has emerged as a threat to international commerce and, in some cases, the stability of weak nation-states that are dependent upon this commerce.

Most of the maritime piracy is conducted by organized crime groups with terrorist or insurgent groups possibly nominally involved in such activities. However, terrorists have plotted the destruction of ships at sea. In 2000, al Qaeda terrorists from Yemen attempted to ram the USS *The Sullivans* with a boat laden with explosives. The attack failed, but later in the year, they were successful in their attack on the USS *Cole.* That attack resulted in the deaths of 17 sailors and considerable damage to the *Cole.* In 2004, the same tactic was used to attack a French oil tanker, the *Limberg*, off the coast of Yemen, and in 2004, Abu Sayyaf, a terrorist group based in the Philippines, claimed responsibility for an explosion on a large ferry that killed at least 100 people. In 2002, the Moroccan government arrested a group of al Qaeda operatives suspected of plotting raids on British and U.S. tankers passing through the Strait of Gibraltar. Intelligence experts believe that al Qaeda has a number of ships, which they have stolen or hijacked. These ships have been repainted and operate with false documentation. It is feared that they will use them to destroy a large oil tanker or cargo ship, which could have a substantial impact on the economy or maritime shipping. A greater security threat is that they might be used to ferry a WMD into a busy port (Luft and Korin, 2004).

Non-Drug Contraband Smuggling

Non-drug contraband smuggling refers to smuggling legitimate goods such as alcohol, cigarettes, textiles, and various luxury goods to evade taxes and tariffs. Smuggling these goods is safer as compared to drug smuggling since the penalties are much less severe. For example, Russia and China have the highest tariffs on luxury goods and the newly created economic elite craves the nuances and trappings of wealth. When smugglers are able to import goods without the tariffs, especially if they are obtained from the originating country where they are less costly or stolen, they are able to realize a substantial profit on the black market. Colombian drug traffickers used money from drug operations to purchase cigarettes and smuggle them into Colombia, avoiding tariffs but resulting in lost revenue to that country. The United States is not immune from such activities. In 2000, FBI agents made several raids in North Carolina and arrested members of a Hezbollah cell who were smuggling cigarettes from North Carolina to Michigan. They made weekly trips, and each trip netted them $3,000 to $10,000. Hezbollah members were able to raise several million dollars with their cigarette smuggling operation. Mohammed Yousef and Chawki Hammound used the proceeds to purchase and ship night vision goggles, mine detection equipment, laser range finders, blasting caps, and other military hardware to Hezbollah operatives (Horwitz, 2004; Mutschke, 2000).

TOC groups in Mexico, Russia, and Asia are involved in transporting and selling stolen automobiles worldwide. There is a high demand for luxury vehicles in the newly rich countries of China and Russia. Luxury cars are stolen from Europe and the United States and then smuggled into other countries where they can fetch substantially more than their value elsewhere. It is estimated that the value of this market is between $10 and $15 billion. It is estimated that 300,000 European vehicles are acquired and disposed of in this fashion each year (U.S. Government Interagency Working Group, 2000). In some cases, those transporting stolen vehicles are also engaged in other TOC activities such as human smuggling and narcotics trafficking.

TOC smuggling is not limited to luxury items. TOC organizations also are involved in smuggling counterfeit goods. Interpol estimates that the trade in counterfeit goods has grown eight times faster than the trade involving legitimately manufactured goods. It is believed that the trade in counterfeit goods represents 6 percent of the world's total trade (Interpol, 2008). Businesses in the United States estimate that the smuggling of counterfeit items costs them between $200 and $250 billion annually. It is estimated that in some sectors of the Chinese economy, 90 percent of the products are counterfeit (Wagley, 2006). Bulgaria is another country that is extensively involved in counterfeit wares. It is at a crossroads for international commerce in Europe, which allows it to easily ship these goods to other countries. There is little doubt that the smuggling of legitimate luxury items and counterfeit products represents a substantial TOC activity.

Counterfeiting

U.S. currency is the most commonly counterfeited currency, because it is accepted in most countries and it tends to hold its value relative to other currencies. Essentially, it is the universal currency. The U.S. Treasury estimates that there is $570 billion in genuine currency in circulation worldwide, with about two-thirds of the currency outside the United States. Advances in computer and print technology have substantially increased TOC groups' ability to counterfeit currency and other financial instruments such as fictitious securities. Drug traffickers, terrorist groups, and other TOC groups are involved in counterfeiting. Some Russian and Italian organized crime groups are principally involved. Moreover, some countries such as North Korea have counterfeited American currency. The greatest problem is that these groups are using counterfeit currency to finance other criminal or terrorist operations.

HS Web Link: To learn more about counterfeit American money, go to *http://www.frbsf.org/ federalreserve/money/ funfacts.html.*

Customs and border protection officers confiscate counterfeit goods coming into the United States. *Source:* http://206.241.31.146/ImageCache/cgov/content/newsroom/highlights/news_5fhighlights/2007/fake_5fgoods_2ectt/v1/image/1/ny_5ffakes_5f210.jpg

Financial Fraud

Financial fraud refers to activities that illegally or improperly obtain money and other valuables from citizens and businesses via some financial scam. Common scams include insurance fraud, lottery fraud, scam business propositions, tax avoidance, offshore investment scams, pyramid schemes, credit fraud, and so on. It is one of the fastest-growing criminal enterprises. Schemes by TOC groups are responsible for stealing billions of dollars annually from citizens, businesses, and government entitlement programs. It has grown because of our dependence on the Internet for financial transactions and because more substantial information about people and their finances is available via the Internet. Also, we continue to move toward a cashless society in which credit, debit, and bank cards are the primary instruments of commerce. Van Dijk (2008) reports that globally, 1 percent of people with credit cards have been victimized by credit card fraud, and more than one-quarter of Internet fraud is perpetrated via credit card fraud. Russian, Nigerian, and Asian TOC groups are principally involved in these activities.

The U.S. Government Interagency Working Group (2000) notes that Russian organized crime groups have penetrated the international banking community, oftentimes using funds derived from criminal enterprises to purchase banks and other financial institutions. This allows them to obtain financial information on individuals and other corporations, launder money, and become involved in insider trading and other financial crimes. They have become involved in Russia's expanding gas and oil industries. Here, they use extortion, steal gas

---

Analysis Box 7-6

Financial fraud, particularly identity theft and the theft of credit card information, is the fastest-growing crime in the United States and the world. There literally are thousands of victims losing millions of dollars each year. Have you been a victim of financial fraud? What have you done to reduce the probability that you will become a victim?

---

and oil and sell it on the black market, and bribe public officials to facilitate these activities. Some estimate that $12 billion annually is moved out of Russia by Russian organized crime groups.

American citizens are the target of a number of fraudsters from countries across the globe. They generally use e-mails, faxes, or letters soliciting donations to charities, invitations to invest in a new highly profitable company, assist in accessing fictitious financial accounts, or advise the e-mail recipient that he or she has won or inherited a large amount of money in a foreign country. Generally, the victim is required to pay upfront fees, taxes, or tariffs for the money to be released to the victim. The fraudster merely keeps the money and the victim receives nothing in return except perhaps a bitter lesson. Victims report losing several million dollars each year as a result of these schemes. Businesses are similarly targeted through stolen credit card numbers and forged identities. A number of Russian TOC groups have been hacking into bank and other financial institutions to steal credit card and personal information.

Environmental Crimes

Environmental crimes consist of the improper or illegal disposal of trash and hazardous waste. Countries across the globe have passed progressive laws controlling the disposal of trash and hazardous waste materials. In many cases, there are not ample legitimate outlets for disposal, or in most cases, the cost of proper disposal is relatively substantial. These conditions provide new opportunities for TOC groups. The U.S. Government Interagency Working Group (2000) estimates that the illegal dumping of trash and hazardous materials is a $10 to $12 billion industry. Organized crime groups in Russia, China, and Japan are principally involved, but other groups are also involved to a lesser extent. Oftentimes, the hazardous materials will be combined with scrap metal or other commodities and shipped out of country. The waste is sometimes shipped to countries with lax laws; in other cases, the waste will be dumped in waterways or buried in desolate areas. Of particular concern is the illegal disposal of radioactive waste. This material could be used by terrorists to build a "dirty bomb."

LINKS BETWEEN TRANSNATIONAL ORGANIZED CRIME AND TERRORIST ORGANIZATIONS

As noted earlier, in numerous instances, there is a convergence between TOC groups and terrorist organizations, and in some cases, it is difficult to discern differences between these two types of organizations. A prime example is narco-terrorism, in which terrorists are trafficking drugs to support their activities, and the terrorists are used by drug traffickers for protection, money laundering, and transportation. This point is amplified by the fact that about one-third of the organizations on the State Department's list of foreign terrorist organizations are also on the list of targeted U.S. drug suppliers (see Schmid, 2003). This section more fully explores the relationships between TOC and terrorist organizations. It is important to understand these relationships when developing enforcement and prevention priorities. Neglecting TOC organizations may allow openings for terrorist groups. On the other hand, if law enforcement agencies can dismantle a TOC group, that may negatively affect affiliated terrorist groups.

There are a number of similarities between TOC groups and terrorist organizations. For example, Schmid (1996) identified the following:

- Both operate secretly and usually from an underground.
- Both use muscle and ruthlessness and produce mainly civilian victims.
- Intimidation is characteristic of both groups.
- Both use similar (although no entirely overlapping) tactics: kidnappings, assassinations, and extortion.
- Both exert control over individuals within the group.
- Both use front organizations such as legitimate businesses or charities.

Later, in a 2003 paper, Schmid identified areas of dissimilarity between TOC and terrorist organizations:

- Terrorist groups are usually ideologically or politically motivated, whereas organized crime groups are profit oriented.
- Terrorist groups often wish to compete with governments for legitimacy; organized crime groups do not. Organized crime desires to circumvent the legal system so that the legal system does not impede the maximizing of profits.
- Terrorist groups relish media attention and oftentimes exert efforts to receive it; organized crime groups attempt to remain in the shadows receiving as little notoriety as possible.
- Terrorist victimization and violence are generally less discriminate than those of organized crime groups.

There is substantial overlap between TOC and terrorist groups, and at the same time, a number of differences. The similarities result in the two types of criminals (based on motivation) having similar modus operandi to the point that sometimes these groups are hard to distinguish from each other. Although organized criminal groups often resort to crimes that produce a monetary reward, they sometimes use violence as a means to this end. Some organized crime groups are more violent than others. For example, violence or the threat of violence is a central part of extortion, which is commonly practiced by a number of TOC groups. Terrorists have political objectives, but TOC groups often have their own quasi-political objectives. They often attempt to corrupt government officials and governments to facilitate their criminal ends. Well-established governments, especially open democracies, tend to be more resistant to intrusion by criminal organizations. Thus, the activities of TOC groups and terrorist groups often parallel, and to some extent, their objectives sometimes overlap.

It should be recognized that there are impediments to TOC groups cooperating with terrorist organizations. The Canadian Centre for Intelligence and Security (2006) has identified several such impediments. First, in some cases terrorist groups and TOC groups that are co-located come into conflict as a result of competition for criminal activities or territories; multiple organizations conducting the same criminal enterprise reduces each organization's margin of profit. Second, both terrorist and TOC organizations demand high levels of loyalty from their members. Alliances with other groups may jeopardize member loyalty, and they increase the probability of government detection or infiltration. Third, a number of terrorist organizations are ephemeral-sporadic—they have the wherewithal, motivation, or resources to conduct only one or a few attacks and do not need outside assistance. Fourth, TOC groups are organized around profits, not politics. They shun the media and any other attention. TOC groups may be unwilling to enter into a cooperative relationship with a terrorist organization because of the potential public exposure. In the long term, it likely would be bad for business. Finally, many traditional crime groups are intensely nationalistic. Even though they commit large numbers of crime, they are loyal to their homeland. Indeed, it is the homeland and its legal and socioeconomic system that provides the TOC group with the opportunities for its profitable criminal activities. Therefore, it likely will be opposed to terrorist organizations that desire to change the status quo. Even though such impediments exist, there still are instances when TOC groups are cooperating and working with terrorist organizations.

In some areas, the connection between TOC and terrorist organizations is blatantly clear. A prime example is the tri-border area of Paraguay, Brazil, and Argentina—an area that is rife with drug trafficking, money laundering, arms smuggling, and other illegal activities. In 1992, Hezbollah detonated a bomb outside the Israeli embassy in Buenos Aires, killing 29 people, and in 1994, it detonated a car bomb attack in the same city, targeting a Jewish-Argentine community center and killing 87. In both cases, evidence pointed to Ciudad del Este, or the tri-border area, as the staging point for the attacks (Shelly and Picarelli, 2005). Sanderson (2004) notes that Hezbollah is not the only Middle Eastern terrorist organization in the area. Hamas and Gamaa al Islamiyah have elements there committing crimes and raising money for terrorist activities. South American terrorist organizations such as the Colombian terrorist group FARC are also present.

Another such area is the border between Pakistan and Afghanistan where al Qaeda is involved in opium production to finance its terrorist operations. Indeed, al Qaeda has developed criminal syndicates throughout Central Asia and North Africa to augment its terrorist campaigns (Sanderson, 2004). A substantial amount of the opium produced in this area is processed by the Kurdistan Workers Party (PPK) and Turkish TOC groups (Canadian Centre for Intelligence and Security, 2006). Given that approximately 90 percent of the world's illegal opium production is in Afghanistan and is largely controlled by al Qaeda and the Taliban, these terrorist organizations must develop links with other terrorist and TOC groups to market the drugs.

In these examples, terrorists work closely with TOC organizations to facilitate criminal activities and raise funds for their worldwide attacks. The intersection of the numerous and varied terrorist groups with TOC groups results in a dangerous cocktail of violence and criminal efficiency. It not only means that TOC groups are jointly working with terrorist organizations but also that terrorist organizations are cooperating with other terrorist groups. Such symbiotic relationships can result in more proficient criminal and terrorist organizations.

Summary

This chapter examined transnational organized crime. It is important to understand this form of criminality because of its relationships, affiliations, and intersections with terrorist organizations. In many cases, terrorist organizations are using transnational crime to raise funds for their terrorist attacks, buy arms and explosives, and maintain their networks. As noted in Chapter 12, it is important that governments reduce funding to terrorist organizations using any means possible. Reduced funding not only will reduce attacks but it also will make it difficult for these organizations to maintain themselves or expand. Moreover, transnational organized crime constitutes a growing and dangerous form of crime. It corrupts governments, leads to governmental ineffectiveness, and results in a socioeconomic structure in many countries that has dire consequences for their populations. It should receive governments' attention because of the harm it does to many societies.

Researchers have found that TOC groups use a variety of organizational structures. Some are classically organized using a pyramid structure with strict command and control, rules, specialization whereby different members are assigned specific tasks, and a strict recruitment system. Other TOC groups are more decentralized, with some of them quite large and encompassing a number of TOC operations across several countries. It is interesting that TOC organizations mirror terrorist organizations in their organizational structures, and in some cases, TOC organizations are integrated with terrorist organizations on some levels. The exact organizational structure often is the result of the environment, criminal opportunities, and the amount of governmental and law enforcement pressure. TOC organizations, as well as terrorist organizations, often become more decentralized when there is substantial law enforcement pressure.

TOC groups are involved in a variety of criminal enterprises. These activities include counterfeiting, trafficking drugs and narcotics, exportation of counterfeit clothing and luxury goods, international transportation of stolen luxury items such as stolen high-value automobiles, money laundering, trading in gems and precious metals, piracy, and environmental crimes. It should be noted that violence and governmental corruption are activities that are commonly associated with these TOC activities. A TOC group's involvement is largely dependent upon opportunities—involvement in some of these crimes is the result of the TOC's location near the resources or a viable market.

It is informative to consider the relationships between TOC groups and terrorism. As noted, they often use similarly constructed organizational frameworks and share a number of other similarities. These similarities represent "pulls" that make it conducive for these two types of organizations to develop alliances for their mutual benefit. At the same time, there are "pushes" that prevent TOC groups and terrorist organizations from developing cooperative relationships. Thus, these relationships remain tenuous and sometimes are forged temporarily; in other cases, they may have a measure of permanence. Regardless, these relationships can facilitate an increase in crime and terrorism. It is vital that governments focus on TOC groups.

The National Intelligence Council (NIC, 2008) prepared a report examining trends in world conditions. The NIC examined projected changes in energy supplies, global warming, population demographics, government stability, and agriculture output. The NIC made one striking finding that is applicable here:

> Concurrent with the shift in power among nation-states, the relative power of various non-state actors—including businesses, tribes, religious organizations, and even criminal networks—will continue to increase. Several countries could even be "taken over" and run by criminal networks. In areas of Africa and or South Asia, states as we know them might wither away, owing to the inability of governments to provide for basic needs, including security. (p. 1)

In essence, future conditions will result in the weakening of a number of nation-states, facilitating the growth of transnational organized crime. In the future, there likely will be more and stronger TOC groups. These groups pose a danger to national security not only in terms of the number of crimes they commit but also in terms of their possibly cooperating with terrorist organizations.

Discussion Questions

1. What is the interplay of street crime, white-collar crime, organized crime, and terrorism?
2. What are the characteristics of organized crime groups?
3. Distinguish terrorism from normal or street crimes.
4. How does transnational organized crime interact with or otherwise affect governments?
5. What factors have facilitated the growth of transnational organized crime? How?
6. There are two economic models explaining the emergence of transnational organized crime. Explain their operation and differences.
7. Compare the various transnational organized crime structures.
8. How do drugs contribute to transnational organized crime and terrorism?
9. How are terrorist groups and transnational organized crime groups similar? Different?

References

Albini, J. (1971). *The American Mafia: Genesis of a Legend.* New York: Appleton Crofts.

Arlacchi, P. (1987). "Large scale crime and world illegal markets." In *Organized Crime: International Strategies.* Report of the International Seminar on Policies and Strategies to Combat Organized Crime held under the auspices of the United Nations and the University of New Mexico, Albuquerque, NM (December 8–11), pp. 47–61.

Bah, A. (2004). "Micro-disarmament in West Africa." *African Security Review,* 13(3). http://www.iss.co.za/pubs/ASR/13No3/FBah.htm (Accessed October 18, 2008).

Canadian Centre for Intelligence and Security (2006). "Actual and potential links between terrorism and criminality." *Trends in Terrorism Series.* http://www.carleton.ca/cciss/res_docs/itac/omalley_e.pdf (Accessed October 31, 2008).

Clarke, R. and G. Newman (2006). *Outsmarting the Terrorists.* Westport, CN: Praeger.

Clinard, M., R. Quinney, and J. Wildeman. (1994). *Criminal Behavior Systems: A Typology.* Cincinnati, OH: Anderson Publishing.

Cockayne, J. (2007). *Transnational Organized Crime: Multilateral Responses to a Rising Threat.* Washington, D.C.: International Peace Academy.

Dishman, C. (2009). "The leaderless nexus: When crime and terror converge." In *Terrorism and Counterterrorism: Understanding the New Security Environment,* ed. R. Howard, R. Sawyer, and N. Bajema, pp. 295–310. New York: McGraw-Hill.

Edwards, A. and P. Gill. (2002). "Crime as enterprise? The case of transnational organized crime." *Crime, Law & Social Change,* 37: 203–23.

Felbab-Brown, V. (2008). *Tackling Transnational Crime: Adapting U.S. National Security Policy.* Washington, D.C.: Brookings Institution.

Finckenauer, J. (2000). *Meeting the Challenge of Transnational Crime.* Washington, D.C.: National Institute of Justice.

Finckenauer, J. and E. Waring. (1998). *Russian Mafia in America.* Boston, MA: Northeastern University Press.

Frantz, D. and C. Collins (2007). "Those nuclear flashpoints are made in Pakistan." *Washington Post* (November 11). http://www.washingtonpost.com/wp-dyn/content/article/2007/11/07/AR2007110702280.html (Accessed August 28).

Friedrichs, D. (1996). *Trusted Criminals in Contemporary Society.* Belmont, CA: Wadsworth.

Glenny, M. (2005). "The lost war." *Washington Post* (August 19). pp. B1, 5.

Horwitz, S. (2004). "Cigarette smuggling linked to terrorism." *Washington Post* (June 8), p. A1.

International Chamber of Commerce. (2010). *2009 Worldwide Piracy Figures Surpass 400.* http://www.icc-ccs.org/news/ 385-2009-worldwide-piracy-figures-surpass-400 (Accessed January 17, 2011).

International Labor Organization. (2005). *A Global Alliance against Forced Labor.* Geneva: ILO.

International Organization for Migration. (2008). http://www.iom.int/jahia/Jahia/pid/748 (Accessed November 21, 2008).

Interpol. (2008). *The Impact and Scale of Counterfeiting.* http://www.interpol.com/Public/News/2004/Factsheet51PR21.asp (Accessed October 25, 2008).

Journal of Commerce. (2009). *Special Piracy Report: By the Numbers.* http://www.joc.com/piracy/special-piracy-report-numbers (Accessed January 17, 2011).

Kenney, D. and J. Finckenauer. (1995). *Organized Crime in America.* Belmont, CA: Wadsworth.

Luft, G. and A. Korin. (2004). "Terrorism goes to sea." *Foreign Affairs,* 83(6). http://www.foreignaffairs.org/20041101faessay83606/gal-luft-anne-korin-terrorism-goes-to-sea.html (Accessed October 20, 2008).

Lyman, M. and G. Potter. (1998). *Drugs in Society.* Cincinnati, OH: Anderson Publishing.

Miller, G. (2009). "Report: Taliban receives less drug money than thought." *Los Angeles Times.* http://www.mercurynews.com/politics/ci_13039875?nclick_check=1 (Accessed August 19, 2009).

Mueller, G. (1998). "Transnational crime: Definitions and concepts." *Transnational Organized Crime,* 4: 13–21.

Mutschke, R. (2000). "Threats posed by the convergence of organized crime, drug traffickers, and terrorism." Testimony of the Assistant Director, Criminal Intelligence Directorate, International Criminal Police Organization-Interpol, before the U.S. Judiciary Committee, Sub-Committee on Crime (December 13).

National Intelligence Council. (2008). *Global Trends 2025: A Transformed World.* Washington, D.C.: Author.

Perl, R. (2003). *Drug Trafficking and North Korea: Issues for U.S. Policy.* Washington, D.C.: Congressional Research Service.

Potter, G. (1993). *Criminal Organizations: Vice Racketeering and Politics in an American City.* Prospect Heights, IL: Waveland Press.

Rabasa, A., P. Chalk, K. Cragin, S. Daly, H. Gregg, T. Karasik, K. O'Brien, and W. Rosenau. (2006). *Beyond al-Qaeda: The Outer Rings of the Terrorist Universe.* Santa Monica, CA: Rand.

Rengert, G. (2003). "The distribution of illegal drugs at the retail level: The street dealers." In *Drugs, Crime, and Justice,* ed. L. Gaines and P. Kraska, pp. 175–92. Prospect Heights, IL: Waveland Press.

Reuter, P. and C. Petrie. (1999). *Transnational Organized Crime: Summary of a Workshop.* Washington, D.C.: National Academy Press.

Rush, G. (1999). *Organized Crime, Drugs and Street Crime.* San Clemente, CA: Law Tech Publishing.

Sanderson, T. (2004). "Transnational terror and organized crime: Blurring the lines." *SAIS Review,* 24(1): 49–61.

Schmid, A. (2003). "Links between terrorist and organized crime networks: Emerging patterns and trends." Terrorism Prevention Branch Office on Drugs and Crime, United Nations, Vienna.

Schmid, A. (1996). "The links between transnational organized crime and terrorist crimes." *Transnational Organized Crime,* 2(4): 40–82.

Shelly, L. (1999). "Identifying, counting and categorizing transnational criminal organizations." *Transnational Organized Crime* (Spring): 1–18.

Shelly, L. and J. Picarelli. (2005). "Methods and motives: Exploring the links between transnational organized crime and international terrorism." *Trends in Organized Crime,* 9(2): 52–67.

Small, K. and B. Taylor. (2005). "State and local law enforcement response to transnational crime." *Trends in Organized Crime,* 10(2): 5–16.

Stanislawski, B. and M. Hermann. (2004). *Transnational Organized Crime, Terrorism, and WMD.* Conference on Non-State Actors, Terrorism, and Weapons of Mass Destruction, CIDCM, University of Maryland (October 15). http://www.cidcm.umd.edu/carnegie/papers/stanislawski_hermann.pdf (Accessed October 31, 2008).

United Nations. (1995). *Results of the Supplement to the Fourth United Nations Survey of Crime Trends and Operations of Criminal Justice Systems on Transnational Crime, Interim Report by the Secretariat.* New York: Author.

United Nations Centre for International Crime Prevention. (2000). "Assessing transnational organized crime: Results of a pilot survey of Forty Selected Organized Criminal Groups in Sixteen Countries." *Trends in Organized Crime,* 6(2): 44–92.

United States Government Interagency Working Group. (2000). *International Crime Threat Assessment.* http://www.fas.org/irp/threat/pub45270intro.html (Accessed September 24, 2008).

Van Dijk, J. (2008). *The World of Crime: Breaking the Silence on Problems of Security, Justice, and Development across the World.* Los Angles, CA: Sage.

Wagley, J. (2006). *Transnational Organized Crime: Principal Threats and U.S. Responses.* Washington, D.C.: Congressional Research Service.

Williams, P. (1998). "Organizing transnational crime: Networks, markets and hierarchies." *Transnational Organized Crime,* 57–58.

Williams, P. and R. Godson. (2002). "Anticipating organized and transnational crime." *Crime, Law & Social Justice,* 37: 311–55.

8

Intelligence and Counterintelligence and Terrorism

LEARNING OBJECTIVES

1. Understand the importance of intelligence and problems associated with its collection.
2. Know the role and functions of the director of national intelligence.
3. Know the kinds of intelligence that are collected.
4. Distinguish the various methods of intelligence collection.
5. Know the members of the intelligence community and their responsibilities.

KEY TERMS

National Security Council

National Intelligence Estimate

National Intelligence Council

Director of National Intelligence

Human intelligence or HUMINT

Signals intelligence or SIGINT

Measures and signatures intelligence or MASINT

Imagery analysis or IMINT

Open source intelligence or OSINT

Central Intelligence Agency

National Clandestine Service

Intelligence Directorate

Science and Technology Directorate

Support Directorate

Defense Intelligence Agency

Department of Energy

Department of Homeland Security

Office of Intelligence and Analysis

State Department

Bureau of Intelligence and Research

Treasury Department

Office of Terrorism and Financial Intelligence

Office of Foreign Assets Control

Financial Crimes Network

Drug Enforcement Administration

Federal Bureau of Investigation

National Security Branch

LEGIT or legal attaches

Global justice initiative

Joint Terrorism Task Force

National Geospatial-Intelligence Agency

National Reconnaissance Office

National Security Agency

Coastwatch Program

Intelligence cycle

Counterintelligence

Domestic industrial espionage

Secure Flight Program

INTRODUCTION

Throughout the early years of the war in Iraq, President George W. Bush and representatives in his administration repeatedly advised that, "We had to get them [the terrorists] over there before they attacked us over here." Although this philosophic musing was used to justify the Iraqi war, with questionable effectiveness, it did signify or at least recognize a need for our intelligence operations to extend well beyond our borders to collect information about those who would attack us or otherwise do our country harm. The 9/11 attacks vividly identified that our intelligence apparatus was sorely lacking as enumerated by the 9/11 Commission (National Commission on Terrorist Attacks, 2004). We needed our intelligence agencies to more effectively identify those individuals and groups who intended to attack us or otherwise do us harm; determine if they had the capability to attack us; and find out about their activities, especially if they were a prelude to an attack. We now are engaged in a global conflict with terrorism as our enemy (see Scheuer, 2004); it is an asymmetric or unconventional conflict resulting in the need for new strategies and tactics. It is unlike any other conflict or war that our country has fought.

The end of the cold war resulted in a paradigm shift in terms of intelligence. During the cold war, we were interested in politicians, governments, armies, and other state activities. Our intelligence apparatus primarily focused on China and the Soviet bloc—they were our enemies. We were interested in learning about their actions so that we could be prepared and able to counter any attacks or other threats. The Soviets were our global enemy. With the fall of the Soviet Union, everything changed. The American military-industrial complex was deemphasized. Congress allocated fewer funds to defense as we attempted to realize a "peace dividend" or savings to fund more domestic programs. The military shrunk in size and fewer resources were allocated to intelligence. We, to some extent, were less engaged at least globally, although we became involved in a number of smaller wars and conflicts across the globe. We exerted few efforts or resources to uncover information about new enemies.

The American embassy bombings in Africa, the attack on the USS *Cole* in Yemen, and the first World Trade Center bombing were the first major attacks on the United States by al Qaeda, but it was the later and more devastating 9/11 attacks that resulted in immediate and massive changes in government and the public psyche. Terrorism immediately became the primary, if not the only, government concern, and within the realm of terrorism, intelligence, or the lack thereof, was jolted to the forefront. Politicians, political pundits, and the mainstream media severely criticized perceived intelligence failures and inadequacies. Indeed, there were pieces and snippets of information about the impending 9/11 attacks that had been collected by a number of intelligence organizations, but they had not been collated and analyzed so that we could successfully identify the impending attack. The National Commission on Terrorist Attacks (2004) documented the many lapses in intelligence gathering and analysis. The primary criticism was

The bombing of the World Trade Center changed our perspective regarding intelligence.   *Source:* AP (01091103335).

that the various intelligence agencies failed to cooperate, share information, and communicate with one another. The intelligence community consisted of a number of intelligence fiefdoms and operated as such. There was no mechanism putting the pieces together and looking at the "big picture."

The 9/11 attacks spurred Congress and the president into action. Enforcement and intelligence agencies were given more powers primarily through the USA PATRIOT Act. Executive orders and laws were passed that authorized and facilitated the sharing of information across intelligence agencies. Enhanced surveillance activities were authorized. Most important, the intelligence community was reorganized with the creation of the position of director of national intelligence (DNI) with the passage of the Intelligence Reform and Terrorist Prevention Act of 2004. The act was legislated to improve the cooperation and coordination of the American intelligence community. Prior to the passage of the act, the director of the Central Intelligence Agency (CIA) supposedly served as coordinator of the intelligence apparatus in addition to his or her duties as director of the CIA. However, the director of the CIA historically had little oversight authority or capability over other intelligence agencies and largely concentrated on managing the CIA. The creation of the DNI supposedly improved our intelligence operations.

Intelligence Failure—What Does It Mean?

As noted, the 9/11 attacks and the 9/11 Commission Report (2004) squarely identified intelligence failures as a significant national security problem. However, this is a broad statement that provides little guidance in repairing the problem. Hypothetically, intelligence failures can occur at multiple levels. First, starting at the lowest level of the intelligence chain, we can fail to collect critical or applicable intelligence information. This problem is discussed in more detail later in this chapter. Second, once it is collected, intelligence agencies fail to recognize its importance, link it with other pertinent information, or otherwise interpret it in a useable policy format. The analysis has shortcomings. Third, intelligence agencies fail to share information, resulting in many incomplete pieces of the same puzzles. The passage of the Intelligence Reform and Terrorist Prevention Act of 2004 was intended to solve this problem. It remains to be seen if this intent comes to fruition. Fourth and perhaps most damning, politicians and policy makers cherry pick intelligence to meet their needs. Several behavioral modes occur here. Policy makers and politicians disregard intelligence that is counter to their beliefs or political positions. The politics of policy formulation trump common good and effective responses. It also results in politicians and policy makers pressuring intelligence agencies' analysts to find the right answers for the wrong questions, often leaving gaps in what we should know about a national security issue.

HS Web Link: To learn more about intelligence failures and their causes, go to *http://www.hoover.org/ publications/policy-review/ article/7217.*

Although in the post–cold war period, we have had gaps in our intelligence-gathering capabilities, particularly human intelligence—field operatives collecting information at ground level—our intelligence agencies have done a reasonably good job of collecting needed information. Further, our intelligence agencies perhaps possess the most skilled analytical capabilities of any country in the world. Our failure has been in the areas of sharing and cherry picking information. For example, in discussing intelligence before the 9/11 attacks, Scheuer (2004) provides a damning indictment of policy makers in the intelligence apparatus and of politicians who consumed the intelligence:

> U.S. intelligence officers—often at the risk of their own lives—had spent most of the decade gathering and analyzing the intelligence that, had it been used fully and honestly, would have allowed U.S. leaders and, indeed, all Americans to know what sort of storm was approaching. Those officers knew a runaway train was coming at the United States, documented that fact, and then watched helplessly—or were banished for speaking out—as their senior leaders delayed action, downplayed intelligence, ignored repeated warning, and generally behaved as what they so manifestly are, America's greatest generation—of moral cowards. (p. ix)

Our intelligence failure was not at the collection and analysis end, but at the consumption end. Politics and careers overshadowed correct intelligence answers and correct effective responses.

THE NATIONAL SECURITY COUNCIL AND THE HOMELAND SECURITY COUNCIL

The **National Security Council** (NSC) was created in 1947 as a result of the National Security Act. It serves as the president's primary forum for considering matters related to national security and foreign policy. In addition to advising the president, the NSC coordinates the implementation of policies across the various federal departments and agencies. In this role, it attempts to ensure that there is consistency in policy implementation.

The NSC is chaired by the president, thus providing the president direct input about national security and intelligence matters. The NSC consists of a number of attendees (both statutory and nonstatutory) including the vice president, the secretary of state, the secretary of the treasury, the secretary of defense, and the assistant to the president for national security Affairs. The chairman of the Joint Chiefs of Staff is the statutory military advisor to the council, and the director of national intelligence is the intelligence advisor. The chief of staff to the president, counsel to the president, and the assistant to the president for economic policy are invited to attend NSC meetings. The attorney general and the director of the Office of Management and Budget are invited to meetings when there are discussions that pertain to their responsibilities or areas of control. In addition, the heads of other executive departments and agencies, as well as other senior officials, may be invited to attend meetings when topics under consideration address their areas of control or expertise (NSC, 2009).

One of the NSC's primary products is the **National Intelligence Estimate** (NIE). The NIEs are written by the **National Intelligence Council** (NIC). The NIC is charged with providing medium- and long-term intelligence-based strategy. The NIC reports to the director of national intelligence and assists in coordinating intelligence products or reporting (NIC, 2009). Nonetheless, the information contained in the NIEs is provided by the NSC. The NIE represents an accumulation of information from the various intelligence agencies about a specific problem. Examples of NIEs include *Trends in Global Terrorism: Implications for the United States* (2006), *Nontraditional Threats to the U.S. Homeland Through 2007* (2002), and *Foreign Missile Developments and Ballistic Missile Threat Through 2003* (2003) (see Richelson, 2008). The NIEs attempt to provide our best information about a specific national security threat. They are not always accurate. For example, Bruno and Otterman (2008) examined the 2002 prewar estimate of Iraq's weapons of mass destruction. They advise that the Senate Select Committee on Intelligence noted that many of the justifications used by the president to go to war were overstatements or were not supported by the intelligence. Even though the NIEs represent our best estimate relative to a given national security threat, they sometimes are not accurate and become problematic when used by policy makers, as discussed in this chapter.

HS Web Link: To learn more about NIEs, go to *http://www.dni.gov/nic/NIC_home.html*.

Since its inception, the NCS has been reorganized several times and its mission expanded or contracted (Brown, 2008). To some extent, changes in the NSC's realm of authority have been made as a result of world conditions; in other cases, different presidents have modified its role based on their perceptions of need. In 2001, President George W. Bush created the Homeland Security Council (HSC). Structurally, the HSC was similar to the NSC with many of the same officials working on both councils. The HSC was constituted to develop and review policies relative to homeland security, which was accomplished by various Homeland Security Policy Coordination Committees. These committees drafted policies for implementation across the various departments within the federal government, including the Department of Homeland Security. Like the NSC, the HSC was involved in intelligence; both groups received intelligence information that was used to develop federal policies.

The creation of the HSC essentially bifurcated the homeland security process: There were now two agencies reporting to the president that had policy authority over national security issues. Wormuth and White (2009) advise that the lack of a single national security advisory body prevented the White House in some instances from being able to act decisively during catastrophes and day-to-day security policy implementation. Stockton (2009) referred this division of powers across the NSC and HSC as a "crippling flaw" (p.1). Wormuth and White recommend that the two councils be merged. Wormuth and White note that there was too little collaboration between the two bodies; the HSC was organizationally weak compared to the NSC, likely the result of the organization being in its infancy, and the HSC had largely been ineffectual.

Analysis Box 8-1

The merging of the Homeland Security Council with the National Security Council was a significant event in terms of managing our security efforts. It resulted in one body having responsibility for examining our security needs. Do you believe that there are differences between domestic and international security needs and, if so, what are those differences? Given that the National Security Council historically was more interested in international threats, do you believe the new format will detract from homeland security?

Essentially, the United States, as a result of the threats imposed by terrorists, should not bifurcate domestic and international security issues. One body should be responsible for all security issues so that consistent, comprehensive policies are developed and implemented. This bifurcation also may have contributed to various intelligence agencies failing to cooperate in sharing information.

In May 2009, President Barack Obama merged the NSC and HSC into one council. As noted earlier, a number of critics had called for the merger. The merger should result in better policy analysis and coordination. Today's conflicts and national security issues are global. It was ineffective to separate domestic and international security concerns—they essentially overlap. Key issues remain, however. First, will the new council provide adequate attention to domestic security? In the past, the international arena has received more attention and importance relative to homeland security. Furthermore, one of the criticisms of the former HSC was that it did not include representatives from state and local governments who ultimately have a tremendous responsibility in preventing and responding to terrorist attacks. They likely will be excluded from the merged council and not have access to information. Second, will there be an increase in coordination and cooperation among the agencies involved in national security? Merging the two councils should clear the way for increased cooperation.

Source: http://www.dni.gov/images/ODNI_seal.jpg

THE DIRECTOR OF NATIONAL INTELLIGENCE

The **director of national intelligence** (DNI) is the titular head of the intelligence community. It advises the president and the National Security Council on intelligence matters related to the national security. Additional duties vested with the DNI include the following:

- Ensure that timely and objective national intelligence is provided to the President, the heads of departments and agencies of the executive branch; the Chairman of the Joint Chiefs of Staff and senior military commanders; and the Congress
- Establish objectives and priorities for collection, analysis, production, and dissemination of national intelligence
- Ensure maximum availability of and access to intelligence information within the Intelligence Community
- Develop and ensure the execution of an annual budget for the National Intelligence program (NIP) based on budget proposals provided by IC [intelligence community] component organizations
- Oversee coordination of relationships with the intelligence or security services of foreign governments and international organizations
- Ensure the most accurate analysis of intelligence is derived from all sources to support national security needs
- Develop personnel policies and programs to enhance the capacity for joint operations and to facilitate staffing of community management functions
- Oversee the development and implementation of a program management plan for acquisition of major systems, doing so jointly with the Secretary of Defense for Department of Defense programs, that includes cost, schedule, and performance goals and program milestone criteria (Office of the Director of National Intelligence, 2009)

These duties squarely place responsibility for managing and coordinating intelligence activities with the DNI. Prior to the creation of the DNI, the intelligence agencies were to a large extent, uncoordinated. There remain some questions relative to the DNI's effectiveness. First, the DNI submits the budgets for the intelligence agencies. In 2008, the intelligence community had more than 100,000 employees and a budget of $47.5 billion (Office of the Director of National Intelligence, 2009). The DNI currently has little control over the agencies' budget formulation or objectives. The agencies submit them to the DNI, who presents them to Congress. For example, 80 percent of the intelligence budget is contained in the Department of Defense. Since the secretary of defense is a cabinet-level position and the DNI is not, it begs the question as to how much control the DNI will have on the overall intelligence budget and its associated objectives.

Second, the DNI has the responsibility of coordinating the agencies comprising the intelligence community. This may prove to be difficult. According to Clarke (2008), significant problems arise with the Department of Defense where the bulk of our intelligence agencies are located and which has the lion's share of the budget. The Department of Defense has been reluctant to relinquish control over its intelligence organs, and indeed, when the DNI was created, then Defense Secretary Rumsfeld fought to keep defense intelligence agencies outside the DNI's scope of control. The Defense Department argues that defense intelligence serves different purposes—it focuses on battlefield intelligence and terrorist and other intelligence is secondary to that purpose. There is some validity to this argument in that the defense role in the war against terrorism is somewhat nebulous and most counterterrorism operations fall outside normal military operations (Morag, 2006). This schism likely will affect the quality of coordination and cooperation among the various intelligence agencies.

As noted earlier, the 9/11 attacks and subsequent legislative and executive changes have resulted in a paradigm shift from an expansive land-war mentality to a more concentrated effort toward combating terrorism and asymmetric warfare. As noted, the Department of Defense retains a "big war" mentality and has been slow to move to a more flexible operational stance, a problem that confronted Defense Secretary Robert Gates in the mid to late 2000s. This philosophy has not only affected intelligence but it also has had an impact on military operations and planning. The armed forces continued to plan for and purchase equipment that would be useful in a large land war, but resisted and developed fewer resources for asymmetric warfare. To some extent, many in the military have not viewed the fight against terrorism as a primary military function (see Clarke, 2008). This initial position hampered our ability to respond to terrorism.

HS Web Link: To learn more about the DNI, go to *http://www.dni.gov/index.html*.

CONCEPTUAL OVERVIEW OF HOMELAND SECURITY INTELLIGENCE

Homeland security has added a new dimension to intelligence. As discussed earlier, in the past, intelligence focused on foreign enemies, and our intelligence activities often centered on foreign lands and activities. Homeland security, on the other hand, is the defense of the American homeland, which substantially expands our collective view of intelligence. This new intelligence perspective is depicted in Figure 8-1.

As shown in Figure 8-1, there basically are four spheres or dimensions relative to intelligence: foreign, domestic, military, and homeland security. In terms of homeland security, the various law enforcement and homeland security agencies are interested in collecting domestic intelligence about impending attacks, terrorists, and terrorist activities. However, since terrorism is substantially international in character, it requires that we look well beyond our borders. Thus, several intelligence agencies within the intelligence community collect foreign intelligence—intelligence about what is transpiring in other countries relative to terrorists and state actions. Military intelligence, on the other hand, has the same view but centers on strategic and tactical military operations. Nonetheless, military perspectives sometimes overlap with terrorist activities, and the military intelligence apparatus obtains information about possible attacks on the United States by terrorists. Finally, as a result of the 9/11 attacks and the need to

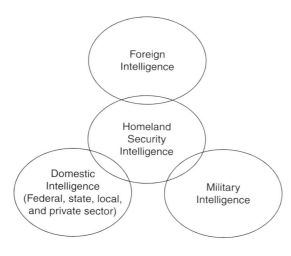

FIGURE 8-1 Framework for Homeland Security Intelligence. *Source:* Masse, T. (2006). *Homeland Security Intelligence: Perceptions, Statutory Definitions, and Approaches.* Washington, D.C.: Congressional Research Service, p. 5.

protect our homeland, local and state police agencies, the first-line homeland defense, have become more actively involved in collecting information about possible terrorists and terrorist plots. Each of these spheres contributes to homeland security intelligence. Part of the intelligence process is to merge or aggregate the information originating from these spheres into coherent information that can be used by policy makers to respond to threats. One of the most significant problems in intelligence sharing occurs here, since many, if not all, intelligence agencies do not like sharing "sources and methods" by which they gather their intelligence with one another, and even more so with domestic law enforcement. There are efforts to combat this problem, but it is still very real and very disconcerting.

TYPES OF INTELLIGENCE COLLECTION ACTIVITIES

Before examining the various intelligence agencies that comprise our intelligence community, it is important to examine the types of intelligence collection activities that agencies use. Many people, when contemplating intelligence, think about James Bond and other similar characters in the entertainment genre. Although governments have spies, they seldom, if ever, are involved in the activities that are displayed on television or in the movies. Indeed, most intelligence activities are mundane; analysts pour over information and attempt to discover answers, trends, and so on. Former DHS Secretary Michael Chertoff (2006) noted,

> Intelligence as you know, is not only about spies and satellites. Intelligence is about the thousands and thousands of routine, everyday observations and activities. Surveillance, interactions—each of which may be taken in isolation as not a particularly meaningful piece of information, but when fused together, gives us a sense of the patterns and the flow that really [are] at the core of what intelligence analysis is all about. . . . We [DHS] actually generate a lot of intelligence . . . we have many interactions every day, every hour at the border, on airplanes, and with the Coast Guard. (p. 1)

As Chertoff indicates, intelligence is the aggregate of volumes of information. It is the sum of the many parts. This sum is achieved only when the necessary information is collected by a variety of agencies and individuals and from a variety of sources. In essence, more comprehensive collection efforts generally result in a more complete intelligence picture. As such, intelligence collection consists of five different types of collection activities (Clarke, 2008; OPSEC, 1996; Richelson, 2008), which will be discussed next.

Human Intelligence

First, **human intelligence or HUMINT** is the collection of intelligence by field agents and other individuals, or human sources. Basically, there are two types of HUMINT. One is clandestine HUMINT, the secret relationships forged between American intelligence personnel and foreign sources. It closely resembles what many perceive as espionage. The other is overt HUMINT, open source intelligence whereby intelligence personnel contact foreign government personnel, read governmental reports, and obtain information that is openly available to the public. Overt HUMINT is most often performed by state department personnel and military attaches and is discussed in more detail later.

FBI agents remove contents from a home following a raid in connection with domestic spying. *Source:* AP (080211018447).

Up until the mid-twentieth century, HUMINT was the primary mode of intelligence gathering. Countries did not have spy satellites or other sophisticated electronics with which to spy on adversaries. Beginning in the 1950s, HUMINT was deemphasized when intelligence agencies began to use technology beginning with spy planes (the U2) and later satellite imaging. The 9/11 attacks demonstrated a significant weakness in our intelligence collection. We had few HUMINT resources, which in large part resulted in our not being able to anticipate the 9/11 attacks, and we had too little information about al Qaeda and other terrorist organizations that desired to attack our homeland (MacGaffin, 2005). Technological spying could not provide us with enough information about terrorist groups since to a large extent, they remain hidden from electronic surveillance. Subsequently, we have increased our HUMINT efforts, and without question, they are the most effective method of obtaining intelligence about terrorist groups. As Betts (2003) notes, "Human intelligence is key because the essence of the terrorist threat is the capacity to conspire. The best way to intercept attacks is to penetrate the organizations, learn their plans, and identify perpetrators so they can be taken out of action" (p. 475). Terrorist organizations or groups evolve or change rapidly. HUMINT, when in place, allows us to collect better and more timely information about their threats.

Analysis Box 8-2

Most of the spy movies and television shows focus on HUMINT. The long-running James Bond movies portray him as involved in HUMINT and getting involved in all sorts of spy-related plots. Do you believe that this genre depicts the actual spy world? How effective would a spy like James Bond be in terms of obtaining intelligence from terrorists?

HUMINT also can be the most problematic, since multiple sources are required to preclude being deceived—information needs to be verified. The Soviets and Chinese, as well as the French and the Israelis, are much better at human intelligence collection than we have ever been.

Today, most HUMINT is performed by the CIA's National Clandestine Service. It operates from our embassies and consulates, which provide it with cover. As embassy or consulate employees, agents of the National Clandestine Service have diplomatic immunity if they are discovered. A number of clandestine officers work under nonofficial cover (NOC). They pose as business persons, scientists, and so on. However, most spying is performed by foreign nationals. American diplomats and other intelligence personnel often recruit these foreign nationals to spy or collect information. They may be opposed to the government or in many cases are attracted by significant payments. Once recruited, they are managed or handled by American intelligence personnel. Most countries rely on this method of collecting intelligence from numerous other countries. As an example, foreign governments likely collect substantial intelligence about the United States by infiltrating our top universities. Universities are open and a source for a considerable amount of information. In addition to scientific information, universities are sometimes involved in numerous defense research projects or projects that can have application in the defense arena.

Signals Intelligence

Signals intelligence or SIGINT includes the interception of electronic communications and deriving intelligence from those communications. These electronic communications consist of a number of different types, including telephone, Internet, facsimile, radio, and radar. The interception of radar allows us to determine the locations of ships, aircraft, and previously unknown military facilities. We monitor telephone and Internet communications in an effort to obtain information about impending attacks and about enemies and organizations. For example, there have been several occasions on which the terrorist threat level has been elevated because of Internet "chatter" among suspected terrorists and terrorist organizations (e.g., see Lumpkin, 2002). All governments and terrorist organizations must communicate for command and control purposes, and these communications potentially can be intercepted. Our SIGINT capabilities have resulted in al Qaeda having to depend less on electronic communications and more on messengers and other forms of face-to-face communications. SIGINT has not prevented the terrorists from communicating among themselves, but it has substantially inhibited them. SIGINT is primarily performed by the National Security Agency.

HS Web Link: To learn more about signals intelligence, go to *http:// www.nsa.gov/sigint/ index.shtml.*

Measures and Signatures Intelligence

The third form of intelligence collection is **measures and signatures intelligence or MASINT,** which falls under the Defense Intelligence Agency. Our government has deployed a variety of electronic sensors throughout the world to gather information. They include radar, infrared, seismic, and radiological detection devices. These sensors are constantly monitored in an effort to collect intelligence on military and nuclear activities. This allows us, for example, to collect information about nuclear programs and nuclear-powered vessels. A spectrographic analysis of a rocket can provide information about the propellant that the rocket is using, which in turn advises of the sophistication of the rocket program. Generally, MASINT is targeted or focused on a location or particular activity. MASINT is extremely important in determining other countries' military capabilities and movements. For example, MASINT is a primary source of information about North Korea's nuclear program. Today, there is a push in the MASINT arena to counter improvised explosive devices (IEDs).

Imagery Intelligence

The fourth form of intelligence gathering is **imagery analysis or IMINT**, which is housed with the National Geospatial-Intelligence Agency. The forerunner of IMINT was the U2 spy plane program, which began in the mid-1950s. The planes flew at 70,000 feet and provided surveillance of the Soviet Union, other Soviet bloc countries, and other countries of interest. For example, it was a U2 plane that provided evidence that the Russians had moved nuclear missiles into Cuba in 1962. Today, our image intelligence has become more sophisticated through satellite imagery. We have deployed satellites that provide significant detail. They are used to monitor government activities in countries such as Russia and China, and they are used to monitor terrorist activities in numerous Middle Eastern countries. For example, we attempt to monitor terrorist movements and training camps in countries such as Afghanistan and Pakistan through imagery. IMINT provides a wealth of information. Unfortunately, up until the 9/11 attacks, the United States overly depended on IMINT and neglected HUMINT. IMINT can provide macro information, but when dealing with terrorists and an asymmetric war, we often need micro information. However, IMINT has been steadily improving with advances in technology, and we are now better able to capture more detailed information through imagery.

A major problem today with IMINT is the commercial availability of imagery information. For example, Google Earth provides image information throughout the world. Terrorists now can search Google Earth and obtain intelligence information about potential targets and countermeasures. Although not as sophisticated as military images, these commercially available sites substantially make infrastructure protection more difficult. At the request of governments across the globe, Google Earth has removed military and other sensitive installations from its maps; nonetheless, it can be used to identify and conduct surveillance on numerous potential terrorist targets.

HS Web Link: To learn more about imagery intelligence, go to *http://www.fas.org/irp/imint/index.html*.

Open Source Intelligence

The final form of intelligence gathering is **open source intelligence or OSINT**. Today, vast quantities of information are available through public or open records, and much of that information is available through the Internet. Intelligence analysts are increasingly using the Internet to collect information. In some cases, it can provide hard intelligence about a specific activity; in other cases, it can be used to collect background information about a problem. Numerous online technical journals provide an abundance of information about conventional weapons, nuclear energy and weapons, and other technology that is useful to a country. For example, some analysts have estimated that the Soviet Union derives approximately 90 percent of its intelligence from open sources (OPSEC, 1996). Most, if not all, terrorist organizations

---

Analysis Box 8-3

Open source intelligence can provide substantial amounts of information about a variety of important security topics, especially considering the amount of information that is now posted on the Internet and is in scientific journals that are being published. Based on your experience reading newspapers and other publications or doing library research, can you identify any materials that may be of interest to a foreign government? Do you believe we should restrict information that is publically available? Why?

---

have websites. They are being monitored and analysts sometimes find information that is useful in the war on terrorism.

This discussion provides an overview of the various types of intelligence collection modes. As can be seen, intelligence is a discipline that uses a number of methodologies and collects vast amounts of information from numerous sources. Once collected, the information must be collated and analyzed. That is, all the pieces must come together at one point so that analysts and policy makers can see the overall or total picture. One of the primary responsibilities of the director of national intelligence is to ensure that this occurs. It has not always occurred in the past, which has led to intelligence failures.

AGENCIES WITHIN THE AMERICAN INTELLIGENCE COMMUNITY

As discussed earlier, the director of national intelligence is now responsible for coordinating our intelligence efforts. Sixteen agencies currently comprise the intelligence community, as listed in Figure 8-2 (Office of the Director of National Intelligence, 2009). Each of the primary agencies will be briefly examined in terms of its role in homeland security.

- *Central Intelligence Agency*
- *Defense Intelligence Agency*
- *Department of Energy* (Office of Intelligence and Counterintelligence)
- *Department of Homeland Security* (Office of Intelligence and Analysis)
- *Department of State* (Bureau of Intelligence and Research)
- *Department of Treasury* (Office of Intelligence and Analysis)
- *Drug Enforcement Administration* (Office of National Security Intelligence)
- *Federal Bureau of Investigation* (National Security Branch)
- *National Geospatial-Intelligence Agency*
- *National Reconnaissance Office*
- *National Security Agency*
- *U.S. Air Force*
- *U.S. Army*
- *U.S. Coast Guard*
- *U.S. Marines*
- *U.S. Navy*

FIGURE 8-2   Agencies within the American Intelligence Network.

Central Intelligence Agency

The **Central Intelligence Agency** (CIA) was created in 1947 with the passage of the National Security Act. The act also created the position of director of central intelligence, a position held by the director of the CIA. The director of central intelligence was tasked with coordinating our intelligence functions. As such, the CIA became the lead intelligence agency (CIA, 2009). However, this was changed in 2004 when the director of national intelligence (DNI) position was created with the passage of the Intelligence Reform and Terrorist Prevention Act. The DNI now is responsible for coordinating intelligence efforts and ensuring cooperation.

Today, the CIA uses a variety of methods to collect intelligence, with an emphasis on human intelligence. As noted, it has operatives stationed throughout the world, making contacts and collecting HUMINT. Once intelligence is collected, the agency is responsible for collating the information and providing answers to questions posed by policy makers in the White House, Congress, State Department, and other executive offices. Essentially, analysts pour through volumes of information looking for relationships and, more or less, connecting the dots. It collects intelligence in foreign countries, whereas the Federal Bureau of Investigation is responsible for collecting domestic intelligence.

Perhaps the best way to understand the CIA is to examine its primary operational components. The agency is divided into four directorates: National Clandestine Service, Intelligence, Science and Technology, and Support. The **National Clandestine Service** is the agency's clandestine arm. It coordinates and evaluates clandestine human intelligence operations across the intelligence community. It conducts clandestine activities to collect information that is not obtainable through other means, and it conducts counterintelligence and special activities as authorized by the president. The National Clandestine Service has operatives in countries throughout the world. The **Intelligence Directorate** provides timely, accurate, and objective all-source intelligence analysis on the full range of national security and foreign policy issues to the president, cabinet, and senior policy makers in the U.S. government. For example, this directorate until recently provided the president's Daily Brief and World Intelligence Review; now there is shared responsibility for these reports, but the directorate still provides substantial input. The Intelligence Directorate is responsible for collating intelligence information and delivering it in a usable form for policy makers. Its analysts pour through volumes of information and use this information to make judgments about policy and strategic issues. The **Science and Technology Directorate** is responsible for the technical support of clandestine officers in the field. It advises the clandestine officers on technical operations and matters that are involved in activities such as audio and video surveillance. This directorate also provides secure communications for CIA personnel and assets. Finally, the **Support Directorate** supports and maintains buildings and infrastructure, ensuring that they have the capacity to operate effectively and securely (CIA, 2009).

The CIA has played an active role in the war against terrorism and has received substantial criticism for some of its tactics. Most notably, the agency became involved in renditions of suspected terrorists and supporters and the operation of "black ops" prisons across the world. Generally, criminals were transferred from one country to another through the process of extradition, a legal process that normally is conducted within the judicial systems of the countries involved. On the other hand, extraordinary rendition or irregular rendition is a process whereby the courts are bypassed and subjects are summarily and unwillingly moved from one country to another and the procedure is a violation of international treaties (see Garcia, 2009). After the 9/11 attacks, U.S. intelligence agencies, principally the CIA, conducted numerous extraordinary renditions of terrorist suspects, often transporting them to countries where the host country would imprison and torture the subjects.

At the same time, the agency was operating black ops prisons or unofficial, secretive prisons in other countries where rendition subjects were held and sometimes aggressively interrogated or tortured, depending on the definition of torture. The primary mode of torture or intensive interrogation was water boarding, which was approved by the White House. The effectiveness of such procedures has been questioned in a number of quarters for its legality and effectiveness. For example, it was reported that Khalid Sheikh Mohammed was water boarded 183 times in one month (Times Online, 2009). In another example, according to a former CIA interrogator, it took only 35 seconds of water boarding to break Abu Zubayduh, a chief recruiter for al Qaeda, who revealed substantial information about al Qaeda terrorist plots (Zagorin, 2007). Yet, it was later learned that Zubayduh actually had been water boarded 83 times. The number of times that these suspects were water boarded, especially Mohammed, brings into question the effectiveness of the technique. Did it take 183 water boarding sessions for Mohammed and 83 for Zubayduh to elicit information? Did the water boarding result in credible or true information? The torture question was further exacerbated when in 2009, it was revealed that the CIA had destroyed 92 videotapes of water boarding (Fox News, 2009). The Obama administration declared that our intelligence and defense agencies will refrain from torture.

Investigators for the European Parliament estimated that the CIA conducted hundreds of unauthorized flights over European territory largely for the purpose of renditions. As an example, a senior prosecutor in Milan, Italy, charged that the CIA abducted a suspect, Abu Omar, in broad daylight in Milan and the CIA flew him to Egypt where he was interrogated (Belifsky, 2006). Several foreign countries have lodged complaints over U.S. rendition and black ops prisons. The rendition program was not new; it began in President Clinton's administration (Lake, 2009). Essentially, the CIA historically has not had assets to collect human intelligence planted within terrorist groups, and renditions and black ops prisons became an alternative method by which to collect needed human intelligence.

It is not widely known that the CIA is also involved in paramilitary operations. For example, the CIA was intimately involved in the 2001 battle at Tora Bora in Afghanistan. The CIA had tracked bin Laden to the area, and CIA personnel and local assets along with military personnel attempted to capture or kill him. Although bin Laden escaped, the battle demonstrated the CIA's paramilitary capabilities. This later became an issue with the 9/11 Commission, which recommended that all paramilitary operations be vested with military special operational forces (Best and Freickert, 2006). However, critics of the commission's recommendation maintain that CIA paramilitary operations assist the agency in collecting human intelligence; the CIA was more flexible and able to respond more quickly than the military; and it is the only agency that is authorized to pay local paramilitary and other groups that work with the United States, as was done with the Northern Alliance in Iraq in the early years of the Iraqi War (House Select Committee on Intelligence, 1996; Weisman, 2001). The military, in too many instances, has been too bureaucratic and has not had the ability to quickly respond to situations calling for rapid paramilitary intervention. Regardless, we see that the CIA is involved in operations that go beyond the collection of intelligence.

HS Web Link: To learn more about the CIA, go to *https://www.cia.gov/*.

Defense Intelligence Agency

The **Defense Intelligence Agency** (DIA) is housed in the Pentagon and is the agency primarily responsible for military intelligence. As such, it focuses on strategic and tactical military operations. It is responsible for providing military-related intelligence and counterintelligence information to the secretary and deputy secretary of defense, chairman of the Joint Chiefs of Staff, and the director of national intelligence. The DIA is the military's equivalent of the CIA, except that the DIA is more directly involved in collecting a wider range of intelligence, including human, signal, scientific and technological, and imagery. In other words, the DIA is concerned with all sources of intelligence whereby information is collected through a variety of means and then collated and analyzed to

Source: http://www.dni.gov/overview.pdf

provide answers to policy, strategic, and tactical questions. Although the DIA is primarily concerned with defense-related intelligence, as a result of the terrorism threat and the level of terrorist activities across the globe, over the past decade, the DIA has applied more efforts to these activities. The trend to a great extent has shifted from traditional wars and battles to asymmetric warfare. As such, the DIA plays a key role in collecting terrorism intelligence, especially in those instances when insurgency operations will affect national security and U.S. military operations (DIA, 2009).

The DIA is concerned with a broad array of security and intelligence initiatives. Vice Admiral Thomas Wilson (2001), then director of the DIA, identified several areas of concern:

- Possible terrorist attacks
- Worsening conditions in the Middle East
- Dramatic changes in the Korean Peninsula
- An expanded conflict between India and Pakistan over Kashmir
- Intensifying disagreements with Russia
- Increased anti-American violence and regional instability, particularly south of the border
- Another outbreak of violence in the Balkans
- Conflict between China and Taiwan (p. 7)

This listing demonstrates the broad and expansive concerns confronting the United States and our military. It is noteworthy that our national security concerns involve problems or conflicts that are dispersed throughout the world. Even though these problems are located on continents far from our shores, they ultimately will have some national security impact on the United States. Finally, the list demonstrates that there is a mixture of conventional as well as asymmetric concerns. Although several of these problems involve countries and the possibility of conventional warfare, most involve terrorism and insurgency. This trend has resulted in new thinking within the

Analysis Box 8-4

The DIA is one of the largest intelligence agencies in the United States, and it is involved in a wide range of intelligence activities. As noted, its primary mission is to collect strategic and tactical intelligence for military operations.

Do you see instances when this type of intelligence would be useful to homeland security? What types of intelligence information does the military need, and what kind of information is vital to homeland security?

Department of Defense as more resources are being devoted to counterinsurgency programming. It also necessitates that the DIA work more closely with other intelligence agencies.

Department of Energy

The **Department of Energy** (DOE) is responsible for maintaining U.S. energy supplies, promoting energy research, and procuring additional sources of energy. As such, nuclear energy is one of the DOE's primary responsibilities. This responsibility includes securing nuclear plants, materials, and by-products, since these materials can be used to construct a weapon of mass destruction. In addition, the DOE ensures the integrity and safety of the country's nuclear weapons; promotes international nuclear safety; advances nuclear nonproliferation; and provides safe, efficient nuclear power plants for the U.S. Navy (DOE, 2009). Naval nuclear power plants are regulated by the DOE since many of the navy's ships are nuclear powered.

The DOE has several intelligence and security programs to fulfill this mandate. First, it has a cyber security program. Since the DOE has a substantial amount of information relative to

Source: http://www.management.energy.gov/images/
New_DOE_Seal_Black_ScreenExampleOnly_ 060208.jpg

The DOE provides timely technical intelligence analysis on all aspects of foreign nuclear weapons, nuclear materials, and energy issues worldwide. *Source:* http://www.intelligence.gov/images/thumbnails/homepage_jobSpotlight_option4.jpg

nuclear energy and weapons, the DOE has a cyber security program to protect this information. Cyber security is important since most nuclear facilities are operated via computer controls and systems. Second, the DOE promulgates security regulations for the nuclear energy industry. These regulations ensure that nuclear materials receive the utmost security. Third, the DOE is involved in preventing the spread of weapons of mass destruction by providing expertise and technical analysis of foreign programs to determine if such weapons can be developed. For example, DOE personnel have been involved in analyzing Iran's nuclear programs. The DOE also attempts to detect nuclear-related activities such as those that have been conducted in North Korea. The DOE plays a key role in the collection and analysis of nuclear-related intelligence. The department's counterintelligence program is designed to collect information about these activities and prevent foreign governments or groups from obtaining materials and information.

HS Web Link: To learn more about the DOE's intelligence operations, go to *http://www.energy.gov/nationalsecurity/intelligence_counterterrorism.htm.*

Department of Homeland Security

The **Department of Homeland Security** (DHS) maintains a sizable intelligence function as part of its operations to provide national homeland security. The DHS's **Office of Intelligence and Analysis** is responsible for coordinating the department's intelligence efforts. In addition to analyzing intelligence information, the office coordinates the intelligence received from DHS agencies, including

- U.S. Citizenship and Immigration Services (USCIS)
- U.S. Coast Guard
- U.S. Customs and Border Protection (CBP)
- U.S. Immigration and Customs Enforcement (ICE)
- Transportation Security Administration (TSA) (DHS, 2009)

As noted in Chapters 2 and 3, the DHS is responsible for protecting the homeland, which is an expansive responsibility. Of particular interest to the department is the protection of our critical infrastructure, as discussed in Chapter 3. The DHS is involved in collecting and using intelligence to achieve this mission. In order to accomplish this mission, the DHS has identified five intelligence priorities:

- Threats to border security, including human trafficking, narcotics smuggling, money laundering, and transnational threats
- Threats of radicalization and extremism, particularly from Sunni and Shiite groups, whereby the department attempts to monitor the processes that attract and indoctrinate potential members
- Threats from particular groups that may attempt to import materials for weapons of mass destruction and people entering or traveling to the United States who may be terrorists or potential terrorists
- Protection of the nation's critical infrastructure, including working with local and state governments and the private sector in developing plans and operational guidelines that safeguard these assets
- Safeguarding against weapons of mass destruction attacks, including the identification of individuals and groups that may become involved in such attacks (DHS, 2009)

Given these five priorities, it becomes obvious that the DHS has a considerable obligation to collect intelligence. For the most part, the five primary operational DHS agencies (listed earlier) have extensive intelligence operations. For example, the U.S. Coast Guard has port and waterways security responsibilities. This is an immense responsibility for preventing all sorts of smuggling, including weapons of mass destruction. The U.S. Coast Guard is also a member of the intelligence community, providing direct feedback to the director of national intelligence. The U.S. Citizenship and Immigration Service interacts with large numbers of illegal immigrants, some of whom may be involved in terrorist or criminal activities. The U.S. Customs and Border Protection has the responsibility for securing our borders and preventing potential terrorists from entering the United States. This requires the collection and analysis of information about people who have entered or who are attempting to enter. U.S. Immigration and Customs Enforcement (ICE) is responsible for investigating all sorts of illegal aliens in the United States, including potential terrorists and criminals. This agency collects a substantial amount of information on these people. Finally, the Transportation Security Administration provides security for our airports and flights, and historically, the airlines have been prime targets for terrorists, resulting in a significant intelligence responsibility. The DHS's Office of Intelligence and Analysis coordinates these intelligence activities.

Complicating the DHS's intelligence mission is its need to work with state and local governments as well as other federal agencies. In the past, intelligence information was shared with other agencies on a "need to know" basis. This resulted in federal agencies being unwilling to work with state and local agencies. Since the DHS has responsibility for securing our national critical infrastructure, it must work with state and local agencies. An important part of this cooperative relationship is the sharing of intelligence. Local and state law enforcement, essentially, are the front line in terms of providing infrastructure protection. One method of sharing intelligence has been the development of fusion centers where local, state, and federal agencies in a geographical area receive and analyze localized intelligence (fusion centers are discussed in more detail in Chapter 14). Moreover, state and local agencies, since they are on the front lines, potentially have numerous opportunities to gather information of local and sometimes national importance regarding terrorist threats.

Source: http://www.state.gov/

Department of State

The **State Department** is responsible for American foreign relations. The department maintains embassies and consulates across the world. These embassies and consulates interact with foreign governmental officials on a daily basis, attempting to solve problems and to ensure that we have the best relations possible with the various countries. As such, the State Department is very interested in the political, social, and economic problems confronting these countries. Within this mix of concerns are terrorist activities, since they may undermine legitimate governments or result in attacks on our country. The State Department actively collects intelligence within these countries relative to political, social, and economic issues. Our embassies and consulates often are the headquarters or operational points for CIA and other intelligence operatives working in these countries.

The State Department's primary unit for intelligence is the **Bureau of Intelligence and Research**. The bureau is a member of the intelligence community and thus shares information with the other 15 intelligence agencies. This provides the bureau with a substantial amount of information on countries. The focal point of the bureau's work is to ensure that intelligence activities support foreign policy and national security purposes. In other words, the bureau is interested in intelligence that advises of activities and changes in a country that could result in shifts in American foreign policy or alert our policy makers on impending international problems. For example, the State Department monitors the political activities in countries such as Pakistan. If the government of Pakistan becomes unstable, it would substantially increase the likelihood that terrorists would obtain nuclear weapons. The State Department must monitor the governments of other countries so that our foreign policies are consistent with prevailing conditions.

In some cases, the State Department is involved in counterintelligence when attempting to change conditions within a specific country (Department of State, 2009). Terrorism and weapons of mass destruction are two primary concerns for the State Department. Regarding terrorism, the State Department monitors terrorist activities within countries, using a range of sources. This information is used by our diplomats to negotiate with governments to enact policies that will reduce terrorist activities and other threats to American national security. The State Department routinely pressures and negotiates with foreign governments for these purposes. The State Department negotiates with foreign governments in an effort to reduce the spread of nuclear weapons and other weapons of mass destruction. The spread of nuclear weapons is a direct threat to the well-being of the United States.

HS Web Link: To learn more about State Department intelligence operations, go to *http://www.state.gov/s/inr/.*

Department of the Treasury

The **Treasury Department** plays a key role in homeland security. As discussed later in Chapter 11, terrorist financing and money laundering are primary concerns in the war on terrorism. We must make every effort to cut off or reduce the funding available to terrorist organizations and their supporters, and the Treasury Department is the lead agency in the attempt to accomplish this objective. The **Office of Terrorism and Financial Intelligence** within the Treasury Department has the responsibility for combating a number of financial crimes and irregularities. Its focus is to provide (1) expert analysis and intelligence production on financial and other support networks for terrorist groups, proliferators, and other key national security threats and (2) timely, accurate, and focused intelligence support on the full range of economic, political, and security issues (Department of Treasury, 2009).

Source: http://www.treas.gov/education/fact-sheets/history/treas-seal.shtml

As the intelligence gathering and analysis arm of the Treasury Department, the Office of Terrorism and Financial Intelligence attempts to safeguard the financial system against illicit uses, including money laundering and the illicit movement of money, and combats rogue nations, terrorists and terrorist organizations, weapons of mass destruction proliferators, money launderers, narcotics organizations, and other national security threats (Department of Treasury, 2009). These objectives are achieved through several mechanisms. First, the **Office of Foreign Assets Control** enforces economic and trade sanctions that have been implemented against different countries and groups. These sanctions are used against repressive regimes and terrorist organizations in an effort to gain compliance regarding trade, human rights, and terrorist activities. For example, we have had sanctions against North Korea because of its nuclear weapons program. We have also implemented sanctions against a number of terrorist organizations, including al Qaeda, Hamas, and Hezbollah. As such, the Treasury Department maintains a list of organizations and countries that are sanctioned by the U.S. government.

The **Financial Crimes Network** (FinCEN) is operated by the Treasury Department and is a network connecting local, state, and federal law enforcement in financial crimes investigations. In the past, FinCEN has focused on a number of financial crimes such as money laundering, drug assets, and fraud. In some cases, these financial crimes are used to facilitate terrorist activities or groups, and FinCEN has taken an active role in this arena.

HS Web Link: To learn more about FinCEN, go to *http://www.fincen.gov/.*

Drug Enforcement Administration

The **Drug Enforcement Administration** (DEA) is the central agency in the United States for combating the worldwide drug problem. One of its primary missions is to interdict drugs coming into the United States from foreign countries. The DEA has agents stationed in 56 countries

Source: http://www.justice.gov/dea/dea_circlelogo.gif

(DEA, 2009). These agents monitor drug activities in the host countries and work with local police agencies to eliminate or reduce the production of drugs and their flow from the host country. The DEA is involved in the collection of homeland security intelligence for two primary reasons. First, the drug problem is international in scope and in some cases threatens to topple legitimate governments. For example, perhaps the greatest national security threat to the United States in coming years is the lawlessness in Mexico as a result of the drug cartels. Some believe that the Mexican government may fail as a result of the narco-terrorism. Second, a number of terrorist groups are now using narcotics trafficking as a way to raise money. For example, a number of terrorist groups including al Qaeda are involved in the heroin trade in Afghanistan. In 2007, the DEA arrested Mohammad Essa for conspiring to import $25 million worth of heroin from Afghanistan and Pakistan into the United States. He was a member of the Baz Mohammad trafficking organization, which is closely aligned with the Taliban and has provided it financial support (MacKinzie-Mulvey, 2007). Thus, drug enforcement is an important part of the war on terrorism and requires a substantial intelligence effort.

The DEA organization contains an Intelligence Division. As noted, there is overlap between drug trafficking and terrorist activities, and in some cases, it is difficult to separate or distinguish the two criminal activities. The inclusion of the DEA in the intelligence community allows the United States to more effectively respond to terrorism by identifying narco-terrorist organizations and money laundering schemes. Other intelligence organizations likely can provide the DEA with information that will assist the agency in attacking large-scale drug trafficking operations, and the reverse is true whereby the DEA may develop intelligence information on drug

Narco submarine captured in Ecuador.   *Source:* http://www.justice.gov/dea/photos/narco-sub/11.jpg

Source: http://www.dni.gov/overview.pdf

trafficking that may assist other agencies in identifying terrorist activities. The DEA, however, has been resistant to efforts by the director of national intelligence to subordinate its intelligence functions. The DEA wants its intelligence apparatus to focus on drug trafficking, which is not always a critical function as identified by the director of national intelligence.

Federal Bureau of Investigation

After the 9/11 attacks, the **Federal Bureau of Investigation** (FBI) made a number of significant organizational changes that resulted in the bureau being more actively involved in counterterrorism. The bureau had received considerable criticism for allegedly not following up leads that may have identified the plot prior to the attacks. This perceived ineffectiveness resulted in calls ranging from reorganizing the FBI to the creation of a new domestic spy service similar to those in other countries (9/11 Commission, 2004; Posner, 2006). The attacks and criticism resulted in a number of organizational and mission changes in the FBI, and today, the FBI has a significant homeland security and intelligence responsibility. Foremost, the FBI is responsible for criminal law enforcement, domestic counterintelligence, and domestic counterterrorism. Essentially, the FBI is responsible for rooting out, identifying, and thwarting terrorist plots that occur on American soil. The FBI is responsible for a vast array of intelligence and counterintelligence operations, including cyber terrorism and crimes, weapons of mass destruction, and counterintelligence.

One of the significant changes in the FBI was the establishment of a National Security Branch, which is headed by an assistant director. The **National Security Branch** contains units that focus on intelligence, counterintelligence, counterterrorism, and weapons of mass destruction.

In addition, the FBI maintains **LEGIT or legal attaches** in a number of countries. These LEGITs are involved in collecting intelligence and counterterrorism activities, especially intelligence about threats or possible attacks on the United States. The FBI has a significant intelligence and counter-terrorism function, since the bureau has the primary responsibility for combating terrorists and attacks on American soil. In the past, the FBI collected intelligence relative to specific cases. Today, however, agents collect a broader spectrum of intelligence information—they collect information about any and all possible terrorists and terrorist events.

In 2009, it was announced that the FBI would initiate the **global justice initiative**, a program whereby FBI agents would interview terror suspects throughout the world (Meyer, 2009). It is reasoned that all terror suspects eventually will be tried in a court of law either in the United States or another country. In the past the CIA's handling of suspects has prevented many of them from being tried due to dubious or coerced evidence. Terrorists were handled as a military or intelligence problem rather than a law enforcement or justice-related problem. The FBI's involvement will ensure that a larger number of such cases can be taken to the courts, especially considering that the agents have long adhered to noncoercive interrogation techniques. Evidence obtained by agents will likely pass judicial scrutiny.

JOINT TERRORISM TASK FORCE The **Joint Terrorism Task Force** (JTTF) is a national, multi-agency organization that has the responsibility of combating terrorist activities in the United States. The JTTF is headquartered in Washington, D.C., but there are 66 field JTTF offices across the United States. They are led by the FBI and the Justice Department. Essentially, the JTTFs are "small cells" of highly trained, locally based investigators, analysts, linguists, SWAT experts, and other specialists from U.S. law enforcement and intelligence agencies. It is a multiagency effort to combine the resources of local, state, and federal law enforcement (DOJ, 2009). Agencies comprising the JTTF are listed in Figure 8-3.

- FBI
- U.S. Marshals Service
- Bureau of Alcohol, Tobacco and Firearms
- U.S. Secret Service
- U.S. State Department/Diplomatic Security Service
- Immigration and Customs Enforcement
- U.S. Border Patrol
- Postal Inspection Service
- Treasury Inspector General for Tax Administration
- Internal Revenue Service
- U.S. Park Police
- Federal Protective Service
- Department of Interior's Bureau of Land Management
- Defense Criminal Investigative Service
- Air Force Office of Special Investigations
- U.S. Army
- Naval Criminal Investigative Service
- Central Intelligence Agency
- State & Local Law Enforcement

FIGURE 8-3 JTTF Member Agencies.

Analysis Box 8-5

The FBI has jurisdiction and responsibility for counter-intelligence on American soil. To some extent, the bureau is the domestic equivalent of the CIA. Perform a search of newspapers and identify a couple of terrorism cases the FBI has made. What kinds of cases does the bureau make? How do these cases fit into homeland security? Does any other agency have similar responsibilities?

Several agencies in the JTTF are also members of the national intelligence community. However, several other agencies that are not members of the national intelligence community have law enforcement responsibilities and may become involved in terrorist-related investigations. In addition, the JTTFs include state and local law enforcement. This comprehensive membership helps ensure that critical intelligence information is shared with agencies that may become involved in a terrorist threat. It also results in all domestic terrorism intelligence being assembled and analyzed in one organization, which results in a more comprehensive and complete examination of information. The inclusion of agencies such as the CIA ensures that international intelligence related to threats to the American homeland is distributed to domestic agencies.

Finally, the FBI is involved in establishing fusion centers at the local level (discussed in more detail in Chapter 14). The fusion centers are composed of FBI agents, other federal law enforcement personnel, state and local police officials, and other public safety officials such as fire and medical emergency. The fusion centers operate in similar fashion as the JTTFs. Personnel associated with the fusion centers provide intelligence information to the group that is disseminated and examined. They focus on possible terrorists and terrorist activities and serve as an early warning system. Information collected at the fusion center level is directed to the FBI and the JTTFs. The fusion centers represent a concerted and coordinated intelligence effort at the lowest level.

National Geospatial-Intelligence Agency

The **National Geospatial-Intelligence Agency** (NGA) is housed in the Department of Defense. It is a combat support agency, meaning that its primary function is to support military operations. However, it now plays a dominant role in counterterrorism and homeland security. Essentially, the NGA acquires and produces imagery and map-based intelligence information in support of national defense, homeland security, and navigation safety. The term *geospatial intelligence* means the exploitation and analysis of imagery and geospatial information to describe, assess, and visually depict physical features and geographically referenced activities on the earth (NGA, 2009). This is accomplished by tasking, whereby imagery is obtained usually by requesting specific images from a variety of agencies and disseminating information to consumer intelligence and tactical agencies.

In many cases, the information collected and processed by NGA is tailored for customer-specific solutions. That is, consumers of intelligence may request specific geospatial information that is provided by the NGA. By giving customers ready access to geospatial intelligence, NGA provides support to civilian and military leaders and contributes to the state of readiness of U.S. military forces. The agency provides other agencies with images and information associated with the images—merging demographic data and information with imagery. NGA also contributes to humanitarian efforts, such as tracking floods and disaster support, and to peacekeeping. This requires that the agency maintain a substantial number of images and maps (NGA, 2009). The NGA also has a cadre of analysts, who are tasked with the responsibility of monitoring and analyzing specific problems such as Iran's battle plans, Russia's strategic rocket forces, and so on.

HS Web Link: To learn more about the NGA, go to *https://www1.nga.mil/Pages/Default.aspx*

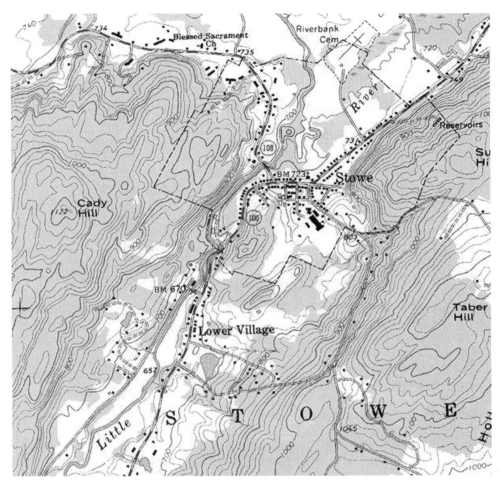

Example of a topographical map produced by the NGA.   *Source:* https://www1.nga.mil/
ProductsServices/TopographicalTerrestrial/Pages/default.aspx

National Reconnaissance Office

The **National Reconnaissance Office** (NRO) is responsible for maintaining our country's system of satellite surveillance. The director of the NRO reports to the director of national intelligence and to the secretary of defense. Satellite imagery plays a key role in military operations, and today, it is important in tracking terrorists and their activities. Moreover, the NRO can provide "real-time" on-the-ground imagery—it allows operatives to actively observe events as they transpire. For example, al Qaeda training camps can be observed and terrorist movements can be identified. Images also provide a wealth of intelligence about activities throughout the world. The agency provides imagery information to a variety of civilian and defense agencies, and the images are used to make tactical and strategic decisions. For example, the NRO manages satellites and listening posts that are used by the National Security Agency to gather signals intelligence. It also provides the National Geospatial Agency with images.

HS Web Link: To learn more about the NRO, go to: *http://www.nro.gov/.*

Source: http://www.dni.gov/overview.pdf

Source: http://www.nsa.gov/about/_images/nsa_logo.jpg

National Security Agency

Up until a relatively few years ago, the **National Security Agency** (NSA) remained a secret agency within our intelligence community. Many joked that NSA stood for "No Such Agency" or "Never Say Anything." Regardless, the NSA is involved in signals intelligence. The agency collects signals intelligence from a variety of sources, including foreign communications, radar, and electronic communications. The agency uses U.S. embassies, ships, aircraft, and other locations to monitor communications. Information is collected in other countries in a variety of languages and dialects, necessitating that the NSA have a large number of language interpreters. As an example, Osama bin Laden and other al Qaeda operatives now must use primitive communications methods, face-to-face, notes, and so on because any electronic communications such as via telephones can be intercepted by the NSA. Obviously, the NSA is concerned with intercepting signals relative to terrorist plots that may occur in the United States. Many of the signals collected are coded, requiring the agency to be extensively involved in code breaking. The NSA collects signals information and provides that information to other members of the intelligence community where it is used to make tactical and strategic decisions (NSA, 2009).

The NSA plays a considerable role in the collection of intelligence. For example, Shorrock (2008) notes that about 60 percent of the information contained in the president's Daily Briefs is derived from intelligence collected by the NSA. The NSA works closely with the NRO in that the NRO operates the nation's satellites and ground stations that intercept signals. A primary consumer of NSA information is the CIA, whose analysts examine signals, telephone calls, and e-mails that are intercepted by the NSA. However, this relationship is not always cordial. For example, the NSA was criticized for not sharing transcripts of cell phone conversations of al Qaeda operatives during the run-up to the 9/11 attacks (see Shorrock, 2008).

Armed Services Intelligence

As noted in Figure 8-1, each branch of the armed services, Army, Navy, Air Force, Marine Corp, and Coast Guard, has intelligence operations that are interconnected with those of other intelligence agencies, especially the Defense Intelligence Agency. The U.S. Coast Guard is part of the Department of Homeland Security and collects and provides intelligence to the Departments of Homeland Security and Defense. The U.S. Coast Guard's mission centers on securing our marine borders and our ports. The U.S. Coast Guard is interested in ships and people who are entering the United States via waterways, and it monitors marine activities. For example, all ships approaching the United States must provide a 96-hour notice of arrival. The agency's **Coastwatch Program** analyzes the manifests for prohibited materials and people who may be on watch lists. The Coast Guard sometimes tasks or directs satellites from the National Reconnaissance Office or the military to observe marine activities and gather intelligence on arriving vessels (Richelson, 2008). The agency works closely with the Customs and Border Protection Agency in securing our ports.

The Army, Navy, Air Force, and Marine Corp have specific intelligence missions that focus on tactical operations. The branches of the military must collect information that assists them when deploying on the battlefield. They are involved in collecting a variety of human, signal, imagery, and technical intelligence. Generally, they are involved in collecting information relative to specific tactical situations. For example, the Army collects information on all sorts of groups in Afghanistan. This information is used to identify enemies, enemy operations, and potential targets, which is especially critical in an asymmetric war. It also collects intelligence on other countries' military operations, since this information is useful in discovering their battlefield strategies and new capabilities. These activities are coordinated with the DIA.

INTERSECTION OF POLICY DECISIONS AND INTELLIGENCE: THE INTELLIGENCE CYCLE

The preceding sections outlined the various intelligence agencies and their operations. As can be seen, the gathering and analysis of intelligence are complicated matters that involve a host of agencies. They involve the collection of homeland security intelligence as well as military and government-related intelligence. They involve civilian agencies as well as military agencies. They center on military and asymmetric threats. Nonetheless, once intelligence is collected, it must be organized into a usable form. This section briefly examines the relationship between policy makers and intelligence. Policy makers are consumers of intelligence, and intelligence is an important ingredient in many of the decisions that are made.

Clarke (2008) and Richelson (2008) have outlined how policy makers intersect with intelligence. It is a five-step process known as the **intelligence cycle** and consists of (1) planning and direction, (2) collection, (3) processing and exploitation, (4) analysis and production, and (5) dissemination, as depicted in Figure 8-4.

Planning and direction refers to the management of the intelligence process and is conducted by the White House, the director of national intelligence, the National Security Council, agency heads, and other consumers of intelligence. Here, consumers request specific information from the intelligence community about a problem, country, activity, or group. For example, the Department of State or Department of Energy may request information about nuclear proliferation in Pakistan, Iran, or North Korea. In some cases, they collect information about specific national security issues; in other cases, they amass information about persons, places,

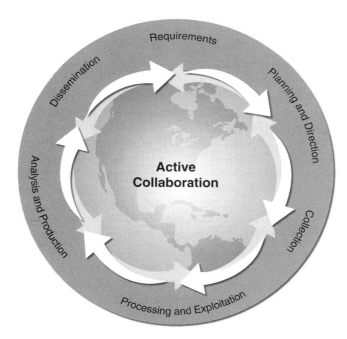

FIGURE 8-4 Intelligence Cycle. *Source:* http://www.fbi.gov/intelligence/images/active_collaboration.jpg

and activities, keeping in mind that specific information about them may be required or requested in the future. Processing occurs when information is collated and stored so that it can be easily retrieved and used. During the analysis and production phase, analysts pour through the information, connect information, and apply the information to specific problems or issues. Finally, the information must be disseminated to policy makers or intelligence consumers. In some cases, the information is provided as a result of specific requests; in other cases, the analysts identify issues and alert the policy makers. For example, the president's Daily Brief, produced by the CIA, is an attempt to keep the president abreast of national security issues throughout the world. Policy makers then apply the information when deciding how to proceed relative to planning and actions.

COUNTERINTELLIGENCE

The preceding sections provided an overview of the intelligence community and its intelligence gathering activities. In addition to gathering information about various enemies, be they individuals, groups, or countries, our intelligence community is also involved in counterintelligence. Richelson (2008) defines **counterintelligence** as, "preventing a foreign government's illicit acquisition of secrets" (p. 394). Within the scope of homeland security, we are not only interested in preventing foreign governments from obtaining critical information but we also want to prevent terrorist groups from acquiring information that may be useful in attacking our critical infrastructure. For example, New York City on several occasions has prohibited photographing mass transit facilities in an effort to prevent terrorists from gaining intelligence that could be used to facilitate an attack. Thus, we are interested in preventing terrorists and sympathetic governments from obtaining information about our counterterrorism activities and potential targets.

The FBI is the primary agency responsible for counterintelligence on American soil. The bureau notes that counterintelligence is its second highest priority, and its importance is derived from protecting the American public from attacks. This is an expansive responsibility. For example, the FBI notes that in the fall of 2003, its counterintelligence division had investigations involving dozens of countries that focused on hundreds of known or suspected intelligence officers who were assigned to enter or travel within the United States. These investigations spanned all 56 field offices. The FBI's counterintelligence priorities include the following:

1. Keep weapons of mass destruction and other embargoed technologies from falling into the wrong hands—whether terrorists or unstable countries around the globe.
2. Protect the secrets of the U.S. intelligence community. Here the FBI investigates people and governments that attempt to infiltrate our intelligence and defense communities to obtain tactical and strategic information.
3. Protect the secrets of the U.S. government and contractors—especially in research and development areas. The FBI helps protect our defense and industrial secrets from foreign countries and agents.
4. Protect our nation's critical national assets—such as our weapons systems, advanced technologies, and energy and banking systems. The bureau's role is to identify the source and significance of the threats and work with the "owners" to reduce any vulnerability.
5. Focus on countries that pose the greatest threat to the U.S. Especially those that want information to further terrorism, economic espionage, proliferation, threats to our infrastructure, and foreign intelligence operations. (FBI, 2009)

Domestic Industrial Espionage

Although the United States is immersed in a war on terror, it should be remembered that terrorism is not the only enemy we face today. Numerous foreign governments compete with us globally and engage in **domestic industrial espionage** whereby they attempt to obtain our military and industrial secrets. There are also enemy states such as North Korea and Iran that would do us harm and likely would cooperate with terrorist organizations. For example, the Chinese maintain a signals intelligence facility in Cuba to spy on the United States. A number of our allies, including Germany, Israel, Japan, and South Korea, have been involved in industrial or defense espionage that was directed against America (Richelson, 2008). The United States spends billions of dollars annually on research and development for defense and industry. When foreign governments obtain this information, they are able to save billions of dollars in research and development; obtain the most sophisticated hardware, software, or equipment; and bring equipment online much quicker. Essentially, industrial espionage undercuts the American economy, posing a critical economic and homeland security threat.

Industrial espionage is a common threat to the United States, with foreign nationals using a variety of tactics to obtain information. Figure 8-5 provides a list of the various tactics used as identified by the Office of National Counterintelligence.

As demonstrated in Figure 8-5, foreign governments use a variety of methodologies in their quest for industrial and defense information and secrets. Moreover, terrorist groups use some of these same techniques when collecting intelligence on American military and civilian operations and personnel. Whereas agents of foreign governments and companies attempt to gain information about industrial or defense technologies, terrorists attempt to obtain tactical information such as troop movements, operations vulnerabilities, and targets.

In addition to a variety of methods of spying on the American industrial and military complexes, a large number of nonimmigrant foreign visitors are involved in this form of espionage. For example, in 2005, there were 22,916 foreign nationals who requested visits to U.S. military and Department of Defense industries, and there were 10,477 such requests for access to

- Targeting U.S. firms for technology that would strengthen their foreign defense capabilities
- Posting personnel at U.S. military bases to collect classified information to bolster military modernization efforts
- Employing commercial firms in the United States and in third counties to target and acquire U.S. technology
- Recruiting students, professors, scientists, and researchers to engage in technology collection
- Making direct requests for classified, sensitive, or export-controlled information
- Forming ventures with U.S. firms in hope of placing collector in proximity to sensitive technologies or else establishing foreign research facilities and software development companies outside the United States to work on commercial projects related to protected programs
- Offering technical services to U.S. research facilities or cleared defense contractors in the hope of gaining access to protected technologies
- Exploiting foreign visits to the United States and collecting at conventions and expositions
- Relying on cyber tools to collect sensitive U.S. technology and economic information

FIGURE 8-5 Spying Techniques Used to Obtain Defense and Industrial Secrets. *Source:* Office of National Counterintelligence. (2006). *Annual Report to Congress on Foreign Economic Collection and Industrial Espionage—2005.* Washington, D.C.: Author.

Analysis Box 8-6

Domestic industrial espionage is a critical problem, especially considering that so much information is stored on computers and foreign hackers are constantly attempting to break into these computers. Many countries, friend and foe, are engaged in such activities, attempting to steal a wide range of information. What industries do you believe would be the probable targets of industrial espionage? What kinds of information would these agents be seeking?

Department of Energy, National Nuclear Security Administration facilities (Office of National Counterintelligence, 2006). A number of countries are represented in these requests, including China, India, Russia, Germany, Colombia, and Japan. Many of those requesting access to these facilities were attempting to collect intelligence information. Moreover, visits to such facilities represent only one type of intelligence collection with many other methods as listed in Figure 8-5 being used on a regular basis. It is apparent that industrial and economic espionage represents a significant threat to homeland security.

Thus, it can be seen that a variety of individuals use different methods to acquire our military and industrial secrets. As noted earlier, when they are successful, it can have a significant economic impact on our country; therefore, this form of espionage is a real threat to homeland security, and we must take the steps necessary to protect such information.

NO-FLY LIST

In many cases, homeland security efforts are invisible to the public. Different programs have been implemented as discussed in Chapter 1, but for the most part, they operate in the background, out of public view. One intelligence-related homeland security program that has received substantial notoriety and is an example of the application of intelligence has been our no-fly list. The no-fly list, now dubbed the **Secure Flight Program**, essentially is a watch list of persons who are not permitted to fly on commercial airlines. It is maintained by the Transportation Security Administration, but various agencies such as the FBI contribute names to the list. Holmes (2009) has identified a number of potential benefits derived from the program. First, such a list can stop or deter potential terrorist plots or hijackings. If potential terrorists believe their name may be on the list, they are deterred from boarding an aircraft and committing an act of terrorism. Second, the list serves to keep certain individuals out of our country. For example, our intelligence agencies have identified a number of possible terrorists. The no-fly list is a mechanism or layer of security that prevents them from entering the United States. At the same time, it may prevent some individuals from leaving the United States. For example, an individual who has ties to a terrorist training camp in Pakistan may be on the list and not permitted to leave the country. Third, Holmes notes that it provides a psychological benefit. That is, the no-fly list may provide citizens with a sense of safety and well-being when they fly. Without this sense of well-being, many citizens may not travel, which would affect our population in a number of ways. Finally, the no-fly list may prevent another costly attack. Since the 9/11 attacks, there have been other attempts by terrorists to use airliners as weapons of mass destruction; in 2006, Scotland Yard arrested 21 people who had plotted to blow up 10 airline flights from London to the United States (BBC News, 2006). Figure 8-6 shows the process used when people are listed on the terrorist watch list.

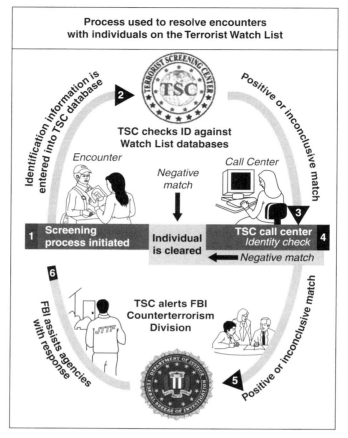

FIGURE 8-6 Process Used to Resolve Encounters with Individuals on the Terrorist Watch List. *Source:* http://www.fbi.gov/ headlines/tscgraphic.jpg

Even though the program may result in a number of benefits, it is questionable as to how effective it is and whether it is cost effective. Holmes (2009) advises that since 2002, the program has cost somewhere between $300 million and $966 million. Using an average amount, it appears to cost in the vicinity of $100 million annually. Moreover, the program is wrought with problems. Primarily, a large numbers of citizens have been prevented from flying who indeed were not terrorists or remotely threats. The problem lies in the no-fly database being a database of names, not people. If it were constructed using people, the database would contain a substantial amount of information such as biomarkers that could be used to identify specific individuals. Since it includes only names, it does not distinguish among people with the same names, there are misspellings, and other problems complicate the process of identifying the targeted individual. In essence, there have been numerous false-positive errors. In some cases, citizens who were mistakenly placed on the no-fly list have sued and won substantial settlements.

One critic of the program referred to it as "security theater" as opposed to actual security or protection (Schneier, 2007). Schneier's point is that the program gives the appearance of providing

Analysis Box 8-7

Obviously the no-fly list is problematic—a number of people have been denied the opportunity to fly because they are on the list incorrectly. There is also the problem of not identifying all those who should be on the list. Have you been prevented from flying or know of someone who has been denied? Given the problems and possible benefits of the program, do you think we should keep it? Why?

some measure of security, but at the end of the day, it is ineffectual and does little to enhance airline safety. It does, however, inconvenience a number of people who are not terrorists or even remotely associated with terrorist activities. Nevertheless, doing an adequate job of screening airline passengers and cargo perhaps is the most effective method by which to ensure air travel safety. The $100 million or so spent each year on the program could be used to enhance security at our nation's airports.

THE GLOBALIZATION OF INTELLIGENCE

Over past decade or so, the relationships and structure of the international intelligence community have evolved. This movement has consisted of what Svendsen (2008) refers to the "homogenization and international standardization" of intelligence (p. 130). Today, there are many more cooperative relationships, formal and informal, in the intelligence community spanning a variety of countries. Old foes are now cooperating in the face of terrorist threats. A new enemy necessitated closer working relationships among a variety of countries. This is particularly true since terrorist groups know no boundaries, and globalization has removed a number of borders, geographical and artificial, that previously provided some measure of security.

During the cold war and immediately preceding the era of terrorism, the 9/11 and other dramatic terrorist attacks in Europe and other areas, most countries' intelligence agencies cooperated sparingly and generally with well-established allies. Countries, to some extent, were aligned by what Huntington (1996) characterized as cultural fault lines as discussed in Chapter 5. During this period, countries knew their enemies and friends, and countries that were not friends were always suspect regardless of their alignment in the world order. To some extent, intelligence arrangements or relationships were tidy and well understood. The end of the cold war and the advent of worldwide terrorism and terrorist organizations resulted in substantial changes in intelligence relationships.

According to Svendsen (2008), the homogenization and international standardization of intelligence have taken several forms. First, there is increased informational sharing across borders and governments. Countries are more willing to share information reciprocally, and given the terrorist threat based on past attacks, there is ample motivation for cooperation. Second, a number of countries, primarily the United States, are involved in training intelligence officers in other countries in areas such as investigations, surveillance, counterterrorism, and so on. Since terrorist groups or cells can appear anywhere, it is to the advantage of countries that are potential targets to enhance intelligence capabilities across the world in an effort to collect more information and potentially prevent a terrorist attack. This training also engenders closer working relationships as countries cooperatively confront terrorists. Third, countries such as the United States are providing technical assistance, often in the form of liaisons who assist or participate in investigations. Such participation often results in more complete investigations leading to arrests or the foiling of a terrorist plot.

The globalization of intelligence is to a large degree in its infancy. Given the current world political dynamics, homogenization and international standardization will continue. This obviously will result in more effective intelligence apparatuses and a more effective response to terrorist threats.

Summary

This chapter provided an overview of our intelligence apparatus and operations and their relationship with homeland security. First, it should be noted that intelligence, especially as it applies to homeland security, is intertwined across a number of levels of government and governmental agencies. Although here we are interested in intelligence that assists in protecting the homeland, it is abundantly clear that it is not a simple matter to separate homeland security intelligence from traditional intelligence activities. Homeland security intelligence is a comprehensive effort examining all facets and types of threats whether or not they are confined within the United States or abroad.

Today, the National Security Council is responsible for advising the executive branch on national security both domestically and internationally. The office of director of national intelligence, created in the wake of the 9/11 attacks, was established to ensure better cooperation among the intelligence agencies and the sharing of information. The director of national intelligence is responsible for coordinating the intelligence operations for 16 different agencies with well over 100,000 employees. These agencies are spread across several federal governmental departments, including Defense, Homeland Security, Justice, State, and Energy. They are involved in several types of intelligence collection, including human, signal, geospatial, scientific, imagery, and open source. The results are a complex myriad of agencies existing in a complex environment that attempt to provide better protection for the homeland. As noted in Figure 8-1, intelligence gathering cuts across several arenas serving a variety of purposes.

Here, however, we were primarily interested in intelligence as it relates to homeland security. In 2002, the White House Office of Homeland Security developed the *National Strategy for Homeland Security*, which provided some sense of organization for homeland security intelligence gathering. This plan is enumerated in Figure 8-7, and it provides insights on the homeland security operations.

The White House Office of Homeland Security is the agency that is primarily responsible for developing policies in the area of strategic response and long-term capacity building. This office coordinates or sets the direction for intelligence and response, which requires substantial interaction across a number of agencies. In 2002, the director of central intelligence (DCI) was involved in several homeland security intelligence operations, but since then, the director of national intelligence has assumed these responsibilities. Now, strategic analysis is performed by the Federal Bureau of Investigation, the Department of Homeland Security, and the director of national intelligence. These three offices are also involved in tactical threat analysis—they attempt to identify ongoing plots and terrorist activities that involve the homeland. The JTTF within the FBI coordinates a substantial amount of intelligence gathering, analysis, and distribution. The Department of Homeland Security is involved in threat analysis, especially threats to critical infrastructure as discussed in Chapter 3. A companion responsibility is to provide warnings when a terrorist attack is suspected.

A recent report by the DNI inspector general found that although progress has been made, numerous problems remain. Specifically, the agencies continue to fail to cooperate and share information (Miller, 2009). This was a problem identified by the 9/11 Commission in 2004 and a subsequent follow-up report issued in 2008. Rarely have we been truly surprised by inadequate information; more often, it has been by our inability to get the information to the right people to connect the dots. The recent inspector general report informs us that much work remains. It is a slow process complicated by the fact that so many departments and agencies are involved in homeland security. Regardless, it is evident that the United States has moved to become much more secure.

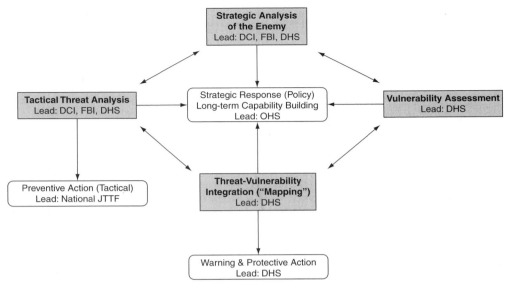

FIGURE 8-7 Roles and Responsibilities of Homeland Security Intelligence and Information Analysis. *Source:* White House Office of Homeland Security. (2002). *National Strategy for Homeland Security.* Washington, D.C.: Author, p. 16.

Discussion Questions

1. Describe how politicians affect intelligence.
2. What is a National Intelligence Estimate? How are they developed? What are some of the problems associated with them?
3. Explain how human intelligence operates.
4. Compare the various types of intelligence collection methods.
5. Describe the purposes and effectiveness of CIA programs such as rendition and water boarding.
6. What role does the State Department have in intelligence and counterterrorism?
7. Compare and contrast the JTTFs with the intelligence network.
8. Describe the intelligence cycle.

References

BBC News. (2006). "Airlines terror plot disrupted". BBC News http://news.bbc.co.uk/2/hi/uk_news/4778575.stm (Accessed March 26, 2009).

Belifsky, D. (2006). "European inquiry says that the CIA flew over 1,000 flights in secret." *The New York Times* (April 27). http://www.nytimes.com/2006/04/27/world/europe/27cia.html?ex=1303790400&en=f28193a7c7a919c0&ei=5090&partner=rssuserland&emc=rss (Accessed February 17, 2009).

Best, R. and A. Feickert. (2006). *Special Operations Forces (SOF) and CIA Paramilitary Operations: Issues for Congress.* Washington, D.C.: Congressional Research Service.

Betts, R. (2003). "Fixing intelligence." In *Terrorism and Counterterrorism: Understanding the New Security Environment,* ed. R. Howard and R. Sawyer, pp. 473–83. New York: McGraw-Hill.

Brown, C. (2008). *The National Security Council: A Legal History of the President's Most Powerful Advisors.* Washington, D.C.: Center for the Study of the Presidency.

Bruno, G. and S. Otterman. (2008). "Backgrounder: National Intelligence Estimates." *Council on Foreign Relations.* http://www.cfr.org/publication/7758/national_intelligence_estimates.html (Accessed March 11, 2009).

Central Intelligence Agency. (2009). *Website.* http://www.cia.gov/index.html (Accessed February 17, 2009).

Chertoff, M. (2006). "Remarks." *U.S. Department of Justice and SEARCH Symposium on Justice and Public Safety Information Sharing* (March 14). http://www.dhs.gov/xnews/speeches/speech_0273.shtm (Accessed January 17, 2011).

Clarke, R. (2008). *Your Government Failed You: Breaking the Cycle of National Security Disasters.* New York: HarperCollins.

Defense Intelligence Agency. (2009). *Website.* http://www.dia.mil/thisisdia/intro/index.htm (Accessed February 17, 2009).

Department of Energy. (2009). *Website.* http://www.energy.gov/nationalsecurity/index.htm (Accessed February 19, 2009).

Department of Justice. (2009). *Website.* http://www.USDOJ.gov/jttf/ (Accessed July 7, 2009).

Department of Homeland Security. (2009). *Website.* http://www.dhs.gov/xabout/structure/gc_1220886590914.shtm (Accessed February 23, 2009).

Department of State. (2009).*Website.* http://www.state.gov/s/inr/ (Accessed February 24, 2009).

Department of the Treasury. (2009). *Website.* http://www.treas.gov/offices/enforcement/oia/ (Accessed February 24, 2009).

Drug Enforcement Administration. (2009). *Website.* http://www.usdoj.gov/dea/pubs/cngrtest/ct120501.html (Accessed March 3, 2009).

Federal Bureau of Investigation. (2009). *Website.* http://www.fbi.gov/page2/may05/ciprimer053105.htm (Accessed March 28, 2009).

Fox News. (2009). "CIA destroyed 92 tapes of interrogations, documents show." http://www.foxnews.com/politics/first100days/2009/03/02/cia-destroyed-tapes-interrogations-documents/ (Accessed March 3, 2009).

Garcia, M. (2009). *Renditions: Constraints Imposed by Laws on Torture.* Washington, D.C.: Congressional Research Service.

Holmes, M. (2009). "Just how much does that cost anyway? An analysis of the financial costs and benefits of the 'no-fly' list." *Homeland Security Affairs*, 5(1): 1–22.

House Permanent Select Committee on Intelligence. (1996). *IC21: Intelligence Community in the 21st Century, Staff Study.* Washington, D.C.: Author.

Huntington, S. (1996). *The Clash of Civilizations and the Remaking of World Order.* New York: Simon & Schuster.

Lake, E. (2009). "Exclusive: Panetta faces rendition queries." *The Washington Time.* (January 15). http:// www.washingtontimes.com/news/2009/jan/15/panetta-faces-rendition-queries/ (Accessed February 17, 2009).

Lumpkin, J. (2002) "Terrorist chatter rises in past week." *Pittsburgh Tribune-Review,* http://www.pittsburghlive.com/x/pittsburghtrib/s_102127.html (Accessed February 9, 2009).

MacGaffin, J. (2005). "Clandestine human intelligence: spies, counterspies, and covert action. In J. Sims and B. Gerber eds. *Transforming US Intelligence.* pp. 79–95. Washington, D.C.: Georgetown University Press.

MacKinzie-Mulvey, E. (2007). "United States announces arrest of Taliban-linked Afghan heroin trafficker on charges of conspiring to import million of dollars worth of heroin." *DEA News Release,* http://www.usdoj.gov/dea/pubs/states/newsrel/nyc051107a.html (Accessed March 9, 2009).

Meyer, J. (2009). "FBI to expand role in terror fight." *Los Angeles Times* (May 22), pp. A1, A17.

Miller, G. (2009). "Intelligence reforms found wanting." *Los Angeles Times* (April 2), p. A14.

Morag, N. (2006). "The national military strategic plan for the war on terrorism: An assessment." *Homeland Security Affairs*, 2(2): 1–14.

National Commission on Terrorist Attacks. (2004). *The 9/11 Commission Report: Final Report of the National Commission on Terrorist Attacks Upon the United States.* New York: W.W. Norton & Company.

National Geospatial-Intelligence Agency. (2009). *Website.* http://www1.nga.mil/Pages/Default.aspx (Accessed March 11, 2009).

National Intelligence Council. (2009). *Homepage.* http://www.dni.gov/nic/NIC_home.html (Accessed July 14, 2009).

National Security Agency. (2009). *Website.* http://www.nsa.gov/about/faqs/about_nsa.shtml (Accessed March 11, 2009).

National Security Council (2009). *Website.* http://www.whitehouse.gov/administration/eop/nsc/ (Accessed February 25, 2009).

Office of the Director of National Intelligence. (2009). *Website.* http://www.dni.gov/who.htm (Accessed January 5, 2009).

Office of National Counterintelligence (2006). *Annual Report to Congress on Foreign Economic Collection and Industrial Espionage—2005.* Washington, D.C.: Author.

OPSEC. (1996). *Operations Security: Intelligence Threat Handbook.* Alexandria, VA: Author.

Posner, R. (2006). *Uncertain Shield: The U.S. Intelligence System in the Times of Reform.* Lanham, MD: Rowman & Littlefield.

Richelson, J. (2008). *The US Intelligence Community.* Boulder, CO: Westview Press.

Scheuer, M. (2004). *Imperial Hubris.* Washington, D.C.: Brassey's Inc.

Schneier, B. (2007). "In praise of security theatre." *Schneier on Security Blog.* http://www.schneier.com/blog/archives/2007/01/in_praise_of_se.html (Accessed March 26, 2009).

Shorrock, T. (2008). *Spies for Hire: The Secret World of Intelligence Outsourcing.* New York: Simon & Schuster.

Stockton, P. (2009). "Beyond the HSC/NSC merger: Integrating states and localities into homeland security policymaking." *Homeland Security Affairs*, 5(1): 1–10.

Svendsen, A. (2008). "The globalization of intelligence since 9/11: Frameworks and operational parameters." *Cambridge Review of International Affairs*, 21(1): 129–44.

Times Online. (2009). "September 11 mastermind Khalid Sheikh Mohammed waterboarded 183 times." *Times Online* (April 20). http://www.timesonline.co.uk/tol/news/world/us_and_americas/article6130165.ece (Accessed April 30, 2009).

Weisman, J. (2002). "CIA, Pentagon feuding complicates war effort." *USA Today* (June 17): p. 11.

Wilson, T. (2001). *Global Threats and Challenges through 2015.* Statement for the record, Armed Services Committee. http://www.globalsecurity.org/military/library/congress/2001_hr/010308tw.pdf (Accessed February 18, 2009).

Wormuth, C. and J. White. (2009). "Merging the HSC and NSC: Stronger together." *Homeland Security Affairs*, 5(1): 1–6.

Zagorin, A. (2007). "Probing the CIA tapes—carefully." *Time Magazine* (December 13). http://www.time.com/time/nation/article/0,8599,1694097,00.html (Accessed March 3, 2009).

9

Homeland Security and Weapons of Mass Destruction

LEARNING OBJECTIVES

1. Understand the definition of weapons of mass destruction.
2. Know the history of the use of various weapons of mass destruction.
3. Be familiar with the types of nuclear threats.
4. Be familiar with the biological agents that can be used as WMDs.
5. Know the nature of chemicals and their use as WMDs.
6. Understand how the various weapons of mass destruction can be delivered and their limitations.

KEY TERMS

Weapons of mass destruction

Biological WMD

Chemical WMD

Geneva Protocol

Nuclear or radiological weapons

Dirty bombs

Bioterrorism

Bacterial organisms

Virus

Toxins

Line source method

Point source method

Blister agents

Blood agents

Choking agents

Nerve agents

INTRODUCTION

In terms of homeland security, the greatest threat to public safety is the potential use of a weapon of mass destruction (WMD). WMDs can be biological, chemical, or nuclear. WMDs have the potential to inflict widespread death, injury, and destruction, especially in heavily populated cities. Moreover, depending on the type of weapon used and its method of deployment, use of a WMD could have a significant negative impact on an economy. Use of a WMD would not only affect the local economy, but its effects could reverberate throughout the nation. For example, exploding a small nuclear devise in a city such as Chicago, New York, or Los Angeles could inflict substantial destruction. Not only would it kill and injure large numbers of people, it would essentially shut the city down for a long period of time, possibly decades. Moreover, it would have other effects. It would overload first responders and hospitals; they would not be able to attend to all the injured and dying. It could have a long-term impact on physical infrastructure. It would substantially affect the economy, having an impact on thousands of persons who were not directly affected by the explosion. In addition, it would have a lasting negative effect on the ecology, making a city uninhabitable. People surviving an attack would suffer health consequences for decades. In essence, in addition to the loss of life and property, use of a WMD would cripple a city, resulting in problems that could last for years.

To some extent, the primary purpose of using WMDs is not the initial death and injuries, but the residual effects that would be more destructive to a country. Destroying a primary communications center might result in initial deaths and injuries and loss of property, but the loss of communications would also have a dramatic impact on society and the economy if the attack resulted in an extended period when communications in a substantial area were disrupted. The detonation of a nuclear devise or the release of the small pox virus at the Port of Long Beach, California, would close the port for an extended period of time and have long-lasting economic ramifications.

Large-scale terrorist attacks enable and strengthen terrorist organizations. The 9/11 attacks demonstrated that a large-scale, destructive attack could be carried out against the United States. The attacks emboldened terrorists and served as an important recruitment tool. It can be argued that the attacks resulted in the proliferation of terrorist groups and cells willing to attack American interests. Al Qaeda was able to achieve a higher level of respect and esteem in the terrorist world because of the attacks. As a result, the war on terror has substantially expanded.

Public support for the war in Iraq was garnered because of a fear that Iraq possessed WMDs. The Iraqis had used chemical weapons in the war with Iran and had used them against the Kurds in Northern Iraq. They previously had attempted to develop nuclear facilities, but these were destroyed by the Israeli military in 1981 (see Vandenbroucke, 1984). There was unsubstantiated evidence that Iraqi officials attempted to purchase yellow cake uranium in Niger, and the country reportedly had substantial chemical and biological weapons programs. It was feared that Iraq would provide these weapons to terrorists, especially al Qaeda operatives. The professed rationale for the war was to protect Americans from attack. The administration of President George W. Bush adopted a preemptive policy worldwide, and this policy was directed at preventing terrorists from obtaining WMDs.

Some believe that terrorists have long sought access to WMDs because of their destructive capabilities (see Cochran and McKinzie, 2008). The *National Strategy for Homeland Security* (Homeland Security Council, 2007) advises that the desire to inflict catastrophic damage on the

United States has fueled a desire to acquire WMDs. There is no doubt that some terrorists and hate groups have a desire to use WMDs against the United States, and it is the mission of homeland security to remove or reduce the opportunity for obtaining and using them in this country. This is a monumental task requiring substantial resources and planning.

HS Web Link: To learn more about the definition of WMDs, go to *http://www. fbi.gov/hq/nsb/wmd/ wmd_definition.htm.*

Although the United States through the Department of Homeland Security and other federal agencies has pursued initiatives to prevent attacks, it should be remembered that nuclear and radiological attacks represent the greatest threats. Harigel (2000) advises that citizens and military personnel can be protected from chemical and biological attacks. People can be inoculated to protect them from most biological weapons, and individuals can be evacuated or provided protective clothing that reduces or eliminates the effects of chemical attacks. Nuclear attacks, on the other hand, are indiscriminate and have widespread effects. If a nuclear attack were to occur, little short of evacuation could protect people. He notes that in actuality nuclear weapons are the only truly WMD.

As noted, there are biological, chemical, and nuclear WMDs. Each type of WMD posses a different set of threats. However, what is a WMD? The federal government has defined **weapons of mass destruction** as

Any explosive, incendiary, poison gas, bomb, grenade, or rocket having a propellant charge of more than four ounces [113 g], missile having an explosive or incendiary charge of more than one-quarter ounce [7 g], or mine or device similar to the above. (2) Poison gas. (3) Any weapon involving a disease organism. (4) Any weapon that is designed to release radiation at a level dangerous to human life. This definition derives from US law, 18 U.S.C. Section 2332a and the referenced 18 USC 921. Indictments and convictions for possession and use of WMD such as truck bombs, pipe bombs, shoe bombs, cactus needles coated with botulin toxin, etc. have been obtained under 18 USC 2332a.

This is a legal definition that is promulgated in federal statutes. The law is designed to be all-inclusive. Congressional intent was to allow prosecutors to pursue any case remotely associated with the use of a WMD or terrorism. This definition also includes conventional weaponry. Truck bombs, pipe bombs, and shoe bombs are included, although they generally use conventional explosives as opposed to a biological, chemical, or nuclear agent. Cameron and Bajema (2009) advise that WMDs simply are weapons that can inflict massive casualties and destruction. They note that there is debate over the definition of WMDs, as the term originally referred to advanced military weapons, not crude or makeshift weapons most often used by terrorists. For the most part, this chapter will focus on biological, chemical, and nuclear WMDs.

Analysis Box 9-1

Congress has defined WMDs very inclusively, including a number of different weapons that may be prosecuted. The statute covers nuclear devices as well as pipe bombs. Should these less lethal weapons be considered in the same statute as radiological weapons? Should possession by a terrorist group receive more attention as opposed to other criminals possessing such weapons? Why?

HISTORY OF THE DEPLOYMENT OF WMDS

WMDs present a substantial problem and generate a great deal of fear. The government and populace tend to treat them as a new phenomenon, but WMDs, although very crude ones, have been used for centuries. An examination of their historical use provides a foundation to better understanding how they are used and their destructive capacities. This section examines the historical use of biological and chemical weapons of mass destruction. Nuclear WMDs are not examined here, as they are a relatively new phenomenon with a limited history.

Historical Precedents for Biological WMDs

A **biological WMD** is defined as the use of a bacteria, virus, or other biological pathogen to attack or deliberately infect people, livestock, or crops. Various forms of biological WMDs, often very crude, have been used for centuries. In 184 B.C.E., Hannibal of Carthage hurled pots containing vipers onto the decks of enemy ships, and in 1495, the Spanish attempted to give wine spiked with the blood of leprosy patients to their French enemies near Naples. The Greeks as early as 300 B.C. polluted the drinking water of their enemies by dumping the corpses of animals into the wells. In most cases, these early attempts were ineffective, but they demonstrate that biological weapons have a long history (see DeNoon, 2003; Harigel, 2000).

There is a history of using biological weapons in the United States. In 1763, British officers planned to distribute blankets infected with smallpox to Native Americans at Fort Pitt in Pennsylvania. The American Civil War witnessed numerous attempts to use biological weapons. Luke Blackburn of Kentucky sold blankets contaminated with smallpox and yellow fever to Union troops. General Johnson used the bodies of dead sheep and pigs to pollute water during the siege of Vicksburg. Again, the attempts were crude, but they demonstrate that those engaged in war will use any means to defeat their enemies (see DeNoon, 2003; Harigel, 2000).

Even though there was a substantial increase in the use of chemical weapons during World War I (discussed later), there were some efforts to exploit biological weaponry. The Germans attempted to use glanders (an infectious disease affecting horses, mules, and donkeys) and anthrax in Argentina, Mesopotamia, Norway, Romania, and the United States to infect draft animals, horses, and mules that were destined for use by the Allies in the war effort. The Germans were accused of attempting to start cholera epidemics in Italy and Russia. They also attempted to introduce fungi to Allied wheat crops (see DeNoon, 2003; Harigel, 2000). Again, these efforts were ineffective and had little impact on the intended victims. However, they spurred interest in biological weapons, and many countries including France, England, Canada, Japan, Germany, and the United States began experimenting and developing biological weapons after the war.

HS Web Link: To learn more about the history of biological weapons, go to *http://www.aarc.org/ resources/biological/ history.asp*.

More recently, in 1950, the East German government accused the United States of scattering Colorado potato beetles over its crops. From 1962 to 1996, Cuban officials accused the United States 21 times of attempting to use biological weapons against them. Their charges included the use of Newcastle Disease against poultry, African swine fever aimed at pigs, tobacco blue mold disease to affect the country's tobacco industry, and sugarcane rust disease against the sugar industry (Zillinskas, 1999). These allegations and attacks demonstrate that biological warfare can be waged against farm crops and livestock, as well as people. Such attacks can cause food shortages and adversely affect a country's or region's economy.

The United States has used chemicals to attack plant life. The United States used herbicides on a limited scale during the last year of the Korean War (Stockholm International Peace Research Institute, 1971), and the United States extensively used the herbicide Agent Orange in the Vietnam War to clear protective and battle areas around troops. Approximately 77 million liters of the chemical were sprayed across the country (Van-Taun, 2005). The use of Agent Orange in the war resulted health problems for American troops and the Vietnamese people.

In reality, there is little or no evidence that countries have been successful in using pests and plant diseases to attack food supplies and livestock. It is difficult to mount an effective attack given the geographical dispersion of food and livestock. An attack may be successful in a given area, but it is nearly impossible to have a substantial impact on a country. For the most part, Zillinskas (1999) advises that plant or crop infestations have been the result of newly introduced pests and diseases that arrived in counties as a result of food shipments or commerce.

The most recent and notable biological weapons attack occurred in the United States in 2001 when several letters laced with anthrax were mailed from Princeton, New Jersey, to several people on the East Coast. Letters were mailed to the editor of a Florida tabloid, the *Sun*; they were mailed to the New York television network offices of ABC, NBC, and CBS. Traces of anthrax were found in the offices of the New York governor, and two such letters were mailed to two United States senators. The attacks created a panic as no one initially knew how many anthrax letters ultimately would be mailed. Moreover, the mailings seemed to be indiscriminate, with victims ranging from ordinary citizens to media personnel to politicians. The attacks resulted in the deaths of five people and a total of 19 people developed anthrax infections. Approximately 10,000 people were administered antibiotics as a result of the attacks, and the United States produced and stockpiled large quantities of antibiotics to counter anthrax. The attacks also resulted in a wave of "hoax" letters. During October and November following the attacks, more than 550 hoax letters claiming to contain anthrax were mailed in the United States. Most were sent to abortion clinics (Snyder and Pate, 2002). It was not until 2008 that FBI investigators were able to identify the perpetrator, who worked in a military bio-weapons laboratory at Ft. Detrick, Maryland.

Finally, it should be noted that individuals rather than international groups have committed terrorist attacks using biological weapons. These attacks generally consist of a single and very specific target as opposed to multiple attacks targeting large numbers of people, such as the 2001 anthrax attacks, during which anthrax was mailed to several individuals. Also, citizens, not international terrorist groups, most often commit domestic biological attacks. These attacks usually involve unsophisticated biological agents. For example, in 1984, members of a cult contaminated salad bars in 10 Dalles, Oregon, restaurants with a strain of salmonella. The cult leaders were eventually arrested and jailed. In 1996, someone laced cattle feed with chlordane, a pesticide.

HS Web Link: To learn more about the salmonella attack in Dalles, Oregon, go to *http://www.efilmgroup. com/News/Bioterrorism- in-Oregon.html*.

In 2003, a supermarket employee deliberately contaminated ground beef with an insecticide. Nearly 100 people became ill as a result of the incident (James Martin Center for Nonproliferation Studies, 2006). It seems that periodically disgruntled people will resort to biological warfare to make a political statement or to obtain revenge for some perceived wrong. But, for the most part, biological attacks are uncommon.

FBI technicians examine a letter tainted with anthrax and sent to Sen. Tom Daschle.   *Source:* http://www.fbi.gov/headlines/anthrax_evid1.jpg

Historical Precedents for Chemical WMDs

A **chemical WMD** is a manufactured highly toxic chemical that can sicken or kill humans or animals or destroy plants. Human and animal exposure can occur through inhalation, transdermal or exposure to the skin, or ingestion. Biological warfare dates back more than 2,500 years, but the use of chemical warfare also has a long history. As early as 1000 B.C., the Chinese used arsenic smoke, and in 431 B.C.E. during the Trojan War, the Greeks used a mixture of sulfur and pitch resin to produce suffocating fumes (DeNoon, 2003; Harigel, 2000). The recognition of the devastation that chemical weapons cause resulted in a number of attempts to control their production and use. In 1874, the Brussels Convention made an effort to control them, and these efforts were expounded upon during the First Hague Peace Appeal in 1899 (Harigel, 2000).

These early attempts to control chemical warfare were disregarded, and chemical weapons were used extensively in World War I. In 1915, the Germans used canisters of chlorine gas at the battle of Ypres in Belgium. The gas resulted in the deaths of 5,000 French troops and injured another 15,000. Subsequently, both sides began using poisonous gas and developed more deadly varieties. Ultimately, mustard gas, which burned the skin and lungs, was developed and deployed. Both sides used the gas and it resulted in 91,000 deaths and 1.2 million people injured. Estimates are that 124,000 tons of chemicals were used in the war (Meselson, 1991).

Harigel (2000) advises that even though the use of these weapons resulted in massive casualties, it was generally recognized that they were ineffective as a military weapon. The inhuman consequences on soldiers and civilians resulted in a loss of support for war efforts and retaliation. In 1925, the **Geneva Protocol** was signed; it prohibited the use of asphyxiating poisonous gases and bacteriological methods of warfare. The Geneva Protocol, however, did not prohibit the development and stockpiling of these weapons. Regardless, it is the cornerstone of today's prohibitions preventing biological and chemical warfare.

Although well intended, the Geneva Protocol has not prevented the use of chemical and biological weapons by signatories and non-signatories alike. During World War II, Japan used chemical weapons against China, and Italy used them against Ethiopia. They most likely used these weapons because China and Ethiopia could not retaliate since they did not have chemical weapons. Saddam Hussein used chemical weapons against Kurdish minorities in Iraq and against Iran between 1980 and 1988; it estimated that 5 percent of the Iranian casualties were the result of chemical warfare and that 45,000 soldiers were exposed to mustard gas during the Iraqi-Iranian war (Harigel, 2000).

HS Web Link: To learn more about the history of chemical warfare, go to *http://www.cbwinfo.com/ History/History.html.*

Although there were treaties prohibiting the use of biological and chemical agents, countries continued to develop them. The cold war resulted in new developments in biological and chemical weapons. A number of new toxins were developed, including VX, a nerve gas that can kill if a single drop were applied to the skin. Other toxins including sarin were developed during this period. Chemical agents became more toxic and dangerous. They saw little use, but Soviet troops used them in Afghanistan after their invasion of that country. As a result of the proliferation of state-sponsored weapons programs, the toxicity of these new agents was increased, making it easier to commit a terrorist act with more lethal consequences.

One example of terrorists using chemical weapons involved attacks in Japan. In 1995, the Japanese cult Aum Shinrikyo released containers of sarin gas on several subway trains in Tokyo. The containers were placed in five different bags in plastic containers. The containers were ruptured using an umbrella, and the contents leaked onto the floor of the trains where they evaporated and were inhaled by passengers. The attacks resulted in 12 deaths and several thousand people were injured. This was the second deadly attack conducted by Aum Shinrikyo. The group previously drove a truck containing sarin to a residential neighborhood in Matsumoto and remotely released the gas, causing seven deaths and injuries to about 1,000 people (Olson, 1999).

There are several examples of the presence of ricin, a toxin extracted from the castor bean, in the United States, although there are no instances of the chemical's use. In 1995, members of the Minnesota Patriots Council, an extremist antigovernment organization, were arrested for plotting the murder of a U.S. marshal. They had planned to sprinkle ricin on the door handles of the marshal's vehicle as well as on the car heater fan (Center for Defense Information, 2003). In 2008, the police and paramedics were called to a Las Vegas hotel room where a guest had become ill. He later slipped into a coma. A subsequent search of his room resulted in the discovery of vials of ricin. The police also discovered caster beans from which ricin is made and a copy of the *Anarchist's Cookbook.* Several civilians and police officers received medical treatment as a precaution (Thevenot and Mower, 2008).

THE THREAT OF NUCLEAR WEAPONS OF MASS DESTRUCTION: DESTRUCTIVENESS, POTENTIAL FOR USE, AND AVAILABILITY

One of the public's greatest fears is that a terrorist group or rogue nation will use weapons of mass destruction against the United States. Although there may be groups with the desire to launch a nuclear attack, few have access to these weapons or the logistical support necessary to carry out an attack. Likewise, although there may be a number of "rogue" nations willing to supply these weapons or otherwise assist terrorists with a WMD attack, there are strong deterrents to rendering such assistance.

Some people claim that today the world is a much more dangerous place than it was in the past. During the cold war, enemies were known and well understood. Officials comprehended where attacks might emanate, built defenses, and prepared for attacks. Essentially, nations developed a nuclear and conventional weapons stalemate. All sides understood that a nuclear war could lead to total annihilation. Today, the circumstances have completely changed. Unlike during the cold war era, terrorist groups remain hidden in many countries, blending in with populations that do not necessarily desire to instigate war. To some extent, terrorists believe this provides them with a modicum of cover and prevents the United States from retaliating should they mount an attack. After the 9/11 attacks, the Taliban provided al Qaeda sanctuary in Afghanistan, believing the United States would not intercede or violate its national boundaries. Moreover, some of today's terrorists are willing to risk total obliteration in order to "defeat" the United States. These circum-stances, it is argued, clearly result in a greater level of danger. As our brief review of the history of WMD illustrates, however, these "new" threats may be more a matter or perception than a new historical precedent. In any case, WMDs present a vexing problem for homeland security.

Basically, there are three general types of WMDs, nuclear, biological, and chemical. First, there are **nuclear or radiological weapons.** A nuclear or radiological attack can be mounted in

FBI SWAT team member is checked for possible radiological contamination as part of a drill.
Source: http://www.fbi.gov/headlines/chemical061407.jpg

several ways. First, an aggressor could obtain a nuclear weapon, smuggle it into the United States, and detonate it. Second, the perpetrator could combine radiological materials with a conventional explosive device and ignite it, hoping to spread radiological materials across a wide area. A third method is to use conventional explosives or attacks on nuclear facilities or materials in the United States, resulting in the spread of radiological debris. In terms of biological weapons, numerous viruses, bacteria, and biologically based poisons could be used to attack a city or area. Finally, many chemicals could be weaponized and deployed against a population. Each of these WMDs are examined next.

NUCLEAR AND RADIOLOGICAL WMDS

Of all the weapons of mass destruction, nuclear devices raise the most concern. Even a small nuclear weapon detonated in a large city would result in catastrophic destruction and vast casualties. Moreover, the presence of nuclear materials—radiation—would result in long-term problems for any country. An excellent example of how devastating this could be is the meltdown of the Chernobyl nuclear plant in the Ukraine in 1986. One of the plant's reactors exploded. After the initial explosion, a number of additional explosions resulted in the release of radioactive materials. These materials drifted over parts of Europe, Russia, Ukraine, Belarus, and even into the United States. The disaster resulted in more than 300,000 people being evacuated. The amount of radiation released was far greater than the radiation released as a result of the bombing of Hiroshima or Nagasaki (World Nuclear Association, 2008). Twenty years after the disaster, the facility remains closed and parts of the area remain evacuated because of radiation contamination.

Nuclear Bombs or Weapons

Only nine countries are reported to possess nuclear weapons: United States, Pakistan, Israel, China, England, France, India, Russia, and North Korea. Together, these countries possess approximately 22,500 nuclear weapons or bombs (*Ploughshares*, 2011). Essentially, a nuclear device can be constructed from highly enriched uranium or plutonium. There are two ways terrorists could acquire a nuclear weapon. First, they could steal or purchase one that has been constructed by a nuclear power. Second, they could acquire the materials and construct a weapon. The Union of Concerned Scientists (2006) advises that of the two options, terrorists are more likely to attempt to acquire the materials and construct a device. If terrorists are able to acquire all the necessary components, it is not difficult to construct a nuclear weapon.

Only a relatively small amount of nuclear materials are required to build a bomb. A crude weapon could be constructed from 40 to 50 kilograms of enriched uranium. A more sophisticated device could be constructed from about 12 kilograms of highly enriched uranium or 4 kilograms of plutonium. Many countries have the knowledge and capacity to build nuclear weapons.

The Spread of Nuclear Material and Information

Most notably, North Korea and Pakistan pose nuclear challenges. North Korea remains isolated from the rest of the world and is a very poor nation. North Korea does possess nuclear weapons and technology. The fear is that it will resort to selling nuclear materials or weapons on the black market to raise currency or to cause problems for the United States. North Korea has routinely used its nuclear technology to gain economic concessions from the United States and other countries. It is feared that if the United States begins to refuse its demands, North Korea may begin selling nuclear technology. More problematic is the fear that North Korea might sell nuclear technology and materials regardless of international overtures. There are many rogue states and groups that seek nuclear weapons.

Today, Pakistan is particularly problematic as it is a nuclear power with 30 to 100 nuclear weapons (Broad and Sanger, 2008). In 2008, Pervez Musharraf (the president of Pakistan and an alleged American ally) was forced to resign, resulting in a degree of instability. During the same time, Islamic terrorists become more active as the government weakened and faced an array of social and economic problems. It is feared that instability in Pakistan increases the probability that radicals within the government might gain control and provide nuclear weapons to terrorists such as al Qaeda or the Taliban. The Pakistani regions bordering Afghanistan seem ungovernable and are the home to Osama bin Laden and his al Qaeda network. Al Qaeda has undeterminable numbers of sympathizers in Pakistan, including government officials working in the intelligence apparatus. In fact, Osama bin Laden has better relations with many of the tribal leaders and some intelligence agents than does the Pakistani government.

Pakistan has a history of sharing nuclear bomb-making information with other countries. In 2004, Abdul Qadeer Khan, an engineer and founder of Pakistan's nuclear program, admitted to sharing nuclear technology and equipment with Libya, Iran, and North Korea. Kahn and his associates developed an international network to smuggle parts and technology out of the country. After his confession, Kahn was convicted in Pakistan but pardoned the next day by President Musharraf. Kahn allegedly sold the technology and materials for several million dollars. After his release, Kahn maintained that Musharraf was aware and involved in all the transactions. It is not entirely clear as to the amount of information and technology that were transferred or the full count of countries that received the assistance (Frantz and Collins, 2007).

This was not the end of Pakistan's involvement in smuggling nuclear technology. In 2008, the president of Switzerland announced that the government had destroyed files documenting the business dealings of Swiss engineers suspected of helping smuggle nuclear technology. The American Central Intelligence Agency (CIA) had requested that the files be destroyed. For four years, the CIA had collaborated with the Tinner family, who operated a Swiss engineering company to sell nuclear materials and technology on the Kahn black market network. Tinner had been working with Kahn since the 1990s. The CIA paid the Tinners as much as $10 million. The material in question included bomb-making designs, centrifuges, and other equipment required for a nuclear program. As a result of Tinners' cooperation, the CIA intercepted equipment destined for Libya and Iran. In some cases, the equipment was sent to the United States and sabotaged before proceeding to its destination. Experts believe that the program was the primary reason Libya abandoned its nuclear weapons program. In Iran, the defective equipment resulted in an explosion that destroyed 50 centrifuges. This slowed Iran's progress but did not result in putting a halt to its nuclear program (Broad and Sanger, 2008). The relationship with the Tinners yielded information about those involved in the nuclear black market and nations receiving defective equipment. It also shows, however, that there remains a vibrant black market, and nuclear weapons information and material are being obtained by nonnuclear nations.

Many are concerned that Russia could be a source of nuclear materials. Several Russian and old Soviet nuclear sites have low levels of security, making them attractive targets for theft or

Analysis Box 9-2

Pakistan is a nuclear state, and it is embroiled in a great deal of conflict internally and externally. Of the greatest concern is that the Taliban control large portions of the country and numerous radical Muslims are sympathetic with jihad. Pakistan represents a place where terrorists may have access to nuclear weapons or materials. Currently, the United States is working with Pakistan to combat the Taliban. How great a threat do you believe Pakistan is in terms of providing terrorists with nuclear weapons? Should the United States conduct more combat operations in Pakistan to defeat the Taliban to reduce the nuclear threat? Why?

terrorism, especially in those countries that broke from the old Soviet Union. Russia has more than 1,000 metric tons of military-grade highly enriched uranium. After the fall of the Soviet Union, a number of organized crime groups formed in Russia, oftentimes headed and staffed with former KGB officers. Many of these organizations have morphed into transnational organized crime cabals networked across the world. Given the amount of money at terrorist groups' disposal, there is concern that these groups may attempt to procure weapons or nuclear materials, and Russian organized crime might be in a position to provide these materials.

The potential for losing nuclear materials is not limited to nation-states. Highly enriched uranium is used to fuel more than 100 research centers worldwide in dozens of countries. These sites include military, industrial, and academic facilities. They are involved in a variety of research projects ranging from medicine to military. Although most of these sites have small quantities of nuclear materials, they often have less security as compared to government-controlled weapon sites. For example, many universities have nuclear research programs, and the security for these materials is at minimum levels at best. These sites represent a potential source of radioactive material.

Smuggling Nuclear Weapons and Materials

Nuclear weapons on American soil are closely guarded by the military, and the Domestic Nuclear Detection Office within the Department of Homeland Security (DHS) monitors the movement and smuggling of nuclear materials in the United States and worldwide. It would be extremely difficult for terrorists to obtain a weapon in the United States. Given America's security standards for nuclear weapons, the most likely scenario is that terrorists will attempt to smuggle a nuclear weapon or weapons' materials into the United States. The United States works with a number of nations to secure nuclear weapons and materials; nonetheless, a substantial amount of radiological materials have been lost, stolen, or otherwise unaccounted for in this country alone. The General Accounting Office found that between 1955 and 1977 several thousand kilograms of nuclear materials had gone "missing." Some of the missing materials likely reflect accounting errors rather than actual losses, but these figures demonstrate at least lax control and accounting (GAO, 1977). The United States, however, has superior controls and accounting for its nuclear materials as compared to countries such as Russia and Pakistan.

ABC News conducted experiments to determine how well American port security was in terms of detecting nuclear material smuggling. On two occasions the network investigators shipped containers containing a small amount of spent uranium, which is radioactive, into the United States. Terrorists may understand that they cannot smuggle large amounts of nuclear material into the United States and consequently attempt to import several small batches. Customs officials examined the cargo because the material was being shipped from Muslim countries but did not find the spent uranium. At the time, customs officials were using first-generation radiological detection equipment. The ABC News exercises demonstrate a need for more effective radiological detection devices at the borders (Cochran and McKinzie, 2008). As noted in Chapter 1, the DHS is working toward the development of more effective detection devices.

If terrorists attempt to smuggle nuclear materials into the United States to construct a nuclear device, they will face a number of challenges beyond security. Terrorists most likely would be forced to make a crude weapon. Such a weapon would be rather large, weighing a ton or more and would require a large amount of highly enriched uranium or plutonium. Transporting the materials would be difficult. The terrorists would have to mask the radioactive materials so that they would not be discovered by radiological detection devices and to protect themselves from radiation exposure. This would result in an extremely large device. Moreover, they would have to assemble a team with the technical ability and equipment to construct the device. In addition to obtaining the highly enriched uranium or plutonium, they would have to acquire a number of bomb parts. It would be extremely difficult to obtain or manufacture a triggering device and other parts necessary for the weapon. These challenges substantially reduce the likelihood that terrorist will be able to detonate a nuclear device in the United States.

HS Web Link: To learn more about how terrorists may acquire nuclear materials, go to *http://www.nps.edu/Academics/centers/ccc/publications/OnlineJournal/2007/Aug/williamsAug07.html.*

Terrorist Attacks Using Dirty Bombs and Attacks on Nuclear Facilities

Methods other than the detonation of a nuclear weapon could create substantial damage: (1) a dirty bomb and (2) an attack on a nuclear power plant or nuclear facility.

Dirty bombs use conventional explosive materials but are wrapped in or contain radioactive material. The radioactive materials are dispersed as a result of the conventional explosion producing contamination. A dirty bomb does not necessarily have to contain highly enriched uranium or plutonium. It could contain radioactive waste products that are produced at commercial power plants, medical centers, or research facilities. Radioactive waste sites generally have fewer security precautions as compared to locations that house highly enriched uranium or plutonium.

There have been attempts to use a dirty bomb. In 1996, Islamic rebels from Chechnya planted a device in a park in Moscow. Although not detonated, it contained dynamite and cesium 137, a by-product of nuclear fission. If the bomb had been detonated, it would have spread radioactive materials into the surrounding area. In 2002, Abdullah Al Muhajir, also known as Jose Padilla, was arrested by federal authorities for plotting to construct and detonate a dirty bomb in the United States. FBI agents arrested Padilla at Chicago's O'Hare Airport. He had a suitcase with $10,000 in cash, and he had undergone dirty-bomb-making training in Lahore, Pakistan. Agents believed he was on a reconnaissance mission for a future dirty bomb attack (Krock and Deusser, 2003). Since terrorists have used dirty bombs in the past, it is plausible that they will resort to them in the future. Numerous facilities contain large amounts of nuclear material, such as nuclear power plants. Crashing a large aircraft into or using large amounts of explosives at a nuclear power plant could have the same effects as a dirty bomb except the effects would be of a much greater magnitude. Such an explosion could cause the reactor core to melt down (such as occurred at Chernobyl) or spent fuel waste to be spread across a large geographical area. The Chernobyl accident resulted in the release of radiation that was several hundred times the amount of radiation that was released as a result of the atomic bombs dropped on Hiroshima or Nagasaki. The effects could be devastating, and the cleanup could take decades.

Security remains a concern for most nuclear plants. There are 104 such facilities in the United States, and they are geographically dispersed throughout the nation. In addition to an air attack, these plants are susceptible to acts of sabotage or ground attack. These plants have

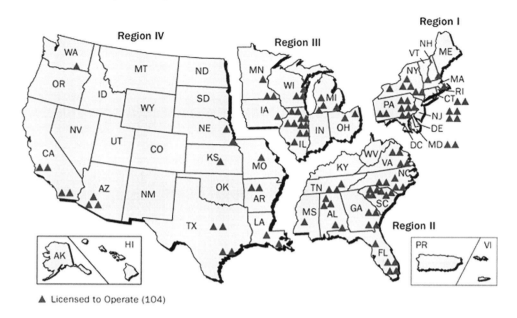

Map of the United States showing locations of operating nuclear power reactors.   *Source:* http://www.nrc.gov/images/info-finder/reactor/reactors-map.gif

security, including electronic monitoring, armed guards, and fencing for perimeter security. But these levels of security may prove inadequate, especially if attacked by a group of motivated, well-armed terrorists. Essentially, terrorists could cause a disaster by using a relatively small amount of conventional explosives to rupture one of the plant's reactors. There have been a number of mock or red team attacks on some of America's nuclear facilities, and although the results are classified, some estimate that the security failed about 50 percent of the time (Project on Government Oversight, 2001).

There is some evidence that power plants have been targeted by terrorists. In August 2003, police in Toronto, Canada, detained 19 Pakistani-born men who had been under surveillance by Canadian authorities. Several had taken flying lessons, been involved in surveillance-like activities, and had filed a flight pattern over a nuclear power plant (Brown, 2003). In March 2003, National Guard troops were dispatched to the Palo Verde Nuclear Power Plant about 50 miles east of Phoenix, Arizona. DHS Secretary Tom Ridge advised that a serious and credible threat had been received. In addition to the troops, a U.S. Customs and Border Protection Black Hawk helicopter was also sent to the scene (Fields, Davis, and Schlesinger, 2003). Although no attacks occurred, these cases demonstrate the serious problem of safeguarding nuclear facilities.

Analysis Box 9-3

The United States and the world are facing an energy shortage. It has been advocated that the United States build more nuclear power plants to supply electricity to our growing population. Building additional plants will increase the security risk. Should we build more nuclear plants? Do the advantages outweigh the disadvantages? In this case, does the need for energy outweigh the need for homeland security?

Determining adequate levels of security was discussed in Chapter 3. The first step in critical infrastructure protection is the determination of the required level of security for a given asset. Given that nuclear and radiological attacks present the greatest problems and possibly disastrous outcomes in terms of homeland security, it is imperative that all facilities with nuclear and radiological materials have the highest security standards—nuclear facilities have not achieved this standard.

Palo Verde Nuclear Generating Station, Unit 1.   *Source:* http://www.nrc.gov/info-finder/reactor/palo.jpg

BIOLOGICAL WEAPONS OF MASS DESTRUCTION

Biological weapons pose a different set of problems for homeland security. Although there are many difficulties in weaponizing biological agents, they are less cumbersome and easier to use than nuclear materials. Also, like radiation, biological weapons do not know borders. The release of biological agents causing disease in one country could easily spread the disease to other countries as a result of animal, plant, and human migration and the winds. The bird flu is a good example. This disease spread from migrating birds and affected animals and people in several Asian countries. Another example is the swine or H1N1 virus that spread across the globe in 2009. Biological WMDs are becoming even more problematic as research advances and information spread across the world. Most of us are very familiar with the stockpiling of biological weapons, but perhaps the greatest fear is the development of new organisms.

Biological terrorism represents a threat to the United States and the rest of the world. Currently, more than 100 counties have the capacity to produce biological weapons on a large scale (Sauter and Carafano, 2005). A number of contagions could pose a real health threat to large numbers of people. Given diseases such as small pox and anthrax, there is the potential to infect large numbers of people over a vast geographical area. Containment perhaps is the greatest issue, along with prevention. There is a great deal of speculation that terrorist groups possess or are attempting to possess biological weapons. Substantial publicity and public fear resulted in 2001 when anthrax was mailed to several locations causing several deaths and injuries.

There is some confusion over what constitutes bioterrorism. Ackerman and Moran (undated) define **bioterrorism** as, "the use by non-state actors of micro-organisms (toxins) to inflict harm on a wider population." Cameron and Bajema (2009) advise that biological weapons "employ living micro organisms (pathogens) or toxins produced by living organisms to attack human beings, animals, and/or plants" (p. 271). These definitions include use by terrorist groups and other groups such as organized crime or hate groups. It should be remembered that biological toxins can be used for a variety of rationales with the same outcome—death, panic, fear, and economic devastation. Moreover, the targets for a biological attack may not be humans; there have been instances when toxins were used to destroy crops and livestock. This exemplifies how biological warfare or acts can have devastating effects on living conditions and local economies.

Types of Biological Weapons

Different biological agents could be used as a weapon of mass destruction. Essentially, there are three general categories of biological agents: bacterial organisms, viruses, and toxins. Figure 9-1 provides a breakdown of the various organisms associated with these three categories. The Centers for Disease Control and Prevention (CDC) has developed a priority system in terms of national risk. Those in the A category are high-priority agents that are rarely seen in the United States, but they can (1) be easily transmitted among people, (2) result in a high mortality rate, (3) result in a public panic or social disruption, and (4) require special action for public health. Category B agents (1) are moderately easily disseminated, (2) result in moderate morbidity and low mortality rates, and (3) require special medical response actions (CDC, 2008).

BACTERIAL ORGANISMS   **Bacterial organisms** cause diseases such as anthrax or the plague. Bacteria are a group of usually single-celled organisms that come in many different shapes, sizes, and forms. They live almost anywhere on earth, including on humans. Many forms of bacteria are not dangerous, but some release toxins that can cause diseases. Each year hundreds of people die

Bacterial	CDC Classification
• Plague	A
• Anthrax	A
• Q fever	B
Viruses	
• Smallpox	A
• Viral equine encephalitis	B
• Viral hemorrhagic fevers	A
Toxins	
• Botulism	A
• Ricin	B
• Staphylococcal enterotoxin	B

FIGURE 9-1 Biological Agents by Class. *Source:* Centers for Disease Control and Prevention. (2008). *Bioterrorism Agents/Diseases.* http://www.bt.cdc.gov/agent/agentlist-category.asp (Accessed September 2, 2008).

from bacteria that grow in body tissue and cause infections. Bacteria-borne diseases are not transmitted from human to human but generally occur as a result of eating contaminated food or the victim consumes the bacteria via inhalation, drinking water, or other liquids. For example, the 2001 anthrax attack in the United States resulted in only eight deaths. The disease did not spread from human to human. To contract the disease, one had to breathe in or otherwise consume the anthrax spores. For bacteria to be used as a biological weapon, the bacteria would have to be spread over a large area, and victims would have to come into direct contact with the bacteria.

HS Web Link: To learn more about biological diseases and agents, go to *http://www.bt.cdc.gov/agent/agentlist.asp.*

VIRUSES Viruses can cause a host of dangerous diseases, including ebola, HIV, hepatitis, smallpox, avian influenza, and SARS. Viruses are also responsible for a number of less serious medical ailments, such as the common cold, influenza, chickenpox, and cold sores. A **virus** is a microscopic living organism that can grow or reproduce only inside a host cell or living animal. Unlike bacteria, viruses are spread from human to human; a prime example is influenza with outbreaks occurring each year. Most viruses are eliminated by a person's immune system. Although antibiotics are sometimes given to people infected with a virus, they have no effect on the virus. A number of antiviral drugs have been developed targeting individual viruses. Antiviral vaccines produce immunity to specific or groups of viruses.

In terms of biological WMDs, viruses are the most problematic. Since they can spread across a population, they often are difficult to contain. Each year Americans experience an influenza outbreak, and thousands of people contract the virus with a number of older and younger people dying. Of all the possible biological WMDs, smallpox is the most dangerous. A number of years ago, smallpox was virtually eliminated through vaccinations. Today, there are only a few cases of smallpox and they generally occur in third-world counties. Essentially, the disease has been absent for so long and Americans no longer receive vaccinations, making many highly susceptible to the disease. One of the homeland security initiatives has been to stockpile smallpox vaccine, should there be an outbreak. It would, however, take a considerable amount of time for the populace to be vaccinated, allowing substantial time for the disease to spread.

Analysis Box 9-4

Numerous viruses are dangerous. Currently, the most dangerous is smallpox. It is deadly and it can spread rather quickly. Given its potency, should we begin to inoculate all American citizens? Does the cost of inoculating Americans outweigh the benefit of not having to be concerned with the disease in the future?

An outbreak of smallpox in Yugoslavia perhaps illustrates the problem. In 1972, a number of people contracted smallpox. Prior to the outbreak, no one in Yugoslavia had contracted the disease since 1930. Although a vaccine for the disease had been available for years, people had not received it because smallpox was essentially nonexistent in Yugoslavia and many other countries. Upon learning of the outbreak, the government declared martial law. A number of villages were blockaded to prevent the virus from spreading. The army quarantined thousands of people who had come into contact with those infected with the disease. In about two weeks, most of the population was vaccinated and the epidemic came to an end. A total of 175 people contracted the disease and 35 died (Preston, 1999). The release of smallpox in large population centers would be even more difficult to control, and it would result in larger numbers of casualties. The Yugoslavia incident, however, demonstrates that quick action can substantially reduce casualties.

TOXINS   Although considered biological weapons, **toxins** actually are not biological substances. They are not living organisms like bacteria or viruses, but they are derived from plants and animals. They are biologically derived poisons or toxins and include botulinum toxin, which is derived from a bacterium; ricin, which is derived from the caster bean plant; and saxitoxin, which is derived from marine animals. Toxins are not alive and cannot multiply like bacteria or viruses and therefore have the same contact effect associated with chemical weapons. They have little value as a weapon of mass destruction. They are difficult to produce in large quantities and numerous chemical weapons are more easily obtained and deployed.

How Biological Weapons Work

Victims of a biological attack can be exposed via three potential routes: (1) contact with the skin, (2) gastrointestinal, and (3) pulmonary. Agents that come in contact with the skin are the least dangerous. The skin provides an excellent barrier against most of these agents except mycotoxins. However, mucous membranes, abrasions, or other lesions may provide a portal of entry for bacteria, viruses, or toxins. Contamination of food or water supplies allows for a potentially significant gastrointestinal exposure. In terms of water contamination, this type of exposure is limited by the direct effects of water dilution and treatment, which inactivate or significantly weaken most microbes and toxins. For this to be a viable method for contamination, the agent must be introduced near the end user in extremely large amounts. Food, on the other hand, is more susceptible to contamination. The agent can be applied directly to the food and later consumed. Exposure via the inhalational route is the most effective mode of delivery for biological agents. Aerosol clouds containing microbes or toxins are not detectable by the senses. Aerosol dispersal mechanisms, however, are limited by the weather (wind, rain, sunlight, and temperature). Nonetheless, aerosol dispersal has the potential for causing widespread illness and death depending on the size of the weapon (Jagminas, 2008).

Biological weapons create a number of problems. The most significant is that they can be deployed, and it may be days or weeks before the deployment becomes evident. A virus must

Foot-and-mouth disease pyre, Devon, UK, 2001. *Source:* http://www.aphis.usda.gov/vs/
pdf_files/safeguarding.pdf

grow and spread within the host population, resulting in a delay before symptoms are evident. Bacteria will affect victims more rapidly, but there likely will be a delay in their discovery. Terrorists could deploy the weapon and disappear before the attack becomes evident. The CDC and other state and federal agencies are constantly monitoring the environment for possible attacks or outbreaks of diseases. Essentially, these agencies watch for the following conditions:

- Large epidemics with unprecedented numbers of ill or dying
- Immunocompromised individuals demonstrating first susceptibility and rapid progression of disease (although equal affliction of previously healthy individuals also may be a clue)
- Particularly high volumes of patients complaining primarily of similar symptoms that are associated with an escalating mortality rate
- Unusual or impossible vector for transmission for that particular region (occurrences where a particular disease normally cannot be easily transmitted)
- Multiple simultaneous outbreaks
- Epidemic caused by a multidrug-resistant pathogen
- Reports of sick or dying animals or plants
- Single case of disease by an uncommon agent (smallpox, inhalational anthrax) (Jagminas, 2008)

Creating Biological Weapons

Biological weapons are more dangerous than chemical weapons, primarily because they are relatively easy to produce or obtain. Biological agents are not biological weapons. Mere possession of an agent—bacteria, virus, or toxin—does not make it a weapon. The agent must be "weaponized."

There are four requirements to weaponize a biological agent. First, the payload or agent must be obtained. Moreover, it must be obtained in sufficient quantities, depending on the agent, so that it will have the desired impact. Second, it must have a container or structure that allows delivery. That is, it must be packaged so that it can be effectively delivered to a target. The payload must remain intact and be dispersed when deployed. Third, it must have an adequate delivery system. For example, for anthrax to be used as a weapon of mass destruction, the delivery system must spread the bacteria over a large geographical area. The delivery system cannot destroy the biological payload. If viruses or bacteria were to be deployed using an explosive charge, the subsequent explosion very likely would destroy or kill the agents. This limits the delivery systems that terrorists could use. Finally, the terrorists must have a competent delivery-dispersal system. The system must be functionally capable of delivering the biological agent over a desired area (Jagminas, 2008). Even if terrorists are able to attain a biological agent, it remains difficult to use it as a weapon of mass destruction.

HS Web Link: To learn more about the dispersing of biological agents, go to http://www.fema.gov/ areyouready/ biological_threats.shtm.

There are two likely methods of dispersing a biological weapon, line source and point source. The **line source method** is the most effective dispersal system. An example is a truck or air sprayer that moves perpendicular to the wind during an inversion (when air temperature increases with altitude and holds surface air and pollutants down). Inversions normally occur at dawn, dusk, or night. The line source method results in the biological agent being effectively dispersed over a large geographical area. The **point source method** uses small packets or containers of the biological agent deployed in a saturation mode in multiple locations. The packets or containers must have a dispersal mechanism as well as the biological agent. Their effectiveness depends on the dispersal mechanism. Agents may be introduced into buildings' heating–ventilation–air conditioning systems or via food or water contamination. This method requires that a number of packets or containers be strategically located across a large geographical area (similar to the method used by the Japanese cult, Aum Shinrikyo, in the Tokyo subway attack discussed earlier). The point source method is less dependent on metrological or weather conditions as compared to the line source method but requires the planting of the agent in multiple locations.

Threat Assessment and Biological Weapons

Threat assessment was discussed in Chapter 3. The level of threat plays a key role in critical infrastructure protection. If a target is desirable to a terrorist group, obviously more resources should be used to protect it. Several variables comprise the threat assessment. This decision-making matrix provides information on how to possibly prevent attacks. If asset vulnerability is reduced, the target is no longer desirable or too difficult to attack. Reducing the means to conduct an attack also impacts the probability of attack. It is a complicated affair to deliver a biological attack of the magnitude that would have a significant impact on the United States. It also assumes that terrorists want to use biological weapons, but this may not be the case. For example, a smallpox outbreak in the United States could easily spread to Middle Eastern countries where there are

---

Analysis Box 9-5

Biological weapons can be used in a variety of locations. Terrorists would likely attempt to use one where there are large numbers of people in order to create the largest number of problems and casualties. Which locations or gatherings in your community would be likely targets if terrorists decided to attack? Does your community have the medical facilities and staff to deal with such an attack?

fewer mechanisms for controlling the outbreak. An attack on the United States could result in far more casualties elsewhere.

Several factors are useful in assessing the threat of bioterrorism. First is the value of the asset to the defender. For example, an agricultural target may not be desirable because of America's immense agriculture infrastructure. An agricultural attack may result in some losses, but in the end, it very likely will have little impact on America's economy or food supply. A second impediment to using biological weapons is the potential harm of the biological agent. As noted, it is difficult to develop a biological weapon, even if the terrorists possess the agent. With the exception of viruses such as smallpox, it is difficult to construct a biological weapon that can have widespread effects. The outbreak of smallpox in Yugoslavia discussed earlier highlights this point. Although it was a serious medical problem, authorities were able to contain and eliminate it with only a few fatalities.

WMDs have been politicized to the point that any attack, no matter how minor, may cause public hysteria. Perhaps a better strategy would be to realistically describe their potential and advertise the resources that would minimize their impact. People want to know that the government can respond to these emergencies. A third issue is vulnerability to biological weapons. Threat assessments need to be conducted. Vulnerability to biological weapons is not even. Some countries are more vulnerable to some biological weapons and some areas are more vulnerable than others. Vulnerability analyses may assist in identifying potential targets or areas that require additional protection. Fourth is the capability to conduct a bio-terror attack. Acquisition of agents and the construction of an effective delivery device are rather difficult, especially a system that can result in significant casualties. Most experts agree that technology has resulted in it being easier to construct a biological weapon; nonetheless, it remains quite difficult. Moreover, even if terrorists have the technology and motivation, it is questionable if they can construct a weapon capable of significant impact.

Perhaps the greatest concern regarding biological WMDs is new strains of viruses that might be created through DNA modification. Although the use of biological weapons is prohibited by treaties, these laws do not apply to all countries and do not ban the possession of these weapons. Many counties continually work to develop more effective biological weapons through cloning and DNA manipulation. Sultan (undated) summarizes the problem,

> Currently, it is recognized that bio-engineering techniques give immense power to its exploiter. If scientists today can resurrect dormant viruses, or through the use of transgenic expression techniques, create new and more resistant strains against the naturally occurring diseases, such knowledge in the hands of the unscrupulous could lead to unforeseen catastrophes. From a bio-weapons point of view these techniques can lead to the manufacture of infectious virulent strains, resistant to the available antibiotics and immune systems, leading to the possibility of the spread of drug-resistant diseases. (p. 6)

CHEMICAL WEAPONS OF MASS DESTRUCTION

A chemical weapon contains inorganic substances that can have an effect on living processes and can cause death, temporary loss of performance, or permanent injury to people, animals, and plants. Numerous chemicals are toxic to humans, animals, and plants, but not all of these chemicals can be weaponized. Thus, chemicals can be classified in terms of their potential for use as a weapon. In addition to chemical warfare weapons, industrial toxic chemicals and materials pose a danger and can be used for limited purposes as chemical weapons. Cone (2008) estimates that there are 82,000 chemical compounds that are used in commerce. Many are highly toxic, whereas others present little or no threat. A 2000 Environmental Protection Agency study found that at least 123 American chemical plants contain enough dangerous chemicals that, if released by one plant, could result in millions of deaths (EPA, 2000). A substantial quantity of chemicals at these plants could present a threat.

Numerous chemical releases have caused death and destruction. In 1984, the release of methyl isocyanate at a Union Carbide factory in Bhopal, India, resulted in 2,500 deaths and 200,000 people becoming sick. The release was the result of sabotage by a disgruntled employee (Muller, undated). In 1989, an accidental release of gases at a Phillips 66 chemical plant in Houston, Texas, resulted in an explosion with a force of 2.3 kilotons. The explosion killed 23 and injured 130 people. The explosion deposited debris in adjoining neighborhoods 9.5 kilometers away. Each year, rail accidents, pipeline ruptures, and traffic crashes result in the releases of toxic chemicals. These incidents demonstrate that the chemical industry poses a significant problem that could be exploited by terrorists.

For the most part, the public is concerned with terrorists using chemical weapons. As noted, chemical weapons have a long history in warfare. Although they have been used by nation-states in times of war, terrorist or political groups seldom use them. Like biological weapons, chemical weapons are difficult to deploy. They must have high levels of toxicity to have an effect, but at the same time, they cannot be too toxic whereby terrorists cannot effectively deploy or handle them. For the most part, terrorists have depended on conventional explosives to carry out attacks. Conventional explosives are easier to obtain, control, and deploy. Nonetheless, chemical weapons must be considered in homeland security planning.

Although literally thousands of chemical compounds are toxic, only about 70 may be useful as a chemical weapon. Today, the most common chemical weapons to be concerned with are sarin and ricin. Figure 9-2 contains a listing of the basic categories of chemical weapons.

Several toxic compounds are contained within each of these categories, which are based on the type of action or impact they have on the victim. For the most part, vomiting agents, irritants, and psychotropic compounds are not satisfactory for use as a chemical weapon. The mortality rate associated with these substances is extremely low. If terrorists desire to use a chemical weapon, they likely will select one that is extremely toxic and has the capability to kill large numbers of people.

BLISTER AGENTS   Blister agents are intended to come into contact with the victims' skin. When deployed, blister agents often result in a low mortality rate, but they cause burns and blisters to the skin. Blister agents contain acid-forming compounds that burn the victim. They

Blister Agents
Blood Agents
Choking Agents
Nerve Agents
Tear Gas
Vomiting Agents
Psychotropic Compounds

FIGURE 9-2   Types of Chemicals That Can Be Used in Chemical Attacks.

can be deadly when the agent is breathed by the victim. They cause irritation to the lungs, eyes, and airway. The most common blistering agent is mustard gas, which was used extensively in World War I. Saddam Hussein used mustard gas in the Iraqi-Iranian war, and it was estimated that 45,000 people were exposed to the agent. There are several varieties of mustard gas. Lewisite is another common blister agent. Blister agents and the precursor chemicals used to make them are monitored under the Chemical Weapons Act.

BLOOD AGENTS   **Blood agents** are chemical weapons that when consumed prevent the body from using oxygen. For example, arsine causes intravascular hemolysis that may lead to renal failure, whereas cyanogen chloride/hydrogen cyanide directly prevents cells from utilizing oxygen. The cells then use anaerobic respiration, creating excess lactic acid and metabolic acidosis. There is speculation that al Qaeda has experimented with cyanide gas. Egan (2001) reports that Ahmed Ressam, an al Qaeda operative, told authorities that the terrorist group experimented with poisonous gases on dogs. It was believed the gases were cyanide.

CHOKING AGENTS   **Choking agents** have similar effects on their victims as do blister agents. Choking agents are acid based and have an effect on the respiratory system, flooding it and often resulting in suffocation. Most choking agents are deadly, depending on the amount of the agent consumed by the victim. The most common choking agent is chlorine, which was first used in World War I by the German army. Chlorine is one of the most commonly used chemicals in manufacturing (Cone, 2008). It is transported throughout the United States by rail and truck, and these tanks could easily be ruptured by conventional explosives. If chlorine were released in a heavily populated area, it could result in substantial casualties. However, any explosion likely would destroy a large portion of the gas, and since it has a distinct odor, it would be quickly identified and the area could be evacuated. Moreover, this point source dispersion is not an effective method of delivering a chemical weapon.

NERVE AGENTS   Nerve agents are the most dangerous of chemical agents. **Nerve agents** inactivate certain enzymes affecting neurotransmitters in the brain. They result in the nervous system becoming inactive, which affects all biological systems. Their effects are almost immediate and death can occur in minutes. They can be inhaled or absorbed by the skin, depending on the agent. There are two primary categories of nerve agents: G-series and V-series. The G-series agents were developed shortly after World War II. They include agents such as sarin, tabun, and soman. These agents are deadly and their release would result in high mortality rates. G-agents dissipate fairly quickly, and, therefore, their danger is from inhalation, not contact. Only sarin has been used in a terrorist attack. The Japanese cult Aum Shinrikyo manufactured the agent and deployed it in 1994 and 1995. In the 1995 attack, cult members released the agent on a Tokyo subway, causing 12 deaths and several thousand people were injured (Olson, 1999).

V-agents, relative to G-agents, are more persistent. That is, they remain in the environment for a long period of time, increasing the likelihood that people will be exposed to the agent through contact. Moreover, only a minute amount of the agent is required to kill a victim. The V-agents comprise the most dangerous class of chemical weapons. It is doubtful that terrorist groups will use VX. Its manufacture is extremely complicated and dangerous due to its toxicity, and this toxicity represents a substantial impediment to terrorists.

HS Web Link: To learn more about VX gas, go to *http://www.bt.cdc.gov/agent/ vx/basics/facts.asp.*

There are other classes of chemical agents, including tear gas, vomiting agents, and psychotropic compounds, but these agents generally dehabilitate rather than result in death or serious injury. They are of little use as a WMD. Different countries' military establishments have experimented with psychotropic drugs, but they are of little use as a WMD. It is interesting, however, that over the years there have been threats in the United States to place psychotropic drugs such as LSD in water supplies, but this has not occurred. If done, it would have little impact, given the volume of drugs that would be required to have any real effect.

Creating Chemical Weapons

As with biological weapons, the effectiveness of a chemical threat is to a large extent based on the delivery system. Many experts believe that chemical weapons cannot produce the same level of casualties as nuclear or biological weapons. To have a significant impact, thousands of pounds of a chemical would have to be effectively released. In essence, if such a weapon could be constructed, an effective attack would be capable of causing only hundreds to a few thousand casualties. A primary difference between chemical agents and biological agents is that the chemical agents have an immediate effect. This results in crippling any response or providing any warning to civilian populations, exacerbating the situation.

Advantages of Chemical Weapons

Chemical weapons have distinct advantages. First, they are relatively inexpensive to produce or procure as compared to biological or nuclear weapons. It does not require a highly sophisticated laboratory to construct chemical weapons, and many of the base chemicals required to manufacture these weapons are readily available. Chemical weapons are easier to use than biological weapons, because they are more stable and containable. Their delivery systems are more manageable, and to some extent, they can be used for specific geographical targets.

The manufacture of some chemical weapons is not overly difficult, and information on their manufacture is readily available given the information contained in scientific journals and on the Internet. The manufacture of chemical agents is similar to the process used to manufacture insecticides. However, even though these agents can readily be made, it still requires a substantial degree of technical sophistication and facilities. Some chemical weapons are easier to manufacture than others. For example, deadly chlorine gas can be made by combining Drano and Clorox liquid bleach. Although easily made in small quantities, the gas would be difficult to manufacture in stable, usable large quantities. Other chemical weapons are more stable and can be manufactured in small amounts and later combined into a larger payload. It appears that if a terrorist wanted to inflict significant casualties, he or she would use some type of nerve agent, which appears to be the most effective.

Weaponizing Chemicals

The American-Israeli Cooperative Enterprise (undated) advises that there are four ways by which a terrorist group could acquire a chemical weapon:

1. Manufacture the weapons
2. Acquire commercially available chemicals that can be used as weapons
3. Theft of chemical munitions from the military
4. Provision of chemical weapons by a state sponsor

As noted, some chemicals are easily manufactured, but they often can be made only in small quantities. Other more dangerous chemical weapons are extremely difficult to manufacture, making them prohibitive. In terms of the second means in the list, ample amounts of chemicals are manufactured and shipped throughout the United States and the rest of the world that are used in manufacturing and agriculture. In some cases, these chemicals can be used to make chemical weapons; in other cases, they are of sufficient toxicity to serve as a chemical weapon. Of course, these chemicals are to some degree monitored by governmental agencies. Thus, attempts to purchase large amounts of them, especially if the purchaser did not have a record of purchasing or using the chemicals, likely would result in suspicion and government investigation. Nonetheless, Parachini (2006) notes that terrorists currently have the capacity to make crude chemical weapons including mustard, sarin, and VX.

It should be remembered that the U.S. military has large stockpiles of chemical weapons stored in secure facilities. However, the military also possesses large amounts of aging chemical weapons left over from World War II and the Korean War, and these weapons are stored in numerous locations that have lower levels of security. They have been targeted for destruction, but legal entanglements have prevented their disposal in some cases. There also may be large amounts of chemical weapons that could be obtained in other countries. The old Soviet Union had large stockpiles, and some of these weapons are now in the possession of countries less committed to their security. Large quantities of military-grade chemical weapons throughout the world could be purchased on the black market and smuggled into the United States.

Finally, there is the possibility of a nation-state supplying chemical weapons to a terrorist group. The world always has large numbers of conflicts with various nations having an interest in their outcome. In other words, states have political motivations to supply weapons to terrorist groups, especially when the state believes it is in its best interest. Once the weapons are supplied to the terrorist group, the supplying nation has little or no control over their use.

MEANS OF DELIVERY Even though the manufacture or acquisition of chemical weapons may not be difficult, delivering the weapon is quite difficult. First, it would require a large volume of a chemical weapon to have significant effects. Transportation would be highly complicated, given the potential for leaks and other transportation problems. Also, security throughout the world is much more intense than in years past. The potential for discovery is far greater.

Second, dispersal of the agent is problematic. For example, if terrorists intended to produce an event that would result in 5,000 to 10,000 casualties, they would have to deploy large amounts of the agent to achieve the effect. There is a substantial amount of loss during delivery due to weather conditions, windage, humidity, and so on. Most likely, a chemical weapon would be used in an area with a high concentration of people, such as a sports arena, shopping mall, or educational facility. Regardless, it is likely that such an event would not lead to large numbers of casualties. It is interesting to note that Sunnis and Shiites did not used chemical weapons during their sectarian war in Iraq even though such weapons exist in the country and region. One possible explanation is that chemical weapons do not have the utility or effects as do explosive devices.

An example of where chemical weapons have been used is illustrative. In 1990, Tamil Tigers used chlorine gas against a Sri Lanka government installation. They released the gas so that it would drift over the fort. The chlorine gas killed 60 governmental soldiers, but it also drifted back over the Tamil Tiger rebels. Since the attack, the Tamil Tigers have not used chemical weapons in this fashion. They found that the gas attacks resulted in a substantial loss of support from the Timal populace (Parachini, 2006). In the end, the backlash was more damaging than the fruits of their attack.

In summary, chemical weapons do indeed pose a threat. However, many problems are associated with their use that will be difficult for terrorists to overcome. It appears that if chemical weapons are used, they will be used with small concentrated targets resulting in relatively few casualties.

Analysis Box 9-6

Currently, the United States is embroiled in an asymmetric war in Afghanistan. It consists of Taliban insurgents attacking American troops and then fading into the countryside. Our troops are at a significant tactical disadvantage. Do you think we should use chemical weapons especially to protect our troops? Should we use nonlethal chemical weapons to accomplish this purpose? What are the ramifications if we did use these weapons?

FACTORS CONSTRAINING TERRORISTS FROM USING WMDS

Historically, a number of factors have prevented terrorists from using WMDs. First, they potentially can produce large numbers of casualties, but for the most part, this is not necessary for the terrorists to send their message. Multiple terrorist events regardless of the number of casualties often send a stronger message. Another factor is that mass casualties could result in a loss of political support. After the 9/11 attacks on the United States, the nation received support from countries across the globe. This support was essentially squandered as a result of the U.S. invasion of Iraq. If terrorists kill large numbers of civilians, it likely will result in diminished support for them and their cause. Even countries that support their cause will be pressured to abandon support. For terrorists to succeed or receive concessions from their enemies, they must have some level of support from the population and other countries.

Nonetheless, some groups may not necessarily prescribe to these constraints, but there are other facts that prohibit the use of WMDs. It has been questioned if WMDs would be used by a Muslim terrorist group in Israel, since many Muslims are integrated throughout much of Israeli society. The use of a WMD in Israel would likely kill many Muslims. This may not be a constraint in the future, since many extremists advocate that citizens must be willing to suffer and sacrifice if victory is to be achieved. This is witnessed by the numerous suicide bombers in the Middle East. The invasions of Afghanistan and Iraq upped the ante. They have infuriated people across the Middle East. Add to that the 2006 invasion of Lebanon by Israel and Israel's treatment of the Palestinians in 2009, and it seems that the region is ready to explode. As the level of anger increases, so does the probability of extremists attempting to obtain and use WMDs.

A number of factors determine whether a terrorist group has the capacity to use a WMD, including the following:

1. *Organizational capabilities.* It would require a sophisticated organization (vertically and horizontally) to develop or otherwise obtain WMDs. Most terrorist groups do not possess this capability. They remain fairly small with limited resources. They have a cell structure as opposed to being complex organizations with varying levels of specialization.
2. *Financial resources.* The procurement, development, transportation, and use of a WMD require substantial resources, depending on the WMD that the terrorists are attempting to procure. Moreover, the whole operation would require substantial resources over an extended period of time, including financial support from acquisition to deployment. There likely are few, if any, groups that have this level of resources without state sponsorship.
3. *Logistical resources.* Logistics refer to the transportation and storing of materials. The supply chain for WMDs can be a half-world long, potentially crossing a number of countries. As a result of the 9/11 attacks, the United States and other countries have substantially increased their assault on and monitoring of terrorist networks, which increases the likelihood that such a supply chain would be broken.

4. *Knowledge/skill/acquisition.*   The use of WMDs requires a high level of knowledge and skill. It is not a simple matter to acquire and deploy a WMD. A terrorist organization can (a) acquire the knowledge and skills via training and education or (b) use personnel with the requisite skills from an outside group. Even though there is a wealth of technical information available, this does not always equate to an ability to acquire the materials, skill, and delivery mechanisms and transport them to a target. In other words, even if technical knowledge is possessed by a terrorist, he or she may not have the experience to transfer that knowledge into a workable WMD.

5. *Materials and technology acquisition.*   There are many examples of biological microorganisms in the world and amounts of chemicals that could be used as a WMD. Obtaining the biological agents, chemicals, or nuclear materials in the quantity necessary to build a WMD is another matter. There always is the possibility of obtaining these materials from the old Soviet Union or another state; it would be difficult to obtain a large enough supply for a devastating attack. Moreover, these materials are highly volatile and there always is the possibility of accidental release or other problems during construction, transportation, and deployment.

6. *Production.*   In terms of chemical and biological WMDs, the production of the materials needed for a sizable weapon would be extremely difficult. It requires a fairly large facility with difficult-to-obtain equipment. If a terrorist group uses substandard equipment and expertise, it substantially increases the possibility of leakage, detection, and accidents.

7. *Weaponization and delivery.*   As noted earlier, the weaponization of chemical and biological agents is difficult, as is the construction of a nuclear device. A biological or chemical weapon can be developed that potentially could destroy a whole city. However, this is an extremely difficult, if not impossible, task. Even if the biological or chemical agents are developed, it is a completely different matter to acquire an effective delivery system. There are many factors that constrict a terrorist group's ability to develop an effective delivery system.

8. *State sponsorship.*   A number of countries would consider assisting terrorists in attacking the United States. However, there also are numerous constraints on these countries, particularly retaliation and the possibility that the weapons could be accidentally released in their own country or used against their country. International condemnation is also a key factor.

IDEOLOGICAL MOTIVATIONS TO ACQUIRE AND USE WMDS

There are several reasons why a group or nation-state might acquire and possibly use WMDs. Some groups see these weapons as meeting their ideological desires. For example, racist or religious groups may use them to further their ideological objectives. Racist groups might use them in an attempt to wipe out their perceived enemies. Some religious groups may see these weapons as a means to bring about the apocalypse. Political turmoil in Africa, Asia, and South America may result in an insurgent group using a WMD against the government. For example, the world has seen a number of genocides in Africa and Eastern Europe. This hatred may be compelling enough to use a WMD.

Possession of WMDs could be seen as a way of enhancing a state's or group's prestige in a region or in the world. North Korea has developed nuclear weapons, and this essentially has forced the United States and other countries to deal and negotiate with North Korea. Iran may be in the process of developing nuclear weapons. This has resulted in Iran having higher levels of prestige within the region. Iran is now seen as a central player in Middle Eastern political affairs. This has forced the United States to have to deal with the country. WMDs, especially nuclear weapons, provide a country with more leverage in the world community.

There are strategic motivational factors for using WMDs. For example, the use of bioweapons or chemical weapons could result in a specific objective: (1) mass casualties, (2) economic damage, (3) target contamination, (4) disruption of the enemy's ability to conduct business, and (5) the undermining of public confidence in the target government. When used strategically, these weapons are seen as one attack mode that can be coupled with others. At the same time, constraining factors include the perception that the use of these weapons may be counterproductive, leading to reprisals and alienation of support groups. States are not likely to use WMDs because of the fear of retaliation and the stigma associated with their use.

RELATIVE DESTRUCTIVENESS OF WMDS

This chapter has focused on the three basic categories of WMDs: nuclear, biological, and chemical. Each type of weapon presents a unique set of problems to nation-states. Each has the potential to cause mass casualties and disrupt a nation's or region's economy. Each requires a homeland security strategy and countermeasures. However, we find that some WMDs are more deadly and disruptive than others. As an example, although there are numerous possible biological weapons, at this point it appears that the smallpox virus would be the deadliest and of the greatest concern. Of course this does not consider any new biological weapons that might be developed in laboratories as a result of altering DNA. Although chemical weapons pose a danger, at this point it appears that militarized chemical weapons such as VX, sarin, and ricin present the greatest danger. These chemical weapons have been developed by countries' military and are not easily made by terrorists, although the Japanese terrorist group Aum Shinrikyo manufactured sarin gas and deployed it in Tokyo. It appears that nerve gases pose the greatest danger among chemical weapons. Finally, nuclear WMDs, especially nuclear bombs, pose the greatest danger. They can do more harm than biological or chemical WMDs.

A United Nations (1993) study examined the relative impact of hypothetical nuclear, biological, and chemical attacks. Essentially, the study found that a one-megaton nuclear device if dropped from a bomber might kill 90 percent of unprotected people over an area of 300 square kilometers. A 15-ton chemical weapon might kill 50 percent of the unprotected people in a 60 square kilometer area. Finally, a 10-ton biological weapon would kill 50 percent of the people in a 60-kilometer area and make 50 percent ill within an area of 100,000 kilometers. These figures demonstrate the potency of the three WMDs.

WEAPONS OF MASS DESTRUCTION PROLIFERATION

The preceding sections have outlined the dangers of WMDs. As noted, numerous WMDs can potentially harm people in the United States. A primary objective of homeland security is to keep WMDs out of the terrorists' hands, and if they are able to obtain them, to keep them from being smuggled into the United States. Currently, nine countries possess nuclear weapons. However, Iran may be in the process of acquiring the capability to construct nuclear weapons, and Iranian officials could share bomb-making plans and materials with other countries. North Korea has shared

---

Analysis Box 9-7

The United Nations study provides us with benchmarks in terms of the destructiveness of various WMDs. Which of the various WMDs is most dangerous? Why?

technology with Iran and possibly other countries. The Pakistani nuclear scientist A. C. Khan provided information to several nations, and it is not known how many countries received his assistance. It is very likely that the future will witness a spread of nuclear arms across the world (Lugar, 2005), and as more counties acquire these weapons, the probability that they will be deployed increases.

HS Web Link: To learn more about countries that have been involved in nuclear technology, go to *http://www.nationmaster. com/graph/mil_wmd_nuc- military-wmd-nuclear./*

Currently, a limited number of countries possess nuclear arms, but numerous countries possess chemical and biological weapons. For example, the James Martin Center for Nonproliferation Studies (2002) has identified 29 countries that are suspected to have or have had biological or chemical weapons programs. A number of these counties are embroiled or cursorily involved in conflicts: Sudan, Iran, Iraq, Myanmar, Libya, North Korea, Pakistan, and Syria. Many of the countries with biological or chemical weapons programs have weak central governments, which increases the probability that WMDs might fall into the hands of terrorists. The breakup of the Soviet Union resulted in the creation of numerous weak nation-states that have a desire to possess these weapons and weak central governments to control them once they have been obtained. It appears that WMDs will continue to proliferate, ever increasing their danger to America and the world.

Summary

This chapter explored the problem of weapons of mass destruction. WMDs represent a threat to the United States and the world; preventing their use and responding to an incident where WMDs have been deployed are the primary objectives of homeland security. WMDs pose the greatest threat to America in terms of fatalities, health, and economic well-being. The United States must develop strategies that reduce the likelihood of their deployment and be prepared should the fail-safe system prove to be inadequate, and as noted in Chapter 1, our country has been working on a number of WMD countermeasures.

Of the three categories of WMDs, nuclear weapons constitute the greatest threat. They potentially can cause the greatest harm in terms of loss of life and economic disruption. They essentially can destroy a whole city or region. Moreover, if deployed, a nuclear attack can devastate an area for many years, having long-term effects. The United States is working with a number of countries to prevent terrorists from obtaining these weapons. Moreover, homeland security is attempting to secure the borders to prevent terrorists from smuggling a device into the United States.

A second nuclear scenario is the destruction of a nuclear facility, such as a nuclear power plant. These facilities could be attacked using a small airplane or by a small group of well-armed terrorists. The destruction of a nuclear power plant could have the same effects as

a small nuclear device, as evidenced by the Chernobyl nuclear meltdown in the Ukraine. Finally, terrorists could obtain nuclear waste products, which have little security, and construct a dirty bomb. These three scenarios represent real threats to the United States.

Terrorists can use a host of biological weapons . Most notably, anthrax has already been used in the United States. The attack left eight Americans dead and several injured. Numerous bacteria, viruses, and toxins can be used as biological weapons, and there are research programs worldwide that are possibly developing more toxic and deadly forms of bacteria and viruses. The biological agent that presents the greatest concern is the smallpox virus. A small amount of the virus spread across several locations could create a substantial epidemic. However, one of the homeland security initiatives discussed in Chapter 1 is the stockpiling of vaccines.

Finally, a number of chemicals can be used for weapons of mass destruction. They range from pesticides to VX gas. Over the years, a number of chemical weapons have been used, most notably during World War I and the Iraqi-Iranian war, and the Iraqis used them against the Kurds in Iraq. Many of the chemical weapons that have been used in the past are not suitable as a weapon of mass destruction. The biggest concern is with newer chemicals such as VX, sarin, and ricin. These are deadly chemicals that have a high kill rate.

Even though terrorists may possess nuclear, biological, or chemical materials, it remains daunting to weaponize the material, and it is a complicated process to deploy such weapons. It requires significant technological knowledge and support system. It also requires a highly developed organization, and most terrorist organizations do not have the ability to deliver a significant WMD. This is especially true since 9/11. The United States and other countries around the world have substantially increased their efforts to prevent terrorists from acquiring and deploying WMDs. This does not mean that they will be unable to do so, but today it is infinitely more difficult.

It is a complicated matter to deploy a WMD, especially in the United States, but it is not insurmountable. Figure 9-3 provides a flowchart of the actions that would be required of terrorists.

This discussion demonstrates that deploying a WMD is a complicated affair. Fortunately, most terrorist groups do not have the capacity to undertake this endeavor. Nonetheless, vigilance must be taken to ensure that the homeland security system maximizes security.

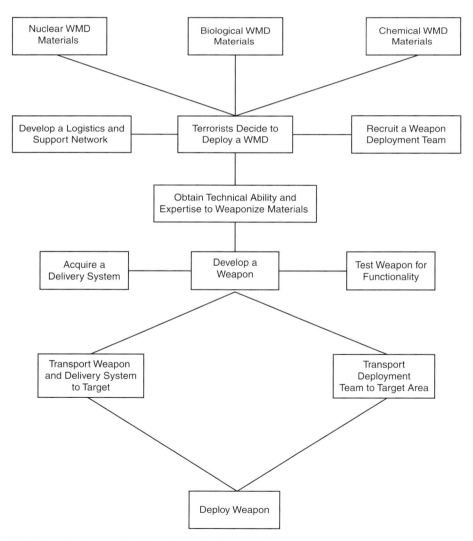

FIGURE 9-3 Process for Terrorists to Deploy a WMD.

Discussion Questions

1. What is a WMD? How do public perceptions of WMDs differ from legal definitions of these weapons?
2. Which WMDs are the most dangerous and why?
3. Describe ways in which nuclear or radiological materials can be used as WMDs.
4. Describe the historical use of WMDs.
5. Compare bacteria, viruses, and toxins in terms of their use as a WMD.
6. Describe the three types of biological agents that can be weaponized. Which is the most dangerous?
7. Compare point source and line source biological and chemical WMD dispersion.
8. Describe the constraints on terrorist groups preventing them from using WMDS.

References

Ackerman, G. and Moran, K. (undated). "Bioterrorism and threat assessment." Stockholm, Sweden: Weapons of Mass Destruction Commission. http://www.wmdcommission.org/files/No22.pdf (Accessed January 17, 2011).

American-Israeli Cooperative Enterprise. (undated). *Chemical Terrorism.* http://www.jewishvirtuallibrary.org/jsource/Terrorism/chemterror.html. (Accessed January 17, 2011).

Broad, W. and D. Sanger. (2008). "In nuclear net's undoing, a web of shadowy deals." *New York Times* (August 25), p. A1.

Brown, D. (2003). "Canada arrests 19 as security threats." *Washington Post* (August 23), p. A20.

Cameron, G. and N. Bajema. (2009). "Assessing the post 9/11 threat of CBRN terrorism." In *Terrorism and Counterterrorism: Understanding the New Security Environment,* ed. R. Howard, R. Sawyer, and N. Bajema, pp. 267–87. New York: McGraw-Hill.

Centers for Disease Control and Prevention. (2008). *Emergency Preparedness and Response: Chemical Categories.* http://www.bt.cdc.gov/agent/agentlistchem-category.asp (Accessed September 3, 2008).

Center for Defense Information. (2003). *CDI Factsheet: Ricin* (February 7). http://www.cdi.org/terrorism/ricin-factsheet.cfm (Accessed August 5, 2008).

Cochran, T. and M. McKinzie. (2008). "Detecting nuclear smuggling." *Scientific American*, 298(4): 98–104.

Cone, M. (2008). "A hazardous dependency: Chemists are hindered in creating safer ingredients for products." *Los Angeles Times* (September 19), pp. A1, A16.

DeNoon, D. (2003). "Biological and chemical terror history: Lessons learned." http://www.webmd.com/content/article/61/67268.htm (Accessed August 20, 2008).

Egan, T. (2001). "A nation challenged: The convicted terrorist; Man caught in 2000 plot is helping investigators." *New York Times* (September 27). http://query.nytimes.com/gst/fullpage.html?res=9403EFD9113AF934A1575AC0A9679C8B63 (Accessed September 4, 2008).

Environmental Protection Agency. (2000). *Chemical Accident Risks in U.S. Industry—A Preliminary Analysis of Accident Risk Data from U.S. Hazardous Chemical Facilities.* Washington, D.C.: Author.

Fields, G., A. Davis, and J. Schlesinger. (2003). "US is pressed to boost role in private-sector security." *Wall Street Journal* (March 21), p. A4.

Frantz, D. and C. Collins. (2007). "Those nuclear flashpoints are made in Pakistan." *Washington Post* (November 11). http://www.washingtonpost.com/wp-dyn/content/article/2007/11/07/AR2007110702280.html (Accessed August 28, 2009).

Government Accounting Office. (1977). "Commercial nuclear fuel facilities need better security." Cited in J. Stern (2003). "Getting and using the weapons." In *Terrorism and Counterterrorism: Understanding the New Security Environment,* ed. R. Howard and R. Sawyer, pp. 158–74. New York: McGraw-Hill.

Harigel, G. (2000). "The concept of weapons of mass destruction: Chemical and biological weapons, use in warfare, impact on society and environment." Paper presented at the Conference on Biosecurity and Bioterrorism, Rome (September 18–19).

Homeland Security Council. (2007). *Strategy for Homeland Security.* Washington, D.C.: Author.

Jagmanis, L. (2008). "CBRNE: Evaluation of a Biological Warfare Victim." *EMedicine.* http://www.emedicine.com/emerg/topic891.htm (Accessed September 2, 2008).

James Martin Center for Nonproliferation Studies. (2006). *Chronology of CBW Incidents Targeting Agriculture and Food Systems 1915–2006.* Monterey, CA: James Martin Center for Nonproliferation Studies. http://cns.miis.edu/research/cbw/agchron.htm. (Accessed August 22, 2008).

Krock, L. and R. Deusser. (2003). *Dirty Bomb: Chronology of Events.* Nova. http://www.pbs.org/wgbh/nova/dirtybomb/chrono.html (Accessed August 28, 2008).

Lugar, R. (2005). *The Lugar Survey on Proliferation Threats and Responses*. Washington, D.C.: Author.

Meleson, M. (1991). "The myth of chemical superweapons." *Bulletin of the Atomic Scientists*, (April): 12–15.

Muller, R. (undated). *A Significant Toxic Event: The Union Carbide Pesticide Plant Disaster in Bhopal, India, 1984.* http://www.tropmed.org/rreh/vol1_10.htm (Accessed September 21, 2008).

Olson, K. (1999). "Aum Shinrikyo :Once and future threat." *Emerging Infectious Diseases*, 5(4): 513–16.

Parachini, J. (2006). "Putting WMD terrorism into perspective." In *Homeland Security and Terrorism: Readings and Interpretations,* ed. R. Howard, J. Forest, and J. Moore, pp. 31–42. New York: McGraw-Hill.

Ploughshares. (2011). *World Nuclear Stockpile Report.* http://www.ploughshares.org/news-analysis/world-nuclear-stockpile-report (Accessed January 17, 2011)

Preston, R. (1999). "The demon in the freezer: How smallpox, a disease officially eradicated twenty years ago, became the biggest terrorist threat we now face." *New Yorker* (July 12): 44–61.

Project on Government Oversight. (2001). *U.S. Nuclear Weapons Complex: Security at Risk.* http://www.pogo.org/p/environment/eo-011003-nuclear.html#anchor2 (Accessed August 28, 2008).

Sauter, M. and J. Carafano. (2005). *Homeland Security.* New York: McGraw-Hill.

Stockholm International Peace Research Instittute. (1971). *The Problem of Chemical and Biological Warfare, Vol. I.* New York: Humanities Press.

Snyder, L. and J. Pate. (2002). *Tracking Anthrax Hoaxes and Attacks.* Monterey, CA: James Martin Center for Nonproliferation Studies. http://cns.miis.edu/pubs/week/020520.htm (Accessed August 23, 2008).

Sultan, M. (undated). "Biological terrorism: The threat of the 21st century. *The Institute of Strategic Studies, Islamabad.* http://www.issi.org.pk/journal/2001_files/no_4/article/2a.htm (Accessed September 8, 2008).

Thevenot, C. and L. Mower. (2008). "Guns, anarchy text found in room with ricin: LV police say terrorism not motive despite discovery." *Las Vegas Review-Journal.* http://www.lvrj.com/news/16142962.html (Accessed August 23, 2008).

Vandenbroucke, L. (1984). "The Israeli strike against OSIRAQ." *Air University Review.* http://www.globalsecurity.org/wmd/library/report/1984/vanden.htm (Accessed August 21, 2004).

Van-Tuam, N. (2005). *Agent Orange and the War in Vietnam.* New South Wales, Australia: Garvan Institute of Medical Research and Univesity.

World Nuclear Association. (2008). *Chernobyl Accident.* http://www.world nuclear.org/info/chernobyl/inf07.html (Accessed August 26, 2008).

Zillinskas, R. (1999). "Cuban allegations of biological warfare by the United States: Assessing the evidence." *Critical Reviews in Microbiology*, 25(3): 173–27.

10

Cyber Crime and Terrorism

LEARNING OBJECTIVES

1. Identify the methods of attacking cyber infrastructure.
2. Distinguish between cyber crime and cyber terrorism.
3. Consider the various sectors within America that are vulnerable to cyber attacks.
4. Identify the types of information that terrorist groups post on their Internet home pages.
5. Examine how terrorists use the Internet.
6. Understand the federal cyber counterintelligence agencies and their operations.

KEY TERMS

Cyber space

Physical or conventional attack

Electronic attack

Malicious code

Hacking

Hackers

Backdoor

Botnet

Denial of Service Attack

Phishing and spoofing

Robot or Zombie

Trojans

Virus and worms

Cyber terrorism

Cyber warfare

National Cyber Response Coordination Group

Netwar

Cyber Action Teams

Computer Crimes Task Forces

Internet Complaint Center

National Cyber Security Division

National Cyberspace Response System

Cyber Risk Management Program

INTRODUCTION

The topic of cyber terrorism has received a great deal of attention and notoriety (see Clarke, 2008). Agency administrators, politicians, and the media have devoted a substantial amount of discourse to the topic. The discussion has been integrated with other terrorist threats and scenarios, making it a real issue for large numbers of people. There are ample examples of what might happen if cyber terrorist acts occur, and there are examples of hackers attacking a number of computers and databases. However, we must distinguish between the possible, the plausible, and the real. In other words, how real is a cyber attack, what kind of attack could occur, and what are the consequences of such an attack? These questions must be examined rationally, and realistic policies and counter-measures must be developed. It begs the question, how catastrophic can such an attack be relative to our national well-being?

Cyber terrorism and cyber attacks have been linked to al Qaeda, other terrorists, criminal groups, and countries. The U.S. government reported that Iraq had Iraq Net, which was set to attack American computer systems (see Stohl, 2006). When U.S. troops captured al Qaeda computers in Iraq, they often discovered complex information about nuclear plants, water systems, and so on. There is no evidence that al Qaeda has used this information to launch a cyber attack against these assets, but the possibility persists. Clarke (2003) advises that seized computers belonging to al Qaeda and other terrorist groups indicate that their members are working with hacker tools, resulting in substantial risk. In 2010, Dennis Blair, director of national intelligence, warned Congress that intelligence indicates that al Qaeda is endeavoring to increase the number of cyber attacks on the United States (Mazzettii, 2010). Al Qaeda and other terrorist groups may believe that cyber attacks would be more effective than physical attacks in terms of economic damage to the United States.

It is important to note that terrorist acts can occur across a broad spectrum of targets. In Chapter 3, the *National Infrastructure Protection Plan* (DHS, 2006) was examined. One of the primary categories of infrastructure addressed in the plan was cyberspace and its related technology. The average American does not fully comprehend or appreciate the impact that the Internet and other communications centers have on our society. A substantial amount of our commerce, daily activities, work, and leisure is conducted through the Internet. It touches everyone's life on a daily basis. The Internet and communications systems encompass a substantial amount of telecommunications hardware and software that is vulnerable to attack and hacking. Communications centers located in some of our major cities control the telephone and Internet communications for large portions of states and in some cases several states. Individual servers or communications sites handle large volumes of this traffic. These facilities and activities are likely targets of terrorists and other computer hackers. An attack on our cyber and communications system, depending on the proportion of communications that are affected, could have disastrous effects on American society.

Before proceeding further, it is important to define **cyber space**. Essentially, it is the world communications domain consisting of vast amounts of hardware, software, and data and information. Some see it as the data and information that freely flow across the globe, but here, cyber space also includes the equipment that facilitates the flow of information. Barlow (1990) has equated cyber space to America's Wild West:

> Cyberspace in its present condition has a lot in common with the 19th Century west. It is vast, unmapped, culturally and legally ambiguous . . . hard to get around in, and up for grabs. Large institutions already claim to own the place, but most of the actual natives are solitary and independent, sometimes to the point of sociopathy. It is, of course, a perfect breeding ground for both outlaws and new ideas about liberty. (p. 1)

Analysis Box 10-1

Terrorists use a variety of methods to attack their enemies, and many are very destructive, including car bombs, armed attacks, and suicide bombers. In many cases, these attacks result in numerous casualties. Do you think a cyber attack would be as destructive? Why?

Barlow's analogy is absolutely correct. Cyber space is vast, so vast that we have yet to harness or comprehend its future potential. We are totally dependent upon it as it intrudes into every aspect of daily life. He is also correct in noting that there is little or no control over most of this technology. It is an open system used freely by individuals, businesses, corporations, governments, criminals, and terrorists. It was built to facilitate use with little thought given to security and the implications of breaches of security. Clarke and Knake (2010) advise that this lack of control and security can result in disasters that are far worse than any other kind of attack—our nation and the world can be brought to their knees as a result of cyber attacks.

METHODS OF ATTACKING CYBER INFRASTRUCTURE

Basically, there are three methods for attacking computers and our cyber infrastructure: physical, electronic, and malicious code (Wilson, 2005). First, a **physical or conventional attack** can be mounted against a facility with the aim of destroying its infrastructure. At the beginning and during the Iraqi War, the United States often targeted communications facilities to impede Iraqi army communications and command functions. When al Qaeda attacked the World Trade Center and Pentagon in 2001, the attacks destroyed communications systems that were linked globally (Marlin and Garvin, 2004); the destruction of these communications systems greatly impeded the public safety response. Coordination of the various responding agencies was hampered, and communications among the various responders were substantially limited. Physical attacks can temporarily destroy communications capabilities, disrupting a number of important activities including recovery.

According to Wilson, a second type of physical attack is an **electronic attack** or electromagnetic pulse, whereby an electrical charge occurs near the computer or server hardware. Essentially, the electromagnetic pulse results in high energy that overloads circuit boards, computer chips, and other electronics. Memory can be erased, software can be disrupted, and hardware can be electronically destroyed. Small, portable electromagnetic devices could be used in a limited fashion to attack cyber infrastructure, but there are no examples of this type of attack.

Third, the most common form of attacks on cyber infrastructure and systems is **malicious code**. Malicious code can disrupt a computer's or network's operation. Moreover, it can spread from one computer to another, resulting in large-scale problems or losses. Several tools are used in such attacks.

Tools Used in Hacking and Cyber Attacks

Attacking computers and infrastructure using some form of intrusive code or program is referred to as **hacking**. Essentially, it does not matter the mode or intent behind the computer or network intrusions; all attackers will use similar methods of hacking. Furnell and Warren (1999) define **hackers** as, "persons who deliberately gain (or attempt to gain) unauthorized access to computer

HS Web Link: To see an example of hacking information on the web, go to *http://www.hackingalert. com/hacking-articles/ hotmail-hacking-guide.php.*

systems" (p. 29). All instances of hacking result in an array problems for the victimized computer system and its owners.

Vulnerability increases as developments in hardware and software outstrip security mechanisms, although there are continuous efforts to develop security measures. The Internet is increasingly being used in every sector throughout the United States and the world. Deregulation of industries and the need to net greater profits have led to an increased reliance on cyber systems as they add efficiency and effectiveness to the governmental or business enterprise. As an example, many utility companies use computerized systems to control and monitor the flow of electricity, natural gas, and water with substantial information flowing across the Internet. Moreover, many systems use off-the-shelf software, whereby an industry purchases its controlling software from one vender. This creates vulnerability. If hackers break into one system, they have the knowledge and tools to invade other similar systems. They in essence can have industry-wide access.

Rattray (2003) notes that hackers are more knowledgeable and sophisticated in their hacking, whereas the knowledge and skills required of hackers to break into systems have declined. A number of countries have established schools to teach hacking (Clarke and Knake, 2010). These countries want a steady supply of technically savvy people who can attack other countries' computer systems or gather intelligence. Moreover, there are numerous sources for hackers to learn about hacking methods with a substantial amount of information posted on the World Wide Web. A number of terrorist groups and others including hackers post this information on the

Net surfers crowd a Beijing Internet café. Many hackers use similar cafés.   *Source:* AP (9611150443).

Backdoor	Code inserted in a program that allows someone to gain access to the program or secure computer. Backdoors are commonly inserted in programs to allow programmers access. Criminals and hackers often insert backdoors in programs to obtain data or to control the computer. A backdoor can also be inserted with the introduction of a worm.
Botnet	A group or network of computers that has been commandeered by hackers to attack other computers or systems for illegitimate purposes. The computers operate in unison and are controlled by the hacker.
Denial of Service Attack	Sometimes referred to as blockades or virtual sit-ins, these attacks initiated by a number of computers making multiple requests that cause the targeted computer or system to become overloaded, with the result that it slows down or crashes. Such attacks are usually originated with a botnet.
Phishing and spoofing	Deceptive e-mails and websites are used to entice a user to provide personal or financial information for fraud or identity theft.
Robot or Zombie	This is a computer that has a Trojan or worm inserted that allows someone other than the legitimate owner to control the computer remotely. Botnets are composed of robot computers.
Trojans	These are viruses or worms that appear to be software upgrades, share programs, help files, screen savers, and pictures such as pornography that once opened run in the background causing damage or allowing an illegitimate user to control the computer.
Virus and worms	These are executable programs that are inserted into a computer program via Trojans or hacking. They typically are meant to harm the computer by altering files or data. They often delete, modify, or corrupt data and files.

FIGURE 10-1   Commonly Used Hacking Tools.

Internet. There is a virtual library for hackers. Thus, there is a range of sophistication relative to computer hackers from the novice to the expert to the nation-state.

Weimann (2004), Kane (2011), and Clarke and Knake (2010) have identified the primary tools used by hackers to attack computers and data systems. Some tools are designed to infiltrate a computer system, whereas others attempt to gain sensitive financial or personal information from individuals. Figure 10-1 provides a listing and brief description of the various tools and methods.

As noted in Figure 10-1, a number of these tools are used in conjunction, whereas some can operate independently. They can be used by hackers, terrorists, or governments to attack the United States or to steal defense or industrial secrets. The number of attacks is substantial and increasing each year. For example, in 2008, the Department of Defense reported that there had been 54,640 attacks on its computer systems, a 20 percent increase from 2007 (U.S.-China Economic and Security Review Commission, 2009). There is an increasing number of cyber attacks on every sector of business, industry, defense, government, oil, power, and so on. It is likely that each year hundreds of thousands of attacks are launched. Clarke and Knake (2010) warn that cyber attacks can be just as devastating as conventional weapons or even a WMD attack.

Analysis Box 10-2

As noted, hackers use a variety of methods to attack computers. They attack individual computers and they attack networks. If you use the Internet, you connect to a network. Botnets and zombie computers seem to be the most troublesome attacks. Has your computer ever been hacked? Do you know if your computer is being used as a zombie? How do you know? Do you have any virus protection software and how effective is it?

WHAT IS CYBER TERRORISM?

To some extent, it is difficult to define cyber terrorism, since it encompasses such a wide spectrum of activities, victims, and perpetrators. Weimann (2005) defined it as "the use of computer network tools to harm or shut down critical national infrastructures (such as energy, transportation, government operations)" (p. 130). On the other hand, Pollitt (undated), defined cyber terrorism as, "the premeditated, politically motivated attack against information, computer systems, computer programs, and the data that results in violence against noncombatant targets by subnational groups or clandestine agents." **Cyber terrorism** is the merging of cyberspace, which is a virtual world where computer programs function and data move, and terrorism, the premeditated, politically motivated violence perpetrated against noncombatant targets by subnational or clandestine groups. Although cyber terrorism can be performed by a nation-state, it generally is used by groups that advocate some cause against a perceived or real enemy. It is used to cripple, cause terror, or have an economic impact on a state or group of people.

There is widespread disagreement relative to the threat posed by cyber terrorism. Some homeland security personnel have referred to it as an "impending Pearl Harbor," great danger, or significant threat, whereas others see it more as a minor inconvenience or at least a threat that has been overstated and popularized (see Carafano, 2008; Lewis, 2006; Rattray, 2006; Stohl, 2006; Wilson, 2005). Those who affirm cyber terrorism as a real danger note our substantial dependence on the Internet and networks and their intrusive relationship with all aspects of society, including commerce, public welfare, finance, and defense. There are many avenues for disruption and numerous targets. On the other hand, those who downplay the threat of cyber terrorism believe that cyber attacks by terrorists do not meet their objectives—large-scale destruction, multiple casualties, or psychological advantage. These results are better achieved with a car or truck bomb! Cyber intrusions by terrorists (although few have been documented) just add to the problem of constant hacking activities, and effective defensive countermeasure systems must be developed to deter hacking and intrusions of all sorts.

National Security Agency personnel monitor cyber traffic.   *Source:* AP (060125032460).

DISTINGUISHING HACKING, CYBER CRIME, CYBER TERRORISM, AND CYBER WARFARE

Hacking, cyber crime, cyber terrorism, and cyber warfare are multidimensional, interconnected problems. A number of crimes and problems are associated with cyber space. The Internet is used to commit a variety of crimes by nation-states, terrorists, and nonterrorists or criminals. Crimes and terrorist acts can emanate from across the globe, including from the United States. They can include the theft of information ranging from financial or personal records to military intelligence and industrial espionage. They can alter or destroy computer systems, adversely affecting our critical infrastructure. Such acts can be conducted by governments, terrorists, professionals, or novice hackers and can target hardware, software, or data files. In essence, cyber crime and terrorism represent a significant challenge to homeland security and law enforcement.

As noted earlier, cyber-related attacks can come from a variety of actors with different motivations. Figure 10-2 provides a breakdown of the different types of cyber criminals, their motivations, and their threat actions.

Figure 10-2 provides a typology of those who would attack computer systems. Hackers are those individuals who attempt to penetrate computers and networks for the challenge. Their attacks essentially are to test their computer skills. In some cases, they will attempt to create damage, but for the most part, their efforts merely are tests of their skills. Computer criminals are motivated by financial reward. They may hack into a computer to steal data such as credit card information or personal information that could be used for gain. In some cases, they may attempt to blackmail a business or group using illegally obtained data or information. Terrorists are more nefarious, and their intentions generally center on creating damage or harm to an enemy. As noted, there is no evidence of cyber terror attacks on the United States, but there is evidence that attempts have at least been contemplated. Industrial espionage, as discussed in Chapter 8, involves individuals, companies, and governments with the primary motivation being financial. Theft of trade secrets can reduce product or systems development costs and result in marketing advantages. Countries are involved in industrial espionage as it provides information about another country's infrastructure and defense capabilities and allows for a reduction in weapons and other systems development.

Cyber Crime

A variety of crimes are conducted or facilitated via the Internet. Many of these crimes are sophisticated property crimes and others support terrorism. Taylor and his colleagues (2006) provide a number of examples of these crimes as noted in Figure 10-3.

This listing demonstrates that the Internet has become a tool that can been used to facilitate a wide range of criminal acts. Perhaps the most common crime is phishing. Millions of Americans receive countless e-mails requesting financial information or their involvement in some kind of financial scheme. The perpetrators are attempting to entice the e-mail recipients to provide financial information or to send money so that some large amount of money in a foreign country can be processed or split between the e-mail sender and the victim. They may also attempt to obtain personal information for identity theft purposes. In some cases, the sender may install a worm that sends victims' financial or personal information to the e-mail sender.

There have been numerous instances in which hackers have accessed retailers' computers and stolen thousands of credit cards' information. For example, in 2009, Heartland Payment Systems reported that its system was broached for an undetermined period of time. The company processes 100 million credit card transactions a month. The number of stolen credit card numbers could not

Type of Cyber Criminal	Motivation	Threat Actions
Hacker	• Challenge • Ego • Rebellion • Curiosity	• Hacking • Systems intrusions • Unauthorized access • Theft
Computer Criminal	• Destruction of Information • Illegal access to information • Monetary gain • Unauthorized data alteration	• Fraud • Cyber stalking • Theft of information • System alteration • Spoofing
Terrorist	• Blackmail • Destruction • Exploitation • Revenge	• Facilitate attacks • Information warfare • System attack • System penetration • System tampering
Industrial Espionage	• Competitive advantage • Economic espionage • Trade secrets	• Economic exploitation • Information theft • Intrusion on personal privacy • Social engineering • Access to proprietary or technology information
Insiders (Employees)	• Curiosity • Ego • Intelligence • Monetary gain • Revenge • Cover up other crimes or errors	• Assault or attacks on employees • Blackmail • Access to proprietary information • Computer abuse • Fraud and theft • Input of false or corrupted information • Interception of information • Destruction of systems or data
Countries	• Intelligence and espionage • Incapacitate systems • Political intervention • Economic destabilization • Cyber warfare	• Hacking • System intrusions • Information losses • Denial of service • Attacks on infrastructure

FIGURE 10-2   Types of Cyber Criminals.   *Source:* Adapted from Stoneburner, G., A. Goguen, and A. Feringa. (2001). *Risk Management Guide for Information Technology Systems.* Special Publication 800-30. Washington, D.C.: National Institute of Standards and Technology.

be determined. In another case in 2007, 45 million credit card numbers were exposed over a three-year period when hackers accessed retailer TJX Companies' computer files (Krebs, 2009).

In addition to common crimes, some hackers attempt to break into systems to cause damage. In 2000, denial of service attacks against Yahoo, CNN, eBay, and other e-commerce sites were estimated to cost more than $1 billion (Denning, 2000). In 2002, there was a one-hour attack on the 13 root servers that control Internet domain names. The attack resulted in eight of the servers going

1. Attacks on financial institutions, businesses, and industries, including military installations
2. Cyber stalking
3. Obscenity, including child pornography
4. Child molestation (obtaining contacts)
5. Sex tourism, in which pedophiles seek underage victims
6. Distribution of digital hate (websites and e-mails), especially by hate and terrorist groups
7. Communications among criminal and terrorist groups
8. Gathering of intelligence information on potential targets
9. Identity theft
10. Money laundering

FIGURE 10-3   Criminal Acts Facilitated via the Internet.

off-line, disrupting Internet service (Lewis, 2002). In 2001, the Code Red worm was launched and infected thousands of computers, resulting in an estimated $2.6 billion in damage. Other recent worms included Code Red II and Nimda. In 2000, a virus infected 1,000 computers at the Ford Motor Company, resulting in the computer system being shut down. The system received 140,000 contaminated e-mails in three hours—an example of a denial of service attack (Lewis, 2002).

The FBI in conjunction with the National White Collar Crime Center operates an Internet fraud-reporting center. Figure 10-4 shows the distribution of complaints that are received.

As noted in Figure 10-4, several Internet scams and fraudulent crimes are conducted on the Internet. The most commonly reported complaint is FBI scams, in which someone alleging that

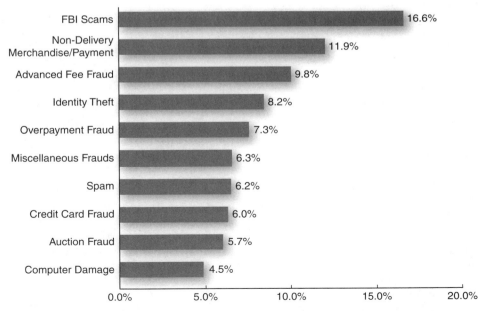

FIGURE 10-4   Distribution of Internet Fraud Complaints.   *Source:* Internet Crime Complaint Center. (2010). *2009 Internet Crime Report.* National White Collar Crime Center. http://www. ic3.gov/media/annualreport/2009_IC3Report.pdf (Accessed August 5, 2010).

he or she is from the FBI requests information from citizens. More than 6 percent of the complaints are for spam, and in many cases spam is used to infect computers with a virus.

Cyber Warfare

Cyber warfare is an attack by one nation-state on another nation-state. It is cyber terrorism conducted by a country. The incidence of cyber warfare has become more common over the past decade with most of the attacks associated with Russia and China (Clarke and Knake, 2010). An attack may serve several purposes:

- Gain economic or military intelligence
- Test another country's defenses
- Cripple another country's weapons systems
- Cripple another country's military communications systems
- Cause economic chaos
- Military posturing or political bargaining

In 2009, a number of government and commercial infrastructure sites in the United States and Korea were attacked via the denial of service method. Sites in the United States included the Treasury Department, Secret Service, Federal Trade Commission, New York Stock Exchange, Nasdaq, and the *Washington Post*. Clarke and Knake (2010) report that some of the sites were hit with as many as 1 million requests per second, effectively shutting them down. In Korea, government sites, banks, and an Internet security companies were targeted. It was estimated that 166,000 computers in 74 countries were used in the Korean attacks. The attackers used robot or zombie computers linked to a botnet. The attacks emanated from North Korea (Sang-Hun and Markoff, 2009).

Northern Command personnel monitor Internet traffic. *Source:* AP (03051505929).

Analysis Box 10-3

Markoff and Shanker found that the United States had prepared for a cyber attack on Iraq but did not initiate the attack. Rather than launching the cyber attack, the U.S. military bombed critical communications centers.

Do you believe the government was correct in not launching the cyber attack? Given the Russian experiences in Georgia and Estonia, do you think cyber warfare is an important part of the military arsenal?

In November 2008, a series of attacks were launched from Russia on the U.S. Central Command, the command that is responsible for conducting the Iraqi War. It could not be determined if the Russian government was directly involved in the attacks. Defense officials noted that their computers are constantly bombarded by attacks, but the November attack was especially intrusive, with the attackers using malware (malicious software that attacks computers) that may have been developed specifically to attack military computers (Barnes, 2008).

There are ample examples of similar types of attacks. In August 2008, Russian troops invaded neighboring Georgia. Preceding and during the attacks, the Russians launched a number of cyber attacks on the Georgians, affecting their ability to respond to the Russian invasion. The Russians created a cyber quarantine. It was the first instance in which a cyber attack was used in conjunction with a shooting war. Previously, in 2007, the Russians were accused of launching a massive cyber attack against Estonia. According to Carafano (2008), the assault affected a number of Estonia's public and private information networks with massive denial of service attacks. The attacks targeted the websites of Estonian banks, telecommunication companies, media outlets, and government agencies. Estonia's defense minister described the attacks as a national security situation.

HS Web Link: To learn more about how Russia used cyber warfare in Estonia, go to *http://www.wired.com/politics/security/magazine/15-09/ff_estonia?currentPage=all.*

In 2009, it was announced that the United States had prepared a cyber attack on Iraq's financial system computers prior to our invasion in 2003. The Pentagon and American intelligence agencies, however, were not given the authority to conduct the attack for fear of collateral damage. It was feared that the attacks would have a rippling effect on other countries' computer systems and possibly disrupt financial markets and operations in other countries (Markoff and Shanker, 2009).

These attacks demonstrate the growing use of cyber warfare. In Georgia, cyber attacks served as a force multiplier for the Russians. These attacks often result in a cost of millions of dollars as victims of the attacks must repair the damage; invest in new security software; and in some cases, remove systems and replace them with new, more secure ones. Cyber attacks on government and other facilities will continue. It is likely that most, if not all, countries are involved in cyber warfare, although these efforts certainly are masked. In 2010, the U.S. military created a Cyber Command headed by a four-star general. The command is tasked with preparing and conducting cyber warfare. The Air Force reportedly transferred 30,000 troops to support cyber warfare (Beaumont, 2010). These troops are being used to monitor cyber systems and develop defenses for cyber attacks. Cyber attacks are now seen as a necessary part of warfare, and the U.S. military and intelligence complex is involved in developing the tools for upcoming wars (see Graham, 2003).

POINTS OF CYBER ATTACKS

President George W. Bush appointed Richard Clarke as his first special advisor on cyberspace security. After the 9/11 attacks, cyber security quickly became a primary homeland security concern. Clarke echoed these concerns, often advocating the need for security improvements.

- Centers for Disease Control and Prevention, which coordinates the nation's response to biological attacks, including identification and mediation. An attack could curtail our ability to recognize an attack and respond to it
- The nation's interconnected financial network, including FedWire, which is the system used by the Federal Reserve Banks to transfer funds. An attack could disrupt financial transactions
- Computer systems controlling water and waste disposal plants and operations. Cyber attacks could contaminate water supplies or create shortages.
- Computer systems that control our dams. An attack could result in flooding or water shortages.
- Networks and systems that control America's power grids. An attack could result in power shortages across large sections of the country.
- A concerted attack on various computer control systems in a large city such as New York City, Chicago, or Los Angeles effectively shutting down the city.
- The 25 or so computer sites that control the flow of data and information over the Internet across the nation affecting all segments of society including commerce.
- The communications network, which includes emergency response communications.
- Transportation communications including air traffic control, rail, and public transportation.

FIGURE 10-5   Cyber Critical Infrastructure.

During a security briefing, Clarke described the areas of most concern relative to cyber terrorism. They are listed in Figure 10-5.

A number of experts have questioned whether a cyber attack can have a devastating impact on America. However, a number of politicians and experts recognize that a cyber attack can serve as a "force multiplier." For example, U.S. Representative Jane Harman, a member of the House Intelligence Committee's panel on terrorism and homeland security stated, "What I fear is the combination of a cyber attack coordinated with more traditional terrorism, undermining our ability to respond to an attack when lives are in danger" (cited in Squitieri, 2002). Should terrorists coordinate a cyber attack with a conventional or nonconventional attack—bombings or WMD attack—our ability to respond to the attack would be substantially hampered. The cyber intrusion likely would increase the destruction caused by the bombing or WMD attack. Reflecting on the 9/11 attacks in New York City, the response was greatly hampered because of radio communications inoperability after the emergency communications center was destroyed in the attack.

CYBER TERRORISM

Cyber terrorism has been defined as the merging of cyberspace, which is a virtual world where computer programs function and data move, and terrorism, the premeditated, politically motivated violence perpetrated against noncombatant targets by subnational or clandestine groups. However, Denning (2001) advises that for an attack to be considered a cyber terrorist attack, it must "be sufficiently destructive or disruptive to generate fear comparable to that from physical acts of terrorism. Attacks that lead to death or bodily injury, extended power outages, plane crashes, water contamination, or major economic losses would be examples." Much of terrorists' current cyber activities do not meet this benchmark. These activities are more akin to hacking. Indeed, Wilson (2005) advises that there have not been any documented instances of significant cyber terrorism. Nonetheless, it is likely to occur in the immediate future.

HS Web Link: To learn more about terrorists' capacity to launch such attacks, go to http://www.fas.org/sgp/crs/terror/RL33123.pdf.

Analysis Box 10-4

The previous discussion advises that it would be difficult for terrorists to launch a significant cyber attack on the United States, but there are those who believe that terrorist cyber attacks are a credible threat. Do you believe our cyber infrastructure is protected from such attacks? Do you believe the threat of these attacks is credible?

Cyber terrorism is attractive to terrorists. Weimann (2004) advises that several advantages make cyber terrorism appealing. First, it is relatively inexpensive. The terrorist needs only a computer and expertise. Second, it is anonymous. Given the worldwide web, it is difficult to determine where a threat originated. Third, the number of targets is enormous and includes governments, industry, universities, public utilities, airlines, and so on. The numerous critical infrastructure targets include utilities and water supplies. Fourth, it does not require physical training, traveling, and the physical risk associated with other types of terrorism. Fifth, it potentially can affect thousands if not millions of people. These advantages mean that terrorists likely will use cyber attacks in the future.

Finally, it should be noted that terrorist organizations will not have the cyber warfare technical skills that governments do. Admittedly, terrorists have a number of highly educated and trained personnel at their disposal. They likely have significant experience with cyber attacks and have conducted some attacks with mixed results. However, governments have two distinct advantages that terrorist organizations cannot overcome. First, governments can allocate millions of dollars to the development of cyber security and warfare—in some cases, resources are virtually unlimited. For example, the National Cyber Security Initiative was originally funded at $6 billion, and the funding is increasing (Brewin, 2008). Other countries that are targets of cyber attacks by terrorists also have a wealth of resources. Terrorists cannot compete in the area of development; they have relatively few resources for cyber attacks.

Second, countries such as the United States have a wealth of expertise. America has the world's strongest engineering and computer science programs within its vast array of universities, and large numbers of cutting-edge research and development companies are located in the United States. For example, Shorrock (2008) notes that approximately half of our intelligence operations (approximately $50 billion annually) are contracted to these private companies, and they have close working relations with government agencies such as the CIA, NSA, National Reconnaissance Office, and the Defense Intelligence Agency. A large part of their mission is electronic intelligence gathering, but at the same time, they are developing cyber security measures. This represents a substantial amount of cyber security technical power. No other country or organization can match it. It is questionable as to how much of this technology filters down to nonintelligence government and private entities, but it is likely that these countermeasures ultimately will be integrated into these sectors.

PHYSICAL ATTACKS ON COMMUNICATIONS INFRASTRCTURE

There has been substantial discussion relative to terrorists hacking into computers and stealing information or disabling them with viruses and worms. However, some consideration should be given to the physical destruction of communications infrastructure. As noted earlier, conventional physical and electromagnetic attacks can disable or destroy software and hardware systems. Communications infrastructure that controls communications and the Internet is distributed across the United States. In many cases, these facilities are unprotected or have minimum levels of security. One or more of these facilities may become the targets of terrorist attacks. Again, it appears that there is sufficient engineering overlap and redundancy so that it would be extremely difficult to bring down the complete system or even a major portion of the system. However, the greatest threat would be if terrorists launched a cyber attack in conjunction with a conventional attack.

In 2006, the Business Roundtable commissioned a report examining how to strengthen our cyber terrorism preparedness. The Business Roundtable is an association of CEOs from America's largest corporations. They represent companies comprising one-third of the value of the U.S. stock market. They actively pursue technological innovation and have a vested interest in ensuring that the Internet is not breached.

The group advises that the primary problem is that our nation is not prepared to reconstitute the Internet after a massive disruption. The Internet essentially is housed in a number of facilities that could be vulnerable to a coordinated attack. The government is responsible for various aspects of the Internet. However, there is no governmental policy on how and when the government would intervene to reconstitute portions of the Internet as a result of attacks. Although the **National Cyber Response Coordination Group** is responsible for coordinating Internet emergencies, it appears that no action plan is in place should such an emergency arise. For the most part, private companies have plans dealing with emergencies that affect their Internet venues, but this essentially represents piecemeal coverage. In other words, the nation is not prepared to enact a coordinated, comprehensive response to a significant breach in the Internet.

The Internet is the backbone for a number of critical communications functions that affect commerce, banking, public safety, and government in general. A significant breach could have significant long-lasting detrimental effects on our economy, defense, and society in general. We have a vested interest to ensure that it is protected and as secure as possible, and we must ensure that an adequate response to breaches exists and is ready to implement.

SIGNIFICANT CYBER GAPS

The Business Roundtable committee identified several critical gaps. First is a lack of formal trip wires to indicate an attack is underway. We do not have formal mechanisms to quickly identify breaches. Second is a lack of accountability and clarity on which institutions provide reconstitution support. Essentially, there is no workable action plan. Third, there is a lack of resources for institutions to reconstitute the Internet infrastructure should a breach occur. Although Congress allocates funding for the Internet, none of the monies are allocated or kept in abeyance should a significant breach occur.

The primary responsibility for reconstructing the Internet should there be a breach rests with the private sector. The government oversees and to some extent regulates the Internet, but the private sector actually runs and operates it. Companies have responsibilities to ensure that the Internet is reconstituted as seamlessly as possible. Companies must also establish a single point with the authority to reconstitute the Internet should there be a breach. In addition, companies should have a strategic plan that establishes priorities when reconstituting an Internet breach. Third, companies need to have early warning systems in place that quickly notify managers of problems so that corrective actions can take place as soon as possible. Finally, consistent protocols should be developed so that companies and industries can coordinate their efforts.

In the end, we face a number of possible problems should there be a significant breach in the Internet. This is problematic given the importance the Internet has relative to American and

Analysis Box 10-5

The Business Roundtable identified a very important problem. Most of our Internet and cyber infrastructure is controlled by the private sector. Most of the developmental efforts are to expedite the flow of information with little regard for security. A number of cyber experts note that the government should take more control by promulgating more regulations. Do you believe the federal government should force the private sector to install more costly security hardware and protocols?

international life. Nonetheless, our experience shows that this may not be a major problem. Lewis (2006) notes that Hurricane Katrina in 2005 resulted in New Orleans and large portions of the Gulf region being taken off-line. He notes that if the political consequences are managed, there is little impact as a result of such large or massive disruptions.

Lewis (2006) advises that once an attack occurs, systems operators immediately respond with countermeasures. For an attack to have any measure of impact, it must have a high level of redundancy. It must target several computers or servers in the system, and it requires a sustained, successful re-attack to overcome system operators' countermeasures. Relatively speaking, it is fairly easy to have a short-term impact on a system, but it may be exceedingly difficult to have a long-term impact, especially on well-secured systems. There have been no credible cyber terrorist attacks (Wilson, 2005), demonstrating the difficulty in successfully mounting such an attack.

Don Jackson, director of intelligence at SecureWorks is pictured outside the security operations center of his company, which manages security information systems for corporations worldwide. *Source:* AP (100702128636).

DETERRING CYBER INTRUSIONS AND ATTACKS

Given the magnitude of the potential problems associated with cyber attacks, it is obvious that much needs to be done to improve security. Kane (2011) has identified several changes that would improve security. First, remove cyber anonymity. Procedures should be implemented to ensure that e-mail and message senders and sender locations are easily identified and traceable. This would be a substantial deterrent to many hackers. Second, mandate that institutions use and constantly update security software. They too often update their security software after a breach, which is too late. Third, minimize the amount of time that computers are online. This reduces the possibility of malicious code being introduced to computers. At the same time, require Internet providers to scan computers within their user networks for robot or zombie software. Fourth, institutions and Internet providers should periodically check their computers for worms and other malicious code to ensure that it is not transferred to end users. Fifth, centralize reporting of computer breaches and intrusions. Although different institutions and some industries such as defense collect hacking information, there should be a national clearinghouse that could warn end users of potential problems and recommend solutions. Such a clearinghouse could also identify hackers and notify law enforcement to take action. Finally, we need better mechanisms for reporting hacking so that trends and modus operandi can be identified.

Clarke and Knake (2010) advise that the most significant problem in deterring cyber attacks is that there is no agency responsible for combating them. The Department of Defense and the military branches are currently implementing and enhancing security within defense, but there is no coordinating or controlling body over civilian applications. For example, the Department of Homeland Security's National Cyber Defense Division has two primary objectives: (1) build and maintain an effective national cyberspace response system and (2) implement a cyber-risk management program for protection of critical infrastructure (DHS, 2008). Clarke and Knake advocate that the division should do more in terms of enhancing security and protection. The DHS should be given more power to mandate some of the changes advocated by Kane discussed earlier.

TERRORISTS' USE OF THE INTERNET

The World Wide Web is an innovation that has substantially affected everyone's life. Almost everyone uses the Internet, including terrorists to further their causes. There is little regulation of the Internet, so to some extent, terrorists are free to use it for a variety of purposes. Periodically, different countries will attempt to exert some controls. For example, in the recent past, major companies such as Goggle and Yahoo have cooperated with the Chinese government to limit access to certain materials that the government believes is subversive. In the United States, there have been efforts to limit or control pornography. In most cases, controls have been ineffective. For example, the federal government may attempt to limit pornography in the United States, but these efforts have failed when challenged in court, and pornography can still be accessed from other countries. Thus, we effectively cannot limit groups from using the World Wide Web.

Terrorists increasingly are using the web and engaging in what Arquilla and his colleagues (2003) refer to as **netwar**,

> an emerging mode of conflict and crime at societal levels, involving measures short of traditional war, in which the protagonists use network forms of organization and related doctrines, strategies, and technologies attuned to the information age. (p. 101)

- Easy access
- Little or no regulation, censorship, or other forms of government control
- Potentially large audiences spread throughout the world
- Anonymity of communication
- Fast flow of information
- Inexpensive development and maintenance of a web presence
- A multimedia environment (ability to combine text, graphics, audio, and video to allow users to download films, songs, books, posters, etc.)
- The ability to shape coverage in the traditional mass media, which increasingly use the Internet as a source of stories

FIGURE 10-6 Why Terrorists Are Drawn to the Internet. *Source:* Adapted from Weimann, G. (2004). *Cyberterrorism: How Real Is the Threat.* Special Report. Washington, D.C.: United States Institute of Peace.

They coined the term *netwar* because many terrorist groups have moved from a hierarchical structure to a network of cells and organizations. Many countries, in the wake of the 9/11 attacks, have stepped up counterterrorism efforts, resulting in terrorist organizations assuming a more covert, dispersed organization. There has been an increase in religious terrorist organizations (see Hoffman, 2006), and these groups or cells are dispersed across countries and continents. Current conditions necessitate a networked communications and coordination system that can best be serviced by the web. Arquilla and his colleagues also note that netwar best describes how terrorists are able to use the Internet for multiple purposes.

Today, virtually all terrorist organizations maintain a website. There literally are hundreds of websites spewing hate and propaganda. In the past, policy makers have concentrated their efforts on conventional terrorism methods and largely neglected how terrorist groups are using the web, but this is changing as policy makers and counterterrorism experts see how terrorists are now using the web. Essentially, the Internet is an important tool used by terrorist groups to further their causes and accomplish a number of objectives. Weimann (2004) has identified a number of attributes that are useful to these groups. They can be found in Figure 10-6.

Overview of Terrorist Websites

The Internet is used by extremist groups of all stripes and from across the globe. Groups ranging from the Ku Klux Klan on the right to socialist revolutionaries have websites espousing their ideology. The Internet has been used extensively by Muslim extremist and terrorist groups. The following are only a few of the groups using the web:

1. Middle Eastern groups include Hamas, Hezbollah, the al Aqsa Martyrs Brigaes, Fatah Tanzim, the Popular Front for the Liberation of Palestine, the Palestinian Islamic Jihad, and the Kurdish Workers' Party.
2. European groups include the Basque ETA movement, Armata Corsa (Corsican Army), and the Irish Republican Army.
3. Latin American groups include Peru's Tupak-Amaru (MRTA), the Shining Path, the Colombian National Liberation Army, and the Armed Revolutionary Forces of Colombia.
4. Asian groups include al Qaeda, the Japanese Supreme Truth (Aum Shinrikyo), the Japanese Red Army, the Liberation Tigers of Tamil Eelam, the Islamic Movement of Uzbekistan, the Moro Islamic Liberation Front in the Philippines, the Lashkare-Tiba of Pakistan, and the rebel movement in Chechnya.

HS Web Link: To learn more about the Hamas website, go to *http://www. qassam.ps/*.

A number of these groups will post information using different languages so that a maximum number of viewers can have access to their propaganda. For example, Hamas and Hezbollah have English versions on their websites. Moreover, the number of terrorist and extremist groups using the web increases exponentially.

These websites often contain a substantial amount of information and serve a number of purposes. Weimann (2004) researched these websites and identified the following elements as fairly consistently included on extremist and terrorist websites:

1. History of the organization and its activities
2. Review of its social and political background
3. Accounts of its accomplishments and exploits
4. Biographies of its leaders, founders, and heroes
5. Information on political and ideological aims
6. Criticism of its enemies
7. Up-to-date news about the group's activities
8. Maps of territory controlled or areas of conflict with enemies

Generally, these groups do not discuss their terrorist campaigns on their websites, with the exception of Hamas and Hezbollah. They tend to concentrate on the social and moral bases for their legitimacy. The avoidance of violence and terrorist tactics is an effort to build the organization's image. Hamas and Hezbollah, on the other hand, often provide statistics on the number of their enemies who have been killed and lists of dead martyrs. They appeal to more militant individuals in hopes of recruiting them for their cause.

Audiences

Terrorist groups engage in public relations campaigns. They must disseminate information to recruit new members. Information dispensed to the general public is also used to solicit funding and to generate public support. An analysis of the websites' content revealed that the groups were targeting three different audiences (Weimann, 2004).

The first audience is current and potential supporters. Websites allow the group to communicate its message to members and to recruit new members. Providing constant information and propaganda helps maintain a level of commitment. Hats, tee shirts, and other items with the group's slogans and insignias are also marketed to help show a presence in the target area. The website is also used to demonize the group's enemies, helping to maintain commitment to the cause.

The second audience is international public opinion. Many of the websites are posted in different languages so that they can reach a wider audience. This allows individuals who are not directly involved in the movement, but who have an interest, to gain information about the group's current affairs. These websites are also aimed at journalists. The website can be used to feed positive information about the organization and its activities and to demonize enemies

---

Analysis Box 10-6

Search the web and find a terrorist website such as the ones operated by Hamas or Hezbollah. Eight different elements are present in terrorist websites. See how many elements are contained in the website that you identify.

to journalists and the larger population. The groups hope the websites can mediate some of the negative publicity that they receive elsewhere.

Finally, these websites are aimed at their enemies. Information on the sites is used to demoralize the enemy. They attempt to convince citizens who are not directly involved in the conflict but who are aligned with the enemy to morally question their leaders' objectives and tactics. It is an attempt to generate debate or divide constituents in enemy camps. The websites attempt to deconstruct the rationale used by the opposition to create uncertainty.

How Terrorists Use the Internet

Terrorists use the Internet for a variety of purposes, often depending on the targeted audience. For the most part, Weimann (2004) has identified eight distinct uses.

PSYCHOLOGICAL WARFARE   The Internet is a convenient tool for conducting psychological warfare. Terrorists can use the Internet to spread disinformation about their enemies. This can undermine their efforts to secure support and materials to wage war. It is also used to instill fear. Accounts, pictures, and videos of attacks and deaths are used to develop a sense of hopelessness on the part of the enemy. For example, al Qaeda often releases information about impending massive attacks on the United States. McNeal (2007–8) found that al Qaeda and other terrorist groups release exaggerated statistics relative to the number of Americans killed in Iraq and Afghanistan and videos depicting executions of Americans. Such information also raises the morale of the group's fighters. In essence, terrorist groups attempt to create cyber fear, which has had a profound impact. Realistically, the 9/11 attacks on the World Trade Center and the Pentagon had more of a psychological impact on this nation, despite the casualties or economic consequences. This is not meant to belittle the large number of deaths, but the attack had a profound effect on our collective psyche. Essentially, people lost confidence in government, air travel, and the economy.

PUBLICITY AND PROPAGANDA   The Internet contains a wealth of information. When people read documents from the Internet, they too often believe the information to be correct or true. However, there is no vetting process for information that is posted on the Internet. People essentially can say whatever they desire. Thus, the Internet is ripe with unbridled verbiage of all sorts. Terrorists have direct control over the content of their websites and essentially can target a number of audiences.

Terrorists use three structures to justify their rhetoric. First, they note that they have no choice but to resort to violence. This appeals to others who are resigned to the social, political, and economic conditions. Terrorists can argue that governments or other enemies are exacting greater harm on society as compared to the terrorists' violence. Terrorists portray themselves as being persecuted, and that their violence is aimed at the persecutors. The objective is to convince others to evaluate how they are being treated, or how they perceive they are being treated, and join with the terrorists overtly or covertly.

Second, they attempt to portray themselves as freedom fighters who were forced into action. They portray the enemy, especially target governments, as ruthless, hostile, and violent. They often point to social, injustice and economic ills suffered by the terrorists and their supporters, whereas the government is corrupt and wasting money on its friends. The propaganda is in terms of the "common man against the rich criminals."

Third, they often mix the rhetoric of peace and nonviolence on their websites. This is to insinuate that they desire only a peaceful existence whereas the other side only makes war against the downtrodden. This posture also is used to solicit support from a variety of quarters, including the international community. As Thomas (2003) notes, the Internet

> empowers small groups and makes them appear much more capable than they might be, even turning bluster into a type of virtual fear. The net allows terrorists to amplify the consequences of their activities with follow-on messages and threats directly to the population at large, even though the terrorist group may be totally impotent. In effect, the Internet allows a person or group to appear to be larger or more important than they really are. (pp. 115–16)

DATA MINING   The Internet has exhaustive information on almost everything, and terrorists can use the Internet to collect intelligence on their enemies. In many cases, descriptions and maps of targets can be obtained from the Internet. For example, Goggle now offers satellite images of all locations in the United States and many other countries. In 2006, the Islamic Army in Iraq circulated information on how to aim rockets at U.S. military sites using Google Earth (Eisler, 2008). The Internet provides information about employees, operations, and infrastructure that can be used to develop intelligence for targets.

FUND-RAISING   The Internet can be used to distribute propaganda to increase the level of sympathy for a cause. It can entice support. The Internet can be used to solicit contributions from a group, region, country, or worldwide. Oftentimes, these sites provide bank codes through which money can be deposited. There are ample examples of when terrorist groups have used this ploy to raise money in the United States.

RECRUITMENT AND MOBILIZATION   The Internet is a useful tool in recruitment. Indeed, it is commonly used by governments and business and industry throughout the world for this purpose. Terrorists often post propaganda with religious decrees and anti-American rhetoric. They often have chat rooms where they attempt to convince recruits to join their cause. These chat rooms allow for a fairly intimate contact from thousands of miles away. For example, McNeal (2007–8) notes that the six Muslim men convicted for planning a terrorist attack on Fort Dix in New Jersey were recruited via the Internet. They had viewed videos of Osama bin Laden preaching inspirational messages. Recently, there have been a number of Americans who have been drawn to terrorist groups, and it is believed they were enticed via information contained on terrorist websites. For example, in 2010, two Americans were arrested at a New York airport as they tried to leave the country and join an Islamic terrorist group in Somalia (Levey and Baum, 2010); in 2009, five Muslim Americans from Virginia, Ulmar Farooq, Ramy Zamzam, Waqar Khan, Ahmad Mini, and Amein Yemer, were arrested in Pakistan where they had traveled seeking training as jihadist guerillas (Schulte, 2010). Many similar cases indicate that terrorist websites are fairly effective in recruiting new members, even Americans.

NETWORKING   The Internet allows for terrorist groups such as Hamas and al Qaeda to maintain contact with individual cells and individual members. E-mails and other information can be sent from any location with Internet access. Since e-mails can be routed through a number of servers across several countries, it becomes difficult to locate their origin. The Internet also makes it possible for groups to better communicate and coordinate activities with other like-minded groups. This networking is especially critical when these groups coordinate an attack.

SHARING INFORMATION   The web has numerous sites that contain information that can assist terrorists. These sites contain information on bomb making, tactics, poisons, assassinations, anti-surveillance methods, and so on. In many cases, the information is very detailed. To some extent, the Internet serves a valuable online training and education function for terrorists.

PLANNING AND COORDINATION   Al Qaeda operatives extensively used the Internet to coordinate their 9/11 attacks in New York and Washington. In many cases, terrorists use plain language or unsophisticated codes on open sites . In other cases, the terrorists are using secure websites, making infiltration difficult. Regardless, the Internet serves as an easy, convenient platform for coordinating their activities.

It is important for us to enhance our monitoring of the Internet. Since it is open, we too may be able to glean valuable intelligence information from it. Anyone can post anything no matter how inflammatory or untrue, and we cannot control content. We are now fighting information with information—increasing our postings and websites to counter the incorrect information that is being posted by the terrorists.

AGENCIES CHARGED WITH COMBATING CYBER TERRORISM

The FBI and the Department of Homeland Security are charged with investigating and countering domestic cyber terrorism. The Department of Defense is also involved in cyber security from an international perspective especially as it related to defense.

FBI's Cyber Crime Division

The FBI is charged with investigating cyber crimes, including cyber terrorism. The bureau's mission is

> first and foremost, to stop those behind the most serious computer intrusions and the spread of malicious code; second, to identify and thwart online sexual predators who use the Internet to meet and exploit children and to produce, possess, or share child pornography; third, to counteract operations that target U.S. intellectual property, endangering our national security and competitiveness; and fourth, to dismantle national and transnational organized criminal enterprises engaging in Internet fraud. Pursuant to the National Strategy to Secure Cyberspace signed by the President, the Department of Justice and the FBI lead the national effort to investigate and prosecute cybercrime. (FBI, 2008)

In order to accomplish this mission, the FBI has created three units: Cyber Action Teams, Computer Crimes Task Forces, and Internet Complaint Center. The **Cyber Action Teams** (CATs) consist of highly trained computer forensics and malicious code experts. The CATs investigate cyber threats nationally and internationally. As an example of how the CAT teams operate, in 2006, CAT teams were sent to Turkey and Morocco to investigate Zotob, a malicious code designed to steal credit card information. The CAT teams worked with

An FBI agent working in the computer forensics lab.   *Source:* http://www.fbi.gov/headlines/ccctf200.jpg.

Turkish and Moroccan authorities to arrest the perpetrators. The virus resulted in a large number of computers crashing in several countries. **Computer Crimes Task Forces** are teams of FBI agents who work with other federal and state law enforcement tracking down sexual predators, scammers, and other criminals by back-tracing e-mails and posing as online victims. Finally, the **Internet Complaint Center** is a joint operation between the FBI and the National White Collar Crime Center to receive complaints from victims of Internet fraud.

The FBI has been involved in controversial surveillance programs. Under Section 216 of the USA PATRIOT Act, the FBI can conduct warrantless eavesdropping of Internet traffic. In 2002, the FBI launched Project Carnivore, which allowed the bureau to monitor Internet traffic, some suggest indiscriminately (see Ventura et al., 2005). The bureau used Carnivore three times in 2002 and six times in 2003. The program was used to investigate alleged extortion, arson, teaching of others how to make and use destructive devices, alleged mail fraud, controlled substance sales, providing material support to terrorism, and making obscene or harassing telephone calls within the District of Columbia (Poulson, 2005). The FBI received a substantial amount of pressure and criticism from Congress and civil liberties groups, resulting in the program's discontinuation. However, the FBI has continued the practice using vender-developed software. Regardless, it appears that the majority of the FBI's investigations do not involve cyber terrorism, so it is questionable as to how involved the bureau is in this arena.

HS Web Link: To learn more about the FBI's cyber investigation activities, go to *http://www.fbi.gov/cyberinvest/cyberhome.htm.*

Department of Homeland Security's National Cyber Security Division

The Department of Homeland Security conducts cyber security operations through its **National Cyber Security Division**. The division has two primary objectives: (1) build and maintain an effective national cyberspace response system and (2) implement a cyber risk management program for protection of critical infrastructure (DHS, 2008). The DHS is organized into two programs or areas to carry out this mandate: National Cyberspace Response System and Cyber Risk Management Programs. The **National Cyberspace Response System** consists of three components. First, the Cyber Security Preparedness and the National Cyber Alert System and US-Cert are notification systems detailing current cyber threats. They are designed to alert the computing community of impending attacks. The National Cyber Response Coordination Group consists of 13 federal agencies, and the group will help coordinate the federal response to a nationally significant cyber-related incident. The Cyber Cop Portal is a portal that is accessed by investigators worldwide, and it provides information relative to electronic crimes and investigations.

The **Cyber Risk Management Program** is designed to evaluate cyber risk levels, implement cyber protective measures, and prioritize funding. One of the primary programs here is Cyber Storm, which is a nationwide cyber security exercise that occurs every two years. Cyber Storm attempts to assess levels of preparedness capabilities in case of a cyber incident of national significance. Cyber Storm was the Department of Homeland Security's first cyber exercise testing responses across the private sector as well as from international, federal, and state governments.

HS Web Link: To learn more about the Department of Homeland Security's cyber security, go to *http://www.dhs.gov/ xabout/structure/ editorial_0839.shtm.*

Even though there are areas of duplication in the FBI's and DHS's programming, it appears that the FBI has the primary responsibility of investigating cyber crimes and terrorism, and the DHS is charged with monitoring the cyber infrastructure and providing national and international law enforcement with information about cyber attacks and prevention measures.

Summary

This chapter examined cyber terrorism, and cyber crimes received some attention since they often are intermingled in terms of discussions and investigations. As noted in the *National Infrastructure Protection Plan* (2006), cyber resources are one of the primary infrastructures that require protection. Our cyber and communications system represents a national nervous system by which business, social, and security activities are conducted and coordinated. Our cyber system is crucial to our nation's well-being since we depend so heavily on the Internet communications infrastructure.

There is debate over the extent and dangers posed by cyber terrorism. Government, technology groups, and others have advocated that our cyber security is lacking substantially. They advise that we are vulnerable to a variety of attacks from across the globe. Numerous studies document cyber intrusions and the potential costs incurred by them. However, critics of this position aptly note that there is no evidence substantiating that American infrastructure assets have been attacked or victimized by cyber terrorists. Indeed, there are thousands of attacks on American computers and networks on a daily basis, but these attacks originate primarily from nonterrorist hackers and groups who attempt to gain access to financial information or play a game by planting malicious viruses, code, and worms. Even though these attacks are not terrorist originated, the outcomes are the same—we must protect our cyber infrastructure. We must continually invest in software and hardware that protects our massive networks from intrusions.

The Internet has become a tool used by terrorists, and all the major terrorist organizations have websites to promote their organization and activities. These websites play a key role in terrorists' recruitment, communications and coordination, and fund-raising. The Internet has substantial appeal to terrorists since it serves many purposes and is an inexpensive tool requiring little training. The Internet and these websites allow terrorist groups to communicate with a variety of audiences, spewing their propaganda unabated. Essentially, it is the most effective communications modality used by terrorists. The United States and other countries engaged in the war on terrorism likely have not devoted enough resources to counter terrorists' use of the Internet.

Finally, the two federal agencies primarily engaged in securing our cyber infrastructure are the Federal Bureau of Investigation and the Department of Homeland Security's National Cyber Security Division. The FBI is responsible for investigating incidents of cyber terrorism, but the bureau is also responsible for investigating a host of other cyber criminal activities. For the most part, it appears that the bureau focuses on these other cyber responsibilities. On the other hand, the National Cyber Security Division is responsible for communicating cyber threats to the computing community and coordinating responses should there be a significant breach in our cyber infrastructure.

Discussion Questions

1. Distinguish cybercrime, terrorism, and warfare.
2. Describe the methods of attacking cyber infrastructure.
3. Why would a cyber attack be appealing to terrorists?
4. How do terrorists use the Internet?
5. What kinds of extremist groups have websites and how do they use them?
6. How do terrorists use the Internet?
7. Compare the FBI and DHS is terms of their mission relative to cyber crime and terrorism.

References

Arquilla, J., D. Ronfeldt, and M Zanini. (2003). "Networks, netwar, and information-age terrorism." In *Terrorism and Counterterrorism*, ed. R. Howard and R. Sawyer, pp. 96–119. New York: McGraw-Hill.

Barlow, J. (1990). *Crime and Puzzlement: Desperados of the Data-Sphere.* http://www.sjgames.com/SS/crimpuzz. html (Accessed June 8, 2010).

Barnes, J. (2008). "Pentagon computer networks attacked." *Los Angeles Times* (November 28), pp. A1, A30.

Beaumont, P. (2010). "U.S. appoints first cyber warfare general." *Observer.* http://www.guardian.co.uk/world/2010/may/23/us-appoints-cyber-warfare-general (Accessed June 15, 2010).

Brewin, B. (2008). "Cost of cybersecurity to triple, panel reports." *Nevgov.* http://www.nextgov.com/nextgov/ng_20080519_1961.php (Accessed November 29, 2008).

Business Roundtable. (2006). *Essential Steps to Strengthen America's Cyber Terrorism Preparedness.* http://www.comw.org/tct/fulltext/0606bizroundtable (Accessed November 28, 2008).

Carafano, J. (2008). *When Electrons Attack: Cyber Strikes on Georgia a Wake-up Call for Congress.* Heritage Foundation. http://www.heritage.org/Research/NationalSecurity/wm2022.cfm (Accessed November 28, 2008).

Clarke, R. (2008). *Against All Enemies.* New York: RAC Enterprises.

Clarke, R. (2003). "Vulnerability: What are al Qaeda's capabilities?" *PBS Frontline.* Cyberwar. http://www.pbs.org (Accessed March 21, 2009).

Clarke, R. and R. Knake. (2010). *Cyber War: The Next Threat to National Security and What to Do about It.* New York: HarperCollins.

Denning, D. (2001). *Is Cyber Terror Next?* http://essays.ssrc.org/sept11/essays/denning.htm (Accessed June 15, 2010).

Denning, D. (2000). "Cyberterrorism." Testimony before the House Armed Services Special Oversight Panel on Terrorism (May 23): 1.

Department of Homeland Security. (2006). *National Infrastructure Protection Plan.* Washington, D.C.: Author.

Department of Homeland Security. (2008). National Cyber Security Division. http://www.dhs.gov/xabout/structure/editorial_0839.shtm (Accessed December 2, 2008).

Eisler, P. (2008). "Google Earth helps yet worries government." *US Today* (November 6). http://www.usatoday.com/tech/news/surveillance/2008-11-06-googleearth_N.htm (Accessed December 5, 2008).

Federal Bureau of Investigation. (2008). Webpage. http://www.fbi.gov/cyberinvest/cyberhome.htm (Accessed November 28, 2008).

Furnell, S. and M. Warren. (1999). "Computer hacking and cyber terrorism: The real threats in the new millennium?" *Computers & Society*, 18: 28–34.

Hoffman, B. (2006). *Inside Terrorism*. New York: Columbia University Press.

Kane, J. (2011). "Virtual terrain, lethal potential: Toward achieving security in an ungoverned domain." In *Toward a Grand Strategy Against Terrorism*, ed. C. Harmon, A. Pratt, and S. Gorka, pp. 252–81. New York: McGraw-Hill.

Krebs, B. (2009). "Payment process breach may be largest ever." *The Washington Post* (January 20), p. A1.

Levey, N. and G. Baum. (2010). "Two N.J. men held on terror charges." *Los Angeles Times* (June 7), p. A6.

Lewis, J. (2006). "Cybersecurity and critical infrastructure protection." In *Homeland Security: Protecting America's Targets (Vol.3)*, ed. J. Forest, pp. 324–28. Westport, CT: Praeger Security International.

Lewis, J. (2002). *Assessing the Risks of Cyber Terrorism, Cyber War and Other Cyber Threats*. Washington, D.C.: Center for Strategic and International Studies.

Markoff, J. and T. Shanker. (2009). "U.S. weighs risks of civilian harm in cyberwarfare." *The New York Times* (August 2), pp. 1, 9.

Marlin, S. and M. Garvin. (2004). "Disaster-recovery spending on the rise." *Information Week* (August 9), p. 26.

Mazzetti, M. (2010). "Senators warned of terrorist attack on U.S. by July." *New York Times* (February 3). http://www.nytimes.com/2010/02/03/us/politics/03intel.html (Accessed June 14, 2010).

McNeal, G. (2007–8). "Cyber embargo: Countering the Internet Jihad." *Case Western Reserve.* http://www.usdoj.gov/criminal/cybercrime/cyberstalking.htm (Accessed November 28, 2008).

Pollitt, M. (undated). *Cyberterrorism: Fact or Fantasy.* http://www.cs.georgetown.edu/~denning/infosec/pollitt.html (Accessed November 28, 2008).

Poulson, K. (2005). "FBI retires carnivore." *Security Focus.* http://www.securityfocus.com/news/10307 (Accessed December 2, 2008).

Rattray, G. (2003). "The cyberterrorism threat." In *Terrorism and Counterterrorism: Understanding the New Security Environment*, ed. R. Howard and R. Sawyer, pp. 221–45. Guilford, CT: McGraw-Hill.

Sang-Hun, C. and J. Markoff. (2009). "Cyberattacks jam government and commercial web sites in U.S. and South Korea." *New York Times* (July 9), p. A4.

Schulte, B. (2010). "5 Va. men facing terrorism charges in Pakistan write of 'noble' motivation." *The Washington Post.* (May 16): A16.

Shorrock, T. (2008). *Spies for Hire: The Secret World of Intelligence Outsourcing*. New York: Simon & Schuster.

Squitieri, T. (2002). "Cyberspace full of terror targets." *US Today* (May 5). http://www.usatoday.com/tech/news/2002/05/06/cyber-terror.htm (Accessed November 28, 2008).

Stohl, M. (2006). "Cyber terrorism: A clear and present danger, the sum of all fears, breaking point or patriot games." *Crime, Law, and Social Change*, 46: 223–38.

Taylor, R., T. Caeti, D. Loper, E. Tritsch, and J. Liederbach. (2006). *Digital Crime and Digital Terrorism*. Upper Saddle, NJ: Prentice Hall.

Thomas, T. (2003). "Al Qaeda and the internet: The danger of cyberplanning." *Parameters*, 33(1): 112–23.

U.S.-China Economic and Security Review Commission. (2009). *2009 Report of the U.S.-China Economic and Security Review Commission to Congress*. Washington, D.C.: U.S. Government Printing Office.

Ventura, H., J. Miller, and M. Deflem. (2005). "Governmentality and the war on terror: FBI project carnivore and the diffusion of disciplinary power." *Critical Criminology,* 13: 55–70.

Weimann, G. (2005). "Cyber terrorism: The sum of all fears?" *Studies in Conflict and Terrorism*, 28: 129–49.

Weimann, G. (2004). *Cyberterrorism: How Real Is the Threat*. Special Report. Washington, D.C.: United States Institute of Peace.

Wilson, C. (2005). *Computer Attack and Cyberterrorism: Vulnerabilities and Policy Issues for Congress*. Washington, D.C.: Congressional Research Service.

11

Terrorist Financing

LEARNING OBJECTIVES

1. Know how the terrorists financed the 9/11 attacks.
2. Understand the difference between money laundering and terrorist financing.
3. Know how the United States is attempting to reduce terrorist financing.
4. Be familiar with how terrorist organizations raise money.
5. Be familiar with how terrorist groups move money.
6. Understand identity fraud and identity theft.
7. Know how breeder documents work.

KEY TERMS

Money laundering

Terrorist financing

Due diligence

Financial Action Task Force on Money
 Laundering

Zakat

Hawala

Identity fraud

Identity theft

Real ID Act

Breeder document

INTRODUCTION

The United States, as well as other countries, is engaged in an all-out effort to combat terrorism. These efforts are being applied on a number of fronts using a variety of strategies and tactics. Our efforts are not restricted to battlefields such as those in Afghanistan, but they also involve multiple strategies in the economic arena. Terrorism is a cancer on the world, and one method by which to defeat it is to starve it—deny or eliminate the funding terror organizations require to operate. If terrorist finances can be substantially reduced and in some cases eliminated, it will contribute to our successes on other fronts. Today, the U.S. government is using a variety of means to reduce the amount of funds available to terrorist organizations. It is a difficult task since these organizations have developed a variety of means to raise money for their deplorable acts. Methods used by terrorists to raise money include (1) criminal activities such as bank robbery, kidnapping, extortion, and narcotics trafficking; (2) donations from local and foreign supporters; (3) assistance from supportive nation-states; (4) contributions from wealthy individuals and organizations; (5) white-collar crime; and (6) revenues from legitimate businesses. Nonetheless, we must press on and "drain the swamp" or eliminate as many funding sources as possible.

Globalization has substantially hindered our efforts to reduce terrorist financing. Globalization has led to the free flow of information and money across countries with few limitations. Weintraub (2002) advises that more than $1 trillion a day is transferred via our international banking and finance system. This vast amount of money and number of transfers are making it increasingly more difficult to distinguish legitimate transactions from those that are associated with illegal enterprises such as terrorist financing—it is akin to searching for a needle in a haystack. Essentially, there are few international boundaries today, and a number of countries are safe havens for money laundering and illegal finance. Transnational organized crime groups have taken advantage of these conditions, and terrorist organizations have followed. They are adept at hiding their money within this complex of financial transactions.

Prior to the 9/11 attacks, the federal government had done very little to counter global money laundering. Partisan politics held these financial issues in a congressional logjam. For the most part, the Democrats were interested in greater oversight or control with laws aimed at tax evaders and white-collar crime. The Republicans, on the other hand, were opposed to federal laws on the grounds that such laws were intrusive, and they favored the deregulation of the American and world finance systems. They were also opposed to such legislation since it likely would target wealthy individuals and corporations (see Malkin, 2002; Weintraub, 2001). Thus, it was only after the shock of 9/11 that Congress and the president pursued money laundering and terrorist financing in earnest. Even then, there were gaps in policies. Shortly after the 9/11 attacks, President George W. Bush pledged to Congress that his administration would starve terrorist organizations, and in fact, officials had frozen almost $200 million in assets belonging to suspected terrorist groups and fronts. Although all sorts of groups and countries had been targeted by these renewed tactics, the government neglected to take any action against Saudi Arabia's assets, even though a substantial amount of terrorist funding came from the Saudis. The Saudis were seen as allies, and the Bush administration did not want to embarrass them (Armstrong, 2004; Prados and Blanchard, 2004). Indeed, some question governments' willingness and ability to counter money laundering (Naylor, 2006). This late and haphazard attack on terrorist funding created an open window for terrorists to move substantial amounts of money by which to organize and orchestrate attacks.

Limiting terrorist organizations' finances by the United States and other countries represents an important tool in the war against terrorism. Depriving terrorists of money can contribute to two important outcomes. First, it can directly or indirectly affect a terrorist organization's leadership, morale, and legitimacy. If funding is reduced, it likely will result in a reduction of support from members, other terrorist organizations, and the community at large. Terrorist organizations' wealth or access to money is demonstrable of their relative power. Without this wealth, they are seen as being weaker by their constituents and enemies. It can lead to organizational instability. Second, it may have strategic implications. It may force a group to alter its intentions—the group may not have the resources to carry out a planned attack. Strategically, the group then must abandon its plans or opt to attack a less desirable target. Both of these scenarios are positive in that they result in less destruction (Financial Action Task Force, 2008).

For the most part, we have measured our successes in defeating terrorist financing by the amount of terrorist money that has been seized. Levitt and Jacobson (2008) advise that this is an inadequate strategy:

> Unfortunately, the metrics most often used assess efforts against terrorist financing—the total amount of money seized and the overall designations—are both inadequate and misleading. The Achilles heel of terrorism financiers is not at the fundraising end, but rather at the *choke points* critical to laundering and transferring funds. It is impossible to "dry the swap" of funds available for illicit purposes, but by targeting key nodes in the financing network, we can constrict the operating environment to the point that terrorists will not be able to obtain funds where and when they need them. (p. 3)

This chapter examines these issues in detail. As Levitt and Jacobson note, the transfer of funds or money laundering is different from raising capital. These activities are distinguished here. This chapter provides information on the financing process and how money is laundered or moved from legitimate sources to terrorist organizations. The various federal agencies involved in countering terrorist financing (attacking choke points) are examined as well as the tools that we currently are using to reduce the flow of money to terrorist organizations. The methods used by terrorist organizations to raise money are examined. For the most part, this chapter focuses on al Qaeda's financing since this group has the most developed system; it is the most dangerous terrorist organization; and it has been examined extensively. First, the money trail for the 9/11 attacks is outlined.

TERRORIST FINANCING OF THE 9/11 ATTACKS

The 9/11 Commission (2004) thoroughly investigated the financing of the 9/11 attacks. It is illustrative to examine how the 9/11 attacks were financed since it illuminates several of the methods used by terrorists to acquire and move money. It also demonstrates the complexity of money movement and the difficulty for governments to identify and intercept terrorist financial movements. The terrorists and their supporters use the world's enormous global financial system to mask their operations. As a corollary, governments, including that of the United States, must implement procedures that examine even relatively small money transfers. The 9/11 Commission estimated that the attacks cost between $400,000 and $500,000, and the money was moved using several transfers of only several thousand dollars.

Although investigators did not learn where the money originated, it appears that the 9/11 attacks were financed largely through the terrorists' Hamburg cell and coordinated by Khalid

Sheikh Muhammad. The Hamburg cell received its funding from al Qaeda. The hijackers, selected from various al Qaeda training camps, were pilots and muscle men. The pilots received additional flight training in the United States, and the muscle men were given training to enable them to physically control passengers and commandeer the airplanes. As they moved from one country to another, they received payments of a few thousand dollars to cover expenses. At one point, several of the hijackers received $10,000 each to purchase forged identity documents and travel from Saudi Arabia to the United States.

According to the 9/11 Commission, approximately $300,000 was deposited in bank accounts in the United States. The money was moved here by (1) bank transfers to U.S. banks, (2) hijackers carrying traveler's checks into the United States, and (3) credit or debit cards used to access foreign bank accounts. The money was used for pilots' lessons and living expenses. A substantial amount of the money came from two financers in the United Arab Emirates. The money was wired to a number of American banks, including banks in California, New York, Florida, and Oklahoma, and in some cases, the money moved through Canadian banks. Money also was wired to the terrorists through Western Union.

HS Web Link: To learn more about the financing of the 9/11 attacks, go to *http:// www.9-11commission.gov/ staff_statements/91/1_ TerrFin_App.pdf*

After the attacks, there was some speculation that at least some of the funding came from within the United States. However the 9/11 Commission found that "no credible evidence exists that the hijackers received any substantial funding from any person in the United States" (p. 138). They were funded by al Qaeda and its supporters using an intricate money-laundering scheme and avoiding detection by authorities.

The 9/11 attacks show the intricacy of funding such attacks. Since they were funded with multiple transfers of relatively small amounts of money, terrorist financial operations can be very difficult to detect, so difficult that they were hard to disentangle until after the fact. It appears that terrorists, especially al Qaeda, are adept at using a variety of funding sources to finance their plots. The mechanisms to discover and disrupt terrorist financing before 9/11 did not fail; they essentially were not designed to uncover the type of transactions that financed the 9/11 attacks.

The 9/11 Commission advised that it is unlikely that terrorist financing can be stopped. That would require a collaborative, effective response from a number of countries, which is unlikely. Terrorists will always seek out and find loopholes or cracks in these systems, which was the case with the 9/11 attacks. They also will use informal methods outside the financial system to move money. An evaluation of different countries shows that a number of them are not taking the actions required to halt terrorist money laundering or transfers. Thus, we continue to negotiate between freezing assets and following the money to collect terrorist intelligence. Gaining international compliance in countering terrorist funding is required if we are to choke their funding and have a measure of success.

Analysis Box 11-1

The 9/11 Commission questions whether we can stop terrorist funding. It advises that perhaps it is better to follow the money—much like we do in organized crime and drug cases. On the other hand, others advocate that we should make every effort to stop terrorist funding. In your opinion, which strategy, stopping the funding or following it, would be the more advantageous? Why?

DISTINGUISHING TERRORIST FINANCING AND MONEY LAUNDERING

Essentially, when attacking terrorist financing, authorities are concentrating on two primary activities: fund-raising and moving or laundering the money. It is important to distinguish these two activities since prevention and enforcement approaches to each, in some cases, are different. Even though terrorist financing and money laundering represent two entirely different activities, they sometimes are interconnected. **Money laundering** is an activity whereby ill-gotten fruits are cleansed—illegally derived funds are moved through the financial system and returned legitimate. Roberge (2007) notes that money laundering is a three-step process: (1) the illegally derived money is placed into the financial system; (2) it is layered or moved through the financial system, usually internationally, and intermingled with legitimate profits and monies to hide its provenance; and (3) it is returned and reintegrated into the legitimate economy. Historically, money laundering has been used primarily by organized crime and corrupt politicians. Today, terrorist groups have developed extensive financial networks to launder their money. Money laundering from all sources is sizable. For example, Roberge notes that 2 to 5 percent of the global gross domestic product is laundered annually.

Whereas money laundering is a process whereby illegal monies are moved into the legitimate economy so that they cannot be identified by authorities and used by terrorists, **terrorist financing** is the mechanisms used by terrorists to raise funds, which are discussed later in this chapter. Organized crime figures and political despots are interested in moving money into the legitimate economy. Terrorists are not interested in doing so; they attempt to raise funds, transfer them without impediment or interception, and spend them for their terrorist activities. The difference is that terrorists are interested only in moving the money from one point to another. They generally are not interested in money laundering or making the money appear legitimate. This results in increased difficulty in identifying terrorists' funds.

Terrorists must move funds from one country to another to facilitate their global activities. For example, prior to the 9/11 attacks, Osama bin Laden and al Qaeda moved money to banks in several U.S. states to finance the attacks. Once deposited, the hijackers withdrew the money. In this case, the money was laundered in that it did not raise any suspicions on the part of American authorities. The 9/11 Commission found that approximately $300,000 passed through American banks (National Commission on Terrorist Attacks Upon the United States (2004)). Prior to the attacks, the money-laundering controls in place at the time focused on drug trafficking and large-scale financial fraud, and the 9/11 terrorists made a number of transfers of relatively small amounts. The money being transferred for the 9/11 attacks essentially arrived under the radar. Afterwards, the U.S. government intensified its efforts to restrict the unabated movement of money (implement more effective choke points), especially money that was suspected of being linked with terrorists.

FEDERAL MECHANISMS USED TO COUNTER TERRORIST FINANCING AND MONEY LAUNDERING

After 9/11, the American government endeavored to deprive terrorists of the funding necessary to carry out future attacks. Prior to 9/11, several laws focused on money laundering. For the most part, these laws were enacted to target organized crime and large-scale narcotics trafficking. For example, the Money Laundering Control Act of 1986 created several offenses focusing on money laundering. The Bank Secrecy Act of 1970 (BSA) required an institutional accounting of large

Police escort a suspect in an operation against a group suspected of financing and recruiting Islamist militants near Barcelona, Spain. *Source:* AP (08101601868).

currency transfers. The Treasury and the Federal Reserve developed regulations requiring record keeping for financial activities such as wire transfers. The USA PATRIOT Act amended the Bank Secrecy Act and required banks and other financial institutions to practice **due diligence**—they were required to determine the sources of financial transactions, creating a paper trail for any subsequent investigations.

Immediately after 9/11, President Bush issued an executive order freezing the U.S. assets of 27 different entities suspected of being terrorist organizations or of collaborating with terrorist organizations. The order also prohibited American financial transactions with these entities and had international implications. The administration believed that terrorists had few

1. The Central Intelligence Agency gathers, analyzes, and disseminates intelligence on foreign terrorist organizations and their financing arms.
2. The Bureau of Customs and Border Protection and the Bureau of Immigration and Customs Enforcement are responsible for enforcing financial laws and regulations at the border.
3. The U.S. Secret Service is responsible for investigating terrorist financing involving counterfeiting.
4. The Bureau of Alcohol, Tobacco, Firearms, and Explosives investigates terrorist financing and activities involving alcohol, tobacco, firearms, and explosives.
5. The Drug Enforcement Agency investigates terrorist financing involving drugs.
6. The Federal Bureau of Investigation investigates all aspects of foreign activities and collects intelligence information within the United States.
7. The Bureau of Economic and Business Affairs leads U.S. efforts to develop strategies to obtain international cooperation.
8. The Office of the Coordinator for Counterterrorism coordinates U.S. counterterrorism policy and efforts with foreign governments to deter terrorist financing.
9. The Executive Office for Terrorist Financing and Financial Crime develops and implements the National Money Laundering Strategy as well as other policies and programs to prevent financial crimes.
10. The Financial Crimes Enforcement Network (FinCEN) consists of regional centers that coordinate federal, state, and local financial crime investigations and intelligence.
11. The Internal Revenue Service investigates terrorist financing with an emphasis on charitable organizations.

FIGURE 11-1   Federal Agencies Combating Terrorist Financing.   *Source:* Government Accounting Office. (2003). *Terrorist Financing: U.S. Agencies Should Systematically Assess Terrorists' Use of Alternative Financing Mechanisms.* Washington, D.C.: Author.

assets in U.S. institutions. Thus, President Bush made the order fairly encompassing, giving the United States the power to freeze foreign banks' accounts in the United States when those banks failed to share financial information with U.S. investigative agencies or refused to block terrorists' accounts. The U.S. government is able to enforce this provision, at least to some degree, since foreign banks must conduct business with the American banking and financial system as a result of the global economy. It fell upon the Departments of Treasury and State to enforce the order. This action laid the groundwork for a comprehensive assault on terrorist financing (see Zagaris, 2004).

Subsequent to the early efforts to control terrorist financing, a number of federal agencies have been assigned new duties that focus on this issue. Figure 11-1 provides a listing of the agencies and their responsibilities.

On its face, this conglomeration of agencies seems to address all the pertinent issues. However, Winer (2008) notes that there are considerable gaps in our policies, and Stana (2004)

Analysis Box 11-2

An examination of the various federal agencies involved in attempting to stop terrorist financing shows that it is a complicated affair. As noted, some have suggested that a czar be appointed to coordinate these activities, especially in light of the importance of controlling terrorist financing. Should we appoint such a czar? Why? Do you believe that a terrorist financing czar would be more effective than our director of national intelligence?

A total of $207 million was seized in Mexico City—the largest drug cash seizure ever.
Source: http:// www.justice.gov/dea/programs/money.htm

advises that these agencies face continuing coordination challenges. Indeed, the current arrangement is akin to our conglomeration of intelligence agencies. The intelligence agencies were so fragmented and reluctant to cooperate and share information that Congress at President Bush's urging created a director of intelligence or intelligence czar whose purpose is to ensure that our intelligence efforts represent coordinated effort. Given the importance of reducing terrorist funding and the number of agencies involved in this task, it may serve national interests to create some type of oversight or coordination authority for our anti-terrorist financing operations to ensure that we have a maximum effort.

U.S. Enforcement Actions

A number of changes were made in the financial enforcement landscape as indicated in Figure 11-1. The U.S. Treasury Department created a task force with representatives from the FBI, IRS, Customs, and other agencies to coordinate anti-terrorist financing. The Treasury Department also increased the power and scope of the Financial Crimes Enforcement Network (FinCEN), allowing law enforcement investigators to have readily accessible information on suspect bank accounts. The FBI established the Terrorist Financing Section within its Counterterrorism Division. This section provides investigative support to the FBI's field offices and foreign governments in cases of terrorist financing. The section participated in the disruption of terrorist finance operations in the United Arab Emirates, Pakistan, and Afghanistan, and it was responsible for prosecuting a Hezbollah cigarette-smuggling operation in North Carolina and Michigan (Zagaris, 2004). The DEA began to give more attention to narco-terrorism since terrorist organizations are extensively involved in drug trafficking to raise money. Customs and Border Protection and Immigration and Customs Enforcement are

HS Web Link: to learn more about the FBI's Terrorist Financing Section, go to *http://www.fbi.gov/page2/ may04/051104terrorfinance. htm*

responsible for securing our borders. One of their responsibilities is to focus on the transfer of money and valuables coming into and going out of the United States. The Internal Revenue Service was charged with investigating Islamic charities, a primary source of income to terrorist organizations. As demonstrated, several federal agencies concentrate on a number of financial activities that could involve terrorist financing.

Financial Action Task Force on Money Laundering

In 1989, the United States in cooperation with the other G-7 nations, established the **Financial Action Task Force on Money Laundering** (FATF), which is headquartered in Paris. Originally, FATF was concerned with money laundering and transfers emanating from the narcotics trade. In 2001, FATF's mission was expanded to include attacking terrorist financing. Today, the FATF has 34 members (FATF-GAFI, undated). It attempts to place pressure on nonmember nations to accept FATF's measures that reduce terrorist financing and money laundering. The FATF uses two strategies to gain compliance. First, if nations do not comply with the standards, the organization will name them and attempt to shame or pressure them into compliance. When this does not result in compliance, the FATF can recommend sanctions against noncompliant nations. Although there are about 130 complying nations, some nations have not pursued money laundering and terrorist financing in earnest (FATF-GAFI, undated). Moreover, a number of countries' governments do not have the ability to police their finance and banking systems, which makes enforcement difficult. Nonetheless, a patchwork system currently is in place, and some inroads have been made in thwarting terrorist finance activities.

MEANS AND METHODS OF TERRORIST FINANCIAL TRANSACTIONS

In the aftermath of the 9/11 attacks, there was speculation that Osama bin Laden was financing the attacks and his terrorist network with his personal fortune. His family has substantial wealth from a well-established construction company in Saudi Arabia. It was estimated that his fortune ranged from $25 million to $300 million (Lee, 2002). However, subsequently it was discovered that his family had not given him large sums of money, and indeed, as result of being cut off by his family, he had only a few million dollars. This was not nearly enough money for him to finance his extensive operations. He had to resort to a host of activities to maintain a constant flow of money to maintain his al Qaeda network.

Nevertheless, bin Laden does have a vast financial network. He has a number of holdings, including trading firms, construction companies, an agricultural production and export company, and a furniture-making company. He invested $50 million in a Sudanese bank but was forced to sell his stake when the United States and Egypt pressured the Sudanese government to expel him. He has investments in Mauritius, Singapore, Malaysia, the Philippines, and Panama and bank accounts in Hong Kong, London, Dubai, Malaysia, and Vienna. He also has hundreds of millions of dollars secured in real estate and elsewhere (Lee, 2002). Even without his family fortune, he has been successful in raising money for his terrorist causes.

To some extent, terrorist funding includes a variety of tactics and strategies at the macro and micro levels. At the macro level, large-scale terrorist organizations such as al Qaeda, Hamas, and Hezbollah solicit or raise funds for a variety of purposes, including the funding of their extensive networks that span several countries. This funding comes primarily from charities, benefactors, and transnational organized crime activities. The funding of local cells often is intended to finance specific terrorist events. The micro level includes local cells that may or may not be affiliated with a larger terrorist organization. In some cases, local cells, whether affiliated or independent, will engage in

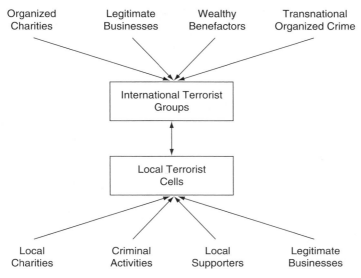

FIGURE 11-2 Sources and Relationships for Terrorist Funding.

fund-raising. They operate legitimate businesses, engage in crime, and have relationships with local charities and supporters. Generally, the local cells will use the money to sustain themselves and fund localized terrorist-related activities. They sometimes will transfer or contribute money to other cells or the terrorist organization with which they are associated. Figure 11-2 shows the funding relationships.

As shown, terrorist financial transactions are a complicated matter. They are multifaceted and involve a number of stages and participants. Through intelligence gathering or trial and error, terrorists often identify cracks or loopholes in financing regulations and move their monies accordingly. For the most part, terrorist financing consists of three distinct operations: (1) earning or acquiring resources, (2) moving or laundering the money, and (3) storing or banking the money until it is needed. Figure 11-3 outlines this process and the various mechanisms associated with each operation.

Alternative financing mechanisms	Earning	Moving	Storing
Trade in commodities			
Illicit drugs	X		
Weapons	X		
Cigarettes	X		
Diamonds	X	X	X
Gold		X	X
Systems			
Charities	X	X	
Informal banking		X	
Currency			
Bulk cash		X	X

FIGURE 11-3 Terrorist Alternative Financing Operations and Mechanisms. *Source:* Government Accounting Office. (2003). *Terrorist Financing: U.S. Agencies Should Systematically Assess Terrorists' Use of Alternative Financing Mechanisms.* Washington, D.C.: Author, p. 10.

EARNING AND ACQUIRING RESOURCES

As noted earlier, a variety of methods are used by terrorist organizations to acquire resources. These methods are elaborated on in this section.

Donor Support of Terrorism

Numerous wealthy patrons in the oil-rich Middle East countries and Gulf States support terrorism. Osama bin Laden received some of the financing for the 9/11 attacks from patrons in the United Arab Emirates. In addition to the wealthy supporters, terrorists receive a substantial amount of money from imams at mosques who divert donations to terrorists or their facilitators.

HS Web Link: To read more about how the United States is attempting to attack donations to terrorists, go to *http://www. icnl.org/knowledge/ijnl/ vol6iss2/special_5.htm*

There is widespread animosity against America and Israel, and this animosity fuels hatred and support for the terrorists. It is not known exactly how much al Qaeda receives, but the UN Security Council (2002) estimated that individual wealthy donors provide the organization with approximately $16 million annually. Given that al Qaeda's annual budget is approximately $30 million, it appears that donations account for approximately half of its financial needs. Other terrorist groups receive considerable financial support from donors.

Criminal Activity

Terrorist groups across the world have a long history of using criminal activities such as robberies, extortion, and kidnapping to fund their activities. In the 1970s, the Symbionese Liberation Army, an American left-wing terrorist group, kidnapped newspaper heiress Patti Hearst; rather than ransoming her, her captors had her become part of the group's crime spree that included bombings and bank robberies to support the group's activities. More recently in the United States, a number of right-wing extremist groups have attempted to finance their operations through bank robberies; these groups also plotted terrorist attacks including bombings and murders.

Criminal activities have long been part of terrorist groups' portfolio of activities in South and Central America. Today, Mexico is close to anarchy; criminals and narco-terrorists routinely kill, kidnap, and extort money from citizens, politicians, and businesspeople. The problem stems from Mexico's inability to intervene in wars between the various drug cartels that provide illegal drugs to the United States. FARC, a terrorist group in Colombia, has a long history of

HS Web Link: To read more about the Mexican drug problem, go to *http:// projects.latimes.com/mexico- drug-war/#/its-a-war*

kidnapping, holding, and ransoming people, especially foreigners. It is estimated that in 2008, the group was holding more than 700 people including 40 high-profile victims (BBC America, 2008). The Shining Path, a terrorist group in Peru, has also engaged in kidnapping. Kidnapping in the region has been used to supplement narco-terrorism activities. Terrorist groups and cells worldwide commonly participate in these criminal activities.

In some cases, they participate in large-scale criminal enterprises. In Chapter 8, the relationship between transnational organized crime and terrorist organizations was discussed. As noted there, terrorist groups' activities often parallel or are similar to transnational organized crime activities especially in narco-terrorism and weapons smuggling. Terrorism also results in unusual criminal opportunities. For example, after the Khobar Towers bombing in Dharan, Saudi Arabia, in 1996, a number of prominent Saudis met in Paris where they conspired to pay al Qaeda and bin Laden to refrain from mounting attacks in Saudi Arabia. It is alleged that the Saudi royal family has also made such payments (Lee, 2002). Whereas common criminals extort money from businesspersons and individuals, some terrorist groups extort money from countries and multinational conglomerates.

The narcotics trade represents an important business for terrorist organizations. Numerous significant or powerful narcotics transnational organized crime groups and terrorist organizations are involved in narcotics trafficking in South and Central America. However, it is also prevalent in Asia and Africa. There is disagreement as to whether al Qaeda and the Taliban are involved in the opium trade (see Lee, 2002). When the Taliban came to power in 2000 in Afghanistan, it banned poppy production. It is questionable how effective that was since large portions of the country were ruled by warlords. Nonetheless, these drug trafficking networks remained and are even more vibrant today. In 2000, the DEA estimated that Afghanistan produced more than 70 percent of the world's opium, as displayed in Figure 11-4.

Many speculate that the Taliban, along with al Qaeda, began to raise funds from the opium trade after the United States and its allies invaded Afghanistan after the 9/11 attacks. In 2007, the DEA arrested Mohammad Essa for conspiring to import $25 million worth of heroin from Afghanistan and Pakistan into the United States. He was a member of the Baz Mohammad trafficking organization, which is closely aligned with the Taliban and has provided it with financial support (MacKinzie-Mulvey, 2007). The FBI (2002) has maintained that the al Qaeda network annually receives millions of dollars from the opium trade in Asia and Africa. Al-Qaeda smuggles the opium through Central Asian countries to countries in East Africa. Given al Qaeda's wealth, worldwide organization, and financial demands or needs, al Qaeda very likely is extensively involved in the narcotics trade but is not the only terrorist organization involved in narcotics trafficking. In 2002, federal agents broke up a methamphetamine ring in a dozen U.S. cities that funneled proceeds to Hezbollah (Kaplan, 2006).

HS Web Link: To read more about the Afghanistan poppy production problem, go to *http://www.csmonitor.com/ World/Asia-South-Central/ 2010/0112/How-US-is- tackling-opium-trade-in- Afghanistan-poppy-heartland*

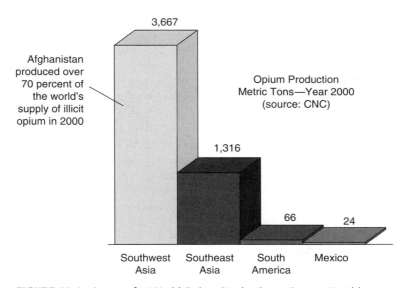

FIGURE 11-4 Sources for World Opium Production. *Source:* Hutchinson, A. (2001). "Statement before the House Government Reform Committee, Subcommittee on Criminal Justice, Drug Policy and Human Resources" (December 5).

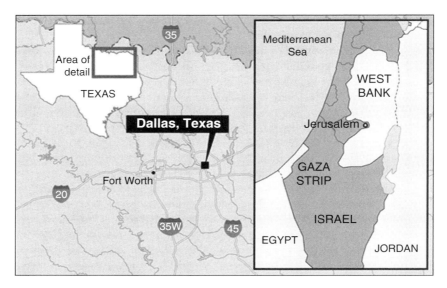

The Holy Land Foundation, based in a Dallas suburb before it was shut down in 2001, provided about $12.4 million in funding to Hamas-controlled organizations in the West Bank and Gaza.   *Source:* http:// www.fbi.gov/headlines/ hlf_map112508.jpg

Charities

A number of terrorist organizations have used charities to raise money. For example, the Irish Republican Army for decades had charities operating in the United States that raised money to finance its attacks in Northern Ireland and England. Left-wing and right-wing groups worldwide solicit and accept donations to finance their operations. However, in the Muslim world, charities are more institutionalized. **Zakat**, or alms giving, is one of the five pillars of Islam—charity is a religious duty for all Muslims (Comras, 2005). Charity is practiced extensively with numerous Muslim charities worldwide. For example, Saudi Arabia and the United Arab Emirates have no formal income tax system and charities represent the primary mechanism for humanitarian projects. In many third-world countries with dysfunctional governments, charities often are more influential than government entities since they are able to provide scores of citizens with assistance. For example, Hezbollah in Lebanon and Hamas in the Gaza Strip are terrorist organizations that are engaged in providing assistance to the population. This assistance engenders greater levels of support for their activities, including terrorism. It also enables them to seek and receive significant charitable donations.

HS Web Link: To learn more about Zakat and Islamic giving, go to *http:// www.zpub.com/aaa/zakat-def.html*

Islamic-based charities are numerous and dispersed across the world. About one-fifth of all charitable organizations are Islamic, and they disperse several billion dollars annually (Looney, 2006). These charities gain widespread acceptance in the Muslim world because they not only provide humanitarian aid, but also further and cement Islamic religious and cultural philosophies. Charities are a tool by which to counter or reduce foreign influence on Islamic culture. They help solidify xenophobic attitudes.

The plight of the Palestinian people has been a rallying point for many charities and givers. It has resulted in substantial donations primarily to Hamas and Hezbollah, two organizations that are recognized as terrorist groups. Other groups are also collecting money on behalf of the Palestinians. Outrage in the Muslim world over the Israeli-Palestinian conflict has resulted in substantial anger, and this has led to numerous and increased donations from the wealthy and the poor. Most of these charities are legitimate, but some have collected or given money to terrorist organizations. Others serve to collect money solely for terrorist organizations. For example, the 9/11 Commission (2004) found that "entire charities under the control of al Qaeda operatives. . . may have wittingly participated in funneling money to al Qaeda" (p. 170).

Charities have been used extensively by bin Laden to obtain substantial resources for his al Qaeda organization. According to Kohlmann (2006–7),

> Standing orders were left by bin Laden to keep all transactions involving charitable groups in cash only. . . these NGOs [non-government organizations] were manipulated as a secret laundry to make al Qaeda's financial network virtually invisible. The charities would then create false documentation for the benefit of unwary donors, purportedly showing that the money had actually been spent on orphans or starving refugees. According to some former employers of these organizations, upwards of 50% of their total funding was secretly diverted to al-Qaeda and Osama bin Laden. (pp. 2–3)

The terrorists then use the money for a variety of purposes including waging war, financing attacks, purchasing arms and explosives, and daily living expenses for terrorists and cells.

Charities have been successful in providing terrorist groups with a substantial amount of untraceable resources. They, to some extent, represent a repository for cash. The charities also serve other functions. Kohlmann (2006–7) advises that the charities are effective in recruiting new jihadists. As a part of their appeal, the charities emphasize the misery, repression, and injury suffered by Muslims. The charities then solicit donations and "deeds." The deeds often include not only humanitarian assistance, but also actions and a jihadist commitment to remove the repressors or enemies and restore Islam to greatness. The charities also allow affiliated terrorists to travel internationally without the usual hindrance; association with a charity facilitates obtaining required travel documents.

As noted, these charities exist throughout the world, including the United States. A good example is the recently closed Holy Land Foundation (HLF) of Dallas, Texas. It was estimated that the HLF raised $13 million in the United States in 2000, claiming that the funds were for the care of needy Palestinians. Evidence shows that a portion of this money went to Hamas (see Looney, 2006). Although Hamas is involved in humanitarian activities, particularly in the Gaza Strip, it likely used some of this money for its attacks on Israel. It is interesting that it took a multinational investigation, spanning 11 years, to close the HLF (Henifin, 2004). In a similar case in 2008, former congressman Mark Siljander was indicted in Kansas City for lobbying for an Islamic charity that was funneling money to terrorists. Siljander received $50,000 from the Islamic American Relief Agency to lobby the Senate Finance Committee to have the charity removed from the panel's list of suspected terror fund-raisers. The charity paid Siljander money that was stolen from the U.S. government (Schmidt, 2008). These cases demonstrate the extensive and complicated nature of charity operations. They also show that terrorists are raising money on American soil—money that sometimes is used to attack us.

Analysis Box 11-3

Policing charities is a particularly difficult problem given that all sorts of charities exist and operate in the United States as well as other countries. The discussion of the Holy Land Foundation in Dallas shows that it is a slow process. Should the United States enact laws that better control charities? Is it politically feasible to enact such laws since the laws would affect all other charities? What kinds of laws would you favor?

It was not until after the 9/11 attacks that the United States became serious about dealing with Muslim charities that supported terrorism. Prior to 9/11, they were seen as malevolent, but causing little harm. However, the 9/11 attacks resulted in renewed interest in all forms of terrorism funding, and the passage of the Anti-Terrorism Act of 1996 provided the primary mechanism to scrutinize these charities. The act has been used to choke funding to terrorist organizations.

The United States and other countries have received substantial criticism for their efforts to close Islamic charities. Critics maintain that these charities provide a substantial amount of humanitarian service in areas that desperately need assistance. However, the problem remains that many of these charities are intertwined with terrorist organizations and activities, and it is extraordinarily difficult to separate those that are genuinely providing humanitarian services from those that are funding terrorism. Even more problematic is that some of the charities are providing humanitarian aid while funneling some of their resources to terrorist organizations. The U.S. policy is that "it is better to be safe than sorry."

This discussion demonstrates that it is difficult to deal with Islamic charities. They are well organized and extensively involved across the globe. The Soviet Union's invasion of Afghanistan in 1976 resulted in the formation of dozens of Islamic charities to assist the Afghan people. Many of these same charities exist today and are collecting money for the Taliban and other terrorist organizations. Thus, some Islamic charities have decades of experience in developing proficient organizations that provide humanitarian aid and fund wars. They also have uncovered and use procedures to evade government scrutiny.

Legitimate Businesses

Criminal groups have often used the money obtained from criminal enterprises to invest in legitimate businesses. In the United States, youth gangs have invested in car washes and automobile trim businesses using money derived from the drug trade (Decker, Bynum, and Weisel, 2004). Larger and more sophisticated groups often gravitate to large legitimate business since they often have the financing capital. As noted, al Qaeda has been involved in an assortment of legitimate businesses in several countries, including mining, diamonds, trading firms, construction companies, an agricultural production and export company, and a furniture-making company. As another example, al Qaeda has been involved in the honey-trading business. Honey is an important commodity in the Middle East and essentially is part of the culture. However, Miller and Gerth (2001) maintain that in some cases, the honey exportation business was used as a front by terrorist groups for smuggling guns, money, and drugs. Regardless, these examples point out that terrorists can maximize the utility and financial return when operating legitimate businesses, and terrorist organizations readily grasp business opportunities to raise funds. Lee (2002) provides additional examples:

According to FBI documents, a Madrid al Qaeda cell ran a home repair company that provided masonry, plastering, and electrical services, as well an enterprise that restored and resold dilapidated vehicles. The cell's activities also included a criminal repertoire— credit card and document fraud, as well as street crime such as home burglary and car theft. A Singapore-Malaysia al Qaeda cell sold medical supplies and computer software but also engaged in bank robberies, violent assaults, and kidnappings. (p. 11)

MOVING OR LAUNDERING MONEY

As noted in Figure 11-2, terrorists move or launder their money in several ways: (1) precious commodities such as gold and diamonds, (2) banking and wire transfers, (3) informal banking or hawaladars, and (4) bulk cash. When engaging in their financial operations, terrorists also work with or interact with other players such as transnational organized crime groups, supporters of terrorist organizations or religious or political causes, and government officials.

Precious Commodities

Precious commodities represent a funding source for terrorist groups, and they are a convenient method by which to move large sums of money. For example, Lee (2002) notes,

> Diamonds, it should be noted, are a particularly attractive commodity for smuggling operatives. They don't set off alarms at airports, they can't be sniffed by dogs, they are easy to hide, and are highly convertible to cash. Also, diamonds have a high value-to-weight ratio: a pound of average quality diamonds is valued at approximately $225,000. A pound of $100 dollar bills is worth in the neighborhood of $45,000, and a pound of gold, at $300 an ounce, is worth $4,800. (p 12)

It appears that Osama bin Laden has used precious stones (diamonds) to raise money and to move it from one country to another. He supposedly obtained millions of dollars over a three-year period through precious stones. Abdullah Ahmed Abdullah, a top bin Laden advisor, was in contact with diamond dealers who represented Sierra Leone's Revolutionary Front in 1998 and bought uncut diamonds from the group. Al Qaeda operatives then transported the diamonds to Europe and other countries where they were sold for sizable profits (Farah, 2001). In another case, two al Qaeda companies, Tanzanite King and Black Giant, exported large quantities of uncut tanzanite from Kenya to Hong Kong, enabling al Qaeda to make large amounts of money (Block and Pearl, 2001). It is likely that terrorist organizations across the world use precious commodities to move and bank their assets; given the complexity and scope of the commodities trade, it is extremely difficult to trace these assets.

Banking and Wire Transfers

Terrorists frequently wire money from one bank account to another. American and Western banks often have strict controls over such transactions, whereas banks in many third-world and Middle-Eastern countries often have insufficient control mechanisms. Moreover, some of these banks willingly facilitate these transfers for ideological reasons or profits. The FBI tracked $90,000 in wire transfers from the United Arab Emirates to New York and Florida bank accounts. The money was accessed by the 9/11 hijackers (FBI, 2002). The U.S. government has been active in pursuing illegitimate funds; for example, the U.S. Treasury Department fined the U.S. arm of UBS AG $100 million for funneling $5 billion to countries such as Cuba, Iran, and Libya, and the Riggs Bank was fined $25 million for failing to report unusual transactions. The amounts of these fines demonstrate how much illicit money is being transferred or laundered by financial institutions (Weiss, 2005). These actions also demonstrate that numerous legitimate banks have substantially and willingly been involved in terrorists' financial networks in the past. It is unclear to what extent they may still be involved in these activities. The U.S. government continues to monitor and attempt to control these financial transactions.

Banks in Muslim countries operate differently from Western banks. First, there is weak governmental oversight of banks in these countries, as well as in a number of other developing countries. This results in many transactions not being scrutinized by any government regulators, facilitating their use by terrorist organizations. The money made by banks generally is used for internal projects or given to charities (Basile, 2009). Many of these banks have Sharia boards that allocate some of these excess funds to charities; it is very likely that some of this money ultimately is transferred to terrorist organizations.

Money Brokers or Hawaladars

There is a time-honored informal, underground banking system within the Muslim world known as **hawalas**. These are alternative remittance systems that involve the transfer of funds or assets from one individual to another using an informal banking system (see FATF, 1999). As noted in Figure 11-4, a simple hawala consist of four steps. Essentially, someone desiring to send money to a person in another country simply contacts the hawala. The hawala then contacts a hawala in the destination country, and the hawala in the destination country delivers the funds without the funds leaving the originating country. This results in a deficit between the two hawalas. The accounts are frequently settled at some future point in time when someone in the destination country wishes to transfer funds back to the originating country.

The hawalas have a number of advantages for their users. They allow funds to be transferred within a very short time, sometimes in a matter of minutes. There are no written records of the transfers; all actions are made on an informal basis. This results in participants not having a tax burden or government scrutiny as a result of the transfers. Those participating in hawala money transfers remain anonymous since the transfers are usually conducted using coded passwords. They are resilient in that they are not affected by economic downturns or war. Finally, hawalas are a less expensive means for people to transfer money as compared to the international banking system, especially when small amounts of money are being transferred.

McCusker (2005) and Lee (2002) have identified variations on the hawala system. These variations are sometimes used to even accounts. The first is under-invoicing. Here, a hawaladar in one country will send goods to a hawaladar in another country, but the goods will be invoiced for less than their value. The hawaladar receiving the goods will then sell the goods at market value, recouping what he or she was owed by the hawaladar who shipped the goods. The second variation is over-invoicing. Here the hawaladar ships goods to another hawaladar who owes him or her money, but the invoice is for a greater amount than the value of the goods. The receiving hawaladar pays the bill, which corrects the financial imbalance. On paper these transactions appear to be legitimate business transactions and there is no evidence of the money transfers.

Given the simplicity of the hawala system, one would assume that it is used sparingly. However, it is used extensively in Muslim countries and some Asian countries. Sander (2003) found that in 2002, $80 billion was remitted through this informal banking system by people living in developing countries. It represented the second-largest flow of capital to these countries

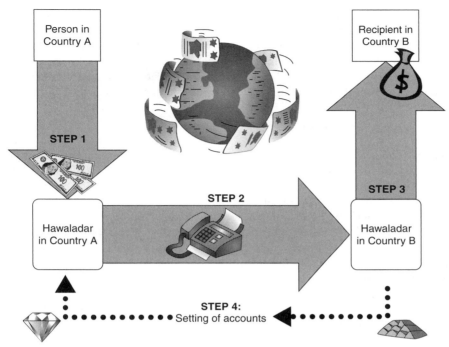

STEP 1. A person in Country A would like to send money to a recipient in Country B. The person in Country A contacts a hawaladar, a hawala operator, in Country A and gives the operator money and instructions to deliver the equivalent value to the recipient in Country B.

STEP 2. The hawaladar in Country A contacts the counterpart hawaladar in Country B via fax, e-mail, telephone. or other method and communicates the instructions.

STEP 3. The hawaladar in Country B then contacts the recipient in Country B and through varification by some code passed from the person in Country A to the recipient in Country B, delivers the equivalent value (in foreign currency of some commodity), less a transaction fee, to the recipient in Country B.

STEP 4. Over time, the accounts between the two hawaladars may become unbalanced and must be settled in some manner. Hawaladars use a variety of methods to settle their accounts, including reciprocal payments to customers, physical movement of money, wire transfer or check, payment for goods to be traded, trade or smuggling of precious stones or metals such as gold and diamonds, and invoice manipulation.

FIGURE 11-5   Interworkings of a Simple Hawala.   *Source:* Government Accounting Office. (2003). *Terrorist Financing: U.S. Agencies Should Systematically Assess Terrorists' Use of Alternative Financing Mechanisms.* Washington, D.C.: Author, p. 18.

behind foreign investment. Officials in Pakistan estimated that at least $7 billion enters that country each year through this alternative remittance system (Lee, 2002).

As noted, the hawala system is used by numerous people for all sorts of transactions. It is used primarily by average people, but the system also is being used to transfer funds for terrorist activities. As discussed earlier, al Qaeda has an extensive network across the globe. The hawala system allows the group to transfer large amounts of money undetected. Other organizations are also using this system. For example, the Colombians are using the hawala system to launder approximately $5 billion annually. U.S. officials note that thus far they have had little luck in tracing the transactions or seizing assets. In another case, in 2002, approximately 390,000 kilograms of U.S. honey were shipped to the United Arab Emirates, Saudi Arabia, and Kuwait. The importers in those countries paid 35 percent over the U.S. price or cost (over-invoicing) yielding funds in excess of $257,000. It could not be determined if the money was used for terrorist activities in the United States, but two of the honey exporting companies are on a terrorist list (Lee, 2002). According to the FBI, some of the money used to finance the 9/11 attacks was transferred to the United States using hawalas (GAO, 2003). The hawala system presents a significant challenge to U.S. and world authorities who are attempting to reduce terrorist financing.

STORING OR BANKING MONEY

The previous sections described the methods by which terrorist organizations acquire and move money. Al Qaeda and other terrorist organizations accumulate varying amounts of wealth, in al Qaeda's case, millions of dollars since its annual budget is approximately $30 million. As noted, these terrorist organizations as a result of these activities accumulate cash and numerous products such as agriculture goods, precious gems and metals, and disposable goods. These goods represent financial resources, but they are not necessarily fluid; they cannot always be converted to cash quickly to finance an operation or sustain a cell. Terrorist organizations develop a business model whereby they estimate their cash flow needs and develop a timely process or method to convert these goods into cash. The hawalas likely are used for some of this conversion. It is also likely that these terrorist organizations retain large amounts of bulk cash since cash is readily accessible and immune from seizure by governments, which might occur if the money were deposited in some banks. They likely concentrate on accumulating goods such as diamonds and precious metals that can be sold fairly quickly.

SAUDI ARABIA'S FINANCING OF TERRORISM: AN AMERICAN CONUNDRUM

Saudi Arabia is perhaps America's closest ally in the Middle East. The United States has maintained close relations with the Saudi kingdom, which sells large quantities of oil to the United States. There have been cases when the Saudis have increased oil production when other OPEC nations were reducing production in an effort to increase prices. President George W. Bush was friends with members of the royal family. There have been instances when the United States tempered its policies in order to maintain warm relations with the Saudis. Our relations and dependency on the Saudis have become problematic since a significant portion of funding in the Middle East for extremism and terrorism comes from the Arabian Peninsula. Although countries such as Iran, Libya, and Syria outwardly promote terrorism, Saudi Arabia has been responsible for a substantial portion of the covert bankrolling of these movements.

In addition to being America's closest ally in the Middle East, it is also the most conservative, and to some extent, the most radical. This extremism has its roots in Wahhabism, Saudi Arabia's brand of Islam. According to the Middle East Media Institute (cited in Gold, 2003),

> Wahhabism leads, as we have seen, to the birth of extremist, closed, and fanatical streams, that accuse others of heresy, abolish them, and destroy them. The extremist religious groups have moved from the stage of *Takfir* [condemning other Muslims as unbelievers] to the stage of "annihilation and destruction," in accordance with the strategy of Al-Qa'ida—which Saudi authorities must admit is a local Saudi organization that drew other organizations into it, and not the other way around. All the organizations emerged from under the robe of Wahhabism.

Analysis Box 11-4

Dealing with Saudi Arabia obviously is a difficult problem for American foreign policy. Saudi Arabia is a friend and ally, although a weak one. We must also understand that the actions that the Saudis can take are limited by their political culture. Should the United States forsake Saudi oil and push for more action in countering terrorism? Would the American people understand that higher prices for oil is the price for more effectively fighting terrorism? What policy should the United States adopt?

These radical roots run deep. Not only has Wahhabism spawned Islamic terrorism, it also made a significant contribution to al Qaeda's beginnings. Indeed, bin Laden is Saudi as were 15 of the 19 attackers in the 9/11 attacks. Bin Laden's ties to Saudi Arabia have resulted in extensive Saudi financial and psychological support for Al Qaeda and other terrorist groups.

HS Web Link: To read more about Saudi Arabia and terrorism, go to: *http://www.jcpa.org/jl/vp504.htm*

Saudi Arabia, with an abundance of oil money, has been extensively involved in charities with significant amounts of this money going to terrorists in numerous countries, including Afghanistan, Palestine, Bosnia, and Chechnya. The Saudis have operated a number of charities, some of which are rather large, including the International Islamic Relief Organization (IIRO) and the Charitable Foundation of al-Haramain. Bin Laden's brother-in-law ran the Philippine offices of the IIRO and the brother of Ayman al-Zawahiri (second in command in al Qaeda), was employed in IIRO's Albanian office. The Charitable Foundation of al-Haramain funded al Qaeda operations in Southeast Asia. Additionally, it is estimated that more than 50 percent of Hamas's funding comes from Saudi Arabia (Gold, 2003).

In 2003, Saudi Arabia experienced a number of suicide attacks that resulted in the Saudis examining terrorist funding more closely. The government began to crack down on extremists in the kingdom and more closely monitor charitable organizations. However, Gold asserts that officials become concerned only with charitable activities within the kingdom and had little concern for their activities outside the country. Money laundering laws were enacted, but again, they applied primarily to money laundering within the kingdom, and they were not comprehensive enough to stem the flow of money to external terrorist groups and activities. The United States has continued to apply pressure on the Saudi royal family, but the royal family is so interdependent with the Wahhabi religious structure that it is questionable if there will be significant results. Indeed, in 2008, Stuart Levey, a treasury undersecretary, reported to a U.S. Senate Committee that Saudi Arabia remains the location where more money is going to terrorism, to Sunni terror groups, and to the Taliban than any other place in the world.

The United States is in a predicament—Saudi Arabia remains the primary source for terrorist funding—but because of our dependence on oil and Saudi support in the Middle East, there is little that can be done. As long as the Saudis fund terrorism, terrorism likely will remain a vibrant destructive force.

IDENTITY FRAUD AND THEFT

A major problem is identity fraud and theft, which are two different but interrelated problems. **Identity fraud** is the process of using a false identity or another person's identity to obtain goods, services, or money. **Identity theft**, on the other hand, is the procuring of this false identity regardless of its use. In most cases, identity theft is used to commit identity fraud, but in some cases, it is used by criminals and terrorists to establish false identities and escape detection. Identity theft and fraud are criminal activities that are closely linked to terrorist financing. In many cases, terrorists will use assumed identities to cover money trails. This helps reduce the possibility that authorities will discover the money or be able to link the money to a terrorist group or activity. Additionally, terrorists engage in identity theft to provide clandestine cover. In this regard, they use identity theft for three purposes:

1. *Avoid watch lists*—Many terrorists and possible collaborators have been identified and their names are on terrorist watch lists that serve to monitor their travel and prevent them from traveling in some countries. They assume new identities to avoid being discovered or to allow them to travel to other countries.
2. *Obscure their whereabouts*—Terrorists often use one or more different identities, especially when conducting terrorist-related activities, which makes it more difficult for law enforcement to trace or apprehend them.
3. *Gain unauthorized access*—Some terrorists or suspected terrorists are barred from entry into certain countries or from using mass transportation such as air travel, and false identities allow them to frustrate such limitations.

Identity theft, not only in terms of terrorism, but also in terms of other financial crimes, has resulted in numerous governmental and private actions to prevent it from occurring. Identity fraud has grown exponentially primarily as a result of the Internet. A substantial amount of commerce is being conducted via the Internet, which has led to the fraudulent acquisition of personal data or information. Moreover, numerous personal identifier databases that are linked to the web are not adequately protected with fire walls. For example, many state and local governments post databases with personal information on the Internet as a part of their open records programs (most notable is real estate information). This has resulted in large numbers of nefarious individuals attempting to commit some form of identity theft using information gathered from the Internet.

HS Web Link: To learn more about identity theft and fraud, go to *http://www. justice.gov/criminal/fraud/ websites/idtheft.html*

Real ID Act

Perhaps the best-known effort to counter identity fraud and theft is the **Real ID Act**, which establishes national standards for driver's licenses. In the past, there has been no uniformity in driver's licenses, and consequently, border security officers and other law enforcement officials would not necessarily know if a driver's license was a forgery, especially if it came from another state and the officers were not familiar with that state's license format. At a minimum, drivers' licenses must contain,

1. A photo identity document (except that a non-photo identity document is acceptable if it includes both the person's full legal name and date of birth)
2. Documentation showing the person's date of birth
3. Proof of the person's Social Security account number (SSN) or verification that the person is not eligible for an SSN
4. Documentation showing the person's name and address of principal residence

Additionally, before issuing a driver's license, the states must verify the information. Congress passed the Real ID Act in an effort to reduce the amount of identity theft and fraud.

HS Web Link: To learn more about the Real ID Act, go to *http://www.dhs.gov/files/laws/ gc_1172765386179.shtm*

In the United States, a driver's license is the primary form of identification. It is used to process all sorts of transactions. Controlling driver's licenses is important

---

Analysis Box 11-5

A driver's license is an important identification document in the United States, and the states have different standards, making it difficult for police officers and other officials to identify valid and counterfeit licenses. Should Congress require the states to implement Real ID? Given the federal budget deficits, should Congress fund the states to implement the act? Should American citizens be required to carry some type of national identification card? Why?

---

because they often serve as a breeder document that can be used to obtain other forms of fraudulent identification. Civil libertarians are opposed to these national requirements; they see the uniform driver's license as a form of a national identification card. Several of the states have voiced opposition, with some refusing to implement the law because of the expense. Nonetheless, a standardized biometrically readable driver's license likely will reduce identification theft and fraud.

Breeder Documents and the Mechanics of Identity Fraud

Gordon and Willox (2003) have identified the mechanics or process by which terrorists and criminals attempt to develop a false identity. They begin by creating a new identity, often by providing fictitious personal information or assuming the identity of another person. The fraudulent identity is then used to obtain a **breeder document**, usually a Social Security card, driver's license, passport, or birth certificate. This allows the individual to obtain other fraudulent documents. When this occurs, there often is no victim and the identity theft is not reported to authorities. There are ample websites that advertise these fraudulent documents and books that describe how they can be obtained, and there are always corrupt officials who will sell the documents.

Once the breeder document has been obtained, other breeder documents can be obtained. These documents then are used to create an identity to obtain other forms of identification and to access financial systems. There are cases in which charlatans have assumed a homeowner's identity and sold the home or property, thereby committing bank fraud. The documents are often used to obtain government benefits such as unemployment (when a false nonexisting employer is used), welfare, and other governmental benefits. In some cases, terrorist groups have raised large amounts of money in this manner by using multiple fictitious identities. Since most of the information on entitlement programs is confidential, there are few investigations unless the investigation is initiated as a result of other wrong-doing. In other cases, fraudulent documents have been used to obtain visas and green cards.

Once an individual has created an identity, he or she can more easily become involved in a variety of criminal activities. Most important, since the identity is false, it becomes more difficult to apprehend the perpetrator. Terrorists can use these identities to obtain money, launder money, export money for terrorist activities, fund terrorist activities within the United States, purchase arms, and move across borders. The identities can be used in smuggling and trafficking drugs and weapons, which is a lucrative financial endeavor for terrorists. In some cases, the fraudulent identities are passed on to illegal aliens who are smuggled into the United States.

The FBI recovers dozens of fake identification documents, including Social Security cards, UN ID cards, and birth certificates from three states. *Source:* http://www.fbi.gov/headlines/krarh.jpg

TERRORISTS' FINANCIAL NEEDS

As mentioned earlier, terrorism requires a substantial amount of funding. The CIA estimates that al Qaeda raises approximately $30 million a year (Looney, 2006; Naylor, 2002), which results in a substantial budget for the organization. This would appear to be insurmountable in terms of the number and types of terrorist activities that could be financed, especially considering that the 9/11 attacks cost al Qaeda less than $500,000 (9/11 Commission, 2004). Levitt and Jacobson (2008) note that the London subway and bus attacks that killed 52 people cost an estimated $15,000. The Madrid subway attack and the attack on the USS *Cole* in Yemen each cost approximately $10,000. It seems that terrorist attacks are rather inexpensive relative to al Qaeda's overall operating budget.

However, al Qaeda and other terrorist organizations, depending on their size and scope, have a significant operational or maintenance budget. Documents seized by the U.S. military show that one branch of al Qaeda in Iraq spent more than $175,000 in a four-month period with only about half the expenditures for weapons. Documents also show that al Qaeda is very bureaucratic, requiring receipts for almost all of subordinates' expenditures, which is dangerous since such records can be discovered by the group's enemies, providing important intelligence information (see Levitt and Jackson, 2004). In fact, parts of this paper trail have been uncovered by investigators, and they provide some insights into the organization's financing. What is important is that al Qaeda is "tightfisted" with its money. Even though the organization has a budget of approximately $30 million per annum, it has massive expenses. Reportedly in 1995, when Ramzi Ahmed Yousef was arrested for the first bombing of the World Trade Center, an FBI agent reminded him that his attack was unsuccessful. Yousef retorted that if he had enough money and explosives, the World Trade Center would have been leveled (Levitt and Jacobson, 2008). This demonstrated that he did not have the resources necessary to successfully carry out the attack.

It seems that al Qaeda's $30 million is spread thin across a number of fronts. Indeed, the group has numerous expenses and overhead. It must pay its fighters and in many cases provide sustenance for their families. It must train fighters in its camps, resulting in considerable expenditures. In many cases, it must pay local officials and corrupt politicians; for example, al Qaeda has been able to maintain bases in Pakistan by bribing or paying a number of the tribal chiefs. It has been estimated that bin Laden paid as much as $20 million to the tribal chiefs (Lee, 2002). In reality, al Qaeda and other terrorist groups have tremendous expenditures, requiring a significant cash flow. It appears that eliminating at least some of this flow of money would have significant repercussions on terrorists' activities.

Summary

This chapter examined terrorist funding. To a large extent, this chapter focused on Osama bin Laden and al Qaeda. This does not mean that other terrorist organizations are not involved in raising funds; indeed, there are numerous such networks across the globe, perhaps several hundred such organizations. However, al Qaeda was examined more closely here because it represents the largest and most sophisticated and problematic terrorist network in the world. Through its various enterprises, it raises approximately $30 million a year (Looney, 2006; Naylor, 2002). A number of narcoterrorist organizations in South and Central America have more substantial revenues, but the fruits of their activities relate more to greed than terrorism; they often use terrorist acts to facilitate their ability to realize financial gains. Terrorist organizations such as al Qaeda raise money to directly support terrorism.

Terrorist funding is a process with three distinct phases: (1) earning or acquiring resources, (2) moving or laundering the money, and (3) storing or banking the money until it is needed. Al Qaeda and other terrorist groups have developed extremely complex and effective financial networks. Terrorist organizations such as al Qaeda are akin to multinational conglomerates.

They use a variety of techniques to raise money, including criminal enterprises, common crimes, legitimate businesses, charities, and donations from wealthy patrons.

The existence of these multiple funding sources makes it difficult to reduce terrorist funding. When authorities are able to effectively intervene in one area, it appears that other sources are available to take up the financial slack. Moreover, Looney (2006) notes that when countries enact tougher anti-terrorist funding initiatives, the terrorists move their operations to countries that are less restrictive. Indeed, the 9/11 Commission (2004) suggests that it is impossible to eliminate terrorist funding, and that a better strategy might be to follow the money. Terrorist groups and activities might be identified by following funding sources—the money trail can provide significant intelligence information. On the other hand, Levitt and Jacobson (2008) advise that terrorist groups have extremely large organizational maintenance costs and that eliminating a portion of their finances likely would cause the groups operational problems. Regardless, it is important that the United States and other countries continue to reduce terrorist funding.

Discussion Questions

1. Terrorist financing consists of two distinct activities. What are they and how do they operate?
2. Terrorists have alternative financing mechanisms. Distinguish among earning, moving, and storing resources.
3. How does a hawala operate?
4. Describe the relationship between the United States and Saudi Arabia and how Wahhabism affects Saudi Arabia and that relationship.

5. What are breeder documents and how do they function?

6. Describe how the terrorists funded the 9/11 attacks.

7. What is the Real ID Act? How effectively has it been implemented?

References

Armstrong, D. (2004). "Charity cases." *Harper's Magazine*, 308(1846): 81–83.

Basile, M. (2009). "Going to the source: Why al Qaeda's financial network is likely to withstand the current war on terrorism financing." In *Terrorism and Counterterrorism*, ed. R. Howard, R. Sawyer, and N. Bajema, pp. 530–47. New York: McGraw-Hill.

BBC America. (2008). *New Kidnappings in Colombia*. http://news.bbc.co.uk/2/hi/americas/7188509.stm (Accessed December 13, 2008).

Block, R. and D. Pearl. (2001). "Underground trade: Much smuggled gem called tanzanite helps bin Laden supporters—bought and sold by militants near mine, stones often end up at Mideast souks—deal making at the mosque." *The Wall Street Journal* (November 18), p. A1.

Comras, V. (2005). "Al Qaeda finances and funding to affiliated groups." *Strategic Insights*, 4(1).

Decker, S., T. Bynum, and D. Weisel. (2004). "A tale of two cities: Gangs as organized crime groups." In *American Youth Gangs at the Millennium*, ed. F. Esbensen, S. Tibbetts, and L. Gaines, pp. 247–74. Long Grove, IL: Waveland.

Farah, D. (2001). "Al Qaeda cash tied to diamond trade, sale of gems from Sierra Leone; rebels raised millions." *The Washington Post* (November 2), p. A1.

Federal Bureau of Investigation. (2002). "Financing of terrorism and terrorist acts and related money laundering." *Briefing* (September 30).

Financial Action Task Force. (undated). *Homepage*. http://www.fatf-gafi.org/pages/0,3417,en_32250379_32235720_1_1_1_1_1,00.html (Accessed December 11, 2008).

Financial Action Task Force. (2008). *Terrorist Financing*. http://www.fatf-gafi.org/dataoecd/28/43/40285899.pdf (Accessed December 10, 2008).

Financial Action Task Force. (1999). *1998–1999 Report on Money Laundering Typologies*. Paris: Author.

Gold, D. (2003). *Saudi Arabia's Dubious Denials of Involvement in International Terrorism* (Number 504, October 1). Jerusalem: Jerusalem Center for Public Affairs. http://www.jcpa.org/jl/vp504.htm (Accessed January 1, 2009).

Gordon, G. and N. Willox. (2003). *Identity Fraud: A Critical National and Global Threat*. Utica, NY: Economic Crime Institute.

Government Accounting Office. (2003). *Terrorist Financing: U.S. Agencies Should Systematically Assess Terrorists' Use of Alternative Financing Mechanisms*. Washington, D.C.: Author.

Henifin, D. (2004). "What took so long? Closing the Holy Land Foundation: A case study in counterterrorism." A paper presented at the National War College.

Kaplan, K. (2006). "Tracking down terrorist financing." *Council on Foreign Affairs* (April 4). http://www.cfr.org/publication/10356/ (Accessed December 17, 2008).

Kohlmann, E. (2006–7). *The Role of Islamic Charities in International Terrorist Recruitment and Financing*. Copenhagen: Danish Institute for International Studies.

Lee, R. (2002). *Terrorist Financing: The U.S. and International Response*. Washington, D.C.: Congressional Research Service.

Levey, S. (2008). *Undersecretary for Terrorism and Financial Intelligence Stuart Levey Testimony Before Senate Committee on Finance*. http://205.168.45.51/press/releases/ hp898.htm (Accessed January 17, 2011).

Levitt, M. and M. Jacobson. (2008). *The Money Trail: Finding, Following, and Freezing Terrorist Finances*. Washington, D.C.: The Washington Institute for Near East Policy. http://www.washingtoninstitute.org/templateC04.php?CID=302 (Accessed December 23, 2008).

Looney, R. (2006). "The mirage of terrorist financing: The case of Islamic charities." *Strategic Insights*, 5(3).

MacKinzie-Mulvey, E. (2007). "United States announces arrest of Taliban-linked Afghan heroin trafficker on charges of conspiring to import million of dollars worth of heroin." *DEA News Release*. http://www.usdoj.gov/dea/pubs/states/newsrel/nyc051107a.html (Accessed March 9, 2009).

Malkin, L. (2002). "Terrorism's money trail." *World Policy Journal*, 19(1): 60–71.

McCusker, R. (2005). "Underground banking: Legitimate remittance network or money laundering system?" *Trends & Issues in Crime and Criminal Justice* (No. 300). Sydney: Australian Institute of Criminology.

Miller, J. and J. Gerth. (2001). "Trade in honey is said to provide money and cover for bin Laden." *The New York Times* (October 11), p. A1.

National Commission on Terrorist Attacks Upon the United States. (2004). *Monograph on Terrorist Financing* (Staff Report). http://govinfo.library.unt.edu/9/11/staff_statements/9/11_TerrFin_Monograph.pdf (Accessed December 11, 2008).

Naylor, R. (2006). *Satanic Purses: Money, Myth and Misinformation in the War on Terror.* Montreal: McGill-Queen's University Press.

Naylor, R. (2002). *Wages of Crime: Black Markets, Illegal Finance, and the Underworld Economy.* Ithaca: Cornell University Press.

Prados, A. and C. Blanchard. (2004). *Saudi Arabia: Terrorist Financing Issues.* Washington, D.C.: Congressional Research Service.

Roberge, I. (2007). "Misguided policies in the war on terror? The case for disentangling terrorist financing from money laundering." *Politics,* 27(3): 196–203.

Sander, C. (2003). *Migrant Remittances to Developing Countries.* London: Bannock Consulting. http://www.dai.com/pdf/Migrant_Remittances_to_Developing_Countries.pdf (Accessed December 16, 2008).

Schmidt, R. (2008). "Ex-Rep Rick Siljander indicted." *The Los Angeles Times* (January 17). http://www.latimes.com/news/nationworld/nation/la-na-indict17jan17,1,1025865.story?track=rss (Accessed December 18, 2008).

Stana, R. (2004). *Investigating Money Laundering and Terrorist Financing: Federal Law Enforcement Agencies Face Continuing Coordination Challenges.* Washington, D.C.: Government Accounting Office.

United Nations Security Council. (2002). *Second Report of the Monitoring Group Established Pursuant to Security Council Resolution 1363 (2001) and Extended by Resolution 1390 (2002).* (August 22), p. 3.

Weintraub, S. (2001). "Disrupting the financing of terrorism." *The Washington Quarterly,* 25(1): 53–60.

Weiss, M. (2005). "Terrorist financing: The 9/11 Commission recommendation." *CRS Report for Congress.* Washington, D.C.: Congressional Research Service.

Winer, J. (2008). "Countering terrorist finance: A work, mostly in progress." *Annals, AAPSS,* 618: 111–32.

Zagaris, B. (2004). "The merging of the anti-money laundering and counter-terrorism financial enforcement regimes after September 11 2001." *Berkeley Journal of International Law,* 22: 123–58.

12

Border Security and Immigration

LEARNING OBJECTIVES

1. Understand the relationship between immigration and border security.
2. Know the patterns of illegal immigration to the United States.
3. Be familiar with our philosophies and methods of border protection.
4. Know the responsibilities and actions of DHS agencies involved in protecting our border and interior.
5. Understand how we control or monitor the flow of goods and people across our borders.

KEY TERMS

Climate migrants

Countries of special interest

Prevention

North American Complementary Immigration Policies

Interdiction

Deterrence

Secure Border Initiative

SBInet

Project 28

US-VISIT

Non-visa or Visa Waiver Program

Secure Electronic Network for Travelers Rapid Inspection

NEXUS program

Maritime Transportation Act of 2002

Transportation Workers Identification Credential program

Customs-Trade Partnership against Terrorism program

Container Security Initiative

INTRODUCTION

This chapter examines border security and immigration. Border security has become a critical component of homeland security. We must secure our borders to ensure that terrorists do not enter the country and that weapons of mass destruction are not smuggled across our borders. In the past, our borders have been rather permeable with scores of illegal immigrants entering the United States annually with little effort. They have come from all points on the globe, and they arrive by land, sea, and air. The majority of these illegal immigrants seek employment, a better life, or escape from tyrannical conditions in their home country. They have not wished to do our country any harm; they simply wish to participate in the American dream. However, as a result of terrorism and the conditions in the Middle East and elsewhere, today there are numerous terrorists who would come to America to cause our citizens and infrastructure harm. They wish to repeat the attacks of 9/11. They possibly will use the same routes that are used by good-intentioned migrants.

For these reasons, we must vigilantly secure our borders. We actually cannot determine how many people are presently in the United States illegally. There are numerous estimates. The federal government estimated that in 2006, between 11 and 12 million illegal aliens were living in the United States. In 2004, the Center for Immigration Studies estimated the number to be 10 million, and the Federation for American Immigration Reform places the number at more than 13 million (FAIR, 2008). These estimates have a range of 3 million. The fact that we cannot accurately identify the number of illegal aliens currently living in our country vividly demonstrates that we have had little control over our borders. If we do not control who enters or leaves our country, we likely expose ourselves to terrorist attacks. This realization has resulted in a number of homeland security initiatives. Principally, we are concerned with border control, immigration, and the false documentation that is used to illegally gain entrance into our country.

Border Patrol agent pats down an illegal alien before returning him to Mexico. *Source:* http://www.cbp.gov/xp/cgov/newsroom/multimedia/photo_gallery/afc/bp/28.xml

IMMIGRATION

Border security and immigration over the past several years have become hot political issues. A number of cities and counties have experienced large increases in the number of legal and illegal immigrants settling in their communities. Many of these communities heretofore were fairly homogeneous with little ethnic diversity. This recent immigration has resulted in a substantial amount of xenophobia and anger toward immigrants. Congress has been considering a number of bills to restrict or otherwise control illegal immigration, particularly along our southern border with Mexico. In 2010, Arizona passed SB1070, which gave the police authority to investigate and detain suspected illegal aliens. Moreover, at least 16 states at the time were considering similar legislation (Markon and McCrummen, 2010). It has become a heated political topic. The anxiety and angst revolve around the two issues surrounding illegal immigration and border reform: (1) securing our borders from would be terrorists who may illegally enter the United States from a variety of other countries and (2) dealing with 11 million or so undocumented aliens who currently reside in the United States.

One side proposes that we secure our borders and expel the illegal aliens. They believe that we cannot develop and implement an effective immigration policy until we have achieved this level of security. Their opponents advise that many of these illegal aliens are productive, having jobs and paying taxes. They further advocate that several sectors of our economy, particularly agriculture and unskilled labor, require this illegal workforce—Americans cannot be recruited to perform many of these tasks. Although securing our borders is an important task, it is questionable if all the illegal aliens can be deported. Can we realistically identify and deport the 11 million illegal aliens who currently reside in the United States? Such a task would be insurmountable and cost prohibitive. Immigration policy is an issue that is separate from border control, and both policy issues should be approached simultaneously, but separately.

The dispute in Congress has stalled immigration reform, but Congress has funded border security on a piecemeal basis. The Department of Homeland Security is currently implementing additional security measures at various locations on our border. Implementation of security measures has been conducted on a cost-benefit basis. That is, those areas where the greatest amount of illegal entry occurs have been receiving enhanced security measures, although it is currently envisioned that we ultimately will obtain total border security. Security is provided with a combination of physical and electronic barriers. Even though today homeland security focuses on border control, it should be remembered that immigration policy is intertwined with border security, and immigration policy cannot be neglected if we are to achieve security.

ORIGINATING COUNTRIES OF AMERICAN IMMIGRANTS

When discussing immigration, most people refer to those illegal aliens coming from Mexico. Such discussions make it appear that Mexican immigration is our only border problem. However, even though a large number of Mexican nationals are illegally immigrating to the United States,

---

Analysis Box 12-1

Immigration is a thorny issue eliciting emotion from both sides. There are those who want to shut down our borders and remove all illegal aliens. On the other side, there are those who say we need them for a number of jobs that Americans will not do. It is a real conundrum. What should we do? Many advise that we should not tackle immigration before we secure our borders. Is this possible? How should we proceed?

large numbers of people are coming from other countries. Figure 12-1 shows the origin of legal permanent residents immigrating to the United States from 2007 to 2009.

Figure 12-1 shows only legal permanent residents; it does not show illegal immigrants since this information cannot be collected. However, it is constructive to examine the legal permanent residents since the percentages will reflect illegal immigration to some extent. Approximately 14.6 percent were from Mexico, and Central and South American countries

(Countries ranked by 2009 LPR flow)						
	2009		**2008**		**2007**	
Region/country of birth	Number	Percentage	Number	Percentage	Number	Percentage
Total	1,130,818	100.0	1,107,126	100.0	1,052,415	100.0
REGION:						
Africa	127,050	11.2	105,915	9.6	94,711	9.0
Asia	413,312	36.5	399,027	36.0	397,834	37.8
Europe	105,398	9.3	103,719	9.4	106,495	10.1
North America	375,236	33.2	393,253	35.5	339,355	32.2
Caribbean	146,127	12.9	137,098	12.4	119,123	11.3
Central America	47,868	4.2	50,840	4.6	55,926	5.3
Other North America	181,241	16.0	205,315	18.5	164,306	15.6
Oceania	5,578	0.5	5,263	0.5	6,101	0.6
South America	102,878	9.1	98,555	8.9	106,525	10.1
Unknown	1,366	0.1	1,394	0.1	1,394	0.1
COUNTRY:						
Mexico.	164,920	14.6	189,989	17.2	148,640	14.1
China	64,238	5.7	80,271	7.3	76,655	7.3
Philippines	60,029	5.3	54,030	4.9	72,596	6.9
India	57,304	5.1	63,352	5.7	65,353	6.2
Dominican Republic	49,414	4.4	31,879	2.9	28,024	2.7
Cuba	38,954	3.4	49,500	4.5	29,104	2.8
Vietnam	29,234	2.6	31,497	2.8	28,691	2.7
Colombia	27,849	2.5	30,213	2.7	33,187	3.2
South Korea	25,859	2.3	22,405	2.0	26,666	2.5
Haiti	24,280	2.1	26,007	2.3	30,405	2.9
Jamaica	21,783	1.9	18,477	1.7	19,375	1.8
Pakistan	21,555	1.9	19,719	1.8	13,492	1.3
El Salvador	19,909	1.8	19,659	1.8	21,127	2.0
Iran	18,553	1.6	13,852	1.3	10,460	1.0
Peru	16,957	1.5	15,184	1.4	17,699	1.7
Bangladesh	16,651	1.5	11,753	1.1	12,074	1.1
Canada	16,140	1.4	15,109	1.4	15,495	1.5
United Kingdom	15,748	1.4	14,348	1.3	14,545	1.4
Ethiopia	15,462	1.4	12,917	1.2	12,786	1.2
Nigeria	15,253	1.3	12,475	1.1	12,448	1.2
All other countries	410,726	36.3	374,490	33.8	363,593	34.5

FIGURE 12-1   Origin of Legal Permanent Residents Coming to the United States.   *Source:* Office of Immigration Statistics. (2010). *U.S. Legal Permanent Residents: 2009.* Washington, D.C.: Author.

contributed an additional 26.7 percent. It is also noteworthy that 36.5 percent came from Asian countries. Although immigrants from Mexico receive the greatest amount of publicity, they represent a small percentage of the total. Although illegal aliens from Mexico are problematic, numerous illegal immigrants from a variety of other countries pose similar problems.

HS Web Link: To learn more about globalization and immigration, go to *http://www.globalissues.org/article/537/immigration*

Additionally, the U.S. Census Bureau (2000) reports that more than 31 million, or approximately 10 percent of the U.S. population, are foreign born, with about 40 percent naturalized as citizens. These statistics demonstrate that America has a long history of immigration, with a substantial number of people coming to our country each year, and they are being integrated into our society. It will be difficult to curb this trend.

Indeed, we likely will experience increased immigration. Several factors will contribute to this trend. The National Intelligence Council (2008) examined a number of world problems, one of which was migration. Shortages in food, energy, and water will result in increased world migration. The council estimated that climate change and human demand would drastically affect food production and the availability of water, resulting in shortages in numerous countries. This problem may result in as many as 200 million **climate migrants** who are displaced. These climate migrants will be moving to a number of countries, including the United States. It is questionable if walls will be able to keep them out. The council did, however, note that world economic power of Western Europe and the United States is in decline, and countries such as Brazil, India, China, Iran, and Turkey will assume a more substantial economic footprint. This may result in increased migration to those countries.

Illegal immigration is not the only rationale for securing our borders. There remains a possibility that weapons of mass destruction (WMDs) or WMD material will be smuggled into our country. A substantial portion of the drugs coming into the United States enters through Mexico from South America. Drugs such as cocaine, heroin, methamphetamine, and marijuana come overland from Mexico. Thousands of pounds of drugs enter the United States each year from across our southern border. Obviously, if such large quantities of drugs can be smuggled across the border, it likely would not be difficult to smuggle WMD material into our country. The smuggling routes and mechanisms are already in place.

In addition to illegal immigration, there is a substantial amount of human trafficking in which women and children are sold as prostitutes or forced to work in sweatshops. They are smuggled into the United States as well as a number of other countries. They become virtual slaves to their handlers or owners with little hope of having a normal life. Their living conditions often are worse than those of their former countries. They are deprived of liberty and rights. This is morally repugnant, and maximum efforts should be exerted to curtail this crime problem, and increased border security is one method of accomplishing this objective. This problem was explored in more detail in Chapter 8.

Analysis Box 12-2

Although most of the illegal aliens flowing into our country are from Mexico, large numbers are coming from other countries. Many of these illegal aliens are dangerous—for example, gangs from Central America and Asia and organized crime from Russia and Europe. Yet we do not consider these groups when we discuss illegal immigration. Should we change the discussion to include these groups? Would this change the focus of the debate? How should we proceed in the future?

Finally, as a result of competing drug and crime cartels, Mexico has witnessed a substantial increase in the level of violence, violence that literally is out of control with several thousand homicides annually. Walsh (2009) reported there were 5,367 narco-homicides in 2008. Multiple homicide victims are discovered almost on a daily basis. Politicians, police and military officials, and reporters have been murdered almost indiscriminately. Kidnapping has become a common occurrence. In a number of cases, this violence has spilled over into the United States with Americans being killed on both sides of the border. Since Mexican drug operations are tied to drug traffickers in the United States, it is likely that this problem will worsen in the future. Enhanced border security might aid in keeping these problems from spilling over into the United States. Moreover, enhanced border security might reduce the amount of drugs coming into our country; tighter border security certainly would make it more difficult to smuggle drugs across the border. A reduction in the flow of drugs across the border might lead to a reduction of violence in Mexico, a collateral benefit.

BORDER SECURITY ISSUES

It is a considerable task for the United States to control its borders—they are rather extensive. The United States shares a border with Mexico that is approximately 2,000 miles in length, and our border with Canada is about 5,500 miles long. Additionally, Forest (2006) advises that the United States has 26,000 miles of navigable rivers and waterways and 12,383 miles of coastline. We also have hundreds of major airports that serve approximately 120 million passengers leaving and entering the United States each year and approximately 4,000 marine ports and terminals. Given the sheer magnitude of our borders, it is a considerable task to secure them. In fact, it is questionable if the United States has the personnel and resources to do so. Nonetheless, we have implemented a number of programs to accomplish this task, and we must implement programs that at a minimum provide a large measure of security.

As noted, there is considerable controversy over the number of illegal immigrants coming into the United States. The problem from a homeland security perspective is that there is evidence that potential terrorists are illegally entering the United States from Mexico and Canada. Generally, these people will travel to a third country such as Brazil and then travel to Mexico or Canada. Mexico is particularly problematic because of the number of illegal immigrants entering our country and the number of human smuggling rings that exist in Mexico and stretch well into South America. As noted in Figure 12-3 presented in a later section, more than 1.1 million illegal immigrants are apprehended each year on our southern border. Once in Mexico, aliens will contact a human smuggling operation to secure passage into the United States.

The border with Canada is also problematic. Although there are only about 7,300 apprehensions each year, the border is extremely long and often desolate and unprotected. Terrorists and illegal aliens entering from Canada often attempt to obtain documentation, often forged, and simply cross into the United States. Once in the United States, they often travel to some predetermined location and possibly link up with other potential terrorists or become integrated into immigrant communities. Another problem is that Canada historically has had less stringent immigration policies as compared to the United States. This may result in terrorists immigrating to Canada, obtaining documentation, and then traveling to the United States.

HS Web Link: To learn more about illegal immigration, go to *http://www.cis.org/illegal*

Border Protection agent watches for illegal aliens attempting to cross the border.
Source: https://help.cbp.gov/

Illegal Border Migration: A Case Study in Tucson

Substantial numbers of illegal aliens enter the United States from Mexico; more than 1.1 million were apprehended in 2006. Figure 12-2 shows the various routes used by illegal aliens to enter the Tucson, Arizona, area from Mexico. Notice that within this fairly limited geographical boundary, numerous entry points are used by hundreds of illegal aliens. The number of entry points in the Tucson area indicates that there are thousands of entry points between our ports of entry that must be sealed.

HS Web Link: To learn more about the Tucson area border patrol, go to *http://www.cbp.gov/xp/cgov/border_security/border_patrol/border_patrol_sectors/tucson_sector_az/stations/tucson.xml*

As can be seen using the Tucson example, the border is extremely porous. There are numerous entry points across the border with most of the entry points close to towns and cities. Entering the United States in a populated area like Tucson makes detection much more difficult since the illegal immigrants often blend in with the indigenous population. Moreover, a substantial number of legal crossings occur on a daily basis, and ferreting out the illegal migrants becomes a considerable task. Also, if preventive or detection efforts are enhanced at one point, it is not difficult for these migrants to quickly travel to another point to attempt entry. Displacement will remain a problem regardless of efforts.

Border Apprehensions

According to the Department of Homeland Security, in 2006, the U.S. Customs and Border Protection agency apprehended about 1.1 million illegal aliens at our southern border. As noted in Figure 12-3, the vast majority of apprehensions occurred on our southern border. There were relatively few apprehensions on our Canadian border; indeed, there were more apprehensions along our coasts. The statistics also show that the overwhelming majority of apprehensions were

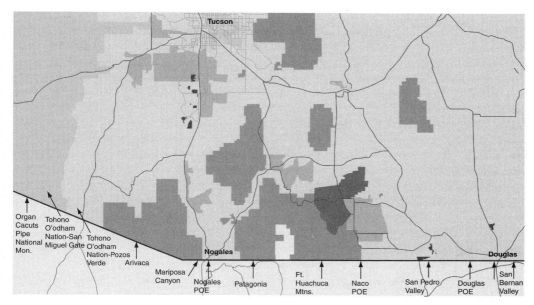

FIGURE 12-2 Tuscon, Arizona, Area Illegal Border Crossing Points. *Source:* Adapted from Ordonez, J. (2006). "Modeling the U.S. Border Patrol Tucson Section for the deployment and operations of border security forces." Masters Thesis, Naval Post-Graduate School, Monterey, CA.

of Mexicans, followed by people from other South and Central American countries. Most of the apprehensions were of adult males, although there was a number of juveniles and females apprehended. Many likely were traveling to the United States to seek employment.

Terrorist Infiltration via Illegal Immigration

There is a fear that terrorists are intermingling with immigrants to enter the United States. The number of illegal immigrants other than Mexican in origin has steadily increased over the past several years. In 2005, of the 1.2 million illegal immigrants apprehended by Customs and Border Protection, 165,000 came from countries other than Mexico. Of that number, 650 came from **countries of special interest.** There are 35 special interest countries, including Iran, Jordan, Lebanon, Syria, Egypt, Saudi Arabia, Kuwait, Pakistan, Cuba, Brazil, Ecuador, China, Russia, Yemen, Albania, Yugoslavia, and Afghanistan, that have been identified by our intelligence community as countries that could export individuals to the United States to commit acts of terrorism (Majority Staff of the Committee on Homeland Security, 2006).

The Committee on Homeland Security further reported that each year hundreds of illegal aliens from countries known to harbor terrorists or promote terrorism are routinely encountered or apprehended attempting to enter the United States via smuggling routes. For example, Mahmoud Youssef Kourani pleaded guilty to providing material support to Hezbollah. He had paid Mexican coyotes (human smugglers) to smuggle him into the United States. He then established residency in the Lebanese community in Dearborn, Michigan. The committee (2006) further found,

> Just recently, intelligence officials report that seven Iraqis were found in Brownsville, Texas in June 2006. In August 2006, an Afghani man was found swimming across the Rio Grande River in Hidalgo, Texas; as recently as October 2006, seven Chinese were apprehended in the Rio Grande Valley area of Texas. (p. 29)

Characteristic	Border							
	Total		Southern		Northern		Coastal	
	Number	Percent	Number	Percent	Number	Percent	Number	Percent
Gender								
Total	1,189,108	100.0	1,171,428	100.0	7,343	100.0	10,337	100.0
Male	969,955	81.6	955,037	81.5	6,319	86.1	8,599	83.2
Female	219,124	18.4	216,370	18.5	1,016	13.8	1,738	16.8
Unknown	29	-	21	-	8	0.1	-	-
Age								
Total	1,189,108	100.0	1,171,428	100.0	7,343	100.0	10,337	100.0
Adult (18 over)	1,074,462	90.4	1,057,665	90.3	6,992	95.2	9,805	94.9
Juvenile (17 and under)	114,569	9.6	113,701	9.7	347	4.7	521	5.0
Unknown	77	-	62	-	4	0.1	11	0.1
Country of nationality								
Total	1,189,108	100.0	1,171,428	100.0	7,343	100.0	10,337	100.0
Mexico	1,023,930	86.1	1,016,434	86.8	4,080	55.6	3,416	33.0
Honduras	52,760	4.4	51,889	4.4	202	2.8	669	6.5
EL Salvador	39,308	3.3	39,004	3.3	100	1.4	204	2.0
Brazil	31,072	2.6	30,843	2.6	134	1.8	95	0.9
Guatemala	22,593	1.9	21,807	1.9	233	3.2	553	5.3
Nicaragua	3,922	0.3	3,826	0.3	13	0.2	83	0.8
Cuba	3,262	0.3	129	-	20	0.3	3,113	30.1
China	2,200	0.2	1,987	0.2	179	2.4	34	0.3
Canada	1,020	0.1	33	-	983	13.4	4	-
Other	9,041	0.8	5,476	0.5	1,399	19.1	2,166	21.0

FIGURE 12-3 Points of Entry and Demographics for Illegal Aliens Apprehended at the U.S. Borders. *Source:* Wu, A. (2006). "Border apprehensions: 2006." *Fact Sheet* (November). Washington, D.C.: Department of Homeland Security.

The director of the FBI has confirmed that there are individuals from countries with an al Qaeda presence who are changing their surnames to Hispanic-sounding names and obtaining false Hispanic identities. They are learning Spanish and attempting to immigrate to the United States as Hispanics (Mueller, 2005).

Many of these questionable individuals who are slipping across the border are being assisted by human smuggling organizations in Mexico. Salim Boughader Mucharrafille, a businessman in Tijuana, Mexico, was convicted of illegally smuggling more than 200 Lebanese into the United States, some of whom had ties to Hezbollah (Associated Press, 2005). In 2004, Immigration Customs Enforcement apprehended Neeran Zaia, who smuggled Iraqi, Jordanian, and Syrian nationals. The aliens would be smuggled from the Middle East to staging areas in Central and South America. From there they would be smuggled into the United States (Schoch, 2006).

A critical problem has been Venezuela. According to the Majority Staff of the Committee on Homeland Security (2006), Venezuela is providing support to radical Islamic groups.

The government has provided thousands of cedulas (equivalent to our Social Security cards) to people from places such as Cuba, Colombia, and Middle Eastern countries that host terrorist organizations. These documents allow them to obtain Venezuelan passports and in some cases visas to the United States. Many terrorist organizations are currently operating in Paraguay; their members can travel to Venezuela, obtain documentation, and then attempt to enter the United States.

There is no estimate of the number of terrorists or persons from terrorist-friendly countries who are entering the United States. However, terrorists generally have access to large amounts of cash, allowing them to hire the best or most efficient smuggling services in Mexico and South and Central America. Consequently, a greater percentage likely succeeds in entering the United States as compared to others who attempt to improperly enter the United States.

BORDER PROTECTION PHILOSOPHY AFTER 9/11

According to Riley (2006), the 9/11 attacks and the magnitude of our extensive borders have resulted in a new philosophy regarding border protection. This new philosophy has two components. First, we have pushed the borders out and away from our shores. Our border security was insufficient so we implemented border or security measures in countries where people and material originated before entering the United States. For example, if we check the identities of U.S.-bound passengers in these originating countries, we likely can intercept terrorists, undesirable or suspicious persons, and illegal aliens before entry. The same philosophy applies to goods and material being shipped to the United States. Inspecting them at their origination point would reduce contraband, drugs, and possibly WMDs from entering our country. These measures are intended to remove threats before they reach our shores. They also reduce the bottleneck of goods and people awaiting inspection at our borders. They are discussed in more detail in this section.

Second, we began profiling people and goods at their originating point. Profiling was seen as a method of reducing the workload and the distractions from inspecting large numbers of people and material at ports of entry. We have identified safe originating points and those points that are suspect or lack required levels of security. For example, some countries, such as England, have more effective intelligence and security. People traveling from more secure countries require less scrutiny as compared to travelers from other countries. Some countries control cargo shipments more effectively, resulting in a measure of ensured safety for the cargo when it reaches the United States. American officials can become more efficient by concentrating more efforts on insecure areas. This does not mean that safe points are neglected since security programs have been implemented in those areas. Profiling also allows us to identify those people and material that should receive more consideration.

The new philosophy outlined by Riley focuses on prevention. **Prevention** is the most important part of any strategy to subjugate aggression or terrorism. A critical part of military strategy is to deploy resources to prevent an enemy from attacking—defense and protecting critical assets are of paramount importance. Our national drug control strategy deploys personnel in foreign countries to interdict drugs and prevent them from coming into the United States. The U.S. Department of State works with countries to prevent terrorist groups from succeeding in those countries. Thus, prevention should be an important and integral part of our border protection strategy. The USA PATRIOT Act gives law enforcement more investigative powers to intercede in terrorists operations to prevent such acts. Even though prevention is routinely recognized as an important strategy, prevention in border security strategies historically has not been predominant.

In 2001, new policies were implemented that attempted to change immigration policies. A part of these policies was to deny entry, detain, prosecute, and deport aliens associated with or suspected of engaging in terrorist activities. Foreign students were barred from taking courses that contained sensitive material. Databases were used to locate and apprehend suspected terrorists or supporters of terrorism inside the United States. The **North American Complementary Immigration Policies** called for the United States to work with Mexico and Canada to develop compatible screening protocols at our borders. These protocols facilitate the identification of persons who would do harm to the United States as they entered from Mexico or Canada. This goal was not accomplished, as the Department of Homeland Security focused on border hardening (Smart Border Initiative), which did little to assist in monitoring persons coming across our borders.

HS Web Link: To learn more about immigration policies and terrorism, go to *http://www.fas.org/irp/ offdocs/nspd/hspd-2.htm*

Patrolling Border Patrol agent scans for illegal aliens.   *Source:* http://www.cbp.gov/xp/cgov/newsroom/ multimedia/photo_gallery/afc/bp/37.xml.

Part of the problem was defining prevention. Prevention became operationalized as interdiction or physically preventing people, especially terrorists, from entering our country. Prevention also includes interdiction and deterrence. **Interdiction** is an attempt to stop a plot once it has begun. **Deterrence,** on the other hand, occurs when potential terrorists believe that defenses are insurmountable and therefore do not attempt intrusion. Deterrence cannot be easily measured, as discussed in Chapter 3; consequently, agencies become less interested in it. Although elements of prevention, interdiction, and deterrence are contained in our current policies, they are piecemeal and no comprehensive system currently is in place.

Secure Border Initiative

During the 1990s, the U.S. Border Patrol changed tactics. The agency began to emphasize deterrence over apprehension. Several programs were implemented, including Operation Hold the Line, Gatekeeper, and Safeguard. These programs placed personnel and equipment as close to the border as possible, and their primary objectives were to deter or prevent illegal crossings and to break up smuggling rings as opposed to apprehending illegal aliens after they crossed the border, which previously had been the policy. The deterrence strategy resulted in a reduction in illegal border crossings as measured by apprehensions. Moreover, the programming resulted in higher levels of public support on the part of American border residents.

The shift in strategy brought criticism from conservatives who believed the programs were too weak; they resulted in fewer apprehensions, and they mistakenly viewed apprehensions as the best measure of security. Liberals criticized the programs because they were too intrusive into community affairs. Others believed that the programs went beyond the Border Patrol's mandate—the Border Patrol should not be involved in immigration issues. As a result of the criticisms and politics, programming became less vigorous. Our policies again began to emphasize apprehension as opposed to prevention and deterrence. Disbanded smuggling operations again became operational, and there was an increase in the number of illegal aliens crossing the border (Bach, 2005).

The 9/11 attacks on the World Trade Center and the Pentagon resulted in a renewed interest in border security. However, the agency again concentrated on interdiction, not deterrence or prevention. That is, organizational effectiveness was measured by the number of apprehensions. The agency also concentrated on locating illegal immigrants and removing them once they were prosecuted. It is without question that interdiction leads to substantial public attention and media recognition, but it is not as efficient as prevention. Also, the costs associated with identifying, tracking, prosecuting, and deporting illegal aliens are quite substantial, costs that are not associated with an effective prevention program. A comprehensive prevention program including cooperation with the Mexican and Canadian governments is by far the most promising strategy. Unfortunately, such a strategy has not come to full fruition.

Border security became an explosive political issue as thousands of illegal migrants streamed across our southern border. As an example, in 2005, Governor Bill Richardson of New Mexico and Governor Janet Napolitano of Arizona declared a state of emergency as a result of the number of illegal aliens crossing their borders. Arizona, in 2010, passed a strict immigration law designed to control illegal aliens. Duncan Hunter, chair of the House Armed Services Committee, proposed building two parallel walls stretching from the Pacific Ocean to the Gulf of Mexico, although Michael Chertoff, then secretary of the Department of Homeland Security, advised that such a fence would be cost prohibitive (Global Security, undated-a). Some have referred to this idea as the "great wall of Mexico" (Global Security, undated-b). The cost and debate resulted in a compromise whereby physical barriers and Customs and Border Protection agents were

increased, and other forms of border monitoring were deployed. The primary program implemented by the Department of Homeland Security to secure our borders has been the **Secure
Border Initiative** (SBI), which is a multiyear project that attempts to secure our
northern and southern borders. The SBI is intended to be comprehensive, addressing
a number of deficiencies that have led to increased illegal immigration. According to
the DHS, the primary components of the SBI include the following:

HS Web Link: To learn more
about the SBI, go to *http://
www.dhs.gov/xnews/releases/
press_release_0794.shtm*

• More agents to patrol our borders, secure our ports of entry, and enforce immigration laws;
• Expanded detention and removal capabilities to eliminate "catch and release" once and for all;
• A comprehensive and systemic upgrading of the technology used in controlling the border,
  including increased manned aerial assets, expanded use of UAVs, and next-generation
  detection technology;
• Increased investment in infrastructure improvements at the border—providing additional
  physical security to sharply reduce illegal border crossings; and
• Greatly increased interior enforcement of our immigration laws—including more robust
  worksite enforcement. (DHS, 2005)

Increase in Customs and Border Protection Agents

Prior to the 9/11 attacks, the Border Patrol was woefully understaffed given that the agency was
responsible for securing about 7,500 miles of border. In 2005, the Customs and Border
Protection agency received funding to increase the number of agents to about 3,000.
Additionally, the Immigration and Customs Enforcement (ICE) agency received funding to

Illegal immigrants are placed in holding facilities before they are returned to Mexico.
Source: Photo by Gerald L. Nino. http://www.cbp.gov/xp/cgov/newsroom/multimedia/
photo_gallery/afc/bp/35.xml

increase the number of investigators by approximately 250 agents. The funding increase also resulted in the hiring of 400 new Immigration Enforcement agents and 400 detention officers. These agents and officers are involved in investigating illegal immigrants within the United States. The ICE fugitive teams collect apprehended illegal aliens for deportation. Even with these increases, it remains questionable if there are ample agents to adequately secure our borders given the vastness of the problem.

Expanded Detention and Removal Capabilities

In the past, ICE has not had the personnel or facilities to hold and process all the illegal aliens who were apprehended. To some extent, as a result of these shortages, the bureau had a policy of catch and release. This resulted in few apprehended illegal aliens returning to their home countries. Funding was provided to increase the bed space in detention facilities by 2,000 to a total of approximately 20,000 beds or spaces. The Department of Homeland Security has been working with other federal, state, and local agencies to develop innovative strategies to increase holding or bed space, for example, holding detainees in local jails. The increased capacity prevents detainees from being released before deportation. Basically, when detainees are released before deportation, many blend into society, fail to appear at their deportation hearings, and remain illegally in the United States.

HS Web Link: To learn more about the detention of illegal aliens go to *http://trac.syr. edu/immigration/library/ P737.pdf*

Another impediment to controlling illegal immigration has been the length of time it has taken to deport or remove illegal aliens. Deportation has taken months and even years in some cases. Extended detentions result in occupied bed spaces at holding facilities, reducing the number of detainees that can be held. The SBI gave the Department of Homeland Security legislative authority to expedite the deportation of some classes of illegal aliens. For example, anyone apprehended within the previous two years is subject to expedited removal. The Department of Homeland Security has implemented this policy at all ports of entry and between ports of entry only along the southwest border for aliens apprehended within 100 miles of the border. The program was applied to the southwest border because this area has the highest levels of illegal immigration. Expedited deportation has resulted in less strain on the system.

Improved Technology

Given that the United States has about 7,500 miles of border, it is impossible to protect them solely with personnel. The Department of Homeland Security has implemented two strategies to improve border security: increased number and effectiveness of infrastructure

---

Analysis Box 12-4

There are legal processes that must be followed when deporting illegal aliens. Our country has bestowed certain rights on them. Consequently, some deportation proceedings take a considerable amount of time, requiring that the illegal aliens be detained. There are those who believe they should not be given these due process rights but should be deported immediately without lengthy hearings. On the other side, civil rights advocates maintain that American should recognize the rights of everyone in our country. Should we expedite the removal of illegal aliens? Should we disregard their rights?

barriers, discussed later, and electronic surveillance commonly referred to as SBInet. **SBInet** entails the deployment of radar, unpiloted aircraft systems, ground surveillance radar, unattended sensors (magnetic, acoustic, and motion), and camera towers to track the movement of people and vehicles at the borders. SBInet represents a virtual wall to be used in less populated areas.

The first phase of SBInet was dubbed **Project 28** and encompasses a 28-mile stretch of the Arizona border. Once implemented, other areas will be protected by SBInet technology. Project 28 has resulted in the construction of a virtual fence. Essentially, when people and vehicles attempt to cross the border, cameras and other sensors will detect the intrusions. Communication towers broadcast real-time electronic images and information to a communications center. Once an intrusion is detected, the cameras are manually controlled, which allows the operator to change angles and zoom in on the intruders, collecting pertinent information for federal agents. The information including images is transmitted to patrolling agents via laptop computer (Richey, 2007). The system is designed to allow border agents to intercept all the people attempting to illegally cross the border.

High-tech equipment used to see and hear approaching illegal aliens.   *Source:* http://www.cbp.gov/xp/cgov/newsroom/multimedia/photo_gallery/afc/bp/13.xml

Project 28 and SBInet have encountered a number of problems. First, Richey notes a number of technical difficulties. Project 28 represents a comprehensive, technically complicated system. Boeing, the primary contractor on the project, has experienced technical difficulties, especially with system integration. The second impediment is Project 28's costs—it is projected that SBInet will cost a total of $8 billion through 2013 with maintenance after 2013 costing more. Moreover, there is no guarantee that there will not be significant cost overages or that the system can be functional as initially designed (Strohm, 2007). Although SBInet and Project 28 are ambitious attempts to secure the border, at this point it is highly questionable if they will come to fruition.

Increased Infrastructure Protection (Fencing)

Customs and Border Protection has been constructing and maintaining barriers along the Mexican border since 1991. These barriers, for the most part, have been limited to urban areas. Two types of fencing have been used. One is primary fencing that is located directly on the border in a number of urban areas. In many cases, the primary fencing has been constructed from steel landing mats—army surplus landing strips from the Vietnam War. The other is Sandia fencing or secondary or triple fencing that has been constructed in the San Diego area. The presence of two or three layers of fencing is more daunting to those who would attempt to cross the border. In addition to the fencing, vehicle barriers have been constructed in some areas (see Nunez-Neto and Vina, 2006). As of December 2008, Customs and Border Protection planned to have a total of approximately 370 miles of pedestrian fence and 300 miles of vehicle fence completed, under construction, or under contract along the southwest border (CBP, 2008).

The U.S.-Mexican border; the United States is on the left side of the photo.   *Source:* http://206.241.31.129/ImageCache/cgov/content/newsroom/photogallery/border_5fpatrol/07_2ectt/v3/image/1/bp007_5f270.jpg

There has been considerable criticism of building walls and fences. If you build a 20-foot fence, illegal aliens attempting to enter the United States will build a 21-foot ladder. In addition to climbing these fences, illegal aliens can dig tunnels under them. It is highly questionable if a fence, especially one several miles or several hundred miles long, can be constructed in such a fashion that it cannot be breached. Moreover, the costs of such a fence have been estimated to be between $300,000 and $500,000 per mile (Nunez-Neto and Vina, 2006). Currently, it appears that they are somewhat effective in fairly short spans in urban areas where they are supplemented with patrol personnel.

The application of technology and physical barriers attempt to seal our borders. Past programs have used physical barriers and increased border patrols in high-traffic areas. Operation Gatekeeper was implemented in San Diego, Operation Hold-the-Line along the border in El Paso, and Operation Safeguard in Arizona. The number of illegal aliens crossing the border in these areas was substantially reduced as a result of these concentrated resources. However, there is some evidence that the numbers were "cooked" by Border Patrol officials. In 1996, members of the Border Patrol union in the San Diego area filed a lawsuit alleging that officials had ordered agents to not make arrests so as to give the impression that the programs had reduced the number of illegal migrants (Global Security, undated-b). Keeping illegal aliens out of our country still remains a conundrum.

Enhanced Enforcement of Immigration Laws: Interior Enforcement as Deterrence

Another area of border security is deterrence through enforcement. The USA PATRIOT Act allows the use of immigration laws by various authorities when investigating terror suspects. Consequently, the majority of terrorist investigations have not led to convictions on terrorism charges, but for immigration violations. Oftentimes, it is easier for authorities to make an immigration case than a terrorism case. Terrorism investigations have morphed into immigration enforcement. For example, in 2005, Wagdy Mohamed Ghoneim voluntarily left the United States for an undisclosed Middle Eastern country. Ghoneim was an influential Islamic cleric in Orange County, California, who was suspected of giving speeches and raising money for groups with terrorist connections. He was not charged with any crime associated with terrorism, such as providing material support for terrorist groups. Rather, Immigration and Customs Enforcement officials charged him with immigration violations. Ghoneim left the country rather than fight the immigration charges (Reyes, 2005). Such actions have resulted in immigrant communities in the United States becoming less cooperative with federal authorities when investigating terror suspects and activities. They also fear deportation as federal agencies cast a wider net in terror-related investigations.

Traditional immigration enforcement has hinged on three principles: (1) workplace enforcement whereby illegal immigrants are removed and deported, (2) lengthy detention to convince immigrants to not enter the United States illegally, and (3) mass removal of illegal aliens to eliminate incentives for them to find work. This strategy has not worked. Too often when illegal aliens are removed from the workplace, there are others to replace them. Detention and removal have become cumbersome and expensive processes, making them ineffective. Moreover, many of those deported often return within a short time. Some illegal aliens have been removed multiple times. A California study showed that more than half of illegal immigrants arrested and incarcerated for felonies often returned to the same city and committed new felonies. It is obvious that traditional tactics have been unreliable.

More effective prevention strategies include focusing on smuggling or human trafficking operations and programs that thwart illegal aliens from gaining employment. Smuggling operations account for large numbers of illegal aliens entering the United States. Interdicting these operations can have an exponential impact on the number of illegal immigrants entering the country. We also must develop effective systems that allow employers to determine if potential employees are here legally. However, critics argue that strategies should focus on apprehension and deportation—a strategy that provides media publicity but is ineffective in terms of reducing the overall numbers of illegal immigrants in the country. Deterring illegal immigration became less important than apprehension and "bean counting."

ICE has stepped up its enforcement of illegal immigration. The agency has focused on two primary areas. First, ICE has concentrated on identifying and removing illegal aliens from the United States. Second, the agency has focused on illegal alien employment. Officers have performed a number of investigations that have resulted in the detention of illegal aliens working without documentation and citations issued to employers who have employed them.

With 11 million or so illegal immigrants in the United States, it is impossible to remove all of them. Therefore, ICE (2008a) has established priorities for removal:

- Identify and process all criminal aliens amenable for removal while in federal, state, and local custody.
- Enhance current detention strategies to ensure no removable alien is released into the community due to a lack of detention space or an appropriate alternative to detention.
- Implement removal initiatives that shorten the time aliens remain in ICE custody prior to removal, thereby maximizing the use of detention resources and reducing cost.

As a result of these priorities, ICE has been concentrating on the removal of illegal migrants who have been arrested or have committed crimes. In most cases, ICE will require those convicted of crimes to serve their sentences before initiating removal proceedings. In 2008, ICE identified and charged more than 221,000 aliens in jails for immigration violations—more than triple the number charged in 2006. Currently, the United States does not have a nationwide jail/prison reporting system that identifies the number of criminal aliens in the United States. ICE uses various data sources and estimated the number to be about 300,000 to 450,000 criminal aliens who are potentially removable and are detained each year at federal, state, and local prisons and jails (ICE, 2008a). When removing incarcerated illegal aliens, ICE first gives the highest priority to those individuals who have been arrested or convicted of serious crimes.

The accelerated deportation of some of these criminal illegal aliens has resulted in a cost savings for several states. Early deportation results in fewer days in jail. It costs a jail or prison about $95 per day to house an inmate. At one point, the state of Arizona had turned over 1,300 inmates for deportation. The state claimed that this policy had saved approximately $17 million. New York State had turned over about 2,000 inmates who were deported for a savings of $141 million (Bazer, 2008).

As noted, ICE has stepped up enforcement of the prohibition from hiring undocumented aliens. ICE has visited and reviewed employment records at a number of businesses and employers. This is being accomplished primarily by its **Worksite Enforcement Unit.** This unit focuses on

Egregious employers involved in criminal activity or worker exploitation. This type of employer violation will often involve alien smuggling, document fraud, human rights

A Border Patrol agent uses a computer word translator to assist in determining the needs of this illegal immigrant. *Source:* http://206.241.31.146/ImageCache/cgov/content/newsroom/photogallery/ border_5fpatrol/32_2ectt/v1/image/1/bp032_5f270.jpg

abuses and/or other criminal or substantive administrative immigration or customs violations having a direct nexus to the employment of unauthorized workers. Worksite investigations also encompass employers who are subjecting unauthorized alien workers to substandard or abusive working conditions. Also included in these types of investigations are employers who utilize force, threat, or coercion, such as threats to have employees deported in order to keep the unauthorized alien workers from reporting the substandard wage or working conditions. (ICE, 2008b)

ICE has operationalized this philosophy by conducting raids on various employers. Here, ICE officers conduct checks of employees to determine if they are legally authorized to work in the United States. For the most part, these raids have focused on employers who hire unskilled and semiskilled employees, for example, the agriculture, food services, manufacturing, and meat-processing industries. There are numerous examples. In May 2008, ICE officers raided an electrical equipment plant in Laurel, Mississippi, and arrested 350, and in the same month, a raid at a kosher meatpacking plant in Iowa netted 400 (*USA Today*, 2008). Generally, those arrested do not have documentation or have forged or false documentation. The problem is pervasive as exemplified by an incident in 2008. A firm that was contracted to clean then Homeland Security Secretary Michael Chertoff's home was found to be using illegal aliens. After the discovery, the firm was fined $22,880 (Hsu, 2008). The raids have received a substantial amount of criticism. Such raids often

HS Web Link: To learn more about ICE's Worksite Enforcement program, go to *http://www.niu.edu/law/ faculty/columns/ SchmallLorraine_8_20_08.pdf*

Analysis Box 12-5

The previous sections discussed the various means that we are using to secure our southern border, including personnel, electronic surveillance, and fencing methods. Additionally, we are increasing the enforcement of immigration laws in the workforce. There are prob- lems associated with each of these methods. How should we secure the southern border? Which methods do you believe have the greatest potential to be effective? Can we really secure our border?

---

separate families. For example, a mother and father may be detained and no arrangements are made for any children in the family. In some cases, family members become destitute since the wage earner is incarcerated. It is also problematic when children are U.S. citizens and their parents are illegal aliens.

The United States Citizenship and Immigration Service (USCIS) is responsible for providing visas to aliens who desire to work in the United States. Basically, those individuals possessing student visas, guest worker visas, and permanent resident or green cards are allowed to be employed on a limited basis. Also, employers can initiate proceedings to employ a foreign national by completing paper work with the USCIS. Additionally, USCIS has developed a computerized system to check the employment status of foreign nationals. The system *E-Verify* requires that employers and foreign employees be registered with USCIS. Currently, approximately 65,000 employers participate in the program. Since 2006, 12 states have begun requiring employers to use the system when hiring. A major problem confronting E-Verify is its accuracy rate, which is approximately 94 percent (Marks, 2008). A number of employers and verified employees have complained about the problem—it has resulted in employers not being able to hire verified employees on a timely basis. For example, between January and July 2008, Intel, one the nation's largest employers, had 12 percent of its 1,360 new hires rejected by the system. Intel appealed 143 of the rejections and all were found to be legal U.S. residents (Frank, 2009).

FORMULATING A COHERENT POLICY FOR BORDER SECURITY

The Secure Border Initiative has several elements that have been implemented. However, it appears that each initiative is being implemented independently of the others. Wermuth and Riley (2007) advise that this uncoordinated, patchwork effort has lead to a number of problems. Moreover, it is rather expensive and very likely not cost effective. In some cases, when technology is involved, we do not know if it will operate at our expected levels of effectiveness. Wermuth and Riley point out that a number of improvements must be made. First, we must remember that we are managing border risk, not eliminating it. It is virtually impossible to totally seal our borders, and decisions must be made relative to the level of effectiveness that we need and the expense that we are willing to endure.

Second, we need to develop evaluative matrices. That is, we must measure the level of program effectiveness. For example, what impact have the current arrangements had on illegal migration? Are they working? We may be funding and implementing programs that in the end do not achieve our goals. To this end, what are our goals? Politicians discuss border security in terms of totally sealing them from illegal aliens, but this is impossible. What levels of security do we what to achieve in the end? Do current and planned programs achieve this level of security?

We must be able to answer these questions; therefore, we must develop meaningful outcome or evaluative measures.

Third, Wermuth and Riley advise that we need a comprehensive and well-thought-out roadmap. This essentially means that we must examine current and planned efforts and ensure that they are integrated into a cohesive border security effort. This means that we must install security measures at insecure points that effectively deal with the problems at that point. It also means that all the security measures must be integrated into a working system, and any inadequacies in the system must be understood and considered. This applies not only to physical and electronic barriers, but also to human security measures. When there are limitations on physical and electronic security systems, it might be necessary to use Customs and Border Protection and Customs Enforcement personnel to fill the gaps. Regardless, we must understand how all these programs or pieces fit into a logical and working secure border system.

US-VISIT

A major problem with immigration and foreigners visiting the United States is ensuring their correct identification. As discussed earlier, there are ample examples of possible terrorists obtaining false documents to enter our country. Statistics indicate that identity fraud is a prevalent problem, especially at our borders. The U.S. General Accounting Office, in a report to several committees of the House of Representatives, detailed the problem (Stana, 2002). Figure12-4 shows the number of falsified documents presented by illegal aliens that were intercepted by immigration officials at our borders between 1998 and 2001.

The data contained in Figure 12-4 show that border officials intercept more than 100,000 people with fraudulent documents each year. The total number of people with such documentation is not known, since it must be assumed that officials are not able to intercept everyone carrying a fraudulent entry document. The data do demonstrate that there is a significant problem and measures need to be taken to ensure the integrity of documents as people leave and enter the United States.

Type of document	Fiscal year 1998	Fiscal year 1999	Fiscal year 2000	Fiscal year 2001
Border crossing cards	30,631	30,797	38,650	30,419
Alien registration cards	28,137	33,308	34,120	26,259
Nonimmigrant visas	13,551	18,003	17,417	21,127
U.S. passports and citizenship documents	14,546	22,142	17,703	18,925
Foreign passports and citizenship documents	11,245	14,695	15,047	15,994
Reentry permits and refugee travel documents	271	1,107	153	702
Immigrant visas	790	663	447	597
Total	**99,171**	**120,715**	**123,537**	**114,023**

FIGURE 12-4 Number and Type of Fraudulent Documents Intercepted by INS Inspectors. *Source:* Stana, R. (2002). *Identity Fraud: Prevalence and Links to Alien Illegal Activities.* Washington, D.C.: Government Accounting Office.

The 9/11 Commission recommended that we need better controls over identification procedures to make it more difficult for terrorists and others to enter the United States. One program addressing this problem is the **US-VISIT** program. The United States has deployed the US-VISIT program to collect biometric data (fingerprints from two fingers) on persons entering and leaving the United States. The program can help identify those individuals who overstay their visas. It can identify persons who are using someone else's identification. Such a program serves first to verify one's identity. Second, it is used for identity discovery: to learn the identity of people who are using posing as someone else (Morgan and Krouse, 2005). The use of biometric data can serve to deter possible terrorists from attempting entry into the United States.

Travelers to the United States come from visa and non-visa countries. **Non-visa or Visa Waiver Program** countries are those in which travelers are not required to obtain a visa. They must possess a passport that contains machine-readable biometric data, which can be accessed at ports of entry to assure identity. In visa countries, travelers are required to visit an American consulate or other visa-issuing point to obtain a visa. Applicants are photographed and their fingerprints are scanned as part of the visa-issuing process. At that point, the information is checked against a watch list of known criminals and suspected terrorists. Visas are denied to individuals who are on this watch list or who have suspect documentation. Upon arrival to the United States, their fingerprints are again scanned to assure proper identification; this reduces the probability that terrorists or other undesirables will obtain another person's visa. Non-visa travelers are scanned when they enter the United States, and their biometric data are examined. DHS noted that US-VISIT is now operational for entry at 115 airports, 15 seaports, and 154 land border ports of entry (Bain, 2008). Ortiz and his colleagues (2006) advise that the system should be expanded to not only include ports of entry, but also border crossings along the Mexican and Canadian borders.

HS Web Link: To learn more about the US-Visit program, go to *http://www. ice.gov/pi/news/factsheets/ visit051903.htm*

Support for the program has diminished because it has not produced the expected results and its expense. Proponents of the program overstated its potential. Since the number of potential terrorists is comparatively small, it seems that the system likely will produce modest results. However, the system does have substantial potential to monitor the comings and goings of people entering the United States. It also allows consular offices abroad to better screen applicants. There has been a drop in the number of people applying for visas to enter the United States, and US-VISIT may be the stimulus for this drop. Persons using fraudulent documents may be dissuaded from attempting entry. In other words, US-VISIT seems to have a preventive effect.

Ortiz and his colleagues (2006) note that there are numerous technical difficulties with the system. A major difficulty is that the biometric database created by the US-VISIT process is not compatible with the FBI's Integrated Automated Fingerprint Identification System. A major problem is that the two systems do not communicate with each other. Another problem is that prints from only two fingers are collected with the US-VISIT program, whereas the FBI system has a full set of prints; it is proposed that in the future a full set of prints will be scanned (Morgan and Krouse, 2005). The integration of the two systems may result in the identification of larger numbers of undesirables attempting to enter the country. Nonetheless, Ortiz and his colleagues (2006) note that the system is in its infancy. As the system matures with future development, it should become more accurate and effective in identifying those who are traveling in and out of the United States. This system also has a measure of deterrence—undesirables and potential terrorists maybe dissuaded from attempting to travel to the United States.

Border Protection agent checks vehicles coming into the United States.   *Source:* https://help.cbp.gov

VEHICULAR SCREENING AT BORDER CROSSINGS

The previous sections examined securing our borders with a focus on people. However, as a result of the North American Free Trade Agreement (NAFTA), trade barriers between the United States, Mexico, and Canada were virtually dissolved, resulting in a tremendous amount of cargo entering the United States at our borders. Canada and Mexico are our two largest trading partners. According to Ackleson (2005), 11.6 million trucks and 16 million cargo containers cross our land borders each year. Additionally, millions of passenger vehicles cross the border each year. This traffic results in a substantial workload for Customs and Border Protection personnel when attempting to screen vehicles. Delays at borders can substantially affect commerce and the costs of goods coming into or leaving the United States.

The Customs and Border Protection agency has implemented several programs designed to expedite the flow of vehicular traffic. First, the **Secure Electronic Network for Travelers Rapid Inspection** (SENTRI) has been implemented on our border with Mexico. SENTRI users are allowed to use special traffic lanes and generally bypass the inspection process. Participants must enroll in the program and pass a criminal background check. SENTRI participants are low risk and generally cross the border repeatedly. The program allows Customs and

Border Protection personnel to concentrate their inspection efforts on vehicles that are not verified. The **NEXUS program** is similar to SENTRI, but it has been implemented along the Canadian border. These programs are evolving as technology enhancements become available. For example, in some instances automatic vehicle identifiers are being used. The identifier information is electronically scanned, and the resultant information is checked with a database. This same technology is being applied to trucks carrying cargo, which has substantially reduced the delay in crossings for these vehicles. At some point, there likely will be widespread use of facial recognition programs to check people as they cross the borders.

HS Web Link: To learn more about the SENTRI program, go to *http://www. cbp.gov/xp/cgov/travel/ trusted_traveler/sentri/ sentri.xml*

PORT AND MARINE SECURITY

Our 77 ports are vast complexes with extremely large numbers of personnel and machinery primarily engaged in the loading and unloading of materials from cargo ships. Two billion tons of freight move in and out of our ports annually, representing 99 percent of our international trade (Bentzel, 2006; Bullock et al., 2005). In 2000, the Interagency Commission on Crime and Security in U.S. Ports reported substantial levels of crime, trade fraud, alien smuggling, importation of drugs and other contraband, environmental crimes, and cargo theft occurring at our ports. The commission also concluded that vulnerability to terrorist attacks was high, and there were no standard security procedures in place. This report and the 9/11 attacks resulted in the passage of the **Maritime Transportation Act of 2002.**

A number of maritime security measures have been enacted as a result of the act. First, the Coast Guard has begun conducting assessments of our ports for security problems and potential vulnerabilities. Second, the **Transportation Workers Identification Credential program** has been enacted. The program mandates that all persons in a port area must have an identification card that is only issued upon a background investigation. This program is similar to the one used for employees at our nation's airports. Third, a centralized maritime intelligence center was mandated by the act, but thus far, it has not been operationalized. Currently, the Coast Guard, Navy, TSA, and Customs and Border Protection all operate separate intelligence functions. In the future, these operations will be merged into one entity. Fourth, the act mandated that all ships passing through U.S. waters must carry transponders so that high-interest and suspect vessels can be tracked. Finally, the act mandated high levels of security for cargo coming into the United States. This is carried out by the Transportation Security Administration and Customs and Border Protection, both within the Department of Homeland Security. Containers coming into the United States are subject to X-ray or gamma imaging to identify WMDs or WMD material. Two programs have been implemented to enhance cargo security prior to its arrival in the United States: Customs-Trade Partnership Against Terrorism (C-TPAT) program and the Container Security Initiative (CSI).

C-TPAT and CSI

The **Customs-Trade Partnership Against Terrorism program** (C-TPAT) is a program that attempts to guarantee the security of cargo at the originating country. Foreign companies verify their supply chain for security and are allowed to ship material with minimum inspections or

One of many container ships coming to the United States each day.   *Source:* http://help.cbp.gov

HS Web Link: To learn more about the Customs-Trade Partnership Against Terrorism program, go to *http://www.cbp.gov/xp/cgov/ trade/cargo_security/ctpat/ what_ctpat/ctpat_overview. xml*

fast tracking. Shippers, importers, brokers, manufacturers, and warehouses adhere to security protocols as established by the Customs and Border Protection agency, and they allow periodic inspections of facilities. These inspections ensure that procedures are being followed. The **Container Security Initiative** (CSI) is a program whereby Customs and Border Protection agents are positioned at major ports throughout the world and inspect cargo destined for the United States. These two programs result in less congestion at U.S. ports of entry. They effectively distribute the workload over a larger geographical area, thus reducing bottlenecks.

These security measures are not without their critics. Security measures compromise commerce systems by increasing the time and costs of shipments. This often results in pressure on security systems. Shippers, manufacturers, and wholesalers often lobby for expedited procedures. Moreover, the political climate in the United States places emphasis on sealing our borders—interdiction and capture. Many prefer that we harden our borders. Consequently, there is constant political pressure on programs such as C-TPAT and CSI.

Summary

This chapter explored a number of issues relative to securing our borders and immigration controls. As noted, immigration control and border security are two different problems, but they are intertwined politically and operationally. Compounding the problem is the impact of various programs on the flow of commerce—economic interests lobby for programs that do not impede the flow of goods and criticize programs that negatively affect this flow. This intermingling of policy perspectives has resulted in a hodgepodge of programs that theoretically operate seamlessly. Nonetheless, we must concentrate our efforts on border security to keep potential terrorists and WMD materials out of the country. This goal certainly is most important, and it should trump immigration and economic concerns.

In terms of immigration, an immense volume of people enters and leaves the United States each year by land, air, and sea. The vast majority of these travelers adhere to laws and procedures. However, a number of people attempt to sneak into the United States, especially across our southern border. Most are seeking employment or a better life, but there are some who are potential terrorists, criminals, or other undesirables. Through the Secure Border Initiative, we are bolstering immigration policies through border security. Here, we currently are deploying electronic monitoring and fences, in an effort to control migration and force migrants to use legal procedures to enter. We also have increased the number of Customs and Border Protection agents to secure our borders.

Many would argue that it is virtually impossible to secure our borders and keep illegal aliens out of the country. They suggest that a more effective program would be to deny illegal migrants employment, thus removing the incentive for their coming to America. The Immigration and Customs Enforcement agency has stepped up its enforcement of the nonemployment of illegal aliens and has made numerous raids on businesses across the country. Indeed, in 2007, the number of illegal aliens coming across the border was reduced, but this likely had more to do with economic conditions than enforcement—only time will tell. If we are able to prevent migrants from entering the United States through employment enforcement, it will reduce the number crossing our borders, making control more manageable.

The US-VISIT program has been implemented to monitor the comings and goings of people entering the United States. It has resulted in our collecting biometric information on visitors. It is being linked to databases so we can verify the identity of these travelers. It has not resulted in the apprehension of a large number of people, but perhaps its greatest benefit is its deterrence effect. With the program in place, people who should not be admitted to the United States are less likely to attempt entry.

Currently, we do not have a clear solution to our border and immigration problems. We do, however, have a number of programs in place that attempt to solve this intricate puzzle, and these programs hopefully will result in larger measures of security. We must realize that national security is relative; regardless of programming, there always will be people slipping into the United States. We can never achieve total security, but we can implement programs that to the extent possible provide us with the maximum level of security.

Discussion Questions

1. Describe the patterns of immigration into the United States.
2. Distinguish between border security and immigration.
3. Riley describes a new border protection policy consisting of two components. Explain how they operate and complement each other.
4. Discuss the issues for programs such as Operation Hold the Line.
5. Discuss the elements contained in the Secure Border Initiative.
6. One of the methods of enhancing border security has been the construction of fences and other types of barriers. Describe these efforts and their effectiveness.
7. According to Wermuth and Riley, what improvements need to be made relative to border security?

References

Ackleson, J. (2005). "Border security technologies: Local and regional implications." *Review of Policy Research*, 22(2): 137–55.

Associated Press. (2005). *Terror-linked Migrants Channeled into U.S.* http://www.9/11securitysolutions.com/index.php?option=com_content&task=view&id=39&Itemid=38 (Accessed December 26, 2008).

Bach, R. (2005). "Transforming border security: Prevention first." *Homeland Security Affairs*, 1(1): 1–15.

Bain, B. (2008). *DHS to Expand US-VISIT Biometric Data Collection.*. http://www.fcw.com/online/news/154728-1.html (Accessed December 29, 2008).

Bazer, E. (2008). "Deporting some inmates proves a break for states." *USA Today* (March 28), p. 3a.

Bentzel, C. (2006). "Port and maritime security." In *The McGraw-Hill Homeland Security Handbook*, ed. G. Kamien, pp. 631–48. New York: McGraw-Hill.

Bullock, J., G. Haddow, D. Coppola, E. Ergin, L. Westerman, and S. Yeletaysi. (2005). *Introduction to Homeland Security*. Burlington, MA: Elsevier.

Customs and Border Protection. (2008). *SBI Programs.* http://www.cbp.gov/xp/cgov/border_security/sbi/about_sbi/sbi_programs.xml (Accessed December 28, 2008).

Department of Homeland Security. (2005). *DHS Fact Sheet: Secure Border Initiative.* Washington, D.C.: Author. http://www.dhs.gov/xnews/releases/press_release_0794.shtm (Accessed December 26, 2008).

Federation for American Immigration Reform. (2008). *How Many Illegal Aliens.* http://www.fairus.org/site/PageServer?pagename=iic_immigrationissuecentersb8ca (Accessed December 20, 2008).

Forest, J. (2006). "Protecting America's borders and points of entry: An introduction." *Homeland Security Protecting America's Targets, Volume 1*, pp. 1-18. Westport, CT: Praeger.

Frank, T. (2009). "Trying to verify employee IDs: Opponents cite flaws in use of federal database." *USA Today* (February 6), p. 3A.

Global Security. (undated-a). *US-Mexico Border Fence: Great Wall of Mexico Secure Fence.* http://www.globalsecurity.org/security/systems/mexico-wall.htm (Accessed December 27, 2008).

Global Security. (undated-b). *Operation Gatekeeper Operation Hold-the-Line Operation Safeguard.* http://www.globalsecurity.org/military/ops/gatekeeper.htm (Accessed December 27, 2008).

Hsu, S. (2008). "Cleaning firm used illegal workers at Chertoff home." *Washington Post* (December 11), p. A1.

Immigration and Customs Enforcement. (2008a). *Secure Communities: A Comprehensive Plan to Identify and Remove Criminal Aliens.* http://www.ice.gov/pi/news/factsheets/secure_communities.htm (Accessed December 28, 2008).

Immigration and Customs Enforcement. (2008b). *Worksite Enforcement.* http://www.ice.gov/pi/worksite/index.htm (Accessed December 28, 2008).

Majority Staff of the Committee on Homeland Security, Subcommittee on Investigations. (2006). *A Line in the Sand: Confronting the Threat at the Southwest Border.* Washington, D.C.: Author. http://www.house.gov/mccaul/pdf/Investigaions-Border-Report.pdf (Accessed December 26, 2008).

Markon, J. and S. McCrummen. (2010). "Arizona immigration law SB 1070—judge blocks some sections." *The Washington Post* (July 29). http://www.washingtonpost.com/wp-dyn/content/article/2010/07/28/AR2010072801794.html (Accessed August 19, 2010).

Marks, A. (2008). "With E-Verify, too many errors to expand its use." *Christian Science Monitor* (July 7). http://www.csmonitor.com/2008/0707/p02s01-usgn.html (Accessed December 28, 2008).

Morgan, D. and W. Krouse. (2005). *Biometric Identifiers and Border Security: 9/11 Commission Recommendations and Related Issues.* Washington, D.C.: Congressional Research Service.

Mueller, R. (2005). *FBI FY 2006 Budget Request: Hearing before the House Committee on Appropriations.* Written Statement (March 8).

National Intelligence Council. (2008). *Global Trends 2025: A Transformed World.* Washington, D.C.: Author.

Nunez-Neto, B. and S. Vina. (2006). *Border Security: Barriers Along the U.S. International Border.* Washington, D.C.: Congressional Research Service.

Ordonez, J. (2006). *Modeling the U.S. Border Patrol Tucson Section for the Deployment and Operations of Border Security Forces.* Master's Thesis. Monterey, CA: Naval Post-Graduate School.

Ortiz, D., S. Pfleeger, A. Balakrishnan, and M. Miceli. (2006). *Re-visiting US-VISIT: U.S. Immigration Processes, Concerns, and Consequences.* Santa Monica, CA: RAND.

Reyes, D. (2005). "Islamic cleric leaves country after lockup." *The Los Angeles Times* (January 4), p. B7.

Richey, J. (2007). "Fencing the border: Boeing's high tech plan falters." *CorpWatch.* http://www.corpwatch.org/article.php?id=14552 (Accessed December 27, 2008).

Riley, J. (2006). "Border control." In *The McGraw-Hill Homeland Security Handbook,* ed. D. Kamien, pp. 587–12. New York: McGraw-Hill.

Schoch, R. (2006). "Setting post 9/11 priorities at the Bureau of Immigration and Customs Enforcement." Hearing before the Subcommittee on National Security, Emerging Threats and International Relations of the House Committee On Government Reform (March 28).

Stana, R. (2002). *Identity Fraud: Relevance and Links to Alien Illegal Activities.* Washington, D.C.: Government Accounting Office.

Strohm, C. (2007). "Lawmakers wary as secure border initiative nears launch." *Government Executive.* http://www.govexec.com/story_page.cfm?articleid=37138 (Accessed December 27, 2008).

USA Today. (2008). "350 suspected illegal workers arrested in Miss. plant raid." http://www.usatoday.com/news/nation/2008-08-25-raid_N.htm (Accessed December 28, 2008).

U.S. Census Bureau. (2000). "Profile of selected demographic and social characteristics for the foreign-born population." http://www.census.gov/population/cen2000/stp-159/foreignborn.pdf (Accessed December 20, 2008).

Walsh, M. (2009). "Mexico murders soar as drug violence spirals out of control." *Telegraph.* http://www.telegraph.co.uk/news/worldnews/centralamericaandthecaribbean/mexico/4217538/Mexico-murders-soar-as-drug-violence-spirals-out-of-control.html (Accessed August 18, 2010).

Wermuth, M. and J. Riley. (2007). *The Strategic Challenge of Border Security.* Santa Monica, CA: RAND.

13

The Response to Homeland
Security Incidents

LEARNING OBJECTIVES

1. Understand the significance of Hurricane Katrina in terms of emergency response.
2. Know how the *National Response Framework* operates.
3. Know how the Stafford Act affects the federal response to emergencies and events.
4. Understand the workings of the National Incident Management System.
5. Be able to discuss how incident command operates in an emergency situation.
6. Be familiar with our medical response to disasters and other emergencies.

KEY TERMS

Mitigation

Risk management

National Response Framework

Layered response

Exercising

Tabletop exercises

After action reports

Emergency Support Functions and Support
  Annexes

Stafford Act

National Incident Management System

Common operating picture

Incident command system

National Disaster Medical System

National strike teams

INTRODUCTION

In Chapter 1, we noted that one of the primary responsibilities of homeland security was to "respond to and recover from significant homeland security incidents." Obviously, our first priority is to prevent incidents that result in significant damage and loss of life. However, we must recognize that this objective may not always be met. We are likely to suffer from future terrorist attacks, and numerous natural and human-made disasters result in significant destruction. An important part of homeland security is to prepare an orderly and effective response to such events.

To a large extent, when we consider homeland security, we focus on terrorist threats and attacks. However, as DHS (2010) and Bellavita (2008) advise, numerous types of destructive events must be considered or responded to using our homeland security response mechanisms. These events include terrorist attacks, fires, floods, earthquakes, tornados, hurricanes, and human-made events such as explosions at chemical or nuclear facilities. In essence, we need to have effective response mechanisms that are capable of mediating the impact of all sorts of large-scale disasters. Although the Department of Homeland Security was created and a number of response mechanisms were implemented as a result of the potential for future terrorist attacks, they have become important response mechanisms for any and all disasters that may befall us. When considering response, we must include these other potential problems, and in actuality, at some level, the response to a natural disaster will contain many of the same operational elements as does a response to a terrorist attack. Moreover, there is a greater likelihood of disasters occurring relative to terrorist attacks. A number of major disasters require a federal response.

HURRICANE KATRINA: HOMELAND SECURITY'S FIRST REAL TEST

On August 29, 2005, Hurricane Katrina hit landfall directly on New Orleans and the Gulf coast. The storm was so powerful, a category five storm with sustained winds of more than 175 miles an hour, that it not only devastated New Orleans, but for the most part destroyed communities all along the Gulf coast in Louisiana and Mississippi. It was the worst natural disaster in recent American history. Approximately 1,840 people died and the storm resulted in more than $80 billion in damages. Numerous breaches in the city's levee system caused widespread flooding throughout New Orleans, displacing thousands of residents. Neighboring communities were also flooded, making evacuation and relief efforts more difficult. The damage was so extensive that people had to be evacuated to cities in a number of other states. Indeed, New Orleans and many other communities have never fully recovered from the storm. Today, New Orleans is a shadow of its former self—many residents were unable to return to their homes and devastated areas still remain in parts of the city.

HS Web Link: To learn more about Hurricane Katrina, go to http:// thinkprogress.org/ katrina-timeline

Katrina was a foreseeable catastrophe. It was common knowledge that the levees were weak and likely would be breached if hit by a powerful storm. Moreover, portions of New Orleans are located below sea level, and with the city's close proximity to the Gulf of Mexico and Lake Pontchartrain, it was only a matter of time before catastrophe struck. These known factors should have resulted in better preparation, but unfortunately prior knowledge did not result in a more effective response. In fact, many would evaluate the response as disastrous.

The federal agency with primary response responsibility was the Federal Emergency Management Agency (FEMA), which had become a part of the Department of Homeland Security when President George W. Bush established the new department. In addition to FEMA, a number of other local, state, federal, and private agencies responded, including the dispatching of more than 50,000 National Guard troops and 20,000 active military personnel

FEMA employee surveys debris for removal. *Source:* http://www.photolibrary.fema.gov/photolibrary/photo_details.do?id=23889

(Pickup, 2006). The 9/11 attacks had lessened the importance of FEMA—the Department of Homeland Security was concentrating on preventing and responding to terrorist attacks. As a consequence of this organizational perspective, FEMA was pushed down into the bowels of the department's bureaucracy. There, it received little support and a substantial level of neglect—it was operating in a top-heavy bureaucracy that was unprepared for major disasters or problems.

FEMA's response was deficient across the board with numerous failures and few successes documented. Problems with FEMA's response abound. For example, Sobel and Leeson (2006) highlight several problems. The Red Cross attempted to go into New Orleans to deliver much needed relief supplies but was prevented from doing so, FEMA confiscated emergency hospital supplies that were destined for a New Orleans hospital that had more than 100 critical care patients, and a Florida emergency response team was able to assist in Mississippi long before FEMA could effectively respond. CNN (2005) reported on similar problems. While fires raged in New Orleans, fire equipment was delayed because FEMA required firefighters to attend training sessions on community relations and sexual harassment. Water trucks were not allowed in the devastated area because they did not have the proper paperwork. Not only was the initial response botched, but numerous scandalous reports surfaced for months later with criticism of the temporary trailers FEMA bought for displaced residents and the ineffective distribution of food, water, and vouchers. Without a doubt, FEMA's and the Department of Homeland Security's responses to Katrina were a disaster. They raised serious questions as to whether these agencies could adequately respond to a WMD attack on one of our cities. They also pointed out the necessity to substantially improve our emergency response mechanisms at all levels.

FEMA received a substantial amount of blame for the less than adequate response to Katrina. However, it should be noted that the city of New Orleans and the state of Louisiana shared a measure of the fault. Officials in New Orleans refused to evaluate the city on a timely basis, and the governor largely remained out-of-play until the situation had become a significant disaster. Essentially, the city and state did little until it was too late. This demonstrates that state and local governments must be more actively involved in planning responses prior to a disaster.

HS Web Link: To learn more about FEMA's response to Katrina, go to *http://www.fema.gov/ hazard/hurricane/ 2005katrina/index.shtm*

RESPONSE GOALS AND OBJECTIVES

In 2010, the Department of Homeland Security elaborated on the objectives for ensuring resilience to disasters. The DHS identified the following objectives:

- Mitigate hazards
- Enhance preparedness
- Ensure effective emergency response
- Rapidly recover (pp. 59–64)

Since 2005, the Department of Homeland Security has attempted to develop plans that would result in emergency response operations that would be more coordinated and effective in meeting the objectives it identified. Today, the foundation for our emergency responses is enumerated in the *National Response Framework* and the *National Incident Management System*. These plans in combination attempt to provide a framework from which to respond to significant national emergencies. It is important to realize that our planning and response mechanisms focus on "all hazards," including terrorist attacks.

The *National Response Framework* provides guidance on responding to terrorist attacks and catastrophes. It focuses on the relationships among the federal, state, and local governments and their obligations. However, before discussing the *National Response Framework*, it is instructive to discuss mitigation. **Mitigation** is a process whereby we attempt to reduce the impact of hazards, terrorist attacks, natural disasters, or human-made disasters before they occur. Mitigation often includes **risk management**, a process of hardening or increasing the safety features associated with critical infrastructure as discussed in Chapter 3. We can reduce the impact of an event if preventive actions are taken previously. For example, if we had attended to flood protection measures in New Orleans, the impact of Hurricane Katrina might have been mitigated or reduced. Mitigation measures are often legislated or mandated by executive orders in building codes, safety requirements and so on. For example, the state of California now has strict building standards that reduce the amount of damage that occurs as a result of earthquakes, and other standards or building codes that reduce the likelihood of fires and damage as a result of fires. Florida has codes that are designed to reduce the amount of damage in the event of a hurricane. As discussed in Chapter 3, target hardening and other mitigation measures should be enacted as part of our efforts to protect critical infrastructure assets.

Analysis Box 13-1

Risk management includes making decisions about actions that should be taken. Decisions are often limited by the amount of resources and the magnitude of the disaster. In terms of responding to a disaster such as Hurricane Katrina, what should be the priorities? How would you establish priorities if you had limited resources—that is, not enough resources to address every priority?

Fire services are a critical part of the homeland security response.   *Source:* AP (080328028099)

NATIONAL RESPONSE FRAMEWORK

The *National Response Framework* was an effort by the Department of Homeland Security to clarify the roles and responsibilities of those who are involved in responding to a significant catastrophe. Schneider (2008) advises that the mismatch between expected roles and responsibilities and actual performance has resulted in gaps in responding to critical incidents. That is, citizens and units of government have different expectations, especially those who are the victims of a disaster or who are responding to these victims, as compared to how governmental units sometimes see their responsibilities. Perhaps the greatest disconnect is between federal authorities and local citizens. The *National Response Framework* attempts to clarify responsibilities and ensure that we have more coherent responses to events.

It should be noted that the federal government sees any response to a catastrophe, whether it is a terrorist attack or a natural disaster, in terms of a **layered response**. Although stated obtusely, this essentially means that local governments are responsible first and state governments second for responding to some catastrophe. This is exemplified by language commonly used in response plans—the federal government will respond to catastrophes and disasters that are of a "significant national emergency." This language and perspective serve to prevent the federal government from assuming responsibility for every mishap, especially those that are minor in nature. Units of local and state governments must take responsibility and control lesser disasters. At the same time, this language allows the federal government to delegate a large measure of responsibility to local and state governments even for major incidents. Here, the federal government sees itself in a supplemental or supportive role. Local and state governments seldom have the resources or capacity to

Analysis Box 13-2

Response to disasters and other events consists of a layered response with local authorities being responsible for minor events, state governments intervening in medium-sized events, and the federal government responding to major disasters and events. What types of events should remain under the purview of local authorities? What types of events should include a state response? Finally, what types of events require federal assistance? Can these events be easily distinguished?

adequately respond even to a catastrophe of medium magnitude. The federal government's, and especially the Department of Homeland Security's, philosophy to some degree abdicates and delegates responsibility and blame—the federal government can diffuse blame in cases such as Hurricane Katrina using this federalist perspective.

The *National Response Framework* was developed as a result of the political reaction to its predecessor, the *National Response Plan*. Lindsay (2008) identified a number of deficiencies with the original plan. First, there was confusion over the federal role in catastrophes relative to state and local responsibilities. The federal role, especially considering that the Department of Homeland Security sees itself in a supporting role, was not clearly articulated. This resulted in response voids when the plan was set in motion. Second, it was overly bureaucratic and difficult to apply in operational terms. Finally, it was not a true operational plan as it identified relationships among various agencies but failed to provide specific operational guidance.

NATIONAL RESPONSE FRAMEWORK: AN ANALYSIS

Philosophically, the *National Response Framework* was designed to improve on the *National Response Plan*, and it addressed the *Plan*'s shortcomings. Primarily, the *Plan* was confusing and failed to clarify agency roles. The chain of command was bureaucratic and cumbersome (Birkland and Waterman, 2008). On the other hand, the *Framework* has a national, rather than a federal government, focus; it attempts to integrate federal, state, and local activities rather than focusing exclusively on federal responsibilities. It serves as an outline of activities and does not provide specific policy and operational directives, which can be a shortcoming if agencies do not develop procedures and enact them. Lindsay (2008, p. 5) provides an overview of the *Framework*'s doctrine, which is provided in Figure 13-1. The doctrine consists of five principles that provide the boundaries of the federal response.

HS Web Link: To view the *National Response Framework*, go to http:// www.fema.gov/pdf/ emergency/nrf/nrf-core.pdf

Local Responsibilities Under the *National Response Framework*

When an incident occurs, local authorities will be the first responders. They will have the immediate responsibility of controlling and responding to the event to reduce the loss of life and property. This is a complex endeavor for large or small jurisdictions, because all the elements in an effective response must be present. They must have a multitude of resources at their disposal including governmental and private agencies, for example, public health, law enforcement, disaster relief, utilities, waste management, fire, American Red Cross, and so on, as depicted in Figure 13-2. Even though local authorities may receive support from state and federal officials, depending on the magnitude of the incident, it may be several days before this support arrives. That support may be fragmented and in some cases deficient as exemplified by past disasters. Consequently, responsibility falls squarely on local officials and their immediate response.

1. Engaged Partnership: the NRF advocates for open lines of communication among various emergency management entities and for support partnerships during preparedness activities so that when incidents take place, these various entities are able to work together.
2. Tiered Response: responses to incidents begin at the local level. When local capacity is overwhelmed, state authorities assist the locality. Likewise, should the state be overwhelmed, assistance from the federal government is requested.
3. Scalable, Flexible, and Adaptable Operational Capabilities: as incidents change in size, scope, and complexity, there needs to be a corresponding change in the response apparatus.
4. Unity of Effort Through Unified Command: a clear understanding of the roles and responsibilities of each entity is necessary for effective response. Moreover, effective response requires a unit of effort within the emergency management chain of command.
5. Readiness to Act: all emergency management agencies, to the extent possible should anticipate incidents and make preparations to respond swiftly to them.

FIGURE 13-1 *National Response Framework's* Philosophical Doctrine. *Source:* Department of Homeland Security. (2008a). *National Response Framework.* Washington, D.C.: Author.

Local elected officials must ensure that a functioning plan of action is in place. This has not occurred or has occurred haphazardly in many jurisdictions. Local leaders are more concerned and consumed by the daily operations of government—delivering services to the populace. When a plan exists it often is outdated or untested (Donahue and Tuohy, 2006). For example, the city of New Orleans had emergency response plans for storm and hurricane events, but they were of little value or were disregarded when Katrina struck. The plan's shelf life had expired through neglect and inattention. Hurricane Katrina was of such magnitude that plans were of little use. Nonetheless, a jurisdiction should have an emergency manager who is responsible for coordinating and controlling the jurisdiction's response to an emergency situation. A major part of this

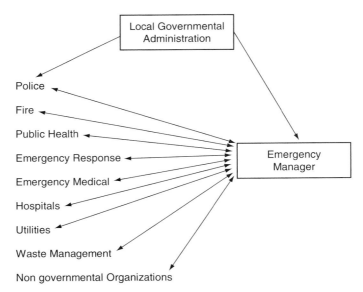

FIGURE 13-2 Local Emergency Response Organization.

coordination and control is ensuring that a workable response plan is in place. This response plan must be scalable, that is, applicable to any event regardless of size or magnitude.

HS Web Link: To view the variety of resources available to state and local governments in the event of a disaster, go to *http://www.usa.gov/Government/State_Local/Disasters.shtml*

State Responsibilities Under the *National Response Framework*

The governor is the chief executive officer for the state. He or she is directly responsible for ensuring that a state has an organizational framework and capacity to respond to a terrorist attack or catastrophic event. Overall, state command and coordination for such events are usually delegated to a state emergency management agency, state homeland security director, or commander of the state police or highway patrol. Large states will have all three operational entities, whereas smaller states may have only one of these offices.

The state has several responsibilities in terms of preparing for and responding to catastrophes. First, the state must effectively communicate event information to the public. This communication serves to assist in coordinating and controlling people in the response area. People need guidance and information in a catastrophe. These efforts reduce panic in the affected area and especially in unaffected areas. People generally want to know what is happening and what they should do when such events occur. As an example, initially there were few official communications in New Orleans in the aftermath of Katrina; this served to exacerbate the situation.

Second, the governor can activate the National Guard, state police, and other resources. (The National Guard is a state's primary emergency resource in large catastrophes.) These resources are required in all but the most minor events. Third, the state coordinates mutual assistance plans with other states. For example, a number of Western states have mutual aid compacts to provide assistance in large fires. Such compacts should be in place should a state experience other types of disasters. Finally, the governor is responsible for communicating requests for federal assistance. Generally, federal assistance is not provided until such a request is made, usually through the Federal Emergency Management Administration.

As noted, the state machinery includes a state director of homeland security and a director of state emergency management. The state homeland security director is responsible for developing a statewide homeland security plan. The plan is fairly broad, focusing on both prevention and response. It generally details different programs that are funded and relationships among state and local agencies with regard to prevention. The director of state emergency management, on the other hand, is concerned with responding to incidents. This office maintains a network of local emergency response managers and capabilities. This office will coordinate state emergency management activities at an incident site, coordinating with the local emergency management personnel. However, it should be noted that in many of these incidents, state resources, especially when the National Guard is activated, represent a substantially larger response than that available from most local resources.

Analysis Box 13-3

As noted, a significant event, depending on its nature, can require the services of a large number of agencies and community-based organizations. If a large chemical spill occurred at an industrial area in your hometown, what agencies would be required to respond? Would outside assistance be required? Who would be in charge of the response?

The National Guard assists citizens with flood control.   *Source:* http://www.fema.gov/medialibrary/photographs/43232

Federal Responsibilities Under the *National Response Framework*

As noted in the *Framework*, the president is responsible for leading federal response efforts when a terrorist attack or other catastrophe occurs. The president's National Security Council provides national strategic policy advice on incident response preparation and how the federal government should proceed during such incidents. For example, the White House Office of Homeland Security developed the *National Strategy for Homeland* Security, which was discussed in detail in Chapter 1.

The secretary of homeland security is the federal officer who is responsible for incident management. On a daily basis, he or she is responsible for prevention, preparation, response, and recovery operational preparedness. The secretary is responsible for developing and maintaining the overall homeland security architecture using policies that are developed by the president's various advisors. FEMA coordinates federal disaster relief when incidents occur. Depending on the nature of the incident, a variety of other federal agencies may become involved in the federal response. If the incident is the result of a terrorist attack, the FBI will conduct a criminal investigation. Large-scale or incidents of significant magnitude may result in the military being activated, as was the case in Hurricane Katrina. The secretary of defense authorizes the use of military assets in domestic catastrophes at the direction of the president. The military would play a key role in WMD attacks in terms of decontamination, evacuation, quarantine, and logistical support.

As noted earlier, the *National Response Framework* uses a layered or tiered response, whereby federal resources are deployed only when local and state resources are unable to adequately deal with the effects of the incident. In some cases, the federal government may take control of an incident. The Department of Homeland Security (2008a) in the *Framework* identifies four scenarios when the federal government assumes command and control:

1. A federal department or agency acting under its own authority has requested DHS assistance.
2. The resources of the State and local authorities are overwhelmed and Federal assistance is requested.
3. More than one federal agency has become substantially involved in responding to the incident.
4. The Secretary has been directed by the President to assume incident management responsibilities. (p. 25)

RESPONSE AS DICTATED BY THE *NATIONAL RESPONSE FRAMEWORK*

According to the *Framework*, a response to a terrorist attack or other catastrophe is a multistage process consisting of (1) preparation, (2) response, and (3) recovery. Continuous planning and development must occur across all three stages if an adequate response to an event is to occur.

Preparation

The preparation stage consists of a cycle of activities that includes planning, organizing, training, equipping, exercising, and evaluating. Figure 13-3 demonstrates this cycle.

PLANNING   First, planning must occur at all levels: local, state, and federal. This planning must be a continuous process. As Schermerhorn (2008) notes, "When planning is done well, it creates a solid platform for the other management functions" (p. 184). One cannot manage, lead, organize, or control a situation without foundational planning. Planning allows organizations to respond effectively across the life cycle of a potential crisis. This planning must be inclusive, detailing the roles and responsibilities of various agencies, including nongovernmental agencies; the collection and use of intelligence information; mutual aid compacts; policy and procedure requirements; and so on. Planning should address specific events such as WMD attacks, hurri-

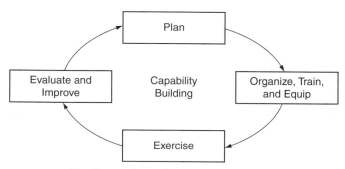

The Preparedness Cycle Builds Capabilities

FIGURE 13-3   The Preparation Cycle.   *Source:* Department of Homeland Security. (2008a). *National Response Framework.* Washington, D.C.: Author, p. 27.

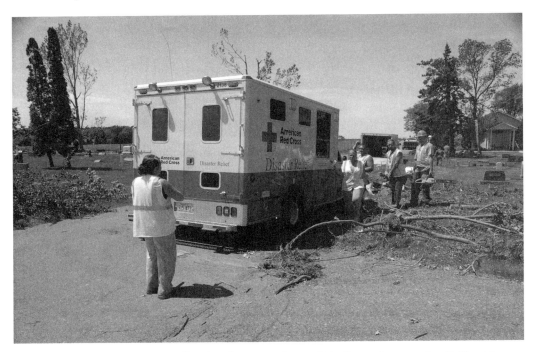

Medical services are necessary in all major disasters.   *Source:* http://www.fema.gov/medialibrary/collections/904

canes, tornados, earthquakes, floods, and fires. Planning should be flexible, addressing a variety of events, and it should be scalable to meet the requirements of events of varying magnitude. Planning should be comprehensive and include tactics addressing preparation to recovery. Since planning encompasses responses from a number of agencies and organizations, it must be ongoing since structural arrangements in some of these organizations will change and evolve over time. The plan must be contemporaneous, reflecting current organizational arrangements, capabilities, and commitments.

Preparation requires considerable pre-event planning. The Department of Homeland Security has developed a number of action or operational plans that will be implemented when an event of national significance occurs. However, successful implementation requires that all the possible scenarios are considered. Preoperational planning must be comprehensive. To this end, the Department of Homeland Security has developed a number of planning areas, which are provided in Figure 13-4.

First, note that the various planning or action areas contained in Figure 13-4 address a multitude of events, including terrorist attacks that may include different types of weapons. Officials must plan for all sorts of scenarios or events. Second, the focus of preparedness is on the emergency management response process with a variety of response and recovery elements addressed. Third, preventive planning must occur to prevent future terrorist attacks and to address mitigation. This process must continue even in the wake of an attack since terrorists often follow up with additional attacks. Fourth, note that considerable planning must occur to ensure that situations are managed. Poor management, as in the case of Hurricane

1. Animal Health Emergency Support	20. Mass Care (Sheltering, Feeding, and Related Services)
2. CBRNE Detection	21. Mass Prophylaxis
3. Citizen Preparedness and Participation	22. Medical Supplies Management and Distribution
4. Citizen Protection: Evacuation and/or In-Place Protection	23. Medical Surge
5. Critical Infrastructure Protection	24. On-Site Incident Management
6. Critical Resource Logistics and Distribution	25. Planning
7. Economic and Community Recovery	26. Public Health Epidemiological Investigation and Laboratory Testing
8. Emergency Operations Center Management	27. Public Safety and Security Response
9. Emergency Public Information and Warning	28. Restoration of Lifelines
10. Environmental Health and Vector Control	29. Risk Analysis
11. Explosive Device Response Operations	30. Search and Rescue
12. Fatality Management	31. Structural Damage Assessment and Mitigation
13. Firefighting Operations/Support	32. Terrorism Investigation and Intervention
14. Food and Agriculture Safety and Defense	33. Triage and Pre-Hospital Treatment
15. Information Collection and Threat Recognition	34. Volunteer Management and Donations
16. Information Sharing and Collaboration	35. WMD/Hazardous Materials Response and Decontamination
17. Intelligence Fusion and Analysis	
18. Interoperable Communications	36. Worker Health and Safety
19. Isolation and Quarantine	

FIGURE 13-4 Homeland Security Planning Initiatives. *Source:* Department of Homeland Security. (2005). *Interium National Preparedness Goal: Homeland Security Directive 8: National Preparedness.* Washington, D.C.: Author, p. 7.

Katrina, results in a failed response and recovery. Today, event management is guided by the National Incident Management System, which is discussed later. Finally, considerable planning should occur that results in the inclusion of personnel from a variety of governmental agencies as well as nongovernmental groups. To a large extent, our planning and action plans have been guided by the *National Strategy for Homeland Security* (Office of Homeland Security, 2002) as discussed in Chapter 1.

HS Web Link: To learn more about the national preparedness guidelines, go to *http://www.fema.gov/pdf/government/npg.pdf*

An effective response is well organized, and this organization must occur at two strategic levels. First, agencies and organizations that are involved in response should have the organizational capacity to maximally respond. This necessitates that each organization has its organization, procedures, and action plans in place. As the saying goes, a chain is only as strong as its weakest link. Second, substantial planning must be conducted to ensure that all involved agencies' responses are coordinated. Any response to an incident will include a number of federal, state, local, and nongovernmental agencies. They must have specific roles and objectives that in combination represent a comprehensive, effective response. In some cases, the federal government and the states use pre-scripted operational assignments to ensure that their response is adequate. Incident management organization is addressed in the National Incident Management System.

ORGANIZE, TRAIN, AND EQUIP The Department of Homeland Security has developed a comprehensive program to train and equip incident responders. States have received block grants for equipment, and this money has been budgeted to state and local homeland security efforts. The department has developed a number of first responder training courses, focusing on all aspects of disaster response and management. Local and state governments must ensure that personnel receive adequate training. Without proper training, first responders will not be able to function successfully. Moreover, state and local agencies are expected using different event scenarios in their training. Different events necessitate different responses.

EXERCISE   An important part of preparation is **exercising**, whereby first responders respond to a mock event or disaster. The mock event depicts a specific scenario such as a biological attack or a large-scale conventional attack. The event is scripted to include casualties and destruction. In some cases, communications, roadways, and other physical attributes are deemed destroyed or otherwise not useable. Once the situation has been constructed, first responders are notified. The response is then monitored to determine proficiency and any gaps or problems that might occur. The mock exercise is a test of organizations' ability to apply their response plans. This evaluation identifies needed changes in procedures and operations, and it is the only way to identify deficiencies other than a response to an actual situation.

Donahue and Tuohy (2006) advise that although exercising is an important or even critical part of incident response preparation, exercises often fail to provide us with useable evaluative information. In most, if not all cases, exercises are conducted in a sterile environment or in a bubble; they do not mimic reality. In some cases, scenarios often are sterile and devoid of some of the intricate details and problems that might occur in a real situation; in other cases, the scenarios are overly complex and convoluted to the point that they are unrealistic and too difficult to mount a satisfactory response. First responders in these exercises generally are volunteers or are paid overtime. The personnel actually working at the time of the exercise are not involved and remain on their regular assignments, creating an artificial situation in which we really do not know how a response will progress. Since exercises are expensive, they generally are conducted on the cheap, a limitation that directly affects outcomes and lends a degree or artificialness to the exercise. Also, as a result of expense, exercising occurs infrequently, another stumbling block to enhancing proficiency.

EVALUATE AND IMPROVE   The final stage in the preparation process is evaluation. We must continually evaluate our responses and response mechanisms. We must ensure that we are prepared to meet whatever challenge befalls us. This reinforces the need for a continuous planning process. In some cases, we can conduct **tabletop exercises**: An exercise is conducted on paper by reviewing procedures to determine if they produce the desired outcomes.

HS Web Link: To learn more about table top exercises, go to *http://www. acp-wa-state.org/ meetingsdoc/october2007/ 04%20Tabletop%20Exercise %20Handbook%20Example. pdf*

Here, a simulated catastrophe is declared. Response procedures are examined to identify the number of first responders required for the incident. The process for mobilizing the necessary personnel, whether they are on or off duty, is examined. All aspects of the response—police, fire, emergency medical, hospital, decontamination, and so on—are examined. The tabletop examination provides insights into how well the various agencies respond, coordinate, and alleviate the situation. The tabletop exercise is an excellent method for testing procedures.

We can also review after action reports from previous responses to emergencies to determine effectiveness. **After action reports** are completed by agencies after responding to some catastrophe or disaster. These reports serve as critiques, listing what went right and deficiencies in the response. A review of these reports over time may assist in identifying potential problems. However, this process has two deficiencies. First, each responding agency completes its own after action report focusing on its response. The reports do not provide a comprehensive picture of what occurred. Cooperation and

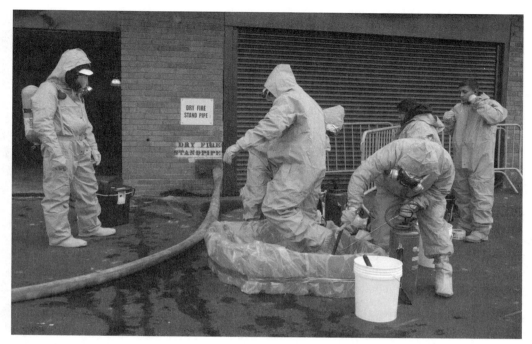

Emergency personnel must practice all aspects of disaster control.   *Source:* AP (04031405280)

coordination among the agencies are not addressed or examined to the extent necessary for a clear evaluation. Second, when writing the reports, personnel often highlight the actions that were successful and deemphasize deficiencies. Nonetheless, after action reports can provide crucial feedback.

Response to an Incident

The mechanics of responses to incidents is addressed in the Department of Homeland Security's National Incident Management System, which is addressed in some detail later in the chapter. Nonetheless, when an incident occurs, it triggers a number of processes and procedures on the part of a number of agencies. It requires substantial communication across a variety of agencies at all levels of government. It requires that efforts be comprehensive and coordinated. This means that support needs must be identified and requests for support must be made expeditiously. Local officials must immediately notify state officials, and when a situation is of sufficient magnitude, federal authorities must be notified. Any delays in requests for assistance result in exaggerated problems.

The *Framework* identifies a number of immediate actions at the scene that must occur:

- Those injured must be evacuated.
- People in convalescent homes and hospitals must also be evacuated.
- Safe shelters for victims and those who are evacuated from the affected area must be identified and made ready.

- Arrangements for food and water must be made.
- Search and rescue operations must commence immediately to reduce the incidence of injuries and fatalities.
- Treatment facilities for the injured must be established.
- Hazards such as fires or contamination must be contained.
- In some cases, quarantines must be established and maintained.
- Arrangements must be made to ensure the safety and health of the first responders.
- Provide information to the public.

All of these activities must occur in short order, which requires substantial coordination and a lucid command operation. It also requires that workable procedures be in place ready for activation.

Recovery

For the most part, recovery is the responsibility of FEMA. The types of assistance required for the recovery stage vary from community to community—community attributes to some extent dictate needs as well as the type of disaster. Flooding will require a different recovery assistance matrix as compared to a WMD attack. Moreover, there are short-term recovery considerations and long-term recovery considerations. Short-term needs refer to the restoration of services such as transportation, utilities, food, shelter, and government programs. Long-term needs, on the other hand, may take months or even years to meet and refer to the redevelopment of affected areas. For example, as of 2010, many areas in New Orleans had not fully recovered from the effects of Hurricane Katrina. Long-term recovery essentially is rebuilding the community so that it functions as it should.

As noted, FEMA is the primary federal agency involved in recovery. It often provides a range of federal assistance. Depending on the type of incident, roads must be reconstructed; permanent housing must be built; schools, government buildings, and medical facilities must be established; and so on. In some cases, funding comes in the form of grants and loans; in other cases, individual citizens receive payments to assist them in recovery. FEMA has several programs, including the Disaster Housing Program that provides housing, reimbursement of expenses for temporary shelter, and repair of homes; Individual and Family Grants that address victim housing needs; Small Business Administration Disaster Loans that are made to affected businesses; Disaster Unemployment Assistance, a program that expedites unemployment benefits and legal services; and FEMA's Public Assistance Grant Program, which provides funds to local and state governments to assist in the resumption of services (Bullock et al., 2005). Recovery, depending on the magnitude of the incident, can cost millions or even billions of dollars.

CRITIQUE OF PAST RESPONSES AND THE *NATIONAL RESPONSE FRAMEWORK*

Organizational philosophy likely is a significant impediment to an effective response as outlined in the *National Response Framework*. The Department of Homeland Security is a highly centralized, bureaucratic organization. Requests often must filter through several layers of bureaucracy before decisions are made. Organizational imperatives and political perspectives often intercede in the decision matrix as opposed to making decisions solely on the basis of the problem at hand. This often creates incongruence between outcomes and needs or problems. On the other hand, the department has delegated or decentralized operational responsibilities to the lowest levels—local and state governments (layered response). Generally, there virtually are no or weak lines of communication between the department decision makers and operatives in the field. Even in the gravest situations, this often leads to disconnect and less than satisfactory solutions. These same problems often exist in the relationships between state and local governments.

Reviews of the *Framework* have been mixed. Lindsay (2008) notes that since its inception, it has been used sparingly, but discussions with emergency response personnel note that federal involvement in disaster relief has improved. Officials in Texas, reporting on the federal efforts with Hurricanes Gustav and Ike, indicated that the federal effort was "good." Nonetheless, there were some snags. State officials reported that local officials had the responsibility of establishing points for the distribution of supplies, but local officials responded that they were unaware of this responsibility. As noted, the *Framework* is as labeled, a framework, and does not provide specific procedures. The absence of specifics may continue to result in confusion. The Department of Homeland Security has developed several Support Annexes (discussed later) that provide more procedural detail, but they are incomplete. Finally, it should be noted that thus far, the *Framework* has been applied in disasters of the moderate range. It has not been applied in a Katrina-like situation. Questions remain as to how it would perform in a higher magnitude disaster.

Donahue and Tuohy (2006) conducted a study of incident managers to determine what mistakes normally occur during responses. They report that we tend to continue to make the same mistakes. To some extent, our emergency response and other governmental agencies do

Emergency medical services are an important part of a response.

not have the capacity to learn. These authors conducted focus groups with a number of incident managers to identify why mistakes and problems occur, and the group identified a number of issues. First and perhaps foremost, uncoordinated leadership generally was present. In many instances, multiple, conflicting, and isolated command structures were present during the response. Second, communications often failed, inhibiting responses. It was noted that such failures were not always technical in nature—most responders have some of the latest communications technology. The problem arose because of a lack of a system whereby various agencies could communicate and coordinate activities—procedural problems. Third, most incidents are plagued by weak planning. Too often, plans are outdated, fragmented, or superficial and do not provide detailed guidance. Fourth, responses often were hampered by resource constraints. A situation of any magnitude will require substantial volumes of resources. In many cases, the resources are not available or they cannot be deployed effectively. Finally, most events are hindered by poor public relations. People understandably want information on what is occurring and what they should do. Information that is useful to the victims or those affected seldom is forthcoming. To some extent, this leads to some level of anarchy. An effective response requires citizen cooperation, and this cooperation cannot occur without direction from the officials responsible for responding to the incident. These issues reinforce the need for agencies to adhere to the tenants outlined in the *National Response Framework* and the need for specific procedures.

EMERGENCY SUPPORT FUNCTIONS AND SUPPORT ANNEXES

As noted, one of the criticisms of the *National Response Framework* is the absence of specific procedural guidelines. The **Emergency Support Functions and Support Annexes** (Department of Homeland Security, 2008b) were developed to at least partially remedy this problem. The annexes are broken down into 15 different emergency support function areas, as listed in Figure 13-5.

The annexes are designed to provide guidance while completing various recovery operations at disasters. Essentially, they provide a listing of federal resources and the mechanisms by which they can be activated. Moreover, responsibility for coordinating the federal response

- Transportation
- Communications
- Public Works and Engineering
- Firefighting
- Emergency Management
- Mass Care, Emergency Assistance, Housing, and Human Services
- Logistics Management and Resource Support
- Public Health and Medical Services
- Search and Rescue
- Oil and Hazardous Materials Response
- Agriculture and Natural Resources
- Energy
- Public Safety and Security
- Long-Term Community Recovery
- External Affairs

FIGURE 13-5 Support Function Areas Addressed in the Emergency Support Functions and Support Annexes.

is vested with an emergency support function coordinator (ESF coordinator), and each area has a separate ESF coordinator. The primary ESF coordinator is located in the federal agency that will have the most significant role, for example, the transportation ESF coordinator is located in the Department of Transportation. As noted, our national emergency response is predicated on a layered approach whereby requests for assistance emanate from a local jurisdiction, as dictated by the Stafford Act as discussed later. Once a need is established, the annexes provide the federal government with guidance on how to proceed in using federal resources.

Perhaps the best way to examine these resources is to explore one of the annexes. For example, the public works and engineering ESF coordinator is located in the U.S. Army Corps of Engineers. Activities conducted as a result of this ESF includes assessment of damage to public works and infrastructure, contracting for support for life-saving and life-sustaining services, providing technical assistance, providing emergency repair of damaged public infrastructure, and implementing FEMA Public Assistance and other programs (DHS, 2008b, p. 17). Even though the U.S. Corps of Engineers has overall coordination responsibility, other federal agencies are available to assist, depending on the nature of the disaster and the scope of damage.

The guide advises that federal, state, and local officials should identify priorities, cooperatively identify support needs, and track the status of response and recovery activities. Again, however, it remains questionable if the annexes and the *Framework* provide adequate procedural guidelines. That is, is there sufficient detail in the planning to guide local, state, and federal officials when responding to an incident? Without adequate guidance, there invariably will be delays and gaps in the provision of services. Future responses should be monitored carefully to identify any procedural deficiencies, and the annexes and the *Framework* should be duly adjusted.

PROCEDURES FOR ACTIVATING FEDERAL ASSISTANCE IN AN EMERGENCY

The federal government and its many departments and agencies possess a multitude of resources that can be deployed to assist local and state governments in the event of a terrorist attack or other disaster. These resources are not deployed automatically but are activated as a result of a state request and federal deployment procedures as described in the Stafford Act. When an incident occurs that exhausts local and state resources, the state can request assistance from the federal government. The **Stafford Act** essentially authorizes the president to provide support to the states in such emergencies. Figure 13-6 charts this process.

When an incident occurs, local first responders provide initial assistance and attempt to mediate the impact of the incident. In minor incidents, local resources are generally sufficient to adequately manage the problem. Incidents of greater magnitude may require the assistance of state emergency operations personnel. If the state cannot provide the level of assistance required to mitigate the situation, state officials will request assistance from the federal government. If a situation is of substantial magnitude, federal resources may be deployed prior to a request from the state. Generally, however, the governor will make a request for assistance to the regional FEMA administrator. Prior to any such request, however, the governor must have activated the state's emergency response apparatus. Once the request is made to the regional FEMA administrator, the administrator and the governor survey the damage to determine its extent and

HS Web Link: To learn more about the Stafford Act, go to *http://www.nyu.edu/ccpr/pubs/Report_StaffordActReform_Mitchell Moss_10.03.07.pdf*

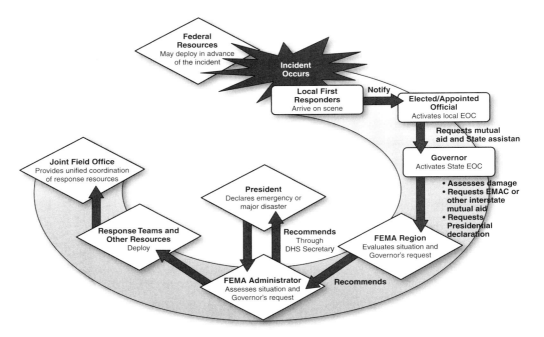

FIGURE 13-6 Process for Obtaining Federal Support in Emergencies. *Source:* Department of Homeland Security. (2008b). *Overview: ESF and Support Annexes Coordinating Federal Assistance in Support of the National Response Framework.* Washington, D.C.: Author, p. 5.

the types of aid that are required to mitigate the problem. The request is then forwarded to the president through the FEMA administrator, and then the president issues a declaration. The declaration allows various federal agencies to provide assistance to the disaster area. The federal agencies involved in the relief effort generally are identified in the Emergency Support Functions and Support Annexes.

In some cases, federal authorities will begin moving emergency resources in place prior to a request. When a large-scale disaster such as a hurricane, earthquake, or flood occurs, FEMA recognizes the level of severity and mobilizes resources so that relief efforts can begin as quickly as possible. A terrorist attack, especially one involving weapons of mass destruction, would result in the immediate mobilization of resources. FEMA monitors incidents and attempts to react as quickly as possible.

Analysis Box 13-4

In order to secure a federal response to a disaster, the president has to declare a national emergency. Generally, a request is made by the governor of the affected state to the regional FEMA administrator. Do you believe this request process as dictated by the Stafford Act is too cumbersome? How do you think FEMA and the president determine if an event is of significant magnitude to warrant federal assistance? Do states attempt to obtain assistance in less significant events?

NATIONAL INCIDENT MANAGEMENT SYSTEM

Thus far, the emergency response programming, particularly the *National Response Framework*, has been addressed in this chapter. An effective and coherent response requires an efficient command and control system. Heretofore, such systems have been somewhat haphazard with little consistency across disaster responses. The Department of Homeland Security (2008b,c) developed the **National Incident Management System** (NIMS) in an effort to ensure some measure of consistency and a more effective response. The system provides guidelines on how incidents are to be managed. The Department of Homeland Security envisions that the *National Response Framework* and the National Incident Management System would interface and provide a cohesive approach to an emergency response.

HS Web Link: To learn more about the National Incident Management System, go to *http://www. fema.gov/emergency/nims//*

As noted, the Department of Homeland Security attempted to develop a system that had continuity. The department identified six attributes for the system, which are listed in Figure 13-7.

The NIMS contains five primary components: (1) preparedness, (2) communications and information management, (3) resource management, (4) command and management, and (5) ongoing management and maintenance. Each of these components is addressed next.

Preparedness

Preparedness centers on a unified approach whereby the NIMS structure is integrated into agencies' emergency operations. Agencies should achieve some level of preparedness relative to communications, resource management, and command. It also requires that agencies are capable of providing varying or scalable levels of service, depending on the magnitude of the incident. Agencies should take stock of their resources, human resources, supplies, command structure, and interoperable relationships among agencies and ensure that they have the capacity to respond to an incident. It also includes the development of plans and procedures, ensuring that first responders are trained and properly equipped, and the development and maintenance of mutual aid agreements for all governmental and nongovernmental agencies. It is most important that all parties potentially involved in an emergency response fully and completely understand their roles and responsibilities. Essentially, preparedness is a matter of coordinating the various components prior to an incident.

- A comprehensive, nationwide, systematic approach to incident management, including the Incident Command System, Multiagency Coordination Systems, and public information
- A set of preparedness concepts and principles for all hazards
- Essential principles for a common operating picture and interoperability of communications and information management
- Standardized resource management procedures that enable coordination among different jurisdictions or organizations
- Scalable, so it can be used for all incidents (from day-to-day to large scale)
- A dynamic system that promotes ongoing management and maintenance

---

FIGURE 13-7 Attributes of the NIMS. *Source:* Department of Homeland Security. (2008c). *National Incident Management System.* Washington, D.C.: Author, p. 6.

Communications and Information Management

Communication is critical to a well-coordinated and effective response. The Department of Homeland Security (2008a) advises that agencies should have a **common operating picture**:

> A common operating picture is established and maintained by gathering, collating, synthesizing, and disseminating incident information to all appropriate parties. Achieving a common operating picture allows on-scene and off-scene personnel— such as those at the Incident Command Post, Emergency Operations Center, or within a Multiagency Coordination Group—to have the same information about the incident, including the availability and location of resources and the status of 373 assistance requests. (p. 23)

An emergency response communications system should have several qualities. First, it must have interoperability—various agencies must be able to communicate with one another. One of the primary impediments in the response to the 9/11 World Trade Center attack was that various first responders could not communicate—fire, police, National Guard, and other responders used different radio channels or frequencies, which prevented them from communicating with other first responder organizations. The problem was exacerbated when the city's communication center was destroyed; it was located in one of the World Trade Center towers (Simon and Teperman, 2001). This was a primary obstruction in recovery efforts. Second, the communications system must be reliable and flexible so that first responders and managers can communicate in all sorts of conditions. Third, communications systems should be resilient and reliable under different conditions, and there should be some level of redundancy so that communications could be maintained if one section or system becomes inoperable.

National Guardsmen deliver supplies during a flood disaster.   *Source:* http://www. photolibrary. fema.gov/photolibrary/photo_details.do?id=40321

Resource Management

It is important to realize that the response to a disaster incident, especially a large-scale incident, requires immense amounts of resources. This includes resources needed for the initial response through recovery. Moreover, these resources must be made available almost immediately. For example, first responders, victims, and the displaced must be fed, housed, and otherwise receive care. In some cases, supplies must be shipped from locations that are hundreds if not thousands of miles from the site. Logistics are complicated, but nonetheless, must be managed effectively. Figure 13-8 graphically shows this process in action.

As shown in Figure 13-8, resource management for an incident is a rather complicated endeavor. Once an incident occurs, requirements must be identified, and there is a wide array of requirements or materials that may be needed to mediate the situation. How many and what types of personnel are needed—military, law enforcement, fire, paramedics, medical, search and rescue, heavy equipment operators, and so on? What types of equipment will be needed—heavy equipment to move debris, communications, temporary shelter for victims and rescue personnel, electric generators, vehicles to evacuate the displaced and injured, and so on? A substantial volume of supplies will be required—water, food, temporary shelter, medical supplies, gasoline for equipment and evacuation vehicles, and so on. Obviously, the type and size of the incident will dictate the resource requirements. Nonetheless, resources must be made available at the scene as quickly as possible to effectively mediate or attend to the situation.

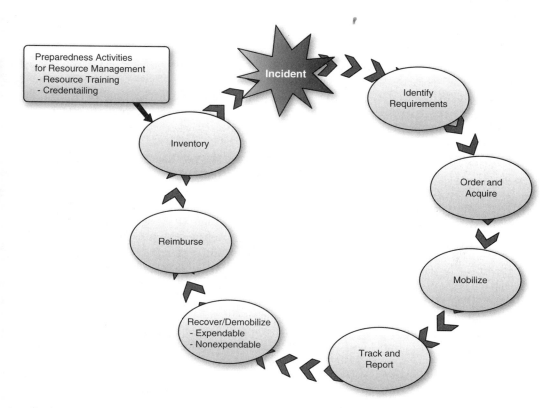

FIGURE 13-8   Resource Management During a Disaster or Attack.   *Source:* Department of Homeland Security. (2008c). *National Incident Management System.* Washington, D.C.: Author, p. 35.

Analysis Box 13-5

It is important for those responding to a disaster that they have adequate resources to respond and mitigate the conditions. This usually requires large amounts of supplies. Agencies often are criticized when they order too many supplies because of the costs or too little supplies resulting in an inadequate response. How can responding agencies determine how many supplies to order? Should they err on the side of too many or too little given today's environment of limited resources?

Once an inventory of resources has been determined, resources must be acquired. Some resources will be available locally, whereas others may have to travel from hundreds or thousands of miles from the site. They must be tracked to ensure that they arrive on a timely basis. Once resources are ordered and acquired, they must be mobilized. That is, there must be an action plan that describes activities, responsibilities, and personnel who are involved in the recovery. Personnel must be matched with equipment and supplies in a deployable manner. The action plan should be of sufficient detail to ensure that all issues and problems are addressed. The plan must be comprehensive and address every detail; omissions often result in problems and in some cases injuries or the loss of life. Moreover, activities must be monitored to ensure that they are consistent with the plan. In some cases, as new problems are identified, the plan and activities will be adjusted. Once the incident has been mediated, there will be an accounting to determine levels and types of expenditures. It therefore is important to track and report on costs and activities. For example, FEMA was severely criticized in the wake of Hurricane Katrina for a number of wasteful expenditures that likely amounted to more than a billion dollars (Hall, 2006).

Once the incident has been controlled and the damage mediated, demobilization occurs. Excess stocks of resources are returned to vendors or stored for the next incident. Emergency response agencies must restock emergency supplies that are used during the initial response to the emergency. Personnel are returned home or sent back to regular service. Finally, government agencies, primarily the federal government, must pay for the expenses associated with the recovery effort.

MECHANISMS FOR REQUESTING AND RECEIVING ASSISTANCE DURING A MAJOR INCIDENT As noted, Figure 13-8 provides the resource management process during an emergency incident. However, it is important to examine the response processes when a disaster occurs. Figure 13-9 shows the flow of assistance and requests for help in a large-scale event. First, note that requests for assistance originate from the local emergency command center. The first response to any incident will include local first responder units and organizations. If the incident is significant, a local command structure will be established to evaluate, control, and respond. A judgment will be made if external assistance is required, whereupon requests will be made to the state and other jurisdictions that have mutual aid compacts with the affected jurisdiction. If state resources are not adequate, the governor will make a request to the regional FEMA director for assistance. FEMA representatives will evaluate the situation, and if warranted, request that the president declare a state of emergency. The federal response often includes assistance from several federal agencies. A joint field office is established to coordinate the federal response, which as noted, includes a wide range of activities and services.

As noted in Figure 13-9, once the assistance begins to flow to the incident, activities can be categorized as coordination and command. From a coordination standpoint, there is an increase in the number of agencies involved in the response as the size of the incident increases. Moreover, the agencies include local, state, federal, and private entities, and they are involved in a range of

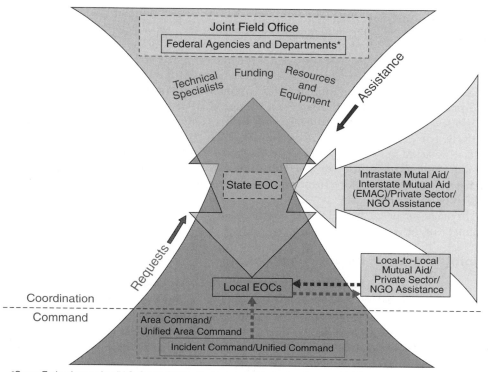

*Some Federal agencies (U.S. Coast Guard, Environmental Protection Agency, etc.) have statutory responsibility for response and may coordinate and/or integrate directly with affected jurisdictions.

FIGURE 13-9   Flow of Requests and Assistance During Large-Scale Incidents.   *Source:* Department of Homeland Security. (2008c). *National Incident Management System.* Washington, D.C.: Author, p. 36.

activities that comprehensively mitigate the problem at hand. Their efforts and responsibilities should fit together like pieces in a puzzle, and if there is a piece missing or services are not delivered as projected or needed, the response will be less than effective. In some cases, agencies do not operate as expected or there are significant delays in their response or initiation of operations. Sauter and Carafano (2005) identify instances when agencies are uncooperative with other agencies or squabble over operations or command and control. If such problems occur, they become problematic for the recovery.

Command and Management at an Incident

The National Incident Management System attempts to standardize incident management for all hazards and incidents across governments. A standardized format results in enhanced operational effectiveness since agencies' roles are predetermined and understood. The primary on-the-ground control mechanism is the **incident command system** (ICS). The ICS is the command center where all efforts to respond to and mitigate an incident are coordinated. Fire and police departments have used such structures for decades when responding to a critical incident. It encompasses agencies, personnel, communications, equipment, procedures, and a unified command structure. When operated correctly, an ICS reduces the probability of errors and affords better coordination of effort. It results in the establishment of overall and agency goals and objectives and results in a cohesive management and operational plan.

HS Web Link: To learn more about the incident command system, go to *http://training.fema.gov/ EMIWeb/IS/ICSResource/ index.htm*

The ICS results in unity of command whereby one individual is identified as being responsible for overall command and coordination. In the past, this has not always occurred; there would be squabbling among the various agency heads or representatives as to which agency was the lead agency. In some cases, it became extremely complicated when local, state, and federal agencies became involved. Implementation of the ICS requires that an incident commander be identified, and the incident commander is responsible for commanding and coordinating all response activities. Even though the ICS is part of the National Incident Management System, questions remain as to whether command will be assumed smoothly and effectively. For example, in most responses, FEMA is charged with coordinating the federal effort, a position assumed by FEMA managers during hundreds of incident responses. However, if the incident involves weapons of mass destruction requiring a response from the military and federal law enforcement officers, it remains to be seen if command will be ideally coordinated or assumed.

In major incidents, the ICS system consists of a number of sections. Figure 13-10 provides a schematic of the workings of a large ICS.

Ongoing Management and Maintenance

In large incidents, the incident commander will have a command staff generally consisting of public information, safety, and liaison officers. The public information officer is responsible for communicating with the public. It is important for response personnel to communicate and advise citizens who are affected by the incident about what is happening, especially in volatile or changing conditions. People need to be informed of evacuation plans and routes, shelter, where to obtain food and water, and how medical care is being provided. One of the early mistakes in Hurricane Katrina was that citizens in affected areas were not given this information in a timely fashion. The public information officer is able to gain citizens compliance and cooperation in the recovery effort.

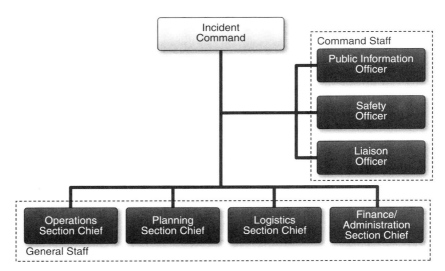

FIGURE 13-10 Incident Command Center Staffing and Organization. *Source:* Department of Homeland Security. (2008c). *National Incident Management System.* Washington, D.C.: Author, p. 53.

The safety officer is responsible for advising the incident commander about safety issues, especially concerning response procedures and personnel. There are always dangers when personnel are working in devastated areas. The safety officer ensures that emergency workers do not take chances or endanger themselves or others. The liaison officer is responsible for maintaining contact with the various agencies involved in the response to ensure that coordination is maintained. The liaison officer is constantly communicating with the various agencies and relaying problems and information to the incident commander.

In addition to these officers, there generally are four section chiefs: (1) operations, (2) planning, (3) logistics, and (4) finance and administration. The operations chief is responsible for the tactical operations. This individual actually coordinates recovery efforts. The planning section chief collects, evaluates, and disseminates information about the incident. This is especially critical in a biological or chemical incident. Also, as an example, when floods occur, the flooding may continue and even increase for several days. It is important to map and plan for changes with the continued flooding. The planning section chief is responsible for keeping other responders updated on such situational changes. The planning chief also is responsible for ensuring that all the necessary equipment is acquired. Finally, this individual must plan for demobilization.

The logistics section chief is responsible for ensuring that necessities such as food, water, shelter, and support are available for emergency workers and victims and those who are evacuated or without adequate supplies and services. The logistics chief is also responsible for ensuring that there are working communications to coordinate relief efforts.

Finally, the finance and administration section chief is responsible for a number of financial activities. First, this chief is responsible for procuring food, water, and other expendables and items

Emergency operations center in San Antonio, Texas, after Hurricane Ike.   *Source:* http://www.fema.gov/photodata/low/38184.jpg

First responder teams participate in emergency drill. *Source:* AP (05050704152)

such as temporary shelter. Orders for material must be placed with a variety of geographically dispersed vendors. If adequate supplies are not acquired, the recovery effort will be substantially hampered. This individual is responsible, at least initially, for processing victims' claims for food, shelter, and other necessities. The financial section chief has a significant pecuniary responsibility, which includes accounting to ensure that funds are spent properly and within legal guidelines.

This section provided an overview of the National Incident Management System. The system provides an operational and organizational structure for responding to critical incidents. It was developed by the Department of Homeland Security to ensure some level of consistency of purpose and coordination during incident responses.

MEDICAL RESPONSE TO CRITICAL INCIDENTS

Hospitals, like police and fire departments, are open and available 24 hours a day. As such, they have come to be seen as an indispensible resource for the public in terms of receiving care in the event of a medical emergency. Hospitals are operated so as to handle a constant flow of traffic or patients. In some cases, staffing will change during certain periods of the year or even days of the week, such as Fridays and Saturdays, when minor spikes occur in demand for services. However, should there be a major incident such as a WMD attack, hospital resources would quickly be

Analysis Box 13-6

It appears that hospitals and medical services throughout the United States are not prepared to respond to a major event such as a radiological or biological attack. Primary care facilities would be quickly overrun with casualties. Given that such events have a low probability of occurring, what should we as a nation do, given that the development of medical services and facilities is a very expense proposition?

overwhelmed. Moreover, unlike other emergencies, the demand for exaggerated levels of medical care would continue for a longer period of time. Medical resources would very quickly be exhausted.

In one study, Treat et al. (2001) surveyed a number of hospitals to determine their readiness should there be an incident such as a WMD attack. The survey showed that 73 percent of the hospital respondents believed that they were not prepared for a nuclear or chemical incident. None of the hospitals reported being prepared to respond to a biological attack. Only one hospital had stockpiled medicines for a WMD attack. Approximately 80 percent of the hospitals reported that their emergency rooms would be able to handle between 10 and 50 victims at a time. The research demonstrated that hospitals in the sample were aware of the potential WMD problems and had taken some actions, but overall, they were not prepared to handle a major event. A significant biological, chemical, or nuclear attack could result in hundreds of casualties that would require immediate treatment.

Steps have been taken to at least partially solve this problem. The Office of Emergency Preparedness in the Department of Health and Human Services has established a **National Disaster Medical System.** The system consists of a number of teams that would respond to medical disasters. Several thousand volunteers comprise various types of teams: disaster medical assistance teams, national medical response teams, burn teams, pediatric teams, crush medicine teams, international medical-surgical teams, mental health teams, veterinary medical assistance teams, and disaster mortuary teams. The teams comprise a national network with some of the teams able to respond within 12–24 hours (Knouss, 2001). Even with the availability of these teams and medical support from other governmental and private entities, a large incident could result in a number of medical care problems.

HS Web Link: To learn more about the National Disaster Medical System, go to *http://www.phe.gov/ Preparedness/responders/ ndms/Pages/default.aspx*

NATIONAL RESPONSE TEAMS

As discussed earlier, the *National Response Framework* and the National Incident Management System were developed by the Department of Homeland Security to provide for a more uniform coordinated response to some hazard or incident. Implementation of these two systems, especially during an event, requires a substantial level of coordination and cooperation among a potentially large number of agencies that may not be immediately available. Past experiences demonstrate that achieving the desired and necessary levels of cooperation likely will fall short of expectations (Donahue and Tuohy, 2006; Sauter, and Carafano, 2005). Although the two systems represent a comprehensive, rational approach to hazard response, they remain cumbersome and at least to some degree, bureaucratic (see Sobel and Leeson, 2006). The systems likely will operate more effectively when small or medium-sized hazards occur, but it is questionable if they can sustain the level of required services in the event of a large-scale hazard.

Emergency medical team prepares for disaster.   *Source:* http://www.phe.gov/Preparedness/responders/ndms/Pages/default.aspx

Crowe (2008) has suggested an alternative strategy, one that could be used as a supplement in the event of a large-scale event. He advocates the creation of **national strike teams**, especially for low-probability, high-consequence events. Since such events occur so infrequently, it is difficult for localities and states to prepare and maintain preparedness for them. Moreover, there is such a wide range of possible occurrences, including floods, earthquakes, hurricanes, tornados, chemical attacks, biological attacks, and nuclear attacks, that it is difficult for jurisdictions to maintain a constant state of readiness since each type of hazard will require, at least to some degree, a different set of response tactics. Crowe provides an excellent example:

> Rather than spending an estimated ten billion dollars nationally to achieve basic bioterrorism preparedness, national mass prophylaxis strike teams could be created and mobilized in association with activation of the Strategic National Stockpile. Each team would be comprised of individual experts who receive training, support, and equipment to establish regional and national teams. The national mass prophylaxis teams would be moved into areas impacted by a bioterrorism attack to provide life-saving medications within the necessary window of twenty-four to forty-eight hours. This would eliminate the possibility that local jurisdictions are unable to provide the equipment and personnel to execute mass prophylaxis in the timeframe required to be life-saving. (p. 3)

Strike teams could be created for different kinds of hazards and dispersed regionally across the nation. By concentrating on the development of these teams as opposed to preparedness in every locale, we likely would have a less expensive, but more effective response to potential events or hazards. Strike teams would result in a paradigm shift. Heretofore, the policy has been that emergency management and response to events was a local responsibility with the state and federal governments providing assistance in the event of major catastrophes. Thus far, the federal government has been reluctant to assume this responsibility. Nonetheless, strike teams appear to have a number of advantages over current policies, particularly a more effective response to low-probability, high-consequence incidents.

Summary

This chapter examined the response to catastrophic events, including natural, human-made, and terrorist originated. In recent years, our country has witnessed a number of such events, particularly the New York City and Washington, D.C., terrorist attacks and Hurricane Katrina on the Gulf coast. Each year numerous natural disasters result in emergency declarations, but most are not of the magnitude of the 9/11 attacks or Hurricane Katrina. Nonetheless, we must be prepared to respond to all sorts of hazards of various magnitudes. This is especially true considering that our country has been attacked, and terrorists likely will attack us again in the future.

All disasters or catastrophes occur in a local community, and as such, local personnel are the first to respond. Today, federal policy places the brunt of responsibility for mediating these occurrences with local and state governments; the federal government sees its role as one of assistance. Obviously, some of these occurrences quickly overwhelm local responders' capabilities, necessitating state and federal assistance. In the past, unified responses—the combined efforts of the many agencies involved in a response—to some degree have been haphazard. In an effort to rectify this situation, the Department of Homeland Security developed the *National Response Framework* and the National Incident Management System.

The *National Response Framework* attempts to provide a framework for responding to hazards. It essentially identifies the numerous agencies across levels of governments that are involved in a response. The *Framework* advises that it is important for roles and responsibilities to be identified and the various responding agencies' efforts to be coordinated.

The *Framework* attempts to identify the pre-event actions such as training, equipping, and organizing that must occur if there is to be an effective response to a hazard. Past responses have shown that coordination and assignment of responsibilities have been two areas that have significantly impeded responses.

The National Incident Management System attempts to ensure consistency in the strategies and tactics used in a response. Whenever a catastrophe occurs, responders must be organized and tactically prepared to respond. The National Incident Management System provides a framework that contributes to consistency and effectiveness in terms of on-the-ground tactics. It enumerates the functions that must occur and where responsibilities are vested. The baseline for a response is the incident command system, and the implementation of the incident command system entails a variety of functions. The system does provide an operating structure that can contribute to the successful response to an event.

Even though the *National Response Framework* and the National Incident Management System provide excellent guidance on responses, gaps and problems remain. For example, we see that our medical capabilities are deficient, especially in the event of a large-scale disaster. Crowe (2008) has suggested that we supplement current strategies with national strike teams. Such teams can be quickly deployed and would have the requisite expertise and equipment required to respond to various types of catastrophes. Regardless, it appears that our response mechanisms are a "work in progress." We must continue to scrutinize our capabilities and their effectiveness in future responses.

Discussion Questions

1. Critique our response to Hurricane Katrina.
2. Describe the functions of the *National Response Framework*.
3. When a major disaster occurs, the federal government will use a layered response. What is a layered response and how does it work?
4. Explain the preparedness cycle that is part of the *National Response Framework*.
5. Exercising is a part of preparation for a catastrophe. What is it and what are the limitations associated with exercising?
6. What are the various procedures by which federal assistance is provided during a disaster?
7. Describe the components and function of the incident command system.

References

Bellavita, C. (2008). "Changing homeland security: What is homeland security?" *Homeland Security Affairs*, 4(2): 1–30.

Birkland, T. and S. Waterman. (2008). "Is federalism the reason for failure in Hurricane Katrina?" *Publius*, 38(4): 692–714.

Bullock, J., G. Haddow, D. Coppola, E. Ergin, L. Westerman, and S. Yeletaysi. (2005). *Introduction to Homeland Security*. Burlington, MA: Elsevier.

CNN. (2005). *Leadership vacuum stymied aid offers*. http://www.cnn.com/2005/US/09/15/katrina.response/ (Accessed January 6, 2009).

Crowe, A. (2008). "National strike teams: An alternative approach to low probability, high consequence events." *Homeland Security Affairs*, 4(2): 1–5.

Department of Homeland Security. (2010). *Quadrennial Homeland Security Review Report*. Washington, D.C.: Author.

Department of Homeland Security. (2008a). *National Response Framework*. Washington, D.C.: Author.

Department of Homeland Security. (2008b). *Overview: ESF and Support Annexes Coordinating Federal Assistance in Support of the National Response Framework*. Washington, D.C.: Author.

Department of Homeland Security (2005). Interim National Preparedness Goals: Homeland Security Directive 8: National Preparedness. Washington, D.C.: Author.

Department of Homeland Security. (2008c). *National Incident Management System*. Washington, D.C.: Author.

Donahue, A. and R. Tuohy. (2006). "Lessons we don't learn: A study of the lessons of disasters, why we repeat them, and how we can learn them." *Homeland Security Affairs*, 2(2): 1–28.

Hall, M. (2006). "Senators hear 'shocking examples' of FEMA waste." *USA Today* (February 13). http://www.usatoday.com/news/nation/2006-02-13-katrina-report_x.htm (Accessed January 29, 2009).

Knouss, R. (2001). "National disaster medical system." *Public Health Reports*, 116: 49–52.

Lindsay, B. (2008). *The National Response Framework: Overview and Possible Issues for Congress*. Washington, D.C.: Congressional Research Service.

Office of Homeland Security. (2002). *The National Strategy for Homeland Security*. Washington, D.C.: Author.

Pickup, S. (2006). *Hurricane Katrina: Better Plans and Exercises Need to Guide the Military's Response to Catastrophic Natural Disasters*. Washington, D.C.: GAO.

Sauter, M. and J. Carafano. (2005). *Homeland Security: A Complete Guide to Understanding, Preventing, and Surviving Terrorism*. New York: McGraw-Hill.

Schermerhorn, J. (2008). *Management* (9th ed.). New York: Wiley.

Schneider, S. (2008). "Who's to blame? (Mis) perceptions of the intergovernmental response to disasters." *Publius: The Journal of Federalism*, 38(4): 715–38.

Simon, R. and S. Teperman. (2001). "The World Trade Center attack: Lessons for disaster management." *Critical Care*, 5: 318–20.

Sobel, R. and P. Leeson. (2006). *Flirting with disaster: The inherent problems with FEMA* (Policy Analysis No. 573). Washington, D.C.: Cato Institute.

Treat, K., J. Williams, P. Furbee, W. Manley, F. Russell, and C. Stamper. (2001). "Hospital preparedness for weapons of mass destruction incidents: An initial assessment." *Annals of Emergency Medicine*, 38: 562–65.

Homeland Security and Policing

LEARNING OBJECTIVES

1. Understand the role of law enforcement in combating terrorism.
2. Know why community policing is an important part of the police response to terrorists.
3. Describe how terrorism and homeland security have affected police organization.
4. Understand intelligence-led policing.
5. Know how police tactics are affected by the threat of terrorism.

KEY TERMS

Community policing

Problem solving

SARA model

Community partnerships

Police liaison officer

Multiculturalism

Public education

Citizen academies

Inventory of the critical infrastructure

Intelligence-led policing

Tactical intelligence

Strategic intelligence

Fusion center

INTRODUCTION

Homeland security represents a major operational area for state and local governments. In the event of a terrorist attack or major disaster, state and local officials are among the first to respond—they represent the "boots on the ground." During this initial response, officials must control the situation and attempt to mitigate damage. It may take days or even weeks, as in the case of Hurricane Katrina, for the necessary federal assets to arrive on the scene. This places a substantial burden on local and state resources, which are limited and often inadequate, especially if there is a substantial event. Additionally, although the federal government has developed plans to prevent attacks, prevention remains a crucial responsibility for local law enforcement that must be considered in the decision-making matrix. Planning must be integrated across political subdivisions of government whereby federal agencies work closely with local law enforcement.

In addition to attempting to mitigate the effects of a terrorist attack, the police are charged with its investigation. A terrorist attack is indeed a crime scene and must be handled as such. Evidence must be collected and safeguarded. Witnesses must be identified and interviewed. If possible, officers must arrest perpetrators or if unable to make an arrest, identify suspects. Even though federal agencies such as the Federal Bureau of Investigation and the Bureau of Alcohol, Tobacco, Firearms, and Explosives likely will be involved in the investigation, if local officers do not play a primary role, they certainly will have a secondary role and be intimately involved in any investigation. As we will discuss, police departments have vast and wide-ranging responsibilities should an attack occur.

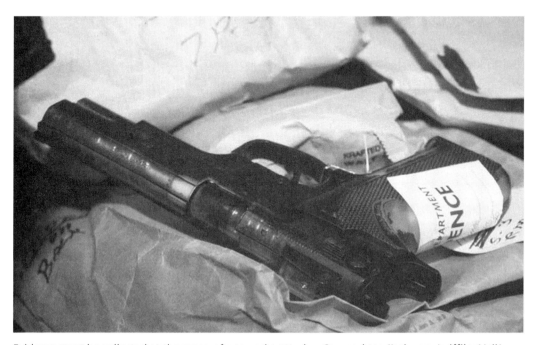

Evidence must be collected at the scene of a terrorist attack.   *Source:* http://ncjrs.gov/pdffiles1/nij/230409.pdf

The federal government has approached homeland security from a top-down perspective. The federal government, to a large extent, has focused on identifying and apprehending terrorist suspects in the United States and abroad. The federal government has moved in the areas of airline security and is mounting efforts in border security. Additionally, the federal government has developed plans to protect critical infrastructure, including the *National Infrastructure Protection Plan,* and provided grants to states to enhance their antiterrorism capabilities, but the federal government for the most part will provide support, not primary responsibility for protecting most infrastructure. This responsibility falls squarely on local law enforcement.

Substantial consternation exists over the role local agencies play in protecting local assets. However, we must "think globally and act locally" (Carter, 2004). Essentially, attacks on a local asset can come from anywhere in the world. Even though many think that terrorist groups that would do harm to America are located mostly in the Middle East, groups across the globe might attack the United States, and groups within our country could mount terrorist attacks against our infrastructure and citizens, as discussed in Chapter 6. Local authorities will assume a large amount of the responsibility to prevent an attack and mitigate its effects should an attack occur. In terms of prevention, many local police departments as a result of community policing have close relations with segments of communities. Community policing plays a key role in preventing terrorist attacks via fostering positive relations with citizens and the collection of intelligence.

COMMUNITY POLICING AND TERRORISM

Community policing, according to most research, is the dominant modality by which police departments deliver services. For example, Hickman and Reaves (2006), using a survey of American police departments, found that almost 70 percent had a mission statement that included community policing, 50 percent had a formal community policing policy as a part of their standard operating procedures, and almost 60 percent had full-time officers assigned to community policing activities. Police departments throughout the country have committed to community policing, and based on its acceptance, it would appear that it has provided departments with dividends.

HS Web Link: To learn more about community policing and terrorism, go to *http://www. homelandsecurity.org/ journal/articles/Scheider-Chapman.html*

Kappeler and Gaines (2009) advise that the two key ingredients in community policing are problem solving and community partnerships. **Problem solving** means that the police will not only respond to calls for service, but will actively attempt to solve the problems that cause calls, disorder, and crime. Goldstein (1979, 1990) advocates problem solving, noting that the police have to go beyond simply answering calls because such activity essentially is wasteful; at the end of the day, nothing is accomplished. The police must root out the causes of crime and disorder and attend to those causes. This results in a safer community. It also reduces police workload since once problems are corrected, they do not result in additional calls or crimes.

The primary mode of operation for problem solving is the **SARA model**, which includes (1) scanning, (2) analysis, (3) response, and (4) assessment (Spelman and Eck, 1989). First, the environment is scanned for potential problems. Scanning can consist of examining crime maps and crime statistics, querying police officers, and talking with people about the problems in their neighborhood. Once problems are identified, they are analyzed. The analysis attempts to identify the magnitude of the problem and its root causes. Additionally, possible solutions are identified. All possible solutions are considered, and the final selection of a solution is based on how well the solution will ultimately solve the problem. Third, the solution is operationalized. This may entail the reassignment of officers, implementation of a new program or tactic, or the implementation of a crime prevention effort. In some cases, the response will consist of several tactics. Finally,

HS Web Link: To learn more about the SARA model, go to *http://www. popcenter.org/about/?p=sara*

once the response has been implemented, it should be assessed to ensure that it in fact solved the problem. Did the symptoms of the problem, calls for service, disorder, or crime decrease? Problem solving is a focused approach to law enforcement, and this focused approach can play a role in combating possible terrorism.

The second ingredient in community policing, **community partnerships**, can play a key role in fighting terrorism at the local level. Community partnerships suggest a positive relationship between the police and the public. Here, the police must foster close, positive relations with all neighborhoods and groups in the community. In some cases, relations must be repaired if problems existed in the past. It means that the police need to listen to people and solicit their input regarding police priorities. In the past, the police have dictated policing priorities without regard to people's perceptions of problems and issues. The police should tackle problems that are of the utmost concern to residents. This means that the police should work cooperatively with community members in identifying and solving problems. Most problems are complex, and viable solutions require community participation. The police must get people involved. Finally, in some cases, the police must work to build communities. Many neighborhoods are in social disarray. The police must identify community leaders in these neighborhoods and work to build these neighborhoods and make them more viable. Essentially, the police must inoculate communities from crime. This means making them stronger and more resistant to the social conditions that contribute to crime and disorder. These conditions will also reap rewards in providing homeland security (see Kappeler and Gaines, 2009).

There are ample examples of where positive community relations have assisted the police when dealing with crime problems. Brown (2007) provides the example of John Allen Muhammad and John Lee Malvo. In the fall of 2002, Muhammad and Malvo terrorized the Washington, D.C., area by randomly shooting and killing several people. The situation was so grave that the government applied all sorts of resources to apprehend them, including roadblocks and surveillance by military aircraft. They were apprehended only after the suspects' vehicle was identified and the information made public; two cooperative community members heard the information and called 9/11 to report the suspects' whereabouts. Many criminal cases are solved as a result of community cooperation, which has long been recognized as an important ingredient in successful law enforcement.

Community Policing and Homeland Security

On its face, it might appear that preventing terrorism at the local level is the antithesis of community policing. That is, a "war on terrorism" requires that police officers use intrusive, aggressive, and militaristic tactics to ferret out terrorists and terrorist plots. Such tactics often alienate people who are the subject of them. Brown (2007) suggests that such tactics may lead to the mistreatment of people. Some police officials may equate the war on terrorism with a military

---

Analysis Box 14-1

It appears that community partnerships are an important part of policing and homeland security. Most communities in America are heterogeneous, with numerous racial, ethnic, and religious groups. Are there any groups in your community with whom the police should attempt to develop better relations? How do they differ from the majority in the community? What actions should the police take to develop better relations?

exercise requiring such tactics. However, we find that preventing terrorism is actually complementary with community policing (Murray, 2005; Pelfrey, 2007). The police, to a large extent, must depend on the public to supply terrorist-related information to effectively thwart local terrorist plots.

The police for the past decade or so have moved to a more militaristic model that is counterintuitive to community policing. This move had its roots in "broken windows" policing (Wilson and Kelling, 1982). Broken windows policing posits that the police should attend to minor crimes and disorder since these problems are the precursors to more serious crimes (see Gau and Pratt, 2008). Disorder results in crime in two ways. First, it demonstrates to potential law violators that there is little or no guardianship—no one is concerned enough to report crime or cooperate with the police should a crime occur. Second, substantial disorder results in an increase in fear of crime and fewer people in public spaces; guardianship is reduced. A number of police departments, including large departments such as New York City and Los Angeles, adopted this philosophy. It was operationalized by having officers concentrate on or take more enforcement actions for minor offenses such as loitering, panhandling, vagrancy, and public drinking and intoxication. Taken to extreme limits, it resulted in zero tolerance policing (see McArdle and Erzen, 2001) whereby the police used little discretion and enforced most if not all laws. It was implemented under the guise of community policing, but in actuality, it resembled traditional law enforcement. Although if used selectively, it could be successful in problem solving, but for the most part, it has been used to generate arrest and citation statistics.

We must consider that terrorists operate by stealth. They attempt to remain hidden until they commit their crimes. Moreover, they blend in with the population. The police must depend on the public to observe and report suspicious activities. In many instances, citizens become aware of suspicious persons and activities before the police. Community policing fosters reporting and cooperation with the public, which are necessary if the police are to prevent a terrorist attack.

POLICING ARAB COMMUNITIES

Historically, the United States has been painted as the world's melting pot where immigrants from all over the world have embarked on new lives. Many came to America to escape political or religious persecution, whereas others came to make a better life for their families and themselves. Although it may be comforting to think of the nation as a melting pot, America is more like a patchwork of people and places. Immigrants coming to America often cleave together for economic and social support. Any large city in America has dozens of ethnic groups oftentimes living in enclaves, which are named after the dominant group living there—"China Town," "Little Italy," or "German Town." These enclaves are an essential part of the country's landscape. Even today, as the nation grapples with protecting the borders, one must remember that for most of us, our ancestors immigrated to this country.

The United States has a history of ethnic tensions, particularly with the African American and Latino populations. Ethnic tensions substantially worsened for people of Arab descent after the 9/11 attacks. There have been numerous incidents in which Arabs were attacked and assaulted. This criminal behavior was not limited to one area, but occurred across the country. Moreover, many non-Arabs were attacked. A number of Asians and people of other nationalities have been mistaken for Arabs and attacked by people with racist views who were frustrated by the 9/11 attacks. Thus, these populations can be a unique problem for law enforcement.

Prior to the 9/11 attacks, one substantial controversy in American law enforcement was racial profiling. Numerous studies showed that African Americans and Latinos were stopped and investigated by police at greater rates than white citizens (Gaines, 2006). After 9/11, the controversy subsided and public opinion shifted to substantial approval for racial profiling for Arab and Muslim people. There was tacit approval for violating civil rights. The rule of law was replaced by hysteria clamoring for security from terrorists or to derive revenge for the 9/11 attacks.

HS Web Link: To learn more about policing Arab communities, go to *http:// www.ncjrs.gov/pdffiles1/ nij/221706.pdf*

Comparatively speaking, the United States does not have a large Arab population. The 2000 census found that approximately 1.2 million Arabs live in the United States. Approximately half of American Arabs are of Lebanese or Palestinian descent. In larger American cities, Arabs constitute less than 1 percent of the population, but a number of cities have substantial populations. For example, Dearborn, Michigan, has the highest concentration with more than 29,000 Arabs, constituting 29 percent of the city's population (American-Israeli Enterprise, 2008). Dearborn has the largest concentration of Arab people compared to any other American city. As a result, it has faced a number of law enforcement challenges and provides a window by which to examine the challenges of policing in Arab communities.

Dearborn's large Arab population attracted a substantial amount of attention, especially from the media. The attention resulted in a great deal of suspicion. The media questioned the patriotism of the Arab population in the city. This attention came not only from the media and racists but also from the federal government. Dearborn's government was acutely aware of the problems resulting from the 9/11 attacks. Mayor Guido warned citizens not to commit hate crimes. Police patrols were increased around mosques, the Arab business district, and schools with large Arab student populations. Police and governmental officials met with community leaders to dispel any concerns that the police would not protect the community. A number of Arab leaders requested parade permits to hold a march in support of the United States after 9/11, but the city dissuaded them from doing so for fear of riots and altercations (Thatcher, 2005). In the end, city officials and the police department saw protecting people as the paramount issue. Human Rights Watch (2002) noted that of six cities with significant Arab populations that it studied, Dearborn responded adequately to the threat of hate crimes. Unfortunately, in many cities, the police and other officials have not been as proactive as those in Dearborn. In November 2001, the U.S. Justice Department announced plans to interview temporary visa holders from countries thought to have a substantial al-Qaeda presence. The purpose of the interviews was to gather information believed to be fruitful in the war on terror. Eventually, more than 300 Dearborn residents were interviewed. The Dearborn Police Department cooperated with the interviews to ensure that they proceeded professionally. City officials were able to convince the local U.S. attorney to make several changes in the interview procedures to reduce the amount of negativity they produced. The interviews received substantial media coverage and again resulted in enhanced suspicions and a great deal of public consternation (Thatcher, 2005). There is no evidence that the interviews produced anything other than anxiety on the part of Arab Americans and advanced racist sentiments.

Henderson, Ortiz, Sugie, and Miller (2008) examined policing in Arab communities. They found four obstacles to positive relations between the police and Arab communities: (1) distrust between Arab American communities and the police, (2) lack of cultural awareness, (3) language barriers, and (4) concerns about immigration status and fear of deportation. It is important for the police to have positive relations with all segments of a community. Given the levels of anger and racism after the 9/11 attacks, it is important for the police to work more closely with Arab communities to foster better relations and to ensure adequate levels of protection for Arab people.

The police must bridge the gap between themselves and Arab and other ethnic communities and reduce distrust. The primary mechanism for accomplishing this is to improve communication.

Individual officers, commanders, and administrators should informally reach out and attempt to establish communications with the minority community. Police officials should also attempt to establish formal contacts and relations. This can be accomplished by implementing community forums and advisory committees such as those formed in cities such as Portland, Oregon; Los Angeles; and Seattle. These meetings should be held in the community as opposed to police or governmental facilities. This instills a higher level of trust. It also engenders greater participation from the community. It is also important for line-level officers to be involved, since they have the most contact with Arab people. Distrust can be reduced when police officials have an open door policy that allows people to voice their concerns; when concerns are voiced, it is important for the police to address them. Hollow responses only antagonize people and contribute to increased distrust. Finally, the appointment of a **police liaison officer** can help to reduce distrust. A liaison officer in effect becomes the advocate for the community. As an advocate, the officer can work closely with community groups, generate support, and identify problems that otherwise may not have been identified. The liaison officer can also help in recruiting Arab Americans for the police department and other governmental positions. Inclusion is one of the most effective means of reducing distrust.

The police have a long history of being accused of lacking cultural awareness. In the 1990s and early 2000s, many police departments developed cultural awareness training programs in the wake of the accusations of racial profiling or "driving while black" controversies. **Multiculturalism**, "the embracing of cultural diversity, a willingness to coexist with people from different backgrounds and cultures, and the celebration of difference, centers on whether [it] divides a society or unifies it" (McNamara and Burns, 2009, p. 7.). When a department polices an ethnic community, it must attempt to embrace cultural differences and unite the community. This is best accomplished by understanding cultural differences and understanding how to treat and interact with people. Police officers must understand that many Arabs do not embrace many aspects of American culture, and in some cases, police behavior is an affront to their beliefs or way of life. Proper training can minimize culture conflict.

Language barriers abound. For example, people in Los Angeles speak more than 80 languages. When there is a significant ethnic population, police departments must ensure that they can communicate with people. In cities with large Arab populations, the department should take steps to provide language training for some of its officers. A number of cities with large Latino populations have developed training programs to teach officers Spanish. Learning the language or at least critical phrases and words can be a significant factor in communicating and developing relations in Arab communities. Departments with large Arabic-speaking populations certainly must have enough translators so that the department can effectively communicate with people, and the departments should produce their critical literature in Arabic. Too often police officers take the view that it is the responsibility of immigrants to learn English and be able to communicate. However, learning a new language takes time, so there is inevitably a communications gap. Police effectiveness depends on good communications, so the police often must bridge this communications gap if they are to be effective public servants.

Another major barrier to effectively serving some ethnic communities is that many people fear that the police will have them deported or otherwise alter their immigration status. Because of this fear and the wedge it creates between the police and the community, a number of police departments have not cooperated with Immigration and Customs Enforcement (ICE) programs requiring police officers to check the immigration status of people. The primary reason for this reluctance is that when the police cooperate with immigration officials, people are less likely to cooperate with the police. As noted earlier, cooperation between the community and the police is essential to effective law enforcement. The police are placed in an awkward position as they attempt to balance immigration laws and gaining community cooperation.

Analysis Box 14-2

The immigration debate in the United States has become rather heated. Some areas, such as Arizona, are strictly enforcing immigration laws; other communities have left such enforcement to the ICE. Those who are not enforcing laws see them as an impediment to law enforcement. Which position do you think is better for American law enforcement? Can these two perspectives be balanced so that both objectives can be met?

HOMELAND SECURITY PUBLIC EDUCATION PROGRAMMING

For a police department to have an effective homeland security program, it must involve members of the community. Terrorist attacks are preceded by unobtrusive activities that include surveillance, dry runs, and the acquisition of the materials with which to conduct the attack. In one study, Smith (2008) found that, on average, terrorists perform 44 such activities prior to an attack. These activities blend into usual daily activities, making it difficult to discern terrorist activities from normal activities. Nonetheless, law enforcement must implement measures that attempt to identify possible terrorists during these pre-attack activities. This requires substantial public cooperation and participation. To gain this community participation, the police must educate the public and provide guidance. Public education is paramount in preventing crime and terrorist attacks.

Public education in the realm of homeland security serves a number of functions, including (1) fear reduction, (2) reduction of community tensions, and (3) encouragement of people to provide the police with valuable information. Police departments must devise several public education programs and plans since every community consists of different ethnic groups, neighborhoods, and population groups. Public education programming must target these groups. One type of program may work with one group, but not with others. Therefore, it is important to ensure that everyone is exposed to this programming and reports suspicious activities to law enforcement. Care, however, must be taken that these programs do not advance racist sentiments or needless fear.

Public education programs should have specific goals. The primary goal is to elicit support and information from the public regarding crime and terrorism matters or intelligence. Not only must the police prepare the public to report suspicious activities, they must also educate them about terrorism. When people are informed, they are more likely to report credible information and are less prone to panic or engage in behavior that results in community problems. Such training should have a component that reduces senseless fear of terrorist attacks. The probability of terrorists attacking any city is close to zero. The police need people to take a rational approach when soliciting their cooperation. Carter (2004: 48) advises that these programs should encourage people to engage in the following behaviors:

1. Know how to observe
2. Know what is suspicious
3. Know how to report
4. Know what to report
5. Know what happens next

Some departments have established **citizen academies** to help educate people (Bumphus, Gaines, and Blakely, 1999). These academies are open to the public and can serve as an excellent tool for informing the public and gaining trust and support. However, not every neighborhood or group may be represented in these academies and the department must devise several different modes for educating the complete spectrum of groups in the community. Other public education modalities include disseminating pamphlets describing what community members can do to assist the police. All public outreach and education programming should include realistic and factual information about the terrorist threat and governmental responses. Finally, community forums and speakers bureaus should be used to impart information. Police departments should approach public education comprehensively. The primary objective of these programs is to get people to report suspicious persons and activities. The police have long used similar programs in the war on drugs and to solicit assistance in apprehending wanted criminals.

Lyon (2002) advises that the police especially should develop programs in communities or neighborhoods that are likely to harbor terrorists. In addition to obtaining information, cooperation from these communities could assist in developing an intelligence network in close proximity to possible problems. For example, the police in Dearborn likely have developed close ties to the Arab community because any possible terrorists in the area will have some ties to the community. Terrorists, be they homegrown or foreign, will likely attempt to integrate themselves into the community to avoid discovery.

A prime example of how public education programs can produce positive results occurred in New Jersey. On May 9, 2007, the Federal Bureau of Investigation (FBI) arrested six suspects who had planned to attack and kill soldiers at Fort Dix. The initial investigative lead was supplied by an alert clerk who was asked to copy a videocassette onto a DVD. The cassette contained footage of the suspects training for their attack. The alert store clerk notified the police, which resulted in an extended FBI investigation and subsequent arrests. This incident exemplifies how law enforcement can obtain valuable intelligence information from the general public.

One of the problems with these types of programs is that in some cases police departments receive many more calls or tips than can be processed. The failure of police to respond to calls results in lowered evaluations of police performance and a reluctance to call the police in the future. Additionally, only a relatively few number of calls result in an investigation. The reporting of "suspicious" persons or possible terrorists becomes even more problematic because some people will make reports based on race and not on actual suspicious activities.

EXAMINING POLICE CALLS FOR SERVICE FOR TERRORIST LEADS

As noted, the police should be interested in suspicious activities. When people observe and report these behaviors, they generally do so using the police department's 9/11 emergency telephone number. Large cities receive thousands of calls each year. It is important for police departments to begin examining these calls for possible terrorist activities. For the most part, this has not been occurring. When a department receives a call about a suspicious activity, the dispatcher will send an officer to investigate. If a crime is not occurring, the officer generally will not do anything. Moreover, these types of calls often receive a low priority so it may be some time before an officer investigates. These suspicious activities generally fall below the radar.

There is a need to develop a mechanism to examine these calls. Hollywood, Strom, and Pope (2008) conducted a preliminary study using Washington, D.C., Metropolitan Police data. They examined 1.3 million calls for service. First, they isolated all calls that included a suspicious person, suspicious vehicle, suspicious package, bomb threat, and other similar calls. This resulted in identifying 100,000 calls. These calls were then examined for other identifiers. They looked for key words such as surveillance, video, photography, taking notes, and using binoculars when examining the suspicious persons and vehicle calls. For the suspicious package calls, they looked to see if explosive ordnance demolition teams were called or if area traffic was restricted. This second round of examinations resulted in 1,200 calls being identified. A more detailed examination resulted in the number being reduced to 850. The other 350 were eliminated as the suspicious activities were explained, as normal work, tourism, misplaced luggage, and so on. The remaining calls were considered possible terrorist activities.

Next, the researchers examined the time of day for the calls and their locations. The calls were also examined to determine if they clustered in a particular area. The researchers then developed a scale to evaluate the calls: (1) atypicality of reported activities, (2) attractiveness of target, (3) whether the call was part of a cluster (multiple surveillance activities), and (4) whether a police report was taken. Applying the calls to the scale resulted in six calls being considered highly probable and several other calls that were highly suspicious. The locations where suspicious activities occurred included bridges, the train station, hospitals, hotels, a military base, and a public safety center.

Although the research did not identify any targets that were ultimately attacked by terrorists, it demonstrated that data mining of police calls for service could produce investigative leads. Future research should focus on automating and refining these techniques. Data produced from such analyses could provide pre- and post-attack information. The research also demonstrates that police department computer-aided dispatch and automated records systems should collect more information than they currently do.

FEMA representative consults with police sergeant while mitigating flood problem.   *Source:* http://www.photolibrary.fema.gov/photolibrary/photo_details.do?id=40336

POLICE EFFORTS TO SAFEGUARD LOCAL CRITICAL INFRASTRUCTURE

Numerous potential infrastructure targets exist in a given location. At some point, local police departments will take **inventory of the critical infrastructure** within their communities. As noted in Chapter 3, the DHS has attempted to develop a national database, but thus far, the efforts have fallen short largely due to a failure to identify workable criteria for the inclusion of specific infrastructure assets as well as political considerations. Communities will need to identify assets and develop response plans, especially given the numerous potential targets that may exist in a given jurisdiction and that attacks on different types of targets present dissimilar challenges to the police and other first responders. Thus, it is important for local police departments to create a catalog or database of all possible terrorist targets in the jurisdiction, especially those that would result in significant damage, loss of life, or economic losses if attacked.

The identification of these critical infrastructure assets serves two primary purposes. First, the database allows the department to comprehensively develop response plans. A police department should have a response plan in place for each of the types of infrastructure locations. These plans should include the roles and responsibilities of all first responders, including hospitals, emergency medical services, utilities, fire, public works, and so on. Second, it results in focusing attention on areas that are of interest to possible terrorists. Once assets are identified, the police department should focus intelligence operations near and around the locations. It is very likely that if a terrorist plans to attack an asset, he or she will conduct reconnaissance. As discussed earlier, reports of suspicious behavior around these locations should be thoroughly investigated. Due vigilance may result in the terrorist being identified before the attack is consummated.

Police departments currently have critical incident response plans for responding to natural disasters, airplane crashes, and many major crimes such as hostage situations. These plans include information about command and control, tactical responses, and use of other support agencies such as disaster, medical, fire, and chemical and radiological personnel. It is important that these plans are consistent with the National Incident Management System as discussed in the previous chapter. These plans are flexible in that they can be used to deploy resources for a host of problems anywhere within a jurisdiction. Police agencies use these plans sparingly as there are only a few instances that call for their application.

Donahue and Tuohy (2006) note that these plans often fail for a variety of reasons, including uncoordinated leadership among the various responding agencies; failed communications, including inoperability of communications systems and a lack of desire for agencies to communicate with one another; weak planning, whereby plans are developed in a vacuum without the benefit of "real-life" experiences; and resource constraints since most emergencies of any magnitude quickly strip a jurisdiction's resources to maintain a maximum response. Donahue and

---

Analysis Box 14-3

There are likely terrorist targets in most communities in the United States. They can be population gatherings, key industries, large businesses, shopping malls, and so on. If you were given the task of identifying possible targets in your community, what would you include on your list? What criteria would you use to include them on the list?

Tuohy note that some of these problems can be overcome through tabletop exercises or drills. However, when these drills occur, critiques are generally conducted piecemeal, with each agency examining its response as opposed to the total response, and the critiques generally focus on what went right as opposed to identifying and documenting failures and problems. Police agencies must examine their critical incident response plans and ensure that they are comprehensive and applicable to terrorist threats or attacks. Pelfrey (2005) advises that planning is the most critical aspect of homeland security. Many departments often are well equipped but do not have adequate plans in place.

Nonetheless, police agencies will begin to catalog the critical infrastructure assets in their communities. Although appearing to be a straightforward process, it likely will be a taxing endeavor as demonstrated by the failed efforts by the DHS to build a national critical infrastructure asset database. Not only must officials identify these assets, they must also examine vulnerabilities. For example, what impact would a bombing of a natural gas transmission line or a petrochemical plant have in a given city? As previously noted, much of this critical infrastructure is privately controlled, and police departments often do not have access to information and the facilities or the technical expertise to evaluate different terrorist scenarios.

HS Web Link: To learn more about private security and policing, go to *http://policechiefmagazine.org/magazine/index.cfm?fuseaction=display_arch&article_id=1048&issue_id=112006*

Partnerships Between Law Enforcement and Critical Infrastructure Security Personnel

Private security is mentioned here because it is a significant force in public security and safety. Each year more is spent on private security than on public police departments, and the private sector employs larger numbers of personnel than public police departments (Morabito and Greenberg, 2005). Policing and private security are not necessarily mutually exclusive domains. For example, Green (1981: 25) has defined the role of private security as, "those individuals, organizations, and services other than public law enforcement and regulatory agencies that are engaged primarily in the prevention and investigation of crime, loss, or harm to specific individuals, organizations, or facilities." This definition shows that there is substantial overlap between private security and the police. Private security continues to grow, and its role in public safety is enhanced as the result of homeland security and terrorism threats.

Many of these private security personnel are assigned to guard much of the critical infrastructure in this country, and this critical infrastructure would likely be a terrorist's target. Historically, there has been little cooperation or communication between the police and private security personnel even though they, to some extent, have parallel responsibilities. However, the threat of terrorism and the need to secure critical infrastructure are beginning to change this perspective. Now, police departments are encouraged to develop formal working relationships with private security firms. Such relations would (1) improve joint responses to critical incidents, (2) coordinate infrastructure protection, (3) improve communications and data interoperability, (4) bolster information and intelligence sharing, (5) prevent and investigate high-tech crime, and (6) devise responses to workplace violence (Ohlhausen Research Inc., 2004).

It is logical for the police to develop and formalize these relationships. The police and private security personnel have common goals, and to a great extent, the private security personnel are more informed about problems, critical points, and vulnerabilities for particular facilities as compared to the police. Many of these facilities have controlled access and activities; therefore, security personnel are more likely to observe people and actions that are out of the ordinary or suspicious and independently or in cooperation with the police investigate them. At a minimum, the police need to be aware of those facilities that are target hardened through private security and have procedures that include private security personnel when responding to those installations.

Partnerships with the police are critical. Some of the activities that must occur are as follows:

1. Cooperative training on the development and implementation of potential terrorist profiles.
2. Mapping potential targets in a jurisdiction to include security assets.
3. Development and coordination of critical incident plans outlining responses to acts of terror and disasters.
4. Better communication between law enforcement and the private security industry.
5. Ensuring that the police and private security share intelligence information as it relates to a specific critical infrastructure.
6. Identifying security assets in the private sector that can be used by police to combat possible terrorists.
7. Identifying the ramifications (destructive, human, and economic) of an attack on specific critical infrastructure assets.

A number of departments now have cooperative relationships with private security. The Dallas Police Department has training workshops for police officers and security personnel. In Las Vegas, police officials meet monthly with hotel security personnel to discuss training, crime, and security problems (Morabito and Greenberg, 2005). To date, most of the partnerships between the police and private security have focused on business districts and retail outlets. Not enough has been done to develop programming with high-value targets such as communications centers, manufacturing facilities, petrochemical plants, and so on. Many of these targets have security operations that are quite sophisticated and elaborate, but the police often know little of their operations. Moreover, many of these facilities have closed-circuit television monitoring that could provide the police with valuable information about possible terrorist operations. The police must do a better job of integrating their operations with area security operations.

Although everyone in law enforcement is well aware of domestic terrorism, few departments have initiated comprehensive planning and programming. Threats of terrorism likely will remain for the next several decades, and the police must enhance their capabilities to respond to them. Private security will play a key role in this new priority.

Local agencies must develop strategies and policies to deal with homeland security and counterterrorism. As noted, it is the local agencies that at least initially will be responsible for response and protection. Police departments will be the first agency to respond to a terrorist attack. If police departments are to effectively deal with terrorist attacks and homeland security issues, they first must have organizational mechanisms in place that facilitate an effective response.

POLICE ORGANIZATION AND TERRORISM

Police departments are complex organizations, and they are structured to facilitate the accomplishment of goals. They have high levels of specialization, and specialized units are created to perform specific functions associated with groups of tasks (Gaines and Kappeler, 2008; Gaines and Worrall, 2011). Given the critical nature of homeland security, it is incumbent on police departments to establish a homeland security unit or in smaller departments, ensure that these tasks are assigned to a multitask unit. The department's structure must be reengineered to ensure that homeland security becomes an embedded activity. Certain homeland security activities must be accomplished. Police departments must be organized so that they can prevent terrorist attacks, or when they are unable to prevent them, they are in a position to mitigate their impact. Given today's climate, the public expects the police to be prepared if an attack occurs.

There is some question as to how rapidly police departments are incorporating homeland security and the war against terrorism in their organizational mantra. For example, DeLone (2007) examined the mission statements for a number of large police departments and found only one department had added this important mission. Marks and Sun (2007) examined references to organizational change and discovered similar findings. Only the larger departments were changing their organization to better incorporate homeland security and terrorism within the organization. Ortiz (2007) examined a number of departments' adaptation of homeland security and found that they incorporated homeland security mechanisms in varying degrees. For the most part, they conducted business as usual. The most significant change was that they exhibited more cooperation with federal agencies such as the FBI and DHS on homeland security issues. The research indicates that police departments have been slow to incorporate homeland security, and it appears that they remain preoccupied with traditional policing responsibilities.

The specific responsibilities for the homeland security unit and its commander should be clearly enumerated. This is accomplished by the promulgation of policies and procedures. The policies will list the responsibilities of the commander and the organizational resources that are available to complete required tasks. Moreover, these policies should enumerate the working relationships with other units in the police department. They should enable the homeland security commander to directly contact other units to obtain information and assistance. A clear chain of command should be established.

As noted, the homeland security unit will have a number of specific responsibilities, including

- Manage terrorist and homeland security information, including intelligence
- Maintain a database of critical infrastructures and their vulnerabilities
- Maintain working relations with critical infrastructure owners, managers, and security personnel
- Maintain liaison with state homeland security officials
- Maintain liaison with federal intelligence agencies such as the FBI and the Joint Terrorism Task Forces
- Coordinate department responses to terrorist events
- Coordinate police activities with those of other first responder agencies
- Identify homeland security training needs for the department
- Conduct or coordinate homeland security–related investigations
- Monitor the readiness of the police department and other first responders in the event of a terrorist attack
- Investigate terrorist attacks or activities

A number of police departments have integrated homeland security into their organization. For example, Figure 14-1 shows the Cleveland, Ohio, Police Department's homeland security structure.

In Cleveland, the Division of Police is organized into four operations with homeland security being one of the major operational areas. The operational area contains seven units divided into three sections. There basically are two types of units within the homeland security operational area: intelligence and operational response units.

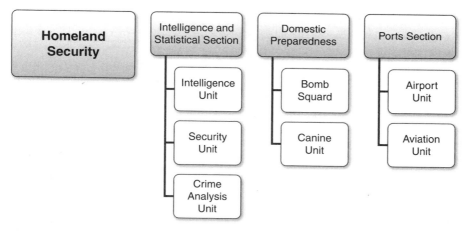

FIGURE 14-1 Cleveland, Ohio, Police Department Homeland Security Organization.
Source: Adapted from http://www.city.cleveland.oh.us/clnd_images/Police/police_org.pdf

Figure 14-2 contains the homeland security Bureau for the Washington, D.C., Metropolitan Police Department.

The homeland security unit in the Washington, D.C., Metropolitan Police Department is much larger than Cleveland's unit. This primarily is because Washington, like a number of other major cities, has a greater potential for terrorist attack. Washington is the nation's capital with numerous domestic and foreign governmental operations and dignitaries. The department therefore must afford greater resources to homeland security.

The Homeland Security Bureau is commanded by an assistant chief and contains two divisions: Special Operations and Intelligence Fusion. The Special Operations Division contains units that would directly respond to a terrorist attack. The unit also contains normal daily operational responsibilities so that personnel's productivity is maximized. The Intelligence Fusion Division contains several units that are involved in collecting and analyzing intelligence. Some units are involved in intelligence within the jurisdiction, whereas other units collaborate with other federal agencies, for example, the Joint Terrorism Task Force (as discussed in Chapter 8) and the D.C. Fusion Center (fusion centers are addressed in more detail later in this chapter).

When establishing a homeland security unit, it is important that the commander have the rank and authority required to not only command the unit, but also to enable him or her to bridge the rank structure to gain cooperation with other units on homeland security activities. Officers assigned to a variety of units should be actively involved in some homeland security activities: (1) patrol, (2) criminal investigation, (3) crime analysis, (4) intelligence, (5) specialized tactical units (SWAT) including hostage negotiators, and (5) community relations and community policing. Members of these units must have a shared vision of the terrorist threat and the department's preventive responses. It is also important that the unit have close working relations with other community service organizations such as paramedics and emergency response, fire, street and road department, and social services. These agencies can provide primary and support services should there be a terrorist attack. Finally, the homeland security unit will be the agency's and jurisdiction's point of contact with state and federal agencies. These state agencies are the conduits for making requests for federal assistance from

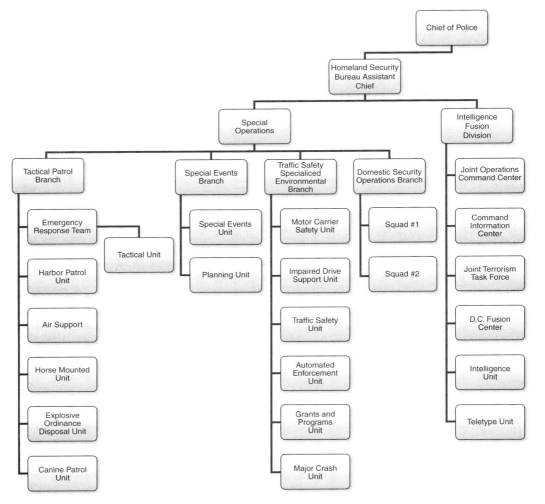

FIGURE 14-2   Homeland Security Bureau for the Washington, D.C., Metropolitan Police Department. *Source:* Adapted from: http://mpdc.dc.gov/mpdc/frames.asp?doc=/mpdc/lib/mpdc/about/org/pdf/MPD_main.pdf&group=1529&open

the DHS. A working relationship must be in place to facilitate any such requests. Having a police department homeland security unit allows for a more immediate state and federal responses should an event occur.

One of the functions of a homeland security unit is to identify and investigate suspicious persons, places, and activities that may be associated with terrorists. Patrol essentially is the "eyes and ears" of the police department. Patrol covers all parts of the jurisdiction 24 hours a day. Patrol officers have the most information about what is occurring on their beats. A working relationship with patrol officers results in more intelligence information being submitted to homeland security analysts. In the same vein, detectives investigating crimes may uncover suspicious activities and forward relevant information to homeland security officials. Crime analysis is a support function within police departments, and essentially, officers assigned to this unit examine crime trends

SWAT teams are a critical component of police homeland security.   *Source:* AP (100721035309)

temporally and spatially. They attempt to identify patterns of crime and behavior. The intelligence unit should work closely with the homeland security unit, or it or some of its activities could be incorporated into the homeland security unit. Intelligence units historically collected information about criminals and groups of criminals. Notably, these units collected information about organized crime, gang activities, and white-collar crime. Today, these units must devote resources to collecting information about possible terrorists and their activities. It is also critical to understand that today terrorist organizations have become intertwined with transnational organized crime, making the investigation of organized criminal syndicates even more important. Specialized tactical units are deployed when there is a dangerous criminal event such as a hostage taking, barricaded person, or drug or gang raid. These units possibly would be deployed should there be terrorist activities. They can collect valuable information during such a deployment that can be used by the homeland security unit to analyze the situation. Finally, community relations or community policing personnel have a substantial amount of direct contact with citizens and community groups. Such contacts can be useful in attempting to identify terrorists in a community. Thus, there are numerous units in a police department that can provide support and information to a homeland security unit.

In addition to establishing the internal workings of the intelligence unit, decisions must be made in terms of relationships with outside agencies, especially other local, state, and federal agencies that are involved in homeland security and antiterrorism investigations. There should be formal agreements specifying the types of information that can be shared. Generally, such

Analysis Box 14-4

Not all police departments have homeland security organizational units. Reasons for this might include the size of the department, the department's budget, and significant crime problems that must be addressed. What factors should a police chief consider when he or she is deciding on developing a homeland security unit within the department? Even if a department does not have such a unit, which of the functions mentioned should be added to other units in the department?

relations are set out in contracts or memoranda of understanding (MOUs) or in mutual aid pacts. A number of legal requirements must be fulfilled for these MOUs to be finalized with most of the regulation centering on maintaining the privacy of records. Federal requirements can be found in 28 CFR Part 23. Should an agency violate these requirements, it opens the agency and the intelligence function to civil litigation and public disclosure. In addition to a possible monetary loss, civil suits often result in the subpoenaing of all sorts of records that likely would jeopardize the unit's operations and intelligence.

As can be seen, the homeland security unit not only has primary functions, but it also serves to coordinate other police resources in protecting a community. This unit is an important addition to a police department in that it will help ensure that the department is ready to respond to a terrorist attack. Its primary responsibility is the collection and analysis of intelligence. Today, intelligence-led policing is the primary operational platform used by homeland security units to accomplish this task.

Officer monitoring crime data and other activities.   *Source:* http://www.ncjrs.gov/pdffiles1/nij/227725.pdf

INTELLIGENCE-LED POLICING

The 9/11 attacks on New York City and the Pentagon demonstrated that any location could be attacked. Even though the probability of an attack on a specific city is extremely low, all jurisdictions must be prepared for the possibility. Threat assessment at the local level implies that local police departments must become involved in identifying potential terrorists and suspect activities, although there is some debate as to whether terror intelligence gathering should be a federal function or should involve state and local agencies (Thatcher, 2005). Currently, police departments are improving their intelligence capacity through intelligence-led policing (Carter, 2004). **Intelligence-led policing** essentially is the enhancement of police intelligence-gathering capability. Most major police departments already have some form of intelligence-gathering capabilities. Intelligence-led policing dictates that departments not only begin collecting information about possible terrorists and possible targets, but that they should also enhance their intelligence-gathering and intelligence-using skills. It is logical to include possible terrorists and terrorist activities, especially considering that narcotics trafficking and other forms of organized crime are used to finance terrorism (Kleiman, 2004; McCaffrey and Basso, 2003).

One of the major difficulties for local departments in collecting terrorist intelligence is that unlike other organized crime groups, little is known about who might be a terrorist and his or her potential activities. For the most part, there is an absence of baseline data or information to guide intelligence and investigative activities. It is too late to gather information about possible terrorists once they have committed a terrorist act. Nonetheless, departments are encouraged to begin gathering information on "persons of interest" who fit some profile of terrorists. As witnessed with the 9/11 attacks, one undiscovered attack can result in the loss of thousands of lives. Local agencies cannot solely depend on the federal government to identify and prevent attacks.

Intelligence-led policing is compatible and complementary with community policing. Police officers across the country are now working more closely with citizens and communities. These relationships represent a vast reservoir of "eyes and ears" for the police. This not only enhances problem solving, but it represents a method to collect intelligence about suspicious persons and activities in a community. Intelligence gathered in the community can be collated and compared to other intelligence to provide a clearer picture of the activities in a jurisdiction. It is important for police managers and supervisors to reinforce this new mandate.

HS Web Link: To learn more about intelligence-led policing, go to *http://www.ncjrs.gov/pdffiles1/bja/210681.pdf*

The Intelligence Process

Essentially, intelligence is "the combination of credible information with quality analysis—information that has been evaluated and from which conclusions have been drawn" (IACP, 2002: v). Carter (2004) provides more depth to the definition:

> In the purest sense, intelligence is the product of an analytic process that evaluates information collected from diverse sources, integrates the relevant information into a cohesive package, and produces a conclusion or estimate about a criminal phenomenon by using the scientific approach to problem solving (i.e. analysis). Intelligence, therefore, is a synergistic product to law enforcement decision makers about complex criminality, criminal enterprises, criminal extremists, and terrorists. (p. 7)

Carter (2004) advises that intelligence analysis should focus on four important questions:

1. Who poses threats?
2. What are the relationships among possible actors?
3. What is the modus operandi of the threat?
4. What is needed to catch the offenders and prevent the incident?

These questions guide investigations and the intelligence process. It is a process that results in the identification of suspects and their co-collaborators, information about how they commit their crimes, and evidence required to make an arrest or prevent a crime or terrorist event. It is critical to homeland security. Although federal agencies such as the FBI are investigating conspiracies, local authorities must be attentive to suspicious activities in their communities, and intelligence-led policing best serves this purpose. The FBI and other federal agencies perform top-down investigations whereas local authorities conduct bottom-up investigations.

Intelligence is a process; it is not merely the accumulation of information and data. Information is collected from a variety of sources and used to produce useful information. Essentially, the intelligence process consists of four steps:

1. Collecting information from a variety of sources.
2. Collating and analyzing the information. That is, it must be organized in a usable format and then analyzed in an effort to garner intelligence or intelligence-related information.
3. Disseminating the information. It is not enough to develop intelligence information; it must also be provided to those who can use it to defeat a terrorist attack or develop policies.

Intelligence is a key component in defeating terrorists at the local level. *Source:* http://ncjrs.gov/pdffiles1/nij/230409.pdf

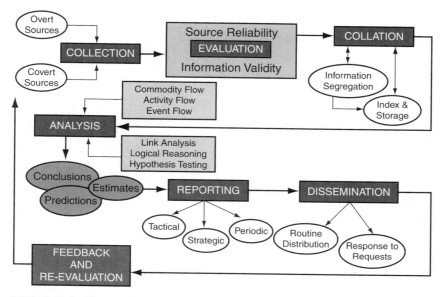

FIGURE 14-3 The Intelligence Process. *Source:* Carter, D. (2004). *Law Enforcement Intelligence: A Guide for State, Local, and Tribal Law Enforcement Agencies.* Washington, D.C.: Office of Community Oriented Policing Services, p. 64.

4. Using intelligence and other information. In some cases, agencies may be provided intelligence information, but fail to use it. In the end, intelligence must be integrated into strategic and tactical operations. This is why it is collected in the first place.

Figure 14-3 proves a diagram detailing the intelligence process.

Intelligence-led policing implies that it be more data driven. Although law enforcement has always been involved in crime prevention, the prevention of terrorist acts is much more critical. Not preventing a burglary is one thing, whereas failure to prevent a WMD attack is another matter altogether. This essentially means that the law enforcement community, at all levels, must be involved in gathering intelligence and using that intelligence to prevent terrorist acts.

Sources of Intelligence Raw Data

It is important to remember that intelligence information can come from a variety of sources. In some cases, a substantial amount of intelligence can be obtained from official agencies such as other law enforcement agencies. For example, the Federal Bureau of Investigation and the Department of Homeland Security maintain terrorist watch lists. A great deal of information can come from a variety of the sources, including

- Travel agents
- Department of Motor Vehicle records
- Property ownership records
- Financial records, including withdrawals and deposits, especially the source of deposits
- Credit card information in terms of what is being purchased and name and address of card holders

- Known associates
- Travel patterns—locally, regionally, and internationally
- Telephone and cell phone records
- Daily or routine activities
- Wiretaps

These activities or sources of information can produce large amounts of raw data. The intelligence officer attempts to collate the information, looking for suspicious patterns that might infer that an individual is involved in a terrorist or suspicious activity. *Link analysis* is one of the most useful methods of analyzing raw intelligence. Basically, a flow chart is constructed showing everyone that a suspect has contact with, and those individuals' contacts are also shown on the flow chart. In some cases, it shows that a suspect is in contact with other people who have relationships with still other suspicious individuals. There may be several degrees of separation, but ultimately the link analysis can identify a number of people who have relationships or who may be involved in a criminal or terrorist conspiracy. Link analysis, more or less, connects the dots and often can provide a wealth of investigative leads.

The old adage "follow the money" has driven a number of criminal investigations, especially those involving organized crime and drug trafficking. The adage is also true for terrorism. In some cases, terrorist or associates of terrorists are engaged in activities to raise money to finance terrorist plots. As discussed in Chapter 11, it is important to stop terrorist financing operations; in some cases, the investigation of terrorist finances leads to information about terrorist plots and activities. It is just as important from an intelligence perspective to focus on ancillary activities as actual terrorist plots and activities.

It should be noted that there are important rules to follow in the intelligence process. First, it is important to ensure that security it maintained. Obviously, terrorists or those supporting terrorist activities want to know if they have come to the attention of authorities, and they likely will take efforts to discover if they have been identified. If they believe that they have been compromised, they very likely will discontinue or alter their activities, thus negatively affecting the ongoing investigations. Along these lines, the media is constantly attempting to collect news information about continuing police investigations. There are those who would reveal information if given the opportunity, regardless of intentions or motivation. Intelligence information should be maintained on secure servers, and strict security should be maintained on any electronic or paper reports that are generated.

Second, one must consider intelligence information for what it is. In many cases, it is unconfirmed information. There may be instances when intelligence information will prove to be reliable; in other cases, it may not. In still other cases, the intelligence may point to a possible crime when indeed no crime has been or is about to be committed. The point is that the police should not base accusations on unconfirmed intelligence information. Before proceeding with charges or invoking criminal justice procedures, the police must establish probable cause. Without meeting this legal standard, the police may accuse an innocent person or reveal an investigation to a suspect before enough evidence has been gathered.

A third point is that intelligence units often collect any information possible. The homeland security unit commander should enumerate the kinds of intelligence information needed. Too often these units collect everything, which equates to little more than nothing. Priorities must be established. Priorities should be based on leads and other information that point to an individual, activity, or location. This is not to say that other information should not be collected, but it infers that there must be priorities and intelligence officers and analysts should pursue these priorities.

HS Web Link: To learn more about police intelligence operations, go to *http://www.it.ojp.gov/documents/LEIU_audit_checklist.pdf*

Intelligence Products

Once intelligence is collected, it must be disseminated to those who can use the intelligence to thwart a crime or terrorist activity. Such reports generally are written for a specific audience—patrol officers, detectives, private security personnel, or the general public. They should be written using the terminology that is commonly used by the group in clear language. If the information is to be useful, it must be understandable. The information should include a time line. That is, when is the event supposed to occur? In order to react, responders must have concrete information. Finally, there should be some follow-up. Intelligence officers or other management personnel should investigate what actions occurred as a result of the intelligence and its dissemination.

Three different products may be needed or used by intelligence officers:

1. Reports that aid in the investigation and apprehension of offenders or terrorists.
2. Reports that provide threat advisories in order to harden targets.
3. Strategic analysis reports to aid in planning and resource allocation.

Crime analysis and intelligence units must have products that are distributed on a regular basis. This ensures a steady flow of information to operational units, and it assists in maintaining contact with the operational units. In addition to the regular products, these units will produce special reports addressing specific individuals, geographical locations, and crime problems.

Tactical and Strategic Intelligence

Intelligence should be used at all levels of the police organization. **Tactical intelligence** is intelligence that is used to guide police operations. That is, if the intelligence unit acquires information about a specific crime or event, then that information will be used to guide officers or detectives to either intercede in the event or apprehend the perpetrators. The use of tactical intelligence is a central part of police problem solving, whereby officers attempt to predict criminal occurrences or patterns and respond to them. McGarrell and his colleagues (2007) and Smith and his colleagues (2006) advise that diligent police investigation and intelligence collection can uncover and prevent terrorist plots. Terrorist attacks are not spontaneous but often are preceded by months of planning, including surveillance by the terrorists. In the United States, about half of the terrorists committing attacks lived within 30 miles of their targets (Smith, 2008). Thus, intelligence can lead to tactical successes.

Strategic intelligence, on the other hand, is used by police managers. **Strategic intelligence** often provides a "big picture." It provides information on how resources should be allocated. It is important when a problem or series of problems occur that there are enough police resources to counter the problems. Strategic intelligence entails examining all potential problems related to crime and potential terrorism and ensuring that resources match the problems. Strategic intelligence is used to determine the number of patrol officers and detectives needed across time. It is also informative about whether the department needs specialized units—is there an adequate workload to justify the unit?

National Criminal Intelligence Sharing Plan

The *National Criminal Intelligence Sharing Plan* (NCISP) was devised to facilitate the exchange of information among criminal justice agencies relative to crime, criminals, and potential terrorists. In the past, numerous impediments prevented information sharing, as exhibited at the federal level. The Department of Homeland Security was created to facilitate operations and information sharing. Some of the problems in addition to a lack of communications include a lack of equipment to develop a national database, lack of standards for intelligence gathering and retention, lack of analysis, and poor relationships among agencies that possess intelligence information. The plan established procedures and lines of communication to facilitate the sharing of information. It essentially removed bureaucratic impediments that had existed.

FUSION CENTERS

The Federal Bureau of Investigation has developed cooperative relationships with state and local agencies across the country by establishing fusion centers. These centers act as multi-agency task forces that gather and analyze intelligence information. The benefit of fusion centers is that they generally are under the direction of the FBI, and the FBI can help ensure that the center's operations are safeguarded and operate within legal restrictions.

Fusion centers are a new innovation in intelligence collection. The **fusion center** is designed to facilitate the sharing and flow of information. The Department of Justice and the Department of Homeland Security (DOJ/DHS) (undated) note that fusion centers are part of a "process [that] supports the implementation of risk-based, information-driven prevention, response, and consequences management programs (p. 2). Essentially, they are an overarching network of public and private entities that are engaged in planning and implementing homeland security programming.

HS Web Link: To learn more about fusion centers, go to *http://www.it.ojp.gov/default. aspx?area=nationalInitiatives &page=1181*

The fusion center provides coordination of all response and counterterrorism elements within a community or metropolitan area. As information or intelligence gathered by local and federal agencies is fed into the fusion center, it is analyzed using the intelligence management model discussed earlier. The fusion center is a comprehensive approach in that it allows for the analysis of information from a variety of sources. It is the most comprehensive manner by which to collect and analyze data for a particular geographical area. Once analyzed, terrorist threat or activity information is generated and supplied to affected constituents. The fusion center also allows for more comprehensive planning and a better coordinated response should a terrorist event occur.

Of critical importance is that the centers include a variety of police, public safety, government, and infrastructure representation. A fusion center can have members from a variety of public and private sectors, and a fusion center's constituency generally is based on the primary public and private institutions that comprise a jurisdiction or metropolitan area. To this end, the DOJ/DHS (undated: 3) has identified the possible participants in a fusion center:

- Agriculture, food, water, and the environment
- Banking and finance
- Chemical industry and hazardous materials
- Criminal justice
- Education
- Emergency services
- Energy
- Government
- Health and public safety
- Hospitality and lodging
- Information and telecommunications
- Military facilities and defense industrial base

- Postal and shipping
- Private security
- Public works
- Real estate
- Social services
- Transportation

The goal is to include all the parties that may be involved in a terrorist attack, and to gain information from all the sources by which to develop strategies and response plans. For example, fusion centers generally include medical and fire department personnel as well as law enforcement personnel. The medical personnel can provide the fusion center with information about suspicious diseases or illnesses—an early warning system for a biological attack—and the firefighter personnel can provide information about suspicious fires or chemical problems.

A number of fusion centers have been constituted. Some are confined to a single city or metropolitan area; some are regional or provide services to a state. Cities and counties have partnered with the Federal Bureau of Investigation to form terrorism early warning groups or fusion centers (Sullivan, 2006). In some cases, they are part of a Joint Terrorism Task Force, which is operated by the FBI. It is critical that the FBI be involved in the fusion center or have some formal relationship with law enforcement personnel since one of its primary responsibilities is to collect terrorist intelligence and investigate terrorist activities.

POLICE TACTICAL CONSIDERATIONS

Previous sections in this chaper addressed some of the administrative and strategic considerations when attempting to implement an effective local homeland security program. A number of tactical considerations should also be mentioned. They focus on responding to a terrrorist attack and officer safety. Since police officers are on the front line, they could become terrorists' targets. Even if they are not the primary targets, they often become victims while responding to terrorist attacks. Indeed, a number of police officers and firefighters lost their lives in the 9/11 attack on the World Trade Center. The threat of terrorism brings new dangers to police officers and firefighters.

Over the past several years, a new trend has developed in terrorism worldwide: a transition from numerous low-level incidents to more destructive attacks. Today, terrorists think in terms of attacks that receive worldwide attention. They seek to show their followers that they can inflict significant harm on their enemies. Their goals are simple: produce mass casualties, attract intense media coverage, cause social unrest, and inflict economic and political harm.

Police officers confronting terrorists in the United States now find themselves vulnerable in six types of situations (Garrett, 2002):

1. *Traffic stops:* Law enforcement lacks prior knowledge of the individual being stopped; the officer may be isolated and the potential terrorist may be in a heightened state of suspicion or anger as a result of the stop.
2. *Residence visits:* Officers are on the extremists' home turf, putting them at a disadvantage; the visit may be routine, but the extremist may not view it as such, and the home may be armed and fortified.
3. *Rallies/marches:* The risk to police usually comes not from the group holding the event, but from protestors, often anarchists who hate the police and believe that the best way to confront the demonstrators is through physical violence.
4. *Confrontations/standoffs:* All such incidents can arise from the three previous situations.

5. *Revenge and retaliation:* A terrorist may be motivated by personal benefit or revenge, such as one who attempts to blow up an Internal Revenue Service office because he or she was audited.
6. *Incident responses:* These can take many forms, ranging from activities of terrorists to acts of nature.

Police departments must ensure that responses to these threats are incorporated into training. Officers must understand and be able to respond to any new threat, especially in terms of officer safety. Since terrorist attacks are very infrequent and have occurred in only a few American cities, most police officers likely are complacent.

Immediate Police Response to an Act of Terrorism

As noted, a number of weapons can be used in a terrorist attack, and the police must be prepared for all of them. Moreover, the police must coordinate their response with that of other first responders such as fire, emergency medical, hospitals, and disaster agencies at the local, state, and federal levels. Obviously, the type of attack will influence the response. For example, a biological attack will necessitate a response that is different from a conventional explosives attack. Nonetheless, there are some guidelines that should be followed. Figure 14-4 provides the general guidelines that law enforcement should follow when responding to a terrorist attack.

The Suicide Bomber: The Police Response

The suicide bomber represents a special problem to law enforcement since such events often involve numerous innocent bystanders and the perpetrator has maximum control over the situation. Suicide bombings have been one of the primary terrorists tactics, as discussed in Chapter 5.

If First on Scene:

- Isolate/secure the scene, establish control zone
- Establish command
- Stage incoming units

If Command Has Been Established:

- Report to Command Post
- Evaluate scene safety/security (ongoing criminal activity, secondary devices, additional threats)
- Gather witness statements and document
- Institute notifications (FBI, explosive ordnance squad, private security, and so forth)
- Request additional resources
- Secure outer perimeter
- Control traffic
- Use appropriate self-protective measures
- Initiate public safety measures (evacuations as necessary)
- Assist with control/isolation of patients
- Preserve evidence
- Participate in a unified command system with fire, medical, hospital, and public works agencies

---

FIGURE 14-4 Law Enforcement's Emergency Response to Terrorism. *Source:* Adapted from U.S. Department of Justice, Federal Emergency Management Agency. (1999). *Emergency Response to Terrorism: Self-Study.* Washington, DC: Author.

They have resulted in numerous deaths of civilians, police officers, and military personnel. They often are planned to inflict the maximum number of casualties. They are a particular threat since they can strike anywhere, necessitating officers from all jurisdictions to be tactically prepared.

When most people think of suicide bombers, they envision people from the Middle East; however, a number of such attacks in the United States have been attempted or carried out by British or American citizens (Spahr, Ederheimer, and Bilson, 2007). In 2001, Richard Reid attempted to ignite explosives in his shoe while flying from Paris to Miami. He was subdued by a fellow passenger. In 2005, a man walked into a federal courthouse in Seattle with a backpack strapped to his chest and a grenade in his hand; police officials shot and killed him. In 2005, a student with explosives in a backpack blew himself up outside a packed university football stadium. Finally, in a controversial incident, U.S. air marshals killed a man at Miami International Airport who claimed to have a bomb. Although these incidents are few in number, they demonstrate that non-Muslim suicide bombers remain a potential threat.

Figure 14-4 provides guidelines for responding to terrorist activities. It is especially important that these guidelines be followed. It is of particular importance that officers ensure the safety of any civilians as well as themselves. This means there should be a maximum evacuation area as it is not possible to gauge the powerfulness of the explosives. Moreover, it is important that the SWAT team and bomb squad be called immediately.

New York City K-9 officer patrols subway. *Source:* AP
(03031804536)

NEW YORK CITY: A CASE STUDY IN LOCAL HOMELAND SECURITY

A terrorist event in the United States is likely to take place in a major city such as New York, Chicago, Los Angeles, or San Francisco. The 9/11 attacks that occurred in New York City raised that city's awareness. City and police officials are acutely aware that their city remains a high-priority potential target for terrorists, with numerous potential targets, including Wall Street; city, state, and federal buildings; sporting events; high-density housing; a mass transit system that carries more than 6.5 million passengers daily; and petrochemical facilities. Consequently, the city has made a number of changes to prevent future attacks or to enable it to respond should a future attack occur. It is illustrative to examine some of the actions New York City has taken, especially considering that the city likely has instituted more safeguards as compared to other cities.

First and perhaps foremost, the New York Police Department (NYPD) has reorganized to include several homeland security elements within the department. The department has more than 37,000 police officers with approximately 1,000 assigned to terrorist duties. One of the tactics used by these officers is the "surge." Essentially, each day about 200 officers are sent to a specific location, usually a potential terrorist target. They surge in the area as a show of strength and deterrence. Officers observe and investigate suspicious persons and activities. Along these same lines, the department has increased the number of bomb-sniffing canines and routinely deploys them throughout the city. The canines serve as a deterrent as well as possibly locating explosive materials.

The city is proactively using counterterrorism tactics in its mass transit system. Each week, NYPD officers conduct more than 300 explosive-screening deployments. Here, officers physically check bags, briefcases, and other containers or conduct an external swab of the containers for explosives reside. NYPD transit bureau supervisors are provided with radiation sensors and random radiological screening occurs on facilities. Various mass transit facilities are inspected daily to ensure that all alarms and access control systems are operational. Canine units are often used in mass transit to detect explosives (Falkenrath, 2007). Essentially, the department has substantially increased its efforts to deter attacks and to detect potential attackers. This is important since some terrorist attacks involved mass transit.

The NYPD is actively involved in gathering intelligence about terrorists and terrorist operations. The department created a Counterterrorism Bureau that has analysts and detectives examine terrorist organizations, potential terrorists, and bomb-making technology. The department has dispatched officers to a number of foreign countries to work with counterterrorism personnel in those countries. For example, when the Madrid bombing occurred, the NYPD officer in Israel was immediately dispatched to Madrid, collected intelligence information, and forwarded it back to the Counterterrorism Bureau. The information collected overseas may likely be helpful in detecting and preventing attacks in New York City. The NYPD Counterterrorism Bureau cooperates with federal agencies but is not dependent on them.

The city is also deploying an array of security hardware. It is initiating the Lower Manhattan Security Initiative, which resembles London's Ring of Steel. Essentially, security cameras are being installed throughout portions of the City. Eventually, there will be about 3,000 cameras with approximately 2,000 owned by private businesses. The London Metropolitan Police Department used similar cameras to identify suspects after the subway bombings in 2005. New York City is also considering movable roadblocks that can be activated remotely should a terrorist or other crime problem occur. In the future, the NYPD may install facial recognition programming to enhance the identification of suspected terrorists or criminals. The city is also installing radiation detection devices around its ports of entry to screen cargo for nuclear materials.

Analysis Box 14-5

A number of civil rights groups have been critical of New York City and other cities because they believe that cameras are a violation of privacy. Further, they believe that the purported benefits do not outweigh the disadvantages. They question if the camera will provide useable information. Should cities install camera systems to observe what is occurring on the streets? How effective are such camera systems in your estimation?

New York is ahead of other major cities in the United States. It has essentially gotten in front of the Department of Homeland Security. City officials see New York City as a plausible target and are attempting to prevent terrorist attacks. This move has resulted in a different NYPD. Counterterrorism is now one of its primary objectives. It is likely that other major cities will follow New York's lead. Most major cities are creating homeland security units, but few are as advanced as New York City's.

Summary

This chapter examined the role of the local police in homeland security. First response to terrorist attacks was addressed in Chapter 13. As noted, homeland security creates new demands on the police. The police must often balance aggressive police tactics when implementing homeland security tactics with maintaining positive community relations. Community policing is not antagonistic to homeland security. Community policing helps build police-community relationships that can result in the provision of intelligence about possible terrorists and their activities. Thus, in a time of a need for homeland security, community policing as a police strategy is even more important, especially when implemented in Arab minority communities.

In order to effectuate homeland security, the police must involve the community. This is accomplished through education programs. The police must provide accurate and useful education. The intent of these programs is not to generate fear, but to provide the public with the tools and understanding by which to assist the police. The public can provide valuable assistance to the police when they identify individuals who may be conducting surveillance on a possible target. This means that the police must educate citizens on observation methods and how to distinguish suspicious activities.

Police departments must be organized in such a fashion that the homeland security function is conducted properly. This generally means establishing a specialized unit within the department or having someone in charge of homeland security operations. Homeland security personnel must have effective working relationships with other units since officers assigned to other units can provide valuable intelligence information. Policies should enumerate the unit's responsibilities and authority. These policies should address all aspects of homeland security, thus ensuring that all important functions are conducted.

Intelligence will play an important role in localized homeland security. This means that the homeland security personnel should be collecting, collating, analyzing, and disseminating intelligence to officers in the department. This function is not foreign to police departments. Many departments have intelligence and crime analysis units that collect information about organized crime, gangs, and drug trafficking. It must be ensured that terrorism intelligence is integrated into this process. Many departments now are joining the Federal Bureau of Investigation and other regional agencies to form fusion centers. These fusion centers operate as regional terrorism intelligence centers. They provide an interface among federal agencies, local law enforcement, and other first responder agencies. This holistic approach results in superior coordination in intelligence and response operations.

Discussion Questions

1. What is community policing and how can it be useful in combating terrorism?
2. Describe the programs in Dearborn, Michigan that attempted to mediate tensions between the public, police, and Middle Eastern community.
3. Homeland security education programs are an important part of preventing terrorism. What types of information should be provided to the public?
4. Describe the relationship between the police and private security relative to homeland security.
5. What functions should a police department's homeland security unit perform?
6. What is intelligence-led policing?
7. Describe the intelligence process.
8. What is a fusion center and how does it operate?

References

American-Israeli Enterprise. (2008). *Jewish Virtual Library*. http://www.jewishvirtuallibrary.org/jsource/US-Israel/arabpop.html (Accessed August 19, 2008).

Brown, B. (2007). "Community policing in post-September 11 America: A comment on the concept of community-oriented counterterrorism." *Police Practice and Research*, 8(3): 239–51.

Bumphus, V., L. Gaines, and C. Blakely. (1999). Citizen police academies: Observing goals, objectives, and recent trends. *American Journal of Criminal Justice*, 24(1): 67–80.

Carter, D. (2004). *Law Enforcement Intelligence: A Guide for State, Local, and Tribal Law Enforcement Agencies*. Washington, D.C.: Office of Community Oriented Policing Servies.

DeLone, G. (2007). "Law enforcement mission statements post September 11." *Police Quarterly*, 10(2): 218–35.

Department of Justice/Department of Homeland Security. (undated). *Fusion Center Guidelines: Developing and Sharing Information and Intelligence in a New Era*. Washington, D.C.: Bureau of Justice Assistance.

Donahue, A. and R. Tuohy. (2006). "Lessons we don't learn: A study of the lessons of disaster, why we repeat them, and how we can learn from them." *Homeland Security Affairs*, 2(2): 1–28.

Frankenrath, R. (2007). Prepared statement of testimony before the Committee on Homeland Security, United States House of Representatives, March 6.

Gaines, L. (2006). "An analysis of traffic stop data in Riverside, California." *Police Quarterly*, 9: 210–33.

Gaines, L. K. and V. Kappeler. (2008). *Policing in America* (6th ed.). Cincinnati, OH: Lexis-Nexis.

Gaines, L. and J. Worrall. (2011). *Police Administration*. Belmont, CA: Delmar.

Garrett, K. (2002). "Terrorism on the homefront." *Law Enforcement Technology* (July): 22–26.

Gau, J. and T. Pratt. (2008). "Broken windows or window dressing? Citizens (in)ability to tell the difference between disorder and crime." *Criminology & Public Policy*, 7(2): 163–94.

Goldstein, H. (1990). *Problem-Oriented Policing*. New York: McGraw-Hill.

Goldstein, H. (1979). "Improving policing: A problem-oriented approach." *Crime & Delinquency*, 25: 236–58.

Green, G. (1981). *Introduction to Security*. Stoneham, MA: Butterworth.

Henderson, N., C. Ortiz, N. Sugie, and J. Miller. (2008). "Policing Arab-American communities after September 11." *Research for Practice*. Washington, D.C.: National Institute of Justice.

Hickman, M. and B. Reaves. (2006). *Local Police Departments, 2003*. Washington, D.C.: Bureau of Justice Statistics.

Hollywood, J., K. Strom, and M. Pope. (2008). *Developing and Testing a Method for Using 9/11 Calls for Identifying Potential Pre-Planning Terrorist Surveillance Activities*. Washington, D.C.: National Institute of Justice.

Human Rights Watch. (2002). *We Are Not the Enemy: Hate Crimes Against Arabs, Muslims, and Those Perceived to Be Arab or Muslim after September 11*. Washington, D.C.: Author.

Kappeler, V. and L. Gaines. (2009). *Community Policing: A Contemporary Perspective* (5th ed.). Cincinnati, OH: Lexis-Nexis.

Kleiman, M. (2004). *Illicit Drugs and the Terrorist Threat: Causal Links and Implications for Domestic Drug Control Policy*. Washington, D.C.: Congressional Research Service.

Lyon, W. (2002). "Partnerships, information, and public safety." *Policing*, 25: 530–43.

Marks, D. and I. Sun. (2007). "Organizational development among state and local law enforcement agencies." *Journal of Contemporary Criminal Justice*, 23(2): 159–73.

McArdle, A. and T. Erzen. (2001). *Zero Tolerance: Quality of Life and the New Police Brutality in New York*. New York: New York University Press.

McCaffrey, B. and J. Basso. (2003). "Narcotics, terrorism, and international crime: The convergence phenomenon." In *Terrorism and Counterterrorism: Understanding the New Security Environment*, ed. R. Howard and R. Sawyer, pp. 206–21. Guilford, CT: Dushkin.

McGarrell, E., J. Freilich, and S. Chermak. (2007). "Intelligence-led policing as a framework for responding to terrorism." *Journal of Contemporary Criminal Justice*, 23(2): 142–58.

McNamara, R. and R. Burns. (2009). *Multiculturalism in the Criminal Justice System*. New York: McGraw-Hill.

Morabito, A. and S. Greenberg. (2005). *Engaging the Private Sector to Promote Homeland Security: Law Enforcement– Private Security Partnerships*. Washington, D.C.: Bureau of Justice Assistance.

Murray, J. (2005). "Policing terrorism: A threat to community policing or just a shift in priorities?" *Police Practice and Research*, 6(4): 347–61.

Ohlhausen Research Inc. (2004). *Private Security/Public Policing: Vital Issues and Policy Recommendations*. Alexandria, VA: IACP.

Ortiz, W. (2007). "Policing terrorism: The response of local police agencies to homeland security concerns." *Criminal Justice Studies*, 20(2): 91–109.

Pelfrey, W. (2007). "Local law enforcement terrorism prevention efforts: A state level case study." *Journal of Criminal Justice*, 35: 313–21.

Smith, B. (2008). "A look at terrorist behavior: How they prepare and how they attack." *National Institute of Justice*. http://www.ojp.usdoj.gov/nij/journals/260/ terrorist-behavior.htm (Accessed August 24, 2010).

Smith, B., K. Damphousse, and P. Roberts. (2006). *Pre-Incident Indicators of Terrorist Incidents: The Identification of Behavioral, Geographic, and Temporal Patterns of Preparatory Conduct*. Washington, D.C.: National Institute of Justice.

Spahr, L., J. Ederheimer, and D. Bilson. (2007). *Patrol-Level Response to a Suicide Bomb Threat: Guidelines for Consideration*. Critical Issues in Policing Series. Washington, D.C.: Police Executive Research Forum.

Spelman, W. and J. Eck (1989). "Sitting ducks, ravenous wolves, and helping hands: New approaches to urban policing." *Public Affairs Comment*, 35(2): 1–9.

Sullivan, J. (2006). "Terrorism early warning groups: Regional intelligence to combat terrorism." In *Homeland Security and Terrorism*, ed. R. Howard, J. Forest, and J. Moore, pp. 235–45. New York: McGraw-Hill.

Thatcher, D. (2005). "The local role in homeland security." *Law & Society Review*, 39(3): 635–676.

Wilson, J. Q. and G. Kelling. (1982). "Broken windows." *Atlantic Monthly* (March): 29–38.

INDEX